GUARDIANS OF THE REPUBLIC

SFC Steven Howd
U.S. Army Reserve Drill Sergeant of the Year
2006

GUARDIANS

☆☆ OF THE ☆☆

REPUBLIC

A HISTORY OF THE NONCOMMISSIONED OFFICER CORPS OF THE U.S. ARMY

ERNEST F. FISHER, JR.

STACKPOLE BOOKS

First published as a Fawcett Columbine Book by Ballantine Books.

Published by
STACKPOLE BOOKS
5067 Ritter Road
Mechanicsburg, PA 17055
www.stackpolebooks.com

Printed in the United States of America

10 9 8 7 6 5 4 3 2 1

Cover photograph courtesy of Soldiers Magazine, Robert Melhorn, archivist.

Cover design by Wendy Reynolds

Library of Congress Cataloging-in-Publication Data

Fisher, Ernest F., 1918-
Guardians of the republic : a history of the noncommissioned officer corps of the U.S. Army / Ernest F. Fisher, Jr.
p. cm.
Originally published: New York : Ballantine, 1994.
ISBN 0-8117-2784-X (alk. paper)
1. United States. Army—Non-commissioned officer—History. I. Title.

UB408.5 F57 2001
355.3'32-dc21

00-067024

CONTENTS

LIST OF ILLUSTRATIONS

FOREWORD

Well may the noncommissioned officers of the United States Army be termed "Guardians of the Republic" as Ernest F. Fisher, Jr., calls them in this book. The Revolutionary War struggles of the Continental Army amply demonstrate the consequences of a shortage of trained and experienced noncommissioned officers. The tactical difficulties of the Continental Army when it contended against the British in battle made the margin of victory for American independence perilously narrow. Those difficulties had many sources, all associated with the necessity of creating an effective army in haste out of inadequate raw materials; but no source of the problem was more important than the absence of a cadre of competent sergeants. As Fisher goes on to explain, such a cadre—once it was achieved—became the cement that held all subsequent American armies together. Without good sergeants and corporals, there can be no effective army. Without competent noncommissioned officers, there can be no sure military guardianship of the republic.

Until the publication of this book, the American noncommissioned officer, as a class of warrior leaders, had never been appropriately studied by military historians. There is no predecessor or parallel to Fisher's book. Either historians have dealt with the Army as a whole, or they have divided their attention between the rank and file in general and the commissioned ranks. Samuel P. Huntington's classic work, *The Soldier and the State: The Theory and Politics of Civil Military Relations*, admirably surveyed the evolution of the profession of commissioned military officership in America in the context of the worldwide and especially German origins of the profession, but never heretofore have we had a detailed and thoughtful historical review of the noncommissioned officer.

As Fisher's work shows, the professional neglect of sergeants and corporals is a paradox in the history of the Army of a democratic society, a paradox in historical treatment mirroring in turn a larger paradox of American democracy. Like Huntington, Fisher is careful to survey the European background of this topic. He informs us that in sixteenth-, seventeenth-, and early eighteenth-century Europe, the distinction between commissioned and noncommissioned officers emerged only gradually. At first, middle-class and even noble youths aspired to the responsibilities and skill of the sergeant, and the sergeant had his place in the hierarchy of ranks that progressed upward with no clear break of the kind that later separated NCOs from those holding commissions. When the distinction did eventually emerge, it was closely associated with differences of social and economic class.

In the United States, with its egalitarian aspirations, the hardening of the line between commissioned and noncommissioned officers should have seemed inconsistent with the nation's democratic values. One of the hitherto largely unrecognized lessons Fisher teaches is that the American military at first tried to escape the European pattern of an emphatic divide between sergeants and lieutenants. Without any real aristocracy, the community spirit infused by the early American militia organizations should have softened tendencies toward European-style distinctions.

General George Washington, however, was a gentleman of aristocratic predisposition and influenced by the hardening of the distinction between ranks in the British army. He only reluctantly accepted the practice of promoting sergeants to officer rank. Thus, there was less journeying from the noncommissioned into the commissioned grades than early American circumstances might have predicted. Still, until the nineteenth century, the possibility remained open that a democratic and egalitarian America might escape the undemocratic and in egalitarian divide in rankings of its military personnel.

It was the development of the United States Military Academy at West Point from 1802 onward that assured a military departure from the professed national values of egalitarianism because it tended to follow the recent European pattern of a hardened barrier between grades. Valuable though West Point was in offering a professional education and instilling a professional ethos among the commissioned officers of the United States Army at a remarkably early stage, this achievement occurred at the expense of a similar professional development among the sergeants. West Point was consciously patterned on European officers' schools, and its borrowings from them included pretensions that the officer was to be a member of the gentlemanly classes. Unfortunately both for an army mirroring American society, and for the fullest possible cultivation of NCO skills, the nineteenth-century Army was just enough isolated from the main currents of American life to permit its commissioned officers to break from the then-existing egalitarian tradition.

While West Point flourished as an officer school, and was followed later by a gradual evolution of higher professional schools for the commissioned grades, systematic schooling of the noncommissioned officers fell into almost complete neglect. Company officers chose their own noncommissioned offices, and how well the latter were taught varied haphazardly from one company to another. Fisher rightly admires the noncommissioned officers of the Old Army of the nineteenth century, particularly the long-service sergeants who indeed provided the cement that held the Army together. But Fisher's ground-breaking insight is that whatever effectiveness the noncommissioned officer corps of the Old Army attained came in spite of the faulty system of company-based selection and training.

The faultiness of the system was too obvious to ignore by the First World War. The new tactics of fire and maneuver, of a general resort to skirmishing tactics and advances in short rushes by small groups of men under covering fire from comrades, escalated the demands for individual initiative and judgment among combat soldiers and NCOs. Haphazard selection and training of sergeants no longer sufficed. World War I therefore witnessed the first attempts toward selecting and training noncommissioned officers beyond the company level, but it did not make enough progress to prevent the NCO corps from being probably the weakest element in the fighting power of the American Expeditionary Forces.

Close on the heels of the breakdown of the old methods of choosing and preparing noncommissioned officers came even more far-reaching changes in the responsibilities and duties of the NCO. The mechanization of the Army during the years between the two world wars heralded a quantum leap forward in the pace of technological change that affected every aspect of military life. Just at the time when the sergeant had to learn to be a more autonomous leader in combat than anytime previously, he also had to become more of a technical specialist in the operation of new and more complex technical equipment. Another of Fisher's main themes is the transformation of the noncommissioned officer from a leader to a leader who was also a specialist in the use of this advanced hardware. While the tactical changes of the World War I era affected primarily the combat role of the NCO, the new post-war military technology made its impact everywhere from the rearmost support echelon to the front line of battle.

The twentieth century clearly called for an educational system for noncommissioned officers to parallel the by-now mature school system for commissioned officers. In the German army, this call was heeded well before World War II, so that in the German army of 1939–1945, the well-schooled proficiency of the noncommissioned officers proved a major source of that force's remarkable flexibility, resilience, and overall combat power. In the United States Army as late as World War II, selection of noncommissioned officers, except for certain technical specialists, remained a prerogative of unit commanders rather than any sort of Army-wide system. There were no schools for noncommissioned officers, except the specialist schools, such as ordnance and signal. Whatever might be said of the necessity to leave some choice of unit leaders up to the unit commander, relegating solely to such commanders the task of selecting and training noncommissioned officers was surely expecting too much of them. The rejection of proposals for sergeants' schools during World War II was a mistake. The noncommissioned officer corps of World War II performed somewhat better than its counterpart in World War I, but only because there was more time for training in general.

At first glance, Fisher appears to be telling a much more encouraging tale of the years after World War II regarding the lessons learned from the war relative to the creation of noncommissioned officer schools that led, ultimately, to the Noncommissioned Officer Development Program and the Noncommissioned Officer Education

System of today. His critical approach becomes quite vigorous in his final pages, where he cites evidence that shows that as teachers of soldiers in units, the Army's noncommissioned officers still do not teach their subordinates as effectively as they should, though the Army training system depends on them to do so. They fail in large part because they themselves are still not taught well enough either in how to nourish leadership in others, or in the technology of the age of electronic war. But, the roots of the difficulty run deeper than that; they return to Fisher's central themes. The turn toward a stronger professional status for noncommissioned officers is probably essential for achieving appropriate leadership capacities and technical skills in the Army of the present and the future.

This may be happening now as Fisher points out in his new Afterword to this 2001 Stackpole edition. No army has ever been better than its noncommissioned officers can make it. The great armies of the modern western countries have always drawn their character from their noncommissioned officers, and the U.S. Army seems to be doing this more and more as the press of technology and the new missions in the post-Cold War era are showing. Indeed, the centrality of the role of the NCO has probably grown even in the relatively short time since the first publication of this book in 1994. Since that time, it has become increasingly apparent that the era of large-scale world wars, and even regional conflicts of the magnitude of the Persian Gulf War, are likely to be rare. Henceforth, the employment of armies will most likely occur mainly in conflicts of small forces, often unconventional in tactics, against terrorists, and in peacemaking and peacekeeping. More and more, units smaller than platoons will have to operate autonomously, with responsibility for decision-making falling to the NCOs and even to the individual soldiers.

The main tendencies of twentieth-century military activities had already moved strongly in that direction, with increasingly lethal weaponry compelling increased dispersal of troops. As we enter the twenty-first century, the political and social circumstances in which armies are likely to act have accelerated the process of pushing responsibility and decision-making down the chain of command. That there is now today better technical and leadership education and greater career incentives for noncommissioned officers says much about the historical accuracy of the analysis presented in this wonderful book.

In *Guardians of the Republic*, Ernest F. Fisher offers a history in unequal detail of the contrasting American approaches toward noncommissioned officership. From the beginning all the way through World War II, the American, British, and German armies contrived to be high-quality fighting forces through most of the nineteenth and the first half of the twentieth centuries. This says much in favor of the national military aptitudes from which their armies arose; it also probably says something about good luck or divine blessings.

The whole history and status of the noncommissioned officers in the United States Army is a story that shows how the role of this unique group developed in ways contradictory to the supposed values of the nation at large, partly because too few American knew enough about what was going on inside the Army. Military historians have been almost as neglectful of the noncommissioned officer as has the general public. Ernest F. Fisher's meticulously researched and critically insightful history is a long-overdue corrective. We may hope that it will be read carefully by enough people that it will help maintain the quality and positive direction that the noncommissioned officer corps has taken in recent years, and that it will continue to aid in the development of the necessary changes in the Army as it seeks to produce noncommissioned officers to meet the technology and leadership challenges facing America in the twenty-first century.

Guardians of the Republic traces that development with detail found in no other study. Whether the current elevation of the standards, training, and status of the Army's noncommissioned officer corps is likely to be sufficient for the work that lies ahead is for the concerned citizen to help decide. With more intensive training of NCOs reinforcing the willingness of the commissioned officers to accord them larger powers, there can be abuse of power as well as an enhanced maturity in the enlisted ranks. For helping us to perceive both the dangers and the opportunities, and to decide where to go next with the selection, training, and organization of our country's noncommissioned officers, there can be no better a foundation than this book.

Russell F. Weigley
September 2000

PREFACE

This history of the noncommisioned officer in the U.S. Army was conceived as a single story. As the research and writing proceeded, however, the narrative seemed to divide itself into two parts—one, the role of the noncommissioned officer as an assistant to the officer in maintaining order and fire discipline in the linear tactics of combat in the nineteenth century, and the other that of the small-unit combat leader and technician of complex weapon systems of the twentieth century. As can readily be imagined, research for two such voluminous themes ranged widely over the entire field of military history.

The research led me to the unsurpassed official collections at the National Archives of the United States in Washington, D.C., and the former Washington National Records Center at Suitland, Maryland. To the staffs of both I owe an immeasurable debt of gratitude. Further valuable material came to light in the excellent special collections of the Military History Institute at Carlisle Barracks, Pennsylvania. To the knowledgeable and helpful staff there I am deeply indebted. Additional important information was made available in the Manuscript Division of the Library of Congress; my special thanks to its staff. The Army Library in the Pentagon building houses the finest and most complete collection of army regulations from the eighteenth century to the present. This collection has been a useful guide in determining U.S. Army policy regarding the role of the noncommissioned officer throughout the Army's history. And finally, to the staff of the Folger Shakespeare Library in Washington, D.C., I owe a debt mere words can never hope to repay. Their collection of original sixteenth- and seventeenth-century military treatises was an invaluable help in tracing the origins of the American military tradition to its European roots.

Numerous officers and noncommissioned officers of the Army have shared with me their wisdom and knowledge, especially in developing the narrative covering the period since World War I. I especially acknowledge the steadfast assistance given me by the late General Harold K. Johnson. Two former Sergeants Major of the Army, William G. Bainbridge and Leon Van Autreve, and many of their fellow senior noncommissioned officers, especially Command Sergeant Major Donald Devaney, have given me skilled help and encouragement throughout the preparation of this history.

As this work was updated for its republication as a Stackpole Books trade paperback, I thank Professor Emeritus Russell F. Weigley of Temple University, author of the monumental classic, *The American Way of War* and other outstanding books, for his kind words in the new foreword; Sergeant Major Larry L. Strickland of the Office of the Deputy Chief of Staff for Personnel at Headquarters, Department of the Army; Command Sergeant Major Daniel K. Elder of Fort Riley, Kansas; Command Sergeant Major (Ret.) Jimmie D. Spencer of the Association of the United States Army; and Maj. Marianna Yamamota, USAR, for their thorough and sound advice on the new afterword. To my dear wife, Else, who only knows how much her love, loyalty, and support have sustained me in this decade-long task, my thanks.

My debts to all those without whose direction and support this book would never have come to completion does not diminish in the least my sole responsibility for any errors of fact and interpretation its pages may contain.

☆☆ PART ONE ☆☆

EUROPEAN BEGINNINGS TO WORLD WAR I

CHAPTER 1

EUROPEAN BEGINNINGS

"The backbone of the Army is the noncommissioned man!"
—*The 'Eathen* (1896) by Rudyard Kipling

Ask any group of reasonably educated Americans to define by example what an Army sergeant is and inevitably someone mentions either the mean-spirited little military bureaucrat, Sergeant Himmelstoss, popularized in the 1930 movie adaptation of Erich Maria Remarque's *All Quiet on the Western Front*, or the conniving Sergeant Bilko, immortalized by Phil Silvers in the 1950s television comedy series *You'll Never Get Rich.*

Other motion-picture images that spring to mind, perhaps no closer to the truth of what a sergeant really is but certainly more flattering to noncoms, are John Wayne's Sergeant Stryker in *The Sands of Iwo Jima*, Burt Lancaster's portrayal of 1st Sergeant Warden in *From Here to Eternity*, Gary Cooper as Sergeant Alvin York, and Jackie Gleason as Master Sergeant Maxwell Slaughter in *Soldier in the Rain.*

No doubt each of these Hollywood stereotypes has had its flesh-and-blood incarnation at some time and in some place during the two centuries and more the United States Army has existed. But these characters were merely quirks in the body military. Not even the U.S. Army itself has a clear idea of what a sergeant is, as its many abortive attempts to define the roles of noncommissioned officers over the years proves.

So what is the Army sergeant, this "backbone of the Army," as Kipling called him, these "muscles and sinews of the corps," those military professionals charged by the seventeenth-century soldier Sir John Smythe "to winne the love of their soldiers by taking great care of their healty and safeties . . . as of their own children"? The modern sergeant Americans have come to love—or hate—traces his origin back to the beginnings of modern warfare, to the period of the late Renaissance in Western Europe.

■ ■

From about the middle of the fifteenth to the beginning of the eighteenth century there occurred in Western Europe a revolution in astronomy, mathematics, and physics that transformed Western cosmology and laid the groundwork for the development of modern science. Not so well known, however, was the concurrent revolution in the military arts and sciences.

As in the other phases of the scientific revolution, the Netherlands were a major center of this activity. Much of what came to be known as the "Dutch" military school was strongly influenced by the thinking of the two leading exponents of neo-stoicism, Justus Lipsius, a professor at the University of Leiden, and the French Protestant reformer John Calvin.

Neo-stoicism, as the name implies, was a Renaissance version of the Greek stoic school of philosophy founded by Zeno of Citium around 300 B.C., which emphasized rigorous moral and physical self-discipline in order to live in harmony with nature and thus achieve true freedom of the spirit. Lipsius and Calvin regarded discipline as one of the most powerful tools in the educational process.

At the same time, systematic discipline, stimulated by drill, training, and military law, came to be regarded as an essential tool in the hands of men with the rank of sergeant and corporal. The first two elements of this triad lay almost exclusively in the hands of these two ranks, while the commanding officer administered military law. Much of this change was the work of a Dutch prince, Maurice of Nassau, prince of Orange (1567–1625), who served as captain general of the provinces of Holland and Zeeland between 1585 and his death. A student of mathematics and the classics while at the University of Leiden, the prince based his most important military innovation—systematic drill—upon Roman precedents.[1]

Before the scientific revolution, warfare had been the sole province of the heavily armed knight mounted on an equally armored horse, for many years a formidable fighting combination that dominated the battlefields of Europe. Fighting in relatively modest arrays, these knights had evolved among themselves over several centuries a highly ritualized and, at the same time, a highly individualistic method of warfare. The military arts and sciences developed concurrently with the scientific revolution over the seventeenth century according to the whims of the princes, to reach its modern form in the eighteenth century. By the end of the seventeenth century this modern form of warfare had virtually replaced the chivalric pattern of combat with well-structured and organized standing armies fighting according to clearly defined and logical principles, widely accepted throughout Europe.

Important elements in this change were the development of an elaborate structure of rank, the lengthening of the chain of command, and the delineation of the status and role of each officer in that chain. At the beginning of this process there had been no agreed-upon distinction made between commissioned and noncommissioned officers. Previously, among officers of a particular military unit there had been simply gradations of authority and responsibility. The practice of distinguishing between commissioned and noncommissioned officers developed gradually over the seventeenth century.*

Military commentators of the sixteenth century generally made no distinction between commissioned and noncommissioned officers; from corporal to colonel all were simply described as officers of a company, battalion, or regiment. A captain or colonel, however, generally was authorized, hired, or "commissioned" by a prince or the ruling council of a city or state to raise soldiers. He would in turn appoint subordinates to assist him.

Early in the seventeenth century, however, a Captain Johann von Wallhausen, commandant of the famed military academy at Siegen founded by Prince John of Nassau, lamented that young nobles and other well-born young men sent by the Protestant princes of Germany to study the first systematic military education of modern times, were unwilling to accept a sergeant's office. They preferred rather the rank of ensign, despite the fact that the sergeant's rank was, in von Wallhausen's opinion, the "most absolute" in the entire regiment. The reason, if there was one, can be found perhaps in the fact that the sergeant dealt directly with the common soldiers, whereas the ensign, who had custody of the colors in garrison and in battle—hence his title—remained aloof from the mundane, daily tasks of training a company or regiment.[2]

In France, however, as late as the eighteenth century, men from the middle classes, the popular elite, and even from the nobility, competed for positions as sergeants. Whenever recruiting was regionally organized and based upon militias, canton systems, or military districts, recruits for positions as subordinate officers (*sous officiers* or noncommissioned officers) were likely to come from the popular elite and from military families—the sons of professional soldiers. This was particularly true for militias in which the military hierarchy most naturally mirrored the local social hierarchy. Under these circumstances, the sons of artisans, farm workers, and day laborers were less likely to be found within the ranks of noncommissioned officers.[3]

During the reign of Louis XIV (1638–1715), however, money came to play an ever-increasing role in the acquisition of military rank as wealthy nobles bought regiments for themselves or their sons, and well-to-do bourgeois bought companies. These military entrepreneurs quite naturally reserved the higher ranks for themselves. This meant that young men without means but interested in pursuing military careers had first to content themselves with the lower ranks or what subsequently became the "noncommissioned" or *sous officier* positions.[4] This situation explains the large number of noncommissioned officers who eventually

***The Oxford Dictionary of the English Language* defines "commission" as "delegated authority to act in the same specified capacity. In the old system of raising forces, a warrant which authorized the holder to raise, equip, and command a body of soldiers in the name of the issuing authority; the warrant by which all officers in the Army from ensign upward are appointed [by the Crown] to the rank and command they hold." Earliest examples of commissioning officers among the English forces are to be found in 1643, 1685, and 1704.

became outstanding generals during the French Revolution and under Napoleon.

Elsewhere in Europe, there continued to be some movement between the two categories of ranks—commissioned and noncommissioned. For example, in Prussia under Frederick II (The Great), noncommissioned officers of middle-class origins and holding engineer or artillery posts in garrison could be promoted to lieutenant rather easily in wartime. In the kingdom of Württemberg, according to a decree of 1754, noncommissioned officers with titles of nobility could become lieutenants after three years of service. Those without titles became eligible only after twelve years of service. In Sweden, overlaps between nobility and commoner frequently took place at the regimental level. Regimental commissioned officers had to have had previous service as noncommissioned officers before receiving their commissions.[5]

Nevertheless, throughout the eighteenth century the schism between commissioned and noncommissioned officers continued to grow as the number of gentlemen without commissions serving in the regiments and companies and the number of commoners serving with commissions, decreased. Monarchs and princes sought by this practice to bind their aristocracies and monied classes more closely to their thrones by reserving for them the higher offices in their armies. This practice eventually separated the commissioned from the noncommissioned officers, as the first came to be recruited exclusively from the gentry and nobility and the latter from among the commoners.[6]

NONCOMMISSIONED ORIGINS

To better understand the significance of these changes, it is helpful to examine the origins of what in time became the noncommissioned officer ranks. From the seventeenth century on, as Wallhausen observed, the development of a potential line of separation had begun between those officers within the military hierarchy who dealt directly with the men and those officers who did not.

The rudimentary origins of the military rank of sergeant are to be found within feudalism, whose military keystone was the armored and mounted knight. Usually landholders performing military obligations in return for land tenancy, the knights had constituted the warrior class of medieval Europe. Standing just below the knight in the hierarchy of medieval society were sergeants, holders of sergeanties, that is, lesser grants of land for which obligations of service mostly civil but also occasionally of a military nature were due. The name "sergeant" derives from the Latin *serviens*—servant—and was used initially to designate petty or lesser officers, generally of the crown, who served in such capacities as royal falconer, huntsman, or tailor.[7]

By the mid-thirteenth century, the service obligations attached to sergeanty had been generally commuted to monetary payments in lieu of service, and that aspect of the rank fell gradually into disuse. As a purely military title or rank, the term "sergeant" did not reappear until the mid-fifteenth century, when the aristocratic traditions of feudal warfare began to dissolve into the larger and less elite formations, composed mainly of commoners—foot soldiers armed with bow or pike.[8]

CHANGES IN MILITARY ORGANIZATION

Such infantry formations had first made their appearance in the late fifteenth century, among the towns and cities of the Swiss cantons. Armed with heavy eighteen-foot lances or pikes, and formed into compact, well-disciplined phalanxes, the new infantry required considerable drilling and discipline in order to hold their positions against the onslaught of charging armored cavalry. Each man had to be thoroughly drilled in the use of the pike and had to be kept in his place during battle by the strictest discipline in order to take advantage of the element of mass.[9]

The older, more experienced soldiers who drilled these men and made them hold ranks in battle as well as on the march were the predecessors of the sergeants and corporals of the *Landsknechte*, mercenary foot soldiers whose prowess was highly prized among the rulers of fifteenth- and sixteenth-century Europe. Instead of wandering about the battlefield looking for a worthy opponent, as the aristocratic knightly warrior had done, each soldier now had to keep his place in ranks and had to fight according to a carefully rehearsed battle drill. For example, in England a royal ordinance of 1528 stipulated that each company of foot was to have a sergeant who was an expert in such drill. This insistence on a stylized battle drill in time reduced the individual soldier's status, as the distinguished British military historian John Keegan has written, "to that of a mechanical unit in the order of battle." The sergeant and the corporal became the pillars upon which this drill, and indeed the battleworthiness of a military unit rested.[10]

Often raised by professional captains under contract or commission to princes or city-states, the closely massed phalanxes of pikemen were the matrix out of which modern professional standing armies developed until gunpowder broke their cohesion toward the end of the seventeenth century. Alongside these formations also grew the territorial militias made up of freemen (small farmers). These militia units were led by men who held their lands by sergeanty, and were therefore of somewhat higher social status than the ordinary farmers whose land holdings were modest and whose tenures less secure. From both types of military service the two basic noncommissioned ranks—sergeant and corporal—emerged.[11]

UPWARD MOBILITY IN RANK

While the evolution of a strictly controlled infantry battle drill tended to fix the soldier in his place on the battlefield, the fifteenth and sixteenth centuries at the same time witnessed the phenomenon of extraordinary upward mobility by many able common soldiers through the ranks of the military hierarchy and into the highest ranks of the landed aristocracy. Mercenary companies occasionally provided opportunities for outstanding corporals and sergeants to rise and in so doing to acquire noble titles and lands from their royal masters. The German poet Friedrich von Schiller described this succinctly in the following couplets from *Wallenstein's Lager:*

Und wer's zum Korporal erst hat gebracht,
Der steht auf der Leiter zur höchsten Macht,
Und soweit kann er's auch noch treiben,
*Wenn er nur lesen kann and schreiben.**

Among those whose military careers illustrate this point is Peter Holzappel. Born in 1585 of a peasant family in Niederhadamar, in Hesse-Nassau, Holzappel served as a common soldier in Holland, then rose through the ranks to become commanding general of the army of Hesse-Kassel from 1633 to 1640. In 1641 the Holy Roman Emperor elevated him to *Graf* or count, and subsequently to *Feldmarshall* (field marshal) of the imperial forces. In 1643, as Count of Melander, he purchased an estate in the province of Jülich-Berg, where he died in 1648. Another example is Johann Aldringen, born in 1591 of a peasant family in the grand duchy of Luxemburg. Aldringen found employment first as a servant in the household of a French noble family. Later he became private secretary of Cardinal Madrucci. In 1622, he joined the imperial army in Innsbruck. By 1625, he had risen through the ranks to become a colonel. At the same time the Emperor made him a baron, and in 1632 a field marshal.† Such spectacular careers were not uncommon during the religious wars of the seventeenth century.[12]

Upward mobility of professional soldiers during the sixteenth and seventeenth centuries was aided by the fact that at the time the ranks of lance corporal, corporal, and sergeant not yet constituted a clearly defined and closed class of noncommissioned—as opposed to commissioned—officers, as was the case in the eighteenth century. Rather, these grades were simply the lower echelons of a military hierarchy that descended from field marshal through general, colonel, sergeant major, captain, lieutenant, and ensign to sergeant, corporal, and lance corporal.

Charged by custom with the instruction and drilling of the troops, sergeants were found in the French army as early as 1485. When Francis I reorganized his army in 1543, he formed five hundred–man companies or bands, as they were sometimes known. A company was commanded by a captain assisted by a lieutenant, an ensign who carried the colors, one sergeant, five corporals, a fifer, and a

*Whoever succeeds in making corporal, Stands on the first rung of the ladder to highest position, And that far can he go, If he can only learn to read and write.

†Still another, although much later example is that of Gerhard Scharnhorst, chief of staff of the Prussian army during the Napoleonic Wars. His father was a free peasant who had risen to the rank of sergeant major.

drummer. Each company or band was raised by a professional soldier with the rank of captain. Thus reorganized, Francis's army became a model for other countries, notably the Netherlands and England. The ranks of sergeant and corporal, thereafter, became permanent parts of the formal military structure.[13]

Before the sergeant took his place in the English army there had been a rank, the "wyffler" or "whiffler" (from "whiffle," a javelin or an ax) whose duties resembled those of a sergeant. Employed during the reign of Henry VIII and well into that of Elizabeth I, the wyffler had the task of instructing soldiers how to use their weapons and maintain the proper distances between the ranks and files of the infantry formations. Under the Stuarts, the duties of this office gradually merged with those of the sergeants.[14]

As already mentioned, the great turning point in military ranks and organization occurred through the influence of Prince Maurice of Orange, military commander of the forces of the Estates of the Netherlands. Prince Maurice enjoyed the important advantage of having access to the wealth of the Dutch merchants in providing for prompt and generous pay for his troops. As one of his contemporaries wrote in a treatise on military organization,

> the first and principall thing that is requisite to assemble and forme an Armie, or Armies, and keep the same in obedience with good effect, is its treasure, to maintain, pay, and reward with severe execution of excellent lawes Militarie.

Daily drill of the troops "practiced year round when on garrison duty, and occupying spare time when on campaign and in the field" characterized Maurice's principles of training. By means of such drill taught by sergeants and corporals, Maurice's troops were able to execute quickly and smoothly those marches and countermarches that gave them such superior effectiveness in battle.[15]

THE SERGEANT'S ROLE AND DUTIES

Prince Maurice conceived of the sergeant and his corporal assistants as drillmasters. These officers were charged specifically with training the men for battle. Such parade-ground commands as "right face," "left face," and "halt," familiar to all soldiers today, had their origin with Prince Maurice.[16] His precepts on training and organization, based on earlier Italian, Spanish, and French practices, were given wide circulation during his lifetime through the writings of a succession of professional soldiers who had turned their hands to the pen as well as the sword.

Their writings clearly detailed the duties and functions of every officer in the military hierarchy, and it is to them that we must turn in order to describe the developing role and status of the sergeants and corporals during the sixteenth and seventeenth centuries. Already at the beginning of this period the ideal had started to emerge of a more humane attitude on the part of officers (including sergeants and corporals) toward their men that can only be described as modern in spirit.

The ideal standard for all in authority, from the general to the corporal, according to Sir John Smythe, a professional soldier of wide experience, was

> to winn the love of their soldiers by taking great care of their health and safeties, as also by action in their own persons, venturing their lives in all actions against the enemie amongst them, and therewith all accompting of them in sickness and health, or wounds received, as of their own children.[17]

This almost family-like relationship between officers and men applied especially to the sergeant and the corporal, who were closest to the ordinary soldiers. This sentiment was echoed by yet another contemporary of Prince Maurice, Robert Barret, who, like Smythe, had also served as a soldier in the French, Dutch, Italian, and Spanish armies. Although Barret was describing the corporal's duties, his words apply equally to the sergeant. An able corporal, Barret wrote, was

> to deport himselfe among them [his men] as a father with his children, his conditions being a patterne unto them asswaging and end [ing] their debates and quarrels, reducing them unto amitie, with loving one another, in such sort that they may be of one will, desire, and ligue.[18]

Wallhausen, like Barret a professional soldier in several armies, declared in the early seventeenth century that the corporal should be as a *Hausvater* (father of the family) to his men, busying himself with maintaining peace and friendship under his command.[19]

The role of the sergeant as linchpin of the company was further underscored by the importance given him by all commentators as the chief disciplinarian of the unit. "In him," Barret wrote, "consisteth the principall parts of the observation of military discipline."[20] So vital was the sergeant's role, Barret averred, that a skillful sergeant was "of so great importance, that more tollerable it were, all the other officers of the Companie (yea were it the Captaine himselfe) to be rawe men and *Bisognios** with little experience and skill, and the sergeant not so; who of necessitie ought to be an expert soldier, and of great spirit and diligence."[21] Moreover, Wallhausen observed that "the sergeant has the most difficult and burdensom office, moreover he must be trained and experienced in all matters relating to war, so that he attains to the offices and honors that mastery of the art of war brings with it."[22]

As a disciplinarian, however, the sergeant was to keep his temper under control, for he ought

> not to slashe or cutt souldiers with his sworde, excepte upon just occasion . . . [rather] if by chance he should be angrie with any souldier of his (in turninge his backe he is to forget that furie) and afterwards sheawe himselfe amiable and loving, and so they [the men] coming to the knowledge of his honoures they shall have the more care not to anger him.[23]

**Bisognio* or *bisonnio*, Italo-Spanish word meaning inexperienced soldier or recruit.

In addition to his role as disciplinarian and drillmaster, the sergeant should also be "the eye, eare, mouth, hand and feet of his superior officers." All commentators agreed that he

> be somewhat lerned, both to write and reade, and to cypher, whereby to keepe a roll or list of all the souldiers of his company, with their several weapons, and have them in memory by names of the *Camaradas*,* and to know distinctly how many *corselets*† and unarmed pikes, with the short weapons, what number of shot, musket, and Calliver; to set with dilligence at an instant all his companie in order as occasion shall cause, and the place wherein he shall be.[24]

The sergeant was also to instruct "the Drummes and Phifes their several sounds, as to how to sound a call, a Troupe, a march swift or slowe, an Alarme, a Charge or a Retriet." In an age when it has been said that the drum was the commander's voice, that is, the basic communications medium for military units, such training was critical.

It was, in Barret's words, also the sergeant's office

> to order and divide the Squadrons [units of from twenty to twenty-five men into which a company was divided] assigning which shall be for the Corps de guard, which for the walles, which for the streetes of the quarter where they are lodged, and which are to accompanie the Colours; and he shall not suffer any souldier to come thither without his Armes fully furnished.[25]

Furthermore, the sergeant was to appoint "those which shall work in the trenches." His role as unit peacemaker and disciplinarian also meant that "if any quarrels or brawles do arise amongst the Companie, it is his part to apprehend the offenders, yet in such sort, that he dismeasure himselfe with none, but execute the same with greatest moderation."[26]

Posting the watch or at least seeing to it that the corporals did so properly, was another of the sergeant's main tasks. A sergeant was, for example, to give the corporals "his opinions in placing the sentinels . . . and to give them the Word [password] with all circumspection and secrecie, as was delivered to him by the Sergeant Major."[27]

Although it was the corporal's job to see that every soldier in his squadron was supplied with powder and shot and so on, it was done under the sergeant's supervision. As for his company's rations, the sergeant was to procure them from the army's stores and "distribute the same unto the Caporals, who are especially to divide it amongst the Camaradas."

In the company commander's absence, the sergeant received his orders from the

**Camarada*, a Spanish word meaning one-half of a squadron, that is, eleven to twelve men. This was the smallest unit of a company and was united for lodging, messing, and friendship. A *Cabo de Camara*, or corporal, commanded the *camarada*.

†*Corslet*, French for the armor of a foot soldier.

lieutenant or, in the latter's absence, the ensign. The sergeant nevertheless was the company's main liaison with regimental headquarters through his daily contacts with the regimental sergeant major. Barret wrote that the sergeant "ought to carrie great respect unto the Sergeant Major," carry out his orders with alacrity, spend as much time in his presence as possible, and listen carefully to his instructions in order to earn promotion himself by following his example.[28]

THE SERGEANT'S EQUIPMENT

To a large degree, the extent of the sergeant's wide range of duties and responsibilities also helped determine his weapons and dress, for all commentators agree that they should not interfere with the performance of his duties. One writer declared that he should be armed only with a halberd (a nine-foot combination spear and battle-ax), sword, and dagger. He continued, "I would not that the Sergeants should weare any long or short tasses [armored skirt pieces designed to protect the thighs] because that their office in marching with their band is to performe the Captain's directions with celerity," and also to march or trot along the flanks, ensuring that the soldiers march straight in their ranks, keep their silence and intervals, and generally comport themselves in a military manner at all times.[29]

Captain Gerat Barry, writing somewhat later, prescribed that the sergeant

> shall go gallantlie with a faire millan [Milan, Italy–made] headpeece, and an extraordinarie good collet [metal collar], and a halbert [halberd] or geneton [small spear]. But by reason of his overmuch travell and paines his armes by no means ought to be havie [heavy], for if they be soe, hardley can he well execute his office.[30]

This concern that the sergeant not be overburdened was a legitimate one, for the eighteen-foot pike normally carried by the foot soldier was hardly a light weapon, especially for someone who had to move about frequently either on the march or in battle. Interestingly, although the infantry abandoned the pike by the end of the seventeenth century, the sergeant continued to carry the nine-foot half-pike or halberd much longer. Noncommissioned officers in the British army carried it well into the nineteenth century. It was last carried in 1876 by the drum major, and the baton this rank still carries may well have been derived from the now-vanished halberd.[31]

When one reflects upon the limited literacy among the general European population of the late sixteenth century, the responsibilities assigned the sergeant assume a degree of education that definitely placed him within the middle class, together with the merchant and skilled craftsman of that time. By the end of the century the sergeant's numerous tasks fully justified the description of him as the linchpin of the company.

THE CORPORAL

To assist the sergeant in the performance of his duties the captain appointed corporals. This rank had been taken over by the English from the French, who in turn seem to have adopted it from either the Italians or the Spanish. Indeed, the term *caporale* is of Italian origin; *il cabo de esquadra*, or chief of the *esquadra* or squad, comes from the Spanish. Late in the sixteenth century corporals began to appear in the ranks of the English county militia.[32]

At that time the office of corporal was a far more demanding one than it became in the eighteenth century. In the earlier period the corporal commanded the twenty-five-man "squadron" of which there were three in each company of foot.

Like the sergeant, the corporal was chosen with great care. As one sixteenth-century writer comments, "when the captain electeth his Caporalls," he should ensure that the man possesses valor, virtue, and experience to such a degree that he will be respected by the men in the ranks. Moreover, he should be mature enough to play the role of a father figure to the men, advising them, settling their quarrels and generally enforcing amity and peace among them.[33]

Somewhat later, other writers also perceived the corporal as "father" to his men as well as peacemaker and personal adviser. Wallhausen also believed that the corporals ought to oversee their subordinates' lives and behavior, their speech and pay, and look after the sick and wounded.[34] The corporal was also to be a teacher of his men,

> he himselfe ensigning and teaching the . . . raw men for, besides that it concerneth every one in particular for his owne defense, and thereby the better to knowe his valour and skill, nothing doth more rejoyce and glorifie a Campe, than the glittering shew and shining of their armor.

Cleanliness and neatness among the men were just as prized then as now, for Barret also advised the corporal to "perswade them to goe neat and cleane in their apparell, but with modestie and profite."[35] The corporal's "father" role was further extended by Barret, who urged him not to permit his men "any prohibited games" lest this reflect badly upon him and bring punishment upon them.

In the presence of his superior officers, however, the corporal was a subordinate, as were his fellow soldiers, but "when alone with his Squadron in any skance,* trench, Ambuscado, or abroad at the watch, or to such other effects, he beareth at that time his Captain's authoritie." And when isolated with his small command, the corporal was to lead it against the enemy just as if he were the company commander himself, for

**Skance*, a Dutch word meaning a small fortress built of turf and earth, commonly used in the Low Countries in the sixteenth-century warfare.

> being at watch or guard in any open place, he is to enscance and fortifie as commodity and the place will permit, to resist the attempt of the enemie, being by them charged, ordering and appointing all his companie to stand with their weapons readie, bent, still, without rumor, and resolute to defende.[36]

It was as corporal of the guard, however, that this officer filled his main role in the company. In this office he was admonished by the same commentator to

> doe his best endeavor to strengthen as such as in him lieth, his little corps de guard, and set out his centinels [sentinels] according to the avenues, or comings on of the enemy: for the cutting off of a centinell, and the surprising of a corps of guard, is of a great importance, and may endanger sometimes the overthrow of the Army.

It therefore behooved the corporal to be very careful and diligent in his duties, visit his sentries often and to "relieve them duely, and not to suffer them to stand too long, especially in cold weather."[37]

Furthermore, the password that the corporal received from the sergeant major must be imprinted on his memory. The corporal was also "to distribute powder, bullets, and match out [to] his squadron . . . and not suffer the holy name of God to be prophaned, or taken in vaine upon his guard."[38]

THE LANCE CORPORAL

Eventually, as had the sergeant, the corporal in turn acquired a soldier to assist him in accomplishing his numerous tasks. The new rank was that of "lance corporal," whose origins, according to one authority, date from the reign of Francis I, a sixteenth-century king of France. When Francis established a territorial militia for his kingdom, he also created in each company a rank specifically reserved for the younger members of the local gentry. This rank was also known as the *lancepesadas*, a term derived from the Italian expression meaning a broken spear or lance. When one of these gentlemen happened to break his lance on his enemy and lose his horse in battle, he was "entertained" under the name of "broken-lance" by "a Captain of a foot-company as his Camerade, till he was again mounted."[39]

THE MILITARY SPECIALISTS

As early as 1591 several specialists with rank somewhat equivalent to that of the sergeant and corporal also began to make their appearance in military formations. Among them were the forage master, the carriage or wagon masters, the quartermaster, and the muster master. In addition, there were with each company of foot two drummers who served as the commander's basic means of communication in garrison as well as on the battlefield. Because of their importance they were usually lodged next to the sergeants. Among their duties were "to parlie with the enemy, to summon their fortes or townes, to redeeme and conduct prisoners, and divers other messages." And so important were their signal codes that if they by misfortune fell into enemy hands, they were to allow "no gyfte, no faire speeches, neither force nor terror [to] cause them to betray any secrets known to them."[40]

Seven years later an even longer roster of specialists was to be found within European armies. These were artillery carters, engineers, carpenters, smiths, founders, armorers, mariners, caulkers, pioneers, and laborers. The latter two groups formed the corps of field engineers whose main duties were to build fortifications or conduct sieges (digging trenches and preparing demolitions). These engineers were placed under the charge of a captain, and during combat soldiers were detailed to protect them from the enemy while they went about their tasks. Artillery was under the supervision of the master of ordnance, and in turn a master gunner was in charge of the guncrews.[41]

During the Thirty Years' War, in addition to the foregoing, there were to be found in Wallenstein's army, among others, such specialists as the *Proviantmeister* (supply sergeant), *Wagenmeister* (sergeant in charge of transport), *Feldschreiber* (a type of field clerk), *Gerichtsschreiber* (clerk for courts martial), *Gerichtsfeldwebel* (sergeant of the courts-martial), and a *Hurenweibel* (a sergeant in charge of the train of camp followers and their offspring—many of these camp followers were whores or unmarried women attached to individual soldiers for protection and care).[42]

THE SERGEANT MAJOR

In addition to the sergeant, corporal, lance corporal, and various specialists, there developed during the sixteenth century another, somewhat ambiguous rank: that of sergeant major. Ambiguous, because in some respects he can be regarded either as the ancestor of the present-day sergeant major, or the predecessor of what became the chief of staff or possibly the operations officer in a military unit. In any case, by the sixteenth century his had become a key position in the army.

The office of the sergeant major had its origins in the fifteenth century. From the beginning, the sergeant major had direct supervision over all the sergeants in the regiment. They were to report to him daily to receive from him the password and other orders for transmittal to the other company officers. The regimental sergeants major were sometimes referred to as the three "corporals of the field," although their duties in no way corresponded to those of the corporals in command of their "camaradas." However, the sergeant major of the army exercised authority over the sergeants major of the regiment. This officer was sometimes called *le sergent de bataille* or *le maréchal* by the French, while the English sometimes referred to him as the "Great Corporal of the Field."[43]

The regimental sergeants major, observed one writer, "receive [their] orders from the Lord Generall himself, or the Lord Marschal, but not commonly from the Sergeant Major General." This would indicate that the regimental sergeant major was indeed a senior officer of the army and therefore cannot be regarded as the predecessor of the modern sergeant major. Yet the duties assigned him by sixteenth- and seventeenth-century writers suggest duties somewhat similar to those of a modern command sergeant major, or possibly an operations officer in a twentieth-century army. The regimental sergeant major was to see to the regimental organization for the march to determine "how many regiments [battalions] of foot and horse are to march under it, and with what ordnance and baggage." And as the troops entered the line of battle, he was responsible for showing them their places and for passing on to them from the sergeant-major general his orders for their positions on the march. In the absence of the sergeant-major general it was his responsibility to see that the order of march and forming for battle was correctly observed. The three brigade sergeants major were under the command of the colonel or general or brigade commander.[44]

The sergeant major also had oversight of logistical matters, for if he "shall find any want of powder, munition or victualls" in any formation of the brigade or regiment, he was to inform the sergeant-major general and, at his orders, draw the necessary ammunition or supplies and see them distributed equally among the companies.[45]

For some contemporaries the man selected for this rank "ought to be a valiant man, an old Soldier, and one that is well experienced in the way of his profession." Others wanted him selected by the general of the army from lists submitted by the colonels on the basis of one per regiment.[46]

The regimental sergeant major took "his orders and commands either immediately from the Generall . . . or from the Marshall, or the Sarjant Major Generall, whether the Regiment be to march in the Avandgard, Battle or Reer." Moreover, a good sergeant major had to have some knowledge "of how the Countrie lies, [in] which the Army is to march."

In the presence of his colonel or his lieutenant colonel, the sergeant major was to act as an assistant to them in overseeing the execution of all orders; in their absence, he had the same authority as the colonel or his lieutenant colonel. This latter point suggests that the sergeant major's role was more analogous to that of a modern chief of staff or operations officer. Some support for this is to be found in the observations of a seventeenth-century writer that once the regiment had been drawn up in divisions, the sergeant major was to give the captains their places, each according to his seniority, "and withall commands the Drum Majour and the other Drummers to beat March, and to move all at an instant." He was also to see that the soldiers kept their ranks on the march and did not straggle. Also while on the march, he was "to keepe as neere the midest of the Regiment as he can" to best observe the order and discipline of its marching and deployment for battle.[47]

Every morning the evening the sergeant major was to report to the sergeant-major general of the army or to the sergeant major of the brigade "to receive the [pass-] Word and orders from him," and pass them on to his colonel or lieutenant colonel and to the sergeants of each company in the regiment.

Even so, the tireless sergeant major's task was not completed with delivering the general's instructions to all the officers of the regiment for

> every night he is to visite all the guards of that regiment, and to keep duely the turnes of their watches, and marches (that one Captain or Company may not do more duty than another) as also in sending out Troupes upon service, to the end that both the honor and labor may be equally divided.

In sum, the sixteenth- and seventeenth-century concepts of the sergeant major's role and status suggest that he was not a commander of troops so much as an agent, or staff officer of the commander, one who saw to it that all the details having to do with the day-to-day administration of a military unit were taken care of for the commander. This suggests the duties of a modern sergeant major.

On the other hand, Johann von Wallhausen, writing about French military practice, believed that the sergeant major ought to be chosen only from among the older and finer-appearing captains. He should, above all, be alert and industrious. For that reason, von Wallhausen declared he ought to be about middle age—forty-five years old. He should not be given a company to command or be placed among the company commanders, for his duties would not allow that. Instead, he should occupy a position within the regiment as the colonel's deputy. As such, the lieutenants, ensigns, and sergeants of the companies should be subordinate to him and, if necessary, he should also be able to remind the captains of their duties.[48]

As mentioned above, for the English and the French there was yet a higher grade of sergeant major, respectively dubbed as the sergeant major of the army or *maréchal de bataille*. Despite these different terms they described essentially the same office. The regimental sergeants major were under his supervision. He in turn was to take his orders from "the Lord Generall or Marshall . . . for all watches and Guards that are to be placed, and upon the change of quarters or a remove he is to march with the Lord generall or Marshall in the Avantgard." After seeing the troops settled, he was to visit them and give orders to the three sergeants major or "grand corporals of the field." Afterward, whether he went himself or sent some other "chiefe officer of the field" to inspect the troops, he was to inform the lord general or marshal of any discrepancies himself.[49]

Like the regimental sergeant major, the sergeant major of the army seemed not to have had a counterpart in the armies of antiquity. Although military writers of the sixteenth century were familiar with fourth century (A.D. 388–391) writings of the Roman military historian Flavius Vegetius' *De Re Militari*, their interest in it was essentially antiquarian.[50] In the Roman legion the officer whose duties most nearly resembled those of the sergeant major in the sixteenth century was the chief overseer of the camp, whom Vegetius describes as not being "an officer of great authority." Rather, he was an experienced soldier selected for the position because of his ability to teach others how to set up camp, build fortifications, and organize baggage trains.[51]

THE ENGLISH MILITIA

Since the traditions and practices of the English county militia, rather than those of the standing army, were first transplanted to the English colonies of North America, it is useful to examine them here. Eventually the military policy of the new republic that was to rise across the Atlantic grew largely out of this tradition, more than from that of the highly professional standing armies of Europe.

By the time the Stuart kings turned their attention to the improvement of training and organization of the county militia in the early seventeenth century, the roles and functions of what became the noncommissioned officers—the sergeant major, sergeant, corporal, and lance corporal—had been rather well defined. The experience of the western division of the Northamptonshire county militia helps give a picture of organization and training of county militia units. Numbering 103 men, in addition to the captain the militia company also included one lieutenant, an ensign, two sergeants, and five corporals. However, since the annual militia muster lasted only three days, unit training left much to be desired. This situation so concerned Charles I that shortly after he ascended the throne in 1625 he took steps to improve the training of county militia. To train the raw levies, the king brought veteran sergeants over from the English expeditionary force stationed in the Netherlands—likely the first example in history of what modern soldiers call reserve component duty. Eighty-four of these sergeants were distributed among the counties by twos or fours, depending on the size and number of the units to be trained.

Going from company to company, these sergeants trained both officer and noncommissioned officers in the drill and maneuver of their troops. Originally the Crown planned that these sergeant-instructors were to remain in England for only three months, but some continued on duty until 1629. Thereafter, the king required of the county militia regular periods of drill to be held throughout the year. These drills were performed under the supervision of professional soldiers such as the sergeants. Thus, professional traditions and standards were eventually merged with those of the militia, a pattern repeated in the colonies.[52]

After the Stuart Restoration in 1660, the Crown took another step toward the improvement of the military system: the organization of a national, or country-wide militia. The lord lieutenants of the counties retained their authority to call out the militia and to arm, equip, and organize the troops, but the Crown acquired a larger measure of control by selecting as commissioned and noncommissioned officers those who were then serving or had served with the standing or regular army. Specifically sergeants were to be appointed only from among men who had served in the regular forces for at least one year. This requirement, however, was later modified to substitute a year's service in the militia for service in the regular army.[53]

The sergeant's continuing importance was commented upon by an eighteenth-century writer on military organization, observing that "the sergeants, even in regular regiments, are of the utmost use and importance, but in the militia [they] constitute the muscles and sinews of the corps." Although the ratio of sergeants to enlisted men in militia units was one to twenty—higher than in the regular service—the writer thought that the ratio should be further increased "by the diminution of some of the higher commissioned officers," thereby echoing the sentiments of a military writer some two hundred years earlier concerning the key position occupied by the sergeants.[54]

This position was likewise echoed on the Continent by no less an authority than the Marshal Hermann Maurice Comte de Saxe, who had led the French armies during the War of the Austrian Succession (1740–1748). The marshal declared that the noncommissioned officer was the one "on whome the excellence of the infantry totally depends."[55]

By the end of the seventeenth century, officers, selected by the sovereign from among noble families, had become a reflection of the aristocracy in England and throughout most of Europe. Standing between this officer class and the common soldiers were the sergeant and his assistant, the corporal, who became a sort of middle class in the command structure of all Western armies, both professional and militia. Over a period of four hundred years the feudal office of sergeanty had been transformed from one of obligation to a feudal monarch in the form of either military or civil service in exchange for land tenancy into a military caste with well-defined status, role, and titles. It was toward the end of this period that the militia of the British North American colonies adopted those military traditions and titles that had crossed the Atlantic with the first colonists and the British armed forces.

Unlike the hierarchical society of old Europe, however, the new society emerging between the coast and the Appalachian Mountains of North America lacked an hereditary and privileged landed aristocracy from which the commissioned officers of Britain and Europe were being increasingly drawn. Furthermore, the New World's vast lands and resources awaiting settlement and exploitation offered a promise of upward mobility unknown to old Europe's more structured society since the sixteenth century. While in no way blurring the manifest distinctions between commissioned and noncommissioned officers in the Continental Army formed in 1775, these conditions would help to shape in that army a noncommissioned officer corps somewhat different from that which developed in British and European armies.

Noteworthy in the writings described earlier in this chapter are the high standards set for noncommissioned officers. These standards called for skilled, brave, and humane teachers and leaders of men placed in their charge. The callous brutes occasionally portrayed in popular literature were generally exceptions to an ideal that remained alive throughout the military history of both Europe and America.

CHAPTER 2

BUILDING ON THESE BEGINNINGS 1775–1785

Before 1775 the nascent military institutions of England's North American colonies had been essentially those of Great Britain. Probably the earliest example of a formal, written authority or commission from the Crown to raise and command troops in time of emergency was that granted to the commanders of militia units raised in 1609. As was the custom with military commanders so commissioned, they selected men to assist them in carrying out their tasks. These were officers and noncommissioned officers in a very real sense. Since that time the terminology "officers and men" has been the expression used in North America to distinguish between the status layers of the military hierarchy that was eventually to develop into the army of the United States. As late as the 1950s a well-known student of military organization observed that the enlisted men "are a part of the organization bureaucracy but not of the professional bureaucracy, for their's a trade, not a profession."[1]

THE ENGLISH TRADITION

In the second half of the eighteenth century two military traditions emerged and formed the foundations of the United States Army. These were the English militia tradition and the Prussian military tradition. The first, though of only limited success in England, traced its origins to the post-Restoration Militia Acts of 1661, 1662, and 1663. Limited in military effectiveness, the militia, based on this legislation, performed only as an amateur political police and riot-control force. This fact and the continued perceived military threats from abroad eventually caused the British to place their primary reliance upon a standing army instead of a national militia, maintained in peace as well as wartime.[2] Moreover, the county militia in England had a troubled history, virtually collapsing during the 1630s, when the American colonies were being established.

Nevertheless, the British took steps to improve their militia rather than abandon it altogether. In 1757 Parliament enacted the Militia Act, which replaced the earlier militia system and set up a new one in its place. Each county was required to support the militia out of taxes raised locally and to raise a fixed quota of men by compulsory ballot. The well-to-do, however, could hire men to substitute for them, thus compromising the universal personal obligation embodied in the legislation.[3]

The act had established property qualifications for commissioned officers, so therefore control passed out of the hands of the great landowners into those of the county squirearchy. In a sense, a similar qualification already existed for the standing army through the purchase system, which gave an officer property rights to his commission. Since the mid-seventeenth century the political expedient of entrusting command of the army to men of some established position in society—that is, men of property—had been widely accepted by politicians of all shades, including the leaders of the militia. The propertied classes regarded this practice as providing a degree of protection from an abuse of authority by the Crown. And when the colonists of British North America turned to the task of establishing their own army, they too accepted this principle as providing protection from abuse by a central authority. This meant that in both the provincial militia and later the Continental Army commissioned rank went almost exclusively to men of property, while men of more modest means filled the enlisted ranks.[4]

This militia system and the principles upon which it rested accompanied the British colonists to North America, where it was unevenly established within the several provinces. The system's training and organizational elements were embodied in a manual published in 1759 and entitled *A Plan of Discipline for the Militia of the County of Norfolk*, a treatise in wide use, especially in the New England provinces.[5] Together with another treatise on militia training, the so-called *Manual of 1764*, popularly called "the *Sixty-Four*," these publications laid the groundwork for the militia training within the American colonies prior to the War of Independence.[6]

It is to the pages of these manuals, especially that of the Norfolk County militia, that we must turn to determine the role and status of the noncommissioned officers at that period. As befitting the tactics of the time, much of this book was devoted to the manual of arms required for the men to deliver a relatively high volume of fire on command. Such training, of course, was largely in the hands of experienced noncommissioned officers.

Spaniards had been the first to originate the manual exercise of firing by command. The French, in turn, had adopted the Spanish drill with muskets. However, the practice of firing by platoons appears to have been an innovation of the great Dutch commander Prince Maurice of Orange. This too was adopted by the French and, in turn, by the English. Initially, when troops used heavy muskets with matchlocks, the manual of arms had been conducted in open order with a three-foot interval between each soldier. But when the matchlocks became obsolete and the much lighter firelocks came into use, the ranks closed up. This enabled Frederick the Great of Prussia to modify the old manual so that his troops, drawn up in three ranks, could fire in close order at the rate of five to six times per minute. The English, though much impressed by the Frederician drill, nevertheless modified it to suit the peculiar requirements of their militia units "to teach men who are, in general, incapable of much attention, entirely unused to arms, awkward, and many of them grown stiff with age and hard labor; and with but a very few days on a year allowed . . . for that purpose [training]."[7]*

In English militia units the officers, almost all of whom were country gentlemen, carried—as did the private soldiers—the flintlock or fusee, as it was known. The sergeants, whose duties had changed little since Prince Maurice's day, were armed with the halberd. Since the sixteenth century, this weapon had become primarily a badge or symbol of the sergeant's authority as well as a means of holding troops in ranks under fire. Only occasionally was the halberd employed as a weapon and then in a manner similar to the bayonet. Otherwise, the manual of arms prescribed for the weapon was similar to that for the flintlock. For example, the Norfolk manual prescribed that "when the officers stand with their fusees ordered, the sergeants are to order their halberts [*sic*]. When the officers carry their fusees on their right arm, the sergeant were to carry the halberts [*sic*] advanced. When the officers carry their fusees in the right hand, the sergeants are to carry their halberts [*sic*] clubbed, taking their cue from the officers."

Counsel given officers by the Norfolk manual suggests that they, rather than the noncommissioned officers, many of whom would be inexperienced men in a militia unit, had to bear a major portion of the burden of teaching the raw recruits the manual of arms. Townshend began his manual with the following advice:

> We must recommend to all gentlemen, who intend to act as militia officers, to arm themselves with a great deal of patience, as they must expect to find many of the countrymen infinitely awkward and stiff; especially those who are turned of thirty years of age, and have been used to very hard labor.

Townshend went on to point out that the militia officer could expect to encounter men with "a great want of apprehension and memory, and an amazing difficulty of understanding," and others, "lazy, careless," and inattentive. The only way to overcome these difficulties, the manual advised, "is to be cool and sedate, and to teach the men *with great good nature and gentleness*; and at the same time however, keeping up such a kind of deportment and behaviour, as will shew them that they are under the command of a superior, and inspire them with respect."

From this it is clear that the Norfolk manual, as was later to be the case with General von Steuben's drill regulations, envisioned officers as the initial drill instructors. Eventually the noncommissioned officers took over these tasks. Officers led the platoons and saw that the files were closed and the ranks dressed, while

*The introduction of artillery onto the battlefield and the distribution of small-caliber field pieces among the infantry was one of the main causes of the adoption of linear tactics, eventually in three ranks, with the cavalry covering the flanks.

the sergeants looked to the flanks in all wheeling movements and saw that the rear ranks kept closed up to the front. Also "they must halt at once with their platoon, and step off with their feet together with them."

Then as now, the sergeants were to prepare their units for inspection by the commanding officers, for "as soon as the sergeants have seen, that the men are properly dressed and accoutered, they are to draw them up in a single rank, divided into three equal parts or divisions." These they were to present to the officers to inspect, "to see that the serjeants have done their duty." Following the inspection, "the serjeants are to post themselves on the right of the front rank, in a line with the men; the corporals are to be posted on the right of the front and rear ranks. . . ."

The Norfolk plan provided a simple organizational structure for militia units and their drill, including firing exercises, that enabled militia to engage in battle according to eighteenth-century practice. Yet when the time came to organize the Continental Army, the widely varying adaptations by the several colonial militias of earlier principles and practices, made it difficult to identify precisely the influence of the Norfolk Plan in the army as organized in 1778.

THE STANDING ARMY

In any case, there were other influences at work—among them those of the British regular forces. Many colonists, both officers and men, served on occasion under such British commanders as, for example, Major General James Wolfe, whose instructions to young officers, as well as his orders as commander, are illustrative of this influence.[8] Because of the relatively frequent turnover of personnel in the British army—compared with other European armies—commanders like Wolfe were frequently forced to employ their junior officers instead of noncommissioned officers in recruit training. Until competent noncommissioned officers had been developed, Wolfe required his younger officers "to make themselves perfect masters of the exercise of the firelock, that they may be able to assist in training the young soldiers in arms . . . and one of the subaltern officers was to be constantly with the recruits when they exercise, to see that they are properly instructed." This suggests that even after capable noncommissioned officers had been selected, they were closely supervised by the company officers.[9]

When Wolfe had experienced noncommissioned officers he expected them to assume full responsibility for their detachments. They were, in Wolfe's words, "to be answerable for the behavior of [their] men . . . and if [they] failed or neglected to confine or punish such as are guilty of crimes . . . [they] will be punished for suffering such irregularities." Sergeants commanded detachments numbering from ten to twenty men, and subalterns commanded detachments larger than twenty but fewer than thirty. As the number of men doubled, the number of officers was to be doubled: a captain commanded fifty to a hundred men, but for any number over a hundred, he was to be assisted by three subalterns and five sergeants.

Then as now, the sergeant also had numerous administrative duties. Sergeants of companies (presumably a type of first sergeant), made out all discharge papers, furloughs, and passes. Company sergeants also checked their men periodically for broken or missing equipment, kept a record of losses, and submitted regular reports to the company commander. Both sergeants and corporals were "to give account in writing to the commanding officers of their companies the manner in which the different squads mess, the number that eats together, the houses where they diet, whether in their quarters or out, specifying the persons' names that entertain such soldiers as do not eat in their quarters." The sergeants also inspected the troop quarters daily. But apparently as a double-check, Wolfe required that his subalterns also inspect the troops' quarters daily, between nine and eleven P.M., "not always trusting to the reports of the sergeants." Moreover, the battalion or regimental adjutants selected "three or four good sergeants that can write well" to serve as orderly sergeants and as messengers.

Furthermore, noncommissioned officers always wore their side arms: sergeants their short swords and corporals their bayonets. They were to have their other weapons within reach, the sergeants their halberds, the corporals their firelocks and ammunition. And, so as not to hinder their movements or cover their sidearms, noncommissioned officers were "not to put on their great coats between troop beating [reveille] and tattoo, unless the weather should be remarkably bad."

These symbols of authority notwithstanding, Wolfe cautioned his noncommissioned officers not "to presume to excuse any man from the review [exercise] . . . or to take upon himself an authority that does not belong to him." Corporals were urged to be careful "to warn the men for exercise, and all other duties." For the corporal who failed to do so "shall be broken."

One of the noncommissioned officer's most important duties was the guard. Here they continued to play the key role as they had for centuries. The regimental guard consisted of one sergeant, two corporals, one drummer, and thirty men. The sergeant of the guard was "responsible for return of arms and accouterments." And as with a negligent corporal "any sergeant in the officer's absence that suffers [allows] neglect of duty will be broke." Moreover, the good noncommissioned officer had the full support of his commanding officer, for Wolfe ordered that "any soldier who insults a noncommissioned officer, either in barracks or upon duty shall be put into the dungeon in irons, until he be sufficiently convinced that modesty, sobriety, and obedience become the character of a soldier."

General Wolfe, like most great commanders before him, fully appreciated the importance of excellent noncommissioned officers. He urged his regimental and company commanders to use great care in their selection. His commanders were "to find out and distinguish the men who have the best capacities, and are most diligent and obedient, that the Regiment may be supplied with able sergeants and corporals . . . for by this means the corps will be constantly furnished with good noncommissioned officers, upon which the discipline of it does in a great measure depend."

In battle the sergeant, in General Wolfe's words, was to be the commissioned officer's substitute and as such was expected to take command of the unit if his commander fell. So strongly did Wolfe feel on this point that he directed that if the sergeant "does not take upon him the immediate command in case the officer falls, such serjeant will be tried for his life as soon as a courtmartial can be conveniently assembled."

Before the battle was joined, and as the regiment or battalion approached the enemy, Wolfe saw the sergeant essentially as a file closer. In Wolfe's words, "the officer in command of a platoon is to be at the head of his men, looking frequently back upon them to see that they are in order, the serjeant, in the meanwhile, taking his place in the interval." At the battalion commander's signal, just before the battle was to begin, the officers moved to the flanks of the platoons where, armed with flintlocks, they could join the battle. The sergeants, in the rear of the platoons, together with the lieutenants and ensigns, were "to complete the files, keep the men in their duty, and to supply the places of the officers or serjeants that may be killed or dangerously wounded." Bringing up the rear also enabled the sergeant to check straggling. Wolfe ordered that if a soldier quit his rank or attempted to flee, he "is to be instantly put to death by the officer that commands that platoon, or by the officer or serjeant in the rear of that platoon." While there remained an officer or noncommissioned officer left alive to command, Wolfe added, "no man is to abandon his colours."

COLONIAL ADAPTATION

General Wolfe's orders and practices were not unfamiliar to British colonists in North America, because during the Anglo-French wars of the mid-eighteenth century, volunteers and militiamen raised among the Atlantic provinces of the empire served alongside regular army units. Some three thousand volunteers from the colonies fought under British command in the disastrous expedition of 1739 against Cartagena, the main Spanish port in Colombia. A combined force of British regulars and colonials captured the French fort at Port Royal, Nova Scotia, in 1710, and in 1745, a Massachusetts-sponsored expedition of colonials captured the French fortress of Louisbourg, on Cape Breton Island. Ten years later, Virginia militiamen marched and fought alongside regulars during General Braddock's ill-fated expedition to Ft. Duquesne.

From these shared battle experiences officers and noncommissioned officers of the militia and volunteer units gained some familiarity with British practice and tradition and came to look upon them as models of organization and discipline. Consequently, George Washington, both as a colonel in the Virginia provincials and later as general of the Continental Army, initially looked to British standards as models for the improvement of training and discipline for the forces under his command.[10]

Not only were the standards of the British regulars admired but those of the

British county militia were held in high esteem by officers of the Continental Army as well. "The American States should," General Nathaniel Green wrote in December 1776, "establish their Militia upon the British plan; they would be a much better body of troops. . . . [A] militia upon the British establishment are a respectable body of troops, and afford a great internal security to the State. They are subject to such a degree of discipline and order as renders them formidable."[11]

Officers of the pre-revolutionary colonial militia usually had read such treatises as Humphrey Bland's *Treatise on Military Discipline*.[12] A copy of this book was in Washington's private library. First published in 1772, Bland's treatise was considered the leading English tactical manual of the day. Read in the southern and middle colonies, it was used in the training of the local militia of Henrico County, Virginia, as well as the city of Philadelphia. But in the northern colonies, Townshend's 1759 *A Plan of Discipline* was used.[13]

These books agreed upon the importance of able noncommissioned officers in upholding the discipline of military formations. While serving with the Virginia provincials at Ft. Cumberland in September 1755, then-Colonel Washington recognized this by the care he exercised over the selection of noncommissioned officers for newly formed militia companies. He instructed his company commanders to recommend only "such men of their companies as they think fit for Sergeants and corporals for the new companies." He added that none of the officers should recommend any but "such as they can vouch for their behaviour."[14]

Militia training in the northern colonies, unlike that in the plantation-dominated South, was somewhat tempered by the fact that distinctions between officers and men did not prevail in the rural militia of New England (as they did in much of the South) due in part to the levelling influence of numerous small property owners.[15] In the North, the private soldier's company officers and noncommissioned officers were "not infrequently his intimate friends or even his social inferiors, men who had devoted their time to the local militia organization and had become familiar with drill and tactics, while he, perhaps was busy with other matters." Moreover, it was not uncommon for regimental or company officers to give their sons or younger brothers noncommissioned rank. In other instances, companies elected their own officers and noncommissioned officers.[16]

It is therefore not to be wondered that New Englanders, especially in the first years of the War of Independence, placed an inordinate amount of faith in the invincibility of their militia and came to rely too confidently upon raw and undisciplined levies whose sole qualification for a soldier's calling was their patriotism.[17]

This rather naïve faith in the citizen soldier was not shared by General Washington who, when he took command of the army from General Artemus Ward in 1775, soon brushed aside the egalitarian structure of the New England militia tradition and instead imposed upon the new army the standards of the British regulars. Henceforth there was to be a greater distinction between officers and men even in the militia units of the New England provinces; "everyone knew his place and kept it on pain of receiving thirty to forty lashes."[18] In the minds of Washington and his generals the precepts of Wolfe and the British regular army took precedence over those of the Norfolk discipline.

Both as a colonel of the Virginia provincials and as Major General Braddock's aide-de-camp, Washington followed the British practice of enforcing different disciplinary codes for officers and enlisted men. For example, in an order of the day published on May 1, 1756, at Winchester, Virginia, he cautioned his command against permitting recruiting irregularities by warning that "any commissioned officer who stands by and sees irregularities committed and does not endeavour to quell them shall be immediately put under arrest. Any noncommissioned officer, present, who does not interpose shall be immediately reduced and receive corporal punishment."[19] Corporal punishment for enlisted men but not for officers was a manifest expression of aristocratic privilege then prevailing in European armies.

In August of that same year, Colonel Washington, in terms Wolfe would have approved, made clear just what he expected of his noncommissioned officers. They were expected to be "diligent in their Duty: Those who are found to be the least remiss, will be punished. They are also to answer for the misbehaviour of the men under their command." And, lest any man be tempted to malinger, the same order directed the sergeant major "to receive the names of the absent and sick men; to search after the first and conduct the latter to the Hospital, to be examined by the Doctor; who is ordered to receive and enter the name of none without just cause; nor entertain any longer than the nature of the Disorder requires."[20]

Although Washington had high regard for the importance of the sergeant in a military unit, he shared with Wolfe and other officers of his time a certain distrust of noncommissioned officers' ability to carry out their tasks without careful supervision by commissioned officers. He instructed his company commanders to "divide [their] men into as many squads as there are sergeants, and make it the duty of each sergeant (who is to keep the Roll of their necessaries for that purpose) to see that the men of his squad have their clothes, arms, and accouterments always together, and in good order. This method I recommend as an alleviation of *but not an excuse for the officers to neglect this duty themselves* [emphasis added]."[21]

As volunteer units flocked to join Washington's army at Cambridge in the spring of 1775, some of his generals such as Charles Lee and Horatio Gates, who had seen service as officers with the British regular forces, attempted with varying degrees of success to develop out of these disparate elements "an American regular army essentially in the image of the British regulars."[22] Part of this effort involved the establishment of standard tables of organization for the Continental Army and the variegated volunteer units assembled in Cambridge. At that time all units had the same company enlisted grades—sergeants, corporals, musicians, and privates. However, there were no provisions for noncommissioned officers on the battalion or regimental staffs. During the remainder of the year, Washington and his staff developed a standard table of organization for the infantry regiment modeled on that of the British army. To each regimental or battalion headquarters was added a noncommissioned element, including a sergeant major, a quartermaster sergeant, a drum major, and a fife major, all appointed by the regimental commander. Each regiment had a headquarters staff and commanded eight companies. In turn, each company had eight noncommissioned officers—four sergeants and four corporals as well as two musicians (drummers or fifers) and seventy-six privates.[23]

Throughout the Continental Army's history, however, there were chronic shortages of personnel, especially among experienced noncommissioned officers. Consequently, the tables of organization were adjusted from time to time to match the availability of personnel. For example, during the winter of 1778–1779, the enlisted strength of each company was reduced to three sergeants, three corporals, two musicians, and fifty-three privates. But in January 1781, the number of sergeants was increased to five in each company and the number of privates to sixty-eight.

The organization and enlisted strength of the artillery and cavalry units varied somewhat from the infantry regiments that made up the major part of the army. Taken into service in the summer of 1775, the Massachusetts regiment of artillery set the pattern for artillery units. In each of its ten authorized companies (the term "battery" had not yet been adopted) there were, as with the infantry regiment, four sergeants and four corporals, but to this were added specialists enjoying noncommissioned status—six gunners and six bombardiers. Thirty-two matrosses, or privates of artillery, made up the rest of the company enlisted strength. Later in the year, when the regimental strength was increased to twelve companies, two musicians (a drummer and a fifer) were added to each company. In 1778 the artillery regimental headquarters acquired the same noncommissioned staff as the infantry regiment, while the noncommissioned strength of each company was increased to six sergeants and six corporals. The number of privates was increased to fifty-six. Three years later, however, each of the artillery regiments was reduced by three companies, and the enlisted strength of each was also reduced from eighty-two to fifty-six, with a proportionate reduction in the noncommissioned grades.[24]

The cavalry regiment as organized in 1777 had a regimental enlisted staff that included two specialists—a saddler and a trumpet major—but no sergeant major or quartermaster sergeant. Each company (the term "troop" would not be adopted until after the Civil War), however, had one quartermaster sergeant, one drill or staff sergeant, one trumpeter, one blacksmith, four corporals, and thirty-two dragoons, or privates. In the reorganization of 1778–1779, one sergeant and one corporal as well as twenty-two dragoons were added to each company. The number of noncommissioned officers remained unchanged when six more privates were added to each company in 1781.

As noted earlier, when Washington assumed command of the Continental Army he sought to apply the same strict disciplinary measures that he had observed among the British regulars and had earlier employed in the Virginia provincials. When, for example, a Sergeant James Finley was found guilty by a general court-martial for "expressing himself disrespectfully of the Continental Association and drinking General Gage's [a British commander] health," the court sentenced him to "be deprived of his Arms and Accouterments, put in a Horse Cart, with a rope around his neck and drum'd out of the Army and rendered forever incapable of serving in the continental Army." Throughout the war corporal punishment, usually flogging with the cat-o'-nine-tails, reduction to the ranks in the case of noncommissioned officers, and on rare occasions, execution, were widely employed with offenders against the good order and discipline of the Continental Army.[25]

THE SOLDIER'S PAY

Washington's concern for the behavior and discipline of noncommissioned officers was matched by concern for their pay, a factor that had a profound influence on both. On October 31, 1775, Washington issued a general order listing pay due the several noncommissioned grades of the Continental Army. Each noncommissioned officer and soldier was "to be paid by the Kalender [*sic*] Month, at the present rates; to wit—48 shillings to the sergeants, 44 to the corporals, drums and fifes, and 40 to the privates, which pay it is expected will be regularly distributed every Month." From this each soldier was expected "to pay for his Cloathing, which will be laid in for him, upon the best terms it can be bought; to do which, a Stoppage (deduction from pay) of 10 Shillings a month will be made, until the Cloathing is paid for." Not only was each man to pay for his own clothing, but he was to "furnish his own Arms (and good ones)." If he were unable to do so, arms were found for him for which "he is to allow 6 Shillings for the use thereof during the Campaign." Each soldier was also allowed two dollars ("continentals") if he brought a good blanket with him, and he was to "have liberty to carry it away at the end of the campaign."[26]*

The following summer, as the army became better organized and more structured, Washington also raised with the Continental Congress's Board of War and Ordnance (the lineal ancestor of the War Department) the question of providing extra pay for such specialists as the drum and fife majors, as well as the sergeants major and quartermaster sergeants. The latter two grades were only partially compensated for their additional responsibilities by exemption from "common duties," but this was not the case with the drum and fife majors. Although their duties set them apart from the common soldiers, and they were regarded somewhat as noncommissioned officers, they lacked any command status and, of course, enjoyed no extra pay. The commander in chief therefore proposed "that additional allowance of a dollar per month should be made to their several pays as now estab-

*It is virtually impossible to calculate the true value of the shilling or Continental dollar at that time, as inflation rapidly eroded the value of both throughout the Revolution. The figures given are of value only to compare the pay of one rank with that of another.

lished, as a sufficient compensation and satisfaction for any extraordinary trouble attending their offices."[27]

The Continental Congress readily agreed to this proposal and on July 25, 1776, declared that "[Congress] in consideration of the Sergeants-Major, Quartermaster-Sergeants, Drum and Fife Majors, not having pay adequate to their service, and hoping that it will excite them to Vigilance and Industry, have pleased to increase the pay for them . . . One Dollar per Month, to commence on the 16th Inst." In spite of congressional action increasing the sergeants major pay, these noncommissioned officers still lacked that authority over their fellow noncommissioned officers enjoyed by their counterparts in the British army. It was not until 1833 that the company first sergeant's pay was increased to a degree commensurate with his responsibilities.[28]

NONCOMMISSIONED OFFICER INSIGNIA

Early in the new army's history there also arose the problem of selecting identifying insignia for the noncommissioned officers. As late as July 1775, the Continental Army was without standard, army-wide uniforms. This made it very difficult to distinguish commissioned from noncommissioned officers and the latter from private soldiers. At the commanding general's suggestion, a temporary expedient was adopted: a strip of red cloth for sergeants and a green one for corporals sewn on the right shoulder.[29]

But such was the poverty of the Continental Army that it was not until May 1782 that the Army's quartermaster was instructed "if practicable, to obtain worsted shoulder knots for the noncommissioned officers." The sergeants were to be distinguished by one on each shoulder, the corporals by one on their right. In the meantime, the noncommissioned officers had to make do by substituting a piece of white cloth until the worsted knots became available. The problem was apparently solved by September of that year when a general order noted that the sergeants and corporals were "sufficiently distinguishable by the badges of their respective Grades."[30]

RECRUITING PROBLEMS

When Washington assumed command of the army around Boston in 1775, he found to his delight that many of the men gathered there "were proved soldiers experienced in the French and Indian Wars." Many of these men were substantial New England farmers and artisans. The muster rolls of Connecticut, New York, and Pennsylvania also show a large proportion of married men, who had been among the first to enlist. Confident that from these a competent corps of noncommissioned officers could be drawn, Washington concentrated on selecting officers of the highest quality to lead them.[31]

However, the initial enthusiasm that caused substantial farmers and skilled workmen to flock to the colors early in 1775 soon diminished as prospects of a lengthy war moved many of these to return to their farms and shops. This situation became so rampant by August of that year that General Washington wrote the president of the Council of Massachusetts Bay, "By the general return made to me for last week, I find there are great numbers of soldiers and noncommissioned officers who absent themselves from duty, the greater part of whom, I have reason to believe, are at their respective homes in different parts of the country."[32]

Almost ninety thousand men enlisted in 1776, but by 1781, the yearly number of recruits fell to below thirty thousand. The Continental Congress had no choice but to resort to a draft or quota system, assigning each state a quota of men to be raised for service. In any case, General Washington began to decline offers of volunteers, describing them as "uneasy, impatient of command, ungovernable."[33]

The draft system also failed to provide men of the same quality and enthusiasm as in the early years. Some southern states, to meet their quotas, even compelled criminals to serve, and throughout the states prisoners of war, including Hessians and British as well as Loyalists and some enemy deserters, were also recruited. Although Congress attempted to halt this practice early in the war and ordered the discharge of such men already enlisted, many state authorities simply ignored the order.[34] This situation certainly dampened Washington's hopes of maintaining a competent corps of noncommissioned officers for his army.

Not only the poor quality of recruits but chronic delays, many quite long, in the issue of pay, clothing, and rations plagued the army throughout the war. Inadequate pay, usually in arrears, plagued the Virginia militia. For example, in 1781 it had not been paid for two years. A depreciating currency and deplorable health standards combined to produce an inordinately high desertion rate among the troops. One historian has estimated that at least one third of the Continental Line (regulars) and at least half of the militia enrolled during the war deserted. In the face of such difficulties as well as "fiercely independent spirit among the officers and men," amounting almost to anarchy, "it is surprising that Washington and his generals ever succeeded in creating a battle-worthy arm."[35]

A good deal of the credit for doing so can be given to General Friedrich Wilhelm von Steuben. His appointment in 1778 as the second inspector general of the Army "set on foot great improvements in tactics, regulations, and discipline," and marked a turning point in Washington's efforts to make of the Continental Line a force capable of meeting British regulars on the field of battle.[36]

THE PRUSSIAN TRADITION

With the assignment of Baron von Steuben to General Washington's staff the second of two military traditions—the Prussian—merged with that of the British to help build the foundations of what was to become the United States Army. Steuben brought with him a thorough knowledge of Prussian army regulations and traditions. Although many British officers had also acquired a familiarity with them through their association with the Hessians and other German mercenaries, von Steuben's unique contribution was his ability to adapt these regulations and traditions not only to the temperament and abilities of the human material he had to work with within the Continental Army, but also to graft them successfully onto the body of the English militia tradition as it had evolved in North America.

Most of these traditions can be tracked back to Frederick William I, the soldier-king father of Frederick the Great. They were codified in two documents, one a memorandum prepared for the crown prince by his father's close friend and associate Prince Leopold I of Anhalt-Dessau, and the other Frederick William's own regulations for noncommissioned officers, published in March 1726. The first was known to von Steuben only through its influence on Frederick the Great, who seems to have taken it to heart. The second was well known to every officer and noncommissioned officer in the Prussian service. The old king* placed so much importance on it that he declared that every noncommissioned officer in the Prussian service should carry a sturdy, leather-bound copy with him at all times. If by chance the noncommissioned officer lost his copy, he was reduced to private and sentenced to three years' imprisonment at hard labor.[37]

Prince Leopold's instructions were characterized by an astonishing degree of psychological insight into the difficult art of human relationships. The prince urged upon his royal student humanity and patience with his subordinates extending down to the ranks. The traditional picture of a brutal Prussian corporal beating an awkward soldier with his stick does not emerge from the pages of this memorandum. Prince Leopold urged Frederick to select officers and noncommissioned officers of steadfast and honest character—men not given to excesses in drinking and gambling. Since Leopold had characterized the *Feldwebel*,† the senior noncommissioned officer of the company as *die Mutter der Kompanie* ("the mother of the company"), he regarded sobriety and patience as vital characteristics of a good *Feldwebel* because everything in the company went through his hands. And through him the company commander was informed as to the condition of his men, their state of training, and their morale.[38]

That Frederick as crown prince took this counsel to heart is seen in his own observation that "the love of enlisted men for the service rests essentially upon their dependence on their superiors. Never will a superior be hated whose energy matches *the goodness of his heart* [emphasis added]."[39] This humane ideal was not out of place in the Age of Enlightenment, whose traditions von Steuben shared with Frederick the Great. Throughout much of the eighteenth century the path of advancement in the Prussian service for a noncommissioned officer to commissioned rank lay open not only to nobles but to a few outstanding men from the ranks. Class lines in the Prussian army, tested to its limits by the Seven Years'

*It is of interest to note that Frederick William I was Frederick William von Steuben's godfather.

†The term *Feldwebel* is derived from *Feld Weybel*, or *Feldwaibel (Weib)* or "field woman" in English, hence "mother" of the company.

War, had not stratified in Frederick's day to the extent they would later in the century.

As late as 1726, in his *Regulations for Noncommissioned Officers of Infantry*, Frederick William I, who saw himself as *vornehmster Korporal* ("superior corporal") of his army, declared that "if a noncommissioned officer, who is not a noble, but has great merit and an open mind, as well as good appearance and has served at least twelve years and is not addicted to brandy, he can be recommended for promotion to second lieutenant." This regulation applied to peacetime as well as during war. In Frederick the Great's army a considerable number of noncommissioned officers were promoted under this regulation during the Silesian Wars (1740–1742, 1744–1745) to make up for the heavy losses among the commissioned officers. In the 1760s, however, as Frederick paused to digest his victories, he dismissed almost all of the commissioned officers who had earlier been noncommissioned in an effort to reduce the debts incurred during the wars. Many nobles, among them von Steuben, were also involved in this reduction in force.[40]

Through his service under Frederick the Great, von Steuben was certainly familiar with these traditions and practices and consequently had little difficulty adapting himself to the American environment. His ability to draw upon his fund of experience in the Prussian service helped him immeasurably to instill military discipline in men far removed from the social controls of European society, but without inciting them to mutiny. Tact, humanity, and good humor were personal qualities that, when combined with his military knowledge, made von Steuben an outstanding teacher of men and in his own right, *der vornehmster Korporal* of the Continental Army.

Von Steuben soon realized, however, that unless the rate of personnel turnover, especially among capable noncommissioned officers, could be stabilized, even an enlightened and humane approach to training and discipline such as he envisioned would be insufficient to enable him to develop a disciplined and trained army. "Not a Continental officer, I fear, will be left in the field, if he must every six months become a drill sergeant," he remarked.[41] Washington too echoed this complaint, observing that

> our officers are reduced to the disagreeable necessity of performing the duties of Drill Sergeants to them [the recruits] with this mortifying reflection annexed to the business, that by the time they have taught these men the rudiments of a soldier's duty their service will have expired and the work recommenced with a new set . . . our discipline has been much hurt, if not ruined, by such constant changes.[42]

About the time of von Steuben's appointment, Congress sought in May 1778 to check the turnover rate by promising to pay at the end of the war, $80 to every noncommissioned officer and private soldier "who had enlisted or would enlist during the contest."[43] By war's end, however, Congress's failure to make a distinction between compensation proffered noncommissioned officers and the private soldiers rose to haunt both Congress and the Army. Yet the offer did have an immediately favorable short-term effect. By October 1778, Washington's army had enlisted 14,998 men for the duration of the war, while an additional 12,101 had been enlisted for shorter periods, making a total of 27,099 men under arms. Confident now that he had some prospects of a reasonably stable force with which to work, von Steuben turned his attention to the training of an army capable of meeting and defeating British regulars in battle.[44]

A typical regiment of infantry with which von Steuben had to work included in addition to 30 commissioned officers, a sergeant major, a quartermaster sergeant, 27 sergeants, a drum major, a fife major (these latter two, although without command duties, were considered noncommissioned officers in rank), and 27 corporals. Private soldiers numbered 477, making a total of 585 officers and men in the regiment that, as in the British army, was actually a battalion by today's standards—the two terms being employed interchangeably throughout the eighteenth century.[45]

Until the implementation of von Steuben's general orders in 1778, training doctrine and practice depended largely upon the experience of the commanding officer or the particular military manual consulted by the officer in charge of training. As the Continental Line prepared to enter the decade that culminated in victory, von Steuben's drill manual, or the "Blue Book" as it was popularly known, for the first time gave the American army an armywide standard of training, organization, and tactics. The Blue Book's influence dominated organization and training in the new army until well into the second decade of the nineteenth century.

General von Steuben regarded the company commanders as the initial figures in imparting these teachings to the army; thereafter, the noncommissioned officers took over. Well aware that the conditions of life in British North America had evolved a society less class-conscious than that prevailing in Britain and Europe, von Steuben sought to foster a close and direct bond between officers and men according to the ideals expressed earlier in the century by Leopold of Anhalt-Dessau. Initially, von Steuben preferred the company officers, as had Wolfe, rather than noncommissioned officers, as supervisors of the training of the raw recruits. The inspector general wished to avoid the traditional practice of giving the "awkward squad" to the sergeants for instruction.[46]

Although company officers at first played the key role in recruit training, it is obvious from a reading of von Steuben's regulations that he intended to create a corps of noncommissioned officers with duties and responsibilities similar to those he had observed in the Prussian service. For this reason the new inspector general emphasized "the qualifications of the noncommissioned officers, particularly the one who is proposed for the first sergeant of the company."[47]

"The choice of noncommissioned officers," von Steuben wrote, "is an object of greatest importance: *The order and discipline of a regiment depends so much on their behaviour, that too much care cannot be taken in preferring none to that trust but those who by their merit and good conduct are entitled to it* [emphasis added]." Note the similarity of this sentiment with those expressed by military commentators of the sixteenth and seventeenth centuries. Von Steuben continued:

> Honesty, sobriety, and a remarkable attention to every point of duty with a neatness in their dress, are indispensable requisites; a spirit to command respect and obedience from the men, and expertness in performing every part of the exercise, and an ability to teach it, are also absolutely necessary; nor can a sergeant or corporal be said to be qualified *who does not write and read in a tolerable manner* [emphasis added].[48]

Subject to the inspector general's supervision, the company commander determined the selection of the noncommissioned officers for his unit. He was, in von Steuben's words, "to divide his company into four squads, placing each under the particular care of a noncommissioned officer, who is to be answerable for the dress and behaviour of the men of his squad."[49]

Furthermore, the company commander "must keep a strict eye over the conduct of his noncommissioned officers; oblige them to do their duty with the greatest exactness; and use every possible means to keep up a proper subordination between them and the soldiers; for which reason he, the company commander, must never rudely reprimand them in the presence of the men, but at all times treat them with proper respect."[50]

Von Steuben's regulations also required the company commander to keep what came to be known in army records as a unit "descriptive book," the ancestor of the morning report. In this book were entered the name and description of every noncommissioned officer and soldier of the company; his trade or occupation before entering the army; the place of his birth and usual residence, where, when, and for what term he enlisted; discharges, furloughs, copies of all returns, and every casualty that happens to the company.[51]

Drawing upon long-established Prussian tradition, von Steuben considered the sergeant major as "the head of the regiment's noncommissioned officers." He was never to connive "at the least irregularity committed by them or the soldiers, from both of whom he must exact the most implicit obedience." In a very real sense, the sergeant major was also the regimental adjutant's assistant, similarly acquainted with "the interior management and discipline of the regiment, and the manner of keeping rosters and forming details."[52]

In like manner, the quartermaster sergeant was to be the assistant to the regimental quartermaster and, in the latter's absence, take over his duties; and "when the army marches to see that the tents are properly packed and loaded, and accompany the baggage." Furthermore, while on the march the quartermaster sergeant was to oversee the "wagoners" that they "commit no disorders, and that nothing is lost out of the waggons."[53]

But it was to the company first sergeant, the American equivalent of the Prussian *Feldwebel*, that von Steuben directed most of his attention. This noncommissioned officer, chosen by all the officers of the company, was, as he had been since the seventeenth century, the linchpin of the company. The discipline of the unit, the conduct of the troops, their exactness in obeying orders, and the regularity of their manners "in large measure depend upon his vigilance." The first sergeant, therefore, had to be "intimately acquainted with the character of every soldier of the company, and should take great pains to impress upon their minds the indispensable necessity of the strictest obedience as the foundation of order and regularity." His tasks of maintaining the duty roster in an equitable manner, taking "the daily orders in a book kept by him for that purpose and shew[ing] them to his officers, making the morning report to the captain of the state of the company, in the form prescribed; and at the same time acquaint[ing] him with many things material that may have happened in the company since the preceding report," all closely resembled the duties of a seventeenth-century sergeant,[54] and, one might add, to those of a twentieth-century first sergeant.*

Since the first sergeant was responsible for the entire company, he was, in von Steuben's words, "not to go on any duty, unless with the whole company; but is to be in camp or quarters, to answer any call that may be made." On the march or on the battlefield, the first sergeant was "never to lead a platoon or a section, but is always to be a file closer in the formation of the company, his duty being in the company like the adjutant's in the regiment."[55]

Proper behavior on the part of the noncommissioned officers, as envisioned by von Steuben, bore no similarity to the caricatures in popular literature of the bellowing, bullying sergeant whose very presence strikes terror into the heart of the soldier. Von Steuben's sergeant was cast rather in the humane tradition of Prince Leopold. According to von Steuben, "they [the sergeants] cannot be too circumspect in their behavior toward the men by treating them with mildness, and at the same time obliging every one to do his duty." Continuing on a cautionary note, Steuben wrote that the noncommissioned officers should nevertheless avoid too great familiarity with the men, for thereby "*they* [the N.C.O.s] *will not only gain their love and confidence, but be treated with proper respect; whereas by a contrary conduct they forfeit all regard and their authority becomes despised* [emphasis added]."[56]

The rigid parade-ground formations that eighteenth-century armies took with them into battle fully justified the high standard that von Steuben demanded of his noncommissioned officers. Although the commissioned officers of the company actually led the men into battle, it was the noncommissioned officers, taking "care to keep the ranks and files properly closed" when every human instinct encouraged straggling or caused the men to bunch in terror, who really prevented military formations from deteriorating into armed mobs. When enemy fire, usually at

*The first sergeant also kept the company descriptive book under the captain's supervision. The army maintained these books until about the first decade of the twentieth century, when they were finally replaced by the morning report and other forms used to describe the individual soldier.

ranges of less than two hundred yards, tore gaps in the ranks, it was the noncom who "must exert himself to dress and complete them afresh, with the utmost expedition." Furthermore, "he must keep the greatest silence in ranks [that orders might be heard] see that the men load well and quick, and took good aim." He was moreover to "do all in his power to encourage the soldiers, and use the most vigorous means to prevent any from leaving the ranks, unless wounded."

It is evident from the foregoing that the noncommissioned officer provided the cement that held the long ranks together under fire, which even under eighteenth-century conditions of warfare could be quite devastating.[57]

Von Steuben's vision of the noncommissioned officer in garrison was outlined in a general order that Washington issued to the army at von Steuben's behest. It read:

> Sergeants and corporals are to set example for the men. Delinquent noncommissioned officers are to be reduced to the ranks. We want a clean Camp, clean Cloathes, well-dressed victuals. However deeply involved in rags our army may be we still can do our best to appear decently attentive to our behaviour in these regards.

As if to give particular emphasis to keeping the appearance of rank and file neat, the "noncommissioned officers are to see that they [the men] wash their hands and faces clean every day and oftener when necessary. And if any river is nigh and the season favorable, the men should bathe themselves as frequently as possible."[58]

STATUS AND PRESTIGE FOR NONCOMMISSIONED OFFICERS

Whether or not to award meritorious noncommissioned officers with commissions did not concern von Steuben, but it did Washington, who as commanding general of the army could not escape making decisions on this question. There seems no doubt that Washington and many of his generals believed, as did their counterparts in the English squirearchy, that commissioned officers should be drawn solely from the propertied classes. It was their belief that the liberties of that class could be assured only through its control of the army. Historical experience in England and elsewhere convinced them of this.

Moreover, Washington's concern about achieving professional standards precluded in his mind completely free movement from the ranks to commissioned status. As he wrote to the Board of War and Ordnance in late July 1776, "promotions by succession are not meant to extend to noncommissioned officers further than circumstances of good behaviour and etc. may direct." However, on occasion Washington yielded, albeit reluctantly, to the wishes of his regimental commanders and authorized the promotion of "some old Sergeants worthy of a preference in the nomination for commissions."[59] In approving such promotions, Washington acted, most likely unwittingly, in the tradition of Frederick the Great, who promoted outstanding noncommissioned officers during wartime to commissioned rank.

Yet it was a practice the commander in chief followed with caution and, in so doing, he set the pattern for the United States Army for many years to come. In August 1776, after acting favorably on a recommendation of the Virginia representatives in the Continental Congress to promote eleven sergeants to commissioned rank, Washington added that he was "much adverse to the promotion of noncommissioned to regimental Officers but upon particular merit or extreme necessity, and nothing would make me consent to a further nomination, but a desire to give all the Colonels an equal chance of providing for a few of the most meritorious of their Serjeants."[60]

In addition to Washington's loyalty to the principle that officers be drawn from the propertied classes, there was another pragmatic element in his desire to restrict the practice of promoting meritorious sergeants to commissioned rank. That was a perceived shortage of capable noncommissioned officers in many units, for "in some corps [there was] an insufficiency of noncommissioned officers, in others an improper distribution of them; some companies having more than their complement; others less." He continued:

> Since *the regularity of service greatly depends on having a sufficient number of good noncommissioned officers* . . . where there is an overplus, these ought to be given to those companies which have not their proportion, and their places supplied in the companies from which they are taken, by the same number of private men drawn from those to which they are annexed. By this method one company will not be benefited at the expense of another. But where there is a deficiency in some companies and no excess in others, the former ought to be made good by new appointments [emphasis added].[61]

Fully appreciating the importance of good noncommissioned officers to "the regularity of the service," Washington and von Steuben also recognized the importance of upholding their authority. In his *Regulations*, von Steuben admonished officers never to "rudely reprimand [noncommissioned officers] in the presence of the men, but at all times treat them with proper respect."[62] Moreover, meritorious performance was acknowledged not only by occasional promotion to commissioned rank, but also by distinctive decorations to be worn on the uniform. A noncommissioned officer or soldier who had served honorably for more than three uninterrupted years was to enjoy the right to "wear upon the left sleeve of the uniform coat a narrow angular piece of cloth the color of the regimental facing."[63]

For six years of service, a rarity in the Continental Army, a parallel stripe of the same color could be added. Here is the ancestor of the venerable and well-known "hashmark," or service stripe worn by senior noncommissioned officers and men. Another equally well-known decoration—the Purple Heart—also had its origin about the same time. It was initially called the Badge of Military Merit and awarded for unusually meritorious service—plus an unblemished record—not for wounds. Edged with narrow lace or binding, the Purple Heart, either of silk or cloth, was worn with the coat facing over the left breast. Only three were awarded by Washington—all to Connecticut sergeants.[64]*

Not only was merit and status recognized by additions to the uniform such as decorations and stripes, but noncommissioned rank was also distinguished by equipping the sergeants with a sword. At the time Steuben wrote his *Regulations* noncommissioned officers of other armies were gradually changing from the traditional halberd to a short sword. Consequently, Steuben stipulated that the noncommissioned officers of the American army be armed with the sword as a side arm.[65]†

Unfortunately, an army that could only with the greatest difficulty feed and clothe itself found it difficult to quip noncommissioned officers with swords. Nevertheless, in February 1780, Washington called the Board of War's attention to this shortcoming, noting that "by regulations the noncommissioned officers are to be armed with swords as a mark of distinction and to enable them the better to maintain authority due their stations." Washington went on to remind the civil authorities that "this necessary arrangement has not yet been carried into execution."[66]

However, captured arms stored at Albany might help solve the problem, Washington wrote, "by some returns I have seen there appears to have been a considerable number of Hessian hangers [a short, usually curved sword] at Albany, though I find no mention of them in the last returns of the Commissary of Military Stores. I presume the Board know where they are and I should think it would be adviseable to have them and any others that may be brought to the Army [and] distributed."[67]

Two weeks later he learned that the "Hessian swords which were at Albany [had been] ordered down to Fishkill with an intention to deliver them out to the noncommissioned officers of the Artillery and Infantry, but that on arrival they were found stripped of their mounting [brackets on the scabbard with which to hang the sword on the belt] which having been brass, had been taken off to cast into Gun Mountings and for other purposes." There was some hope, however, that these brass fittings could be replaced with iron and the swords then issued to the army. It was not until August 31, however, that Washington was able to announce in a general order that "a small number of sabres and belts having arrived for the noncommissioned officers, application is to be made immediately for ten swords for each regiment, vizt. one for the Quartermaster Serjeant and one for the First Serjeant of each company. The Bayonet belts now in the hands of those Serjeants are to be turned in."[68]

*The award was allowed to lapse after the Revolution. It was revived in 1932 in honor of Washington's bicentennial by War Department General Order 3. Army Regulations 600-45, August 8, 1932, prescribed that the medal could be awarded "for acts or service prior to February 22, 1932," specifically to those who had previously been awarded a service citation certificate (issued for meritorious conduct or gallantry not performed in actual combat) or wound chevrons.

†The halberd, traditionally carried by sergeants in European armies, was also carried by sergeants in the Continental Line.

In addition to enhancing the authority and prestige of the noncommissioned officer with appropriate side arms, Washington and von Steuben were also concerned about providing them suitable quarters. Instead of being billeted with the private soldiers there was to be "one tent for the noncommissioned officers of each company, and one for every six men. The tents of the noncommissioned officers and privates are to be pitched in two ranks, with an interval of six paces between the ranks, and two feet between each tent; the tents of the noncommissioned officers to be in the front rank, to the right of their companies, the Battalion left." Each noncommissioned officer had a list of his company's tents, with the names of the men quartered in each. A quarter of an hour after tattoo the noncommissioned officers visited their respective squads to see "that they are all present and retired to rest, and make their report to the commanding officer of the company."[69]

THE SERGEANT'S DEMANDS

As the war drew to an end in the spring of 1783, the status and prestige of the noncommissioned officer to which Washington and von Steuben had given so much attention became a political issue as Congress prepared to demobilize the Continental Army. The issue arose partly from the fact that the noncommissioned officers were, in Washington's words, making "new and unusual demands of compensation for their services." Noncommissioned officers of the Continental Line were the most articulate spokesmen for these demands, which extended "to a Claim of Half-Pay or Commutation, upon demobilization, for the noncommissioned officers of that Line." In some respects this agitation called into question the long-established principle that control of the army was to rest in the hands of the propertied classes of society. Such a threat existed, it was believed, if enlisted men could claim the same privileges, in terms of compensation, as commissioned officers.[70]

There were grounds for Washington's concern. Only a year before, two noncommissioned officers of the Connecticut Line had been tried and acquitted by a general court-martial for "endeavouring to excite a Mutiny in the Connecticut Line and also not discovering an intended Mutiny to their officers when they knew a plan was laying and a Combination forming to carry it into execution."[71] There had also been similar unrest among the men of the Pennsylvania and New Jersey lines, who briefly mutinied under the leadership of their sergeants in attempts to call congressional attention to their grievances. Although Washington steadfastly believed that noncommissioned officers were not entitled to compensations approaching those of commissioned officers, he nevertheless believed that they should be granted compensation exceeding those of the rank and file and urged Congress to reach a compromise with them before news of the peace and forthcoming demobilization reached the troops and caused widespread unrest throughout the army.[72]

As if to underline the urgency of their demands, the noncommissioned officers of the Connecticut Line sent a formal petition to Washington soliciting half-pay upon demobilization. This would have established a sort of professional corps of reserve noncommissioned officers. Washington refused, however, to accept the petition because, he claimed, it had not reached him through proper military channels. Yet even as he did so, he informed one of his generals that "I shall take it into Consideration."[73] Apparently impressed with the noncommissioned officers' arguments, Washington eventually forwarded their demands to the president of the Continental Congress with the observation that "considering its subject and the manner of Expression, I think it is not improper to transmit it to your Excellency, to be laid before Congress."[74] In his covering letter transmitting their demands to the president, he wrote,

> The Difference mentioned, between them [the noncommissioned officers] and the soldiers, in their Cloathing and Allowance of Lands (especially the latter), I think very pertinent and will be found to be conformable to the practice of European Nations, and is particularly exemplified in the Grant of Lands, made by the British proclamation, alluded to by the Sergeants. Independent of this practice, the reason is well founded, as it serves to prompt that Pride of military distinction, which is necessary to the Sergeant, to raise him to that superiority over the Soldier which it is his duty to observe; and without which, he will not be able to maintain that Respectability in his Station, which the nature of his Command requires; and which, in all well disciplined Armies, is very essential to the Service. I submit it to the Consideration of Congress; and to their Wisdom I leave its decision.[75]

It is clear from the tone of Washington's communication regarding the petition that his concern for the status and prestige of the sergeants had, if anything, been enhanced during the war. He had come to realize, as had generations of combat commanders before him, that able noncommissioned officers are essential to effective military operations. Throughout seven years of war, battalion and company officers' leadership, vital though it was, could not have kept the soldiers in ranks without the help of small corps of experienced and loyal noncommissioned men. It was they who had kept steady the ranks of the Continental Line at critical junctures in the Army's fortunes. Despite chronic personnel turbulence in all units, long-term noncommissioned officers proved to be the cement that held together the flimsy structure of the Continental Army through good times and bad. Not only the regulars, but the militia units felt the influence of their example and leadership.

However, with victory at hand neither Congress nor the several states were willing to support a professional military class, commissioned or noncommissioned, nor to enhance the status of the professional soldier. Except for a brief confrontation between members of Congress and dissidents of the Philadelphia garrison led by noncommissioned officers, nothing came of the sergeants' demands, in spite of General Washington's endorsement. Congress demobilized the Continental Army and with it collapsed the hopes of the noncommissioned officers for special recognition and compensation for their wartime services.[76]

With the signing of the Treaty of Paris on September 20, 1783, formally ending the War for Independence, it was clear that the new nation had no immediate intention of maintaining a professional army either in the British or European traditions. Instead, the new nation at first reverted to those militia traditions that the colonists had brought with them from their homeland. Most members of the Continental Congress believed that the Continental Army had been created only to fight the war. That war now over, the Army was no longer needed.

General Washington acknowledged that the new nation neither needed nor could it afford a standing army comparable to the Continental Line. He proposed in January 1790, however, that all able-bodied young Americans be given peacetime training in a nationwide citizen army similar to that of the Swiss Confederation.[77] But nothing came of that plan.

On October 18, 1784, in accordance with a proclamation of Congress of June of that same year, the Continental Army was disbanded and passed into history.

In a resolution of May 26, 1784, Congress turned over to the state militias the task of garrisoning the few remaining western outposts. Congress further directed that all troops remaining in federal service, including all officers above the rank of captain, be discharged—except for twenty-five privates to guard an army depot at Ft. Pitt (now Pittsburgh) and fifty-five privates on similar duty at West Point, New York. No mention was made of noncommissioned officers for these detachments. Actually, these men were little more than watchmen or custodians. Many were old, invalided soldiers who had no other place to go. Henry Knox, a brigadier general of artillery who had served as commander in chief since Washington's resignation on December 23, 1783, was thereupon honorably discharged and the rank of commander in chief abolished. Also discharged were all officers of the 1st American Regiment of Infantry stationed at Ft. Pitt under the command of Colonel Henry Jackson.[78]

The formal military structure of the Continental Army that had developed since 1779 was no more, but the *Regulations* written by von Steuben still remained, and on their basis a new army and a new noncommissioned officer corps was to be built. In the period from June 3, 1784—when the regular army was created—to 1821, what regular or militia forces remained to the new republic would use von Steuben's famed Blue Book as guide for the organization and training of the noncommissioned officers. The standards he had set for the noncommissioned officers of the Continental Army continued to guide the U.S. Army into the first decades of the new century.[79]

MASSACHUSETTS ARTILLERY REGIMENT, 1775 *

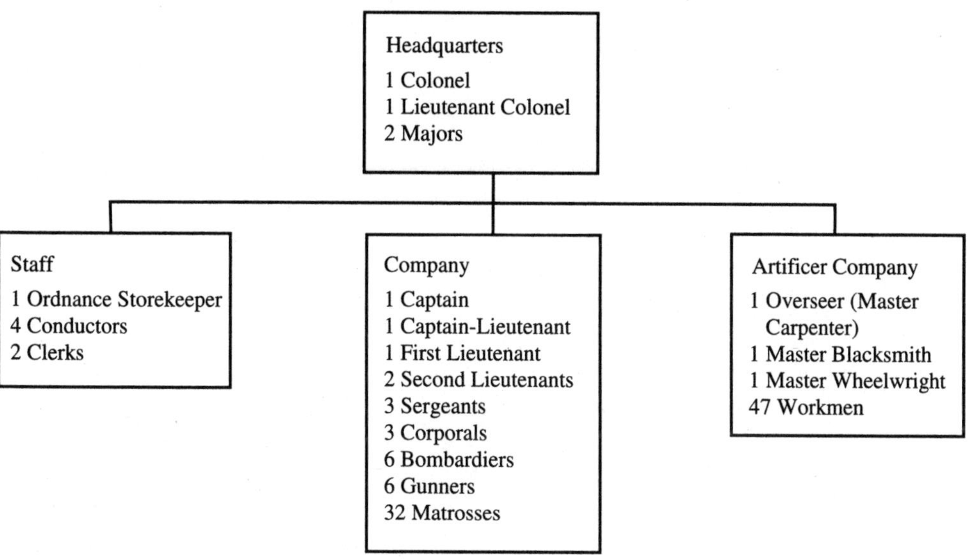

a. Ten companies were authorized; some were actually organized.
*Wright, p. 14

INFANTRY REGIMENT, 1776 *

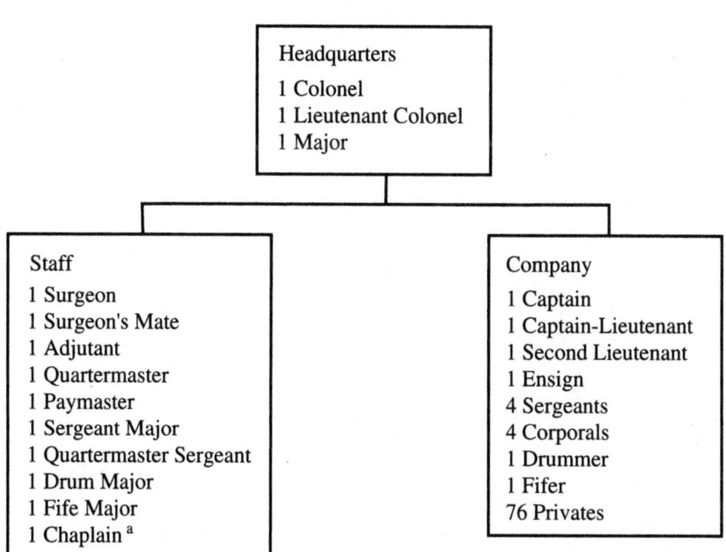

a. One per two regiments, January 16–June 28, 1776; thereafter, one per regiment.
b. Subdivided into four squads, each with a sergeant, a corporal, and nineteen privates.
*Wright, p. 47

ARTILLERY REGIMENT, 1776 *

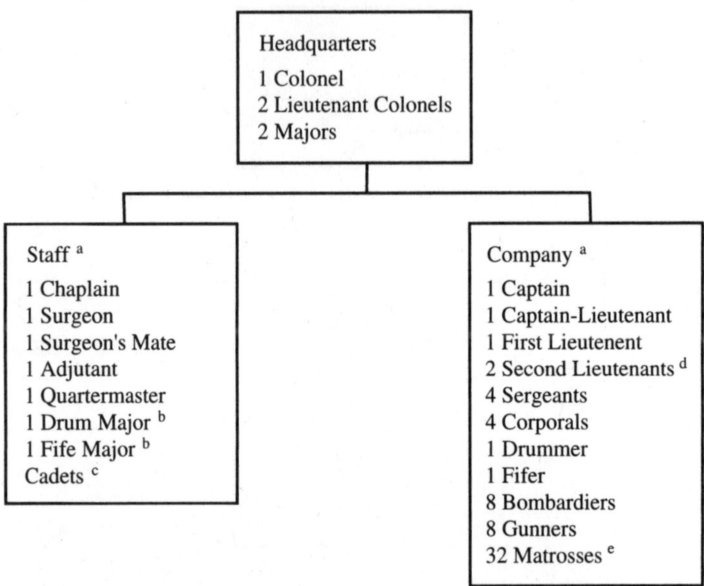

a. These structures are conjectural. The separate company authorized on 28 October 1775, for the Hudeon Highlands was identical except that it had 60 matrosses.
b. Added on June 1776.
c. At least 2 volunteers training to become second lieutenants.
d. One performed duties of fireworker.
e. Privates. Bombardeers and gunners were specialists receiving higher pay.
*Wright, p. 53

LIGHT DRAGOON REGIMENT, 1777 *

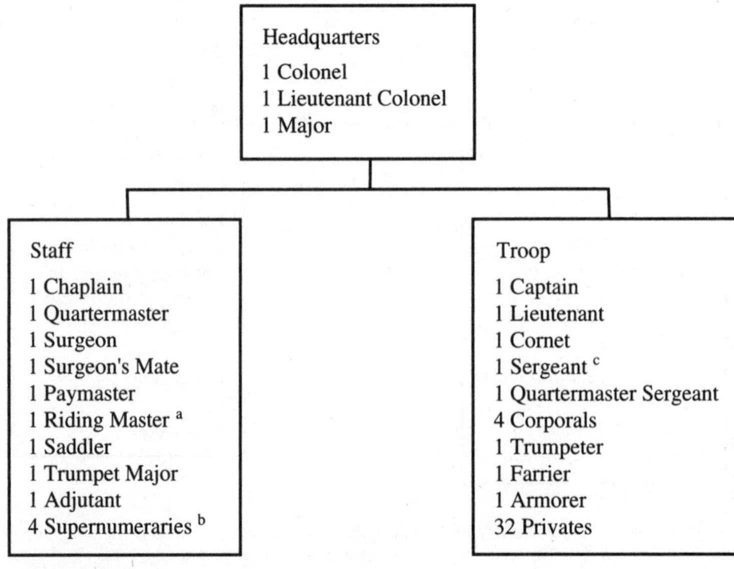

a. Instructor in horsemanship.
b. Cadets undergoing training.
c. Variously designated orderly sergeant or drill sergeant.
* Wright, p. 107

INFANTRY REGIMENT, MAY 1778 *

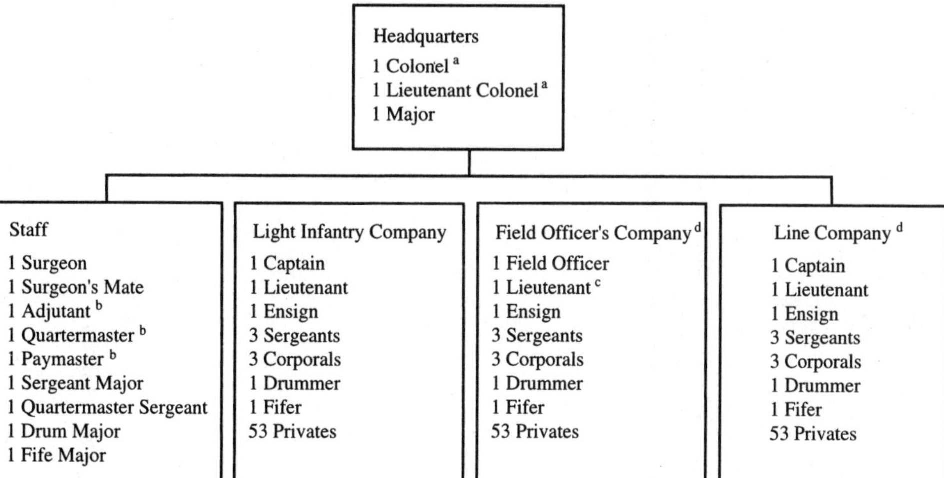

a. Or a lieutenant colonel commandant.

b. Performed by company officers.

c. Lieutenant of colonel's company was designated captain-lieutenant.

d. In regiments with 3 field officers, 3 line companies. In those with only 2 field officers, 6 line companies.

* Wright, p. 127

AN INFANTRY REGIMENT DEPLOYED IN TWO BATTALIONS, 1779 *

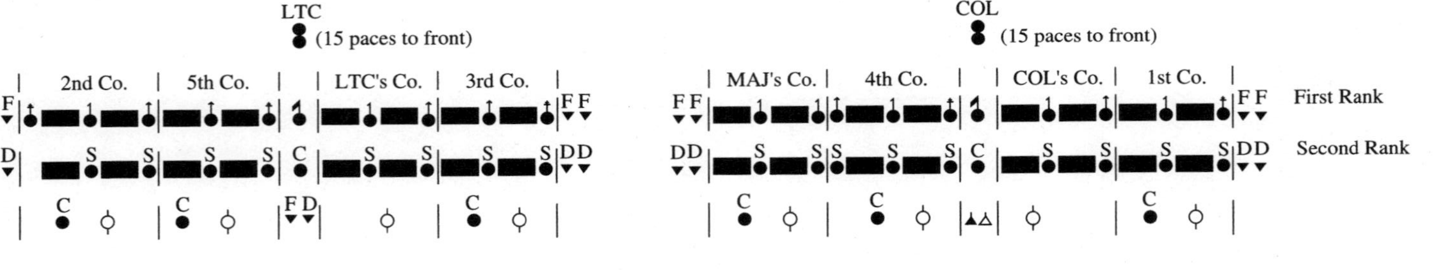

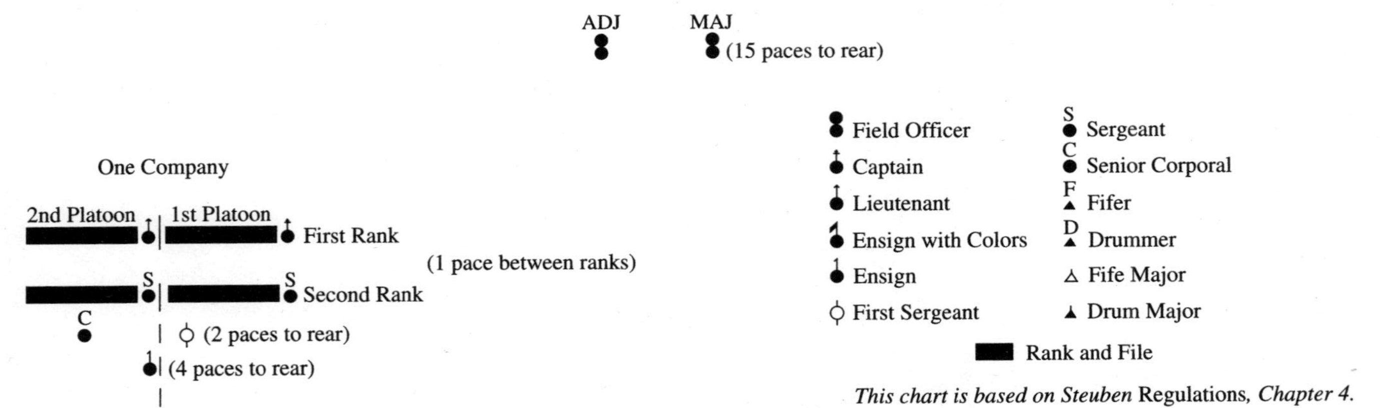

This chart is based on Steuben Regulations, *Chapter 4.*

*** Wright, p. 141**

CHAPTER 3

ADOPTION OF NEW PRINCIPLES

For the first few years following the War of Independence, Congress, beset with the problems of nation building, paid scant attention to the armed forces. The Continental Army had been demobilized, and Congress turned over to the militia of the several states the task of guarding the new nation's frontiers, especially those of the northwest—or Ohio—territories where powerful Indian tribes challenged the advancing line of settlement.

Surviving noncommissioned officers of the Revolution had returned to civilian life and were dispersed among various militia units where, together with former commissioned officers, they maintained as best they could some semblance of minimal military training based on von Steuben's *Regulations*. Inasmuch as historical experience had demonstrated the vital importance of a corps of capable, professional noncommissioned officers to the success of a military unit, Congress's decision not to maintain such a corps but instead rely upon the *ad hoc* training methods of the militia boded ill for any future contest of arms.

Meanwhile, beyond the Atlantic there arose out of the ferment of the French Revolution and the Napoleonic Empire new precepts of military organization and tactics that in time rendered obsolete many of those that much of von Steuben's *Regulations* rested upon. Many of these new principles were embodied in *Les Réglements Conçernant l'Éxercise et les Manoeuvres de l'Infantrie, du 1er. Aout, 1791*. General Alexander Smythe of the U.S. Army prepared an abridged version of these regulations and published it in 1812 with the approval of the War Department for use by the Army. Thus, the French tradition, as it had evolved during the wars of the French Revolution and the Napoleonic Empire was added to the earlier British and Prussian traditions.[1]

To General Smyth's abridgment of *Les Réglements* was added William Duane's *Handbook for Infantry; containing the First Principles of Military Discipline* of 1813. The French system as interpreted by Smythe and Duane was officially codified in 1815 by a board of officers under Brevet Major General

Winfield Scott. This work, known familiarly thereafter as "Scott's Exercises," soon supplanted von Steuben's *Regulations* in the regular Army.

Meanwhile, Congress requested the president to prepare and submit for approval "a military system of discipline for the Infantry of the Army and Military of the United States." But the Army, occupied with campaigns that were not going very well, was unable to comply. Consequently, during the War of 1812, insofar as tactical instruction of troops was concerned, every officer was a "law unto himself." Nevertheless, then-Colonel Scott, using makeshift translations of the French system, trained two brigades of Major General Brown's division at a camp near Buffalo, New York in 1814. How well the Americans were trained was proved by the comment of the British general commanding the troops opposing them in their first battle, who when he saw them advancing exclaimed, "Those are regulars, by God!"[2]

It was during Scott's training of his troops at Buffalo, therefore, that the French tactical system was first introduced into the U.S. Army. Slightly modified, the French drill and tactical instruction were adopted by the War Department and known throughout the regular service as "the system of 1815." By 1820, it had been adopted by the militia as well.

REGULAR AND MILITIA

Before a uniform drill and tactical instruction system could be put into general use, Congress first had to decide upon the relationship between the regular Army and the militia in carrying out the military policies of the new nation. This was among the first questions debated by the Continental Congress after the War of Independence. It was an important issue because the role and status of the noncommissioned officer were affected with those of the regular Army.

The question was not an easy one to decide, because the establishment of a peacetime military ran directly counter to an ardent anti–standing army tradition inherited from seventeenth-century England. In the words of one student of this tradition, it had "played a part in the indictment of Great Britain, in the Declaration of Independence, in the coming of the Revolution, and in the creation of a Constitution with a Bill of Rights. At the end of the eighteenth century, it acted as a brake on the power of the Executive."[3]

This tradition had its legal and literary embodiment in the widely read legal *Commentaries* of William Blackstone, which appeared between 1765 and 1769. Often cited throughout the colonies, they had a lasting influence on political leaders of the new nation. In his *Commentaries* Blackstone described the locally controlled militia rather than the standing army as a safeguard of "the constitutional security of the nation." By the end of the eighteenth century, Americans as well as Englishmen were in general agreement that a large standing army was incompatible with freedom. This sentiment remained for many generations a basic assumption of almost every American political figure.[4]

It was against this background that Congress turned over to a committee chaired by Alexander Hamilton the problem of recommending the form a peacetime military establishment should take. At the committee's request, General Washington prepared a study entitled *Sentiments on a Peace Establishment.* In it he outlined his recommendations concerning the military needs of the United States.[5]

Like most Americans of his day, Washington considered a large standing army in time of peace hazardous to the liberties of the nation. Yet a few regular troops were "not only safe, but indispensably necessary," he wrote. Such a force, he observed, should number no more than 2,631 officers and men, sufficient for garrisoning the vital fortress at West Point, the magazines, "and our northern, western and southern frontiers." This small force was to be composed of Continental troops rather than state militia. They would look to Congress, not the states, for their orders, pay, and supplies. The bulk of this army was to be composed of infantry numbering 1,908 men and organized into four regiments. In Washington's view, organization of militia units was to have been entirely uniform throughout the United States, as it had been in Britain. "Each Regiment," he observed, "should be composed of two Battalions, each Battalion to consist of 4 Companies and each Company, as at present, of 1 Captain, 1 Lieutenant, 1 Ensign, 5 Sergeants, 3 Corporals, 2 Musicians, and 65 Privates."[6]

General Washington foresaw no difficulty in recruiting this number of men. In any case, the three-year men still in the Continental service were expected to make up the force initially. Thereafter, he envisioned that "when the soldiers from the War have frolicked among their friends, and find they must have recourse to hard labour or a livelyhood . . . I am persuaded numbers of them will reenlist upon almost any Terms." This would have sufficed for maintaining a peacetime army, but not in wartime.

In such circumstances, Washington admitted the basic defense force must be based on a militia system, enrolling all able-bodied men between the ages of eighteen and twenty-five. His espousal of this view placed Washington in the classic Whig position—supporting a citizen militia as opposed to a large standing army. The ensuing debate in Congress between the advocates of a large regular establishment and reliance on a citizen militia was a distant echo of the century-old political issue between the Whigs and Tories in Britain.[7]

In eighteenth-century England a large standing army had been perceived as strengthening the Crown, and the United States, having just achieved its independence from the British Crown, was reluctant to re-create a central authority similarly reinforced. Ironically, even as political interest in the militia question was dying out in Great Britain toward the end of the century, it was becoming a major issue in the new nation being created from the former British colonies.[8]

In June 1783, after studying Washington's recommendations as well as those of several of his associates, Hamilton's committee submitted to Congress a plan for the organization of the peacetime military establishment but "with a more ambitious militia program." Opposition to the plan developed within Congress, which ultimately rejected it. Sectional rivalries and political and economic questions caused debate to drag on until April 1, 1785, when Congress finally resolved

> that it is necessary that a body of troops consisting of 700 regular noncommissioned officers and privates be raised for the term of three years, unless sooner discharged, for the protection of the northwest frontiers, to defend the settlers on the land belonging to the United States from the depredations of the Indians and to prevent unwarrantable intrusion thereon, and for guarding the public stores.[9]

In addition, the states were to furnish—on the basis of a quota system—recruits for a mixed regiment of infantry and artillery. This regiment was to consist of eight infantry and two artillery companies. The pay scales established for this force suggest the rather low status of the noncommissioned officer: only one dollar more than the pay of a corporal and only two more than that of the private soldier:

Lieutenant Colonel	$50.00 per month
Major	$45.00 per month
Captain	$35.00 per month
Lieutenant	$26.00 per month
Ensign	$20.00 per month
Surgeon	$45.00 per month
Surgeon's Mate	$30.00 per month
Sergeant	$ 6.00 per month
Corporal	$ 5.00 per month
Musicians	$ 5.00 per month
Private	$ 4.00 per month

On the other hand, among the commissioned officers there were far wider differences in pay, denoting the different degrees of responsibility and authority. The slight differences of pay among the enlisted ranks indicated that in establishing the pay scales little note had been taken of the sergeant's significantly larger responsibilities and duties as compared with those of a private soldier. The sergeant's low pay and the slight difference between what he and the private soldier received was not calculated to add prestige to the sergeant's office.

Meanwhile, in spite of the advocacy of Washington, Hamilton, and Knox for a federally regulated militia, Congress failed to pass a militia law until May of 1792. In doing so, it did not set nationwide standards, as Washington had recommended, other than prescribing that the states were to organize and train their militia units according to von Steuben's *Regulations*. Otherwise, training and discipline were left entirely up to the states. Henceforth, the state militia rather than the minuscule regular force established in June 1784 was the predominant military force of the new nation in terms of numbers.* However, the regulars, with the advantage of

*Not until 1940 did Congress complete the military structure recommended by Washington when it accepted the principle of *compulsory* military training and service in time of peace.

professional leadership from both commissioned and noncommissioned officers, ultimately proved their superiority in battle.[10]

TESTING THE NEW ARMY

With the passage of the Northwest Ordinance in 1787, the states had ceded to Congress their claims to the western territories between the Appalachian Mountains and the Mississippi. The ordinance gave the federal government responsibility for policing and defending these territories and thrust upon the small regular Army even greater responsibilities than those contemplated by the Hamilton Committee when it submitted its recommendations to Congress in 1783. In April 1790 accordingly, Congress reluctantly increased the existing 700-man regular force to 1,216, enlisted for three years and organized into a regiment of infantry and a battalion of artillery.

There were to be four sergeants and four corporals in each company. Monthly pay for these two noncommissioned ranks was set at $5.00 and $4.00 respectively, with deductions for clothing and hospital stores. Each of the sixty-one privates in a company received $3.00, with similar deductions. Some idea of congressional esteem for the Army can be obtained by comparing the pay scales of 1790 with those established in 1785. In addition to the higher pay that had been authorized previously, enlisted men received a ration of bread, meat, and spirits (usually whiskey) plus a small amount of vinegar, soap, and candles. Each man was also annually issued a hat, two pairs of overalls, socks, and four pairs of shoes. Neither overcoat nor underwear were issued.[11]

Congress acted just in time, for in the fall of 1790 a military expedition consisting of militia and a few regulars had been virtually destroyed by Indians in the northwest territories. A year later George Washington, now president of the United States, dispatched a second expedition under the command of Major General Arthur St. Clair to put a stop to the Indian depredations against the settlements.

Numbering some two thousand men—six hundred regulars, six hundred militia, and eight hundred enlisted volunteers—this *ad hoc* force was as badly trained as it was insufficient for the task. After a belated start, St. Clair and his men left Ft. Washington (near present-day Pittsburgh) and advanced deep into Indian territory, where they fell into an ambush on November 4, 1791. Almost half the force was lost—632 killed and 264 wounded. These losses exceeded even those of Long Island and Camden, two of the bloodiest battles of the War of Independence. One historian, commenting on the ambush, observed, "want of discipline and experience of the troops," mainly among the ill-trained militia, was the cause of the defeat.[12]

Troop behavior during this campaign demonstrated that neither the militia nor the regulars had developed sufficient numbers of professional officers or noncommissioned soldiers capable of maintaining march discipline and holding the men in ranks under fire. Given the reduction in pay for all ranks provided for in the legislation of 1790, this is not to be wondered at.

Reaction to this disaster was not long in coming. In March 1792, Congress, in an act "making further and more effective provision for the protection of the frontiers of the United States," authorized recruitment to increase to full strength the two regiments of infantry and the battalion of artillery—the units then making up the regular Army. Provision was also made for the first time since the Revolution for a regimental sergeant major and a regimental quartermaster sergeant, each to be paid $7.00 per month. Pay of the other noncommissioned ranks remained unchanged.[13]

In December 1792, on the basis of this legislation, the President appointed an experienced officer of Revolutionary War fame—"Mad" Anthony Wayne—to organize and command a new force designated the Legion of the United States. Although Congress authorized 5,120 men, recruiting proceeded so slowly that only 3,692 men had signed the rolls by November 1794.

General Wayne divided his legion into four 1,280-man sub-legions, each a balanced force composed of infantry, artillery, and cavalry. These strength figures were never actually reached, however. At the same time, the infantry companies increased the number of noncommissioned officers to six sergeants and six corporals, in addition to two musicians and eighty-one privates.

For the training St. Clair had neglected, General Wayne assembled his men on the banks of the Ohio, just outside Pittsburgh at a camp he named Legionville. Separated from the distractions of Pittsburgh, then a brawling frontier community, the legion trained for about a year under Wayne's watchful eyes.[14]

Determined to create a professional military organization, General Wayne set high standards for both officers and men of the legion. He saw to it that each company commander received a copy of von Steuben's *Regulations* and adhered to it strictly in the training of his men. Anxious to avoid some of the tribulations of the Continental Army, Wayne made sure that all men were well clothed. He issued needles, thread, and patches to ensure that the men maintained their clothing properly. As if to emphasize his determination, Wayne directed that any company conspicuous of slovenliness would be detailed to perform camp fatigue duty until its appearance improved. Individual private soldiers who displayed unshaven faces and soiled uniforms were punished with twenty lashes.

Noncommissioned officers were treated with greater consideration. Unlike Washington, Wayne did not apply the same punishments to his noncommissioned officers as he meted out to the ordinary soldiers. Reprimands were the most widely employed corrective for sergeants. Reduction to the ranks was considered severe enough for all but the most serious offenses. This was a practice that continued for many years. Illustrative was the case of a Sergeant Hopkins, who, like many others of this rank, kept a woman. Relations between the two were not always harmonious, and the resulting screaming and yelling frequently disturbed the patients in the nearby post hospital. When the surgeon, a Dr. Carmichaels, attempted to remonstrate with the sergeant, Hopkins threatened and abused him. Summoned to the scene, the guard took both Sergeant Hopkins and his woman into custody. Judging the sergeant's conduct both "insubordinate and wicked," a court-martial sentenced him to be reduced to the ranks.

Serious military offenses were another matter. For example, General Wayne did not hesitate to hang a sergeant for desertion. Otherwise, though, he did what he could to protect his senior enlisted men from the wrath of the civilian authorities. When one sergeant was sentenced by the civil court to pay a $3.00 fine, suffer fifteen lashes, and obtain someone to guarantee his good conduct for six months for having abused a local magistrate, Wayne intervened to get the indignity of a flogging remitted. Wayne knew the value of a good sergeant and did much to enhance his prestige and authority. By the time his legion prepared to take to the field in the spring of 1794, Wayne had developed a corps of able noncommissioned officers.

In the autumn of 1793, Wayne led his legionnaires, accompanied by 1,600 mounted Kentucky militiamen, to the southwest branch of the Maumee River, where they passed the winter at a post named Ft. Jefferson. The following summer the legion went on campaign, vigorously harassing the Indians and finally bringing them to bay on August 20 at the Battle of Fallen Timbers. There, Wayne's well-disciplined regulars charged with the bayonet and broke the Indian center. This victory gave the young army "its first model of excellence."[15]

The territory north of the Ohio now pacified, the Legion of the United States had served its purpose. Accordingly, on May 3, 1796, an act of Congress dissolved the legion with the actual deactivation taking place on October 31. Henceforth the regular Army consisted of four regiments of infantry, two companies of light dragoons, and the existing corps of artillery and engineers, all under the command of a major general with a brigadier as deputy.[16]

ATTEMPTS TO IMPROVE THE SERVICE

Following the deactivation of Wayne's legion, Brigadier General James Wilkinson became ranking officer in the regular establishment. Although lacking in professional integrity and loyalty to the Army,[17] Wilkinson nevertheless attempted to maintain professionalism within the Army by insisting that distant garrisons along the frontier spend more time "on soldierly work" and refrain from "cropping" or tending their gardens.* This order produced a marked change on some far-flung posts. For example, with von Steuben's *Regulations* in hand, the noncommissioned officers of the five companies stationed at Ft. Detroit during the summer of 1797 drilled their men daily from five to seven A.M., eleven A.M. to one P.M., and four until six P.M. "under the supervision of 2 officers who were regularly detailed for the purpose."[18] One can guess that little energy remained for gardening following these drill sessions.

*At many posts the troops spent a good bit of time during the growing season cultivating the land in the vicinity of the garrison in order to supplement their meager rations.

Greater emphasis on systematic training alone does not, however, make a dependable professional army. Some improvements had also to be made in enlisted pay and living conditions. Congress soon realized that if good men were to be recruited and kept in service, pay and pensions had to be improved. Accordingly, in 1795 all enlisted men who had served in the War of Independence were granted a $5.00 monthly pension for maximum disability, with correspondingly smaller amounts for lesser disabilities. In 1808 similar pensions were extended to non–Revolutionary War veterans. In 1797, meanwhile, Congress also sought to improve enlisted pay, directing that pay "should never be more than two months in arrears." A year later the pay of each enlisted grade was increased $1.00 per month, and rations were increased as well.

Some changes were also made in identifying noncommissioned grades. In March 1799 the Revolutionary War shoulder knots were abandoned for shoulder straps. Henceforth, all noncommissioned officers wore red worsted shoulder straps as designation of rank: staff sergeants one on each shoulder, line sergeants one on the right, and corporals one on the left shoulder. In 1801 a measure was adopted that caused considerable resentment among the older officers and senior noncommissioned officers—a requirement to wear the hair short. Many older men, deeply proud of their queues—symbolic of the military professional—resisted losing them. One old noncommissioned officer reportedly insisted that upon his death his queue be allowed, in a last measure of defiance, to protrude from his coffin.[19]

Some thought had meanwhile been given to improved professional education for both officers and noncommissioned officers. During the War of Independence, Congress had authorized the creation of a "Corps of Invalids," composed of disabled veterans who, in return for maintenance, served as a garrison for West Point and also to train young aspirants there for commissions in infantry regiments. By 1784, however, most of the corps had drifted away, leaving behind only thirty-eight "invalids," too penniless or disabled to travel. However, though the corps had been dispersed, the idea of somehow utilizing West Point as a training site persisted.[20]

At first, what was eventually to become the military academy at West Point had been envisioned as a school for the training of sergeants as well as cadets. In a recommendation submitted to President Adams in January 1800, the secretary of war, James McHenry, stated that the Army needed enough sergeants to fill the requirements for a fifty thousand–man force. These noncommissioned officers were to alternate between the military academy and troop duty.[21] Nothing came of this recommendation, at least as far as the training of sergeants was concerned. In 1802, however, Congress created a separate corps of engineers consisting of seven officers and ten cadets. This corps was assigned to West Point to serve as the academy staff for the training of commissioned officers only. By 1812 the academy had graduated eighty-nine officers, sixty-five of whom were still on active duty at the time the second war with Great Britain began.[22]

Cadet training, however, included all the duties of noncommissioned officers and privates as well as the duties of an officer. For the first time an infusion of professionally trained junior officers came into the Army. These young officers, under such leaders as Winfield Scott (himself not a West Point graduate), took over some of the duties formerly assigned to senior noncommissioned officers, greatly subordinating the role of the sergeant to that of the officer. However, it was not until the appointment of Sylvanus Thayer as superintendent in 1817 that the military academy truly came into its own as a professional school. Since the noncommissioned officers were dependent upon commissioned officers for their selection and training, improvement in the professional standing of the latter inevitably improved the professionalism of the former.[23]

Although Congress voted to raise volunteers and to increase the size of the regular Army in late 1811, on the eve of war with Britain, it still remained far below its authorized strength—less than seven thousand men, mostly dispersed in scattered frontier garrisons often too small even to conduct battalion exercises. As had been the case during the War for Independence, a sustained war effort by the new nation had to be built on volunteer companies with amorphous common militia behind them.[24] This represented the consensus of Congress, as shown in the Militia Law of 1792. Little had changed since then.

Some idea of the quality of that militia can be seen from an account of a militia muster published in the *Norfolk Gazette and Publick Ledger* on August 31, 1807. The correspondent wrote:

> A little before one the captain, who I shall distinguish by the name of Clodpole, gave directions for forming the line of parade. In obedience to this order, one of the sergeants, the strength of whose lungs had long supplied the place of drum and fife, placed himself in front of the house and began to bawl with great vehemence, "All Captain Clodpole's Company to parade here," says he, "and you all that han't guns, fall into the lower end!"[25]

IMPOSING A NEW DISCIPLINE

Ill-prepared though the nation's armed forces were on the eve of war, there were officers such as Scott, then commanding a brigade on the Niagara frontier, who were determined to create trained and disciplined professionals out of the raw recruits assembled under their command. Using "a tattered old copy of the French regulations issued by Napoleon" as well as Duane's *Handbook for Infantry* as his guides, Scott began to act as his own drill sergeant, as had von Steuben a generation before at Valley Forge.*

He first instructed his officers, who in turn instructed their noncommissioned

*Although employing Duane's *Handbook*, Scott preferred the French *Réglements*. In 1814, General Scott, as chairman of a board appointed to draw up new regulations, discarded Duane as archaic and wholly adopted the French system as developed by Napoleon. (See C. W. Elliott, *Winfield Scott: The Soldier and the Man*, pp. 147, 190.)

officers in the school of the soldier and in squad, company, and battalion tactics. For two months, at a training camp just outside the village of Buffalo, Scott maintained a ten-hour duty day for his troops. As might be expected, some found this more than they could endure. But undeterred, Scott brooked no interference with his task of producing troops trained to professional standards. When increasing desertions threatened to undermine his training program, Scott did not shrink from taking stern measures—including ordering several executions.[26]

Scott's preference for Napoleonic doctrine notwithstanding, Duane's *Handbook* was still the official regulation for the U.S. Army, and Duane, as had von Steuben, placed great emphasis on the administrative role of the noncommissioned officer.

In Duane's words, "the order and good conduct of the company" depended upon the noncommissioned officers, and they should be "selected from among the most orderly and best qualified men." Within the company each sergeant was in charge of a squad that established its own mess, over which he presided. In addition, the sergeant was responsible for the cleanliness of his men, their clothing, arms, and quarters. Every morning each sergeant prepared two copies of his morning report and presented them to the company first sergeant, who in turn gave one copy to the company commander and retained one for himself. Weekly reports concerning the condition of the men and their equipment were given to the regimental sergeant major. Company sergeants also performed orderly duty, essentially acting as an assistant to the officer of the day. The roster for this duty was maintained by the regimental sergeant major.[27]

As for the corporals, Duane considered them deputy sergeants, taking charge of the squads when in quarters. They also kept rolls for duty and details, helped train recruits in the manual of arms, and instructed them in caring for their arms and equipment, as well as for their provisions and ammunition. At tattoo both sergeants and corporals called the roll and posted guard. In the latter task the senior corporal had the choice of route after an equal distribution had been made.

Although the noncommissioned officer played an important administrative role in Duane's *Handbook*, Duane was less inclined than von Steuben had been to give the noncommissioned officer a role in tactical instruction and training. Close-order and parade-ground drill and maneuvers were basic elements of nineteenth-century battlefield tactics, but Duane was reluctant to entrust noncommissioned officers below the rank of sergeant major or first sergeant with them. Duane believed that noncommissioned officers "seldom know more than to imitate what they have seen or heard of, and teach [the tactical principles] mechanically."

Tactical training, according to Duane, should be in the hands of the commissioned officer, for "the first object of him who wishes to become a military man" is to master the tactical principles, and this mastery was the exclusive province of the commissioned grades. Shorn of his tactical role, Duane's noncommissioned officer was not likely to be carrying "a field marshal's baton in his knapsack" after Napoleon's famous dictum.

By involving the commissioned officer more directly in recruit training, Duane hoped to enhance its quality. He wrote that "the chance of finding noncommissioned officers who can clearly comprehend and explain the principles of good discipline, is not one in twenty; from which cause it is twenty to one that the recruits are imperfectly or erroneously taught."

Duane observed with approbation the relatively humane practices of the armies of revolutionary France, "In which no man is ever beaten with a cane." In Duane's words, when recruits in their confusion blunder, the officer-instructor "must react unlike the traditional drill-sergeant, but with patience and a little good humored raillery, which will excite pride and not contempt." The harsh discipline of many eighteenth-century armies, Duane observed, was inconsistent "with reason and humanity." The drill instructor, Duane wrote, "should be of a cheerful but firm disposition, more disposed to laugh at rude mistakes of the first drills, than to use opprobrious language." Instruction, he added, should be given "in familiar and persuasive language, as advice rather than command; always with good temper and kindness . . . abuse never." Duane believed that commissioned rather than noncommissioned officers could better maintain these standards. This represented a change of the original principles of the seventeenth-century military commentators.

On the march, however, Duane's sergeants functioned in a traditional manner. Of the four sergeants and eight corporals in an infantry company, only the corporals carried muskets. The sergeants were primarily occupied with keeping the men in ranks. Together with some commissioned officers, the sergeants formed a supernumerary rank four paces to the rear of the last rank of the company. The duty of these sergeants was "to attend to the good and close order of the ranks . . . and to attend to the disabled in action."

The sergeants also assisted the officers in maintaining troop control under fire. In battalion formations sergeants took positions on the flanks of each company, where they covered the officers stationed there. These were the same positions occupied by the sergeants in close-order drill.

On parade four of "the most respectable sergeants" formed the color guard. The ensigns, bearing the colors, formed a rank with two sergeants on each side as color guard; two additional sergeants covered the rear.

Unlike von Steuben, Duane believed that each company should have a sergeant major—actually a first sergeant—who "would conduce to the perfection of discipline." Such an arrangement, Duane declared, greatly lightened the duties of the battalion sergeant major who "has charge of the details of sergeants, corporals, privates and musicians for every service, guards, drills, fatigues . . . and is an indispensible aid to the adjutant." In addition, the battalion sergeant major "should be a complete master of all the exercises of the battalion from the first drill to the movements in line of battle." This latter represented an enhancement of his role over that of his counterpart in eighteenth-century warfare.

Company descriptive books, maintained throughout the early years of the United States Army's history, tell much of how the noncommissioned officers actually carried out these largely administrative duties in garrison and in the field. That of Captain C. Hartell's company of the 27th Infantry Regiment, stationed along the Niagara frontier during the War of 1812, is typical.

At reveille 1st Sergeant Thorne was "to divide the company into squads, each to be conducted by a noncommissioned officer who will hold accounted [*sic*] for the good and orderly conduct of his squad." As for the squad leader, "when one or more of his squad is turned out for Guard, he will inspect them and their arms, see that their clothing [*sic*] be clean, arms in good order, flints good and well fitted, ammunition sufficient and in good condition."[28]

The first sergeant was to "furnish himself with a roll [roster] of the company and also a squad roll." Captain Hartell also enjoined the private soldiers of his company to "pay due respect to noncommissioned officers—on being asked a question [of a noncommissioned officer] they will answer promptly 'yes Sir' or 'no Sir' as the case may require, and always pay the same deference towards them." The noncommissioned officers in turn closely supervised the troop quarters. For that purpose, the first sergeant detailed "an orderly corporal . . . daily to inspect company rooms several times in the course of a day."

In Captain Hartell's order detailing a noncommissioned officer "whose duty it shall be to teach New Recruits the Manual Exercises and instruct them how to clean their arms and accoutriments [*sic*] and see that they perform this duty each for himself," can be seen the facets of a modern drill sergeant's duties.

When in October 1814 the good citizens of New Utrecht, New York, complained of depredations by soldiers from the local garrison on their property, the post commandant directed that "a trusty noncommissioned officer and two privates will therefore be selected each day from each regiment whose duty it shall be patrols [*sic*] on the Ground in the vicinity of their Regiment, take up all stragglers and send them into camp for examination." When soldiers went into town to patronize the local merchants, a "noncommissioned officer [was to be] detailed by the adjutant to see that good order is strictly kept, and he will be held responsible for the conduct of the men, and order every man, as soon as he had reasonable time to take his purchases, to his quarters."*

Training for both commissioned and noncommissioned officers was regular and systematic even at isolated army posts. The commanding officer of the 9th Military District, with headquarters at Sackets Harbor on the Niagara frontier during the War of 1812, directed that

> Officers' drill will take place during the sitting of the General Courts Martial at half past three o'clock p.m. on the grand parade. Sergeants' drill will also take place hereafter at Eleven o'clock a.m. precisely when all sergeants of duty will attend on the grand parade and be drilled by such of the noncommissioned officers of Captain Swearingen's and Captain Smith's companies as may be there present for that pur-

*This description resembles the duties of military police in modern armies, but note that only noncommissioned officers performed these duties.

> pose. And the sergeants will be particular in communication to the corporals whatever instruction they may receive at such drill.

Sergeants major were required to attend during the whole time of the drill "but in a supervisory capacity only" to see that the men behave with utmost order and propriety."[29]

It is clear from these excerpts that officers were charged with maintaining professional standards among their troops. This discipline bore fruit on July 5, 1814, against British regulars along the Chippewa Creek near the Canadian border, and on July 25, at Lundy's Lane. In these two engagements the long months of rigorous training by General Scott and his officers were fully justified. These battles were unique in that they were "the only extended open field actions of the war in which the Americans fought at least as well as British veterans," and called forth from the opposing British commander the exclamation.[30]

In the same year, not content to rest upon such laurels, the Army adopted new infantry drill regulations designed to bring organization and tactics more in harmony with those of the Napoleonic tradition with which Scott was familiar. In 1814 an Army board under his presidency prepared a new set of regulations to replace those of Duane, which had been the only common basis of the army organization and tactics during the recent war with Great Britain. In time the new infantry drill regulations, as noted earlier, became known as *Scott's Infantry Drill Regulations* or *The System of 1815*, and provided guidance for the army throughout the war with Mexico and into the first years of the Civil War.

SCOTT'S INFANTRY DRILL

As outlined in Scott's regulations and exercises, infantry drill and maneuver concentrated on moving company- and battalion-sized units from column to line, from which a large volume of fire could be directed at the enemy (a tactic favored by Napoleon and his marshals). Swift and precise execution of rather complicated maneuvers or evolutions enabled a commander to move large numbers of men rapidly into linear formations.

Based as they were on Napoleonic tradition, Scott's regulations provided the United States Army with little tactical guidance during the nonconventional Seminole Wars in Florida or against the nomadic Indian tribes of the Western plains. Not until the war with Mexico (1846–1847), did the regular Army have an opportunity to employ these tactics against an army organized and trained along European principles. Led by a new generation of officers who had largely received their professional training at West Point, the U.S. Army distinguished itself in this brief and victorious war—the first outside the borders of the new nation.

Then as now, a lethal volume of firepower was the supreme desire of all field commanders, from company to regiment. Scott's *Regulations* enabled commanders to maneuver their units on the battlefield so as to control large amounts of musket fire on command. With the evolutions described in the *Regulations* in mind, one can imagine the impressive sight made by a regiment moving from march column onto the field by battalions and there deploying on line to deliver a rolling pattern of musket fire across a thousand-man front. In the execution of such evolutions noncommissioned officers played key roles in helping to maintain precise and orderly movement of the company, battalion, and regiment. As color sergeants, color guards, and guides, many noncommissioned officers performed gallantly on the battlefields of Resaca de la Palma, Buena Vista, Churubusco, and Molino del Rey, to name a few of the many American victories in the Mexican War.

The *Infantry Drill Regulations* of 1815 placed ultimate responsibility for the training of company noncommissioned officers in the hands of the company commander, assisted by his subalterns. This instruction included the school of the soldier and of the company. At the conclusion of this phase of training, each noncommissioned officer was expected to have an accurate knowledge of the exercise and use of the infantry weapons, "the manual exercise of the soldier and of the firings and marchings." As a check on the effectiveness of this training at the company level, the field-grade officers of the regiment and the adjutant, assisted by the sergeant major if qualified, periodically assembled the noncommissioned officers for the purpose of drill—a review of the school of the company—and to teach tactical theory.[31]

Thereafter, when casualties or promotions reduced the noncommissioned ranks, the company first sergeants oversaw the training of the newly appointed sergeants and corporals. Senior commissioned officers of the regimental staff, according to the regulations, were "to be attentive in seeing this duty diligently discharged."

The regimental color guard, composed of noncommissioned officers (the ensign no longer carried the colors), also received considerable attention from officer instructors because of the color guard's importance as the element by which the regiment was guided on the march and on line. Regimental commanders frequently drilled the guard as well as the battalion guides "in the practice of marching in the order of battle or in the line." The sergeant of the color guard was instructed to give the most scrupulous attention "to the habit of prolonging, without varying to the right or the left, a certain given direction [usually designated by the regimental commander], and of maintaining, with the utmost precision, the length, as well as the cadence of the step."

The importance of the noncommissioned officer in maintaining these formations can be seen in the following. When the company was drawn up on line the captain placed himself to the front and on the right flank. The first sergeant then took his place in the rear rank, covering the captain. In this position he was designated as the covering or replacing sergeant and guide for the right flank. The other sergeants marched as file closers. Corporals, according to their height, were placed on the right and left flanks of their companies and in the rear, in preference to the front rank.

The sergeant major's post was to the left of the battalion, and the major whom he was to assist was stationed opposite the center of the left wing. The quartermaster sergeant was posted in a line with the front rank of the pioneers and three paces to the right of them. The regimental color guard consisted of a sergeant and three corporals; this sergeant commanded the color guard and marched between the two sergeants carrying the national and regimental colors. Because of the importance of their roles, these three sergeants were selected personally by the regimental commander.

Inasmuch as companies, battalions, and regiments maneuvered as units in serried ranks, it was of surpassing importance that these ranks moved in proper order and in harmonious relationship to one another. For their successful execution, these maneuvers depended upon thoroughly trained noncommissioned officers acting as guides. Two of the most important were designated as "general guide of the right and general guide of the left." They had to be "particularly qualified in the accuracy and precision of the step and in prolonging without deviation, a given direction of line."

When the companies moved from column to a battalion line, the color sergeant, marching between the national and regimental colors, assumed a particular importance in keeping the colors on the proper course as the battalion advanced. The three noncommissioned officers of the color guard marching in the center of the formation constituted the basis of alignment. If for any reason the color sergeant, instead of marching perpendicular to the battalion front, followed an oblique direction, the entire battalion would slant on line, bulge out, and lose its original alignment.

Beginning in the center and increasing in proportion as the false line of direction deviated from the true, crowding and jostling would take place on one wing and a breaking and opening of files occur on the other. It was therefore of utmost importance that the color sergeant marched on a line at right angles to the original front and the basis of the battalion alignment was always perpendicular to the line of direction on which the color guard marched.

Although this drill was taught and endlessly rehearsed on parade grounds throughout the Army, its significance lay in the fact that it was also the battlefield drill. When units marched into battle, they moved from column onto line and maneuvered on the field of battle in rigid conformity to this drill. In this drill the senior noncommissioned officers played key roles in making these often intricate maneuvers move in an orderly fashion. Orders were given by the commanding officers, but it was the noncommissioned officer who saw to it that the ranks remained steady and the files closed up.

Thus was the noncommissioned officers' combat role as enhanced under the French system, not so much as an actual leader of men, but as the key assistant in executing the maneuvers ordered by the troop commander. For this reason, the government soon took steps to write into law a greater awareness of the noncommissioned officers' importance and status within the Army.

ENHANCING THE NCO'S STATUS

In 1841 Congress, by means of several changes in the regulations, took steps to enhance "the station and respectability" of the noncommissioned officer. Taking cue from von Steuben's admonition to his officers of almost seventy-five years before, the new regulations cautioned all officers not to reprove noncommissioned officers in the presence or hearing of privates lest the authority and respectability of the noncommissioned officer be weakened in the eyes of his subordinates. At all times admonition was to be conveyed in mild terms, without exposing the individual to ridicule, whatever his rank. If the situation required stronger disciplinary measures than mere verbal admonition, noncommissioned officers were placed under arrest in separate quarters, but never confined with private soldiers.[32]

Perhaps one of the most innovative among the measures designed to enhance the noncommissioned officer's image was a regulation published in 1841 that enjoined all company commanders to give their attention to the organization of a separate mess for their noncommissioned officers "when circumstances of the service permit." Unfortunately, this latter clause meant that separate messes were rarely established, for as late as 1906 some Army reformers were still advocating a separate mess as a means of enhancing the status of noncommissioned officers. A separate mess nevertheless was considered in theory "highly desirable for the maintenance of the respect and authority due the noncommissioned officer."[33]

A change that affected all ranks by reducing some disciplinary problems for noncommissioned officers was the gradual elimination of rum, brandy, and whiskey from the daily ration. A proposal to pay a cash allowance in lieu of the liquor issue was introduced in Congress in 1830. With the rise of the temperance movement, President Andrew Jackson declared on October 25, 1832, "that coffee and sugar were to be substituted for the allowance of rum, whiskey, or brandy."[34] Six years later Congress, in a bill to increase the military establishment, confirmed the presidential action, although coffee did not completely replace liquor until the Civil War.[35]

Such relatively minor changes did not alter the fact that the noncommissioned officers' opportunities in the Army were nevertheless far more limited than those of the commissioned officer. The former remained locked into his regiment for his entire career as it remained the appointing authority for a noncommissioned officer and, for all practical purposes, his permanent place of assignment while in the Army.

No noncommissioned officer or private soldier could be transferred in grade from one regiment to another without the previous authority of the general in chief of the Army. Such authority, moreover, could only be obtained by the regimental commander through the adjutant general—a lengthy process rarely indulged in. Consequently, to protect their grade, senior noncommissioned officers had little choice but to remain with the same unit throughout their military careers, unless they were commissioned or appointed ordnance sergeants. These men often became almost legendary figures in their respective regiments as generations of officers came and went, while the old sergeants stayed on as seemingly indestructible fixtures, held in awe by both officers and enlisted men.[36]

CHAPTER 4

ENHANCING THE NONCOMMISSIONED OFFICER CORPS

When, on February 13, 1815, official Washington learned that war with Britain had ended with the signing of the Treaty of Ghent on Christmas Eve 1814, Congress was as quick to respond to the cessation of hostilities as it had been after the War of Independence—doing what the enemy forces could not do—significantly reducing the size of the United States Army. The post-war Army was authorized a strength of ten thousand men, exclusive of a corps of engineers. The bulk of this force consisted of eight regiments of infantry of ten companies each. Each of these companies had a captain, a first and second lieutenant (the latter taking the place but not the duties of the ensign), four sergeants, four corporals, two musicians (who ranked as noncommissioned officers), and sixty-eight privates.[1]

In an effort to stimulate enlistments at the beginning of the war, Congress had significantly increased the pay of all ranks: sergeants major and quartermaster sergeants to receive $9.00 per month; sergeants $8.00; corporals $7.00; senior musicians or teachers of music $8.00; and simple musicians $6.00. The private soldier's pay was only $5.00 a month, compared with the artificer's, or military mechanic's top-enlisted-specialist pay of $10.00 a month. But by an act of December 12, 1812, Congress increased enlisted pay to $12.00 for sergeants major and quartermaster sergeants; $11.00 for sergeants and senior musicians; $10.00 for corporals; $9.00 for ordinary musicians; and $8.00 for privates. As before, the artificer, a category that included blacksmiths, farriers, and saddlers, continued at the top of the pay scale with $13.00 per month. These rates remained unchanged until the 1830s, when the ferment of Jacksonian democracy produced a favorable climate within Congress and the country for again increasing army pay.[2]

In the autumn of 1817, John C. Calhoun took over the duties of secretary of war, just as the Army was completing the reorganization directed by Congress in 1815. About the same time, Sylvanus Thayer became superintendent of the military academy at West Point. Thayer set about improving the training of the cadets, thus assuring the small Army of a corps of professional officers. The new secretary and superintendent each in his way saw that the Army rested on a thoroughly professional cadre of officers and noncommissioned officers, for Scott's earlier victories at Chippewa and Lundy's Lane gave abundant proof of the value of such men.[3]

In spite of earlier congressional authorization for a 10,000-man army, when Calhoun became secretary of war the regular Army had a strength of only 8,200 men. In May 1820, Congress reduced the Army's authorized strength to 6,000, leaving the secretary with no choice but to focus on maintaining only a small professional cadre of officers and enlisted men capable of being fleshed out in wartime with thousands of volunteers. Although acceptance of the concept of an expandable army had to wait another century, Calhoun repudiated Washington's long-standing militia principle and sought to replace it with the dictum that a professional military uniquely possessed military value. This point was, as one historian has expressed it, the "one result of the War of 1812 that would reverberate through the next century of American military history."[4]

Small though it was, the U.S. Army was henceforth a thoroughly professional institution. Increasingly, its officer corps was composed of graduates of the military academy. This fact had a two-fold effect on the noncommissioned officers: Professionally trained officers meant better noncommissioned officers because the former trained and groomed the latter. Also, by filling the commissioned grades with academy graduates, the Army effectively limited movement from the ranks into the commissioned grades. This left even the most able enlisted men with little choice but to remain with the noncommissioned corps if they chose a military career.

During this euphoric interlude between the War of 1812 and Andrew Jackson's presidency in the 1830s, the small professional Army, scattered over a vast region and divided into numerous and of necessity small garrisons, watched over the frontiers of the young republic. At best, life in these garrisons was tedious. Other than the routine duties of administering and maintaining a military unit and post, a good part of an officer's time was spent serving on frequent courts-martial. Many offenses that today would be dealt with in the company through nonjudicial punishment were then often disposed of by courts-martial. For their part, noncommissioned officers spent their time in the routine training and housekeeping chores of garrison life.

THE NONCOMMISSIONED OFFICER'S STATUS

In general the noncommissioned officer, who was trained and selected by the commissioned officer, continued to be treated far better than the private soldier. For example, a noncommissioned officer was rarely deprived of his whiskey ration as a disciplinary measure, but for the rank and file this was almost always appended to other punishments such as hard labor in chains or flogging. Among the noncommissioned officers, corporals seemed most likely to run afoul of regulations.

Neglect of duty and conduct unbecoming a soldier—usually due to drunkenness—were the most frequent charges they faced, with reduction to the ranks for varying periods of time being the most common punishment.

Such was the fate of Corporal Fish of the Baton Rouge garrison one hot July day in 1821: for absenting himself from guard mount he was "suspended to the ranks for one month."[5] Sometimes administrative rather than legal tangles hazarded a noncommissioned officer's position, as when it was discovered by an adjutant that there were more noncommissioned officers in a company than were authorized by regulations. Those junior and excess to authorized tables of organization were forthwith reduced to the ranks without prejudice.

Not only corporals but also sergeants sometimes incurred the heavy hand of a court-martial. In Captain Ferdinand Z. Amelung's company book can be traced the fall and redemption of a certain Sergeant Lain, who in the summer of 1818, while stationed with the 1st Infantry Regiment at Baton Rouge, sold whiskey to the privates of the company. The regimental court-martial ordered Sergeant Lain struck from the roll of sergeants and mustered as a private as of June 26.[6] His disgrace was brief, however: Four days later, Captain Amelung, taking advantage of the fact that he and part of his company were on detached service at Bay Fêche, Attakapas, Louisiana Territory, restored Lain to his old rank. As he did so, Captain Amelung wrote, "It is hoped that his Indulgence will stimulate not only Sergeant Lain but also all the noncommissioned officers towards a zealous performance of their duties."

This act of leniency did not end Captain Amelung's problems, because two weeks later, when he returned to his base camp at Nova Iberia, near Baton Rouge, he found that during his absence "considerable disorder and misconduct had taken place." Among the punishments meted out at that time, was the reduction to the rank of a Corporal Oliver Butler for two weeks for "repeatedly furnishing Private Charles Thomas with his own ration of spirits when said Thomas was under confinement at Camp Nova Iberia."

Apparently Butler took his reduction in good stride and soon proved his worth once again, for the corporal was later "promoted to the rank of Sergeant . . . to take rank from the first day of August."

NONCOMMISSIONED OFFICER PROMOTIONS

Until the outbreak of the Civil War there was no major change in the enlisted grade structure of the Army, but there were noteworthy developments within the small regular force that emerged from Secretary Calhoun's stewardship. Under the tutelage of a growing body of professional officer graduates of West Point, the army's organization became more systematic and stereotyped. Throughout the period 1815–1861, there was also a conscious effort on the part of the officer corps to enhance the prestige and authority of the noncommissioned officer "and to provide for more gradation and specialization with the grade structure of the post, regimental and company level." In the Army, the garrison post was the principal service agency, the regiment the primary field headquarters, and the company the main tactical element. For much of the century the noncommissioned officer structure developed around these three bodies.[7]

In both the infantry and artillery the enlisted grade structure was standardized, with one regimental sergeant major, one quartermaster sergeant, and in the infantry two principal musicians in each regiment. Artillery companies had four sergeants and four corporals, three artificers, two musicians, and forty-two privates, while each infantry company had four sergeants, four corporals, two musicians, and forty-two privates.[8]

The Army regulations of 1821 and 1825 first established a systematic method of noncommissioned officer selection. Appointment of both company and regimental noncommissioned officers was the prerogative of the regimental commander. However, in the case of company noncommissioned officers the regimental commander was generally expected to accept the company commander's recommendation unless there were overriding reasons not to do so.[9]

These regulations also specified that "every noncommissioned officer will be furnished with a certificate of his rank, signed by the colonel and countersigned by the adjutant—assimilated, as near as may be, to the commission of an officer." Appointments of noncommissioned officers were also announced in regimental orders, after which these men could not be degraded "except for incapacity, or misconduct proven before a court and if found guilty of a slight offense, the punishment shall not exceed reduction to the ranks."[10] The regulations simply codified a long-standing practice.

To encourage company morale by holding out the prospects of advance, when practicable the "selection of company sergeants was to be made from the corporals." However, when appointments to the rank of corporal or promotion to sergeant were made from one company into another of the same regiment, they had to be made with the approval of the captain into whose company the new noncommissioned officers were transferred.[11]

The grade of lance corporal, long recognized in practice though not in statute, also acquired legal status under these regulations. A private thus selected commanded squads or detachments consisting of privates only or containing other lance corporals junior to himself. Neither his pay nor duties as a private, however, changed. However, the appointment placed him in line for promotion to corporal when a vacancy occurred. These appointments were also announced in regimental orders, and the man was thereby entitled to a badge of rank that could not be removed except by judgment of a court-martial. Some years later similar provisions were made for the appointment of lance sergeants from among the corporals of a unit.[12]

DESIGNATION OF RANK

Together with standardization of procedures in the selection and appointment of noncommissioned officers came changes in the designation of rank among them. By March 1815, the noncommissioned officer's shoulder straps in use since the War of Independence had been abandoned in favor of "wings" on the shoulders of coats worn by light infantry units. These wings had their drawbacks, and after several years of experimentation with various types of rank designation the Army adopted chevrons.

The regulations of 1821 prescribed chevrons to be worn on the sleeve of the uniform, points down, as a means of designating noncommissioned rank. Sergeants major and quartermaster sergeants wore authorized worsted chevrons on each arm, above the elbow; sergeants and senior musicians wore them below the elbow; and corporals were given a single chevron on the right arm, above the elbow. Chevrons for the infantry were white and artillery yellow. Officers continued to wear epaulets.[13]

In 1833 shoulder straps made a brief comeback, but three years later chevrons returned to the duty uniform, this time for good. Changes were also made in the noncommissioned officer dress uniform when slashings (stripes), similar to those already worn by commissioned officers, were added to the sleeves. Slashings of gold lace were prescribed for officers, of worsted wool for sergeants.[14]

IMPROVEMENT OF PAY AND LIVING CONDITIONS

Changes in regulations concerning the enlisted grade structure and rank designation for enlisted men were accompanied by recommendations for improvement of their pay and living conditions. Foremost among those pressing for such improvements was Major General Jacob Brown, Winfield Scott's commanding officer on the Niagara frontier during the War of 1812. In a letter to the secretary of war in 1825, General Brown wrote:

> If in a country like ours it shall be considered most wise to maintain, in time of peace the small military establishment which is now authorized, I trust there is good cause to believe that the people will see and feel the importance of making that establishment as perfect as might be expected from the unequaled materials on which the nation has to draw.[15]

Central to making the small professional Army "as perfect as might be expected" was, in General Brown's view, "the advancement of the noncommissioned officer grades of the army." The key to obtaining and retaining "the talent and ability requisite in the station of a noncommissioned officer," Brown wrote, "was an adequate pecuniary emolument"—in short, better pay. The social prestige attached to the commissioned rank gave to officers a "ready passport to the highest circles of society." But such was not the case with the noncommissioned officer, who together with his commissioned counterpart shared equal responsibility for "the moral and physical efficiency of the rank and file. Indeed," Brown continued, repeating a seventeenth-century dictum, "there is no individual of a company, *scarcely excepting the captain himself, on whom more depends for its discipline, police, instruction, and general well-being, than on the first sergeant* [emphasis added]." Brown concluded:

> It is a grade with cares and responsibility. Its duties place the incumbent in constant and direct contact with the men, exercising over them an influence more the powerful as it is immediate and personal; and all experience demonstrates that the condition of every company will improve or deteriorate nearly in proportion to the ability and worth of its first sergeant.

Congressional response, however, was less than enthusiastic. The first increase in pay following General Brown's plea had to wait until 1833, when a new pay scale—the first since 1802—was established for the Army. For example, members of the regimental noncommissioned staff—the sergeant major, quartermaster sergeant, and chief musician, were henceforth paid $16.00 per month (five years later this was increased one dollar); the company first sergeant, $15.00; all other sergeants $12.00; artificers $10.00; corporals $8.00; and musicians and privates $6.00 (five years later increased to $8.00). It is noteworthy that the artificer was no longer more highly paid than the sergeants, reflecting a more abundant supply of skilled workmen available for recruitment. Perhaps most important in terms of remuneration was the provision to give each enlisted man serving continuously for ten years 160 acres of land on expiration of his service and an extra ration for each five years of service. In the thirty-one years since 1802, Army pay just about doubled, yet was still hardly sufficient to keep pace with increased costs in a rapidly growing country.[16]

THE ORDNANCE SERGEANTS

In 1832 Congress reestablished the ordnance department by separating its function from that of the artillery. Not to exceed two hundred and fifty men, the department, in addition to the usual noncommissioned grades, consisted of six grades of specialists. These were, in order of rank, master workmen, armorers, carriage makers, blacksmiths, artificers, and laborers. At the same time, Congress also created the rank of ordnance sergeant. One ordnance sergeant was appointed for each military post. These men were selected from among those sergeants of the line with at least eight years of military service.

The ordnance sergeant received and preserved the ordnance, arms, ammunition, and other military stores. For this he was paid an additional $5.00 per month over his regular pay as a sergeant, thereby making him second only to the master workman in pay. There was an additional intent in the congressional action establishing this grade: to offer "a reward to those faithful and well-tried sergeants who have long served their country, and of thus giving encouragement to the soldier in the ranks to emulate them in conduct, and thereby secure substantial promotion."[17] This was the first of several attempts, culminating in the creation of warrant officer in the twentieth century, to work out a means of rewarding and recognizing able noncommissioned officers without fully elevating them to the commissioned ranks.

In the years that followed, the adjutant general's files bulged with numerous applications from older noncommissioned officers applying for appointments as ordnance sergeant. With the accompanying recommendations from their commanding officers, these applications tell a great deal about the noncommissioned officers of that day.

Sometimes ordnance sergeants were transferred from one post to another "for the good of the service"—making them the first noncommissioned officers to be transferred without loss of rank. There were others who were occasionally relieved for incompetence. In many cases these applications tell stories of the concern and compassion that most commissioned officers felt toward enlisted men who had given the Army years of loyal service.[18]

One such case was that of Sergeant Van Camp, ordnance sergeant at Ft. Winnebago, Wisconsin. When, early in 1846, Army headquarters in Washington raised the question of abandoning the old fort, Brigadier General George M. Brooke, then commanding officer of the 3rd Mounted Rifles stationed in St. Louis, Missouri, strongly urged against the action, arguing that the fort would be needed until the Winnebago and Menominie Indians "had been removed to their intended and permanent homes." In any case, the only expense involved in keeping the post open was that of keeping an ordnance sergeant there. The present ordnance sergeant [Van Camp], General Brook stated, was "a worthless drunkard even when the post was occupied by a garrison and, I presume, never sober since the troops left." Brooke recommended Van Camp's replacement with Ordnance Sergeant Horn, then at Ft. Howard, Wisconsin. General Brooke recommended him "as a most sober and excellent person to be placed [at Ft. Winnebago]."[19]

Fortunately for Sergeant Van Camp, Brigadier General Brady, commanding officer of the 4th Military District, in which Ft. Winnebago was located, sprang to his defense. General Brady countered Brooke's criticism of Van Camp with the observation that he (Brady) did "not know a more efficient Ordnance Sergeant in the Army than Sergeant Van Camp." True, Brady added, he "does sometimes drink more than is good for himself [but] I shall take measures to ascertain that what his habits have been since the troops left [Winnebago], and if they have been bad, I would respectfully suggest that he be removed to Mackinac where there is no ordnance sergeant, and where under the eye of the commanding officer he would do well."

General Brady defended Van Camp because of the sergeant's length of service and "the excellent service he had rendered as sergeant." Van Camp had, Brady added, enlisted in 1812 and served honorably throughout that war. Now an old man, Van Camp, "if removed from the Army could not make a living in civil life." This was a sentiment frequently expressed by officers concerning their older professional soldiers.[20]

If it were necessary to relieve Sergeant Van Camp, however, General Brady recommended his *own* favorite, Sergeant Shaw of the 5th Infantry. Honorably discharged from the service, Shaw was then living in St. Louis with his family. He was, Brady declared, "a Sober, industrious man and a good scholar [and] had served through several enlistments with much credit." He would, Brady averred, "be willing to reenlist if that would aid him in procuring the appointment." Eventually Sergeant Van Camp was transferred to Mackinac Island as ordnance sergeant, and Sergeant Shaw and his family moved to Ft. Winnebago instead of Sergeant Horn.

The intemperate Van Camp was not the only ordnance sergeant to run the risk of serious disciplinary action because of his addiction to drink. An inspecting officer visiting Ft. Wood, Louisiana, where a Sergeant Jeremiah Beck was stationed as ordnance sergeant, found him intoxicated and the affairs of the post in disarray. Placing Beck under arrest, the officer informed the commander of the Western District of the situation. The latter sent an officer to Ft. Wood to investigate the charges against Beck and found him "plainly unfit for any separate charge or command from his habitual use of liquor and its encouragement among those under him."[21]

Meanwhile, Beck, sensing that he was no longer competent to perform the duties of ordnance sergeant, submitted his resignation to the commanding general of the Western Division. But in doing so he reminded the general that he (Beck) had "been an old soldier and a long time in the service [had] been mutilated in Mexico [he had lost an arm] in the service of my country, and wish to retire to a peaceful life upon my pension [approximately $8.00 per month] where I may not hereafter be persecuted."[22]

For all his shortcomings, Sergeant Beck was apparently not without friends in high places. A memorandum from the adjutant general to Secretary of War March suggested that although the former had misgivings from the first concerning Beck's fitness for the post, "the appointment was so strongly urged upon the secretary of war from other quarters, as to result in an order, first to enlist then to appoint the discharged soldier [Beck had been discharged following his wounding during the war] Ordnance Sergeant, to the place he now holds with so little credit to himself or advantage to the public." Although the adjutant general recommended that Beck be discharged from the service, the ordnance department managed to have him transferred to another post where, like Van Camp, he was under close supervision. Both Van Camp's and Beck's case illustrate the extent to which the Army would go to spare a loyal and long-service noncommissioned officer the ignominy of a dishonorable discharge when drink threatened to end an otherwise honorable career.

From a study of most of the applications one must conclude that fidelity (length of service) and sobriety as well as a good hand were the primary requisites of an ordnance sergeant. Most applicants had generally served ten to fifteen years and been noncommissioned officers for much of that time. In some cases, there had been interruptions in their service as, for example, in the case of Sergeant Thomas Mulligan, then with a recruiting party in New York City. Mulligan had enlisted in 1832 and had served the whole period of his enlistment with the exception of about four months at its commencement as a noncommissioned officer in the 3d Regiment of Artillery. Discharged as first sergeant of Company D of that regiment in 1837, Mulligan reenlisted in April of 1839 and quickly regained his noncommissioned rank. During the interval between enlistments Mulligan served with the Philadelphia Volunteers in Florida.

Some applicants, such as a Sergeant William Hayes, had already seen service elsewhere—in Hayes's case a three-year stint in the Marine Corps, before joining the Army. Hayes's fifteen years in the Army had been divided between the artillery and the recruiting service and he had been a sergeant for fourteen of those years.[23]

Frequently, long-time first sergeants, seeking less arduous duties for their final years in the Army, applied for appointments. One was Thomas Baldwin, first sergeant of Company D, 4th Artillery, who applied for the post of ordnance sergeant at either Thong's Point, New York, or at Dearborn, Michigan.

Baldwin cited his "service of near eleven years in the 4th Artillery, almost nine of which in grade of 1st Sergeant" as giving him a claim "to favorable consideration." To this his regimental commander added that "Sgt Baldwin is well qualified to perform any duty that may be required of him." The good sergeant had indeed a fine record, having served in both the Florida campaign against the Seminoles and throughout the Mexican War without a day's absence. Actually, First Sergeant Baldwin's own statements rather understated his record, for one of his former commanders wrote from Tampa, Florida, that Sergeant Baldwin was "qualified in a superior degree for the station he solicits, being a man of good education, excellent talents and trustworthy character—the increased size of his family now very naturally prompts the wish for a retirement from active duty of the field."[24]

Another of Sergeant Baldwin's former company commanders briefly reviewed his career as further justification for his appointment to the position he sought. Baldwin enlisted in July 1837 and was promoted to corporal in June of the following year for good conduct in Florida. The next year he made sergeant, and later the same year his company commander appointed him first sergeant—a post he held for the next nine years. When the company was sent to Corpus Christi in 1845 during the Mexican War, Baldwin was selected to act as sergeant major of the artillery battalion, then commanded by a Colonel Childs. In this position Baldwin took part in all the battles except Buena Vista and Cerro Gordo. "It would be difficult," his company commander, Captain R. C. Smead, observed, "to find a noncommissioned officer who has seen or done more service in the Mexican War than he has. He writes a good hand, understands making out all kinds of papers and returns, is a good accountant, and is quick and accurate as a clerk." In fact, Smead concluded, "I consider him well-qualified for the situation of Ordnance Sergeant and from his long and faithful service entitled to it in preference to any other noncommissioned officer that I am acquainted with."[25]

There were other applicants who in addition to the usual qualifications claimed the office because of personal hardship. In such cases, the soldier sometimes bypassed command channels and appealed, as did Sergeant W. R. Wilson, directly to the secretary of war.[26] Wilson requested of the secretary that after ten years of service in the Army, seven as a noncommissioned officer, "the situation of Ordnance Sergeant at Ft. Griswold, Connecticut be given to me." His reasons for wishing the appointment were that "I have a wife in feeble health, a small child, and wife's mother to support, and if I am ordered to Mexico, as is very likely, they will all be left to certain misery and destitution." When one remembers that the sergeant's pay at this time was $13.00 a month and that there were no provisions for dependents accompanying deployed enlisted personnel, the sergeant was not far wrong in predicting dire straits for his dependents during his absence.[27] A note on the routing slip accompanying Wilson's letter stated "not according to regulations." So it would seem that his appeal fell on deaf ears, and the sergeant was sent with his regiment to Mexico after all.

An even more appealing case was that of Sergeant R. T. Jackson, leader of the regimental band of the 6th Infantry. In his letter of application, which, unlike Wilson's, went through channels to the adjutant general, Jackson presented himself as a soldier who had raised a large family during his military career of nineteen years, seventeen of which had been as a noncommissioned officer.

"A desire to promote the welfare of my wife together with my five children," Jackson wrote, "prompts me to take a liberty for which I trust the nature of the case will plead an excuse." For nineteen years he had been a musician in the regimental band and its leader for the past seventeen years. Although as band leader he received "double or nearly so the allowance made by law to an Ordnance Sergeant . . . yet a consideration which to me as a man of family is of great moment and considerably impairs my future prospects in life leads me to seek an appointment of at least half my present income that I may rear and educate a family solely dependent upon my exertions for all they can expect on Earth." This consideration was "the loss of my front teeth so indispensably necessary to the fulfillment of my present duty as leader of the Band [undoubtedly he played a wind instrument] and using as I have done for some time artificial ones at a great expense to myself, I am only able to perform with great inconvenience and oft-times very acute pain."[28]

To this Sergeant Jackson's commanding officer added his recommendation that Jackson "is sober, faithful, and intelligent, he writes an excellent hand and is well fitted for the situation." The adjutant general's military aide added the note that "the sergeant is an old soldier and behaved gallantly and was wounded in the operations before Mexico." Needless to say, a position as ordnance sergeant was found for the faithful band leader and noncommissioned officer.

There were also senior noncommissioned officers such as Sergeant William Smith of Company H, 1st Regiment of Artillery who, feeling the infirmities of age and frequent campaigns becoming too much for him, applied for an appointment as ordnance sergeant, where his duties would be less arduous. In an eloquent letter to the adjutant general, Smith wrote that

> Feeling my good constitution—only in about 11 years once on sick report—fast declining in consequence of the fatigues, exposures, and excitements of the present campaign, particularly through often and sudden changing of climate, I do consider it my duty to myself to try to preserve my health for future service for my voluntarily adopted country, in whose cause I have the honor to serve ten years and six months, and having been entrusted since the 26th December 1838 with the rank of sergeant, therefore, as I must be afraid not to be able to fulfill the duty of soldier in the field for the future to the full satisfaction of my superiors, and to myself, I take the liberty to make use in my behalf, of the privilege assigned to noncommissioned officers in paragraph 185 of the General Regulations of 1847 and beg most respectfully the Adjutant General to have the kindness to take my situation of health, my servitude, and the respectfully enclosed testimonials to my character and ability in favourable consideration by replacing Ordnance Sergeant vacancies, or by appointments for new military posts.[29]

In prose considerably less involuted than that of Sergeant Smith, his company commander declared that he had known Smith for many years and had always known him to be "a man of integrity, industry, and good habits." Moreover, Smith was "a competent clerk and conversant with all kinds of military returns."[30]

To this the regimental commander added that Smith had also behaved gallantly in battle. He had taken part in the battles of Contreras, Churubusco, and the attack on the Belin Gate of Mexico City. During the latter action "Sgt. Smith was right at or near the head of the regiment, all the way up to the arches, until the enemy left the Gate."[31]

There were also senior noncommissioned officers who, for one reason or another—usually age—were ineligible for commissions, but whose commanding officers pushed them for appointment as ordnance sergeant by way of compensation. Such was the case of Sergeant H. W. Miller of Company B, 1st Dragoons. In a recommendation to the regimental commander, Miller's company commander, Lieutenant J. Love, wrote that he had never seen "him the least under the influence of liquor, and my belief is that he never even touches it. He writes a fair hand, and is one of the most accurate clerks I ever saw." Love continued:

> Sgt. Miller was so conspicuous for his good conduct under all circumstances whilst serving with the Army of the West, that every officer of the regular army with that

> division recommended him for a commission that I make this application [in his behalf]. He is now getting too old to serve another enlistment in performance of the active duties of Orderly Sergeant. His term of service expires in April, and he is unwilling to leave a profession in which he has spent the prime of his life. In recommending Sgt. Miller I honestly believe that I am recommending one who is as well if not better qualified than any sergeant in the Army and sincerely hope that his long and faithful service will be rewarded.[32]

The regimental commander enthusiastically endorsed Lieutenant Love's recommendation, pointing out to the adjutant general that of Miller's fourteen years of Army service, twelve had been as a noncommissioned officer. On December 26, 1848, Miller was appointed ordnance sergeant for Ft. Wood, Louisiana, to replace Sergeant Jeremiah Beck who, it will be recalled, had been relieved of that assignment.

Noncommissioned officers whose battle wounds incapacitated them for further active field service were also recommended by their commanding officers for appointment as ordnance sergeants. One solicitious C.O. General A. Shields, who appealed to the adjutant general in behalf of Sergeant Patrick Martin, whom Shields described as "a poor fellow who lost his limb at Churubusco" during which he had conducted himself gallantly. Martin, General Shields continued, "wishes now to be appointed Ordnance Sergeant." His health was excellent, and the loss of a limb was his only disability and would not interfere with his performance of the duties of ordnance sergeant, General Shields assured the adjutant general.[33]

Another old soldier, Sergeant Abraham Garver of the 1st Infantry, then stationed at Ft. Brown, Texas, received the hearty endorsement of his company commander, Captain J. H. La Motte, in his application for appointment. Sergeant Garver had seen twenty-five years service in the Army. Twenty of these years had been as a noncommissioned officer. Captain La Motte wrote the adjutant general in behalf of this "trusty, respectable old soldier" for appointment at some post, preferably along the Rio Grande. The old sergeant, he wrote, had been seriously wounded during the battle of Monterey and had been subsequently offered his discharge with a certificate of disability, which he declined. Garver's wound, Captain La Motte added, would not inhibit him from the performance of the duties of an ordnance sergeant. Furthermore, "he writes legibly—is temperate and exceedingly correct in all his deportment and . . . fully competent to the discharge of the duties of Ordnance Sergeant." This recommendation was sufficient to get the old sergeant the post of ordnance sergeant at Ft. Brown, Texas.[34]

Usually ordnance sergeants, unless relieved for misconduct, remained at their posts until old age or death removed them. In the latter case, the incumbent often left a wife and family to be taken care of, as did Sergeant William Heckle at Ft. Smith, Arkansas, who died on March 26, 1848 "of disease of the lungs," leaving a wife and several children.

Sergeant Heckle's "sudden and unexpected" death deprived the post commander "of the valuable services of a faithful and efficient noncommissioned officer." Because there was a considerable quantity of ordnance and ordnance stores on post, the ordnance sergeant had been required to perform the duties of quartermaster sergeant as well. As the only officer on the post, Lieutenant F. Flint urged the adjutant general to send him as soon as possible a replacement for Heckle. "It is important," the lieutenant wrote, "that . . . he should be a trusty, intelligent, and efficient man, as I am the only officer on post and necessarily compelled to entrust much to irresponsible subordinates." Lieutenant Flint had not long to wait, for Sergeant John Livers of the 4th Artillery Regiment was soon appointed.[35]

Sergeant Livers was later replaced, in March 1848, by Sergeant William H. Ailes, who had served with the 6th Infantry since November 1831. Ailes had taken part in the campaign of 1832, fought on the Sabine River in 1836, in the Florida campaigns of 1838, 1839 and 1840, and on the western frontier until 1848. For several years he had been assigned as clerk at regimental headquarters, at several periods to the ordnance department. At the time of his assignment to Ft. Smith, Ailes was serving as acting ordnance sergeant at Ft. Washita, then Indian Territory in what is now the state of Oklahoma.

CARING FOR OLD SOLDIERS

The number of ordnance sergeant positions in the Army was insufficient to meet the needs of all elderly soldiers disabled by wounds, age, or sickness. In any case, not all of them were qualified for such duty, even if the positions had existed. Typical of the latter type was Sergeant Charles Bussell, late of Company I of the 4th Regiment of Artillery. He enlisted in the Army in 1815, but by 1844 he had decided to apply for a discharge and make his living farming and selling produce to the soldiers stationed at his old post, Ft. Monroe. However, Bussell had not counted on opposition from the regular post sutler to his planned activities on the post. Incensed at this treatment, the old sergeant wrote to both President Polk and General Winfield Scott protesting that he was not allowed to sutle at Ft. Monroe. The present sutler, Bussell complained, "is a crook and a miser." Slaves, he added, were allowed to sell produce for their masters, but he, an old soldier, was unable to sell anything from his farm wagon to the soldiers.[36]

When Bussell realized that his plans to make a living sutling had failed, he attempted to reenlist—without success. His former commanding officer wrote the adjutant general stating that when Bussell requested his discharge, he cautioned the sergeant that he "was advanced in years and once out of the service . . . would find it difficult to reenter it." Now the colonel wrote, "I do not believe there is a single Captain in my regiment who would be willing to receive Bussell as one of his soldiers." The regimental commander added that Bussell still had the privileges of the post market, as had other tradesmen, but that Bussell had misused the favors shown him by evading post orders. The old sergeant in turn appealed in vain to General Scott to help him to reenlist. He wrote, "General, I am now old and worn out in the service. General, if I am enlisted, I shall remain my lifetime in it."[37] Bussell, however, was too old to serve any longer as an efficient soldier, and his appeal fell on deaf ears.

The Army, however, was not entirely lacking in compassion for old soldiers. When Sergeant Michael Moore, for five years the principal instructor of the drummer boys in the Army school of practice, attempted to reenlist, the assistant surgeon at Ft. Columbus, New York, refused to sign the usual medical certificate of fitness "on account of an impediment which the sergeant has in his speech." His commanding officer promptly intervened in his behalf with the adjutant general, pointing out that Sergeant Moore had enlisted as a boy. He had served seven enlistments satisfactorily and, now at the age of forty, to deny him reenlistment because of a speech impediment that had no adverse effect on his performance of his duties as an instructor was manifestly unjust. Moore's commanding officer therefore requested permission to reenlist him without the surgeon's signature. Prompt approval of the request came from Washington, and Moore continued to instruct the drummer boys at Ft. Columbus.[38]

Yet these largely *ad hoc* measures were manifestly inadequate to meet the needs of most aged or disabled soldiers, most of whom were noncommissioned officers. In the republic's early years the lot of such men had not been a happy one. From 1790, when the first military pension had been established, until 1851, the monthly pension for retired or disabled soldiers, regardless of rank, had been increased from $5.00 to only $8.00 per month. Not only were these sums woefully inadequate, but there was no provision for the sheltered care of such men—many of whom were aged—who often needed it.

Commissioned officers had long recognized a need for some kind of care for elderly soldiers who because of the infirmities of age or wounds were no longer able to perform their regular duties. Since 1827 successive secretaries of war urged upon an indifferent Congress that some provision be made for the institutionalized care of disabled or aged soldiers of the regular Army. Although many noncommissioned officers were married men, often with rather large families, most enlisted men remained single throughout their Army careers and consequently had no one to look out for or care for them in their old age. Foremost among Army officers pressing Congress to provide somehow for old soldiers, was General Winfield Scott, who between 1841 and 1849 repeatedly urged Congress to establish a "retreat" or "asylum" for "worn out or decayed rank and file of the Army." Such an institution would, he wrote with a parsimonious legislature in mind, "be supported from the Army itself, in deduction from pay, fines, and Reversions."[39]

In spite of such pleas, not until March 3, 1851, after the war with Mexico, did Congress pass legislation providing for the establishment of a "military asylum for the relief and support of invalid and disabled soldiers of the Army of the United States."

Although Congress authorized its establishment, the support of the asylum, as

General Scott had promised, came largely from the army itself: deductions from enlisted pay (12½ cents per month) and from such windfalls as the $150,000 contribution in lieu of pillage that General Scott levied on the citizens of Mexico City during the war. Scott deposited two thirds of that sum with the Bank of America in New York City, to be held as credit for the army "asylum" or Soldier's Home, as it came eventually to be known. The home was open to "all who had served honestly and faithfully for twenty years in the Army after arriving at the age of 18, or who had been disabled by wounds or disease in the service." The home's first temporary quarters opened on December 24, 1851, in a rented house next door to the Winder Building, the old War Department building, in Washington, D.C. Within a week of its opening, the home had three residents.[40]

In addition to the needs of aged and disabled soldiers, there were also the needs of men on active duty, such as increases in pay. In 1854, Congress increased pay for all grades by $4.00 a month, thereby raising a sergeant's from $13.00 to $17.00. Concurrently, Congress authorized longevity pay for the first time, providing an extra $2.00 per month for a second enlistment and an additional $1.00 for each enlistment thereafter. Since enlistments were for a five-year period at that time—even a gray-headed old sergeant was not particularly well paid before the infirmities of age forced him into the Soldier's Home.

Modest though it was, the soldier's pay was also often in arrears. Although regulations stated that enlisted men be paid every two months, men stationed in remote garrisons or on extended field service in Indian territory sometimes had to wait six months before the paymaster caught up with them.[41]

Since the second war with England, much had been accomplished to improve the noncommissioned officer's status. With the establishment of the U.S. Military Academy at West Point came the professionalization of the officer corps and, subsequently, significant improvement in the selection and training of noncommissioned officers. Greater emphasis on professionalism brought servicewide improvements in pay and living conditions. This included laying the foundations of sheltered care for aged and disabled enlisted men. Many senior and outstanding noncommissioned officers turned their attention to further career enhancement through opportunities for commissions in the regular Army. The war with Mexico provided those opportunities.

CHAPTER 5

PROMOTIONS FROM THE RANKS

Compared with the societies of Europe in the first half of the nineteenth century, American society had developed in a relatively unstructured pattern. Class lines in the new nation were not as identifiable nor as fixed as they were in Europe. Moreover, the vastness of an as yet undeveloped continent held out a hope, if not a promise, of a better life for thousands of Americans striving to improve their standard of living over that of their parents. For some, the small regular Army, scattered though it was over this broad land, offered some opportunity, at least for social advancement, to those men commissioned from the military academy at West Point. There were two other roads to a commission in the regular Army, one through direct appointment by the president, and the other—though rarely used—promotion from the ranks. For the regular Army noncommissioned officer, the latter was usually the only way to become an officer.

However, in the eyes of many both within and without the Army, promotion from the ranks was effectively blocked by the establishment of the United States Military Academy. Indeed, Jacksonians viewed the academy as a deterrent to the advancement of good men from the ranks and therefore as a deterrent to enlistment in the Army of capable and ambitious young men. In the words of an anonymous soldier critic writing in the 1830s, West Point "has rendered the Army very unpopular and odious with the great mass of the people. Young men of character and enterprise rarely enlisted, because they know well, that on a peace establishment, no higher rank that a *Sergeantcy can be obtained* [Italics in the quoted text]."[1]

Moreover, he added in the then popular nativist vein, this situation prevented the government

> during the last twelve years, to obtain a sufficient number of American citizens to complete the necessary complement for the rank and file of our little Army. Hence, as if to render the service still more odious and anti-American, foreigners have been freely received. Certainly half, and possibly two-thirds of the present rank and file

> are the following descriptions,—and we *challenge a refutation* of these statements—viz: English, Irish, Scotch, Welsh, Danes, Swedes, Prussians, Poles, Austrians. Now what "esprit du [*sic*] corps" could be expected in a regiment composed of such materials.

The anonymous soldier then turned to what he saw as the evil effect the West Point–created officer caste had on comradely relations between commissioned and noncommissioned officers:

> There is no social or friendly inter-course between the enlisted man,—no matter if he is a Sergeant,—and the lowest commissioned officer in any way further than relates to their respective duties. There is just as almighty a distance preserved between a Sergeant-Major, who is the highest noncommissioned officer in the service, and a Brevet 2d Lieutenant, who is the lowest commissioned officer,—*a distressingly dignified rank, by the way*—as though it were a sacrilege in the former to presume to approach the latter in a familiar manner. Perhaps some Brevet is ready to excuse himself, that "the enlisted men are not fit for moral associates," for him. We will grant the truth of his excuse in its general reference, and then most respectfully inform him, that the existence of the West Point School, by preventing respectable young men from entering the Army, is at once the author of the evil and the excuse.

An additional legacy of the Jacksonian era—"that education should command no special privileges or considerations"—was widely accepted by many other Americans. In the late 1830s this legacy manifested itself in proposals brought before Congress to authorize the promotion of capable noncommissioned officers to brevet second lieutenants (men serving as lieutenants but without the pay of that grade) and thereby reduce the number of West Point–trained officers on active service in the regular Army.[2]

The issue turned on whether to dismiss present brevet second lieutenants, many of whom had been appointed from civilian life, and to replace them with meritorious noncommissioned officers promoted from the ranks. A resolution to do so was placed before the House Committee on Military Affairs in February 1831. This committee examined "the expediency of authorizing appointments in the line of the Army from meritorious noncommissioned officers of the Army," and found no constitutional restrictions on the president for doing so.

In a statement breathing the very essence of Jacksonian democracy, the committee found it to be "utterly at variance with the genius and spirit of our government to exclude any class of citizens from eligibility to any office." The committee therefore concluded that commissions ought to be given noncommissioned officers whenever "the President considers that their merits and qualifications entitle them to advancement."[3]

There the matter rested until the next session of Congress, when it was taken up again. At that time the committee agreed with its predecessor that it was "unnecessary to invest the President with a discretion to promote noncommissioned officers to second lieutenancies," since he had it already under the Constitution. In the meantime, however, the committee learned that by an act passed on April 29, 1812, the president, when there was no vacancy in the line (that is, no shortage of commissioned officers) was nevertheless empowered to assign to units graduates of the military academy by brevet as second lieutenants, "provided that there shall not be more than one supernumerary [excess to authorized strength] officer in any company at the same time."

Since this applied only to West Point graduates, exercise of presidential authority to appoint noncommissioned officers to second lieutenants enabled such officers to outrank "all brevet second lieutenants previously existing (that is those West Point graduates so appointed) in violation of a principle of military usage so long established that a departure from it, excepting under peculiar circumstances, would be attended with the most injurious consequences" (presumably undermining the morale of academy graduates on active duty). The committee accordingly undertook to circumvent the 1812 legislation by inserting a provision into a bill reported to the House lifting the restrictions on appointment of supernumerary second lieutenants only for academy graduates and giving the president discretion to make such appointments from among either academy graduates *or meritorious noncommissioned officers*.

The committee then resolved

> that the Executive be vested with a discretion to appointment from among the noncommissioned officers of the Army, where they may be found worthy of promotion, a certain portion of the 2d Lieutenants . . . that, in order to enable the President to do this, the Committee further enquire into the expedient of reducing the number of cadets in the Military Academy at West Point and to prohibit the appointment of any cadet [to the academy] who has not yet arrived at the age of seventeen years.[4]

Although the House failed to act on the committee's resolution, Congress had taken another small step toward rewarding meritorious noncommissioned officers with long service.* Yet this action failed to satisfy many senior noncommissioned officers, for in January 1837, five years after the original resolution, twelve noncommissioned officers of the active Army submitted a memorial to Congress requesting that "persons in their grades be promoted to commissions for faithful and meritorious services."[5]

In their memorial the noncommissioned officers declared "the institution at West Point had for the last eighteen years furnished *all*† the commissioned officers for the Army, to the total exclusion of every enlisted soldier, no matter what

*The first step, it will be recalled, had been the act of April 5, 1832, authorizing the grade of ordnance sergeant.

†Italics supplied. Actually, not all commissioned officers were academy graduates. There had always been political appointments of prominent men or their sons to commissions, although in comparison to West Point graduates, they were relatively few in number.

his services, qualifications, of merit have been; which in the opinion of the undersigned, is *contrary to the true spirit of the Constitution of our country, and in opposition to all our republican institutions* [emphasis supplied]."

Continuing their list of grievances, the noncommissioned officers stated:

> when the patriotic soldier seriously reflects that being enlisted excludes him from preferment, and that not one of his grade can ever obtain promotion, either by acts of bravery, or otherwise, and that most of his officers are men who know not the soldier's wants by actual experience, he naturally loses his ambition, and either becomes a miserable outcast, deserts, or quits the Army in disgust. In fact, very few Americans will ever enter the service under such circumstances; and we attribute, in a great measure, the present abandoned and degraded condition of the American soldiery to no other cause, and are consequently led to believe that were a portion of the officers promoted from sergeants, the ranks of the Army would in a few years be greatly improved, and a meritorious and faithful class of officers be added to the Army.

The petitioners were careful not to align themselves with the more radical Jacksonians by adding that they were not "among those who wish for a total annihilation of the Military Academy, for we believe the institution a good one; we ask only for an equal chance with the rest of our countrymen."

Referring to the "principle of military usage" on which the earlier resolution of the House Military Affairs Committee foundered, the petitioners declared that

> Under the usages which have for a long time and do now govern the Army there is no chance for the soldier—not even a vestige of hope that he can under any circumstances rise above the rank of sergeant; he is doomed to serve out a servitude of years, despised and degraded by all his countrymen, notwithstanding his qualifications and merits may be of a superior kind. We therefore look upon those laws, usages, or regulations which totally exclude any class of Americans from the just reward of his merit alike prejudicial to the good of our country and the respectability of the Army.

Turning their attention to the predicament of those among their fellows not likely to qualify for commissions under any circumstances, the petitioners argued that "the pay of the higher grades of the noncommissioned officers should be increased so that they could live respectably with due economy." What they had in mind was the creation of a grade for very senior noncommissioned officers between the enlisted ranks and the commissioned officers—possibly something like the grade of warrant officer that the British,* and much later the Americans, were to adopt.

If this were not possible, the petitioners suggested that the problem might be eased somewhat by giving faithful old officers and soldiers "the exclusive privilege of suttling for the troops, and every other encouragement given to those who risk their lives and property and spend the bloom and vigor of youth in the service of their country, consistent with the good and welfare of our republic."

*The grade in the U.S. Army eventually developed quite differently from that of the British.

This touching memorial went the way of earlier efforts to provide for the promotion of meritorious noncommissioned officers to the commissioned grades. The House referred the petition to the Committee on Military Affairs, which took no further action. The U.S. Army therefore entered the decade of the 1840s with the professional noncommissioned officer's position locked into a hierarchial system from which there was for years—at least until after 1847—no escape into the commissioned grades of the service.[6]

American institutional and legislative reluctance to promote senior noncommissioned officers to commissioned grades was in marked contrast to the practice in the French army during much of the nineteenth century. A French law of 1832 reserved one third of all second lieutenant vacancies for *sous officiers* (noncommissioned officers) with at least two years' experience in grade. Another third was reserved for the graduates of the so-called *grandes écoles*—Saint Cyr and the Polytechnique.* The remaining third the government could appoint as it wished. This legislation remained essentially unchanged until 1881. However, after 1874, noncommissioned officers had first to attend a school for student officers to become eligible for commissions. In actual practice, until 1881 second lieutenant vacancies in the French Army were filled just about equally from the graduates of the *grandes écoles* and from among the *sous officiers*.[7]

Inasmuch as this practice grew out of the French revolutionary experience, it is noteworthy that American revolutionary experience did not produce a similar one. Although under General Winfield Scott's influence the U.S. Army drew heavily upon Napoleonic organizational and tactical doctrine, it indulged only sparingly in the practice of promotion of able and senior noncommissioned officers from the ranks and that mainly during and after the war with Mexico.

While it seemed at the time unjust to many noncommissioned officers, this practice actually helped strengthen the Army's noncommissioned officer corps. Many capable senior sergeants, finding their way to a commission blocked, often remained with the service. While there were many who eventually did leave to seek betterment in civilian life, sufficient numbers remained to provide that hard core of ability and experience from which legends arose during much of the nineteenth century.

WARTIME PROMOTIONS

As generally happens with the onset of war, expansion and attrition created a requirement for commissioned officers beyond that which the military academy could fill. The war with Mexico was the republic's second major conflict of the nineteenth century and consequently revived a long-dormant proposal to grant

*The *grandes écoles* were in some respects the French equivalent of the U.S. Military Academy at West Point.

commissions to outstanding senior noncommissioned officers to help meet these requirements.

As mentioned above, this proposal had been considered earlier, in 1831, but in spite of considerable lobbying by some noncommissioned officers, it was dropped, mainly because the War Department had been unwilling to "dilute" the professional officer corps by promoting from the ranks. But several years later, amidst the patriotic fervor induced by the Mexican War and spurred no doubt by considerable losses among the junior officers, a proposal to award outstanding noncommissioned officers with commissions had better prospects. This time the proposal was adopted by Congress in March 1847 as part of an *Act Making Provision for an Additional Number of General Officers and for Other Purposes*.[8] The specific section referring to noncommissioned officers read:

> That when any noncommissioned officer shall distinguish himself, or may have distinguished himself in the service of the United States, the President of the United States shall be, and is hereby, authorized, on the recommendation of the commanding officer of the regiment to which such noncommissioned officer belongs to attach him by brevet of the lowest grade, to any corps of the army: *Provided*, That there shall not be more than one so attached to any one company at the same time; and when any private soldier shall so distinguish himself, the President may in like manner grant him a certificate of merit, which shall entitle him to additional pay at the rate of two dollars per month.[9]

But even before the passage of this legislation, family and friends, sometimes using what political clout they possessed, on many occasions actively pressed the claims of their particular "distinguished" noncommissioned officer to a commission in the Army. A study of this correspondence in the files of the then–adjutant general of the United States Army, Brigadier General Robert Jones, sheds considerable light on the types of some of the men then serving as noncommissioned officers, their backgrounds, and their relationships to the civilian community.

Some of the noncommissioned officers whose causes were advanced by family and friends were indeed outstanding candidates and deserving of promotion. Others, however, were manifestly unqualified, a fact that nevertheless failed to deter their advocates. An example of the former was the case of Arthur Donaldson Tree, whose brother, Lambert Tree of Washington, D.C., wrote on his brother's behalf to Arthur's regimental commander, Colonel D. E. Twiggs, of the 2d Dragoons.

Colonel Twiggs, one of several regular Army officers who had distinguished himself during the Mexican War, readily responded to Lambert Tree's request with an eloquent endorsement:

> It affords me great pleasure to bear testimony to the conduct and character of your brother. He joined my regiment in 1842, and has since then been constantly under my command. He is as well qualified for a commission in the army as any young man I know of—his habits are good and his attention to duty is without a parallel. I have

> never known a superior to him. I trust you may be successful in your application, although I would much regret to lose him from the regiment.[10]

After first giving the original of Twiggs's letter to his brother-in-law, General William Patton, to place before the president, Lambert Tree sent a copy to Cave Johnson, an influential member of the congressional delegation from Pennsylvania. In his letter to Johnson, Lambert wrote that his brother, now sergeant major of the 2d Dragoons, "was brought up to the mercantile profession, but owing to the depression of the times was thrown out of employment and entered as stated . . . the dragoon service in its earliest organization. He is now about 31 or 32 years of age, of commanding figure, possesses a good education, and clever talents as his letters evince, published in the Union [newspaper]."[11]

Apparently Lambert's persistence in advancing his brother's cause, together with Colonel Twigg's endorsement, impressed the right people. With the entire Pennsylvania congressional delegation supporting him, Arthur Donaldson Tree was appointed a second lieutenant in the 2d Regiment of Dragoons on July 7, 1847.

Not so fortunate, however, were Corporal Herring (like Tree a noncommissioned officer in the 2d Dragoons), Corporal O'Sullivan of the 3d Infantry, and Sergeant Wallace of the 4th Artillery. In Herring's case it was the applicant's father who intervened in behalf of the aspiring noncommissioned officer.

A proud though somewhat indulgent parent, he wrote to Secretary of War Marcy requesting that his son, John D. Herring, be commissioned an officer in the dragoons. "He was," the elder Herring wrote, "born at Flemington, New Jersey, is 26 years of age, had received a liberal education, and by his aspirations in life, manners, conduct, and abilities, is qualified for the station he solicits, and will no doubt perform his duties to the government and his country in an able and honorable manner. He has the reputation of being a good soldier and excellent clerk and is much esteemed."[12]

Corporal Herring's platoon commander, a Lieutenant A. Lowry, was the first to respond to the adjutant general's request for an evaluation of the applicant. Lieutenant Lowry reported to his company commander that he considered young Herring "totally incapacitated for the position he desires to fill . . . he was and is most strikingly deficient, his Clerking qualities avail him but little and, if once esteemed, it cannot be the case now, as he is about to be tried by Court Martial for drunkenness in its most aggravated form."[13]

To this, Captain Merrill, the company commander, added the finishing touch by informing the adjutant general he had never considered Herring an efficient man, "being greatly deficient in that energy of character required for this situation." Merrill concluded, "I would state that however much I might desire the prosperity for corporal Herring and the gratification of his father in seeing him so commissioned in the army, I could not under a full sense of duty say that he even possesses one qualification for a commissioned officer."[14]

Needless to say, Corporal Herring's ambitions went unrealized. There were others, however, who sought to advance the fortunes of sons of local political figures, such as Corporal O'Sullivan.

Whether influenced by rising Whig sentiment in northern Illinois or only out of inordinate pride in a native son, friends of Corporal M. O'Sullivan petitioned Secretary Marcy in his behalf, requesting that he be given a commission. In doing so, O'Sullivan's advocates were not above using veiled political pressure to advance his cause. "You will recall," they declared, "that Corporal O'Sullivan distinguished himself at the battles of the eighth and ninth of May last, and as yet has not been promoted. He is a son of Illinois and we expect something for him from your hands. I doubt not that he will honor any position that you may confer upon him."

The letter continued in a somewhat more threatening tone:

> There has been some considerable feeling manifested [here] because the government has not seen fit to promote him, whilst he has been so highly extolled by all who knew him and his gallant conduct on those trying occasions. Your friends in this state expect that something will be done for him and will be sadly disappointed if there is not. I write this letter because I notice that there were several vacancies [presumably young officers] made by the fight at Monterey.[15]

Stung perhaps by the rather callous reference to the battle of Monterey, Corporal O'Sullivan's company commander, a Captain Bainbridge, replied to the adjutant general's request for a report on Sullivan by noting that "Sullivan, with others of the rank and file of the army, have been absent on the recruiting service, for their respective regiments since July last—in consequence of which, they did not participate in the storming of Monterey." Nevertheless, Captain Bainbridge reported that he had, in accordance with instructions, "made a careful inquiry amongst Sullivan's associates and comrades in reference to his character, habits, and qualifications and find but one opinion expressed upon those points; all of which results in his entire unfitness for the promotion asked for by his friends."[16]

The adjutant general passed this information on to O'Sullivan's cohorts. Needless to say, he was not commissioned, and there is no record of what political retribution, if any, his friends visited upon Secretary of War William Marcy.

Some noncommissioned officers, especially those on recruiting duty, were not above doing some politicking in their own behalf among the local citizenry to advance their applications for promotion to commissioned rank in one of the new regiments then forming for the Mexican War. Taking advantage of the legislation of March 1847 authorizing the granting of commissions to certain distinguished noncommissioned officers, a certain Sergeant Wallace of the recruiting party in Pittsburgh undertook to organize some local support in his behalf. His commanding officer, however, reported to the adjutant general that he had "been informed by Judge Wilkins that a petition in favor of Sgt. Wallace of the Recruiting Party and Sgt. of Company I of the 4th Artillery for an appointment as Lieutenant under the late law increasing the Army was in circulation in town and signed by many of the most respectable citizens. Which the judge informed me his refusal to sign, knowing that there were many noncommissioned officers in the service much more deserving and capable."

His commander added that "Sgt. Wallace is in this situation a passable soldier of good deportment." However, his wife was "a laundress and not one that the ladies [presumably the officers' wives] could associate with." The lieutenant concluded by observing that "Wallace has in some measure become quite a pet with many of the citizens and of late had got somewhat above his business."[17]

It is evident from letters like the foregoing that neither political pressure nor manipulation were sufficient to force open floodgates of promotions in the regular Army for noncommissioned officers to commissioned rank. Even after passage of the legislation in March 1847 authorizing commissions for noncommissioned officers who had distinguished themselves in battle, the officer corps of the regular Army continued to insist on its traditional high standards of character, conduct, and education for admission into its ranks. Of this trinity, distinguished conduct on the battlefield was the essential first step to recognition that might ultimately lead to a promotion.

The several campaigns of the war with Mexico provided many able noncommissioned officers with opportunities to demonstrate their bravery and proficiency. In a few instances noncommissioned officers even found themselves in command of small detachments in combat situations, offering a foretaste of the Indian wars to come.

Such an incident occurred during the 16th Infantry's march to Monterey, Mexico. Apparently, the newly organized regiment was blessed with some able noncommissioned officers, for Colonel John W. Tibbits, the 16th's commanding officer, reported that on the approach march he had

> placed twenty-one men, a sergeant and a corporal as a van guard with muskets loaded and bayonets fixed with orders to proceed the column at the distance of one hundred yards. The guard performed contact maneuver promptly which was remarkable (my command not having as yet had the advantage of the drill even in the school of the company), I myself showed them how and saw them perform the maneuver before I left.

No sooner had Tibbits posted his advance guard than a messenger arrived informing him that Captain Graves "had left the pack mules under the care of Sergeant R. B. McDowell of Company A and ten men mounted on mustangs." Sensing that with the enemy operating in widely scattered bands throughout the area Sergeant McDowell and his men might be in peril, Colonel Tibbits "directed Captains Graves and Brannon with sixty men, ten from each company, to march in quick time to the relief of the sergeant and his men and ordered after them twelve men in ambulances, with a large number of canteens and a few kegs of water, as the weather was very hot and the men had suffered previously for want of water."

The relief party

> found Sergeant R. B. McDowell with seven of his men (two having got ahead and come to camp, and another having been sent by him to apprize me of his condition) defending the train of mules against about seventy of the enemy whom they had kept at bay. They had unloaded the mules and constructed a kind of breastwork with the packages of foods but had not been put to the necessity of resorting to it for protection, but were firing upon the enemy from the outside. On the arrival of Captains Graves and Brannon, and being fired upon by them the enemy retired. The mules were then repacked and brought in safety to the camp before night. I cannot refrain from bringing to the notice of the Executive [the secretary of war] Sergeant R. B. McDowell, and recommending that he be appointed a Brevet 2d Lieutenant for his gallantry and good conduct, as provided by the 17th Section of the Act of March 3, 1847, a position for which he is well-qualified by education and soldierlike appearance.[18]

In spite of this recommendation, Sergeant McDowell's name does not appear among the list of noncommissioned officers submitted by the adjutant general in January 1848 to Secretary of War Marcy. McDowell's name may have been dropped because he fell in a later action, or perhaps the other officers of the 16th Infantry may not have shared Colonel Tibbits's enthusiasm for the sergeant. This was not uncommon, for the officer corps of a regiment had some of the aspects of a gentlemen's club or fraternity.

There were instances when the officers of a regiment vetoed recommendations for promoting certain noncommissioned officers to brevet second lieutenancies. For example, the officers of the 6th Infantry wrote the adjutant general from Mexico City protesting the promotion recommendations for certain noncommissioned officers of the regiment on the grounds "that decided cause of objections to the promotions recommended exist. We allege others, in the existence of bad habits in some, the improper associations of most, and the want of sufficient intelligence and education in all." To commission such men, the officers of the 6th Infantry continued, would "have the effect to place among the commissioned officers of the Army, persons whose characters, habits, associations, and feelings cannot fail to exert a deteriorating influence upon our reputation as a class."[19]

From the 2d Artillery Regiment stationed in Mexico, of a list of several noncommissioned officers cited for gallantry in action, only two were recommended for commissions as having "sufficient intelligence and education and habits of propriety to receive commissions." The regiment could not, however, "present the names of any others in the same terms."[20]

When a noncommissioned officer did possess the necessary qualifications for admission into the corps of officers, however, endorsement usually came from every level of command. For example, a captain of light infantry enthusiastically recommended to his regimental commander a brevet lieutenancy for a Corporal William H. Fitzhugh of his company:

> Corporal Fitzhugh's gallantry at the storming of Chapultepec where he was wounded, his respectable standing in society at home, his liberal education, general intelligence and gentlemanlike deportment give assurance that his appointment will illustrate the excellence of the law which authorized these awards of merit.

To this the regimental commander willingly gave his endorsement, writing that Corporal Fitzhugh "has been distinguished for gallantry, wounded in action, his deportment being that of good soldier and a gentleman and of a good moral character."[21]

During the Mexican War not all promotions of noncommissioned officers to commissioned rank were based on the authorization contained in Section 17 of the legislation of March 3, 1847. Some deserving volunteer noncommissioned officers were promoted simply to fill vacancies caused either by death or resignation. For example, when the office of commissary to the 1st Regiment of South Carolina Volunteers, then on duty in Mexico, was vacated by the death of its incumbent, the officers of the regiment petitioned President Polk to appoint William P. Graves, 1st sergeant of Company I, to that office. Twelve officers of the regiment signed the petition, "believing him to be competent to the discharge of its duties and well deserving of the compliments."[22] President Polk harkened to his fellow Carolinians and Democrats and appointed Sergeant Graves in July 1847.

A resignation in the regiment of light infantry offered opportunity for one of the company commanders, a Captain Charles I. Biddle, to advance the cause of one of his sergeants, John R. Neidy, whom he described as "a young man of 21 years of age, respectable, intelligent, and soldier-like in appearance and feeling and has been distinguished in all the actions and in every other situation for his activity and spirit." Captain Biddle informed his regimental commander that he would be happy to have him as an officer of his own company, either as a brevet second lieutenant or as a full second lieutenant in place of the resignee.[23]

This latter offer was a rare compliment, for noncommissioned officers elevated to commissions were usually not assigned to the same company where they had served as enlisted men, but were transferred to other units within the regiment. Neidy could be appointed, Captain Biddle suggested, either under the recent legislation or by promotion to full second lieutenant in the regular Army, in place of the officer who had resigned.[24]

With such exceptions as sergeants Graves and Neidy, who were commissioned under other provisions, the adjutant general submitted toward the end of the war a consolidated list of meritorious and qualified noncommissioned officers—twenty-nine sergeants and five corporals—recommended for commissions. These men, the adjutant general wrote, "have been selected from the several recommendations of commanders in the field, as seeming entitled to be regarded as candidates for promotion under the 17th Section, the Act of March 3, 1847."

The adjutant general also noted that "many other noncommissioned officers are mentioned for gallant conduct in battle and recommended to favorable consideration, but they do not appear to be designated in such special manner as to warrant their promotion [to commissioned rank]. In some cases they are reported as not possessing sufficient general good character, intelligence, and education, to hold commissions in the Army." Interestingly, very few specialists ratings of that day—laborers and artificers—were included on the lists submitted by commanders in the field and none of them were commissioned.[25]

None of the new brevet second lieutenants, however, saw service during the Mexican War, for Secretary Marcy did not submit their names to President Polk until June 27, 1848. Although the president signed their commissions the following day, the ratifications of the Treaty of Guadalupe Hidalgo ending the war had already been exchanged on May 30. The newly commissioned officers served in a peacetime army. Many, however, took part in the fighting against the Indians on the western frontier and some even served as officers during the Civil War.[26]

While not all noncommissioned officers who had been mentioned with approbation in dispatches possessed the necessary qualifications for commissions, a provision in the legislation of March 1847 provided for such men by stating that a "certificate of merit" could be issued by the president awarding them additional pay at the rate of two dollars per month. This provision was extended to deserving noncommissioned officers who failed to qualify for commissions, but there were exceptions. There were officers who, while acknowledging that their noncommissioned officers had distinguished themselves in combat, nevertheless refused to single out any of them either for commissions or for certificates of merit on the grounds that all men in their units had performed outstandingly.

One such officer was Brevet Major Braxton Bragg, then commanding Company C of the 3d Light Artillery. "The noncommissioned officers and with few exceptions, the privates of Company C, 3d Artillery," he reported, "since I have commanded them have performed the ordinary duties of their respective stations with the most commendable alacrity and zeal." He continued:

> Prior to the passage of the law under which this report is required, the conduct of those engaged in the battle of Buena Vista and in the defense of Saltillo, though not more than was expected of brave soldiers accustomed to victory, was all that could have been desired of men under my command. But I cannot consider any one as having distinguished himself further than this, nor can I designate individuals whose good conduct was so general. The benefits of that law, as I understand it, cannot therefore be extended to any one of my command.[27]

Major Bragg was not the only commander unwilling to single out any of his men for special recognition under the new legislation. Following the battle of Buena Vista, the commanding officer of the 2d Dragoons reported to the adjutant general that while the general conduct of his noncommissioned officers "was soldierlike in the extreme, no act was performed by anyone, deserving of especial notice."[28]

Captain T. W. Sherman of the 3d Artillery was also somewhat reluctant to single out men in his unit for special citation, stating that "the noncommissioned officers and privates of Light Company E, 3d Artillery, behaved so generally well in the Battle of Buena Vista that it would be difficult to discriminate much between them." Nevertheless, Captain Sherman noted, it was "necessary to mention the names of Sgt. Swain and Artificer Austin whose services stood conspicuous, as the result of both distinguished skill and bravery." Captain Sherman wrote that "thanks to their coolness and bravery, and skill in manning the remaining howitzer," he was able to hold his position. However,

> though my opinion of the conduct of Swain remains to this day unchanged as brave and efficient man in battle, yet in consequence of his general lax habits as a noncommissioned officer and gross neglect of duty I was compelled in April last to prefer charges against him, which resulted in him being reduced to the ranks by a Court Martial; and I have also to add that with the exception of his acknowledged merit in battle, I have no confidence in him as a noncommissioned officer and could not therefore recommend him for a commission. I would therefore respectfully recommend that artificer Andrew Austin and Pvt. Edward Swain receive a certificate of merit for their good conduct in the battle of Buena Vista that will entitle them to the extra allowance . . . provided by law.[29]

There were other unit commanders who, while acknowledging that their noncommissioned officers had distinguished themselves "for their gallantry and conduct in battle," declared that "justice to the interests of the service as well as to the men themselves requires that they ought not to receive commissions." Instead, they were recommended for "the beneficial provisions of the Act of Congress in relation to increased pay."[30]

This latter seems to have been the major effect of the legislation on most of the noncommissioned officers who had distinguished themselves during the war. As already mentioned, only thirty-four noncommissioned officers eventually received commissions as a result of their gallant conduct in battle against the Mexican army. Reflecting on the total commissioned officer strength—2,863 (regular and volunteer) of the Army during the Mexican War—the promotion of thirty-four noncommissioned officers to the commissioned ranks had little effect upon the officer corps as a whole.[31]

With the end of the Mexican War the provision established in 1847 no longer provided a satisfactory method of rewarding meritorious noncommissioned service. Accordingly, in 1851 Congress created a procedure for the peacetime promotion of certain noncommissioned officers. There were two steps in the selection process. The candidate had first to pass an examination by a regimental board as prescribed in General Order No. 17, October 4, 1854, before presenting himself before a board convened at the United States Military Academy at West Point. Consisting of professors of mathematics and ethics, as well as the commandant of cadets, this board convened annually, on the first Monday of September, to examine candidates. Those few noncommissioned officers who managed to survive this selection process were then breveted as second lieutenants in the same manner as graduates of the military academy.[32]

This process proved in practice to be as selective as that provided under the earlier legislation, and very few noncommissioned officers won commissions through it. Not until the Civil War, with its enormous demands for manpower, did the situation change. Then, as many state volunteer units were raised, hundreds of former noncommissioned officers of the regular Army were given commissions in them and, as many veterans were later to observe, generally performed their duties with distinction. But such service ended with peace. During the interwar years, noncommissioned officers only rarely advanced to commissions in the regular Army. Neither Congress nor the professional officer corps were likely to press for or tolerate any further "dilution" of this selection process.

The Civil War forced upon both Congress and the professional officer corps some modifications in this process. Subsequently, as with every major war fought by the United States, increasing numbers of outstanding noncommissioned officers were promoted into the commissioned grades. Between the Mexican and Civil wars, pressure from the noncommissioned officers corps continued to urge upon the Army a systematic provision for enabling outstanding noncommissioned officers to win commissions. The issue was to reemerge from time to time until the noncommissioned officer corps in the twentieth century became a professional body in its own right, managed in a manner similar to that of the officer corps.

CHAPTER 6

DIVERSITY AND LEADERSHIP

By the beginning of the 1850s there had emerged within Congress a pattern of concern for the Army that can only be described as one of prewar neglect, wartime support, and postwar indifference.

Just prior to the War of 1812 the peacetime establishment numbered 9,128 men, exclusive of officers. During that conflict the nation raised a force of over 450,000, most of it, however, composed of state militiamen. In the decade following the War of 1812, the Army's strength remained at around 11,600 men. Until the beginning of the 1840s, this was to remain largely unchanged. By 1845, however, it had fallen to only 7,883 and, by May of 1846, to 5,925 men. On the eve of the war with Mexico, the Army enlisted strength was 8,866, of whom only 7,500 were available for field service. During the war, 1,016 officers and 35,009 enlisted men joined the regular Army, swelling its ranks to 42,587. An additional 73,532 men enlisted in the state volunteer units.[1] After the war the old pattern reasserted itself as Congress sharply lowered the regular Army's authorized strength. Because of difficulties in recruitment, the Army's actual strength in July 1859 lagged behind the 18,165 authorized.[2]

In spite of these fluctuations in strength, tables of organization as they related to noncommissioned officers remained rather constant. There was one sergeant major and one quartermaster sergeant per regiment; four sergeants, four corporals, and two musicians for each company. The latter ranked with and were paid as noncommissioned officers.[3]

In 1849 an additional battery was added to the artillery regiment, thereby increasing the number of noncommissioned officers in the artillery by four sergeants and four corporals. There were no changes, however, in infantry and dragoon regiments.

FOREIGN-BORN NONCOMMISSIONED OFFICERS

During these decades of feast or famine in terms of manpower, the small regular Army became increasingly isolated from the mainstream of American life. In the period between the War of 1812 and the Civil War, the bulk of the Army moved from the old Northwest and confrontation with the British along the now-quiescent Niagara frontier to the then-relatively remote trans-Mississippi frontier. This physical isolation in turn bred among the West Point–educated officers and their long-service noncommissioned officers a sense of almost monastic dedication and separation from the civilian population, as the military careerists "cultivated," in the words of one army historian, "specialized skills within a sprawling nation of jacks-of-all-trades."[4]

This aloofness from civilian life in turn cultivated within the civilian population a widespread lack of understanding for the military. A soldier writing of his service during the decade of the 1850s reported that there was little respect for the soldier among the civilians of the eastern cities and towns. There, he was looked upon as an individual "too lazy to work for a living. Only the people of the Western frontiers," he wrote, "appreciated him and understood how much he did toward making the new country a safe place for them to acquire homes and develop the land."[5]

As the Army's physical and mental isolation increased, so did the number of foreign-born in its ranks. This ultimately meant an increase of foreign-born among the noncommissioned officers. This in turn influenced changes in the Army's (and society's) perception of the corps. During the republic's early years there had been few aliens in the ranks, but as the tide of immigration swelled in the 1830s and 1840s, so did the number of immigrants in the Army. During the years 1814–1815, muster and receipt rolls of two representative companies of the 3d Rifle Regiment show only four foreign-born noncommissioned officers—two sergeants, an artificer, and a senior musician. Of these, three came from the British Isles, while the fourth, the musician, came from Italy.

Throughout the nineteenth century the rosters of musicians assigned to the regiments contained a growing percentage of men born in Europe—mainly in Germany and Italy. Since senior musicians ranked with noncommissioned officers, they accounted for a significant number of the foreign-born of that grade.[6]

Many of these noncommissioned musicians were employed as instructors at the Army's school of music, which in the 1840s was located on Governor's Island, New York. The drummer and fifer recruits, or music boys as they were usually known, were assigned to Company B of the island's garrison and placed under the command of the post adjutant. One of those music boys later recalled that the adjutant appeared at his company only on muster days, "leaving the care and management of the 50 or 60 boys to the two sergeants in charge."[7]

One of these sergeants was a Dane, Sergeant Hanke, who lived with his wife in a couple of small rooms on the second floor of the troop quarters. The other was an Irishman, Sergeant Moore, who kept house with his wife and several children on the lower floor of the barracks. Two corporals, Butler and Pfaefle, the latter a German immigrant, acted as assistant instructors. The two sergeants, the music-boy chronicler recalled, remained in service for a combined total of more than sixty years.[8]

From time to time the Army, responding to nativist fears, sought to restrict recruitment of aliens. But the opening up of western lands and the expansion of manufacturing and trade left the Army with little choice but to draw increasingly from immigrants to fill its ranks, especially during the Mexican War. During the mid-nineteenth century, as thousands fled famine and hard times in their European homelands, the proportion of foreign-born recruits in the regular Army rose to 47 percent. Half of this figure was Irish, with Germans making up the majority of the rest.[9]

It was not until the Civil War that the influx of foreign-born soldiers became a flood, but most of these were to be found in the ranks of the state volunteer regiments rather than the regular Army. The state units paid a generous bonus for enlistments and their discipline was considerably less harsh than that of the regulars. In the Union Army, Germans accounted for the largest foreign element, while in Confederate service the Irish made up the major alien portion. Volunteer regiments, composed almost entirely of foreign-born soldiers, usually had noncommissioned officers of the same ethnic group. For example, in a volunteer company of Swedish-Americans from Galesburg, Illinois (the company became a part of the 43d Illinois Volunteer Regiment), all the noncommissioned officers were Swedish-born. Frequently three out of every four sergeants and six or seven corporals in a company were of the same national origin as that characterizing the entire unit.[10]

Occasionally the reverse was true. In the 175th New York Infantry, a part of the nominally all-Irish Corcoran Legion, in one of the companies all the sergeants and seven corporals were German (the eighth corporal was French). Even in units made up of almost entirely native-born Americans, there were to be found some foreign-born noncommissioned officers.

One of these was German-born Sergeant Fredrick Fuger of Battery A, 4th New York Artillery. During the battle of Gettysburg Sergeant Fuger and his battery were defending Cemetery Ridge when Confederate general Pickett launched his famous charge. After all of the battery's commissioned officers had been either killed or wounded and five cannon destroyed by enemy action, Sergeant Fuger continued to fight on with one of the serviceable guns until he and his men were ordered to withdraw. Not all foreign-born noncommissioned officers fought so gallantly, however. The most frequent incidence of desertion among noncommissioned officers during the war occurred among those who were foreign-born.

However, it was the small professional regular Army, both before and after the Civil War, that really provided many immigrants and the native-born alike the adventure and opportunity for which they yearned—to see the fabled lands of western America and there, possibly, to find their fortunes. While fortune eluded most, soldiers of the regular Army nevertheless found plenty of excitement policing the vast western plains.

THE NONCOMMISSIONED OFFICER IN THE INDIAN WARS OF THE 1850s

Throughout the 1850s a swelling tide of western migration confronted the Army with the task of protecting the thousands of settlers struggling over prairie and mountain to new homes in the West. The Army also had the task of protecting the Indians from some of the more unscrupulous adventurers who followed the wagon trains westward.

The number of men available to the Army for these missions did not, however, increase in direct proportion to the numbers of settlers or Indians needing its services. The absolute requirements for men in the various posts left only thirteen regiments available for actual field service. Congressional appropriations since the war with Mexico were sufficient only to keep the Army on a peacetime footing. Consequently, with little more than 11,000 men available for field service, the regular Army had "to prosecute an active and sanguinary war for a distance extending from the 35th to the 46th degrees of north latitude with numerous tribes of hardy and warlike Indians."[11] Not until 1890 were the plains Indians finally subdued. By then the Army had fought twenty-four military operations officially designated as wars, campaigns, or expeditions, and had engaged in nearly a thousand armed clashes with hostile Indians.[12]

Since the end of the Second Seminole War in August 1842, the Army had shifted the bulk of its manpower and its operations to the trans-Mississippi territories. Already in the 1820s and 1830s detachments of mounted riflemen, operating from bases at Jefferson Barracks and Ft. Leavenworth, had begun to protect trading caravans and patrol travel routes across the Great Plains and to show the flag. By the 1840s, the Army's primary operational concern was the protection of the swelling stream of settlers moving in long columns of wagon trains toward Texas and the Southwest from hostile bands of Indians. This westward migration had also long been the focus of growing tension between the United States and Mexico.[13]

The Army sought to prevent Indian hostilities through the traditional display of military force on or beyond the western frontiers. In 1844, the 1st Regiment of Dragoons made a wide circuit through the Indian country. In April of that year, as tensions not only with Indians but with Mexicans increased in the Southwest, the army shifted its sixteen-company reserve force—3d and 4th regiments of infantry—from its base at Jefferson Barracks near St. Louis to the vicinity of Ft. Jesup, Texas. Two companies of each regiment, however, remained on the western frontier, where they too formed a part of that display of military force.[14]

To patrol and show the flag throughout the vast western territories, the Army generally employed company-sized units operating out of a multitude of small frontier posts and camps. Some idea of how thinly spread the Army was is illustrated by the fact that the 11,000 men available for active service in 1859 were stationed in 130 garrisons scattered over three million square miles—from the Canadian border to west Texas. Such dispersal as well as the tactics of the roving Indian bands meant that much of the combat took the form of small-unit operations. These gave able noncommissioned officers frequent opportunity to distinguish themselves in command of units or detachments in instances where there were no commissioned officers available.[15]

Generally, these operations were, in the words of a student of the period, "one fruitless, disheartening pursuit after another." Rather than the better-known battles such as that of the Little Big Horn, they characterized the major part of a soldier's field service at that time.[16] One operation occurred in the spring of 1854 at Ft. Ewell, on the San Antonio road some fifty miles northeast of Laredo, Texas. At the time of the incident all of the garrison's commissioned officers were in the field, except one sick in the post hospital. This left the assistant surgeon, Dr. E. Jones, as senior officer on post. Consequently, when a report arrived telling of an attack by a band of Indians on a wagon train twelve miles away, Dr. Jones had no choice but to send in pursuit a force under the command of noncommissioned officers. This force consisted of three detachments, each under the command of a company 1st sergeant who had been left behind (the other sergeants were already in the field with their companies).[17]

Setting out without a local guide, the three detachments, in Dr. Jones's words, "pressed the pursuit across a country of the most unfavorable kind for 80 miles without a drop of water for either man or horse, and then continued it 25 miles farther, until they overtook the Indians." Overtaken by a superior force, the Indians nevertheless managed to escape into thick chaparral, but in so doing, "lost their plunder, baggage, animals, trophies, and some of their arms."

General Smith, commanding general of the Texas Department, added his own endorsement to Dr. Jones's report, declaring that "the noncommissioned officer in charge of the parties sent out, and the men I know to be as good as any in the Army; and of their ability and disposition to render a good account of the enemy, if they can overtake him I have no doubt." General Smith concluded by placing before the commanding general of the Army "in terms of highest commendation" the names of the three first sergeants: C. H. McHalley of Company D in overall command; John Green of Company B; and John Williams of Company G.

Not only departmental commanders' reports to the Secretary of War, but also the annals of the old cavalry regiments themselves are rich in accounts of noncommissioned officers leading men in combat against the Indians. These reports and accounts have supplied the substance for story and legend for over a century. Foremost among the cavalry units that participated in the operations in the Texas Department in the 1850s was the U.S. 5th Cavalry. It had a long and distinguished record there until forced to leave the department at the outbreak of the Civil War.

Noncommissioned officers played an important role in establishing that record in numerous skirmishes and battles against marauding Indian bands. Some of the more outstanding of these noncommissioned officers commanded units of the 5th Cavalry, for example, 1st Sergeant Walter McDonald who, on February 13, 1857, led a detachment of Company D from Camp Verde in vigorous pursuit of a band of Comanches. Catching up with the Indians on the banks of the Kickapoo Creek, 1st Sergeant McDonald and his men attacked the Indians. After a sharp battle, the cavalrymen defeated the Comanches, killing six and capturing all of their animals at the cost of one private killed and the bugler severely wounded.[18]

On July 2, 1857, Sergeant William P. Leverett, in command of a detachment of the 5th Cavalry, pursued, overtook, and defeated another band of Comanches on the south bank of the Llano River. He and his men captured a number of the Indians' animals together with their entire camp equipage. The enemy warriors, however, slipped away into the chaparral.

In September 1857, a detachment of Company I, commanded by Sergeant Charles M. Patrick, set out from Ft. McIntosh and after a seven-day pursuit and search, came upon a band of Indians encamped near Santa Caterina. Despite a long march, much of it under heavy rains that imposed a severe strain on both men and horses, the cavalrymen managed to preserve their rations and ammunition. For two days of the week-long march, Sergeant Patrick and his detachment covered almost one hundred and sixty miles over mountains and through ravines to keep up with the fleeing Indians.

Once the enemy had been brought to bay, Patrick led the attack until his horse threw him after becoming mired in the mud. Although the Indians took both Patrick and his horse under fire, he survived unhurt, but his mount was killed. His men continued to press the attack, forcing the Indians to withdraw down a deep ravine where they dispersed and concealed themselves in the tall grass. At no loss to themselves other than Patrick's horse, the cavalrymen accounted for six Indian warriors killed or wounded and twelve horses captured.

On January 25, 1858, 1st Sergeant Walter McDonald, with a detachment from Company D, set out from Camp Verde in pursuit of marauding Comanches, who had been committing depredations against the settlements along the San Jeronimo River. After a rapid pursuit lasting four days, 1st Sergeant McDonald brought the Indians to ground on the south branch of the Llano River. During the ensuing skirmish, the cavalrymen killed two of the Indians and recaptured the horses that they had stolen from settlers. Two of 1st Sergeant McDonald's men were wounded during the action.

Not only sergeants, but on occasion corporals commanded pursuit detachments, as did Corporal John Rutter, who with a detachment from Company B, started out on August 25, 1858, from Camp Colorado in pursuit of Indians who had stolen horses from settlers living near the post. In spite of heavy rains, Corporal Rutter and his men rode on for two days with only brief halts to the banks of the rain-swollen Sabano Creek.

Because of the high waters, Rutter's men and horses had to swim the creek. Scrambling up the opposite bank after an exhausting crossing, they found themselves in the midst of the enemy's camp. Because of the wet crossing, only a few of their weapons would fire, so Rutter had no choice but to order his men to charge through the camp. Most of the Indians, taking advantage of the lack of American firepower, forced their way through the cavalry line and escaped. One cavalryman was killed and two horses wounded. Two of the Indians were wounded and all of the stolen horses recovered.

On December 14 another corporal, Patrick Collins, with a detachment from Company I, rode from Camp Ives in pursuit of a party of marauding Comanches and overtook them on the north branch of the Guadalupe River. In the engagement that followed, Corporal Collins and his men killed four of the enemy and wounded others while capturing all of the Indians' animals and equipage.

Late in January 1858, Sergeant Alex McK. Craig, in command of a detachment from Company C, set out from Camp Lawson in pursuit of a party of Comanches who had stolen horses from nearby settlers. Two days later, he and his men overtook the Indians in a thick chaparral on the banks of the Aqua Frio. Immediately charging the enemy, the cavalrymen engaged in a running fight with the Indians for about four miles. During the fight, Craig and his men killed four and severely wounded several of the Indians. All of the stolen horses were recovered.

The most successful operation of the year, however, took place when 1st Sergeant John W. Spangler, commanding a detachment from Company H and a detachment of state troops from Camp Cooper, advanced northward to the Pease, a tributary of the Red River. There, on January 19, Spangler encountered a war party of Comanches. In the battle that followed, the cavalrymen killed fourteen of the Indians, wounded some, and captured three. Forty-five of the Comanches' horses fell into American hands without loss or serious injury to any of 1st Sergeant Spangler's command.

It is interesting to note that in spite of their demonstrated leadership and gallantry in combat operations, none of the names of the noncommissioned officers cited in these narratives are to be found among the forty corporals and sergeants of the 5th U.S. Cavalry who were later commissioned during the Civil War. There may have been several reasons for this. The first is that these men who had performed so well on the southwest frontier during the 1850s may have been too old to qualify for commissions during the 1860s; another is that they may simply have been unable to pass the written examinations given candidates from the ranks; and it may have been that many of these men were just content to continue serving as noncommissioned officers in their units.

Concurrent with the 5th Cavalry's experiences, a thousand miles to the west in the territory of New Mexico, the Army continued to seek out and subdue Indian bands deemed hostile. In the autumn of 1858, an expeditionary force moved against these Indians.

On the night of October 17 a party of five Navajo Indians broke into a corral within two hundred yards of the Army camp near the settlement of Jimez and stole a horse, six donkeys, and seven head of cattle belonging to a Don Francisco Sandoval. When the incident was reported the following morning to the expeditionary force commander, Lieutenant Colonel D. S. Miles, he "immediately started a detachment of 10 men of Company E, Mounted Rifles, under Sergeant John Duffin, with six men of Captain Valdez's company of spies and guides as trailers" after the fleeing Indians. Just before sunset, Sergeant Duffin's party overtook the Indians with their booty. Duffin and his men attacked, killing one Indian, and after a chase of four to five miles, recovered all the cattle and four of the donkeys, which they then returned to Don Francisco's corral.[19]

Meanwhile, the Navajo struck again, in far greater strength, this time in the vicinity of the expedition's headquarters at Ft. Defiance. Reporting the operation, Colonel Miles wrote:

> This morning at 7 a.m. the post herd, with I Company's horses, passed out through Canyon Bonita, as usual, and under a guard of 15 mounted rifles and 10 infantry, when it was suddenly attacked by about 300 mounted Navajo, concealed in ambush. The riflemen performed their duty admirably and resisted with energy, under [their] commander, Sergeant Bernard W. Clark, of I Company, Mounted Rifles [with] all and more than could be expected. His [Sgt. Clark's] conduct was well conceived as honorably and bravely executed, and deserves my warmest thanks. He saved, except three, all of his company horses and a part of the quartermaster's herds, all of the sheep and cattle, but lost about 62 mules.[20]

In spite of this repulse, the Indians did not cease their harassment. On February 8, 1860, the Navajo attacked a detachment commanded by Sergeant Werner of Company C. Assisted by corporals Bailey of Company G and Elwood of Company B, together with forty-one privates of the 3d Infantry, the detachment was guarding the post cattle herd some seven miles from Ft. Defiance. For two hours a force of five hundred Navajo, half of whom were mounted, attacked the men from three sides. Fortunately, the attack did not come as a surprise. Sergeant Werner had posted an advance party in the cover of some woods to watch for the Indians and these men gave warning of the attack. When it began, the advance party withdrew to the main body. There Werner and his men held their ground until reinforcements arrived from the fort. The Indians fled in every direction, leaving ten of their number dead on the field and twenty wounded. Only one of Sergeant Werner's men was wounded.[21]

Texas, meanwhile, remained an important area of operations. On February 9, 1859, Captain R. P. Maclay of the 8th Infantry, stationed at Ft. Inge, a small post near the town of Uvalde, sent Sergeant Maloney and four of his company to escort a party of citizens in pursuit of some Indians who had stolen a number of horses from a Dr. Isobel in nearby Frio Canyon the previous Sunday. On Thursday the men picked up the trail and by the following Sunday, February 13, overtook the Indians. In the skirmish that followed, Sergeant Maloney's men killed three of the six Indians. Of the fifty-eight horses stolen, forty-nine were retaken; seven had been killed by the Indians on the trail and two during the skirmish. Captain Maclay noted in his report to headquarters that "the success of the expedition was due in great measure to the good conduct of Sergeant Maloney and the men under his command."[22] Not all hostile Indians were confined to the Southwest, nor were Army units always successful in combat with them. Far to the northwest, in the Oregon and Washington territories, numerous and powerful tribes, backed into that corner of the continent, fought desperately to stem the tide of settlement lapping at the Pacific shores. On May 16, 1858, a war band of 1,200 Indians attacked three companies of the 1st Dragoons and a company of the 9th Infantry.

Overwhelming the small force, the Indians mortally wounded the two officers in command, Captain Taylor and Second Lieutenant William Gaston. Their commissioned officers gone, the dragoons and infantrymen fought on bravely under the command of the noncommissioned officers. First Sergeant Edward Ball of Company H displayed great courage and determination throughout the action. With a few men he repulsed the assault of a large number of Indians at one of the most important points in the defensive perimeter, thereby enabling privates Francis Poiseu, C. H. Harnish, and James Crozet to rescue and carry off the body of their fallen captain, although they too later fell during the battle.

When the Indians again tried to seize Taylor's body, 1st Sergeant William C. Williams and a few men successfully drove them back, although Williams fell mortally wounded during the action.[23]

These able small-unit leaders matched even the Indians in their ability to live and fight on the high plains. A few of these men have left behind a rich store of diaries, memoirs, and correspondence describing their experiences on the western frontier in the decades preceding the Civil War. From these sources it is possible to determine what kind of men they were, their backgrounds, training, how they came to enlist in the Army, and much about the conditions of military life in their day.

One was Percival G. Lowe, who served a five-year enlistment with the dragoons on the high plains. Raised—as were most recruits—on a farm, Lowe had an inclination for adventure from the start. After leaving his family farm at the age of fifteen, Lowe sold newspapers on the streets of Lowell, Massachusetts, before setting out to sea for three years, which included a stint with a whaling expedition. Leaving the sea, Lowe then learned the daguerreotype business, all the while continuing to satisfy his wanderlust through wide-ranging reading about voyages, travels, campaigns, explorations, and history.

Finding his spirit of adventure thus further stirred, Lowe determined to enlist in the mounted service of the Army, which he hoped would place him "on the great plains of the west, among Indians, buffaloes, and other big game, and the mountaineers and trappers of whom [he] had read so much."[24]

Lowe enlisted in the Army in Boston on October 16, 1849. The regimental descriptive roll listed him as a farmer, twenty-one years of age, five feet eleven inches tall, 175 pounds, dark complexioned, dark-brown hair, gray eyes, and in perfect health; in short, good material for the Army.

Lowe was sent with a group of recruits to the dragoon training center at Carlisle Barracks, Pennsylvania. There he found the noncommissioned officers charged with his basic training were mostly veterans of the Mexican War—seasoned and hardened campaigners, well qualified to train and discipline recruits. His training completed, Lowe was then sent with seventy-four other men to Ft. Leavenworth as replacements assigned to the 1st Dragoons. To assist the regular noncommissioned officers accompanying the replacements, several men were made lance noncommissioned officers especially for the trip. A commissioned officer was in overall command of the group.*

Chief among the noncommissioned officers at that time was the acting first sergeant, a supposed deserter from the British army in Canada, as Lowe described him, "an all-around brute—big, burly and noisy." The commissary for the replacements on the trip and the sole regular noncommissioned officer was a Corporal Wood, who before his enlistment had been a pork packer in Louisville. Failing in business, he had enlisted in the 1st Dragoons and served throughout the Mexican War. Lowe considered him a fine clerk because he understood government accounts and was fully competent to act as quartermaster for the detachment.

Aside from the acting first sergeant, several others among the replacements were foreign-born, most of them from Ireland. Among the latter was a man named Byrns, then twenty-one years old. He eventually rose through all the noncommissioned grades, becoming a second lieutenant in the regular Army at the beginning of the Civil War. Byrns ultimately became the colonel of a volunteer regiment and fell at the head of his troops during the Wilderness campaign.

On March 17, 1851, about a year and a half into his enlistment, Lowe was promoted to corporal. A year later he made sergeant and shortly thereafter became first sergeant of Troop B. At the time of his first promotion, corporals drew $10.00 a month, company musicians and drummers $12.00, sergeants $13.00, and first sergeants $16.00. With his corporal's pay and some money saved from his annual clothing allowance, Corporal Lowe was able to manage fairly well in garrison at Ft. Leavenworth.

In the mid-nineteenth century Army, garrison life was not as perceived by many civilians, just drilling and fatigue details relieved by idleness, drinking, gambling, and brawling. Instead, Lowe and his companions spent a good part of their free time organizing a thespian society and presenting plays for the garrison's officers and their families.† The men also organized dances for members of the garrison

*This was rather common practice in the 1850s. See also *Ten Years in the Ranks, U.S. Army* by Augustus Meyers, pp. 17–18.

†About this time an Irish-born officer, a Second Lieutenant D. H. Hastings, joined Lowe's troop. After serving several years as a first sergeant, Hastings had been commissioned for gallantry during the Mexican War. He eventually retired as a major in the regular Army. See Meyers, *Ten Years in the Ranks, U.S. Army*, p. 41.

and their families as well as for civilians from nearby Weston. Lowe himself, after he became a sergeant, even found time to join the local Masonic lodge at Weston and had enough leisure to attend lodge meetings once a week. Two of Lowe's fellow sergeants were married and lived on post with their families.[25]

Except in cases of very serious offenses, military justice in the form of company punishment was usually left almost entirely in the hands of the noncommissioned officers in garrison. While in garrison at Ft. Leavenworth, Troop B regularly held company courts-martial with three noncommissioned officers sitting in judgment. The court's proceedings were reviewed and acted upon by the first sergeant. Only rarely were the findings of the company court appealed. In such cases, the parties together with the first sergeant, went to the company commander, who heard the complaint. Sergeant Lowe could not recall when the captain ever reversed the findings of his noncommissioned officers. No officer ever attended a company court nor, in Lowe's words, did they want to.

Summary courts were unknown, and few cases reached the general or garrison court. Nor did the noncommissioned officer's responsibility for trial and punishment end with the company courts-martial. There was also the custom at Ft. Leavenworth in the 1850s to detail a noncommissioned officer each month as "provost sergeant." His duty was to work the prisoners in policing the garrison and, on occasion, supervise the digging of graves.

A successful career as a senior noncommissioned officer, Lowe observed, could provide a springboard to launch a man of sober and industrious habits into middle-class society. Certainly it was no drawback, as he recalled, naming several who had made the transition. Ben Bishop, a former 1st sergeant of B Troop before Lowe joined it, retired from the Army and became a prosperous cattle dealer in nearby Weston. Sergeant Lowe visited him frequently when off-duty.

In the winter of 1852, while Lowe was at Leavenworth, 1st Sergeant Hooper of B Troop retired after ten years (two enlistments) of service. With land warrants and some money that he and his wife had managed to save during those years, Hooper moved to Iowa, where he became a prosperous and prominent farmer. Another noncommissioned officer of B Troop was Sergeant John Cuddy, who married a well-to-do Spanish lady upon his retirement and lived many years as a prosperous rancher in California. Another sergeant became a typesetter on the *Missouri Republican* after retirement and one of B Troop's artificers—a farrier—retired and through marriage acquired a large farm in Clinton, Missouri. When the Civil War began, he threw his lot in with the Confederacy and fell as a major at Vicksburg. Sergeant Candy of D Troop eventually became the colonel in charge of the Hampton, Virginia, Soldier's Home following retirement.

As for Sergeant Lowe, at the end of his five-year enlistment he left the Army to become a civilian employee of quartermaster transportation, then finally a private freight contractor, hauling freight over the Great Plains across which he had once ridden as a soldier in the 1st Dragoons.

But there were exceptions to a happy and prosperous retirement for some of

Sergeant Lowe's comrades. Sergeant Cook, the able quartermaster sergeant of the 1st Dragoons during Lowe's enlistment, went on a filibustering expedition to Nicaragua after retiring from the regular Army. The expedition ended in failure, and Cook barely escaped with his life. He eventually found his way to San Francisco, where he died in poverty.

Senior noncommissioned officers sometimes had a voice in the selection of their successors. As Sergeant Lowe prepared to leave the service he selected a Corporal Ferguson as his successor. Irish-born, Ferguson had enlisted during the Mexican War and reenlisted in 1854. Both the troop and its commander knew that it was Lowe's wish that Ferguson take his place, and "all became educated up to the idea and expected it." When Lowe left for his last furlough prior to the end of his enlistment, he left Ferguson as acting 1st sergeant. Unfortunately, not all the troopers were satisfied with the choice, for one night after tattoo roll call, one of the troublemakers stabbed Ferguson to death. The murderer was quickly tried and sentenced to be hanged by a general court-martial composed of commissioned officers.

An account of another noncommissioned officer's experience illustrates the career of a foreign-born recruit entering the Army in the mid-1850s. Born in Prussia, Eugene Bandel attended the local gymnasium where among other subjects he studied botany and classical languages. In 1853, Bandel emigrated to the United States. In September 1854, the nineteen-year-old decided to seek his fortune in the West. By November he arrived in St. Louis, unemployed and broke. In his extremity Bandel enlisted in the United States Army. His first duty station was Jefferson Barracks, where he was assigned to Company E of the 6th Infantry.[26]

In the mid-fifties, when Bandel joined the 6th Infantry Regiment, it was comprised of ten companies of seventy-four men each. Each company had four corporals and four sergeants, one of whom was the first, or orderly sergeant. In addition to the company noncommissioned officers, there were two field musicians, a fifer and a drummer, with each infantry company.

Established in 1826, Jefferson Barracks in 1854 was the headquarters of the Army Department of the West, one of the five military districts into which the country was then divided. When young Bandel arrived in November 1854, Jefferson Barracks was still the starting point for many military expeditions to the Great Plains and the Rocky Mountains. It was to those regions that Bandel and his infantry company were ultimately sent.

Eugene Bandel's foreign birth was not a career obstacle. Within nine months he was promoted to the rank of corporal with pay of $13.00 per month and $50.00 per year clothing allowance from which a careful soldier like Bandel could save a few dollars.*

There were other ways in which a soldier might eke out a few extra dollars to

*A corporal in the cavalry or artillery received one dollar a month more than an infantryman, presumably for the additional skills his duties required.

add to his pay. In Bandel's day, a soldier was not expected to do manual labor for the government unless civilians were not available. If it was necessary to employ soldiers as laborers for more than ten consecutive days—in road building or fortification construction for example—the soldier was paid twenty-five cents extra per day as a common laborer or forty cents per day as a mechanic, carpenter, or blacksmith.

Observing many of his fellow infantrymen in the regiment, Bandel wrote to his parents that they were "men who either do not care to work, or who, because of being addicted to drink, cannot find employment. There are some exceptions to this," he added, "these are mostly Germans, well brought up, some who in Germany were university students and who found themselves [as he had himself] temporarily in a position where it was impossible to secure employment; so that they were thus forced to enter the army. These got on very well, and it is only with such that I have friendly intercourse," he wrote. It is difficult to determine whether Bandel was simply trying to reassure his parents that he was keeping good company or whether he was revealing an ethnic bias.

In spite of this rather aloof attitude, within three years Bandel advanced from corporal to sergeant and eventually to 1st sergeant of his company. He wrote his parents:

> The [to first sergeant] promotion, relieves me of all guard duty, and my duty now consists of the management of all company affairs. The arms, rations, clothing, and all such company property is in my charge. I must make out all company papers; that is, technically, I am responsible for them. Though I have a company clerk under me who attends to all the actual writing, I must look them over [all papers] and sign them. It is also a part of my duty to read all names at company roll call, as well as assign the proper guard shifts and other similar duties. I now have a tent of my own—pay is now increased to $20.00 per month.

As the end of his enlistment drew near, 1st Sergeant Bandel, like many others before him who worked their way westward in the ranks of the regular Army, decided to leave the military and settle in the West. With his discharge papers, Bandel took with him about $300.00 in cash, including expenses for return to his place of enlistment (St. Louis), back pay, clothing allowance, and money saved ($2.00 per month withheld from a soldier's pay and returned to him on discharge). This, he believed, was sufficient to help him get started as a civilian in California.

Accordingly, on July 31, 1861, 1st Sergeant Bandel obtained a furlough for the three months remaining on his enlistment and journeyed from San Bernardino, where his unit was stationed, to the Benicia arsenal, where he expected to find employment. Bandel's grub stake did not last long, however, for he paid over $100.00 for new civilian clothing and travel expenses to Benicia cost him $75.00. Although his first job paid only $2.00 per day, Bandel eventually married, raised a family and worked his way up to the position of master mechanic at the Benicia arsenal.

▪ ▪

Of course, not all noncommissioned officers of the mid-nineteenth-century regular Army were as successful or as self-disciplined as were sergeants Lowe and Bandel. However, from their diaries it is evident that sufficient numbers of their fellow noncommissioned officers managed to thrive in the services as to suggest that the Army did indeed attract some very able men to its ranks—far more than the public has traditionally believed. These men, to become capable noncommissioned officers in the environment the Army offered in those years, had to exhibit qualities of courage and leadership that in civilian life would—and often did after they left the service—enable them to take their places as solid, middle-class citizens in a highly competitive society.

CHAPTER 7

NONCOMMISSIONED OFFICERS IN THE CIVIL WAR

At the outbreak of the Civil War the regular Army numbered only 16,000 men, deployed principally in the departments of the West, where they patrolled the high plains and mountains. This number was soon increased by an act of Congress of July 29, 1861, which raised the authorized strength of the regular Army to 20,334 and eventually to 22,714—an increase of nine regiments of infantry, one of cavalry, and one of artillery. As a result of this expansion, hundreds of regular soldiers were promoted to commissioned and noncommissioned ranks.[1]

This increase in strength, however, was never intended to enable the regular Army to deal with the crisis of secession alone. Unlike the earlier Mexican War, the Civil War was largely fought and won by volunteers. Thus, the noncommissioned officers of the volunteer regiments best typified the wartime noncommissioned officer.

THE VOLUNTEER

Fortunately, many of these men came from civilian pursuits, were quite literate, and had strong family ties. Consequently, they left behind a rich store of correspondence and diaries that proud families and descendants have preserved. In these documents the volunteer noncommissioned officer can be seen either as he saw himself or as he wished others to see him.

The regular Army noncommissioned officer, on the other hand, is generally viewed—as in the past—through the eyes of his officers in official reports and correspondence. More often than the volunteer, the regular Army enlisted man had severed ties with his family and had less education than the more numerous volunteers. For these reasons, the regulars left behind only an insignificant body of correspondence compared with the volunteers. When a regular has left a record, it is more often in the form of memoirs, usually written many years after the war. In some cases regulars who rose through the ranks to become senior officers of the Army have left only brief descriptions of their days as noncommissioned officers, preferring to concentrate on when they were most prominent.

In May 1861, President Lincoln issued a call for 42,034 volunteers, to be raised by the states and organized into 40 regiments for three years' service. So great was the response that by July some 208 regiments had been organized, of which 153 had already been mustered into federal service and 55 more were almost ready to be enrolled. By August of that year there were 485,640 three-year volunteers in service. About one in ten—a sizeable number—of these men eventually became noncommissioned officers.[2]

Eventually 700,000 men enlisted as volunteers in state units, making up some 418 regiments of infantry, 31 of cavalry, and 10 of artillery. Although during the war, with the aid of the draft, a total of 2,666,999 men served either as regulars or volunteers, the total active strength at any one time was never much over the one million authorized by Congress, and the total strength for duty at any one time never even reached that.[3]

Meanwhile, the crisis that was tearing the nation apart had a less serious effect on the regular Army. Its only grave defections came from among the commissioned officers from the Southern states. They could and did tender their resignations when secession of their home states tested their loyalties. Enlisted men, on the other hand, were locked into the regular Army by the terms of their enlistment contracts. Therefore, resignation was not an option for them, regardless of their sectional loyalties. In any case, most regular Army noncommissioned officers at that time generally came from states outside the Confederacy and from social classes with little or no economic stake either in states' rights or slavery.*

Authorized to raise a large volunteer army and to significantly increase the size of the regular Army, the secretary of war faced questions that had troubled his predecessors since the War of 1812—the relative roles to be played in the conflict by the regulars and the state-raised militia or volunteers. Should the regular Army serve as a nucleus or as a model for the volunteer forces, or should it be consolidated with the volunteers, with regulars functioning as instructors and a leavening influence among the inexperienced volunteers?

The first choice would have kept intact the corps of veteran noncommissioned officers; the second would have broken up the regular Army units with certain loss of morale. General Winfield Scott, then the senior officer with the regular estab-

*When Texas seceded in January 1861, the state convention demanded that Major General David E. Twiggs, the department commander, surrender all forts and U.S. government property within the state. Although Twiggs at first resisted this demand, he eventually complied by issuing an "Order of Exercises" that required all troops to evacuate the posts, surrender all public property not necessary to transport them to the coast, and then, retaining their side arms, to concentrate at the port of embarkation, where they surrendered the remaining transportation to self-appointed state agents. The latter severely tested the loyalty of regular Army enlisted men by offering them good pay and liberal bounties if they would enter Confederate service. But, with very few exceptions, the overwhelming majority of enlisted men declined these blandishments. See George F. Prince, *Across the Continent with the Fifth Cavalry*, pp. 95–99.

lishment, advocated the first choice, one that he had adopted with success during the Mexican War. Secretary of War Simon Cameron urged upon President Lincoln the second choice. Lincoln accepted Scott's recommendation.[4]

REGULARS AND VOLUNTEERS

Some former regular Army noncommissioned officers nevertheless found their way into the ranks of the volunteer regiments, where they became highly valued trainers and leaders. A few even won commissions in volunteer units on the basis of their previous military service and experience. Most volunteer units, however, had to train their own commissioned as well as noncommissioned officers. The result was a corps of noncommissioned officers quite different in attitude and tradition than that of the regular Army.

Both regular and volunteer regiments were made up of ten companies. In turn, each of these had three commissioned officers, a captain, a first and second lieutenant; four sergeants, one of whom served as company first sergeant; four corporals; one wagoneer; and 64 to 82 privates. The regimental noncommissioned staff consisted of a sergeant major, a quartermaster sergeant, a commissary sergeant, hospital steward,* and two principal musicians. Although authorized regimental strength ranged from 869 to 1,049 officers and men, actual wartime strength was usually between 375 and 530.[5] When at full strength, the regiment could be maneuvered as two battalions, as had been the practice since the eighteenth century.

Even though both regular and volunteer units had similar organization, there were important differences. One was length of service—one to three years for volunteers, but five for regulars. Furthermore, most states, in order to fill their quotas, offered volunteers cash bounties—some as large as $500. The regular Army could never match this. Further inducements, such as rapid promotions, were offered state-appointed officers and noncommissioned officers. The rank they held in militia units often depended upon their success in obtaining enough recruits to fill out their commands. For example, as more recruits came in, Dennis J. McCarthy of Company H, 104th New York Volunteers, was promoted to second corporal and shortly thereafter to fourth sergeant of his company, all within one year of his enlistment. His monthly pay as sergeant was $17.00, all of which he could keep, unlike the regular, from whose pay $2.00 was deducted each month to be repaid him at the end of his service.[6]

Although the regulars quite naturally benefited from the increased pay that an anxious Congress authorized to stimulate enlistments, this increase was no longer in gold and silver coin, as in the past, but in paper money—the so-called greenbacks—a currency that fluctuated in value. Regulars also benefited as unit strength increased but generally not as rapidly as the volunteers. As the war clouds

*On the eve of the Civil War hospital stewards were advanced ahead of company first sergeants on precedence lists.

gathered, many former noncommissioned officers reenlisted in their old units and quickly regained their former rank, thereby blocking the promotions of many younger men.[7]

Despite the fact that soldiers of the regular units were led by more experienced cadre and were usually somewhat better cared for, most young men preferred service in the volunteers. Their leaders, both commissioned and noncommissioned, were frequently well known to them, often friends or acquaintances from their home communities. In many cases, this acquaintance was on a first-name basis. Frequently, it was the custom for volunteer companies to elect their own officers. Sometimes the regimental commander himself was elected by the men. More often, however, regimental commanders were appointed by the state governor.

Noncommissioned officers selected by political appointees were bound to be of a somewhat different breed than those of the regular Army and therefore stood in a somewhat different relationship to their superiors and subordinates. Furthermore, volunteers frequently clung more steadfastly to the ideals and customs brought from civilian life than the longtime regulars. For example, one sergeant of volunteers wrote to his brother that he did not chew, smoke, or drink "and should not if i [*sic*] was in the Army for twenty years."[8]

Such attitudes were not uncommon among men of volunteer units. That many were friends and neighbors with close ties with the folks at home also served as a measure of control on individual behavior. But as the years of service lengthened, and the rigors of combat grew more severe, these controls weakened.

In the early years of the war a degree of familiarity existed among officers and enlisted men of the volunteer regiments that was unheard of in the tradition-bound regular Army. For example, when several noncommissioned officers shared their tent with a lieutenant of their company shortly after the 83d Ohio Volunteer Infantry Regiment was mustered into service, no objections were raised.[9] Another aspect of this familiarity is illustrated by a corporal of a Pennsylvania volunteer company, who observed that the battalion major was "a neighbor of mine, and he was also a friend, as I courted my wife in his house and she was [then] living with his [the major's] wife and family." Later, that same corporal, when asked by his sergeant to contribute to the purchase of a sword for the company commander, told the sergeant "where he could go, with words suitable to the occasion."

The captain was getting $100.00 per month and the corporal only $16.00, and "they wanted me to help him buy a sword!" the irate corporal declared. But this display of egalitarian sentiment was too much even for the volunteers. "The next day," the corporal wrote, "the sergeant came around and said 'you made a dam fool of yourself yesterday, and Captain Smith won't even let you have corporal's stripes, even if you was [*sic*] a veteran of two enlistments.' " Yet the practice of recruiting units from the same community inevitably created conditions in which the enforcement of much of the traditional regular Army discipline, such as flogging, was difficult, if not impossible. In any case, flogging was abolished early in the war among the volunteer units, and the regulars soon followed suit.[10]

On the other hand, as the war progressed, the volunteers did not shrink from drastic disciplinary measures when such were necessary. A sergeant of the Pennsylvania volunteers, writing from camp near Leesburg, Virginia, on June 21, 1863, told how the entire corps was assembled to see three deserters shot.[11]

Traditionally each state governor commissioned officers in the regiments raised in his own state. However, as the war continued complaints multiplied that under this procedure inferior men were often placed in command over more experienced and able ones. Advancement, the secretary of war observed, should be as in the regulars, based on merit, and "the volunteer soldier should be given to understand that preferment will be the sure award to intelligence, fidelity, and distinguished service." After the heavy casualties of several major battles, state governors under pressure from dismayed voters began to fill many commissioned vacancies in volunteer units with outstanding noncommissioned officers who had demonstrated their competence in battle rather than in politics.

This was the case in the 7th Regiment, Illinois Volunteers. Noncommissioned officers and even in some cases privates who had distinguished themselves were raised to commissioned status. The commander of Company A, Captain Samuel G. Ward, had enlisted as a private. He was later selected to be regimental sergeant major, and after three months in that position was promoted to be commander of Company A. He served well and gallantly in that position until he fell at the battle of Shiloh on April 6, 1862. Following Captain Ward's death, his place was taken by his first sergeant, George W. Wheeler.[12]

After the battle of Allatoona Pass on the eve of Sherman's march through Georgia, other noncommissioned officers and privates were commissioned to take the places of fallen or resigned officers. For example, Sergeant David Leib Ambrose was promoted to be first lieutenant of Company H, Private William E. Norton became commander of Company I, and Private James Crawley became Norton's first lieutenant, taking the place of Lieutenant John E. Sullivan, who fell at Allatoona Pass.[13]

Yet it was difficult to separate the two commissioning practices in every case. Thomas McGregor of the 60th Indiana Volunteers was tendered a commission by the governor of the state for his gallantry during the battle of Arkansas Post in January 1862. His brother Frank, who was also serving in an Indiana regiment but had not been offered a commission, felt that his own deeds had gone unrewarded and decided to accept the proffered help of a prominent citizen of his hometown to see what could be done in his behalf.[14]

Apparently Indiana and Illinois units were more inclined than those from Ohio to follow the secretary of war's advice, for neither Sergeant Frank McGregor nor his friends managed to obtain commissions. Meanwhile, besides Thomas McGregor, there were several other of his fellow noncommissioned officers who received commissions for meritorious service. Among them were First Sergeant William P. Herren, of Company B, 72nd Indiana Volunteer Regiment of Mounted Infantry, promoted to captain; Sergeant Robert Maxwell to first lieutenant; and the company's third sergeant, Charles M. Robinson, to second lieutenant. This seemed to confirm Frank McGregor's lament that "enlisted men in Ohio regiments have not the chance of promotion that those in Indiana regiments have."[15]

Whether true or not, McGregor's statement does suggest that many enlisted men perceived that states did not, as the regular Army had done during the Mexican War, follow a uniform policy for promoting outstanding noncommissioned soldiers. Actually, each state had its own policy and practice in promoting men from the ranks and commissioning officers in general. For its part, the regular Army resumed its policy, largely in abeyance since the Mexican War, of commissioning meritorious and educated noncommissioned officers, most of whom, in the words of one regular Army noncommissioned officer, became "efficient and reliable officers whom the rank and file could respect."[16]

For example, the regular Army's 2d Infantry Regiment promoted several outstanding noncommissioned officers during the war. Among them was the first sergeant of Company B, Daniel W. Burke. Not only was he promoted to first lieutenant, but he also received the Medal of Honor for valor. Burke remained with the Army following the war and eventually retired as a brigadier general in 1899. In addition to Burke, the regimental sergeant major and half a dozen company 1st sergeants received commissions as second lieutenants. This was, by the way, a far greater promotion rate for noncommissioned officers than had been the case during the Mexican War. A senior noncommissioned officer of the 2d Infantry observed that "without exception they made good officers and gave the regiment a better character and standing than the inexperienced civilians that had been inflicted upon us at the beginning of the War."[17]

Another regular Army regiment, the 5th (formerly the 2d) Cavalry, promoted more noncommissioned officers to commissioned rank during the war than had the entire U.S. Army during the Mexican War. A total of fifty-four former enlisted men, of whom forty-three had noncommissioned service, received commissions in this regiment. Some had served with other units during the war but were commissioned in the 5th Cavalry at war's end. One was Charles B. Compton who, before enlisting for three months in the 1st Iowa Volunteer Infantry in May 1861, had been an engineer in civilian life. He was promoted to first sergeant and later to sergeant major of the Iowa regiment until honorably discharged at the expiration of his enlistment on August 21, 1861. He reentered the Army on October 19, 1861, as a captain in the 11th Iowa Volunteer Infantry. In January 1863, he was appointed a major of the 47th Colored Infantry. He was finally mustered out of the volunteer service as a lieutenant colonel in March 1866. In July of the same year he received an appointment as a regular Army major in the 40th Infantry Regiment. He became lieutenant colonel of the 5th Cavalry in July 1879 and its colonel on August 4, 1882.[18]

Occasionally the sons of senior military officers enlisted in the ranks, as did Edwin V. Sumner, son of Brigadier General Edwin V. Sumner, and Alfred B. Taylor, son of Rear Admiral Robert Taylor. Young Sumner served as first sergeant of

Company B of a volunteer battalion known as the "Clay's Guards." This unit was organized at Washington, D.C., in April 1861 for guard duty at the White House and other public buildings. First Sergeant Sumner did not serve long with that unit. In August 1861 he was appointed from at large a second lieutenant in the 1st Dragoons (1st Cavalry). He was promoted to first lieutenant in his regiment the following November and to captain in September 1863. By the end of the war he had become a brevet brigadier general of volunteers. Eventually he joined the regular Army's 5th Cavalry as a captain in April 1866.[19]

Foreign-born immigrants who joined the Army as young men seeking a foothold in the American scene also earned promotions. Irish-born Thomas E. Maley, who enlisted at St. Louis in the old 2d Cavalry (later 5th Cavalry) in May 1855, rose to major before the war was over. Young Maley rode with his regiment to duty in Texas, where on March 8, 1856, as a noncommissioned officer, he distinguished himself "for gallant conduct in combat with hostile Indians along the Guadalupe River." Appointed regimental quartermaster sergeant, Maley served in that grade until the expiration of his enlistment in 1860.

In June of that year Maley was appointed freight and ticket agent for the Illinois Central & Toledo, Wabash & Western Railroad. He held this job until September 1861, when he was appointed first lieutenant and regimental quartermaster in the 6th Pennsylvania (Volunteer) Cavalry. In April 1862 he received a regular Army commission as a second lieutenant in the 5th Cavalry. He was made a brevet major on July 28, 1864, after serving with distinction with his regiment in several campaigns and battles.[20]

There were other noncommissioned officers whose careers were not quite as predictable as that of Major Maley. English-born Henry Baker, participated as a sergeant in General Patterson's Shenandoah campaign, the battle of Falling Waters, and the Maryland and Peninsular campaigns. At the battle of Gaines Mill during the latter campaign, Sergeant Baker carried the regimental colors with gallantry. In August 1862 he was appointed regimental sergeant major, but two months later was appointed second lieutenant. Thereafter, his rise was rapid, reaching major's rank in March 1865. While serving on escort duty with General Grant in November of that year, Major Baker for unknown reasons went AWOL. In January of the following year his name was dropped from the regimental rolls.[21]

One of Baker's predecessors as regimental sergeant major was German-born Gustavus Urban. He enlisted in the old 2d Cavalry in July 1855 and like Thomas Maley, marched with the regiment to Texas, where he served as regimental sergeant major until the expiration of his enlistment in 1860. He immediately reenlisted and was appointed regimental quartermaster sergeant in March 1861. The following September Urban was discharged from his enlistment to accept a captaincy as an assistant adjutant general of volunteers. He then joined Brigadier General Abercrombie and served with him until after the battle of Malvern Hill, when he was recommended for an appointment in the regular Army by General Abercrombie, who in doing so stated: "There are very few, if any, of his rank who have a stronger claim for advancement. His services to me at the battle of Fair Oaks as a staff officer were invaluable."

Shortly thereafter, Urban was appointed a second lieutenant in the 5th Cavalry and as a first lieutenant in July 1862. From September 4 to December 3, 1864, Urban commanded the regiment with bravery and distinction as a brevet colonel. Following the war he reverted to his regular Army rank of captain and served in various expeditions against the Indians. He died on January 11, 1871, at Ft. McPherson, "a highly esteemed and faithful officer."[22]

There were other noncommissioned officers in the Civil War, such as Adolphus W. Greely, who not only won a commission after serving bravely as sergeant, but went on to win fame in positions of great responsibility, in Greely's case as an arctic explorer. During the war Greely served as a private, corporal, and 1st sergeant in the 19th Massachusetts Volunteers from July 29, 1861, to March 18, 1863, when he was appointed a second lieutenant in the 81st U.S. Colored Infantry Regiment. Eventually he was promoted to captain in that unit.

Following the war, Greely received an appointment in the regular Army as a second lieutenant in the 36th (presently 7th) Infantry Regiment in March 1867. Upon a reduction in the Army's strength, Greely was transferred to the 2d Artillery, but the order was soon revoked and he was assigned to the 5th Cavalry on August 7, 1869, and promoted to first lieutenant on May 27, 1873. Eventually, Greely was assigned to duty in the office of the chief signal officer of the Army. It was from that position he in time became a distinguished student of arctic exploration and a leader of expeditions into that region.[23]

Even more widely known than Lieutenant Greely was William F. ("Buffalo Bill") Cody. In 1863 Cody enlisted in the 7th Kansas Volunteer Cavalry, where he was promoted to noncommissioned rank. In this capacity, Cody served as regimental scout after the battle of Tupelo, Mississippi. Honorably discharged after the Civil War, Cody eventually was appointed by General Sheridan as chief scout and guide for the 5th Cavalry in the Republican River campaign of 1869. His later career as world-renowned showman of the American West is too well known to bear repeating here.[24]

While these eight men represent only a small percentage of the forty-three former noncommissioned officers who, with the exception of William Cody, reached commissioned rank in the 5th Cavalry, they are representative of the wide variety in background and education found among the noncommissioned officers of the regular Army both immediately before and after the Civil War.

THE NONCOMMISSIONED OFFICER'S ROLE

Since most volunteers started their military experience fresh from a civilian background and with only the most rudimentary knowledge of things military, they had no choice but to rely heavily on the standard training manuals that long provided the doctrinal basis for training in the regular Army. The importance of these manuals for an understanding of the noncommissioned officer's role in the Civil War lies in the detail with which the NCO's duties were described in each particular manual.

At the beginning of the war there were two training manuals in circulation: General Winfield Scott's by then rather antiquated *Infantry Tactics*, published in 1815; and Colonel William J. Hardee's *Rifle and Light Infantry Tactics*, published in 1855. A third manual, General Silas Casey's *Infantry Tactics*, superseded both by 1862, after changes in weaponry had made Scott's obsolete and Hardee had defected to the Confederacy. The infantry tactics that the Army employed during much of the Civil War were based on the translations of the French *Ordinances* of 1831 and 1845 for the maneuvers of heavy infantry and *chasseurs à pied*, translations prepared by both Scott and Casey.[25]

Like earlier changes in tactical doctrine, the French *Ordinances* represented the latest thinking in post-Napoleonic doctrine based upon a continuing revolution in weapons technology. These changes came about, as General Casey described it, as "a departure from those processional movements and formations in the order of battle which [had] characterized the Prussian school of Frederick the Great." Apart from the influence of changes in weapons technology, Casey observed that Frederician tactics had been discarded "by the ablest tacticians of Europe, and have been violated in all the great actions since the French Revolution."[26]

Thus the three-rank battle line of the mid-eighteenth century was abandoned and the U.S. Army adopted the two-rank linear formation in its stead. This change, Casey claimed, increased the rapidity of the gait as well as the intervals between the battalions and the brigades, but at the same time held the troops in closer order and in control when maneuvering in the presence of the enemy. He wrote that it would also "assure that deployment upon the head of the column was the safest and most rapid means of forming a line of battle." From these changes the brigade ultimately emerged as the basic tactical unit during the war.[27]

General Casey continued Scott's earlier emphasis upon the sergeant's role in maintaining unit direction and cadence. The sergeants, Casey wrote, should also "be well instructed in their duties as battalion guides." The importance of this role to maintaining the order and alignment of formations as they moved from marching column into line of battle was as important in the Civil War as it had been in Mexico. Sergeants, serving as general guides, were chosen from among those "most distinguished for their carriage under arms and in marching." They were to be "respectively denominated, in the maneuvers, the right general guide and the left general guide, and be posted in the line of file closers; the first in the rear of the right flank, and the second in the rear of the left flank of the battalion." Together with the color guard, for which Casey, unlike Scott, preferred corporals instead of sergeants, these general guides played key roles in helping to maintain the alignment and cadence of the ranks as they moved from march column onto the line of battle.

The general guides marched in step with the color rank, each sergeant-guide maintaining himself abreast, or nearly so, with that rank. The importance of maintaining cadence throughout the formation was stressed by both Scott and Casey, the latter observing that nothing contributed more "to fatigue soldiers and derange the interior order of battalions than frequent variations in step." Therefore, general guides on the march and in the line of battle were to indicate to the companies near the flanks the step or cadence of the battalion center.

Both Hardee and Casey gave the noncommissioned officer a major role in the instruction of the recruits in the school of the soldier and of the company. Company officers, however, remained charged with the responsibility of training noncommissioned officers to accomplish these tasks. Casey, for example, placed the entire training of the noncommissioned officer in the hands of the company commander, holding him responsible for both the theoretical and practical instruction of the company noncommissioned officers. The regimental adjutant was responsible for the instruction of the regimental noncommissioned staff. During field training each noncommissioned officer was required, as he explained a movement, to execute it on the ground and in the presence of his company commander.

By designating the captain as the primary instructor of his company, Casey was actually continuing a tradition begun by von Steuben in 1778. Casey—as had von Steuben—regarded company officers as the primary instructors of the squads in the school of the soldier. This meant that while the noncommissioned officers were to train the individual soldier, the commissioned officers were to have the oversight of their training when they were assembled in squads, platoons, and companies. If there were insufficient company-grade officers present, however—and during the Civil War this was often the case—Casey had the company commander employ his better sergeants as instructors, although an officer supervised them when at all possible.

Noncommissioned officers were expected to learn to give commands. "Each command, in a lesson, at the theoretical instruction," Casey wrote, "should first be given by the instructor and then repeated, in succession, by the noncommissioned officer, so that while they become habituated to the commands, uniformity may be established in the manner of giving them." The theoretical instruction of the sergeants "should include the School of the Soldier, the School of the Company, and the Drill for Skirmishers, as well as knowledge of the principles of firing."

As hundreds of volunteer units began organizing, both officers and noncommissioned officers usually started out equally ignorant of military knowledge and blundered along together through varying periods of training and frequently with inadequate equipment.[28] Much of this training took place off duty when the regimental staff, both commissioned and noncommissioned, assembled at some convenient place to prepare themselves for the next day's activities. If an experienced instructor was not available, as occurred frequently, one of the more senior of the commissioned officers presented lessons based on one of the training manuals then current, and emphasized the subjects to be covered the following day.

A corporal in a Massachusetts volunteer regiment noted that the noncommissioned officers of his company had "lessons in tactics every night at the Captain's quarters to fitt [*sic*] them to drill the privates in squads according to the book." A sergeant of an Ohio volunteer regiment observed that "every night I recite with the other first sergeants and 2d lieutenants. We shall finish Hardee's *Tactics* and then study Army regulations."[29]

Not all states depended on such *ad hoc* training for their volunteers. Some, such as Michigan, adopted a more formal system of training for both commissioned and noncommissioned officers. In June 1861, for example, the governor of Michigan designated Ft. Wayne, near Detroit, as a camp of instruction for the 5th, 6th, and 7th volunteer infantry regiments. Officers and noncommissioned officers received their training there prior to the arrival of the recruits. After instruction by the most experienced drill sergeants, chosen from among the cadre, the future troop leaders took turns commanding skeleton formations made up of fellow trainees; the pivot man holding strings or poles across the space normally occupied by privates to represent squads, platoons, or companies.

By the time the recruits arrived at the training camp, the regimental cadres had already acquired a knowledge of the fundamentals of drill and organization as well as some degree of self-confidence in their newly assigned roles. In some instances veteran noncommissioned officers who had served in the regular Army for one or more enlistments took over the training of replacements. The latter drilled intensively in squad and company movements, then were put into their regular units for further training, along with more seasoned comrades, in battalion and higher exercises.[30]

However, the Michigan practice was the exception. More typical was the training of Ohio units described by Brigadier General Andrew S. Burt, looking back on his experience as a sergeant in the 6th Ohio Volunteer Infantry.* He observed that "the lack of self care on the part of our soldiers, those amongst them competent to teach, was a source of utmost anxiety to those in authority. Lucky was the regiment which had some old soldiers as a leven [*sic*] of knowledge, whether he had belonged to the old Army, or was a veteran of the Mexican War . . . according to my experience particularly was the regiment lucky if that leven was an old German soldier."[31]

Many volunteer units had the good fortune, as Burt noted, to include in their ranks veterans of the Mexican War as well as some immigrants with European military training who often helped out as drill sergeants. As one historian has observed, "the aid rendered by foreigners, schooled in the excellent systems of Prussia, France, Switzerland, and other European countries, in training the Union forces was tremendous, and their service in this connection deserves far more recognition than it has received."[32]

*General Burt enlisted in the 6th Ohio Volunteers in April 1861. He subsequently became a sergeant and was later promoted to captain. Before he retired in 1902 after forty-one years of service, he had attained the rank of brigadier general.

The devotion of these foreign-born soldiers to their new homeland is illustrated in the sentiments expressed by Sergeant Fergus Elliott in a letter to his brother shortly before the battle of Lookout Mountain, Tennessee, on November 20, 1863.* "I do not forget that I am a true born Englishman, and never shal [*sic*] as long as I live, but while I am in America I will fight for America, and if England was to interfere on the rebel's side, could fight them as well as the Rebels themselves."[33]

In some instances, because of the language problem, all men of one nationality were concentrated in the same unit, as in the 9th Ohio Volunteer Infantry. Recruited mainly from among the German-settled regions of the state, this particular regiment had in its ranks many noncommissioned officers who had received some military training in Prussia or in one of the other German states before emigrating to America.[34]

A good deal of garrison training consisted of seemingly endless hours of drill on the parade ground in the expectation that the elements of this drill transferred to the battlefield would enable the commanders to maneuver their units rapidly and in order in the face of enemy fire. Even those who had to undergo this often tedious and certainly tiresome drill were sometimes impressed by the overall picture of order and power given by highly disciplined military units.

A noncommissioned officer writing from a training camp near Washington, D.C., described his training with some enthusiasm:

> From 0900 to 1100 there was instruction in the manual of arms, company drill, and maneuvers by company. For two hours in the afternoon there was battalion drill under the colonel's command. [He taught the companies] how to move in concert without getting confused and how to change the line of battle from one point to another. I've always enjoyed seeing a regiment when on battalion drill, every movement is so completed, so scientific.[35]

There was more to a noncom's day than long hours on the parade ground. A representative day could well have been described by Fergus Elliott. In November 1862, Elliott was promoted to orderly sergeant in his company, to take the place of one who had just been commissioned a first lieutenant. As orderly sergeant Elliott found "plenty of work to do."[36]

There was roll call at daybreak; doctor's call at 0630; morning report to be completed and turned in at 0700; guard mount at 0800; and camp drill from 1000–1130. Then there was dress parade at 1630, followed by roll call at sundown, and tattoo "all of which is performed by me," Elliott reported proudly. At that time Sergeant Elliott was sharing a tent with a lieutenant who was under ar-

*Born in Leicestershire, England, Elliott came to the United States with his parents when he was fourteen years old. At the battle of Gettysburg, after two color bearers had been shot, young Elliott was detailed to carry the colors. This he continued to do throughout General Sherman's campaign in Georgia. Later Elliott was promoted to company first sergeant. Following the war, he was employed in Germantown, Pennsylvania. He died in December 1923 at the age of eighty.

rest in quarters, for what charge Elliott does not say. "I have full charge," he added, "of the company in preparation for the regimental inspection."

Quite late in the war it was not unusual for noncommissioned officers to be left in charge of company-sized units after their commissioned officers elected to take immediate discharges to civilian life. For example, after the conclusion of Sherman's Georgia campaign and Johnston's surrender, many regiments that had taken part in that campaign began assembling on Raleigh, North Carolina, preparatory to either mustering out or assignment to occupation duties elsewhere in the former Confederacy. In many cases commissioned officers of volunteer units had been quick to take their discharges and leave entire companies in the hands of their sergeants. From an assembly camp near Raleigh Sergeant Elliott wrote of the 109th Pennsylvania Volunteers that "I was in command of a company of a hundred men or more" during the march to Raleigh. And a Sergeant Tallman wrote that "I was still in command of Company C" when General Grant reviewed the victorious army at Raleigh.[37] Tallman added that "while at Raleigh quite a number of the absent members of our Regiment rejoined us and among them several of our company who had been absent sick or wounded, Lieutenant Butts was one of them and assumed command of Company E which was a relief to us sergeants as we did not want the responsibility without the pay and the honors."

TACTICAL CHANGES

By the time Casey published his manual in 1862, massed rifle and artillery fire from well-prepared field fortifications suggested the desirability, indeed the very necessity, of a less vulnerable tactical formation than the two-rank line of battle advancing in attack. The tactical changes suggested by this challenge ultimately greatly enhanced the combat leadership role of the noncommissioned officer.

Such changes had been forecast in the decades preceding the war by the unique requirements of military operations against nomadic tribes of Indians on the western plains. At that time Army units had been forced temporarily to abandon traditional linear tactics for lines of skirmishers composed of small units operating in open formation.[38] Under such circumstances, as noted earlier, a senior noncommissioned officer might often find himself in command of a unit as large as a platoon.

But when the Civil War began and large armies faced one another in the field, the Army reverted to the traditional European linear tactics. Yet as battle followed battle, and the growing lethality of weapons caused casualty rates to soar, Army commanders came gradually to employ a more open battle order, to reduce the vulnerability of their men to the increased volume and accuracy of enemy firepower. In his manual, General Casey had anticipated this development by outlining the skirmish formation as a supplement to the close-order linear tactics of the traditional battlefield.[39]

During the war both armies came gradually to adopt the more open order described by Casey. From compact battle lines drawn up in two ranks, companies and even battalions moved out in lines of skirmishers. An entire battalion could advance from a line of battle in eight successive lines of skirmishers. Advancing by squads and sections, taking advantage of all the cover and concealment offered by the terrain, skirmishers advanced to within assaulting distance of the enemy positions. Before the final assault, however, Casey's tactics called for the skirmishers to regroup into a battle line and then to close with the enemy.

The central feature of these tactics was the subdivision of the companies and battalions into their constituent parts or fractions, each with its own commander. In some cases this might be a noncommissioned officer. Obviously skirmish tactics greatly enhanced the roles of successive commanders from major down to corporal: The major assumed the functions of a brigade commander; the captain those of the colonel; the lieutenant those of the captain; the sergeant those of the lieutenant; and the corporal, no longer a mere rifleman, took command of the squad.

The officers and noncoms were, in Casey's words, "to see that the men [in line of skirmishers] economize their strength, keep cool, and profit by all the advantages the ground may offer for cover. It is only by this continual watchfulness on the part of all grades that a line of skirmishers can attain success." Officers and sergeants were cautioned by Casey to abstain from taking a part in the firings. They should instead concentrate on maintaining order and silence among the men. The commanders were to see that "the skirmishers do not wander imprudently" and caution them to be calm and collected, not to fire until they saw their targets and were sure they were within range.[40]

Such tactics gave the company commander and his noncommissioned officers considerable latitude "in the management of their commands under fire, and hence an error in judgment in any one may initiate a movement," one experienced Civil War commander remarked, "that may lose a battle."[41] Fortunately, the regular Army possessed numerous officers and noncoms trained in Casey's tactics. The bulk of the Army of the United States, however, was made up of volunteers with little or no prior military training or experience who at first found it difficult to form a two-rank battle line, let alone lines of skirmishers under fire.

But as the war dragged on the volunteer army too became skilled in the use of Casey's skirmish tactics. A good example was an attack in the last weeks of the war by Union forces against the forts defending Mobile. To assault these formidable positions, skirmishers advanced in small groups by rushes, taking advantage of all cover and concealment and digging trenches when necessary. In this manner battalion-sized units managed, in spite of heavy enemy fire, to work their way forward to within assaulting distance of the forts.

While skirmishers advancing in open order by rushes across broken terrain came increasingly to dominate the Civil War battlefield, the long battle lines drawn up in two ranks never ceased to impress both friend and foe. A sergeant of the 11th Massachusetts Volunteer Infantry expressed his feelings at viewing the

Union regiments drawn up in close order at Harrison's Point, on the James River, in July 1862:

> Let cheer upon cheer run along the lines four miles in extent—taken by one regiment before the preceding had finished and all followed by a Tiger. I assure you the effect is electric—how it thrills the senses to feel assured by enthusiastic shouts that plenty of friends are present to back you, and you go forward with a rush lest your pride taunt you of cowardice.[42]

Lined up elbow-to-elbow, shoulder-to-shoulder, in battle lines of two ranks, most men did, as the Massachusetts sergeant observed, draw confidence and strength from close physical contact with their fellows. Under these circumstances the sergeants' task was somewhat lightened—limited to maintaining cadence in the advance, keeping the lines dressed, seeing to it that the men fired on order,* and discouraging straggling.

Illustrative of combat with the linear tactic is an account of the battle of Gaines Mill in 1862 by a corporal of the 2nd Infantry, a regular Army unit:

> Our colors were planted on the very brow of the rise, and we dressed [aligned] to them [the colors] as we did on parade. This brought us in full view of and made us a conspicuous mark for the enemy who were plainly to be seen at the edge of a wood directly in front and about 200 yards away. As soon as they observed us they began firing, but with little effect at first, until some minutes after when they estimated the distances more closely. We lost no time in replying. The command was given to commence firing, to fire at will, and to sight for 200 yards . . . after firing many rounds in our exposed position [we] were ordered to fall back a few paces and to fire kneeling or lying down. The rising ground in front of us now gave us a little protection. I fired a few rounds in a [prone] position, in which it was difficult to reload . . . then I arose and fired kneeling until I heard a sudden command to close ranks and fire by company. This command, I learned afterward, was given because the enemy seemed to form for a charge upon us. We arose and in double ranks began to fire volleys all together, to the command of load, ready, aim, and fire which proved to be very effective, for the Rebels retired into the woods and for a while their firing ceased; then it commenced in a more feeble way, when we ceased firing by company and fired at will again.[43]

THE NCO AS COLOR BEARER

In this military drama, the focal points of the regimental line were the national and regimental colors, carried by experienced sergeants who had demonstrated their skill in maintaining cadence in formation under fire. In his *Infantry Tactics*, Casey observed that "the first element in the march to the line of Battle" and the "color [national] bearer—a sergeant—who must be accustomed to prolong without vari-

*It was most important that all pieces fired simultaneously in order to support the shock action of massed rifle fire on compact masses of men. This was a key element in the linear tactics of the day.

ation, a given direction." The battalion commander, Casey added, could best prevent "the loss of intervals in march line" by frequently drilling the color-bearer sergeants in the skill of prolonging a direction given them by the colonel.[44]

Corporals made up the color guard. They concentrated on maintaining cadence and direction and opened fire only in defense of the colors themselves. The company in whose ranks the colors and their guard marched was designated by Casey the color or directing company. The entire battalion guided on it while in line.[45]

A sergeant of Company E of the 109th Pennsylvania Volunteer Regiment who carried the national colors on Sherman's march through Georgia gave a good picture of just what the color bearer actually did in combat:

> So some one said, Charge. When I lead them with the colors and said, come on 109th and they gave a yell such as they know how to give and away we went as fast as the brushes would let us. [The sergeant does not say at this point whether he was able to keep the line dressed.] We drove them from their positions and chosen ground and with our combined forces drove them by mid-night entirely off the field, capturing 10 pieces of cannon, a great many prisoners.[46]

Later in the campaign this volunteer color sergeant faced an even more challenging situation at the battle of Peach Tree Creek. With the national colors held firmly above the field, Sergeant Elliott stood his ground in the face of a strong enemy attack and managed to rally his men around him to save their regiment from what appeared to be certain rout.

The hazards of the color guard were well known both to volunteers and regulars. When regular Army corporal Augustus Meyers was detailed to serve on the 2d Infantry's color guard following the battle of Gaines Mill in 1862, he observed that "it [the color guard] had its disadvantages, the killed and wounded being always greater in proportion to the color guard than in the companies . . . one of our two color sergeants had been killed and two of the color corporals wounded."[47]

A REGULAR ARMY NCO

Unlike most of his counterparts in volunteer regiments, Corporal Meyers was not content with this modest toehold in the noncommissioned elite. Promotion to company sergeant soon followed, and at twenty-one Meyers became the youngest sergeant in his company. In spite of his youth, Sergeant Meyers was soon detailed as brigade commissary sergeant, a post usually filled by older and senior sergeants. But the fact that so many of the latter in the 2d Infantry had been commissioned undoubtedly accounted partly for Meyers's rapid rise. Although detail to commissary sergeant was usually regarded as a promotion, there was no extra pay involved, and Meyers continued to be carried on his company's muster roll as "absent on special duty."[48]

Sergeant Meyers's supervisor was First Lieutenant Hamilton S. Hawkins, who was acting brigade commissary and quartermaster. Lieutenant Hawkins's chief assistant was Sergeant John W. Clous, quartermaster sergeant of the regular Army's 6th Infantry Regiment, who acted in the double capacity of brigade quartermaster and commissary sergeant. It was to relieve Sergeant Clous of the details of the latter position that Sergeant Meyers was detailed commissary sergeant.*

Under Sergeant Clous's tutelage young Meyers soon became familiar with the rules and regulations of the commissary department and the appropriate forms used for the many accounts and reports required. When in camp, the commissary sergeant had as an office a wall tent furnished with two small field desks and a folding table. His detachment included a clerk and three men to load and unload wagons and to assist in issuing rations.

As the war entered its final months during the siege of Petersburg, Meyers was appointed acting ordnance sergeant. Although he found this job "easier than in the commissary department and the reports and accounts which dealt only with arms, accouterments, and ammunition for the infantry were more simple," ordnance sergeant represented a promotion.

Each morning Sergeant Meyers sent a wagon loaded with 20,000 rounds of cartridges to the front, only a short distance away. A file of the guards, sometimes under Meyers's command, always accompanied the wagon, which remained at the front until dark, distributing ammunition as needed. Before returning to the rear for the night, Sergeant Meyers left behind a supply of ammunition with the troops. Appomattox found him still serving as ordnance sergeant.

VOLUNTEER NCOS

Noncommissioned officers of volunteer regiments, on the other hand, rarely demonstrated the same degree of attachment to the military service as regulars like Meyers and Clous. This was partly because they had enlisted for shorter periods and had no intention of serving a day longer than necessary. Most had no particular fondness for military life. Some even went so far as to desert when they believed they had done their duty. One was Mathew Woodruff of Clark County, Missouri.

When President Lincoln issued his first call for volunteers in 1861, Woodruff enlisted at the age of nineteen in the 2d Northeastern Missouri Volunteer Infantry. As with most wartime volunteers, neither restlessness nor economic need drove him to enlist, as was often the case with regulars. It was enough for him to know

*Sergeant Clous, Meyers's senior by eight or ten years, was a well-educated man who, like Meyers, had served on the western frontier against the Indians. Sergeant Clous was commissioned in December of 1862 and following the war became a professor of law with the rank of lieutenant colonel at the military academy at West Point. At the close of the Spanish-American War he was a brigadier general detailed as judge advocate of the commission formed to settle affairs between the United States and Cuba. John Clous eventually retired as a brigadier general in 1901.

that the Union had been challenged by rebels, and that the president had called for volunteers to defend it.[49]

Following only a few weeks of rather desultory training, Woodruff's regiment merged with another local unit to become the 21st Missouri Volunteers. This unit in turn joined the 6th Division to become a part of the Army of the Tennessee, then commanded by General U. S. Grant. The young Missourian's baptism of fire was a terrible one—the battle of Shiloh. Within a day Woodruff and his comrades became battle-hardened veterans, "not iron disciplined regulars but willing warriors."

Before his three-year enlistment expired Woodruff became first sergeant of Company G, and when his first enlistment ran out, he readily reenlisted for the duration. His unit, now redesignated the 21st Missouri Veteran Volunteer Infantry, fought on throughout the war. Its last battle—one of the last of the war—was at Mobile in April 1865. Severely wounded during that operation, Sergeant Woodruff returned to his home in Clark County on convalescent leave. His brief visit home over, he returned to his unit, now on occupation duty in the South. Nine months later, his morale and health undermined, Woodruff deserted, just three weeks before his unit was mustered out of the service.

Woodruff returned to his home town, married, and settled down to farming and raising a family. Not until 1874 was he able to get his desertion expunged from his service record and thereby qualify for a pension. The war years, his wound, and declining health, however, took their toll. Woodruff died at his home on March 3, 1884, aged forty-two.

There were others, perhaps more representative of the volunteer noncommissioned officer than Sergeant Woodruff. Two of these sergeants, John L. Bailey and Jonathan P. Stowe, were fated to fall early in the war. Henry M. Crocker, Bailey's close friend in the 27th New York Volunteer Regiment, described how Bailey led his small detachment ashore during the Peninsula campaign of May 1862.

> We disembarked from the steamer S. R. Spaulding near West Point day before yesterday, right among the enemy's cavalry, and part of our company was deployed as skirmishers under the command of Sgt. J. L. Bailey.

After a brief fire fight, Bailey's detachment dispersed the enemy cavalry. That night Bailey, apparently short of men, took his place on the picket line with his friend, Crocker. Together they manned an outpost near the woods. "Just as the moon was dropping behind the trees, a couple of Rebs came out of the bushes—Sgt. Bailey challenged them [and] was shot dead."[50]

The second was Sergeant Jonathan P. Stowe, a respected veteran noncommissioned officer in the 15th Massachusetts who perhaps most nearly expressed the feelings of most volunteer noncommissioned officers and soldiers alike when he wrote his family: "You all know that I had never shown any desire for a military life until the force of circumstance placed me where I am and if I can ever live to see old New England again, I will let somebody else fight who likes it."[51]

Several months as a prisoner of war at Libby Prison in Richmond, Virginia, did nothing to enhance Stowe's attachment to military life. Taken prisoner at the battle of Ball's Bluff, Virginia, on October 21, 1861, Stowe was confined in a large tobacco warehouse until the following February when he, together with four hundred other enlisted men and fifteen officers, was exchanged for a like number of Confederate soldiers. After a short furlough at home, Stowe rejoined his regiment near Harpers Ferry in March 1862.

The following September General McClellan brought Lee's army to bay between the Potomac and Antietam Creek. On the 10th of that month Stowe noted in his diary that he had been "ordered to deal out [to his men] two day's rations then fell in . . . put knapsacks in pile and prepare for action."

On September 17, McClellan attacked Lee, and the battle of Antietam began. In spite of his tasks, Sergeant Stowe found moments during the action to make what were to be the final entries in his diary:

> Battle, oh horrid battle, what sights I have seen [and] now see around me . . . I am wounded . . . and am afraid shall be again, as shells fly past me every few seconds carrying away limbs from trees and scattering limbs . . . am in severe pain [his knee had been shattered by a minié ball] . . . how the shells fly. I do sincerely hope that I shall not be wounded again.

As he lay on the ground awaiting the litter bearers, Stowe noted that "we drove them [the enemy] till they got sheltered, then we had a bad place. [Presumably this was where he received his wound.]" Finally overcome by pain, Stowe made his last despairing entry in his diary: "Oh, I cannot write." Eventually he was evacuated to a field hospital, where his leg was amputated on September 20. Unfortunately, the wound failed to heal, and tetanus set in. Sergeant Stowe died in the arms of his brother on October 10, 1862.*

In spite of their lack of previous military experience and a commitment to a military life, numerous records similar to Stowe's demonstrate that the volunteer noncommissioned officer who made up the overwhelming bulk of the noncommissioned officers of the Union armies became as able and courageous leaders of men as their far less numerous regular Army counterparts. For most volunteer noncoms their wartime experiences were never more than an interlude—albeit a traumatic one—in a lifetime, frequently all too brief as in the cases of sergeants Bailey and Stowe. The significance of the volunteer noncommissioned officers' experiences during the Civil War, however, was that they set a pattern for selection and training that remained essentially unchanged through two world wars.

One Civil War veteran summed it up this way:

*As Sgt. Stowe's condition worsened the medical service notified his family, and his brother hastened to his side, reaching the hospital the day he died.

In the hardships, dangers, privations and glories of one good soldier, we have the history of every good soldier who belonged to the Union Army. They all bore the same burdens, fought the same or similar battles, and had adventures identically the same. So with companies and regiments, which are the foundations of armies. The history of one is the history of all.[52]

CHAPTER 8
INDIANS, FOREIGNERS, AND REFORM

"The storm of the Civil War was gone, the citizen armies disappeared, and with the Regular Army all was much as it had been before."[1]

Although this eloquent description was essentially true, following the war there were forces abroad in the land that in the years to come would greatly influence the regular Army in general and the role and status of the noncommissioned officer in particular. As had been the case after the war with Mexico, so it was following the Civil War: Exposure of thousands of Americans to military discipline for the first time, either as volunteers in state units or in the ranks of the regular Army, had spread a belief through ever-widening circles of American opinion that some profound changes and reforms were needed in the Army's treatment of the men who filled its ranks, noncommissioned officers and privates alike. To this belief was added the as yet dimly perceived potential impact that technological change was having upon the armed forces and, by extension, the evolving role and image of the noncommissioned officer in the period 1870 to 1914.

For a time, though, at least on the surface, all appeared to be as it had been in the three decades preceding the Civil War, as the regular Army once again took up the task of pacifying the Indians of the West. Before this task had been completed, the Army, operating from 255 widely scattered military posts, fought 943 engagements against the Indians between 1865 and 1898.[2]

Typical of these isolated frontier posts was one described by a traveler on the western plains in the early 1880s. Nothing today better evokes the image of the post–Civil War West—as generations of American moviegoers have come to know it—than our wayfarer's description of Ft. Fetterman as it appeared to him over a century ago:

> A unique and curious sight is a frontier post upon the Plains. The quadrangle of low, dirt-roofed log cabins enclosing the parade ground, the officers' quarters, more pretentious with their little log piazzas, the house of the commanding officer, for the

> construction of which the largest and straightest logs had been selected, and all nestled down upon the bosom of the great outstretching plain, for a picture that will dwell long in the mind of the beholder. Thus looked Fort Fetterman from the summit of the last ridge.[3]

In this instance the approach to the fort was by stagecoach carrying the travelers from the nearest railroad station, some one hundred miles away.

As before the war, many of the operations launched from posts like Ft. Fetterman involved small units in which noncommissioned officers played key roles as combat leaders. But they had good preparation for such a role because some of them had been commissioned officers during the Civil War. These included some former officers of volunteer units of the Union armies as well as some former Confederate officers (the latter banned by law from commissioned service in the regular Army) who found service as noncoms with regiments assigned to frontier garrisons.

An unusual and therefore atypical example was an all-volunteer force commanded by Major George A. Forsythe known as "Forsythe's Scouts." Former Union volunteer and Confederate officers made up one third of the unit's strength.* This unit's 1st sergeant was W.H.H. McCall, a former brigadier general of volunteers who distinguished himself during the Indian Wars in the defense of Beecher's Island on September 17, 1868.[4]

Not only were former commissioned officers serving throughout the regular Army as noncoms, but also numerous veterans, some of whom could trace their service back to the Mexican War. One historian of the frontier army quotes an officer as observing that these men

> were sturdy old fellows wearing 4 to 6 service chevrons on their arms. They had taken life as it came; Mexico, the Plains, the War . . . and then the Plains again. The Civil War had been the climactic life experience for many of these older soldiers, and little else loomed as significantly in their vocal recollections. These old-timers often had a profound influence on the younger men, and as late as 1886 to 1891, at least two privates of F Company of the 18th Infantry were veterans of the Civil War.[5]

Such men, of course, were a great help to the noncommissioned officers in maintaining discipline and morale.

NONCOMMISSIONED OFFICERS AS SMALL-UNIT LEADERS

The noncommissioned officer of the post–Civil War/Indian Wars Army has become, both in legend and in fact, the archetype of the "tough old Sarge."

The very embodiment of such a man was William Carroll, born on Prince Edward

*The men of this unit were actually on the quartermaster's payroll as civilians, armed and subsisted by the Army but supplying their own mounts.

Island, Canada, in 1845. Carroll enlisted in 1870 at the age of twenty-five in the 4th U.S. Cavalry in New York City under an alias derived from his mother's maiden name, Johanna Lannon. He was known to his army friends as John or Jack Lannon.*

Lannon served five years with I Troop. His next enlistment was with the 3d Cavalry Regiment. Except for a brief period on recruiting duty as an infantryman, Sergeant Lannon remained with the 3d Cavalry, serving with B, F, and C troops for the remainder of his career. In 1898, during the Spanish-American War, as a sergeant with C Troop, Lannon moved to Georgia and Florida en route with his regiment to Cuba. While the regiment was stationed in Tampa, Frederick Remington, the famed artist of the American West, met Sergeant Lannon and made a series of rough sketches of him in the C Troop area. It was Remington who gave to the sketches the title "Old Bill," probably in reference to Lannon's real name. Shortly after the 3d Cavalry landed in Cuba, Lannon contracted yellow fever and died at Siboney, Cuba, on July 24, 1898.[6]

Old Bill's comrades in the regiment characterized him as an "old fashioned NCO (a tough disciplinarian and a superb horseman)." One officer described him this way: ". . . aside from his horsemanship, Sgt. Lannon's most marked characteristics were his loyalty to his organization and his unfailing good humor under trying conditions. A stern disciplinarian, he was nevertheless ready with a smile and jest when roads were muddy, skins damp and cold, rations low. He accepted hardships as part of his day's work." After his father died during his first enlistment, Old Bill, throughout the remaining years of his service, regularly sent his mother money out of his modest pay and visited her during each leave. His last visit home was just one year before his death in Cuba.†

Don Rickey, a distinguished historian of the enlisted man in the Indian Wars, has described the noncommissioned officer's role well by observing that

> most officers left the administration of company affairs in the hands of the 1st Sergeant, who, in turn relied on the duty sergeants and corporals. The enforcement of discipline and the awarding of company punishment were often left to the personal inclinations of those noncommissioned officers who frequently prescribed punishments that were humiliating and, in many cases actually illegal. In some companies discipline was maintained by the fists of the noncommissioned officers . . . in companies containing more than the usual number of toughs, ability as a scrapper was a prerequisite for appointment to noncommissioned status, and a really pugnacious man was sometimes reduced to the ranks for some breach of regulations, but then appointed again because he was able to handle the hardest cases in the company without having to call in official assistance.[7]

*The use of an alias when enlisting was commonplace during the late nineteenth century, when many people considered Army service undesirable.

†In January 1901 his mother began to receive an Army pension of $12.00 a month after old age forced her to quit her job as a serving woman. She continued to live on Prince Edward Island until her death in March 1901. (Emerson)

A noncommissioned officer cast in this mold was Sergeant John B. Charlton, of the 4th U.S. Cavalry. A wild youngster, rebellious of parental authority, Charlton ran away from home and enlisted in Battery K, 1st U.S. Field Artillery. The battery was then commanded by a Captain Graham, later a general, whom Sergeant Charlton described as "the hardest taskmaster who ever wore the blue." Under this admittedly hard discipline, the once wild youngster was thoroughly tamed and became, in turn, a strict disciplinarian. Reminiscing years later, Sergeant Charlton remarked that he talked back to Graham just once, and "he reduced me by order." In the course of time, Charlton continued, Graham "made and broke me so often, that I put my chevrons on with hooks and eyes." Sergeant Charlton was not, however, an exception, for Graham had eight different 1st sergeants in three years. One of them deserted and took thirty-seven men of the unit with him.[8]

Given the large number of Civil War veterans in the regular Army, it was inevitable that many noncommissioned officers were usually men with long periods of service to their credit. In 1894 almost all of the 1st U.S. Cavalry Regiment's sergeants had been in grade for ten to sixteen years, some even longer. An anecdote of that period tells of a twenty-two-year-old lieutenant demanding of his sergeant of the guard, who he thought needed some instruction in the performance of his duties, "How long have you been a noncommissioned officer?" "Twenty-four years the seventeenth of last month, sir," was the old soldier's devastating reply.[9]

These veteran noncommissioned officers, as had their pre-war predecessors, gave a good account of themselves as small-unit commanders in the final decades of the Indian Wars. Among them were such men as Sergeant Michael McCarthy of the 1st Cavalry. Part of a force of four officers and ninety troopers ambushed by Nez Perces under Chief Joseph near White Bird Canyon, Idaho Territory, on June 17, 1877, Sergeant McCarthy was in command of a key point on the right of the line against an overwhelming attack. After gallantly repulsing several assaults, McCarthy and the six troopers under his command were ordered to withdraw. Fighting their way back through the encircling enemy, the men rejoined the rest of the command but continued to fight on during the retreat of the main body. Although Sergeant McCarthy had two horses shot from under him and was finally left for dead, he managed to escape and report for duty after three days of hiding and wandering in the mountains. For his valor and leadership under fire, McCarthy received the Medal of Honor.[10]

In one of the last campaigns of the Indian Wars, Corporal Paul H. Weinert, a gunner of the 1st U.S. Artillery Regiment during the Battle of Wounded Knee, South Dakota, in December 1890, took command after the lieutenant in command fell gravely wounded. Sending one of his cannoneers to the rear with the wounded officer, Corporal Weinert and his second cannoneer manhandled their piece into position and opened fire. Despite heavy rifle fire that riddled the gun carriage and even knocked a round from Weinert's hands as he was about to load, he continued to fire and move his gun into even more favorable positions until the enemy withdrew. For his gallantry and bravery, Corporal Weinert too was awarded the Medal of Honor.[11]

Another incident illustrates stubborn courage in the face of hopelessly overwhelming odds. An obscure commissary sergeant, Amos J. Custard of the 11th Kansas Volunteer Cavalry, was in command of a five-wagon supply train and twenty-five men enroute from Sweetwater Station to the Platte Bridge Station, fifty miles to the east and near the site of present-day Casper, Wyoming, when attacked by a large Indian force. Earlier in his journey, Custard had rejected the suggestion of a thirty-man telegraph patrol from the 11th Ohio Volunteer Cavalry that they join forces at Red Buttes. Custard assumed that his force was strong enough to travel anywhere on the trail between Laramie and South Pass.[12]

The commissary train drew to within three miles of the Platte Bridge Station when, on July 26, 1865, an artillery round fired by the small garrison there alerted Custard to the presence of hostile Indians. Custard first sent a corporal and two privates forward to determine the size and location of the Indian band, and meanwhile ordered his wagons into corral. However, only three of the five managed to do so before the Indians attacked his party. Quickly surrounding the wagons, the Indians overran and destroyed the two that had failed to join the others. But Sergeant Custard and twenty of his men fought on. The post commander at Platte Station refused to attempt relief of the besieged wagon train because he considered the Indians attacking his own garrison too numerous for him to attempt a sally from the fort. George Bent, a French-Cheyenne with the Indians, later observed that Sergeant Custard had selected an excellent defensive position. But after four hours the Indians overran his position and killed Custard and his companions. Of the three-man scouting party, only the corporal managed to reach Platte Station. But Sergeant Custard's resolute defense of his wagon train cost the Indians heavily and forced them to break off their siege of the garrison at Platte Station.[13]

MILITARY RELATIONSHIPS

Diaries, unit records—especially the company descriptive books—tell us that those men who manned the isolated garrisons and patrolled the vast plains of the western frontier were from all classes and nations, although the majority were American-born. In the relatively isolated and restricted social environment of the frontier, educated men from affluent family backgrounds served in company-size units together with illiterate boys from farms too poor to support a large family, and with unemployed laborers from cities and towns no longer able to provide opportunities for adventurous and restless young men.

Occasionally there were even men from ancient noble families in Europe or with degrees from an equally ancient European university. In the ranks of the 12th Infantry in the early 1870s was a bugler who had come from a noble Prussian family and whose brother was a colonel in the Prussian army, and in the 1890s, C Troop, 8th Cavalry, included a graduate of Harvard College.

Former noncommissioned officers of the Army also took up ranching in the far West. One was ex-Sergeant Whaley, the proprietor of a ranch at the mouth of the Big Wichita, near the Red River. Whaley, after discharge, had settled in this country. As had many other noncommissioned officers, he had saved up a little money from his small pay. Sergeant Charlton, who met Whaley in 1872, when troops E and L of the 4th Cavalry had come to protect him and his property from marauding Indians, described him as a "magnificent type of the old dragoon sergeant; he stood about 6 feet 2 or 3 inches in his shoes and was straight as an arrow; was about 45 years of age, right in the prime of life, lean and sinewy; had yellowish-red hair, a long flowing tawny or reddish blond beard. His 1000 acres, ever since the reservation had been located at Fort Sill, had been the stamping ground for Indians."[14]

Regardless of ethnic origin or social status in the widely scattered infantry or dragoon companies, only military rank and worth counted. In Spartan barracks corporals and privates dwelt in one large room, with sergeants usually occupying small cubicles of their own adjacent to the main sleeping quarters.[15] Under such circumstances it was not surprising that company-sized units in their isolation often developed almost familial bonds reminiscent of the German army of the eighteenth century when the first sergeant was the "mother" of the company and the captain the "father."

Keeper of the company descriptive book, the family bible of the unit and closest adviser to the captain in all matters concerning the men, the first sergeant stood at the center of this familial structure. For example, if one of the company wished to speak to the captain, he had first to obtain the first sergeant's permission. Yet there were occasions when the latter used his free time to help his men solve personal problems, as in the case of a 1st Sergeant George Neihaus of the 10th Infantry, who in his free time taught an enlisted man how to read and write. In later years that man became a quartermaster sergeant.[16]

Many a private regarded his noncommissioned officers with awe. From the beginning of his Army career, after the recruiting sergeant enrolled him, he was under the immediate supervision of noncommissioned officers. After a brief period of training at a reception center, the new recruit was sent to his regiment. There the regimental commander assigned him to duty in one of the companies. The first sergeant listed him on the company roster, entered him in the company descriptive book, took him to the barracks where a sergeant assigned him a cot and placed him in a particular squad, whose leader, quite possibly a corporal, undertook his military education and launched him on his career as a professional soldier.[17]

The initial steps in this process were well described by a veteran of the Army of the 1870s. A new recruit, he wrote,

> is soon taught that the order of the youngest corporal in his company is just as emphatic and as much to be observed and as promptly to be obeyed as that of the Cap-

> tain of his company or the Colonel of his regiment. The fact that the young corporal who is in charge of his squad wears the chevrons of a noncommissioned officer, that his appointment to the grade has been approved by the Colonel of the regiment, and a noncommissioned officer's warrant duly issued him, also established another fact, which is, that the Corporal has learned to appreciate and apply two army regulations: First, that "military authority will be exercised with firmness, kindness, and justice," and second, "superiors are forbidden to injure those under their authority by tyrannical or capricious conduct or by abuse language"; otherwise he would not have been appointed a corporal.[18]

FOREIGN-BORN NCOS

Throughout the interwar years, 1866 to 1898, the regular Army continued to be characterized by a high degree of ethnic diversity, although on an average 75 to 80 percent of the enlisted men were native-born. An officer of that period observed that "in no other army were members of so many countries together as in that of the United States. In a single post, even in a single company, the nations of the civilized world were represented . . . not only all nationalities but also all occupations and stations in life were represented."[19]

Numerous descriptive books of Army units during the last thirty years of the nineteenth century bear out these observations. As their titles indicate, these books tell quite a bit about the rank and file. They indicate a higher percentage of foreign-born among the noncommissioned officers than among the private soldiers because foreign-born individuals, as is the case with ethnic minorities today, were more apt to reenlist. For example, the descriptive book of the 12th Infantry Regiment in the 1880s shows that more than half of the noncommissioned officers were foreign-born. These men averaged fourteen to nineteen years of service and thirty to fifty years of age, giving a picture of mature men devoted to the career of professional soldiering and not simply young immigrants, as in the 1840s and 1850s, using the Army as a vehicle for economic advancement in a new land.[20]

Typical of this type of noncommissioned officer was Sergeant Charles A. Windolph of the 7th U.S. Cavalry, who was twenty-four years old at the time of the Battle of the Little Bighorn in June 1876. Born in 1851 in Bergen, Germany, young Windolph first practiced the shoemaking trade with his father. But in the spring of 1870, as the clouds of war darkened the horizon, Windolph left Germany for America to avoid the military draft. Arriving in New York City, he found considerable unemployment. "A good many German boys like myself," he reminisced later, "had run away from the compulsory military service and the Franco-Prussian War, but about the only job there was for us over here [United States] was to enlist in the U.S. Army . . . there were hundreds of us German boys in that same fix."[21]

In 1885 the 12th Infantry regimental sergeant major was a thirty-one-year-old German who had been a baker before his enlistment in 1880. His rise was rapid—by 1884 he had become post quartermaster sergeant and the following year regimental sergeant major, well deserving of the rating given him by his commanding officer: "an excellent, energetic, zealous, and efficient sergeant major." A quartermaster sergeant of the same regiment had been born in England. Enlisting in 1881, he made his rank by 1884. Another quartermaster sergeant had been born in France. A common laborer, he enlisted in 1882 and was appointed quartermaster sergeant from company first sergeant in 1887. Discharged that same year, he later reenlisted and was appointed ordnance sergeant in 1894.[22]

The 16th Infantry descriptive book of the regimental staff, band, and permanent party listed two senior musicians as foreign-born out of a total of seventeen men in the band, three foreign-born on the staff, and two foreign-born out of eight men in the permanent party. Former occupations of these men ranged all the way from laborer to lawyer.[23]

A similar picture emerges from a study of the 4th Infantry's descriptive book for staff and band. Of a total of ten noncommissioned officers on the regimental staff, six were foreign-born—four Germans, one Swiss, and one Irish. The descriptive book of the 4th Artillery staff and band showed that out of twenty-six noncommissioned officers serving between 1865 and 1887 twenty were foreign-born, mostly from Germany and Ireland, thereby maintaining an ethnic pattern that had existed in the regular Army since the 1840s.[24]

Company descriptive books of the Indian Wars and of the Civil War give frequent testimony of the high esteem in which most foreign-born enlisted men were held by their commanding officers. One such foreigner was a twenty-two-year-old Englishman by the name of Reginald A. Bradley who enlisted in the U.S. Army in the years following the Civil War. After first outfitting themselves for life in the far west of America, young Bradley and a friend arrived there in the early autumn of 1888 in search of fortune and adventure. Finding little of either, Bradley soon wearied of the life of a prospector and itinerant cowboy and left his partner in 1889 to enlist in C Troop of the 4th Cavalry, then stationed at Ft. Bowie, Arizona.[25]

Young Bradley found not only many enlisted Germans in C Troop, but that the troop commander, a Captain William Ziriax, was also German-born. Of the troop's noncommissioned officers, all were German except 1st Sergeant Kerr, who had been born of Irish immigrant parents in Tennessee. There were, in addition to Bradley, numerous British-born enlisted men scattered throughout the regiment, whose sergeant major was an Englishman. Many of the English, however, were deserters from the British army in Canada.

Bradley's experience seems to confirm earlier instances in the last days of the Civil War, when entire companies were left pretty much in the hands of senior noncommissioned officers. Typical of one of these companies was that of Captain Benteen, of General Custer's 7th Cavalry. Sergeant Windolph recalled that Benteen "let the first sergeant pretty much run the company; he, Benteen, wasn't always interfering and running the details."[26]

Likewise, C Troop's first sergeant, Bradley recalled, "had everything to do with running the troop . . . officers were supposed to take us out on mounted drill—but often there was just one officer available—so the First Sergeant did it." At such times the troop was divided into two platoons, Bradley added, "and the First Sergeant was always in command of the first platoon and the Duty Sergeant of the second platoon."

"Roll-call was at 9 A.M.," Bradley continued, "and the noncommissioned officers in charge would just walk around to see that the fellows were there." Inasmuch as Ft. Bowie was in the middle of a desert, such a seemingly casual procedure can be explained, for there was simply no place for an AWOL soldier to go in those circumstances."*

In spite of the senior noncommissioned officer's key role in the typical U.S. Army unit of the western frontier from 1870–1890, acknowledgement of it seems not to have followed into retirement, except in story and legend. For example, even though they long survived the Indian Wars, the names of sergeants Bradley, Windolph, and Daniel A. Kanipe,† are not to be found in the membership rolls of the Order of the Indian Wars of the United States, nor were they among the guests attending the annual meeting and dinner of the Order on January 17, 1920. These omissions say much about the status and prestige of noncommissioned officers when they were no longer needed to keep the company or troop running on a day-to-day basis.‡

PROMOTION OF MERITORIOUS NONCOMMISSIONED OFFICERS

Further evidence of the noncommissioned officer's limited status in the eyes of the professional officers was the continuing difficulty of obtaining a commission for even the most meritorious noncommissioned officer in peacetime. The number of all noncommissioned officers—native- and foreign-born—who reached commissioned grade during the period 1870–1890 was quite small, despite the general orders of 1854 and 1867 directing that 174 of the annual vacancies for second lieutenant be filled from among the noncommissioned officers. In the period 1867–1878, only 295 men, exclusive of West Point graduates, were appointed second lieutenants. Of this number, only 36 or one eighth, came from the ranks—the remaining 259 were civilians without previous military experience.[27]

This state of affairs eventually called forth a vigorous protest from many noncommissioned officers who claimed that the act of 1854, establishing promotions of meritorious noncommissioned officers from the ranks, was being flagrantly ignored. In response, Congress on June 18, 1878, enacted legislation stipulating that

*At the end of a five-year enlistment, Bradley was discharged at the Presidio on November 22, 1894, as "a sergeant of Excellent Character."

†Sgt. Kanipe, of C Troop, 7th U.S. Cavalry, carried General Custer's last order to Cpt. Y. M. McDougall "to bring packs up."

‡The membership rolls of the U.S. Cavalry Association for many years did not include noncommissioned officers.

noncommissioned officers "who had rendered outstanding service for at least two years should receive priority, immediately after the graduating class of the military academy in filling officer vacancies." Only after these two sources had been exhausted were appointments to be made from civilian life. This legislation did improve the chance of noncommissioned officers receiving consideration for commissions, for over the next two years twenty appointments to second lieutenant were made from among qualified noncommissioned officers. Percentages of noncommissioned officers commissioned eventually rose in the 1880s to 30 percent—123 out of a total of 366 of non–West Point graduates receiving commissions in the regular Army.[28]

The new procedures established by Congress called for the company or battery commanders to report to their regimental commanders those men with not less than two years of service whom they deemed by education, conduct, and service to merit advancement. Regimental commanders in turn were to forward these names, together with those recommended from their own regimental staffs, to the departmental commanders. These would annually assemble a board of five officers to make a preliminary examination of the noncommissioned officers recommended. After this sifting and winnowing process, those names still deemed worthy of consideration were submitted to the secretary of war. The chief of engineers and of the other staff corps also followed a similar process before submitting names to the secretary, who then convened a board to make the final selections.[29]

It became evident by 1878, however, that vacancies for second lieutenants to be promoted from the ranks of meritorious noncommissioned officers were less than one to a regiment. Regimental commanders and examining boards were cautioned to bear this fact in mind lest expectations for promotions be raised that could not be realized. However, to provide for these meritorious noncommissioned officers who had passed the examining boards but for whom there were no immediate vacancies, the adjutant general furnished each candidate a certificate to that effect. For such noncommissioned officers the title "candidate" was prefixed to their rank on all rolls, returns, orders, and correspondence. A candidate was also entitled to wear on each sleeve of his coat a single stripe of gilt lace similar to that worn by commissioned officers.[30]*

These privileges were temporary, however, terminating within the next calendar year following that in which the certificate was awarded unless succeeding boards of examination renewed their recommendation. For those candidates who, while awaiting appointment, passed the mandatory age limit (thirty years) and hence became ineligible for appointment, there was to be some small compensation. They

*His stripe was to be worn on the upper half of the cuff, and be made of two pieces of gold braid running the length of the cuff and pointed at the upper end, with a small button below the point of the stripe; width of braid, one quarter inch; width of space between braid, one eighth inch. (General Decision, Letter December 11, 1889, 5942 AGO 1889)

were entitled to wear the gilt lace stripe only on the left sleeve "so long as they maintained the same standing and good conduct as noncommissioned officers in the service as at the time of their examination."[31]

Twelve years later the upper age limit for examination was lowered from thirty to twenty-nine, and for candidates appointed directly from civilian life the limit was lowered to twenty-seven. This measure was presumably an effort to prevent boards from examining a candidate who would reach the mandatory age limit shortly after being recommended by the boards.[32]

In June 1892, Congress, in a measure that harked back to Jacksonian populism, modified the legislation of 1878 concerning the promotion of enlisted men to commissioned rank. Henceforth, not only noncommissioned officers but *any* unmarried soldier under thirty years of age and with two years of good service could present himself to the board of examiners of his department. If recommended by the board, the soldier could then appear before the general board at Ft. Leavenworth for a series of competitive examinations. This change not only extended the privilege of consideration for promotion to commissioned rank to privates, but also permitted the soldier himself to initiate the process rather than depend on his company commander. However, by extending the privilege to all enlisted men, the possibility of promotion ceased to be a prerogative of the noncommissioned grades and consequently had an adverse effect on the status of the noncommissioned officers.[33]

ADDITIONAL CHANGES

Although the chances of a meritorious noncommissioned officer being elevated to the commissioned rank had actually changed little between the years 1880 and 1890, that decade nevertheless produced a series of reforms aimed at improving the lot of enlisted men in general and the noncommissioned officer in particular.

Within the Army this reform movement was led mainly by Samuel B. Holabird, quartermaster general from 1883 to 1890. In a sense it was a small part of a series of nationwide reform movements, ranging from civil service reform to the temperance movement. The latter, for example, actually influenced the adoption of the canteen system throughout the Army that, while it had no direct influence on the role or status of the noncommissioned officer, did make his job somewhat easier by taking liquor off post. With the spread of the on-post canteens, the traditional sutlers, or traders, who had been longtime camp followers, were left with only their liquor sales to sustain them. But when in February 1881 President Rutherford B. Hayes forbade the sale of intoxicating beverages at military posts, the last props were knocked out from under the sutler system. That traditional neighbor of the military disappeared only to reappear many years later in a mutated form among the small and sleazy shops and bars that clustered around the main gate of many military posts during and after World War II.[34]

However, far more important for the noncommissioned officers' well-being than taking alcohol off post, was their long-standing complaint for better provision for retirement. Since 1851 the Soldier's Home in Washington D.C., had provided sheltered care for old soldiers of all ranks who through age or disability were unable to provide or care for themselves. But there was no pension system sufficient to support a former soldier after he had retired from active duty, no matter how long his service. At last, in February 1885, Congress passed legislation creating a pension system for retired enlisted men. Upon application to the president, an enlisted man with thirty years' service could be placed on the retired list with the rank he held at the date of retirement. Thereafter, he would receive three quarters of his pay and allowances.

Although such reforms undoubtedly helped to reduce the desertion rate to its lowest since the Civil War, the business panic of 1893 may have played an even more important role in filling the Army's ranks and in keeping the men there for their full term of enlistment. Thanks partly to the Spanish-American War and the Philippine Insurrection (1899–1902), the desertion rate remained relatively low. But in the immediate postwar period scandals relating to the Army surfaced and precipitated demands for further reforms. By 1905 the desertion rate had increased to 10.3 percent. It did not begin to decrease until 1908, when for the first time in thirty-six years the Army raised enlisted pay.

POSTWAR ANTI-ARMY FEELING

These changes occurred during a period of growing anti-military feeling in American society. Beginning in the 1870s, the U.S. Army and the "boys in blue" were no longer the darlings of the public imagination they had been a decade earlier, when Johnny came marching home in triumph from the Civil War. For one, the southern congressional delegation still seethed with resentment over the regular Army's role in the military occupation of the South that ended in 1877. Moreover, the use of the Army and National Guard to quell civil labor disturbances did not endear the military to the urban working classes in many northern and western states. Actually, the main burden of this latter task fell upon the organized state militias—the National Guard—rather than the regular Army. Nevertheless, the former flourished on a wave of parochial martial enthusiasm in the 1870s and 1880s while the regulars languished under a pall of widespread anti-military feeling. By 1877 national indifference to the Army reached such a point that Congress failed to appropriate funds for its support until almost the end of the fiscal year.[35]

This tendency to denigrate the role of the regular Army while romanticizing the role of the citizen soldier helped to foster in the public mind a climate of indifference to the fate of the former. But even more influential and long-lasting was a growing conviction on the part of the increasingly powerful business community in late nineteenth-century America "of the obsolescence of war itself," or "business pacifism," as Samuel Huntington has described it.[36]

Discussing it in terms of the nation's history, Huntington wrote:

> Jeffersonian hostility to the military had been largely confined to the limited institution of the standing army as a threat to republican government. Jacksonian hostility had broadened this to include opposition to a military caste as the enemy of popular democracy. Business pacifism had expanded it still further so that the conflict was no longer one of institutions or social groups, but the fundamental struggle of two entirely different ways of life.[37]

Although there were those both in government and in the Army anxious to improve career conditions for the professional soldier—the noncommissioned officer—there were those among the public, in addition to the powerful advocates of business pacifism of which Huntington wrote, who were quick to criticize many aspects of Army life. Among them were embittered former enlisted men of the Union army and members of the popular press. For them a tyrannical officer and his noncommissioned agent became popular targets of criticism in the last decades of the nineteenth century.

Much of this criticism was found in numerous newspaper articles throughout the country characterizing the typical noncommissioned officer as a tyrant and a bully, aided and abetted by commissioned officers indifferent to the private soldiers' welfare. Numerous letters to the editor in such publications as the *Army and Navy Journal* often "complained that company commanders too often appointed as noncommissioned officers men who did not hesitate to use the severest measures to keep the soldiers in line. As a result, a host of grievances arose against the conduct of those noncommissioned officers, particularly the first sergeants. They were accused of subjecting the men under them to all sorts of persecution with no recourse to justice."[38]

One historian quotes several "old soldiers" as blaming such petty tyrants for the high desertion rate of the Army which, in 1871, had reached eight thousand or one third of the enlisted strength of the Army at that time. Confirmation of this observation also came from General E.O.C. Ord a year later, when he declared that "the noncommissioned officer has almost entire and continuous control over the men, and if, as is often the case, these petty officers are bullies, drunkards, or tyrants, the men desert wholesale." Such comment did not encourage rapid reform, however, for as late as 1907 the inspector general of the Army was moved to comment that for many years a regular Army maxim had been "sustain the sergeant." While admittedly a plausible and sound principle of military discipline, in many instances unconditional adherence to this maxim by the company commander had led to abuse of authority by the noncommissioned officers with a consequent rise in the desertion rate.[39]

Even more devastating criticism, because of its wide circulation among the public, was a series of articles published in August and September 1889 in the *St. Louis Post-Dispatch* by one of its reporters who had spent three months as a recruit at Jefferson Barracks. In addition to the sensational charges against commissioned officers for their mistreatment of their men, the newspaper report also "charged that soldiers were treated brutally by noncommissioned officers without as much as an investigation."

The *Post-Dispatch* series provoked a storm of controversy, with both supporters and detractors of the Army taking up pens to join the fray. A presidential court of inquiry, however, determined that many of the more sensational charges could not be substantiated but found sufficient substance in others to warrant remedial action. Subjected over the years to this type of criticism, some of it unmerited, many veteran noncommissioned officers took advantage of the act of June 16, 1890, which provided for an honorable discharge from the service "at the end of a three year enlistment or by purchase before that time." A veteran officer observed "that a large number of our best noncommissioned officers who have become through years of hard service, efficient and trained soldiers, are daily taking advantage of late General Orders to be discharged."

Occasionally relations between noncommissioned officers and their men did in fact deteriorate into violence. Such violence, however, rarely took the form of outright mutiny but rather covert retribution for real or fancied wrongs. Such was the case of 1st Sergeant Emanuel Stance of F Troop of the all-black 9th Cavalry.

As 1st Sergeant Stance rode with his troop onto Ft. Robinson, Nebraska Territory in August 1885, he could look back on many years of service on the southwestern frontier that included an award of the Medal of Honor while in command of a detachment against the Indians near Kickapoo Springs, Texas, on May 20, 1870. An outstanding example of a noncommissioned officer of the Indian Wars, Stance found himself, as did many of his contemporaries, increasingly at odds with the new type of recruit entering the Army in the late 1880s.[40]

During the next two years worsening relations between noncommissioned officers and the men of F troop resulted in a series of ten incidents involving eight different privates and four noncommissioned officers in a unit numbering only forty-five men. First Sergeant Stance eventually became the focus of this turmoil, which indicated "that rank was a more divisive force than the bonds of race could overcome."[41]

On Christmas morning of 1887, Stance was found murdered on a road outside the fort, apparently a victim of retribution by his own men. Unfortunately, the evidence indicated that for all his excellence as a soldier and noncommissioned officer, 1st Sergeant Stance "was more than a strict disciplinarian," hounding his troops. He condoned similar behavior on the part of his subordinate noncommissioned officers. Tensions developed along the line of the military caste system rather than along racial lines, for the men perceived their 1st sergeant rather than their white officers as their chief tormentor, and the result was the murder of Stance.[42]

In a small way, 1st Sergeant Stance's tragic death symbolized the passing of an era—that period in the Army's history when the noncommissioned officer was the absolute authority in his own small domain. Although many years passed before a new type of noncommissioned officer replaced the old, many in the Army were already developing practices and concepts that in time developed a noncommissioned officer quite different from the "hard-as-nails" Indian fighter of the frontier days. Systematic and structured education of the noncommissioned officer both as technician and professional was the key that in the years to come opened doors to this change.

CHAPTER 9

IMPROVING THE TRAINING OF NONCOMMISSIONED OFFICERS AND THEIR TESTING IN WAR

". . . intellectual ability is not the first requisite of a good noncommissioned officer . . ."

—a U.S. Army artillery officer, 1890

There was growing recognition on the part of some in the Army's command structure during the 1880s and 1890s that because of "the [noncommissioned officers'] ever-increasing importance and responsibility" the noncoms required special education for the proper performance of their duties.[1] Such men should be, in the opinion of the secretary of war, "of a higher average class of men than we have heretofore been able to obtain in the regular service." The secretary then recommended that a school for noncommissioned officers of the infantry and cavalry similar to one that had been in existence since 1824 for the artillery at Ft. Monroe* be established at Ft. Leavenworth.

The Secretary held out little hope, however, for improvement of the noncommissioned officer corps "until the pay attaching to these positions is sufficiently increased to offer an inducement for a good class of men to enlist for the purpose of obtaining them." Adding that while there were many good noncommissioned officers in the service, he concluded that "it is incontestable that the average of intelligence and efficiency is far below what it should be."[2]

These questions—how to train and how to select a new type of noncommissioned officer that the Army of the coming century would require and, having accomplished that, what to pay such men—held the attention of many military thinkers around the turn of the century. Because the Army staff had more control over training and selection of noncommissioned officers than their pay, the discussion revolved around these requirements.

Addressing themselves to a consideration of noncommissioned officer training,

*The Artillery School of Practice was established in 1824 (*American State Papers*, MA III 699–701; WDGOs 10 & 18, 1824), although the first class probably did not meet until 1825.

some military intellectuals, such as Emory Upton and his disciples, looked to European armies for their models. American travelers often returned from abroad with glowing reports of the quality and status of the noncommissioned officer of the armies observed in Europe. These men, one American observer declared after visiting Britain's major army base at Aldershot, were

> magnificent types . . . as they pass through the streets with ringing strides, straight as arrows, neat as soap and water, pipe clay and brush can make them, proud of their profession, and often exercising fully as much authority over the men under them as the best of their officers. Authority of a different kind, perhaps, but with the military maxim, that to be able to command one must be able to obey, so ingrained in their very nature that they are the main stay and dependence of their superiors.[3]

In spite of the British class system, these men enjoyed a degree of acceptance by their officers rarely found in American garrisons, for it was "not an unusual sight to see a game among the officers umpired by some veteran noncommissioned officer skilled in all the intricacies of the national game of cricket."[4]

In the opinion of many American observers the reason for the outstanding European noncommissioned officers lay mainly in the systematic professional training provided in special schools. On the other hand, the U.S. Army at that time had little comparable to offer except for specialized schools for artillerists, hospital stewards, and signalmen. The oldest of these was the aforementioned school for noncommissioned officers of artillery. Because of the technical requirements of that arm, special courses for noncommissioned officers had been offered as adjunct courses for commissioned officers. Some idea of the Army's commitment to this course can be seen in one historian's comment that it was ''continued whenever a qualified instructor was available."

The artillery school was formed originally to train commissioned officers in a two-year course of instruction before they were assigned to artillery units. Enlisted men (noncommissioned officers) were also trained along with them in a parallel course. The school for noncommissioned officers was not, however, a noncommissioned officer's training academy. In any event, the artillery school was phased out in 1835 and not reestablished for twenty-four years.[5]

When the artillery school reopened in 1858, instruction for both commissioned and noncommissioned students was conducted in three departments—laboratory, theoretical, and practical. Examinations were held annually, beginning on September 12 for company-grade officers. The director of the school for noncommissioned officers was a captain assisted by two lieutenants detailed from the companies on post. Scarcely one class graduated before the approach of the Civil War forced suspension of classes and closing of the school.[6]

The school did not reopen until April 1868, as the Artillery School of the United States Army. On the evening before the first postwar class was to begin, the commandant addressed the assembled students—both officers and noncoms—on their course of instruction and its objectives. The noncommissioned officers, he declared, were to be examined each month by the commandant in person, and a report showing the efficiency of each student was to be forwarded to the adjutant general of the Army. Every noncommissioned officer belonging to the five school companies was required to attend the full two-year course. The course was to be both theoretical and practical—the practical course quite similar to that given commissioned officers but emphasizing the duties of the noncommissioned officer. The theoretical phase of the course embraced mathematics, including the entire field of arithmetic. Those men able to do the work went as far as equations of the second degree in algebra.[7]

After thirty years of operations, the school was "temporarily suspended" in May of 1898, upon the outbreak of the war with Spain. But during those three post–Civil War decades the school graduated nineteen classes of commissioned and noncommissioned officers. Eight of these classes had been one-year and eleven were two-year courses of instruction.[8]

Not only did the artillery arm require of its noncommissioned officers a high degree of specialized training in a school environment, but similarly two of the Army's support services, the medical service and the signal corps, also required considerable specialized technical training. The caliber of many of these noncommissioned officers suggests a degree of professionalism equal to or, in some cases, even superior to many comparable and more highly paid positions in civilian life at the time.

MEDICAL SERVICE NCOS

The training of medical noncommissioned officers predated the Civil War. In August 1856 Congress authorized the secretary of war to appoint hospital stewards from among the enlisted men of the regular Army. Those appointed became part of the noncommissioned general staff and a permanent part of the medical department. These men presumably were trained individually by the military contract surgeons for whom they worked.[9]

As early as 1857 the hospital steward was given a distinctive uniform. If color and style bestow status, these men enjoyed an unprecedented degree of prestige during the Civil War. Their hats were decorated with a buff and green cord and an ornament consisting of a gilt wreath with a white "U.S." in the middle. One side of that hat was looped up and fastened with a brass eagle badge, and a feather adorned the other side. The collar and cuffs of the tunic were piped with crimson, and the trousers sported a 1½-inch crimson stripe. On the sleeves were two narrow half chevrons of yellow silk and a caduceus of the same material.

By 1887, when the medical service became the hospital corps, the hospital steward had also taken over nursing duties, in addition to those he had originally been assigned. These latter included pharmacist, record keeper, property man, general manager of a dispensary, and wardmaster. It is therefore not surprising that such work attracted men of potential scientific bent.

One was Hungarian-born John Xantu, who, in addition to his military duties, did significant work in the West between 1870 and 1890 as an outstanding ornithologist. Although his medical training had been limited to his work as hospital steward, he rose eventually to become acting assistant surgeon to the Army's surgeon general, William A. Hammond, with whom he worked for many years. Another former hospital steward was Charles Emil Bendire (1836–1897), who eventually became a commissioned officer. He too made important contributions to ornithology, including a book entitled *Life Histories of North American Birds* published in 1892. Bendire, as a result of his scientific contributions, was made an honorary curator of the Department of Oology* in the U.S. National Museum (the Smithsonian).

An act of Congress in March 1903, however, abolished the grade of hospital steward and provided that henceforth the hospital corps' enlisted ranks would consist of sergeants first class, sergeants, corporals, privates first class, and privates. Their ranks and pay were the same as that formerly given hospital stewards, acting hospital stewards, and privates of the hospital corps. With this legislation "the ancient and honorable title of Hospital Steward passed into history."[10]

SIGNAL CORPS NONCOMMISSIONED OFFICERS

Not only the artillery and the medical services, but also the signalmen had unusual technical requirements that called for a high degree of training for senior enlisted men. Beginning in 1870, for example, when the signal corps became responsible for the national weather service, candidates for training as noncommissioned observers at the many weather stations maintained by the corps throughout the United States were especially enlisted on the basis of educational as well as physical aptitude. So popular was this duty that there was keen competition for enlistment, giving the signal corps the pick of the better educated men.[11]

Each recruit for the signal corps had first to pass a preliminary physical and educational examination. Educational testing was accomplished at the signal school at Ft. Whipple (now Ft. Myer, Virginia) to determine the recruit's ability to spell and write legibly, his proficiency in arithmetic, English grammar, as well as the history and geography of the United States. After completing their training course at the signal school, men assigned to weather stations received on-the-job training in meteorology, their education continuing as assistants on station. As vacancies occurred in the list of sergeants-observers, they were filled by selection from among corporals or privates first class who had served at least one year on station and "who had been distinguished for fidelity and ability in discharge of

*Oology is that branch of ornithology that studies birds' eggs.

their duties." In the words of General William B. Hazen, then chief signal officer, this training "furnished a force of soldiers of superior education and good character" at the many weather stations throughout the United States."[12]

General Albert J. Myer, Hazen's predecessor as chief signal officer, added that the signal corps' central school for technical training had

> made it practicable to put on station duty and in charge of stations only those noncommissioned officers and men who have been drilled, taught, tried and so known to be fit for the labors and responsibilities required of them . . . The self possession of noncommissioned officers in charge of stations, their prompt, concise and reliable reports, rapidly collected in emergencies which have occurred over great extent of territory . . . have received the warm commendation of high executive officials.[13]

In October 1870 the corps sent one sergeant-observer to each of the twenty-five weather stations scattered between the Mississippi valley and the Atlantic and Gulf coasts. A month later the first systematic meterological reports began to come in via telegraph from these stations. Two years later the Congress acknowledged the importance of these observer-sergeants by authorizing the annual appointment one of their number to the grade of second lieutenant. Once appointed, however, there was no further promotion for such officers, for their training was deemed too narrowly focused for general commissioned service.[14]

An act of Congress in June 1887 permanently organized the enlisted force of the signal corps with an enlisted complement of 150 sergeants, 30 corporals, and 270 privates. These men were all to be trained at the signal school at Ft. Whipple before being promoted and assigned to the field. Among them was a Sergeant Will Croft Barnes who, as a first class private, had been assigned as a telegrapher and assistant to Ft. Apache, Arizona, in the 1880s. During an Apache uprising in September 1881, young Barnes displayed extraordinary skill and bravery in restoring, under fire from hostile Indians, breaks in the telegraph line connecting the fort with the outside world. For this action, Barnes, since promoted to sergeant, received the Medal of Honor during a retreat ceremony at Ft. Apache in the spring of 1883.[15]

In marked contrast to Barnes was another weather-observer, Sergeant John T. O'Keefe, who in the early 1880s served as sergeant-observer at the Pike's Peak Station. Unfortunately for O'Keefe's career in the signal corps, his practice of making up weather reports days in advance in order to give himself free time for his numerous drinking binges resulted in abrupt dismissal from the corps. O'Keefe not only made up weather reports to suit his fancy, but with the years this mountain Munchausen became such a renowned teller of tall tales as to enter into the folklore of Colorado.[16]

In 1891 the signal school for enlisted men was transferred to Ft. Riley, Kansas, where it remained until after the war with Spain. At the same time enlisted training left Virginia for Kansas, the signal service, as it was commonly known at the time, was shorn of its responsibility for weather stations, now grown to three hundred nationwide. In 1891, when responsibility for the national weather service was transferred to the Department of Agriculture, the enlisted personnel at these stations were given honorable discharges from the signal corps but remained at their posts as civilian employees of the federal government.[17]

Administration and operation of weather stations, however, had not been the sole duty of the U.S. Army Signal Corps noncommissioned officers. Constructing, operating, and maintaining signal communications during the Civil War within the Army's zone of operations, and, when necessary, intercepting enemy communications, were also tasks frequently performed by signal corps noncommissioned officers. An example of the latter was credited in 1864 to Sergeant John D. Colvin. During operations in the Carolinas, Colvin managed on June 14 of that year to break a code used by the Confederate army. When the Confederates devised another code, Colvin broke that one as well. Sergeant Colvin's commander, Major General John G. Foster, commanding the Department of the South recommended that Colvin "be rewarded by promotion to lieutenant in the Signal Corps, or by brevet, or the medal of honor." Although he did not receive the Medal of Honor, Colvin was commissioned a second lieutenant in 1865.[18]

In 1899 a modest advance in the development of a practical field telephone kit was made by a Sergeant Eccard of the signal corps. The Eccard Kit, as it was known, was an ingenious combination of Bell telephone, Morse key, and battery, using the key for all calling. A single device acted as both transmitter and receiver and as a telegraph sounder. Unfortunately for Eccard's claim to fame, the kit was found too expensive to manufacture for general issue.[19]

There were others who also contributed to signal corps communications in the field. For example, the first heliograph line in the U.S. Army was the work of Sergeant Alvarado M. Fuller in 1878. Fuller supervised the construction of the line between Ft. K. Cogh and Ft. Custer in the Department of the Yellowstone. Fuller's work so impressed the district commander, General Nelson A. Miles, that he made Sergeant Fuller responsible for the establishment of the heliograph network in Arizona during the (Apache) Geronimo campaign of 1886.[20] Fuller was later promoted to second lieutenant.

The skills of signal corps noncommissioned officers trained to man weather stations also made these men valuable members of several expeditions to the Arctic, most notably one led by signal corps Lieutenant Adolphus W. Greely in 1881–1884. Greely's party consisted of two other officers, twenty enlisted men, and a civilian. The expedition was to make regular meterological and magnetic observations as well as a series of exploratory trips from the base camp, designated Ft. Conger. On one of these trips in 1882, a three-man party of Greely's men explored Greenland's northern coast and reached 83° 24″ north, the farthest north reached until that time. One of the members of this party was Sergeant David L. Brainard of the U.S. Signal Corps.[21]

In 1882 a relief ship for Greely's expedition left St. John's, Newfoundland, as planned, but an unbroken ice barrier forced the ship to return without contacting the Greely party. The next summer a second ship attempted to reach the men but was caught in pack ice and sank. Although Greely and his men managed to reach several of the food caches left behind by the unsuccessful relief expeditions, the food was insufficient to sustain the men through the long winter. By the following June there were only seven survivors, including Lieutenant Greely.

On June 22, 1884, a third relief ship, commanded by Commander Winfield S. Schley of the U.S. Navy, reached the Greely party at Cape Sabine. The survivors included Sergeant David L. Brainard,* Hospital Steward Henry Biederbick, Sergeant J. R. Frederick, and two privates. Despite their hardships, these men brought back with them a valuable series of meterological, tidal, magnetic, and pendulum observations. Among the seventeen men who perished during the expedition were five signal corps noncommissioned officers: Sergeant Edward Israel, astronomer; Sergeant George W. Rice, a photographer; and three meteorologists, sergeants Jewell S. Winfield, David S. Ralston, and Hampden S. Gardiner, all of whom died of starvation. The exploits of these men testified to the high degree of specialized training they received as noncommissioned officers.

EXTENDING NCO EDUCATION TO THE COMBAT ARMS: COMPARISONS WITH OTHER ARMIES

As we have seen, throughout much of the nineteenth century professional education for noncommissioned officers in the U.S. Army was limited to meeting the technical requirements of artillery, medical, and signal services. The traditional combat arms—infantry and cavalry—depended almost entirely on *ad hoc*, on-the-job training for their NCOs. As the century drew to a close and the requirements of modern weaponry were becoming more complex and sophisticated, interest grew within the Army to extend specialized education to the noncommissioned officers of all arms and services.

After extensive travel abroad (1875–1876), Major General Emory Upton published a report on the armies of Europe and Asia. This report included some important comparative observations on the education and status of noncommissioned officers. Upton learned, among other things, that all European armies generally accepted the premise "that a good noncommissioned officer can no more be improvised than an officer." Even before he completed his report, Upton decided that upon his return to the United States he would use it "as a vehicle for advancing reform."[22]

Not surprisingly, General Upton found the German army, still savoring its recent triumph over France and the establishment of the German Empire, a paragon of military training and organization. He wrote "the perfection of the German mil-

*Brainard was later commissioned a second lieutenant of cavalry in 1886 and retired as a brigadier general in 1918.

itary system lies less in the military organization than in the exactness which men of every grade, in every branch of service, are trained for the efficient performance of their duties."[23]

The excellence of the noncommissioned officers in the German army impressed Upton particularly. He believed first-rate training, both within a unit and in special schools, was the reason for this excellence. Candidates for promotion to noncommissioned officer rank were first given instruction at the battalion level in reading, writing, spelling, and arithmetic. They were also taught to prepare those reports and returns required especially of noncommissioned officers.

Most of the students were men who, after the completion of their three years' compulsory service, had indicated a preference for the military life by reenlisting. An additional source of candidate noncommissioned officers was a series of preparatory schools for the sons of career noncommissioned officers and privates of the army. These boys were admitted to the schools between the ages of ten and twelve and completed the course at the traditional school-leaving age of fourteen for working-class children.

From these two sources noncommissioned officer candidates were channeled into four schools especially established for the training of infantry noncommissioned officers. At the time of General Upton's visit each of these schools had an enrollment of 496 with a commissioned and noncommissioned staff of 19 officers and 63 men. A fifth school, with an enrollment of 248, had just been established at that time, and a sixth one was soon to follow. Admission was open to graduates of the preparatory schools and to volunteers from the battalion schools between the ages of sixteen and twenty. After completion of the three-year course of instruction, each graduate had to agree to serve an additional four years in the active army.

The course of instruction included infantry tactics, army regulations, preparation of reports and returns, and such other subjects necessary for the student to qualify as a military clerk, sergeant major, or first sergeant. The students had earlier been instructed in the school of the soldier at the company and battalion level in order that they might function as military instructors and leaders themselves.

As in the United States Army, the artillery arm of the Imperial German army had long maintained its own school system for the education of noncommissioned officers. At the higher of these schools the students were taught mathematics, physics, German, the science of artillery, fortification planning, and drawing.

Upton also observed that all major armies in Europe offered greater inducements and privileges than did the United States Army in order to retain the services of senior noncommissioned officers. In Italy, for example, good candidates for sergeant were obtained by a combination of inducements and privileges. Among these were good pay, good training over an eight-year enlistment period, and good retirement. Senior noncommissioned officers who had served twelve years were offered at the end of their service continued employment either with the state-owned railroads or in the various bureaus of the war ministry. In 1874, more than a thousand former noncommissioned officers were so employed. Special privileges for senior noncommissioned officers, such as their own lounges, well lighted, heated, and provided with books and periodicals; separate quarters and mess; and freedom to remain off post until taps, all combined to limit their contact with the men and thereby reinforce their status and authority.

Interestingly, Upton found that authoritarian tsarist Russia obtained most of its junior commissioned infantry officers from among the ranks of meritorious noncommissioned officers. Selected noncommissioned officers attended a two-year course at any one of fourteen academies, one located in each of the provinces of the empire. Upon graduation they were commissioned as infantry officers; about 1,800 graduated annually from the academies for noncommissioned officers into the commissioned grades of the army—an ironic contrast with the more egalitarian society of the United States, where such promotions were rare.

General Upton, reflecting on what he had learned of the European education and treatment of the noncommissioned officer, wrote that it "should impress us with the conviction that, if in future wars we would increase the chances of victory, and diminish the waste of human life, we should devote our attention to the education of our noncommissioned officers of our army."[24]

The questions raised by Upton concerning the selection and training of noncommissioned officers resulted in no immediate innovations, and our objective in examining them here is to provide contrast between the American and European systems. Nevertheless, while Upton's observations failed to result in the reforms he had hoped for, they did stimulate considerable discussion for several years among officers of the regular Army in the pages of professional journals as to how the United States could better provide the education needed to produce the type of noncommissioned officer required for modern warfare. All were in agreement that the traditional system of training and selecting noncommissioned officers was no longer adequate to the Army's needs in the upcoming century. However, none seemed as willing as Upton to adopt the European systems, even contending that "it is not expected nor at all advisable, that our sergeants and corporals hold such exalted positions as we find in most European armies."[25]

Throughout a debate that dragged on from the 1890s into the first decades of the twentieth century, most officers at the company level opposed the establishment of formal schooling for the noncommissioned officer. The company commander's knowledge of his men and his perception of demonstrated worth were regarded as sufficient for the selection of good noncommissioned officers. As one of the more analytical of these officers put it, "for military efficiency, intellectual ability is not the first requisite of a good noncommissioned officer; tact, commonsense, strength of character, thorough honesty and trustworthiness are essentials which can be made more valuable, but cannot be supplied by general education."[26] Yet at the highest command levels voices, including that of the secretary of war, were beginning to doubt whether the traditional *ad hoc* system was adequate for the times and urged the establishment of post schools "where not only instruction by lessons and lectures should be given in matters pertaining to military service, but also in the elementary branches of mathematics, science, mechanics, surveying, engineering, drawing, etc."

The adjutant general of the army noted that "the rapid advance in the army of War requires more study, closer application and greater capacity on the part of noncommissioned officers than in former years." According to the inspector general there had been noted in recent years "a certain deterioration in the instruction and abilities of our noncommissioned officers." At the regimental level the view prevailed that most senior sergeants were men of limited intellectual capacity and, because of their age, no longer capable "of close study, recitation and resulting mental development."

A number of officers presented ambitious outlines for noncommissioned officer courses. First Lieutenant Harvey C. Carbaugh proposed a syllabus for artillerists including instruction in field geometry, use of measuring and meterological equipment, the application of electricity, the general and special properties of bodies, the cause and effect of motion in laying guns, the use and power of machines, and field engineering. He envisioned that this course would apply to noncommissioned officers of all branches, not just artillerymen. He did not see it as a step toward a commission, however, quoting Major Joseph P. Sanger that "however well a noncommissioned officer may do as a second lieutenant, he is almost certain to fail in the higher grades, unless his education requirements are far above those now considered necessary."

To raise the noncommissioned officer to the standard of efficiency demanded by modern warfare and to emphasize the point, very modern in its concept, that noncommissioned rank was in itself a worthy career goal, Lieutenant C. W. Farber suggested the adoption of one of two schemes. The first was a permanent school at some centrally located post, and one corps for each branch of the service.[27]

Officer-instructors would be assigned to these schools for a period of years. Instruction would last eight months and take the form of recitations, lectures, and practical exercises. Qualification and class standings would be determined by examination and successful candidates would be assigned as corporals to regiments where vacancies existed for them. Each regiment would be supplied from this corps, the commanders requisitioning noncommissioned officers as vacancies occurred.

The other proposal was based on a decentralized self-study system more in the American do-it-yourself tradition than the European-style academy system. The success of this scheme, Farber added, depended on the full cooperation of the local post commander, who would have to detail an officer to supervise the studies of the candidates, provide for reasonable facilities and assistance, and set aside specific periods for recitations and instruction.

In any case, either of these noncommissioned educational systems, in Farber's opinion, "would give them a feeling of independence which they can not always attain under the present method of appointment." The day of the rough-and-ready noncommissioned officer had passed, Farber wrote, and the new age demanded a higher degree of professionalism based firmly on a universal military educational system.

In spite of these perceptive recommendations another decade passed before the Army took any significant steps to implement them, for changes of this magnitude occurred only at a glacial pace. Only the threat of a world war and eventually the war itself could quicken it.

Meanwhile, as the decade of the nineties drew to an end, the Army became engaged in what Secretary of State John Hay referred to as "America's splendid little war." Unlike the Civil War, the Spanish-American War was of short duration and involved relatively few men. In a real sense it was the regular Army's war.

SOME NONCOMMISSIONED OFFICERS, REGULARS AND VOLUNTEERS

The United States entered the Spanish-American War with a 25,000-man regular Army, most of which for many years had been scattered in company-sized units in widely separated garrisons. Companies rather than battalions and regiments had been the rule. Consequently most commissioned and noncommissioned experience had been limited to company duty.[28]

Writing of these companies while describing Captain [later general] John Palmer's days at Ft. Sheridan, one historian wrote that

> individual company units were magnificent. Men enlisted for five years. In his [Palmer's] company, no man ever became a corporal until after his first enlistment. The noncommissioned officers were superb and were capable of handling all the administration of the company. We had drill in the morning and dress parade in the afternoon. After the morning drill, except for an occasional tour of guard duty or service on a court martial our [the commissioned officers'] time was our own.[29]

Although they were usually well-trained and disciplined units, few of these companies had ever formed integral parts of either battalions or regiments in tactical exercises. There were no brigades or divisions in the peacetime organization.[30]

The hard core of the Army that crossed the seas to do battle with the moribund Spanish empire and later with Filipino insurgents was essentially a regular force composed of companies whose cement was the noncommissioned officer. These were the men who, in spite of the admitted shortcomings in their selection and training, had held the company-sized units together during the lean prewar years and would continue to do so during the coming war itself.[31]

While these old-time regular noncommissioned officers have left us virtually no record of their wartime service, their more articulate and literate colleagues, the volunteer noncommissioned officers—those who volunteered solely for the duration—have left numerous vignettes of the regulars at work. One was recorded by Corporal Leland Smith, then a volunteer serving with a U.S. Signal Corps photographic detachment in the campaign against the Philippine insurgents.

Smith's detachment accompanied a company commanded by a young lieutenant appointed directly out of civilian life. The company was in pursuit of an insurgent band and was in march column as it approached a bamboo thicket in which the insurgents were suspected to have taken refuge. As the company drew near the thicket, the lieutenant ordered the men to form a company front and to "fix bayonets." While the men did so, the company commander placed himself in front of the line preparatory to leading a bayonet charge into the jungle. Corporal Smith watched in fascination as the company's grizzled old 1st sergeant, aware of the hazards of moving into dense vegetation in this manner, gave the lieutenant a caustic look, then growled to the men, "take off those bayonets." Smith was uncertain whether the lieutenant overheard the 1st sergeant's order. In any case he said nothing, and the company, with bayonets sheathed, moved with greater caution through the bamboo.[32]

Another vignette came from Corporal A. H. Frazier, who in early 1898 enlisted in the 1st Company, U.S. Volunteers, then commanded by a capable West Point graduate. During the Manila campaign, Frazier repaired a broken signal line under fire and was promoted to sergeant for his valor and initiative. Later, a so-called political appointee—a first lieutenant—took command of Frazier's unit. So innocent was he of military training that Frazier observed he did not even know the manual of arms. When Sergeant Frazier was discharged in October 1899,* he purchased a training manual outlining the manual of arms and sent it to the new detachment commander with his compliments.[33]

As for the all-volunteer units, a different picture emerges. It is often true in wartime that very able men, because of poor planning and circumstances, never really get an opportunity to demonstrate the worth of their training. One such picture emerges from the recollections of a Sergeant Guy Gillette of Company M of the Iowa National Guard. Gillette enlisted in 1893 at the age of fourteen, with his father's but not his mother's consent. Over the next five years young Gillette advanced to the rank of sergeant, and it was as a sergeant that he entrained in April 1898 with his comrades from Company M to take part in the war to liberate Cuba.[34]

Commanding Company M was a Captain Edward A. Kreger who had earned a law degree at the Iowa College of Law in Des Moines and was admitted to the state bar in 1897. Soon after settling in Cherokee, Kreger had begun to organize a group of young men into Company M of the 4th Regiment of the Iowa National Guard. Unlike many of the so-called "political appointees," Captain Kreger enjoyed the full confidence of his small command, although his military experience

*Frazier later went on to a distinguished career in the U.S. diplomatic service.

was limited to rising from private to major in the cadet corps of Iowa State College.[35]

Unfortunately, in spite of such able commissioned and noncommissioned officers, Cherokee's "Gallant Company M" got no further than a muddy training camp at Chickamauga, Georgia, where typhoid fever raged through the camp. Sergeant Gillette and his comrades spent three wretched months struggling more to survive the ravages of disease than to train for war. Finally, in late August of the same year, without ever having seen the foe, Company M, or what was left of it, returned to Des Moines, decimated and demoralized, with many of the men bearing the marks of the fever instead of battle wounds. As for Gillette, he was left behind in the military hospital when the rest of his company went home. Pressed into service as a hospital orderly—there having been little for him to do as a sergeant under the conditions prevailing at Camp Chickamauga—he too contracted typhoid fever. Not until the end of October was he well enough to leave for home.

The wartime experience of hundreds of volunteer noncommissioned officers paralleled those of Gillette. America's splendid little war had hardly been a fair test of either their training or ability. Gillette ultimately went on to serve many years as a distinguished U.S. senator from the state of Iowa.[36]

By and large the majority of noncommissioned officers of the relatively modest expeditionary forces of the Spanish-American War performed reasonably well. This was the type of war for which they'd been trained. But the tactical challenges of the conflict were not those envisioned earlier by Emory Upton and his disciples. The dispirited battalions of the moribund Spanish empire or the ragtag Philippine insurgents did not provide challenges suitable for training either officers or noncommissioned officers to meet the armies of the German Empire. It took total war to challenge the adequacy of the U.S. Army's tradition of selection and training of the noncommissioned officer. Then, for the first time, his status and role in garrison and field was placed in sharp contrast to those of noncommissioned officers of the armies of Great Britain and France, as America fought side by side with these two nations in the closing campaigns of World War I.

CHAPTER 10

DECADES OF INDIFFERENCE

THE STRUGGLE TO IMPROVE NONCOMMISSIONED PAY AND STATUS

". . . they cared not a fig whether they remain noncommissioned officers or not . . ."
—an Army staff officer, 1904

Between 1870, when Congress actually reduced Army pay to prewar levels and 1908, when it finally authorized the first Army-wide pay reform, there had been no servicewide change in Army enlisted pay. Of all the changes proposed and discussed in noncommissioned officer selection, education, and pay since the Civil War, none was debated at greater length than the question of a more equitable pay scale for all enlisted men, especially for noncommissioned officers of the line.

The pay crisis of the Army was a phenomenon of the turn of the century. Demographic and industrial changes in America by 1890 had created an entirely different environment for and challenges to the legendary army of the Indian Wars. Before 1898 there had been little difficulty keeping the 25,000-man Army up to strength. Its ranks were largely filled with men having several years' service, if not several enlistments to their credit. All the higher-ranking noncommissioned officers and many of the lower grades were men of long service. Moreover, the desertion rate for the few years preceding the war with Spain was smaller than before or since and the character of the rank and file was perhaps the highest ever enjoyed by any American army up to that time.

There were many reasons for this happy state of affairs. First were the conditions of service. The troops were brought less into contact with the various aspects of civilian life. Army garrisons formed a world apart, and moves were infrequent. The activity of industrial and commercial development had not reached the dimensions it was to assume at the end of the century nor penetrated into the regions of the nation where most of the troops were stationed. Living in one place, moreover, the soldier saw only one side of this activity and was usually unimpressed. In the 1890s, opportunities to improve his condition financially or otherwise tempted him less frequently than they did later. His own pay was relatively greater, its purchasing power was more, and his opportunities to spend it were fewer.[1]

Second was the unit cohesion and élan engendered by long service and satisfaction with the military life in general. Most of these soldiers of the pre-1898 Army had acquired—through long terms in the same regiment, the same company, and with the same comrades, perhaps in the same grade—a pride in their organization and a love of the service that by 1900 had largely ceased to exist. Transfers in the old Army had been infrequent and the violent disintegration of units with the all-pervasive personnel turbulence of a latter day were all but unknown. There existed an *esprit de corps* difficult to measure but nonetheless invaluable.[2]

BACKGROUND OF THE PAY CRISIS

By 1900, however, almost every service and industrial condition had changed. Opportunities for able-bodied and trained men had vastly increased, while inducements to enter the Army remained the same or had relatively decreased. A fall-off in recruitment, retention, and efficiency was the result. The situation became so desperate by 1907 that Secretary of War William Howard Taft in his report that year devoted considerable attention to the situation. His words are worth quoting at length here:

> Today nearly every organization of the line is depleted in numbers. That itself means unpleasant increase in fatigue and loss of interest in military work. It is impossible with two or three squads of men in a company to raise the present prescribed course of training above absurdity in the eyes of either officers or men. Under these conditions it becomes distasteful to the one and disgusting to the other. Moreover, these reduced organizations are made up almost wholly of recruits and men of short service. Even the noncommissioned officers, with decreasing exceptions, are men still in their first enlistment.

The report continued with the same acerbity to describe the decline in the qualifications of the noncommissioned officers in the Army of the day.

> With the passing of the old noncommissioned officer, the enlisted service, in the absence of relief, will enter upon what is likely to prove the last stage of demoralization. Formerly by sheer force of character, superior training, and long service this class built up for itself an artificial status distinct from that of the private soldier and making more for discipline and efficiency than any other one thing. The average noncommissioned officer of line organizations is as ignorant of his duties as the recruits from which he was drawn, and lacks both the force of character necessary for discipline and the ability essential for efficiency. To restore former conditions is beyond hope; but to create a natural and lawful status for this class is not only possible but necessary if the worst fears for the Army are not to be realized.[3]

Continuing his report with an observation that ultimately helped carry the day for an increase in enlisted pay, Secretary Taft acknowledged that recruitment and retention of men for the Army was difficult even in the best of times, but this difficulty was augmented in periods of great widespread prosperity when labor was in high demand—$1.75 to $2.50 a day at the time for a common laborer—and Army pay only $13 a month. Furthermore, the enhanced technical requirements of such arms as the coast artillery made it especially difficult to keep the ranks of that arm filled. Secretary Taft continued:

> This service [the coast artillery] requires for its proper performance a high degree of mechanical skill, and the training necessary to develop the men leads to their acquisition of a considerable knowledge of electricity and a skill in assembling and manipulating various kinds of electrical apparatus in general use in the commercial world. The result is that by the time these men have served one enlistment they have obtained a proficiency which commands much higher remuneration in civil employment than it does in the Army, and they do not reenlist. I think it is quite probable that an increase in the pay of enlisted men, including considerable additional inducement for men to reenlist and such reasonable increases in the pay of noncommissioned officers as would stimulate men to remain in the service and to qualify themselves for these higher positions, would have a markedly beneficial effect upon the recruitment of the Army.

In recruiting young men to fill its ranks, the U.S. Army indeed found itself, as had generally been its lot, competing with wages paid unskilled laborers. The Army traditionally offered such men less money but better food, clothing, housing, and medical care than would have been their lot in civilian life. To recruit in the 1880s required only a very slight upward adjustment in pay. While this sufficed for the rank and file, it was no solution for obtaining and retaining men of noncommissioned caliber. For them the Army had to compete with comparatively better paid skilled workmen and subordinate employees of civil organizations and institutions. These were the foremen, chief clerks, skilled workmen, and mechanics so needed by commerce, industry, and government around the turn of the century. If the Army could not offer such men inducements at least equal to those offered them in civilian life, it could not hope to obtain, still less retain them.

Retention of those few able men whom the Army managed to recruit at that time was, in Secretary Taft's opinion, the key to the selection and training of first-rate noncommissioned officers. His analysis of the problem deserves verbatim inclusion here, for it provided the rationale of the Pay Bill of 1908.

> Once competent NCOs are secured—their retention as long as physically fit for their duties works for efficiency, provided that a reasonable flow of promotions be maintained. Just as in the old Army no cause contributed more to the standard reached then the high class of Noncommissioned Officers developed, so now no cause has contributed more toward demoralization than the inability under existing conditions to secure qualified men for these grades, or to retain them when secured; and so

> nothing would avail more now to restore efficiency than the creation of a body of highly trained Noncommissioned Officers. These are as important to the Army as foremen to factories; as section bosses to railways; as skilled workmen and subordinate officials are to every industrial or commercial enterprise; or as petty and warrant officers are to the Navy.
>
> The same knowledge of their trade, the same abilities, the same qualities of mind, and the same force of character are essential in one case as in the other. Qualified leaders, successful drivers of men, are everywhere in demand. Men who can make other men work have a recognized value above their fellows in the industrial world. The wage value of a man who can make seven other men do the work for which employed, who can train seven other men to a higher productive capacity, who can make seven unskilled laborers skilled, is far higher than that of any of the seven. The Army must compete in the opportunities it offers with the opportunities these classes can find outside.
>
> The noncommissioned officers are men who in civil life would be skilled workmen, foremen, chief clerks, and subordinate officers. If the Army cannot offer them inducement equal to those that civil institutions are glad to offer, it can not hope to secure or retain them. Moreover, the work of these men in the Army when properly performed is itself highly skilled and of great importance. They form a necessary part of the military hierarchy, but have each individual functions requiring with every advance in grade steadily rising ability, knowledge and training. The importance of the work of electricians and machinists in the Navy and Coast Artillery is recognized outside of the service merely from common familiarity with the trades in which these men are skilled. But important as their work is, it is no more important than the work of other high grade noncommissioned officers in the same or different services (especially of the combat arms) for which, though less familiar outside and differently named, an equally arduous training is essential for success. Moreover, all advantages lie with these men in the navy and artillery possessing recognized trades. The opportunities to acquire such trades in civil life are no more than the opportunities of civil life offer for employment if they leave the service. Civil life presents, on the other hand, no opportunities for the acquirement of the skill and knowledge essential for the other noncommissioned grades, nor openings for employment wherein this skill and knowledge would be of direct advantage.
>
> The essential training for these positions is given only by the Government, its results are of use only to the Government, and the Government, in justice to itself and to these men, should make reasonable effort to retain them. The ordinary duties and responsibilities even of a corporal are largely increased over those of a private. The sergeant for efficiency must be more highly trained than the corporal. The duties of a first sergeant or of a regimental sergeant-major demand knowledge, administrative ability, and force of character of the highest order.

This problem had been developing since the 1870s, when the few improvements in Army pay authorized by Congress had been limited to only a few categories of noncommissioned officers whose duties demanded considerable technical training. During General Upton's trip abroad in the 1870s he found widespread agreement among his hosts on the importance of adequate pay and a good retirement system in obtaining and retaining good noncommissioned officers—which the U.S. Army did not have. When Upton submitted his report to the secretary of war in 1877, a private's base pay was $13.00 a month—$3.00 *less* than it had been during the Civil War.[4]

At the turn of the century there had been little or no change in enlisted pay, which remained at $13.00 per month for the first two years of an enlistment with an increase of $1.00 per month for each subsequent year of service through the fifth. For the next five years pay was increased to $18.00 a month. The perennial private—and there were many—could look forward only to an additional $1.00 per month for each subsequent five-year enlistment until he was placed on the retired list.

For corporals, the situation was not much better. Monthly pay ranged from $15.00 to $20.00, depending on length of service. Duty or line sergeants received $18.00 to $23.00, according to length of service, and remuneration for 1st sergeants ranged from $25.00 to $30.00. In addition to these pay scales there was a clothing allowance that amounted to $66.97 during the first year of service, $29.70 during the second year, and $38.32 for the third year, for a total of $134.99. After twenty-five years of good service an enlisted man could apply to be placed on the retired list. After 1885, this occurred at two thirds pay and commuted allowances amounting to $25.00 to $28.00 per month, depending on the man's grade at time of retirement.[5]

Consequently, even as the century moved toward its close, the inequities of Army pay were perceived as an increasing burden to enlisted morale and efficiency. Indeed, in the century's last two decades the situation in the regular Army became so bad that many otherwise capable men declined promotion to the rank of corporal simply because the pay of that rank scarcely compensated for the additional responsibilities. The very modest increases in pay that Congress had seemed likely to approve in 1888 were, in the opinion of then–Secretary of War William C. Endicott, totally incommensurate with the responsibilities of, for example, a first sergeant, and therefore no incentive "to tempt the best and most reliable soldiers to accept the position."[6]

Secretary Endicott declared that the pay of the lowest-ranking noncommissioned officer should not be less than $25.00 per month and that pay for all noncommissioned officers should be readjusted upward from that base to $50.00 or even $55.00 for the highest ranking. Inasmuch as the sergeant was, in Secretary Endicott's words, "the intermediary between the private soldier and the commissioned officer, the line of demarcation between these three classes should be as strongly accentuated downward as it is upward." Justice to the noncommissioned officer and proper regard for the discipline, efficiency, and morale of the Army required this, Endicott concluded.[7]

In spite of Endicott's eloquent argument in behalf of improving enlisted pay, twenty long years passed—during which a war was fought with Spain, an insurrection quelled in the Philippines, and an expeditionary force sent to China—before Congress considered a servicewide increase in enlisted pay for the regular Army. During these two decades, as the cost of living more than doubled, the Army staff devoted considerable time and thought to making a military career more attractive to enlisted men. There was general agreement, however, that any service-wide pay increase must be accompanied as well by improvement in promotion policies for noncommissioned officers if the Army was to obtain and retain the quality of men needed for noncommissioned service.

In 1903, for example, the average pay of skilled workmen in five different trades was $70.00 per month, while the pay of the qualified corporal of the line was only $15.00 per month. Clearly, Army pay scales, set thirty-three years earlier, were out of joint with the times. Yet given the traditional congressional restraints on spending, the Army could not hope to match in dollars the pay of skilled workmen in civilian life. It did, however, offer some inducements with real cash value to the class of men who might normally lack many of these amenities, such as food, clothing, housing, medical care, and pensions—modest as they were.

The attractiveness of Army life therefore rose and fell with changes in the economic conditions in the country at large. In good times the Army with its regimented way of life and traditionally low pay found it difficult to compete with civil employment; in periods of economic depression, recruits were plentiful. During the depression of 1893–1896, on the eve of the Spanish-American War, the supply of recruits so exceeded demand that at one time recruiting officers were instructed to enlist only soldiers with previous good service. It was also during this period that excellent men, anxious to retain their positions, often occupied the senior noncommissioned grades. Consequently, the regular Army entered that war with generally high-quality noncommissioned officers.[8]

After the war the situation completely reversed itself. A postwar business boom raised the pay of skilled workers to such an extent it discouraged both enlistment and retention of highly skilled men, as Army pay rates continued to lag behind those in the civilian trades. For example, the coast artillery corps, with its requirement for technically trained men, found it especially difficult to keep its ranks filled. The difference between Army pay and that of civilian workmen not only made it difficult to recruit good men but to retain them after training them in a particular skill.

Some idea of the growing skills changes in weaponry and technology demanded of noncommissioned officers of all arms and services since the Civil War can be seen in the training programs for noncommissioned officers at the coast artillery school. In December 1899, a class for electricians was established and in October 1902 a school for gunnery specialists was added.* These courses included algebra, geometry, trigonometry, seacoast engineering, mechanical drawing, and photoprinting. Later courses were added for radiomen and firemen with equally challenging academic requirements.[9]

Obviously, if they were paid on a scale significantly less than that of the Navy or of their civilian counterparts in the trades, men with this type of training could not long be retained by the Army. The Navy, with a longer tradition of technical

*In 1901 electrician training was made part of the school of submarine defense and transferred from Ft. Monroe to Ft. Totten, New York.

skills among its enlisted men, had long offered significantly better pay than the Army. For example, a young man enlisting in the Navy and serving for thirty years but not rising to petty officer (noncommissioned) rank could expect to earn a total of $16,760.60 during his career and upon retirement a monthly pension of $59.75. The Army offered a private total pay of only $6,852.00 and a monthly pension of $26.00 after thirty years' service.[10]

Another aspect of noncommissioned pay and morale, especially the latter, was that the pay of privates performing extra duty, usually as laborers on construction projects of only a quasi-military nature, frequently exceeded that of many line noncommissioned officers. It was often to a soldier's pecuniary advantage to remain in the ranks as a private because in some cases he could earn more there than a sergeant major or quartermaster sergeant simply by performing extra detailed duty as a carpenter or mason on projects such as bridge building or barracks construction.

Major W. P. Evans, assistant adjutant general of the Army, wrote in 1904 that a corporal's pay should be at least as great as what a private earned when detailed to nonmilitary work duty. If this rule had been applied to all ranks, corporals' pay would have been raised to $22.00 per month; duty sergeants $30.00; and 1st sergeants as high as that of the best-paid noncommissioned officers.[11]

This situation, moreover, often posed serious disciplinary problems and adversely affected noncommissioned morale. For a private with only a few months' service to draw more pay in a month than a 1st sergeant was particularly galling to a senior noncommissioned officer. Unlike the private, the latter was a trained professional with many years' service who on occasion might be required to take over command of the entire company.

This latter requirement especially irritated senior noncommissioned officers who, in the absence of the company officers, frequently found themselves in charge of the company—but without an officer's pay. This situation arose mainly from a chronic shortage of officers at the turn of the century—to which the secretary of war drew attention in 1904. Heavy calls upon line officers for detail to the general staff, to military schools, recruiting duty, and ROTC reduced the number of commissioned officers available for service with troops. Consequently, many companies were left with only one officer on a regular basis who was often required on special occasions to assist the staff at battalion or regimental headquarters. In such circumstances the company was left in the hands of the 1st sergeant. For example, at a review for the commander of the Colorado Department in 1908, two companies were observed to be under the command of their sergeants.[12]

A staff officer in the adjutant general's office exclaimed in 1904:

> How often have we failed to keep noncommissioned officers keyed up to the proper standard of efficiency because they cared not a fig whether they remain noncommissioned officers or not? How often had we failed to induce our best sergeants to ac-

> cept the diamond of the first sergeant? The difference in pay can hardly be said to be an inducement. Very often the sergeant consents to become first sergeant because the captain wishes him to do so, not because he feels that he will be paid an adequate sum for his increased care and responsibility and for his increased social isolation.[13]

"Modern warfare," this officer continued in a prophetic observation, "has also greatly increased the responsibilities of noncommissioned officers, particularly squad and section leaders. On them would fall, under combat conditions, the control of small units, often of companies." Such men could not be trained in a day. or picked up on any street corner. Echoing Secretary Endicott of sixteen years before, he concluded:

> If you want them you must be willing to pay for them. Let justice be done the faithful noncommissioned officer. We do not ask it for the sake of the noncommissioned officer himself, although much might be said on that score. We ask it solely for the improvement of the service, for the benefit of the people of the United States, for whom the Army is maintained.[14]

To remedy one aspect of this problem, the Army staff suggested the creation of a service (or construction) corps of the regular Army. A bill prepared by the staff in 1905 provided for the organization of such a corps that would include five hundred privates second class, all to be paid at the same rates as authorized for engineers. Such a corps would in effect have increased the combat strength of the regular Army, restoring a corresponding number of fighting men to the ranks. Most importantly, it would have removed the necessity of extra duty and hence of extra pay for privates who volunteered for such duty. Unfortunately, Congress was in no mood for such a radical departure from tradition, and the legislation failed to pass.

Nevertheless, the Army staff continued its search for a remedy to this problem and continued to urge upon an indifferent Congress the necessity of pay reform if the U.S. Army was to keep abreast of the armies of other nations. In matters of pay, most armies set the line separating noncommissioned officers from rank and file above the rank of corporal, who was generally considered to be no more than a selected private. Only the highest noncommissioned grades were regarded in European armies as noncommissioned officers *per se*. In the following table it can be seen that in terms of a corporal's and a sergeant's pay, only the United States Army had failed to make a significant differentiation.

PAY OF NONCOMMISSIONED OFFICERS RELATIVE TO THE PAY OF PRIVATES IN THE PRINCIPAL ARMIES OF THE WORLD[15]

Country	*Corporal*	*Sergeant*	*1st Sgt.*	*Sgt. Maj.*
Japan	3 to 3.75	5 to 8.25	—	9.9 to 20
Russia	1.2	2	8	12

Country	*Corporal*	*Sergeant*	*1st Sgt.*	*Sgt. Maj.*
France	44	144	—	204
Austria	2.46	3.23	—	5.7
Germany	1.7 to 3.27	4.9	8.5	8.66
Italy	1.22	2.28	—	2.9
Great Britain	1.7 to 2	2.33 to 2.61	3 to 3.37	Warrant Officer
United States	1.15	1.38	1.92	2.61

(The figures indicate that the pay, for example of a corporal in the Japanese army, ranged from 3 to 3.75 times that of a private soldier.)

While the Army staff acknowledged that adequate pay alone would not be sufficient in itself to give the noncommissioned officers the status and privilege due their rank, there was general agreement that a more equitable pay scale must be the foundation on which a structure of noncommissioned status and privilege should be built.

However, the staff was well aware of the traditional American distaste for symbols and trappings of caste and privilege. Therefore, it argued that the creation of a more clearly defined noncommissioned class within the Army was "no more inconsistent with democratic theories of government than . . . the creation of armies themselves, for all societies, democracies, monarchies, and autocracies maintained armies." To copy foreign methods, no matter how useful elsewhere, would be disastrous, the staff knew, if they were found to be at odds with the American people's basic instincts. Yet the principle of clear distinctions in rank was essential to discipline in all armies. In any case, distinctions between enlisted men and commissioned officers had long existed in the U.S. Army. A similar though lesser distinction between private and noncommissioned officer would therefore be no radical innovation but would in Army eyes, greatly improve discipline and efficiency.

A solution to this problem long eluded the efforts of the War Department. Nevertheless, in the last years of the nineteenth century some efforts were made to improve the pay of certain of the noncommissioned grades, especially of the noncommissioned staff, and of coast artillery electricians and signal sergeants—men whose technical skills were much in demand both in and out of the service.

POSTWAR DIFFICULTIES

After the patriotic frenzy of the Spanish-American War and the euphoria of victory had passed, enlistments, as noted earlier in this chapter, began to decline, and the desertion rate rose.

There were many sources of dissatisfaction in the first decade of the new century, especially widespread among senior noncommissioned officers. Among them were the lack of on-post housing for their families; too long service requirements before eligibility for retirement (most NCOs preferred either twenty years at half pay or twenty-five years at three-quarters pay); an absence of guaranteed civil service appointment after long and faithful service; and too frequent changes in company officers, especially of the captains. Before the Spanish-American War, in most companies there had been a personal *entente*, or understanding between officers and their men—an *entente* considered vital to contentment and discipline. After the turn of the century this rapport was allowed to disintegrate.[16]

In the opinion of many officers, the continuing loss in the postwar years through retirement and discharge of older noncommissioned officers with their strong sense of professionalism and unit loyalty was leading to the demoralization of the enlisted service. While most officers despaired of restoring former conditions, they were nevertheless convinced that somehow the Army must improve the quality of its noncommissioned officers if their worst fears were not to be realized.

Widespread among the officer corps following the war with Spain (especially those in service with troops) was the belief that conditions, insofar as noncommissioned officers were concerned, were growing steadily worse. Both in quality and quantity the corps was perceived to be degenerating—enough good men were not being recruited and the really able men were not being retained under present pay conditions. This belief engendered a feeling of discouragement that risked descending eventually into indifference. Around the turn of the century this feeling seemed to permeate every company, troop, and battery in the Army and many officers believed if it was not checked, it would threaten widespread demoralization within the units.[17]

RETAINING SENIOR NONCOMMISSIONED OFFICERS IN OTHER ARMIES

Even those nations whose armed forces were sustained by universal military conscription also shared some concern for retaining a significant proportion of trained men following completion of their compulsory term of service. It was from this latter group that capable replacements for the noncommissioned officer corps were drawn. Consequently, the major military powers of Europe, in competition with industry, offered a larger variety of inducements to encourage able men to reenlist.

Their objective was not merely to retain long-term privates but to retain those men who had the capacity to serve as noncommissioned officers. To do this they gave their noncommissioned officers greater status and privilege than before. Some European armies had long led the way in this regard. In Britain, for example, noncommissioned officers had long enjoyed their own quarters, a separate mess, and other privileges unique to their rank. Furthermore, the British army often promoted the most outstanding among the sergeants to the rank of warrant officer, a grade between the enlisted ranks and the commissioned officers. This practice, the British believed, had the advantage of keeping these able men at tasks for which their education and training best fitted them by not pitting them against commissioned officers, who usually had the advantages of a superior education and affluent social background.

Among the continental powers the German empire had perhaps the most advanced system of noncommissioned officer selection and training. Like their British counterparts, the German noncommissioned officers enjoyed separate quarters, mess, and rated a salute from their subordinates. German army noncommissioned officers were drawn from special schools or from the ranks as in the United States Army. With the Germans, however, such men were selected from among those who had been especially encouraged to reenlist with the object of becoming noncommissioned officers. The German army instructed them not only in military subjects but in ancillary fields of study that better enabled them to fulfill their duties as senior noncommissioned officers.

After five or six years of service these men received further instruction intended to prepare them not only for the highest noncommissioned grades but also for positions in the lower ranks of the civil service. Upon completion of twelve years in the active army, the German noncommissioned officer received a bonus the equivalent of $300.00, and upon retirement the right to a permanent post in the lower grades of the German civil service.

Yet even these inducements would have been insufficient to retain capable noncommissioned officers in both the British and German armies had it not been for the fact that their pay, when combined with the benefits unique to the service, was competitive with that of the industrial classes from which these men were drawn. Although military pay alone rarely matched civilian rates, the allowances, service increases, bounties, and other rewards during active service, as well as pensions and guarantees of civil service employment after retirement, helped minimize the actual difference.

U.S. REACTION TO THESE PRACTICES

The failure of the U.S. Army to adopt the provision of assuring civil service appointments for retired noncommissioned officers had long been a source of considerable dissatisfaction among noncommissioned officers who periodically urged upon an indifferent Congress the adoption of this practice. The failure to do so seemed unfortunate, for such men had acquired through long service habits of mind and body, as one military commentator put it, that would be particularly useful in government service requiring some skill and responsibility. In 1906 the Navy's chief of the bureau of navigation, followed a year later by the Army chief of staff, recommended "that men who have served three enlistments be privileged, without examinations, to place their names on the list of civil service appointees, in occupations for which their service (Army or Navy) and their efficiency reports show them to be fitted." Yet even as they submitted their recommendations, the service chiefs seriously doubted (correctly) that Congress would ever adopt such proposals.[18]

Many U.S. Army officers such as Emory Upton, with additional European examples in mind, had long urged that greater efforts be made to enhance noncommissioned officer status and authority, both on and off duty, by delineating more sharply the line of separation between them and the rank and file, not only in terms of pay but also in matters of privileges and amenities. Most American officers, however, drew back from outright advocacy of an Uptonian position by observing that American egalitarian traditions would prevent U.S. Army sergeants from holding such exalted positions *vis-à-vis* the other enlisted men, as their counterparts held in most European armies. Instead, sergeants of the U.S. Army, these officers argued, should content themselves with such modest measures as the provision of separate tables in the company mess, even though almost sixty years had passed since Army regulations had first enjoined this provision with little success upon company commanders. Many also urged that the construction of barracks with private facilities for noncommissioned officers would help to improve their status in the eyes of the private soldier.[19]

To correct the practice of promoting unqualified men, but not the practice of reduction to the ranks upon transfer between units, some officers suggested that when a vacancy occurred among line sergeants of a particular company the three senior corporals be examined by a board consisting of the officers of that company. This examination would have been both written and practical, that is, given both in garrison and in the field. In grading the examinations due weight was to be given each man's service record within the company. The man rated most highly in all three categories would then have been selected to fill the vacancy. This would, it was claimed, "foster among all of the corporals the proper spirit for applying themselves to study." It was expected that only the "most intelligent and capable of the three candidates would be advanced to the status of sergeant." This system worked well, once adopted, as long as there was a surfeit of able volunteers. But with the return of peace after the war with Spain, the Army once again found it difficult to fill its ranks with enough able men for this recently adopted system to function properly.[20]

As for the longtime tradition of reduction to the ranks when a man transferred to another unit from the one that had promoted him to his original rank, some exceptions had developed over the years. For example, noncommissioned officers of the coast artillery corps—sergeants major, sergeants, master electricians, engineers, electrician sergeants first and second class, master gunners, sergeants major junior grade, and firemen—could be transferred from post to post without loss of rank. The reason for this was that they owed their appointments to the chief of artillery rather than to the local unit commander, as in the case of infantry and cavalry. The former selected these men after they passed qualifying examinations under War Department control. This gave the coast artillery corps, also the signal corps and the hospital corps, which were similarly organized, a corps-wide uniformity in qualification standards that noncommissioned officers of the more traditional combat arms lacked, and thus permitted transfer from one unit to another without loss of rank.[21]

Not only could many enlisted men of these corps look forward to eventual advancement to senior noncommissioned grade, but "all unmarried soldiers under thirty years of age who are citizens of the United States, who are physically sound, who have served honorably not less than two years in the Army, and who have borne a good moral character, before and after enlistment," could apply to take examinations for promotion to commissioned rank. There were two examinations, a preliminary departmental one given in March of each year and a final competitive examination the following September, open to those who had successfully completed the first. These examinations were thorough, but not beyond the capacities of a man of good intelligence who had "applied himself with reasonable diligence."

Although the regulations stated that vacancies in the grade of second lieutenant not filled from the current graduates of West Point by the first of July of each year were to be filled "so far as they are available" by enlisted men who had passed the two examinations, few enlisted men actually advanced to commissions by this route. The reasons were that too few men with the potential qualifications were recruited, and too few senior noncommissioned officers could cope with the examinations.

Failing advancement to commissioned rank, there were, however, other inducements to remain in military service. If an enlisted man survived twenty to thirty years of service, he could look forward to admission to the Soldiers Home, if disabled in the line of duty, or after twenty years of honest and faithful service. Moreover, there was a 75 percent pension awaiting him after thirty years of honorable service. Both provisions assured a career soldier a degree of care and sustenance, modest though it was, in his old age unmatched by any offered in civilian life for men of his class at the time. Above and beyond these assurances, there were such things as reasonably comfortable and clean living quarters, good recreational facilities, the post exchange, opportunities of travel and to learn a trade, as well as the educational advantages of some service schools.

In spite of these inducements, the Army chronically failed during the two decades preceding the First World War to enlist the quantity and quality of men authorized by Congress. Through hard experience, the Army was learning the primary role that pay and pay alone played in getting and keeping recruits. The Army staff was well aware that in peacetime the spirit of patriotism and self-sacrifice was not sufficiently widespread to maintain even a small regular Army. To a certain extent, the love of the military life or a spirit of adventure often impelled a man to enlist, but rarely were these motives sufficient to encourage him to reenlist. Individual self-interest was the dominant factor.

Since under normal conditions of service a soldier did not make corporal before his second enlistment, the Army realized that it must offer sufficient pay to encourage a potential noncommissioned officer to reenlist. This was particularly important in developing sergeants whose counterpart was not the average but the higher class of skilled workmen. The pay of a sergeant of the line would therefore had to have been increased from $24.00 to a maximum of $44.00 per month. A

1st sergeant, with even greater value to the service, should have been entitled to higher pay as he was expected to surpass every enlisted member of his company in executive and administrative ability as well as in knowledge of soldiering. This was equally true of the regimental sergeant major. By 1907 there was no longer any doubt in the War Department that such men were worth more pay. They had demonstrated their determination to make the Army their career. Their rewards should be sufficient to encourage them in this resolution. The Army staff recommended that the pay of senior enlisted grades, starting between $33.00 and $36.00 per month, should be increased in the same proportion and at the same interval as that of the corporal and sergeant to a maximum of $56.00 and $60.00 respectively.

PROPOSED AND PRESENT PAY OF NONCOMMISSIONED OFFICERS ENLISTMENT

Grade	$ *1st*	$ *2nd*	$ *3rd*	$ *4th*	$ *5th*	$ *6th*	$ *7th*	$ *8th*	$ *9th*	$ *10th*
Corporal										
Proposed	18	21	24	30	33	36	36	36	36	36
Present	15	18	20	20	21	22	22	23	23	24
Sergeant										
Proposed	24	28	32	35	38	41	44	44	44	44
Present	18	21	23	23	24	25	25	25	26	27
1st Sgt.										
Proposed	33	38	44	47	50	53	56	56	56	56
Present	25	28	30	30	31	32	32	33	33	34
Sgt. Maj.										
Proposed	36	42	48	51	54	57	60	60	60	60
Present	34	37	39	39	40	41	41	42	42	42

In addition to the above increase, the Army staff and the secretary of war recommended provisions for long-deferred amenities designed to enhance the noncommissioned officers' status. These included such things as that long-deferred provision for separate tables in the mess, pending the provisions of separate mess rooms with allowances for suitable table furnishings and additional rations to raise somewhat the standard of such facilities. For single noncommissioned officers, private rooms in barracks were also recommended and for married men, adequate housing on post.[22]

THE ARMY PAY BILL OF 1908

In 1908 Congress finally yielded to Army importunities and passed the first comprehensive Army-wide pay bill since 1870. The act of May 11, 1908 solved the problem that had for so long demoralized senior noncommissioned officers by significantly increasing their pay in relation to that of privates. The Army expected that the greater difference in pay between senior noncommissioned officer and private would, in addition to earlier changes, more sharply delineate the line of division between them and help the Army "retain a good class of noncommissioned officers, and encourage the return to civil life of privates who could not demonstrate their fitness for appointment as noncommissioned officers."[23] Furthermore, remuneration granted the noncommissioned officers in the Pay Bill of 1908 exceeded that recommended a year earlier, in the staff study prepared for the Army chief of staff.[24] Those senior noncommissioned officers possessing such special skills as electrician, engineer, medical technician, and master musician remained as they had for many years the most highly paid, generally earning more than double the pay of sergeants of the line in the combat arms.

RATES OF MONTHLY PAY OF ENLISTED MEN*
ACTS MAY 11, 1908, AND JUNE 3, 1916

Grade and Army of Service	*First Enlistment Period*
Quartermaster Sergeant, Senior Grade—Quartermaster Corps Band Leader—Infantry, Cavalry, Artillery, Corps of Engineers Master Signal Electrician—Signal Corps Master Engineer, Senior Grade—Corps of Engineers Master Hospital Sergeant—Medical Department	$75.00
Hospital Sergeant—Medical Department Master Engineer, Junior Grade—Corps of Engineers Engineer—Coast Artillery Corps	$65.00
Sergeant, First Class—Medical Department	$50.00
Regimental Sergeant Major—Field Artillery Cavalry, Infantry, Corps of Engineers Sergeant Major, Senior Grade—Coast Artillery Corps Quartermaster Sergeant—Quartermaster Corps Ordnance Sergeant—Ordnance Department First Sergeant—Artillery, Cavalry, Infantry, Corps of Engineers Chauffeur, First Class—Signal Corps Battalion Sergeant Major—Corps of Engineers Battalion Supply Sergeant—Corps of Engineers Electrician Sergeant, First Class—Coast Artillery Corps Sergeant, First Class—Corps of Engineers, Signal Corps, Quartermaster Corps Assistant Engineer—Coast Artillery Corps	$50.00
Battalion Sergeant Major—Field Artillery Infantry	$40.00

*Exclusive of U.S. Military Academy band and field musicians.

Squadron Sergeant Major—Cavalry Sergeant Major, Junior Grade—Coast Artillery Corps Master Gunner—Coast Artillery Corps Sergeant Bugler—Infantry, Cavalry, Corps of Engineers Assistant Band Leader—Infantry, Cavalry, Artillery, Corps of Engineers	
Sergeant—Corps of Engineers, Ordnance Department, Signal Corps, Quartermaster Corps, Medical Department Chauffeur—Signal Corps Stable Sergeant—Corps of Engineers Supply Sergeant—Corps of Engineers Mess Sergeant—Corps of Engineers Color Sergeant—Field Artillery, Infantry, Cavalry, Corps of Engineers Electrician Sergeant, Second Class—Coast Artillery Corps Band Sergeant—Artillery, Cavalry, Infantry, Corps of Engineers Musicians, First Class—Infantry, Cavalry, Artillery, Corps of Engineers	$36.00
Sergeant—Artillery, Cavalry, Infantry Stable Sergeant—Field Artillery, Infantry, Cavalry Supply Sergeant—Infantry, Cavalry, Artillery Mess Sergeant—Infantry, Cavalry, Artillery Cook—Artillery, Infantry, Cavalry, Corps of Engineers, Signal Corps, Quartermaster Corps, Medical Department Horseshoer—Infantry, Cavalry, Artillery, Corps of Engineers Musician, Second Class—Infantry, Cavalry, Artillery, Corps of Engineers	$30.00
Corporal—Corps of Engineers, Ordnance Department, Signal Corps, Quartermaster Corps, Medical Department Mechanic—Coast Artillery Corps Chief Mechanic—Field Artillery Musician, Third Class—Infantry, Cavalry, Artillery, Corps of Engineers	$24.00
Corporal—Artillery, Cavalry, Infantry Saddler—Infantry, Cavalry, Field Artillery, Corps of Engineers, Medical Department Mechanic—Infantry, Cavalry, Field Artillery, Medical Department Farrier—Medical Department Wagoner—Infantry, Cavalry, Field Artillery, Corps of Engineers	$21.00

Private, First Class—Infantry, Cavalry, Artillery, Corps of Engineers, Ordnance Department, Signal Corps, Quartermaster Corps, Medical Department	$18.00
Bugler—Infantry, Cavalry, Artillery, Corps of Engineers, Signal Corps Quartermaster Corps, Medical Department Private, Second Class—Ordnance Department	$15.00

There was, however, some concern among the staff that by clearly favoring the senior noncommissioned officers in the pay scale their ranks would eventually be filled with quasi-permanent appointees. Recruits would then have found their path of advancement blocked, as in the years preceding the war with Spain, when there was little movement of personnel within the ranks. In that case, the results might well have spread dissatisfaction among the privates, with a corresponding increase in desertions, a falling off in enlistments, and the formation of a class of time-serving soldiers.[25]

Yet these were worries over future possibilities rather than present certainties. For the present, the majority of the Army staff was satisfied with the Pay Bill of 1908 because among other things it helped the noncommissioned officer corps through the crisis of morale that had plagued it since the 1880s. No less an observer than E. A. Galington, inspector general of the Army, summed it up by writing that "the spirit of the service is more sanguine since the passage of the act increasing the pay of the Army."[26]

Eight years later, on the eve of the United States' entry into World War I, Congress reaffirmed the pay advance of 1908 in the National Defense Act of 1916, while at the same time significantly increasing the size of the regular Army and the reserves. There was not to be another change in Army pay until long after World War I had been fought and won and the vast national army raised to fight it had been demobilized.

CONSIDERATION FOR ESTABLISHING THE GRADE OF WARRANT OFFICER

In addition to the Pay Bill of 1908, there remained the question of how to reward noncommissioned officers with long and distinguished service who had reached the top of the rank scale. Despite the fact that enlisted men could in theory advance through the noncommissioned grades to the highest commissioned ranks, the number of commissioned vacancies were actually so rare that in practice very few enlisted men were so rewarded. Furthermore, in 1907 the conditions of appointment did not permit such promotions to be used as a method of rewarding long and faithful service in the ranks. This being the case, the creation of a new grade, that of warrant officer, was proposed.[27]

Such a grade was envisioned to fall between the noncommissioned and the commissioned officer. It would not have been an innovative step since it had been taken long ago in the small British regular army, whose system resembled somewhat that of the American. Furthermore, the United States Navy also had adopted the grade of warrant officer a number of years before. Secretary of War William Howard Taft had also recommended that the grade of warrant officer be opened to Army sergeants major, first sergeants of battalion and regiments, coast artillery noncommissioned staff officers, sergeants first class of the hospital and signal corps, chief musicians, and post noncommissioned staff officers. He also recommended among the prerequisites for appointment the completion of fifteen years of active-duty service, ten of which were to have been as a noncommissioned officer, five in the grade for which warranted.[28]

The grade of warrant officer was to be not only a reward for long and faithful service, as had long been advocated, but an encouragement for able men to remain in the service. Senior noncommissioned officers would not have been considered eligible for appointment to warrant officer simply on the basis of having reached a higher grade. Exceptions would have been made, if necessary, for such specialists as master electricians in the coast artillery, master electricians in the signal corps, and chief musicians whose skills had been acquired prior to their enlistment. Only a prescribed written examination would have been required of them before appointment.

In his report for 1907, the secretary of war recommended that if the grade of warrant officer were adopted for the Army, the pay should be set at $1,000 yearly at the outset and, as in the case with commissioned officers, increased 10 percent for each five years of service up to twenty years. The maximum pay would therefore have been $1,400.

The Committee of Military Affairs of the House of Representatives began hearings in 1911 on creating the grade of warrant officer in lieu of the grade of post noncommissioned staff officer. However, the rank and grade of warrant officers was not established until the passage of the act of July 1918. This legislation established the Army mine planter service in the coast artillery corps and appointed in it warrant officers to serve as masters, mates, chief engineers, and assistant engineers of each mine-laying vessel. The utilization of warrant officers was further expanded by the act of 1920, which authorized appointment of warrant officers in clerical, administrative, and band-leading activities.[29]

PROPOSALS FOR REFORM OF THE RETIREMENT SYSTEM

The Army staff also undertook studies of the national retirement systems of other nations, as they applied to noncommissioned officers. These studies showed that when compared with those of other military powers, the United States Army's requirement of thirty years service before a man received a retirement pension was unique. Germany and Italy, for example, not only permitted but encouraged their noncommissioned officers to retire with permanent employment in the civil service after only twelve years of active military service. Germany and Austria-Hungary also authorized retirement with full pension at any time after eighteen years; France after fifteen; and in Great Britain there was compulsory retirement after twenty-three years. Japan, on the other hand, retired its noncommissioned officers with pensions when they reached forty years of age.

Unlike most commissioned officers who with advancing years usually had attained a rank making fewer physical demands upon them, enlisted men, regardless of their rank, usually faced the same physical demands throughout their careers. The Army staff therefore questioned the wisdom of the thirty-year retirement. The retention of noncommissioned officers after they were no longer physically fit was a serious impediment to the service, as had been observed when the regular Army took the field in 1898.

It was difficult to set absolute retirement limits because after twenty-five years of service some men remained in better physical condition than others after only twenty years. Therefore, a graded system for retirement by years would be more efficient and fair. Yet if retirements were to be graded by years, they must also be graded in pay. For example, a man with twenty years' service should not receive as much pension as a man with thirty years'. The staff therefore recommended that retirement should be compulsory after thirty years but permitted at any time after twenty if the individual's services could be spared. Retirement after twenty and before twenty-five years should carry half pay; after twenty-five years three-quarters pay of grade. Under such a system, the practice of allowing the computation of double time for war or foreign service adopted in 1900 would no longer be necessary.[30]

☆☆ PART II ☆☆

WORLD WAR I TO THE PRESENT

Since 1775 war or the threat of war has played a major role in the evolution of the noncommissioned officer corps of the United States Army. World War I, with which this second part begins, was no exception. Indeed, as it had on world history and military technology, this war had a greater impact on the Army's image of the noncommissioned man than any of the nation's previous conflicts.

For the first time the Army of the United States, or the National Army as it was then designated, trained and fought in close cooperation with the armies of its allies, Great Britain and France. Thus European attitudes and traditions had considerable influence on the image and role of the noncommissioned officer corps. Furthermore, the tactics of the infamous trench warfare on the Western Front had a profound effect upon the roles of the infantry noncommissioned officers, both Allied and American. Despite postwar neglect that ignored many of the First World War's lessons, the Second World War and America's entry into it found the Army more receptive and innovative in its willingness to create a noncommissioned officer corps able to engage the armies of two of the world's great military powers—Germany and Japan.

The development of the so-called Cold War with the Communist powers prevented the noncommissioned corps from descending into the traditional postwar pattern of neglect that had followed earlier conflicts. Instead, the Army embarked on a series of educational and administrative reforms that survived a partial hiatus during the Korean War, was revived during the operations in Southeast Asia, and eventually reached its culmination in the post-Vietnam decade. Out of these years of turbulence and experimentation emerged a noncommissioned officer corps that is a worthy companion to the commissioned officer corps in peace and war. This then is the story told in this second part: how the Army, its officers, and noncommissioned officers brought this evolution about under the extraordinary challenges of the past seventy years.

CHAPTER 11

WORLD WAR I

YEARS OF CHALLENGE AND CHANGE

With the enactment of the Pay Bill of 1908, the status of the noncommissioned officer improved somewhat, but there still remained too little difference between a private soldier's pay and that of a senior noncommissioned officer. As the clouds of war gathered in Europe, the United States Army took yet another step toward improving the noncommissioned officer's status and prospects for career advancement by lifting the barrier that had traditionally prevented the noncommissioned officers of the combat arms from taking his stripes with him when he transferred to another unit. At least for the duration of the war, a noncommissioned officer could transfer without loss of grade. This liberated him somewhat from his traditional role as the company commander's man, but in 1908 this change was still in the future.

Much of the Army's pre–World War I perception of the noncommissioned officer was to be found in the tradition that maintained the barrier to transfer in grade. Selected and trained by his company commander, his warrant signed by his regimental commander upon the company commander's recommendation, the noncommissioned officer had been always regarded as essentially "belonging" to the company commander. There was much truth in this perception because in a very personal way a man selected for advancement to noncommissioned rank reflected his company commander's judgment and sense of values. The state of affairs in effect locked the noncommissioned man into his particular unit for his entire career and did indeed limit his opportunities for assignment and promotion. In the second decade of the twentieth century, however, the demands of empire and global conflict forced gradual modification of this tradition and practice.

In spite of many years of earnest pleading and argument by advocates of reform, it was ultimately the challenge of mobilization and war that finally brought about needed change, even if it was only temporary. The call to arms in 1917 unified all the land forces of the United States for a moment in history. For the duration, the secretary of war proclaimed the regular Army, National Guard, and National (draft) Army to be an entity—the Army of the United States. But the war was scarcely over when the Army reverted to its tradition of binding the enlisted man back into his parent unit, the unit that initially had given him his rank.

The world war also brought American noncommissioned officers into close contact with their foreign counterparts for the first time. From these contacts both commissioned and noncommissioned officers began to make comparisons that reflected adversely on the status and role of the American noncommissioned officer. Over forty years before, General Emory Upton had pointed out the hazards and disadvantages of the American system of noncommissioned officer selection and training in the face of modern war, but little attention had been paid to his proposals. Now, faced with the unprecedented challenges of world war with its heavy casualties, especially among company grade officers, the U.S. Army, under Pershing's prodding, took steps to enhance the status and role of the sergeant. Like his fellows in Allied armies, the American sergeant would be expected to take over command of platoons or companies in combat when necessary.

EVOLUTION OF TRANSFERS IN GRADE

Since 1912 several regiments of the regular Army had been stationed overseas as so-called "colonial," or permanent, garrisons. The permanent assignment of certain units to the several foreign stations had been proposed in 1911 and formally adopted in 1912.[1] Duty stations ranged all the way from Hawaii, the newly acquired Canal Zone, and the recently conquered Philippines, to an imperial foothold on mainland China at Tientsin. Although commissioned officers were regularly rotated between these garrisons and home service, noncommissioned officers had no such privilege, except through transfer to a stateside unit and reenlistment there as privates. Former sergeants major, first sergeants, and other senior noncommissioned officers had alternated between home service and foreign duty simply by remaining with their regiments when these units were moved. These men had been compensated for extended periods of foreign duty and credited for "double time," that is, two years credit toward retirement for each year spent abroad. However, this practice was discontinued when the foreign garrison policy went into effect around the turn of the century, leaving noncommissioned officers assigned to overseas garrisons with no choice but to remain with their units if they wished to retain their stripes.[2]

The desirability of providing some relief for these men was first brought to the War Department's attention by two company commanders, Captain Dana T. Merrill, of the 10th Infantry stationed in the Canal Zone, and Captain John Mc. A. Palmer, then with the 15th Infantry in Tientsin. The department responded by canvassing commanders of overseas garrisons as to the effect the permanent stationing of units overseas was having on reenlistments. Replies revealed that many able noncommissioned officers of long and excellent service were being lost to the Army because of their unwillingness to commit themselves to indefinite overseas service simply to keep their chevrons. For example, the commanding officer of the 24th Infantry in the Philippines replied that of his noncommissioned officers scheduled to complete their enlistments in November of 1914, 90 percent of them would not reenlist. The main reason given for not doing so among those men who desired to remain in the service was that the choice between remaining overseas indefinitely or returning to home station as privates was intolerable, and therefore a deterrent to reenlistment.[3]

Rather than tamper with long-established tradition, the Army staff sidestepped the issue by recommending only that the appropriations bill for the Army for the fiscal year 1915 restore double-time credit for overseas service, provided, however, that no enlisted man should be retired under this provision whose actual total period of service was less than twenty years. Furthermore, commanding officers of overseas regiments were to report the probable number of noncommissioned officers above the grade of corporal, with three years of continuous service overseas, who would reenlist in their present organizations, provided they could be assured either of a transfer in grade for a period of three years to an organization of their own arm stationed in the United States, or of an equal period of detached service in the United States.[4]

The Army staff remained opposed to the principle of transfer in grade on the ground that the men concerned might not be acceptable to their immediate superiors in their new units. The staff agreed that the efficiency of a noncommissioned officer was a matter better left to the judgment of his immediate commanding officer, and that such transfers, by bringing in men with their stripes from another unit, would have an adverse effect on unit morale.[5]

In taking this position, the staff recognized that regimental, battalion, and particularly company commanders would object to surrendering their time-honored privilege of selecting and training from among their own men their own sergeants and other noncommissioned officers and of using this as a means of encouraging efficiency and discipline within their units.[6]

Transfer in rank from one unit or duty station to another had long been the sole privilege of commissioned officers. The Army also detailed officers from one unit to another without, however, removing them from the roster of their original regiment. For some time, however, this practice had also been followed for senior noncommissioned officers with highly specialized skills in the ordnance department, quartermaster corps, coast artillery, medical corps, and signal corps from station to station or post to post. For noncommissioned officers of the combat arms, however, there was no such opportunity. The number of appeals and complaints to the War Department from men so disadvantaged left no doubt on the eve of the First World War that a solution to the problem had to be found if the Army was to retain many of its most experienced men of the combat arms.[7]

By early 1914 the Army at last came up with a partial solution to this problem. However, it only applied to senior noncommissioned officers of the Philippines garrison. Henceforth, these men were to be selected by the adjutant general for overseas duty from a roster of eligible senior noncommissioned officers. Those returning from the Philippines were to be detailed to vacancies created by the transfer of their reliefs to overseas duty. The purpose of this measure, however, was solely to maintain the Philippines garrison. By no means had the Army adopted on a servicewide basis the principle of unrestricted transfer in grade from unit to unit. This did not come until the United States entered the war, and then only as a wartime expedient used with caution.

With the entry of the United States into the First World War in April 1917, the nation mobilized the regular Army, the National Guard, and, through the draft, a national army. Out of this *levée en masse* a homogenized organization emerged for a brief time—the Army of the United States. In a general order published in August 1918 as the American Expeditionary Force (AEF) prepared to join the Allied offensive on the Western Front, the Army Chief of Staff, General Peyton C. March, declared that "This country has but one Army—the United States Army." All distinctive appellations, such as regular Army, Reserve Corps, National Guard, and National Army were discontinued, and the single term United States Army was exclusively used. Temporary promotions in the regular Army and appointments in its enlisted reserve corps were also discontinued, and were to be made only in the Army of the United States. Commissioned officers and enlisted men were henceforth transferred from one organization to another as the interests of the service required.[8]

At least for the duration, noncommissioned officers, regardless of the source of their warrants, could, at least in theory, be transferred and remain in grade. Yet, whenever during the war there was any challenge to the company commander's traditional prerogative to select his own noncommissioned officers, the Army staff had been quick to reject it. For example, when a suggestion was made in 1918 to improve the quality of noncommissioned officers above the grade of corporal by appointing them at large from the brigade or division on the basis of competitive examination in divisionwide noncommissioned officers' schools, the staff dismissed it as "too radical a change at the present time."[9]

Inertia and tradition combined to defeat the staff's policy even though the early months of mobilization, training, and movement overseas in late 1917 and early 1918 had demonstrated that the traditional practice of noncommissioned officer selection and training had failed to produce both the quality and quantity of noncommissioned officers required for modern warfare. This was substantiated by an inspector general's report in June 1918, which observed that "in no part of our training has there been so pronounced a weakness as in the noncommissioned officer personnel."[10] The report went on to condemn the practice as poor and inefficient even as it had functioned in peacetime.

TRAINING NONCOMMISSIONED OFFICERS FOR COMMISSIONS

As it had in the nation's previous wars the question of commissioning senior noncommissioned officers again became a lively issue. When the Army staff began to study Allied experience during the war's first two years, it soon became evident that trench warfare would exact a heavy toll among junior officers. Although it appeared logical, as it had during the Civil War, to draw upon experienced noncommissioned officers as a source of company-grade officers, the Army staff was reluctant to open the floodgates of commissions to men from the ranks. Nevertheless, when it appeared likely that the United States would eventually enter the war, the staff began to study the feasibility, in the event of mobilization, of selecting from among the regular Army noncommissioned officers those men deemed capable of being trained to serve as commissioned officers of the militia or the reserves.[11]

Early in 1916, at the secretary of war's direction, the Chief of Staff queried the various department commanders to obtain their reactions to a proposal made by Major General John F. Bell, then commanding general of the Western Department. General Bell in a letter to the adjutant general of the Army had pointed out that approximately 20 percent of the regular Army's noncommissioned officers had, in his opinion, the potential for commissioned service in wartime, and should be so trained. They would be, in Bell's words, a significant asset "of immense value to the United States Army." In support of his contention, Bell cited the records of many noncommissioned officers, both regular and volunteer, who had served as commissioned officers in the Philippine Constabulary and Philippine Scouts, or in the U.S. Volunteer Regiments during the Spanish-American War.[12]

Comments received by the Chief of Staff concerning Bell's proposal disclosed that not all his colleagues shared his confidence in or evaluation of the intrinsic worth of the regular Army noncommissioned officer corps. Brigadier General Malcolm M. Macomb, then commandant of the War College, suggested that all commanders of the various service schools first be canvassed as to their views. General Macomb also remarked that some noncommissioned officers might be able to perform useful service as members of the Officer's Reserve Corps on duty with drafted men.[13]

General Macomb's suggestion was readily accepted by the secretary of war, and letters went out immediately to commandants of all service schools and chiefs of the several staff corps. Each respondent was directed to address himself to three questions: whether the special training recommended by Bell be given at the noncommissioned officer's home station or at a central school or academy; the scope of the training and the amount of time to be devoted to it; and the awards of incentives to be given noncommissioned officers (extra pay to graduates, or a commission in the Officers' Reserve Corps, or both).[14]

Among the earliest replies was a favorable one from Brigadier General John P.

Wisser, commanding general of the Hawaiian Department. He declared that the training Bell proposed would fully utilize the latent abilities of the noncommissioned officers. It would if adopted, Wisser added, eventually replace the traditional system of promoting outstanding noncommissioned officers from the ranks. Although Wisser readily acknowledged that the old system had produced some able company commanders, it had failed to produce officers with the education needed for further professional development beyond that rank.[15]

Resurrecting a long-quiescent Uptonian theme and elaborating on Bell's proposal, General Wisser also observed that the experience of European armies suggested the desirability of establishing permanent schools for the general education of noncommissioned officers. At such schools, Wisser continued, the students would be separated from routine Army duties and given opportunities for study and intellectual development that would supply the broader educational background needed if they were eventually to compete with West Point graduates.

In contrast with General Wisser's enthusiastic endorsement and elaboration of General Bell's proposal for noncommissioned officer education for commissioned service, the governing board of the coast artillery schools expressed a deep-seated doubt concerning the academic potential of most senior noncommissioned officers, although the coast artillery corps had some of the most highly trained noncommissioned officers in the service. The board was skeptical of whether these soldiers, able and experienced though they might be, would be capable of meeting the academic standards envisioned by Bell and Wisser. Instead, the board recommended that such training should be broadened to include not only noncommissioned officers, but all young enlisted men who could pass the examination required by the War Department General Order 64, 1915.[16]

The board's recommendations suggest that it believed that the bulk of the students should be young men with educational backgrounds generally superior to that of the average career noncommissioned officer. As a matter of fact, the board rejected the adoption of Wisser's two-year course for noncommissioned officers.

The commandant of the Army schools at Ft. Leavenworth was even less sanguine than the coast artillery board over the proposal to educate career noncommissioned officers for commissions. First of all, the commandant had serious doubts, as had the coast artillery board, concerning the accuracy of Bell's estimate that 20 percent of the noncommissioned strength of the line constituted suitable material for commissioned service—regular or reserve.[17] The commandant declared that over the past few years experience had demonstrated it was exceedingly difficult to find material among enlisted men for efficient noncommissioned, let alone commissioned, officers. Among the reasons for this state of affairs, the commandant observed, were short terms of enlistment and permanent localization of regiments. In some cases men made 1st sergeant even during their first term of enlistment. Although some of these men admittedly had the potential for commissioned service, most lacked, in the commandant's opinion, the training and experience that had marked the noncommissioned officer of an earlier day. A tendency to look back on an assumed "golden age" on the western frontier, when all soldiers were first-class men and all noncommissioned officers outstanding, although lacking a factual basis, was a common attitude among many senior officers in the decades preceding the First World War.

In the commandant's opinion, War Department General Order 64 was the only suitable road to a commission for capable enlisted men, and there was therefore no need to adopt General Bell's proposal. However, noncommissioned officer schools authorized for regiment might, stated the commandant, be expanded in scope to include a preparatory course for the examination provided for in General Order 64. Such a course, he believed, would give ample opportunity to deserving and ambitious noncommissioned officers and other enlisted men to rise in their profession, while remaining on duty with their parent organization where their services were always needed.[18]

Even stronger adverse comment on Bell's proposal came from within his own department. The signal corps' aviation school's commandant, Colonel William A. Glassford, observed that his experience and study of the lessons of war had convinced him that educated young men, rather than senior and experienced noncommissioned officers, made the best junior officers. Furthermore, it was his belief that the educational and physical standards of the regular Army would have to be greatly improved before a significant number of candidates for commissions could be drawn from among the enlisted men.[19]

Neither conscription nor worn-out recruiting practices, Glassford added, would fill the Army's ranks with sufficient noncommissioned officers of the caliber needed for commissioned service. There should be, he continued, but one door open to enter the Army as a commissioned officer, and that was the military academy at West Point.[20]

Eventually Congress passed legislation providing for the appointment of a total of two hundred noncommissioned officers of the regular Army to West Point over a period of years. This, most senior officers hoped, would obviate the necessity of establishing special schools for the training of noncommissioned officers and other enlisted men for commissioned service, as Bell had suggested.[21]

As the United States moved steadily toward participation in the war in Europe, it became evident that even the adoption of Bell's scheme would be unable to supply the National Army with sufficient company-grade officers demanded by wartime mobilization. As Bell's critics had frequently pointed out, the bulk of the Army's younger commissioned officers in wartime would come not from the ranks of senior noncommissioned officers, but generally from among the college-trained men who would, it was expected, flock to the colors in large numbers with the entry of the nation in the war.

Combat experience on the Western Front eventually demonstrated that high attrition among company-grade officers would be met by able noncommissioned officers stepping in to fill the gap. Rather than commissioning large numbers of noncommissioned officers from the regular Army, the staff eventually provided leadership training that would enable senior noncommissioned officers to understudy and in time of emergency step in for a fallen platoon leader or company commander.

When the United States finally entered the world war, the task of selecting and training sufficient noncommissioned officers to train the rank and file and to supervise them on a day-to-day basis became second only to the challenge of training officers to command the new army. To this task the Army turned, even as had the British two years before, when Lord Kitchener's "new armies" of volunteers assembled for training. This training period had been plagued, as was that of the Americans, by an initial lack of experienced officers and noncommissioned officers. Yet within a year these battalions and regiments marched off to war on the Western Front to fight in the first battles of the Somme. The Americans during their training, however, had the advantage of drawing upon British and French battle experience gained since 1915.

SELECTING AND TRAINING NONCOMMISSIONED OFFICERS FOR THE NEW ARMIES

In May 1917, shortly after the April declaration of war, Congress passed both the so-called National Defense Act and the Selective Service Act, authorizing the president both to increase the regular Army significantly and to raise a national army of citizen soldiers through the draft. Despite opposition on the part of the general staff's War College (Plans) Division to a further increase in regular Army strength, the War Department ordered significant increases in regular Army regiments. This meant that instead of releasing officers and noncommissioned officers of the regular Army to assist in the training of the newly raised citizen army, the latter would be forced to draw upon its own resources for training as it had during the Civil War. In the words of a member of that planning staff, "this would repeat the folly of 1861 in 1917."[22]

The War Department decision meant, among other things, that the citizen army would be responsible for the selection and training of thousands of noncommissioned officers. To help meet this demand, the staff combed the retired lists to find noncommissioned officers suitable for recall to active duty until such time as additional noncommissioned officers could be selected and trained. By early 1918, more than 648 retired noncommissioned officers had been recalled to active duty under the provisions of Section 7 of the National Defense Act of 1916 to assist in the training of conscripts. Additional noncommissioned officers, but of untested potential, were expected from the officers' training camps—for those men who failed to complete the course were usually appointed noncommissioned officers in the Army of the United States before being assigned to units.[23]

Recall of retirees and the enlistment of dropouts from the officers' training programs, however, could supply only a small percentage of the number of noncommissioned officers needed for the million-man plus National Army. Although the traditional practice of selection and training noncommissioned officers by the company commander was slow and cumbersome in terms of wartime requirements, it was, nevertheless, the method most widely used, for it conformed with long-standing tradition. Training was on the job, in which a potential noncommissioned officer understudied an experienced noncommissioned officer. This was supplemented by a series of privately printed training manuals designed "to assist the noncommissioned officer . . . by placing before him in brief and compact order a comprehensive idea of the scope of his duties and responsibilities."[24]

These manuals told the prospective noncommissioned officer not only what to do, but how to do his job. Army regulations supplemented these manuals with information concerning current changes in practice and procedure. Appearing between 1902 and 1917, these manuals were essentially books of instruction telling the noncommissioned officer, from corporal to sergeant major, what his duties were in garrison and in the field and how to perform them. The first of this series of manuals to appear had been Captain Stewart's *Handbook for Noncommissioned Officers of Infantry*, published in 1903. Eleven years later the War Department itself entered the field with the publication in 1914 of a somewhat more comprehensive *Manual for Noncommissioned Officers and Privates of Infantry of the Organized Militia and Volunteers of the United States*. In 1917 this publication was superseded by a *Manual for Noncommissioned Officers and Privates of Infantry of the Army of the United States*. There was little difference between the 1914 and 1917 editions save for a citation of Article of War No. 65 in the 1917 manual cautioning enlisted men about insubordinate conduct toward noncommissioned officers—a fitting caveat as the U.S. Army prepared for war. Distribution of the first 400,000 copies began in mid-June of that year, shortly after the United States entered the war. Deliveries on the basis of twenty-six copies per lettered company began at once. Although these handbooks were in the popular American tradition of self-help, it soon became evident that on-the-job training combined with the study of these manuals would not produce the large numbers of noncommissioned officers required by the National Army.

Nevertheless, because of their widespread distribution and use, these manuals had some value, for they told the user much about the Army's perception of the noncommissioned officer's role. In each the role of the infantry noncommissioned officer, which accounted for the overwhelming number of noncommissioned officers, was perceived primarily as assisting the officers of the company "in the instruction, discipline, and care of the other enlisted men." Under the general supervision of commissioned officers, the noncommissioned officer was regarded as the primary instructor in the school of the soldier.

The manuals described an infantry company's roster during the prewar years as consisting of the 1st sergeant, the quartermaster sergeant, four to six line sergeants, and six to ten corporals. Upon the shoulders of the line sergeants fell the

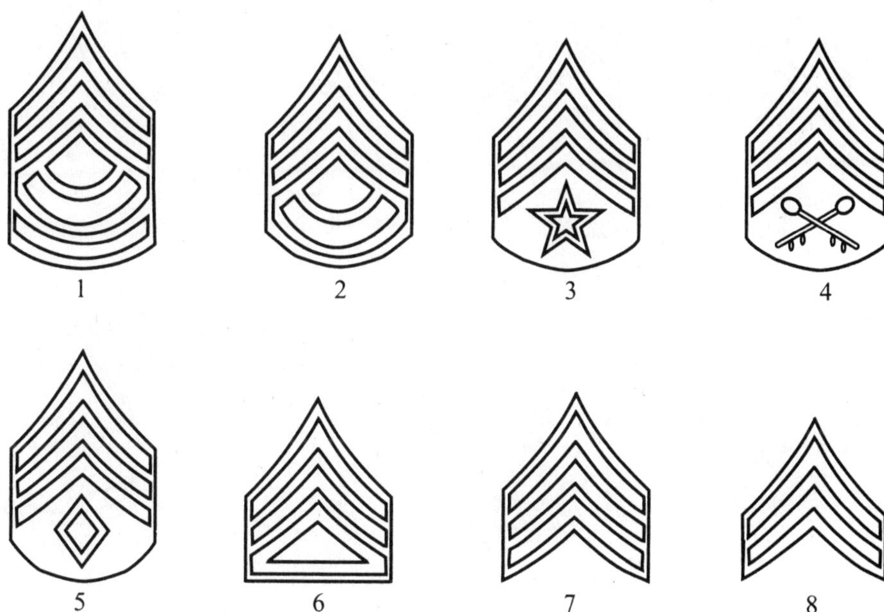

1. Regimental Sergeant Major 2. Battalion/Squadron Sergeant Major 3.Color Sergeant 4. Drum Major 5. 1st Sergeant 6. Company Supply Sgt. 7. Sergeant 8. Corporal

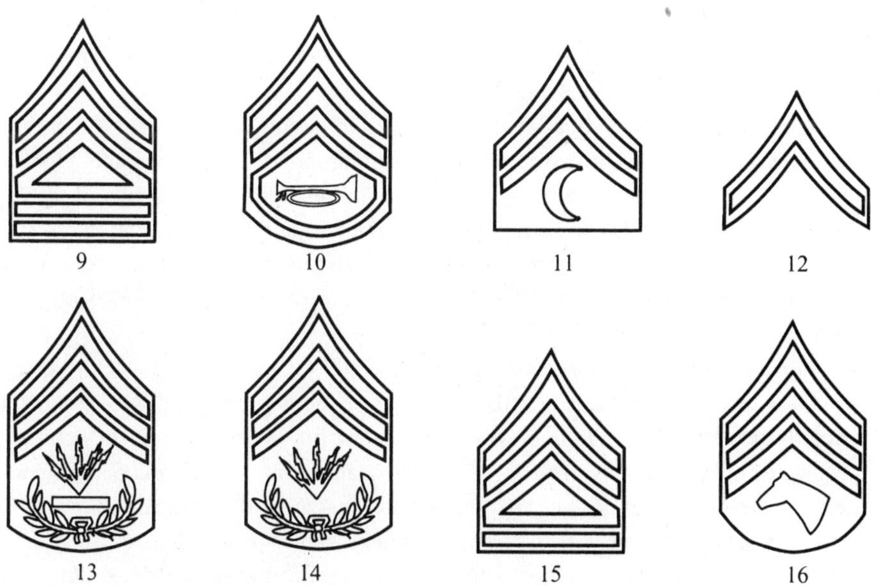

9. Regimental Supply Sergeant. 10. Sergeant of Field Music 11. Mess Sergeant 12. Lance Corporal 13. Electrician Sergeant 1st Class 14. Electrician Sergeant 2nd Class 15. Battalion Supply Sergeant 16. Stable Sergeant

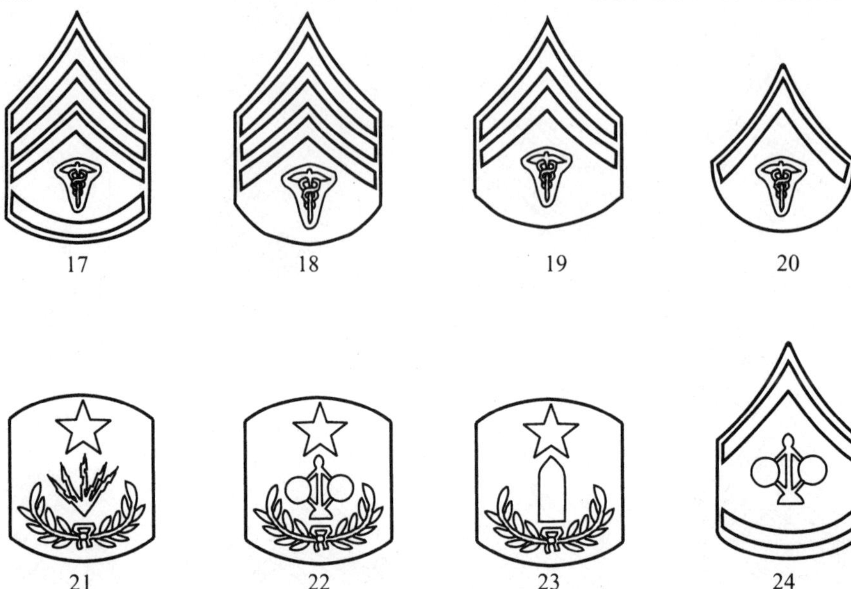

17. Sergeant, 1st Class, Medical Corps 18. Sergeant, MC 19. Corporal, MC 20. Lance Corporal, MC 21. Master Electrician, Coast Artillery Corps 22. Engineer, CAC 23. Master Gunner, CAC 24. Fireman, CAC

task of training and maintaining the integrity of the squads in combat. The squad leader—a corporal—assisted the sergeant.*

Standing as he always had at the apex of this hierarchy, was the 1st sergeant, still selected by the company commander from among the line sergeants "for his excellence of character, capacity to command the respect and obedience of the enlisted men as well as for his intelligence, efficiency, and military bearing." It was he who assisted the company commander in the discipline, instruction, and administration of the company. Moreover, in the absence of the commissioned officers, he took over command.[25]

Another wartime-generated change was the role of the quartermaster sergeant, who had traditionally combined the functions of both supply and mess sergeant. Directly responsible to the company commander for all government or company property, he kept the property books for all quartermaster and ordnance property held by the company. He had also immediate charge of the company kitchen, its storerooms, and the mess hall. Company cooks and men detailed to assist them were under his supervision, but with wartime mobilization all of these duties in-

* In addition to the corporal, each squad contained seven privates.

creased to such an extent that the tasks were now divided between two men, a supply sergeant and a mess sergeant, thus abolishing the rank of quartermaster sergeant.

As wartime training progressed it soon became evident that traditional doctrine contained in the current training manuals and army regulations was insufficient guidance to prepare both commissioned and noncommissioned officers for trench warfare on the Western Front. To make up for this deficiency, Allied training missions began arriving in late 1917 in the United States to provide instruction by men experienced in trench warfare. Assigned to divisional training camps, each mission assisted in tactical training, including instruction in the new tactics and weapons then in use among the Allied armies on the Western Front. In 1915–1916 the British "new armies" had in a similar fashion also drawn upon the battle wisdom of instructors who had survived months of combat at the Front.[26]

The experience of the 7th Division with these Allied training missions was typical. In December 1917 six British and two French officers, each accompanied by a noncommissioned officer, arrived at the division's training camp in Tennessee to begin instruction in the use and care of the automatic rifle and machine gun, gas defense, use of the bayonet and trench mortar, construction of field fortifications, and scouting and patrolling. One officer and two noncommissioned officers from each regiment attended the courses, which lasted from one to six weeks.[27]

Because of the relatively small numbers of Allied instructors involved, the course of study was presented first to the division cadre who in turn trained the recruits. As had been the practice during the Civil War, the cadre spent a good deal of their free time preparing themselves to pass on the new information in preparation for the reception and training of the thousands of men with no previous military experience.[28]

The bearing and skill of many of these visiting noncommissioned officers often attracted favorable mention among American officers. In the words of Major General John F. O'Ryan, commanding general of the 27th Infantry Division, Sergeant Major William Tector of the Leinster Regiment was one of the most experienced instructors of the British army gymnastic corps. His natural ability as an instructor "was so exceptional as to call for some mention. He possessed real qualities of leadership, in that the men developed for him a real affection, although when on duty he was exacting and strenuous in his comments and criticism." Tector had been wounded several times during the war, and this bestowed on him, as it did on many of the foreign instructors, a certain glamor for the young men of the division who were being trained by him.[29]

Through this training assistance, the Americans were able to avoid mistakes such as the British had made when they drilled the "new armies" in the tactics of the Boer War—where an entire battalion formed sections and deployed in extended order, each company led by its commander, with the colonel at the head of the battalion. As late as 1915, British volunteers were still being trained to advance at the walk in open order, and to regard the bayonet as their principal weapon. Such outdated tactics helped to account for high casualties incurred by the British in the war's first two years.[30]

By the time the training program was completed, a total of 167 British commissioned and 165 noncommissioned officers and approximately the same number of French personnel, both commissioned and noncommissioned, had been assigned to various divisions throughout the United States.[31]

Important as this foreign training assistance had been to the existing divisions, it did little to solve the more important problem, which was that of training sufficient noncommissioned officers and specialists for the rapidly growing National Army. As the Allied armies braced themselves in the spring of 1918 for what was expected to be the last great German offensive on the Western Front, the secretary of war directed intensification of noncommissioned officer training by "all regular regiments of infantry in the United States, not yet in divisions." They were to begin at once intensive training of a large number of men, including noncommissioned officers, clerks, cooks, mechanics, and buglers. Each of the twenty-four infantry regiments involved was to develop noncommissioned officers and specialists for at least one additional regiment.[32]

Later, in June 1918, this training was expanded to include the Puerto Rican infantry regiment and all National Army cavalry regiments not yet assigned to the divisions. What was noteworthy about this action is that it was a necessary, though belated, first step in the arms toward taking noncommissioned officer training out from under the company and making it a responsibility of higher echelons, in this case the regiment or division. Each regiment was encouraged to organize a school for the training of noncommissioned officers. All enlisted men presumed to have the necessary intelligence or education to serve in noncommissioned or specialists' grades were urged to attend.[33]

Some regiments, nevertheless, elected to retain the traditional method of on-the-job training by selecting understudies for the noncommissioned staff at regimental headquarters. At the 2d Infantry headquarters, for example, the regimental headquarters staff was duplicated by selected men placed under the current noncommissioned staff for instruction in their duties. The companies were to do the same by selecting an understudy for each of the major noncommissioned positions. There were acting 1st, supply, and mess sergeants, one company clerk, two buglers, and four cooks. These men were actually to take over those positions within their respective companies under the direct supervision of the company officers and the incumbent noncommissioned officer. A part of this training was centralized by requiring all student noncommissioned officers to attend a prescribed weekly course of instructions at the regimental level. In the cases of the acting 1st, mess, and supply sergeants, each company was also to publish orders announcing that these men were serving in these capacities.[34]

Other units—for example the 308th Cavalry Regiment at Camp Harry J. Jones at Douglas, Arizona—centralized training at the very start by setting up regimental schools for the different positions. There was a school for 1st sergeants and troop clerks with a course of instruction consisting of twenty-four one-hour periods. A similar school was created for troop and regimental supply sergeants. Their instruction consisted of sixteen one-hour periods. Similar schools were established for cooks, troop saddlers, horseshoers, stable sergeants, and stable orderlies. Carried away by a zeal for wider education, this regiment even established an enlisted men's school under the direction of the unit chaplain. This was to be a three-month course in such general education subjects as reading, writing, spelling and speaking English, elementary arithmetic, geography, and history of the United States. Two men from each troop were detailed to attend the school.[35]

Other units followed somewhat different patterns. The 10th Infantry at Camp Custer, Michigan, established regimental training schools under the supervision of three commissioned and ten noncommissioned officers. Beginning in mid-July 1918, the schools had been operating for less than a month when the regiment was transferred to a division and split to form the 10th and 77th Infantry regiments. More than half of the students were immediately assigned to the new regiment as noncommissioned officers. The remainder, however, continued their training in divisional schools, for each of the companies was still short about one half of its authorized noncommissioned strength.[36]

The effect of this procedure may be seen in the history of the 7th Division whose enlisted strength constantly changed during its formative and training periods as the regiments were "called upon to furnish nucleus after nucleus of trained and partially trained personnel for the formation of other units." Enlisted personnel were supplied in this way to the 78th and 88th divisions and to the 2d and 3d Division trains, as well as to the ordnance, quartermaster, and other services. It was one of the trying periods in the 55th Infantry Regiment's history, as the "yeast" of the "Old Army" was spread thinner and thinner to leaven the "whole" for the days to come.[37]

An example of this "leaven" is found in the words the author of a popular post-war novel put into the mouth of a regular Army sergeant speaking to a group of replacements:

> "Now listen," began the sergeant, "you're going up to join a unit of the regular army. They don't get drunk there, and they don't go around slugging each other. Orders are given to be obeyed and the men obey them. The noncommissioned officers are respected, and they conduct themselves so as to be worthy of that respect. And there's none of this sneaking off and passing the buck and soaking yourself with rum all the time. I'm telling you this so you won't get in the mill [stockade] the minute you land. You're going to join an outfit where they soldier, and if you want to keep yourself in right, you've got to soldier likewise. Get me?"[38]

Needless to say, in the draft-based National Army such leaven—in spite of retired NCOs recalled to active duty, occasional NCOs detailed from other duties, and some respected foreign "advisers"—remained insufficient to reproduce regular Army standards throughout the service. The Army of the United States had perforce to rely upon the many *ad hoc* unit training programs to produce the needed noncommissioned officers. Under such conditions it was not surprising that wartime experience disclosed that while quantitative goals were met, qualitative goals were not. The reason for this shortfall was that most wartime noncommissioned officer training, in spite of all the suggestions and plans, was either traditional on-the-job training or *ad hoc* unit schooling, both of which were short-term. Such training, partly because of the lack of the time required for it to be more thorough, had stressed the strictly vocational aspects of the noncommissioned officers' duties. It neglected to emphasize their role as leaders of men and to enhance their status in the hierarchy of command. Yet trench warfare required emphasis on the latter two aspects of noncommissioned officer training.

As one historian has observed, out of the major battles along the Western Front during the war's first three years, one perception emerged: that modern battle was the fragmentation of spatial and temporal unities.[39] The Allied armies, however, did not all gain this wisdom at the same time. For example, it took the horror of Verdun to teach the French to break up their advance into small groups. Led by a noncommissioned officer, each small group of infantrymen took advantage of the mist along a river and every fold in the ground while at the same time giving covering fire to its neighbors. Mastery of these tactics enabled the French with modest casualties to overrun the German trenches in their sector during the first battle of the Somme, while the British units, who had yet to learn these lessons, were decimated even before reaching the German lines.[40]

Such tactics, however, placed a far greater burden of leadership upon small-unit commanders—company commissioned and noncommissioned officers—a burden far greater than their traditional training had prepared them to assume. Like their British Allies, the Americans were slow to adopt these tactics. But in the coming battles, the fact that American small-unit commanders, both commissioned and noncommissioned, so distinguished themselves was perhaps more a tribute to their innate courage and resourcefulness than to what little leadership training they had received before the battle.

Quite understandably the Americans entering combat in the war's last year had not yet made these tactics their own, although some aspects of the Civil War and the later Indian Wars had foreshadowed them. In any case, it took the British and French at least two years of fighting on the Western Front to adopt and master these small-unit tactics.

As the war increasingly brought American officers into close and frequent contact with their counterparts among the British and French forces, it became increasingly evident that trench warfare placed far greater demands upon the American noncommissioned officer than he was prepared to meet. Observed differences in the training, status, and role of the American noncommissioned officers and their Allied counterparts soon became a subject of widespread comment among officers of the American Expeditionary Force. A random sampling of company and field grade officers suggests how these differences were viewed. Commissioned officers complained that they were too frequently performing tasks better left to noncommissioned officers. Because these comments illustrate so well the consequences of the American approach to noncommissioned officer selection and training, several are cited verbatim.[41]

First lieutenant of engineers: "Appointment of unqualified men, and arbitrary reductions and reductions on account of change of organization should be minimized in the case of noncommissioned officer."

Second lieutenant, infantry: "Promoting noncommissioned officers from strictly their 'drill side' rather than from their ability to lay out work and handle men."

First lieutenant, motorized transportation corps: "It has been my observation, particularly in the A.E.F. but also in this country that officers are very often put in places and in work which does not require an officer. In other words, officers are given work to perform which could be accomplished by a noncommissioned officer just as well. The doing of this does not work for economy and lowers the position of the noncommissioned personnel. The noncommissioned officers should be given *more power and prestige* [emphasis added]."

First lieutenant, infantry: "There is not sufficient distinction made between noncommissioned officers and privates to cause and maintain proper dignity of the noncommissioned office and usually the noncom himself does not take the proper pride in his office mainly for the reasons stated."

First lieutenant, infantry: "Noncommissioned officers should be given such privileges and treatment so as to make a more distinct difference between the noncommissioned officers and the private. In this way more efficient work can be done by the noncommissioned officers and a higher degree of discipline maintained."

Second lieutenant, engineers: "It is my opinion that noncommissioned officers are not permitted to exercise their initiative sufficiently and that those of higher grade especially should have a wider scope of authority. Closer co-operation between these men and their officers would in my opinion be beneficial to the service."

Captain, field artillery: "The lack of responsibility put on noncommissioned officers, the lack of separation, and of special privileges given them so that they may feel their responsibility. This would also give the private more incentive to work."

First lieutenant, artillery: "Too little responsibility given to noncommissioned officers. [The phrase] 'An officer must be present' attached to many orders takes responsibility from noncoms and causes laziness and lack of initiative on their part. Our noncoms cannot be compared to those of English or French armies for *responsibility, initiative or ability* [emphasis added]."

Second lieutenant, infantry: "One, namely that while our Noncommissioned Officers theoretically have unlimited power and responsibility, practically they have not through a combination of circumstances. Very few of them realize their responsibility and value to the service (this probably is more true in army during past war than in old regular army) and too much fraternization between Noncommissioned Officers and Privates. The value of this is shown by the discipline of the British Army where the noncommissioned officer realizes and uses his responsibility to the betterment of the service."

Captain, infantry: "Training of noncommissioned officers is slighted almost to the point of neglect. Officers, from the Company Commander down, [are] obliged to spend fifty percent of their time and energy in doing the work of noncommissioned officers."

Second lieutenant, field artillery: "Non-coms should have more experience in handling men, rather than officers. They did not have a fair chance to develop initiative, consequently in many cases they fell down."

Lieutenant, machine gun battalion: "Sergeants and Corporals come into a position of responsibility and leadership in action, which their limited peace status poorly prepares them for."

Captain, machine gun battalion: "Our noncommissioned officers are not paid enough or given privileges above the privates that should add the proper dignity to their position."

First lieutenant, artillery: "There is not enough differences [*sic*] in the pay of a private and a noncommissioned officer to cause the men to work for promotion and after promotion to be more loyal."

First lieutenant, infantry: "Too much petty detail work given to officers, work that could be done by non-coms. Noncommissioned officers are not given enough responsibility and deprived of initiative. Officers tied down and restricted by too many petty restrictions. I know one true instance where a Colonel had to get a pass from a sergeant to get off a train and get something to eat."

Second lieutenant, infantry: "Noncommissioned officers should bear more authority. Officers do work of corporal. Non-coms are not sufficiently respected by men and backed by officers. Non-coms are given little or no authority."

Second lieutenant, field artillery: "Too little effort made to develop initiative and responsibility in noncommissioned officers. Too many officers doing corporal's jobs."

Second lieutenant, field artillery: "Higher rate of pay for Sergeants and more prestige for all noncommissioned officers, making their incentive greater and their position more authoritative. A Corporal should receive more than $3 more than a 1st cl. Pvt."

Second lieutenant, infantry: "Noncommissioned officers of infantry are not paid in proportion to the responsibility or intelligence expected of them, have few privileges over the grade of private and their authority suffers in consequence."

The question of the role and status of the noncommissioned officer involved not only the problem of adequate pay but, as can be seen from the foregoing comments, also the overall relationship of commissioned officers to enlisted men.

While a concern for maintaining this relationship at a satisfactory level had historically been an essential element of command, the changing social climate within American society since the turn of the century had heightened this concern. Then, too, there were traditional American attitudes toward authority as reflected in the "letters" of a private to his girlfriend. "I don't like the sargent [sic]," he wrote. "I don't like any sargent but this one in particular . . . sarjents have an idea that if they don't get a lot of fellas to go out to drill with them they don't look popular."[42] While admittedly a humorous comment on Army life, such letters reflected ingrained attitudes that added challenge to the noncommissioned officer's tasks.

For the most part, however, men appointed to noncommissioned grades regarded their elevation not as a relief from the manual labor of the private soldier, but as a serious responsibility. Such a man was Cyril B. Mosher, of the 12th Field Artillery of the 2d Division, who had left Yale University to enlist in the Army. After having been appointed lance corporal, Mosher wrote in a letter to his mother that his duties now consisted of drilling recruits every morning, now in semaphore, calisthenics, dismounted and artillery drill. "This rank," he wrote, "entitles me to my first stripe. I am no longer a buck private but a *noncommissioned officer* [emphasis added]." Mosher was eventually promoted to the rank of sergeant, chief of a gun section. While serving in this capacity he was killed in action in June 1918 during the battle of Château Thierry.[43]

While treating men to preserve their self-respect was generally deemed vital to good morale, many young officers entering active duty for the first time with temporary wartime commissions had little knowledge of the proper methods of dealing with their enlisted subordinates, especially experienced noncommissioned officers. Frequently these inexperienced officers sought to accomplish through public rebuke what could be more efficiently accomplished through a private talk with the subordinate himself. This problem, however, was not entirely confined to the young and inexperienced company-grade officer, but was found at times in others of more experience. Many senior noncommissioned officers often endured in bitter silence, within the hearing of their subordinates, unmerited rebuke not only from a subaltern, but also from senior officers as well. Nevertheless, repeated injunctions in Army literature, dating from von Steuben's day, had branded such practice destructive of both a noncommissioned officer's status with his men and of his ability to enforce discipline among them.[44]

There was yet another aspect to this problem—the noncommissioned officer himself. The practice of commissioning some outstanding regular Army sergeants to help meet the need for more officers to lead the National Army brought forward as their replacements some who were not up to prewar standards. Many of these were assigned to newly formed divisions; in the case of the 89th Division it was usually two to each company of infantry and battery of artillery. These noncommissioned officers, however, were a valuable help in drilling the new recruits as well as in the preparation of the vast amount of paperwork required of a new organization—work entirely unfamiliar to newly mobilized men. As a class, though, many of these noncommissioned officers did not accommodate themselves well to the new conditions of service with draftees or National Guard units. Those who failed to do so proved not to be as valuable as noncommissioned officers as better-educated and more highly skilled men drafted from civilian life, of which there were a number in every company or battery.[45]

American officers had long been familiar with Kipling's dictum that the noncommissioned man is the backbone of the army, and, in a very general way, acknowledged it as a truism. But as contacts between the American and British forces grew during the war, it soon became apparent that practical day-to-day applications of this dictum in the two armies differed widely. Among the British, the noncommissioned officer had long been given privileges and distinction that set him in a class apart from other enlisted men. This, the British believed, enabled the noncommissioned officers to maintain a degree of authority and prestige that he otherwise would not have. The Americans, on the other hand, partly because of differing historical, social, and political traditions, were reluctant to set apart the noncommissioned officer to that degree and did not attach the same importance, as did the British, to privilege, status, and distinctiveness as props to noncommissioned authority.[46]

As a matter of fact those officers who assigned to their senior noncommissioned officers tasks that traditionally belonged to officers were often severely criticized, although able sergeants were quite capable of performing a wide range of these tasks, such as checking daily rations. Such a situation occurred between a division inspector general and Lieutenant John D. Clark of Battery C, 15th Field Artillery Regiment of the 2d Division. Clark reported the following exchange in a letter to a friend.[47]

> "You have checked the rations, have you not lieutenant?"
>
> "Yes sir."
>
> "Did you do it personally?"
>
> "No sir, I had the mess sergeant check them and report to me. Every other night is consumed in a trip to the guns with ammunition, so I have to rely to some extent on [my] noncommissioned officer."
>
> "Don't you know that according to the regulations of the U.S. Army every officer in command of a body of men is required to check the rations personally?"

In spite of General Pershing's efforts to enhance NCO prestige, Army regulations, such as the case of the visiting inspector general, often discouraged officers from more effectively utilizing those noncommissioned officers who were eager and ready to undertake a wider range of duties and assume a greater role in leadership.

In contrast with American tradition and practice, in the British army the mantle of authority and privilege was placed upon the shoulders even of the most junior noncommissioned officers. For example, from the moment a private soldier received the rank of lance corporal—an acting rank with no increase in pay—he found that an important distinction had been made both in his military and social status. With his military status came an authority he did not have before, as well as a social status conferring upon him an exclusiveness and privilege that set him apart from his fellow soldiers. For example, he was no longer allowed to walk with a private soldier, and in most battalions there was a corporal's mess that he might join. Both corporals' and sergeants' messes were allowed to remain open for one hour after lights out. And the lance corporal, together with all other noncommissioned officers, was allowed the privileges of wearing his bayonet when leaving camp and of returning later than private soldiers.

British noncommissioned officers enjoyed other distinctions as well. For instance, the platoon sergeant did not fix his bayonet when his platoon was paraded for inspection. Moreover, it was the custom for general officers when addressing a battalion on parade to commence by saying "Officers, noncommissioned officers, and men," further exemplifying how the British army recognized the three classes. Such was the status of the sergeant major for example, that a battalion commander, when considering promotions among his noncommissioned officers, would regularly ask his opinion before making a decision. Indeed, it was the sergeant major who set the tone, discipline, and power of command for the battalion's noncommissioned officers. A similar relationship also existed between the sergeant major and other noncommissioned officers at the company level.[48]

Under these circumstances it was not surprising that Allied officers viewed the training, status, and role of the American noncommissioned officer with critical eyes. Both British and French military missions, after visiting the first two American divisions to arrive in France, expressed considerable doubt over the effectiveness of the noncommissioned officers they had observed with these units. The British especially were disturbed over the apparent American failure to set the noncommissioned officer apart from the private soldier, as was the case in the British army. This failure, in British eyes, made it impossible for the noncommissioned officer to enforce discipline and to command the respect and instant obedience of the enlisted men under him. The British insisted that to enhance the noncommissioned officer's prestige and status in the eyes of the troops, the former must be given special privileges denied the other ranks.[49]

During the First World War, with its fantastically high casualty rates among company grade officers, the senior surviving British noncommissioned officer had customarily taken command of the company when all commissioned officers became casualties. Since enlisted men in the British army had been trained to regard the noncommissioned officer as a legitimate leader and in a class by himself, such a transition was relatively easy to make.

In spite of quite different attitudes toward noncommissioned officers, American units in similar circumstances on the Western Front had similar experiences. When all company or platoon officers became casualties, senior noncommissioned officers regularly assumed command and continued the fight with skill and courage. While this was remarkable in view of the significant differences in role and status between the British and American noncommissioned officers, most of the credit for this performance may be traced to General Pershing's emphasis on NCO leadership training following the arrival of the first American units in France. British military missions had observed in earlier visits to two American divisions that the noncommissioned officer seemed to exercise little authority over his men. Part of the reason for this was, the British concluded, the practice of throwing noncommissioned officers and privates together in the field and garrison with little regard for difference in rank. This practice was an outgrowth of the attitudes of commissioned officers in the U.S. Army who tended to look upon their noncommissioned officers as just another category of enlisted men and not as subordinate leaders. Foreign observers generally regarded this practice with dismay, commenting that if in peacetime the noncommissioned officer had not achieved a recognized ascendancy and command over his men and was not regarded by them with respect, the men would not instinctively and unquestionably obey and follow him in times of stress and danger.[50]

Adverse comparisons were even made with Russian noncommissioned officers. For example, an American army attaché reported from Petrograd (St. Petersburg) in June 1916 on his observations of recruit training in the Imperial army that "the noncommissioned officers do all the actual work; rarely an officer may be seen, and then only looking on. . . . I never see friction among them [the soldiers] or toward the noncommissioned officers. All hands are 'trying hard.' We can learn a lesson from the Russian Army noncommissioned officers who are capable, patient, self-reliant; they work or drill rapidly and confidently; they do not pause to correct themselves and then 'do it all over again.' The command 'as you were' does not seem to be used at all."[51]

Even American enlisted men, who one might expect would have the most confidence in the noncommissioned officers closest to them did not, according to some observers, have complete confidence in them. "It is true," wrote the wartime commander of the 27th Division, Major General John F. O'Ryan, "that in most companies noncommissioned officers, with great initiative and determination, took over the command of platoons and even companies, and maintained the fight, but from no source will the testimony be stronger than from enlisted men themselves, of the vital importance in combat of the commissioned officer in whose experience and judgment the men have confidence."[52]

Undoubtedly one of the reasons for this lack of confidence was a widely held perception among enlisted men of the ephemeral quality of the noncommissioned officers' stripes. Often the awarding of stripes could be quite a casual affair, as with Corporal Elmer Straub of the 150th Field Artillery Regiment. On October 20, 1918, Straub was seated in his dugout writing a letter when as he noted in his diary, "Lt. Clift came along and stopped in our home and, after looking around a little, informed me that I was now a sergeant, and that 'Pete' was now a corporal; so after I had addressed my letters I sewed on some chevrons."[53]

But once won, these stripes could as easily be taken away, as an old soldier lamented in a postwar novel: "They come and go, stripes do, like leaves in the trees.

I had 'em all, up to sergeant major, 'n' I lost them all too."[54] The hero of the same novel, Sergeant Eadie, observed philosophically while contemplating the loss of his own stripes, "It's all in the game. They say it's healthy for a man to shed his stripes every so often, like a snake sheds its skin. Anyway, I'd get made again when I get back to my outfit." To which his companion replied, "I'm glad that I'm a buck [private]. Nothin' to lose an' no responsibilities. All I got to do is to look after myself." "You've got the right idea," agreed the sergeant, "the easiest thing I know is getting busted and for eight dollars a month difference, I can't see the advantage."[55]

In a message to the Chief of Staff in April 1918, General Pershing, no doubt stung by adverse comparisons and such unfavorable images, recommended that the question of upgrading the training and increasing the status and responsibility of sergeants be studied by the Army staff because of the likelihood that noncommissioned officers would replace the commissioned officers as unit commanders when the latter became casualties. To this end, Pershing suggested that special schools for sergeants be established immediately throughout the Army for the purpose of upgrading their leadership skills and thereby enhancing their prestige vis-à-vis the other enlisted men. The AEF commander also suggested separate messes for sergeants, thereby minimizing familiarity between senior noncommissioned officers and other ranks.[56]

Such was General Pershing's prestige and authority that within weeks the substance of his recommendations concerning noncommissioned officers had gone out over the secretary of war's signature to each department and division commander. These recommendations pointed toward an important servicewide change in the status and role of the noncommissioned officer, and included stressing the element of responsibility in the training of sergeants, and imbuing them with the habit of command and giving them the schooling and prestige to enable them to replace at once casualties among commissioned officers.

Under this guidance, division and other commanders were enjoined to bring to the attention of organization commanders the great importance of improving the status of noncommissioned officers, particularly of sergeants, and of perfecting their training to the highest possible degree. Separate quarters and messing were to be arranged and sergeants were to be extended special privileges. Fraternization with lower ranks was prohibited.

The duties and responsibilities of sergeants were to be "thoroughly represented to them," and they were to be "encouraged to study all subjects connected with their profession." All these measures were designed "to make the sergeant realize that his position is a responsible one, and to inculcate in him the habit of command. He should be encouraged to give his ideas freely when called upon to do so by his officers."[57]

That high-ranking American officers were not indifferent to these recommendations was manifest in remarks made by a senior officer on Pershing's staff following a visit to the Meuse front. "The problems of leadership," he observed, "were those of the junior officer and the noncommissioned officers. Unless they had been wisely chosen and well trained, nothing in the way of orders from the upper echelons was going to do much to improve on the job they were doing."[58] The training programs initiated under Pershing's orders in the spring of 1918 to enhance the leadership potential of noncommissioned officers acknowledged the validity of this observation. An examination of citations for valor in the remaining months of the war suggests that these training programs, with their emphasis on upgrading noncommissioned officer status and performance, had a positive influence.

Whether this *ad hoc* process of selection and training of a corps of noncommissioned officers was responsible for it or not, the AEF produced some outstanding noncommissioned officers, many of whom received high decorations for their initiative and valor. Few of them, however, distinguished themselves in the public imagination as did Corporal Alvin C. York of Pall Mall, Tennessee. Immortalized by actor Gary Cooper in the 1941 motion-picture version of his wartime exploits,* York has become somewhat of an archetypical noncommissioned hero—a man of few words who shoots straight and does what has to be done.

In fact, York's exploits are worth repeating here because they still stand as one of the finest examples of noncommissioned initiative under fire. During an attack mounted by the 2d Battalion, 328th Infantry, 82d Division, on October 8, 1918, York's unit, Company G, found itself pinned down by enemy machine-gun fire. His commander sent a force of four noncommissioned officers, including York, and thirteen privates to work their way around the enemy positions and silence the fire. During this maneuver, the group surprised a force of about 250 Germans, whom they attacked. Mistaking the seventeen Americans for the vanguard of a much larger force, the Germans began surrendering. As they did so, the enemy machine gunners took both groups under fire, killing all the noncommissioned officers in the party except York.

Shrewdly taking a position close to his prisoners, York returned the enemy fire with devastating accuracy. Afraid of hitting their own men, the German fire was largely ineffectual. After a counterattack led by a German officer failed due to York's coolness and deadly marksmanship, enemy morale collapsed completely. When York's little group finally reached the American lines, it had in tow 3 officer and 129 enlisted prisoners from the German 45th Reserve Division. For his heroism York was awarded the French Croix de Guerre and the American Medal of Honor.[59]

There are countless other examples of noncommissioned officers of the AEF who exercised outstanding initiative and valor in France, although not on a scale to rival those of Corporal York. One was Corporal (later sergeant) Walter Rudy of Company M, 356th Infantry, who on the night of September 2, 1918, found himself escorting a detail carrying a large marmite can of doughnuts to a company

* Mr. Cooper won that year's Academy Award for best actor in the title role.

outpost. When an enemy patrol opened fire on the doughnut escort out of the darkness, Rudy coolly deployed his men and killed one of the enemy before forcing the rest to flee into the night. Corporal Rudy later reported to his sergeant that not a doughnut had been lost.[60]

Perhaps more typical of many noncommissioned officers was Corporal Frank R. Dillman, of the 64th Infantry, 7th Division, whose initial reaction when first made corporal was that he "did not have to do manual labor, which pleased me mightily."[61] Committed to the front quite late in the war, Corporal Dillman was not above a bit of "gold-bricking," nor had he proven himself to be an outstanding leader. However, in all fairness he had little opportunity to show his ability for the war ended shortly after he arrived at the front. His desire to avoid manual labor was reflected in an incident described by Dillman.

> When ordered to deepen some old trenches, the boys virtually refused to work except when a commissioned officer was over them, as they were certain that we would be there only a few days. Since I was a corporal and didn't have to dig, I pretended to direct the digging, walking along the trench whenever the officer was around.

This brief vignette illustrates the lack of leadership on the part of some noncommissioned officers at that stage in the war.

Nevertheless, Dillman seems to have rated pretty well with his sergeants for, at one time, as his company moved into new positions, he was placed in command of "our platoon, since I was senior corporal. I was instructed to find places for the 45 or 50 men to sleep, and the officer walked away," leaving Dillman to exercise his initiative. "We billeted for the night," Dillman continued, "in an old dilapidated French trench, the men sleeping almost anywhere on the ground and on the fire step . . . next morning I was up early, for I felt pretty important with a whole platoon on my hands (all the sergeants had gone to the front to get the lay of the land, as we were due to relieve an outfit of infantry.)"

Eventually Corporal Dillman led his men forward and observed that

> as we were upon the line, Glen Crowley, one of our sergeants, called me to Francis X. Orminski, a corporal. Crowley told Orminski to bring his squad of men with him. We gathered around Sgt. Crowley and another sergeant from the outfit we were to relieve; I think that this was part of the 56th Infantry. This sergeant gave us instructions for placing an out-guard, and told us that there was nothing to worry about, that the Germans were over on that hill about 1,500 yards away, that we were to form a line about 75 yards in front of our company, who by this time were in the dugouts just vacated by the retiring company. Orminski placed his squad in line about 10 to 12 paces apart, their rifles loaded and locked, and the men sitting cross-legged on the ground. . . . Crowley and I sat down behind the largest tree we found handy, leaned against it and tried to sleep. We didn't unroll blanket rolls but froze there in our o'coats.

Their hardships had not long to run though, for

> this was the night of November 10, 1918. At about two o'clock in the morning, Cpl. Orminski woke me up and told me it was my turn to take charge of the guard. . . . I called my sentries in at dawn and went back to the line established by L Company the night before.

Although Dillman did not know it at that time, at eleven o'clock that morning the war ended rather quickly for him and many like him.

However, for Sergeant Jones E. Warrell, an artillery forward observer with the 112th Infantry of the 28th Division (Pennsylvania National Guard), the war ended "not with a whimper but a bang."

On November 11, 1918, Warrell was in charge of a six-man artillery intelligence section of the 112th Infantry, manning an observation post in the church tower of the village of Xammes, France. Warrell described the event in his diary:[62]

> I had just come off duty at 9:15 [A.M.] o'clock and was informed of the glad news [the armistice] by my relief. It didn't seem hardly possible, nor believable. At any rate, safety first, so I stayed inside [a root cellar that the section used for its billet and from which it drew supplies]. About 10 o'clock, the fury of the [Allied] artillery bombardment increased, at which time the enemy firing had practically ceased. Promptly at the stroke of eleven, the din ceased, and a strange quiet came over the country, broken only by cheers and the shooting of flares. The great conflict of all time had ended.

With the coming of the Armistice and the rapid demobilization of the National Army, most noncommissioned officers returned to civilian life carrying with them a treasury of these and similar experiences. For the regular Army noncommissioned officers who had accepted wartime commissions, as well as for those who had been promoted into their places for the duration, widespread personnel turbulence would make it difficult for the Army to do much toward maintaining or building upon the wartime efforts initiated by General Pershing to change the status or role of the noncommissioned officer. The interwar years, therefore, were a period of retrenchment and retrogression. It took another world war to revitalize the movement toward reform and change so briefly tested during the period 1917–1918.

CHAPTER 12
ADJUSTING TO POSTWAR AUSTERITY

America's first experience with global war forced the nation to depend on nationwide conscription on a more comprehensive and larger scale than had been the case during the Civil War.* Then, in spite of a largely unpopular draft, volunteers had still formed the bulk of the Army, at least in the North—the South went to the draft early in the war. In the Civil War, however, regular units remained intact, whereas in World War I regular Army units, long understrength, were greatly diluted by large infusions of raw recruits, draftees, and the promotion of more experienced personnel to staff the many new headquarters and command groups created to control and support the expanded Army of the United States.

For many regular Army senior noncommissioned officers this often meant a temporary wartime promotion to commissioned rank—in some cases even to field grade. And for many junior regular Army noncommissioned officers, there was unforeseen advancement to senior noncommissioned grades, to take the places of the men given wartime commissions. All of this had the effect of diluting and destabilizing the noncommissioned officer corps.

This war-induced upheaval within the regular Army NCO corps also had an impact on the peacetime establishment, generating a similar degree of personnel turbulence aggravated by a series of fiscal measures that reduced the regular Army to a fraction of its wartime strength. Attempts to solve these problems engaged much of the Army staff's attention during the decade of the 1920s. The search for solutions was exacerbated by three factors deeply affecting the regular Army's destiny between the wars: the Army Reorganization Act of June 4, 1920; chronic,

*World War I also saw, for enlisted men, the introduction of serial numbers. The first, Number 1, was issued to a sergeant named Arthur B. Green (or Cream or Crean), February 28, 1918. The last enlisted serial number—RA 68118876—was issued to a Private Alan W. T. Okahara at Honolulu June 30, 1969. Serial numbers for officers were not introduced until June 1921, when General Pershing was issued Number 01; a Captain Russell William Nielson was issued the last officer serial number—OF130621. Effective July 1, 1969, all service members began using their social security account numbers in lieu of service numbers.

crippling, congressionally imposed fiscal restraints; and finally, almost a death blow to the Army, the national trauma of a worldwide economic depression.

POSTWAR REORGANIZATION

The Army Reorganization Act of June 1920 amended the Defense Act of 1916, which had set policy for the Army during the war years, and in the words of John W. Weeks, secretary of war, "marked the beginning of a new era in the service of this [War] Department to the country." Although the legislation failed to provide, as the Army staff had recommended, for either universal military training or for the automatic application of the draft in future emergencies, it did afford a definite basis for proceeding with the postwar reorganization.[1]

Essentially, the Reorganization Act dealt with two broad subjects: the kind of army the nation would support and the internal structure of such an army. With the first, the act—driven by the desire of the people and of Congress to have the cost of the government reduced—opted for the traditional policy of providing for a small regular Army augmented in wartime by a large citizen force, presumably drawn from the National Guard and the reserves. Whereas in the past the nation had extemporized such forces after an emergency arose, this new legislation provided for the peacetime establishment and development of these forces through the voluntary service of citizens of military age.[2]

Concerning the question of the Army's internal structure, the act also sought to deal, among other things, with the impact of technological change upon the enlisted grade structure, which by 1919 had reached crisis proportions. The number of enlisted grades had increased by war's end to such an extent as to cloud the distinction, for pay and prestige purposes, between the noncommissioned officer of the line, who exercised leadership authority, and the increasing numbers of skilled specialists, who performed certain technical and administrative duties but had no leadership authority.[3]

Congress attempted to solve this latter problem in 1920 along three different lines. First was by expanding the warrant officer list beyond the Army mine planter service to include the performance of certain administrative and specialist duties. Second, by prescribing seven standard grades into which all enlisted men could be fitted for the purpose of pay and the establishing of both rank and precedence. And third, by setting up a large number of specialist positions in the lower grades that carried additional pay but without additional rank or authority.[4]

EXPANDING THE WARRANT OFFICER CORPS

By legislation in 1920, Congress expanded the warrant officer corps by authorizing appointment of warrant officers in clerical, administrative, and bandleading activities. This time the expansion was envisioned as a reward for those noncommissioned officers who had served as commissioned officers during World War I as well as for deserving senior noncommissioned officers for whom no higher ranks existed. The War Department also supported this expansion for the purpose of having warrant officers supplant field clerks* to perform certain duties at higher echelons in lieu of commissioned personnel.

Appointment and assignment procedures published in 1920 provided for appointments in the Army at large rather than in specific branches. Assignments were authorized at various headquarters and tactical units for clerical, administrative, and supply duties. In 1921 warrant officers were excluded from performance of duties from which enlisted men were also excluded, such as serving as summary courts-martial officer, defense counsel, officer of the day, and assistant adjutant. The act of 1920 authorized 1,200 warrant officers, but an act of 1922 reduced this number to 600, exclusive of the number of the Army mine planter service, which was fixed at 40. Here the numbers remained for many years. Army bandmasters were also exempt from this ceiling.[5]

Expansion of the warrant officer list in the interwar years served to greatly enhance the noncommissioned officer's image. As had long been the case in the British army, this grade had been initially conceived as a means of rewarding senior noncommissioned officers whose experience and skills, while qualifying them for further advancement, did not, because of age and lack of education, qualify them for commissions. For many years the warrant officer grade in the U.S. Army was regarded both as the apex of an enlisted man's career and as a means of retaining in the service outstanding noncommissioned officers who might otherwise have left it.

However, the creation and expansion of the warrant officer grade took place at the expense of the rank of post noncommissioned officer and of the corps of Army field clerks. As early as 1907 there had been those on the Army staff who advocated the creation of the grade of warrant officer, and in 1911 the House Committee on Military Affairs held hearings, albeit unsuccessful, on a bill providing for the creation of the grade of warrant officer in lieu of that of post noncommissioned officer.[6]

These efforts languished until 1918, when Congress finally authorized the grade to meet the highly specialized requirements of the coast artillery's mine planter service. Two years later, when Congress amended the National Defense Act of 1916 with the passage of the Army Reorganization Act of June 1920, the

*Between 1894 and 1916, civilian personnel of the civil service had performed the clerical work of the Army at higher headquarters. In August 1916, the entire class, known as headquarters clerks, had had their status changed by law from civilian to military. Henceforth they were known as army field clerks. At the same time, Congress authorized the secretary of war to select for military service two hundred quartermaster corps clerks with certain qualifications as to length of service to be field clerks of the quartermaster corps. With the entry of the United States into World War I and the rapid expansion of the Army, Congress authorized the appointment of more field clerks. Eventually their number rose to 4,673. (See Memorandum, AGO to ACofS G-1, Subject: Legislation to Permit Appointment of All Field Clerks as Warrant Officers, July 1, 1925, in AG 221.5, Army Field Clerks, Box 484, RG 407, Modern Military Branch, NARA.)

amendment included an expansion of the warrant officer list to 1,120, a number far exceeding the requirements of the mine planter service.

This legislation was mainly the work of Congressman Julius F. Kahn of California, chairman of the House Committee on Military Affairs. His intent, and that of his colleagues on the committee, was to provide for senior noncommissioned officers who had held temporary commissions during the war and who would have suffered financial and other hardships upon their return to the enlisted ranks. For this reason, all appointments to warrant officer under this legislation were initially limited to those enlisted men who had held temporary wartime commissions.[7]

Yet for Secretary of War Newton D. Baker, there were other more pragmatic reasons for establishing the grade. In his view, the primary purpose of the expansion was to provide more economical and efficient administrative services for the larger tactical units in the field by furnishing a class of officers who would be able to accomplish many of the administrative tasks then performed by lieutenants at division, corps, and army headquarters.[8] This dichotomy of purpose between Congress and the War Department caused some confusion in the years to come over the question of the role of the warrant officer vis-à-vis the senior noncommissioned officer.

Through expansion of the warrant officer list, the legislation of 1920 also blanketed in the field clerks and started the process by which the Army field clerks, the successors to the general service clerks who had existed in the Army prior to 1894, passed into oblivion over the next decade. That both Army field clerks and field clerks of the quartermaster corps were to become eligible for appointment to the warrant officer grade seems clear from the text of the act that authorized the secretary of war to make appointments to that grade from

> among noncommissioned officers who have had at least ten years enlisted service; enlisted men who served as officers of the Army at some time between April 6, 1917, and November 11, 1918, and whose total service in the Army, enlisted and commissioned, amounts to five years; persons serving, or who have served, as Army field clerks, or field clerks, QMC; and in the case of those who are to be assigned to duty as band leaders at some time between April 6, 1917 and November 11, 1918, or enlisted men possessing suitable qualifications.[9]

As warrant officers began to take over clerical duties at higher headquarters, increasing numbers of Army field clerks and quartermaster field clerks became surplus. Those who had the necessary military qualifications for field service were appointed warrant officers. Meanwhile, the more than 1,600 field clerks then still on active duty continued in their present status but with designations more accurately descriptive of their actual duties. However, since no more field clerks were to be appointed, they were eventually phased out through attrition.[10]

Henceforth, administrative, clerical, and stenographic work in the field Army was performed increasingly by warrant officers, master sergeants, staff sergeants, and privates first and second class (with specialist pay). These men were trained at vocational schools established at corps area and department headquarters. Following graduation and assignment, they could eventually advance to the rank of warrant officer, and under certain circumstances exercise command, a privilege that the now defunct quasi-civilian field clerks never had. In effect, this policy provided for the first time a systematic progression by which enlisted men could advance through their military career to commissioned officer rank, for that is how the Army regarded warrant officers.[11]

Although the amendment of June 1920 seemed to settle the status of those field clerks not made warrant officers, there were those in Congress eager to integrate the remainder of these men into the permanent establishment as warrant officers. After the war the Army had been anxious to replace them with warrant officers but it had at first no choice except to keep hundreds of clerks on the active rolls because the overwhelming majority of the first warrant officers appointed generally lacked the necessary clerical skills and experience. In the Army's eyes the field clerk grade, never clearly defined by law, had become an anomaly. However, until enough warrant officers could be trained to take over their tasks, two separate and distinct clerical grades existed side by side at corps and army headquarters.

Meanwhile, postwar demobilization and budget cutbacks reduced the number of field clerks from over 4,000 in 1918 to 400 by the end of fiscal year 1921. The following year the number fell to 215, of whom 87 were pre-1916 appointees, the remainder being wartime appointees. Finally, an act of Congress of April 27, 1926, authorized the Army to appoint the remaining field clerks into the warrant officer corps.[12]

Efforts to further enlarge the warrant officer list continued when early in 1929 legislation was introduced in the House of Representatives authorizing the secretary of war to "appoint as Warrant Officers any civilian clerk of the Quartermaster corps who was serving in that capacity on April 6, 1917 and who has continued to serve as such, or in the military service, through the period of the World War and continually thereafter to date." The Army staff, however, opposed using the warrant officer grade for anything but recognition of long and distinguished enlisted service, observing that the proposed legislation would create a new class of eligibles—approximately 317 female and 418 male clerks—and establish a precedent for further legislation seeking the appointment to a military grade of any civil service employee in any bureau or branch of the War Department who might have served in that capacity during the war. The staff feared this would set a precedent permitting other civil service employees to enter the Army under the guise of warrant officers. These objections were sufficient to stop the proposed legislation.[13]

A year later further congressional legislation proposed that quartermaster civilian clerks with commissioned service, varying from less than a month to no more than two years, be made warrant officers. In addition, the legislation proposed to compute civilian clerical service as a basis for longevity and for purposes of retirement. Such legislation, if passed, would have permitted a quartermaster civilian clerk with twenty-five years at his desk and less than a year in an officer's uniform to outrank a warrant officer with more than twenty years' service in the line—all of it military. This bill was, of course, anathema to the regular Army and it did not pass.[14]

The intent of these bills was to provide for old-timers in the quartermaster corps' civilian ranks by having them retired as warrant officers, thereby giving them a more adequate retirement than they would have received from the civil service. But the Army argued that if this were a sound idea for the QMC, the same might be said for civilian clerks in the engineers, the signal corps, the adjutant general's office, as well as in the Chief of Staff's office. If passed, this regulation eventually could have swamped the military service and the retired list with civilians drawing the same benefits as worthy noncommissioned officers of long service and recognized military accomplishments.[15]*

Concurrently with the legislation establishing the warrant officer grade, the act of June 4, 1920, had also established the medical administration corps. This corps was composed of former noncommissioned officers of the medical department who had held wartime commissions in the sanitary corps. During the war many of these men had been employed as adjutants, supply officers, and personnel officers. However, the new appointments to the medical administration corps proved in many instances to be so unsatisfactory that the act was soon amended to authorize only the appointment of civilian pharmacists in the corps, and enlisted men were taken off the eligibility list.[16]

Influenced by this experience, the Army determined henceforth to limit warrant officers to positions that had considerable individual responsibility but no command authority. In addition to clerical duties, these positions included those requiring a high degree of technical skill in the engineers, quartermaster, and signal corps. This policy also had the advantage of enabling the Army to appoint older men—that is, senior noncommissioned officers—as warrant officers, for such positions required little arduous physical work.[17]

Between 1922 and 1935, however, no warrant officer appointments were made other than of bandleaders and Army mine planter service personnel, thereby strongly suggesting that the original intent of using the grade to reward outstanding senior noncommissioned officers was no longer being practiced. Moreover, among the warrant officers only one pay grade existed, except in the Army mine planter service. Although the authorized strength remained at six hundred, legislation after 1922 authorized the appointment of personnel, with certain qualifications, in excess of authorized strength. Not until 1936, because of the depletion of the original lists, were competitive examinations held to replenish the lists of el-

*In the annual appropriations act for the Army and item "pay of officers on the retired list" was one to which both the Army and Congress were particularly sensitive. Since warrant officers were now included on it, the Army was especially anxious not to so overload the list as to arouse adverse comment or action by Congress.

igibles for regular Army appointments. Appointments against vacancies continued to be made from the 1936 list until the beginning of World War II.[18]

RESTRUCTURING THE ENLISTED GRADES

In addition to an expanded warrant officer list, the 1920 amendment to the National Defense Act of 1916 also established a completely new enlisted-grade structure, made up of seven grades. Master sergeants comprised the first grade while 1st sergeants and technical sergeants were in the second. Third grade included only the staff sergeants, and the fourth grade were the line sergeants. Corporals made up the fifth, and privates first class and privates, respectively, made up the sixth and seventh grades. Although there were some high-ranking specialists in the first five grades, most of the civilian crafts, as defined by wartime personnel policies, were now in the last two. Twelve specialist grades were equally divided between the noncommissioned grades to cover the remaining vocational skills required. Approximately 29 percent of the men in these grades were authorized specialist ratings, which enabled them to receive additional pay for their skills without the chevrons reserved for combat arms noncommissioned officers.[19]

The reorganization was not without its critics, as illustrated by two letters to the editor of the widely read service publication of the day, the *Army and Navy Journal*. A reader identified only as "Disgruntled" noted,

> With much chagrin and discouragement among higher grade non-commissioned officers of certain branches of the Service, particularly those of the staff corps . . . what inducement is there for a sergeant of the Medical Department, who has already had to pass an examination for the grade he holds, to try to attain the grade of staff sergeant when he gets no more pay than he is already getting? It can only be hoped that further legislation will right the injustice, as we do not believe it was the intention to reduce the pay of any enlisted man of the Army.

Another critic, this time with the rather intriguing *nom de plume* "Sous Officier, Captif Ballon," expressed the hope that the War Department would recommend

> some adjustment to the reorganization legislation as applies to former sergeants first class who on reenlistment are facing a reduction of more than twenty-five percent of their pay, although they retain assimilated grade of staff sergeant. As an example, base pay of sergeant first class was $51 plus $20 additional re-enlistment pay, plus twenty percent under Act of May 18, 1920; total $85.50. Base pay of staff sergeant after re-enlisting in grade of staff sergeant, Air Service, for example, is $45 plus third fogy [longevity pay] of $13.50, plus twenty percent, Act of 18 May 1920; total $70.20 . . . I can therefore, after seventeen years honorable service re-enlist in my own vacancy with a loss of $58 per month. In all fairness let us say no injustice was intended. Yet the innocent bystander gets bit and will likely become a casualty.
>
> . . . surely the best interests of the Service demand retaining of the old experienced NCO's of ten to twenty years service, men of large ability who have proved their loyalty and courage. A lot of the old-timers are gone, more are going. Surely legislation

in the right direction will keep them in the Service. Let us say a twenty-five year retirement law, double time for service with the AEF, and first of all, a square deal to everybody.[20]

Given the cost-cutting mood of Congress, Captif Ballon's recommendations had little chance of acceptance. To make matters worse, public esteem for the regular Army enlisted man, despite the Army's role in the recent world war, had plummeted so low by the 1920s that eight states even disenfranchised them along with felons, idiots, and the insane. The *World Almanac*, a correspondent to the *Army and Navy Journal* noted, declared that in the states of Indiana, Nebraska, North Dakota, and Ohio soldiers and sailors were disqualified from voting; in Missouri paupers were added to the list along with soldiers while Oregon also denied Chinese as well as soldiers and sailors the vote. Texas disenfranchised military personnel along with those convicted of bribery and dueling as well as paupers. Finally, in West Virginia soldiers and sailors were denied suffrage along with paupers and those convicted of bribery.[21]

NEW STRIPES FOR OLD

Along with the new grade structure went new insignia with which to identify the grades. In August of 1920 insignia were prescribed for all grades, consisting of olive drab chevrons set on a dark blue background that formed an edging around each chevron, arc, and lozenge.[22] This system of enlisted insignia was prescribed by War Department Circular 303, August 5, 1920, and later incorporated into the October 14, 1921 edition of Army Regulations 600-35.

The regulations, however, made one very significant change in the wearing of chevrons, prescribing that they be worn on the left sleeve only. The chief, equipment branch, operations division, Army general staff, explained why in a memorandum to the Chief of Staff, dated July 30, 1920: "The attached memorandum places the chevron on the left sleeve instead of the right. This is in response to a universal demand that the left sleeve is the proper place as that is the side men are passed* and therefore the side their grade should be marked."

The editors of the *Infantry Journal*[23] commented, "We note that this order retains the old system [see below] of having the chevron worn only on one side of the coat. It was hoped that the new order would restore the pre-war custom and authorized the wearing of them on both sleeves."

The War Department quickly realized that the "universal demand" cited by the chief of the equipment branch as justification for continuing this alien system was not of this universe, because War Department Circular 72, March 16, 1921, rescinded it.

Actually, this practice went back to World War I, when on April 30, 1918, the

*"Passed" here means "reviewed," as at inspections and parades.

War Department issued a letter suspending the wearing of chevrons on both sleeves "during the present emergency" and prescribing their placement on the right sleeve only. General Headquarters, American Expeditionary Forces, France, promulgated this change to the uniform regulations by General Orders No. 75, May 18, 1918. The reason this measure was adopted in the first place was simply that the Army quartermaster general was not able to keep pace with the demands of wartime expansion. To furnish enough cloth to provide uniforms for 250,000 men (750,000 yards of cloth) he recommended "that chevrons be worn on one arm only, as is now the case in the Navy and in the British Army."[24]

The troops in France saw the situation through different eyes. The editors of the *Stars & Stripes* opined sardonically:

> The reason is that, if allowed to continue wearing chevrons on both sleeves, our corporals and sergeants would soon become the most hyper-decorated members of the Allied fighting family. Wound stripes, service stripes and chevrons would soon be running thither and yon up and down every non-com's arm, making him look like the great Nubian leopard.[25]

Confused as to which sleeve would be deprived of its chevrons, but nevertheless expressing his dissatisfaction over the new order succinctly and with feeling, an artillery man known to posterity only as "F.D.D.," sent the *Stars & Stripes* the following couplet:

> *They're saving cloth and though they mean no harm,*
> *They're takin' off the chevrons from my good right arm.*[26]

Chevrons are tangible and very visible symbols of a noncommissioned officer's status, experience, and competence in the profession of arms, and to take any away without cause is to strike a severe blow at the good soldier's self-respect. The fact that some officers favored a system that would have such an impact on the postwar Army's enlisted leaders, short-lived as it was, indicates a lack of appreciation for noncommissioned officer morale in some very high Army circles and may explain in part why badly needed reforms in the enlisted career system were so hard-fought and so long in coming during these lean years.

This example was not the last time well-meaning but thoughtless staff officers would tinker with noncommissioned officer insignia, and in later years it would result in needless confusion and weakening of morale, as we shall see in Chapter 17.

The Army staff expected standardization of the enlisted grades would provide a means for solving the problems of rank and grade within the regular Army, small by wartime standards, yet somewhat larger and technologically more sophisticated than the prewar establishment. The first step was to categorize the many new grades and titles that had developed since the war. The accompanying table shows how this was done:

REARRANGEMENT OF THE NONCOMMISSIONED OFFICER STRUCTURE, 1920[27]

New Grade	*Old Titles*
First or Master Sergeant	Regimental Sergeants Major; Sergeants Major, Senior Grade; Quartermaster Sergeants, Senior Grade; Master Hospital Sergeants; Master Engineers, Senior Grade; Master Electricians; Master Signal Electricians; Engineers, CAC; Regimental Supply Sergeants; 25 percent of Ordnance Sergeants authorized in CAC; Band Sergeant and Assistant Leader, USMA Band
Second or 1st Sergeant or Technical Sergeant	1st Sergeants; Technical Sergeants; Hospital Sergeants; Master Engineers, Junior Grade; 75 percent of Ordnance Sergeants, First Class; Assistant Engineers, CAC; Quartermaster Sergeants; Electrician Sergeants, Artillery Detachment, USMA
Third or Staff Sergeant	Squadron and Battalion Sergeants Major, Junior Grade; Battalion Supply Sergeants; Sergeants, First Class; 50 percent of Master Gunners authorized in CAC; Master Gunners, Artillery Detachment, USMA; Assistant Band Leaders; Sergeant Buglers; Electrician Sergeants, Second Class; Radio Sergeants; Color Sergeants; Sergeant Field Musician, USMA
Fourth or Sergeant	Sergeants authorized in all arms and services except those designated as specialists; Company Supply Sergeants; Mess Sergeants; Stable Sergeants; Band Sergeants
Fifth or Corporal	Corporals authorized in all arms and services except those designated specialists; Band Corporals; Corporal Buglers
Sixth or Privates First Class	Privates, First Class, as First designated; Specialists, as prescribed
Seventh or Private	Privates as designated; Privates, Second Class; Specialists, as prescribed

This table also shows how difficult it was to separate those noncommissioned officers who were primarily combat leaders from technicians or specialists. Actually, the new structure succeeded only in separating noncommissioned officers and specialists at the three lowest grades. The first three continued to be made up of many men whose primary functions were technical, although generally they directed others in the performance of these tasks. The establishment of the specialist categories proved difficult—the original directive was amended five times the first year and twice more in 1921, before a final version was completed in September of that year. By that time, there were on the list some 231 vocational skills that could add from $3.00 to as much as $25.00 to a private's monthly pay.[28]

In terms of percentages in each grade, the act of June 1920 fixed the numbers of both noncommissioned officers and specialists in the regular Army. Although still a relatively inflexible system, it was nevertheless an improvement over the old one by which Congress had prescribed every detail down to the exact number of corporals in an infantry company. However, in 1936, Congress further amended the act of 1916 to give the president (and hence the War Department) the power to fix by executive order the numbers and grades and/or ratings of enlisted men. Henceforth, the president issued annual authorizations for the total number of Army enlisted grades. This apparent flexibility, however, had little effect until after the Army began a major expansion in 1940.[29]

The table on page 214 illustrates the relative stability between 1921 and 1939 of the enlisted structure created by the legislation of June 1920. Slightly more than one half (53 percent) of the regular Army consisted of privates first class or privates with specialist ratings. The remainder were about equally divided between noncommissioned officers and specialists. However, the basic premise on which the new structure rested—that noncommissioned grades were to be given only to soldiers in leadership positions, while those performing special technical tasks were to be privates first class or privates with specialist ratings—had been violated from the beginning.

The simplified grading system clarified the situation somewhat, but did not change the fact that a master sergeant might function, depending on the table of organization of his branch or service, under the new structure in much the same way he had under the old—as a regimental sergeant major, ordnance sergeant, or supply sergeant. Master sergeants, essentially specialists with clerical or other technical skills, drew more pay than did 1st sergeants, whose positions depended entirely on their demonstration of outstanding leadership. Furthermore, 1st sergeants could not attain the highest enlisted grades without transferring to the enlisted staff for assignment to tasks for which they all too frequently had little talent. Consequently, that old problem of junior personnel earning more than their seniors resurfaced. The new structure provided that in certain cases privates first class and privates with specialist classification could earn almost as much as master sergeants of the line.* Such inequities increased as the mechanization of the Army called for greater numbers of highly paid occupational specialists in direct competition with industry.[30]

*For example, a specialist first class in the grade of private first class was entitled to $60.00 a month: his $35.00 base pay plus $25.00 a month pay as a specialist of the first class. A master sergeant's base pay at that time amounted to $74.00 per month.

COMPOSITION OF ENLISTED STRENGTH OF THE ARMY, 1921–1939*
(Excludes Philippine Scouts)

GRADE	PERCENTAGE			
	Authorized Act of 1920	*June 30, 1921*	*June 30, 1930*	*June 30, 1939*
Master Sergeant	0.6	0.8	0.8	0.7
1st Sergeant		1.1	0.9	0.7
Technical Sergeant	1.8	0.7	1.2	1.2
Staff Sergeant	2.0	1.6	3.5	3.0
Sergeant	9.5	8.7	9.1	8.8
Corporal	9.5	7.5	9.0	8.4
Private, First Class	25.0	22.7	24.6	26.1
Private	51.6	56.8	50.6	50.8
Flying Cadets		0.1	0.3	0.3
Specialists (as percentage of Privates and PFCs)				
First Class	0.7	Data	0.7	0.7
Second Class	1.4	Not	1.1	1.2
Third Class	1.9	Available	1.6	1.9
Fourth Class	4.7		5.1	5.2
Fifth Class	5.0		5.3	5.5
Sixth Class	15.2		14.5	14.7
Total	28.9		28.3	29.2

FISCAL RESTRAINTS

As happened following all the nation's wars, the post–World War I years witnessed a significant reduction in the Army's enlisted strength brought on by severe budget cuts imposed by Congress. But because of the unprecedented expansion during the war, this reduction was potentially more of a problem than it had ever been before during similar periods of economic retrenchment.

Although many commissioned officers were also adversely affected, the reductions, when they came, posed more of a problem for noncommissioned officers. This arose from the fact that the Army had to do something with all those noncommissioned officers who had accepted commissions during the war. The Army had promoted many junior enlisted men to fill their places and was now faced with the problem of restoring the ex-sergeants to the enlisted ranks they had vacated to accept commissions while at the same time trying to be fair to the men who had served throughout the war in the higher noncommissioned grades and were now rendered surplus by the postwar reductions.

Many senior noncommissioned officers had been fully aware of this hazard during the war and therefore had hesitated to accept the proffered commissions,

**Annual Reports* of the Secretary of War, Fiscal Years 1921, 1930, 1939

although their services as officers were urgently needed by the Army. These men were concerned that by accepting a commission they might jeopardize their regular Army status as senior noncommissioned officers following the war. Consequently, early in the war the Army staff sought to reassure them by undertaking a study to solve this potential problem.

At first the adjutant general proposed simply to reinstate in their former rank those noncommissioned officers who chose to reenlist following wartime commissioned service. As for the men who had been promoted to take their places as noncommissioned officers, they would then be reduced in grade—in many cases to private. While this proposal was simple and direct it was bound to cause considerable turbulence and hardship. Under the adjutant general's proposal, a soldier who had been appointed sergeant major of his regiment or 1st sergeant of his company—to fill a vacancy created by commissioning the incumbent—would be demoted when the former returned. One can imagine the impact this would have had on the demoted man's morale and personal life.[31]

In preparing these plans, all the Army staff had to go on was the National Defense Act of May 1916 that had authorized the discharge of enlisted men to accept commissions in the National Guard, the Officers' Reserve Corps, or the volunteer forces. While the act authorized these men to return to the regular Army upon expiration of their commissions with credit for retirement and continuous service pay, it said nothing specific about reinstating them to their former enlisted grades. It was this oversight that the staff addressed first.

As early as June of 1917 the secretary of war had authorized the chief of the coast artillery to issue, for the period of the emergency, limited warrants in the grades of noncommissioned officers listed in Army Regulations 310—sergeants major, senior and junior grade; master electricians, engineers and engineer sergeants first class; assistant engineers, electrician sergeants second class; firemen, radio sergeants; and master gunners. Men given wartime limited warrants in these grades were to be informed that if those who held permanent warrants elected to reenlist in the coast artillery corps following their commissioned service, a corresponding number of limited warrants would be revoked. The demoted men were then to be placed on the lists of eligible candidates to whom permanent warrants would be issued as they became available.[32]

Meanwhile, Secretary of War Newton D. Baker sought to extend these provisions to the entire Army. He persuaded Congress to amend the National Defense Act of 1916 so that "any former noncommissioned officer who was discharged to accept a commission in the Army of the United States and who reenlists within three months from the date of his discharge as a commissioned officer, shall be restored to the grade held before being discharged to accept such commission." In March of 1918, Congress adopted this as an amendment to the National Defense Act of 1916.[33]

Notwithstanding Secretary Baker's efforts, there remained limitations inherent in the legislation that, as the Army's judge advocate general later pointed out, caused some of these men to lose their noncommissioned status. In an opinion, the JAG declared that

> no distinctions have been drawn between temporary and permanent noncommissioned officers, and the Act itself purports to create none . . . It follows therefore, that a noncommissioned officer, who held only a temporary appointment at the time of his discharge to accept a commission, upon being restored to his former grade, continues merely in his former status of a temporary noncommissioned officer, and he is therefore subject to the appropriate regulations and restrictions pertaining to that character of tenure.[34]

The postwar crisis of excess noncommissioned officers proved even worse than the staff had anticipated. There was not to be just one major postwar reduction in regular Army strength, but a series of reductions and each one sent a shock wave of demotions throughout the noncommissioned officer corps. On the heels of the armistice and demobilization, Congress reduced the regular Army to a target strength of 280,000 by 1920. A year later it fell to 155,000; to 137,000 by 1922; and to 125,000 in 1923. By 1927 congressional indifference to things military brought about a further decline of regular Army strength, to 118,750. The final blow came with the onset of the decade of the thirties and the beginning of the worldwide depression. This forced even greater economies on the Army which, in the words of one historian, had by then become hardly more than a minor school for soldiers.[35]

Although in 1922 the Army dropped 1,000 commissioned officers as surplus, far greater reductions were in store for the noncommissioned officers. Over 1,600 were demoted by the end of 1922, with more reductions to come. It was even worse for married noncommissioned officers, for many had already been reduced at least one grade, and they were far more dependent upon their pay and allowances than were commissioned officers with their greater education and employment opportunities. The average married noncommissioned officer consequently found it very difficult to adapt to his demotion, for even that small difference in pay usually meant the difference between a decent living and real hardship for his family.

For one, the threatened demotion proved too much to bear. On November 2, 1922, Sergeant Major B. H. Nelson, slated to lose his rank on December 13, shot his wife and then himself in their quarters at the Presidio of San Francisco. Nelson was one of the 1,600 noncommissioned officers slated to lose their rank through demotion and despondency over this fact caused him to kill his wife and himself, the official Army board of investigation concluded. Sergeant Major Nelson's suicide was discussed in relation to the threatened demoralization of the morale among noncommissoned officers in the Army and the board memorialized Congress in an effort to save these ranks.[36] Their plight was such as to move at least one general officer to appeal directly to Secretary of War John W. Weeks to urge

Congress to allow the Army to retain these men in their present grades until the budget-induced surplus could be absorbed through normal attrition.[37]

The Army staff hoped to do this by a gradual absorption of surplus noncommissioned officers into vacancies originally provided by the tables of organization of May 3, 1917, but as the wartime emergency came to an end and demobilization got under way, many unforeseen problems arose that made this goal difficult if not impossible to realize.[38] Some of these were of the Army's own making. For example, the War Department had authorized the continuation of warrants for surplus and unassigned noncommissioned officers upon reenlistment following the war. However, between 1919 and 1925, the series of congressionally mandated reductions left the Army with large surpluses of noncommissioned officers, especially in the higher grades. Therefore, many experienced noncommissioned officers who had served as officers during the war found themselves upon their return to enlisted status junior to noncommissioned officers who had risen rapidly as a result of the wartime need for senior noncommissioned officers. This situation, as well as the chronic uncertainty over reductions had an injurious effect on morale and the reenlistment of experienced and desirable men.[39]

Meanwhile, the chiefs of the several technical services modified their regulations governing the appointment of noncommissioned officers in order to readjust noncommissioned grades and specialist ratings and bring them more into conformity with postwar requirements. For example, in the quartermaster corps, all noncommissioned officers from technical sergeants on down were affected. Soldiers holding warrants as technical sergeants, if demoted to staff sergeant, were given warrants in the latter grade with date of rank from November 23, 1913. This enabled them to outrank any of that grade promoted during the war. Those technical sergeants reduced to sergeant were placed on an eligible list by the quartermaster general with first priority for promotion as vacancies occurred. This was also the case with sergeants and corporals as they were demoted. Staff sergeants reduced to sergeant were given warrants with date of rank from April 1, 1917. This too enabled them to outrank those holding wartime warrants.[40]

With the end of the war, the appointing authority for senior noncommissioned personnel was returned exclusively to each of the technical service chiefs. During the war, for example, temporary appointments to the senior grades in the quartermaster corps in the regular Army, National Guard, and National Army had been delegated to commanders down to separate brigade level as well as the commanding general of the American Expeditionary Force. Authority for permanent appointments, on the other hand, remained in the hands of traditional authorities, the secretary of war for the regulars and the quartermaster general for the National Guard.[41] Similar provisions existed for master and technical sergeants of the ordnance corps, who were henceforth to be appointed by the secretary of war upon recommendation of the chief of the corps. The latter in turn had authority to appoint all other ratings within the corps, except in the Philippines Department, whose commanding general had the authority to appoint sergeants and corporals of ordnance.[42] Senior noncommissioned officers of the medical department, medical, dental, and veterinary services, were henceforth also appointed only by the secretary of war, upon recommendation of the Army surgeon general and following successful completion of the prescribed examination. The selection of other ratings was left up to the surgeon general.[43]

ABSORBING EXCESS NCOS

As the Army enlisted strength fell from 175,000 in February to 150,000 in June of 1921, the number of noncommissioned officers surplus to Army requirements continued to rise. Efforts to save the grades of these deserving and able men were greatly restricted in the tables of organization set forth in the National Defense Act of 1916. To deal with this situation the Army resorted initially to two measures—freezing promotions and authorizing servicewide transfers.

The Army suspended all promotions to the first three noncommissioned officer grades but kept open opportunities for promotions in the fourth and fifth grades (sergeants and corporals). The rationale for this was that in many cases the duties of these grades were being performed by acting sergeants and corporals who, in fairness, were entitled to the rank and pay of the duties performed. Having suspended promotions within or to the first three grades, the Army also sought to absorb the existing surplus through servicewide transfers rather than by demoting these experienced men.

As for rated specialists, their qualifications were so numerous and varied that their transfers were left in the hands of local commanders. Since sufficient funds existed to pay the noncommissioned officers and rated specialists only through May 31, 1922, the Army staff expected by that date to have the ratios of noncommissioned officers to other ranks in conformity with the authorized strength of the Army.[44]

An opinion rendered by the judge advocate general in October 1921 gave an added urgency to this plan as the Army sought to beat the May 1922 deadline:

> A noncommissioned officer restored to the grade from which he was discharged to accept a commission in accordance with the Act of March 30, 1918, was not entitled to be carried surplus and in grade if reorganization under a later Act makes his reduction necessary.[45]

In spite of the Army's efforts to soften the impact of the congressionally mandated force reductions, they soon outran the Army's plans and capabilities, as the authorized strength fell to 137,000 in 1922. The worsening plight of many senior noncommissioned officers, especially those who had served as commissioned officers during the war and who had not been appointed warrant officers, was highlighted during an inspection trip by the Army Chief of Staff, John J. Pershing, in

January of that year. The Chief of Staff returned from his trip with strong recommendations from his senior commanders against the reduction of senior staff sergeants on the grounds that "it was so unjust to the individual as to have a very bad effect on morale." Many commanders suggested that a temporary solution might lie in reducing the number of corporals and specialists until ordinary vacancies had absorbed the senior sergeants with long service, many of whom had had commissioned service, often field grade, during the war.[46]

This suggestion was rejected on the grounds that it would result in a top-heavy organization, at variance with that authorized in the National Defense Act of 1916. As long as Congress continued to reduce the regular Army's enlisted strength as frequently as it had done since the end of the war, the Army staff saw no way to avoid demotion of many senior noncommissioned officers, with consequent adverse effect on morale.[47]

Some of the staff, in an effort to soften the blow, now suggested a reduction of senior noncommissioned officers throughout the Army in inverse order or rank—in which a sergeant of five years' service, two of which were in the grade of sergeant, would be demoted before a sergeant of twenty-five years' service, of which ten or fifteen had been in grade. Hallowed tradition, however, stood in the way of this proposal. The promotion or demotion of noncommissioned officers had traditionally been the prerogative of the unit or local commander. Although, in practice, seniority had always been a consideration, it had never been mandatory, and the War Department was not about to change that policy.[48]

The Army staff now reluctantly acknowledged that the only way by which large-scale demotions of senior noncommissioned officers could be avoided would be through legislation. Accordingly, at the direction of the Chief of Staff, the Army's operations directorate prepared a memorandum to be submitted to Congress requesting an increase in the number of noncommissioned officers authorized for the regular Army. Meanwhile, the War Department extended the May 31 deadline to the end of the fiscal year—June 30, 1922—hoping to gain additional time for transfers, attrition, and other adjustments to possibly ameliorate the impact of the mandated demotions. All officers ordering demotions were instructed to lessen the hardships involved by careful selection of those eventually reduced in grade.[49]

In an appeal to the Senate Armed Services Committee, the secretary of war pointed out that reductions of noncommissioned officers, especially in the first three grades, would deprive the Army of "the necessary number of noncommissioned officers to carry on its functions effectively and efficiently." The secretary went on to explain that many War Department activities were of a continuing nature, with a necessary amount of overhead in all branches of the service, just as in any business organization. These activities required for their efficient operation certain noncommissioned grades no matter what the strength of the Army might be.[50]

For example, when enlisted strength was reduced to 150,000, noncommissioned grades had been readjusted accordingly by cutting branches and activities—and in many cases, even tables of organization—far below what they should have been. These measures, the secretary observed, had enabled the War Department to function without asking for an increase in percentages of noncommissioned officers. Further reduction of the Army's enlisted strength, however, without some increase in the percentage of noncommissioned grades, would have caused dangerous shortages and many vital War Department activities would have to have been significantly curtailed.[51]

It was not just a question of maintaining a greatly reduced regular Army whose mission had been fixed by the amendment of the National Defense Act as approved on June 4, 1920. Congress had defined what was known as the Army of the United States that consisted of not only the regular Army, but the National Guard, the Organized Reserves, including the Officers' Reserve Corps and the Enlisted Reserve Corps. The reservoir for these organizations, as provided by the legislation, was the Reserve Officers' and Citizens Military training camps.

In an article written for the *Army and Navy Journal* in April 1922 its Washington correspondent, E. B. Johns, observed that "each of these component parts of the Army of the United States has a definite function and all are interdependent. The failure to appropriate sufficient funds for one of them will eventually break down the entire system and prevent carrying out the purposes of the National Defense Act as it was passed by Congress."[52]

To these arguments the *New York Times* on March 21 declared that "a force of 115,000 enlisted men would be only about 15,000 stronger than that of 1914. Since then the Service has acquired an air corps, modern artillery batteries, a chemical service, a motor organization, a machine gun arm and tank companies. These must all be kept up, or the United States Army will cease to be a modern army."[53]

The War Department's arguments carried some weight with the Senate, which in early December 1922 passed a bill increasing the number of noncommissioned officers of the first three grades. Pending similar action by the House, the secretary of war immediately revoked all orders reducing noncommissioned officers. Orders were amended, changing the effective dates of demotions from December 31, 1922, to March 31, 1923. Rated specialists excess to authorized tables of organization, however, were not so fortunate. They were to be disrated on schedule, by the end of December 1922.[54]

The secretary's action granted at least a temporary reprieve for some 3,907 noncommissioned officers made surplus by then-authorized enlisted strength of 125,000. A breakdown of the 3,907 shows the following:

1st Grade	Master Sergeant	429
2d Grade	Technical Sergeant	829
3d Grade	Staff Sergeant	532
4th Grade	Sergeant	1461
5th Grade	Corporal	656

If the legislation passed by the Senate were passed by the House, authorized strength in the first three grades would have been increased as follows:

Grade	*Current Auth.*	*Auth. S. 4037*	*Increase*
1st	429	922	242+
2d	2250	2582	332+
3d	2250	4229	1729+
Total:	550	7803	2300+

If all vacancies created by the passage of the Senate bill were filled by transfers (except where no excess existed) the effect on demotions would have been:

Grade	*Listed for Demotion*	*Increase S. 4307*	*Excess*
1st	429	242	186
2d	829	322	497
3d	532	1729	−1197
Total:	1790	2300	− 415

These figures indicate that even with postponement of demotions of the noncommissioned officers, originally scheduled for the end of December 1922, and enactment of the Senate legislation into law, there would still have remained a minimum of 683 noncommissioned officers of the first two grades surplus under current enlisted strength figures. To this number must be added those in the first three grades unqualified for transfer to the detached enlisted men's list (DEML),* to which the bulk of the legislated increase would most likely have been allotted. All of this, of course, depended on the passage of the legislation and maintenance of current enlisted strength figures at 125,000. But there was no assurance of either.[55]

In any case, when the House failed to pass the Senate bill, all plans for avoiding the impact of large-scale demotions had to be shelved for the time being. Even the possibility of partially solving the problem of excess noncommissioned officers by transfers among corps and branches held out little hope, as all corps commanders and branch chiefs reported surpluses. Deadlines for demotions were extended a few months, but that was all. The adjutant general could do little but limit transfers to those specifically recommended and urge all concerned "to make the best of an unfortunate situation."[56]

Making the best of an "unfortunate situation" involved such things as determining the relative rank of noncommissioned officers discharged from wartime commissions. While absent from their units as commissioned officers, it will be recalled, their places had often been taken by men formerly junior to them who in many cases had been promoted to noncommissioned grades senior to the ones they held before commissioning. Upon return to enlisted status, these former officers often found themselves outranked by these former subordinates. Inasmuch

*Personnel assigned as orderlies or enlisted aides to general officers as well as instructors for ROTC and the National Guard and recruiting service.

as this problem could not be solved by antedating the appointments of noncommissioned officers, the War Department issued a circular that provided for technical and staff sergeants who had been reduced to grades of sergeant following return to enlisted status to be given warrants as sergeant with date of rank from April 1, 1917. This in effect permitted them to outrank men promoted during their absence as commissioned officers.[57]

In practice, this meant that technical and staff sergeants of the quartermaster corps, for example, who had been reduced to the grade of sergeant would be given warrants as sergeants with date of rank from April 1, 1917, thus permitting them to outrank all those within the grade of sergeant who had been advanced in grade during their absence.[58]

However, quite aside from protecting the seniority of senior noncommissioned officers, the continuing problem of surplus noncommissioned officers in the regular Army remained to be solved. A possible solution—albeit only a partial one—lay in augmentation of the DEML. This last included, as previously noted, details for ROTC duty at educational institutions, as instructors to the National Guard, and to the recruiting service. Since for the most part noncommissioned officers and other enlisted men so detailed were additional in their respective grades to those authorized for the regular Army, the Army staff studied the possibility of increasing the number of enlisted men authorized for the DEML in order to reduce the number of noncommissioned officers to be demoted under WD Circular 275, as amended.[59]

The detail of enlisted men for duty at educational institutions had been authorized under the provisions of the National Defense Act of 1916. Sections 46 and 56 of this legislation established the total number of active-duty noncommissioned officers authorized duty with special units of the ROTC: Not to exceed forty-five for cavalry; ninety for field artillery; seventy for coast artillery; forty for engineers; thirty for the motor transport corps; fifteen for the signal corps; and not more than one per unit from the medical corps. Noncommissioned officers detailed for duty with high schools were chargeable to regular army ratios. However, those detailed to colleges and universities, and they were the most numerous, were additional in their respective grades to those authorized for the regulars, but their number was not to exceed five hundred.

The Army, understandably anxious to present only its best for this duty, required that "the noncommissioned officers detailed for duty at all educational institutions shall be of excellent character, soldierly appearance, sober, dependable, and capable instructors in the basic training of a soldier." They were to have not less than one year's service, at least a grammar school education, and some clerical ability.[60]

However, since the allowable number of noncommissioned officers detailed for duty at educational institutions depended upon the student enrollments, and could in any case not exceed five hundred, there was little likelihood of finding secure positions for excess noncommissioned officers in this category of the DEML.

Turning from the ROTC, the Army staff concentrated on the possibility of increasing the numbers detailed to the politically popular National Guard units in the several states. The first step in this direction came from the Militia Bureau with a request in late 1921 for an increase in the number of sergeant-instructors for the National Guard. At the time of the request there were 36 technical and 1st sergeants; 46 staff sergeants; 388 sergeants; and 81 corporals—a total of 515 men—allotted to the bureau.[61]

What the Militia Bureau had in mind was an exchange of the allotted eighty-one corporals for sergeants, on the grounds that competent enlisted men for instructor duty could not be obtained in any appreciable numbers from regular Army grades below that of sergeant. Corporals and privates first class had not proven generally capable as instructors. Moreover, since even the pay of sergeants made it difficult for them to live in the civilian community, lower-ranking noncommissioned officers found it impossible.[62]

Under the circumstances, the substitution of sergeant-instructors for corporals with a gain of spaces for 81 additional sergeants was the best the Army could expect since Congress had failed to pass legislation (H.R. 12819 and S. 4037) increasing the percentage of noncommissioned officers in the regular Army. This left the total number of noncommissioned officers detailed to the National Guard as instructors unchanged at 551, but increased the number of sergeants from 388 to 469. While the secretary of war was sympathetic to the chief of the bureau's desire for instructors no lower in grade than sergeant, he nevertheless believed that until Congress saw its way clear to authorize an overall increase of enlisted grades (which it seemed determined not to do) there was no chance of this type of remedy for the problem of excess noncommissioned officers.[63]

Rebuffed in 1923, the Militia Bureau, encouraged by congressional action amending the National Defense Act of 1916, returned to the attack the following year. In June 1924, Congress again amended the 1916 legislation and authorized a net increase of 1,987 noncommissioned officers in the first three grades: 237 in the first; 375 in the second; and 1,750 in the third. There was, however, a decrease of 375 in noncommissioned officers of the fourth grade (sergeants), but the fifth and sixth grades (corporals and privates first class) remained unchanged. Total authorized enlisted strength for the regular Army remained, at least for the present, at 125,000.[64]

The chief of the Militia Bureau therefore determined to obtain a certain number of that increase as sergeant-instructors for the new National Guard units. He had strong arguments on his side, for during fiscal year 1925, 120 new units were to be added, and the 1924 authorization of 551 noncommissioned instructors was inadequate to train these additional units. An increase of at least 63 noncommissioned officers (raising the total from 551 to 614), while still far short of the Guard's real needs, was a more equitable distribution of the additional noncommissioned officers authorized.[65]

However, the Chief of Staff offered the Militia Bureau an increase of only fifty sergeants—a total of 601 instead of the requested 614—because the legislation had actually *decreased* the number of sergeants, the rank most needed by the bureau. To make even fifty additional men available, the Chief of Staff explained, would reduce other worthwhile activities by fifty noncommissioned officers. Nevertheless, the Militia Bureau stuck by its guns and recommended that the allowance of sergeant-instructors even be increased to 627 for fiscal year 1927, and to 675 thereafter, subject, of course, to availability of funds.[66]

Not only the Militia Bureau, but the U.S. Army Recruiting Service, sought with every argument it could muster to increase its allotment of noncommissioned officers. As was the case with the National Guard, the recruiting service also believed that its allotment of 900 enlisted men was inadequate for the accomplishment of its mission. Not only was the number assigned insufficient, but the distribution of grades—269 sergeants and above and 631 corporals or lower—was considered unsatisfactory. The recruiting service argued with some justification that a majority, rather than a minority, of its men should be in grade of sergeant or above. In order to do his job properly a recruiter must attain sufficient rank to speak with some credibility concerning the opportunities for personal advancement offered by the Army. Like his counterpart on duty with the National Guard, he must also draw sufficient pay to enable him to live decently in the civilian community and to present a neat personal appearance. Moreover, adequate pay helped keep him free from financial worries so that he might concentrate on his work. Until these problems were solved it would be difficult to get good men to transfer from the line to the recruiting service.[67]

Faced with a requirement for 74,000 enlistments and reenlistments to maintain the Army at its authorized enlisted strength of 125,000 for fiscal year 1924, the secretary of war finally authorized the detail of 271 additional sergeants to the recruiting service. At the same time, the secretary also made available funds for monthly allowances to men on recruiting duty in lieu of quarters and subsistence.[68]

Although the detailing of additional sergeants provided some relief for the recruiting service, it did not solve the continuing problem of too large a proportion of corporals and below on recruiting duty. As far as the adjutant general was concerned, these men had little value as recruiters. Once again, the AG turned to the legislative liaison branch of the general staff in an effort to obtain an increase in the ratios of senior to junior noncommissioned officers in the regular Army.[69]

CHANGING THE RETIREMENT SYSTEM

Another possible means of absorbing excess senior noncommissioned officers had attracted both Army and congressional attention in the mid-1920s. This was a proposal to reduce the years of service required for enlisted retirement from thirty to twenty-five years. Such a proposal would have encouraged many senior noncommissioned officers to take immediate retirement in grade and thus avoid the likelihood of demotion and eventual retirement at thirty years in a lower grade. For various reasons, however, the Army was reluctant to permit retirement with twenty-five years' service. Pressure for change in the thirty-year requirement came instead from enlisted men themselves and from a handful of congressmen who supported them.

Several congressmen, among them two New Yorkers—Hamilton Fish and Isaac Siegel—introduced legislation designed to enable enlisted men to retire after twenty-five years' service. Not only did the legislation call for a reduction in years of service, but also for an increase in retirement pay as well. The first bill, introduced in June 1922, provided for retirement at the expiration of twenty-five years' service regardless of grade held at the time and retired pay of not less than $100.00 per month. A second bill, introduced in December, also called for retirement after twenty-five years' service and a $30.00 per month increase in rates of retirement for all ranks down to and including privates first class. Both bills provided for funding to come from a monthly deduction for the support of the Soldiers Home.[70]

Prior to the act of February 4, 1885 (later amended in 1890, 1907, and 1921) there had been no provisions for the retirement of enlisted men of the regular Army. Disabled men were given modest pensions, and after 1851, could enter the Soldiers Home, but remained on the active-duty rolls and not as retirees. When provision for retirement at three-quarters pay after thirty years of service was finally adopted in 1885, it had been regarded primarily as a reward for long and faithful service and only incidentally to provide for men who had become incapacitated for further active duty. Consequently, the privilege of retirement for physical disability *per se* had never been accorded enlisted men as it had been for officers. Compensation for disability was provided through the War Risk Insurance Act, pensions, or care at the Soldiers Home in Washington, D.C.[71]

Army response to the congressional initiative was negative, despite the possibilities this legislation offered of absorbing some of the excess senior noncommissioned officers. Declaring itself satisfied with the general laws governing retirement, the War Department opposed any attempt to tamper with the present system. Since the policy of enlisted retirement with pay was still relatively new in the Army and at that time not generally accepted for workers in the civilian sector either, the Army was understandably sensitive to possible public criticism of a retired list and to any increases in its numbers and cost. Such criticism might have caused sufficient adverse reaction in Congress to jeopardize the Army's retired list, which had recently been increased with the addition of warrant officers.

The general staff professed to have found in the act of August 24, 1912—which revoked an earlier act of May 26, 1900, that had allowed certain foreign service to be counted as double time toward enlisted retirement—evidence of congressional willingness to tinker with the retirement system to the Army's disadvantage. This suggested to the War Department that Congress would most likely not favor a reduction of the time necessary for retirement of enlisted men. There was yet another consideration—the Army's sincere belief that the thirty-year retirement was both fair and liberal. For example, a man enlisting at the minimum age for enlistment—eighteen—would, after thirty years of service, be able to retire at forty-eight (this at a time when most men continued to work past sixty-five). To authorize retirement under that age would place on the retired list able-bodied men in the prime of life who would render no further service to the government in return for their retired pay and allowances. That would be, in the Army's view (a view that generally mirrored that of late nineteenth-century American society), undesirable from every public standpoint—financial, industrial, and moral. The concept that the soldier with twenty-five years—or even twenty—of service would have *earned* his retired pay lay many years in the future.[72] In any event, the issue soon became moot after Congress failed to consider the legislation.

Not surprisingly, the original impetus for congressional interest in reducing the time required for retirement by enlisted men had come from among the men themselves. Prominent among them had been Sergeant Ernest A. Perry, assigned to the DEML and on duty with the Army recruiting service in Harrisburg, Pennsylvania. Sergeant Perry organized a lobbying effort on a shoestring. With considerable skill he had persuaded the widely circulated *Army and Navy Journal* to provide free publicity in behalf of twenty-five-year retirement. Perry then helped draft a bill (H.R. 12106) authorizing twenty-five-year retirement that Congressman Fish introduced in the second session of the 67th Congress in 1922. The *Army and Navy Journal*, meanwhile, polled its readers and determined that more than 4,500 men favored such legislation. After raising $398.55 through letters of solicitation from among the noncommissioned officers and expending nearly $600.00 of his own funds, Sergeant Perry finally gave up the fight when the Army intervened and ordered him "to discontinue these activities and to return any future contributions."

The adjutant general informed Perry that his attempts to influence legislation were not authorized by the War Department, which regarded such activities as "a breach of regulations and orders." That ended the matter, but the War Department took no further action against Sergeant Perry, since he had in good faith checked with the adjutant general's office before embarking upon his venture and had accounted honestly for all funds received and expended.[73] Nevertheless, the issue lingered on. In 1924, Army Chief of Staff General John J. Pershing directed the staff to review the retirement laws, governing not only enlisted men but warrant officers and field clerks as well, to determine the desirability of any revision or readjustment.[74]

After reviewing existing laws concerning retirement, the staff found them both fair and liberal and recommended against making any revision or readjustment in them. The Army staff also remained opposed to any legislation authorizing retirement of enlisted men for physical disability, preferring rather to rely on suitable pension laws and the Soldiers Home to provide for the care of enlisted men invalided out of the service for physical impairment.[75]

It may well have been that the Army's reluctance to the opening up and examination of the whole retirement system stemmed partly from a desire to protect certain traditional *ad hoc* retirement practices. Often, for example, the company 1st sergeant, when a deserving man was about to retire, would with the company commander's cooperation step down and take a reduction to private—whereupon, the company commander would boost the "professional" private up to 1st sergeant, so he could retire in that grade. Of course the newly minted "1st sergeant" kicked back all the difference in pay to the real "top kick." Although one retired general observed that this practice "was perhaps dishonest . . . it was the Army's way of taking care of its own."[76] It is certainly doubtful whether such ingenious ways of avoiding reform of the retirement system would have survived congressional scrutiny.

There was one exception to the Army's reluctance to tamper with the enlisted retirement list. It continued to look with favor upon some form of special treatment for retired enlisted men who had served as commissioned officers during the war. Since virtually all these men had been noncommissioned officers, such special treatment, in effect, increased retirement pay for many retired enlisted men. The War Department, therefore, supported legislation giving retired enlisted men who had served honorably at least one year during the war as commissioned officers the retired pay and allowances of warrant officers.

The Army expected passage of this legislation to help solve the problem of excess senior noncommissioned officers in the postwar regular Army by raising retirement pay sufficiently to encourage many of these men to retire. A large number of noncommissioned officers were then eligible but were not making application to be placed on the retired list. They were apparently either hoping for promotion to the next higher grade or, failing that, looking for the passage of legislation enabling them to retire with the pay and allowances of warrant officers. The legislation they were waiting for involved an amendment to a bill granting retired warrant officer pay and allowances to noncommissioned officers who had served as officers during the war and who had been placed on the retired list before or during the war. The Army-supported amendment would simply have extended warrant officer retirement to *all* noncommissioned officers, even those presently on active duty, who had served honorably as commissioned officers of the U.S. Army at any time between April 16, 1917, and November 11, 1918.[77] This amendment became law with the passage of an act on June 6, 1924, amending the National Defense Act of 1916.

However, the Army in the last analysis was fighting what may best be described as a doomed rear-guard action to avoid demotion or reduction of many of its senior noncommissioned officers. By the end of 1925 it had become clear that not only was the Congress intent upon further reducing the Army's authorized strength, but intended, as it had following the Civil War, to reduce Army pay as well. This in turn presented the Army staff with the hard choice of either further reducing its noncommissioned officer corps or reducing the overall enlisted strength below 118,750 men. The staff recommended the adoption of the first choice. Reductions and demotions of noncommissioned officers would then be accomplished by having each branch and department bear its *pro rata* share of the cut in noncommissioned grades. The adjutant general nevertheless continued to argue (in vain) for the exemption of the recruiting service from this reduction. It was believed that the service must be maintained at its strength of 900 men in order to enlist the 72,000 recruits needed to keep even a skeleton army up to authorized strength.[78]

Thus did the small regular Army that had organized and helped to lead the conscript National Army to victory in World War I adjust once again to that tradition of postwar neglect that had been its fate after every war since the War of Independence. That some semblance of discipline and tradition always managed to survive this chronic sociopolitical trauma was a tribute to those few officers and men who remained on active duty and carried on in spite of legislative indifference and public neglect.

CHAPTER 13

SYMBOLS AND SUBSTANCE

"MAGNIFICENT MEN" OR "MUDDLE-HEADED NONCOMMISSIONED VETERANS"?

Among the more important factors determining an officer's status within the military establishment is the extent to which he is regarded and treated in law and regulation as a professional careerist. Traditionally the U.S. Army commissioned officers have been transferred, usually for the purpose of career enhancement, from unit to unit or post to post. With few exceptions this was not true of noncommissioned officers. Regardless of how much service they had, they usually remained with the regiment that had given them their original warrant. For an enlisted man, transferring was, as a soldier observed in a noted novel of military life, "comparable to a civilian moving from one city to another. His friends either moved with him or they lost him. Even when he moved from, perhaps, a city that he loved to a city where he was a stranger."[1]

Moreover, commissioned officers could, at the end of their careers or in case of disability, count on transfer to the Army's retired list, where they could live in reasonable comfort and dignity. This also was not the case with noncommissioned officers, especially those incapacitated in line of duty prior to completion of thirty years of service.

Within the U.S. Army the interwar years witnessed a drawn-out struggle against tradition and administrative inertia to extend to noncommissioned officers, through the medium of improved provisions for assignment and retirement, some of the symbols and substance of professional status long enjoyed by commissioned officers. A significant part of this struggle was an effort to win for senior noncommissioned officers the privilege of intraservice transfer without forfeiture of rank. This privilege gave the noncommissioned officer a career flexibility approximating that of the commissioned officer—a radical concept in the pre–World War II Army. The outcome of this struggle was not determined until World War II and its attendant mobilization at last forced tradition and administrative inertia to yield. Improvements in retirement privileges for noncommissioned officers, in spite of numerous and eloquent pleas in the pages of professional periodicals such as the *Army and Navy Journal*, had to await the end of World War II and the onset of the so-called Cold War.

TRANSFERS IN GRADE

As long as most noncommissioned officers were unable to transfer in grade from one organization to another, regulation or legislation—as in the legislation of June 4, 1920—designed to more clearly define and establish enlisted ranks and grades lost much of its importance in terms of the enhancement of the role and image of the noncommissioned officer. An old Army saying, true up until the beginning of World War II, "You leave your chevrons behind you when you move," summed up the bitter irony of the career sergeant's lot as compared with that of the commissioned officer. The officer took his rank with him as he moved from unit to unit during his Army career, whereas the sergeant usually had little choice but to remain throughout his career with the same unit that promoted him, or forfeit his stripes if he transferred.

Policy permitting the in-grade transfer of noncommissioned officers of the first three grades was, as will be recalled, first established early in the century, but only for noncommissioned officers of the coast artillery units on permanent or "colonial" station in the Philippines. Later this policy was extended to coast artillery units in Hawaii and the Panama Canal Zone. The replacement of these noncommissioned officers worked somewhat in this manner: The commander of the overseas department submitted to the adjutant general in Washington a requisition for the replacement of each noncommissioned officer whose tour of foreign service was about to expire; he then called upon the chief of the coast artillery corps for recommendations to replacements; these names were referred to the individual noncommissioned officer's corps area commander, who then issued the necessary orders for overseas assignment.[2]

Such orders usually read as follows:

> Staff Sergeant Doe is relieved from further duty with his organization and will proceed to the Panama Canal Department for a tour of foreign service in that command as replacement for Staff Sergeant John Smith, First Coast Artillery Regiment, who is to be assigned to the Ninth Coast Artillery, Fort Banks, Massachusetts.

The wording of such orders was not construed to require that the replacement be assigned to the same organization the returning noncommissioned officer had come from. Inclusion of the latter's name in the order was only for the purpose of identifying the individual being replaced. Overseas commanders continued to enjoy full authority to assign noncommissioned officers arriving in their departments wherever they wished. It was not necessary to assign the replacement to the same organization from which the man departing had come. The overseas department commanders could shift noncommissioned officers about in grade as required. Commanding generals of the Hawaiian and Philippine departments habitually followed this practice, but the Panama Canal Department commander preferred to assign replacements to the unit of the individual being relieved.[3] In time, other arms and branches were also included in this system of in-grade transfers.[4]

These practices were the fruit of several years of study by the Army staff and resulted in the publication of Army Regulations 615-210, which established on a restricted basis the authority for enlisted transfers in grade. These changes were necessitated by several chronic problems, among them the instability of noncommissioned officer grades within organizations caused by frequent turnovers; inequality of distribution of the foreign-service load; and frequent assignment of misfits to overseas posts because of unsatisfactory classification practices in various types of regiments.

One of the first changes took place in 1912, when the system of replacement on overseas station by organization was changed to one of replacement by individuals. Under this system the regimental commander in the overseas garrison made all noncommissioned appointments locally and then reduced these men to grade of private prior to their return to the States. This system was found wanting, and in 1915 it was changed to permit noncommissioned officers of the first four grades to be sent overseas in grade. This change was not, however, put into practice until 1920.

To support this system, two rosters were maintained, one by the adjutant general for the first three grades, and a second by the regiments for men of the fourth grade (sergeant) and below. This system continued in use throughout the First World War for the so-called "colonial" units, but not for France. In 1921 these rosters were discarded, but noncommissioned officers of the first four grades continued to be replaced in grade. Eight years later the system was changed again to allow transfer in grade to overseas posts only of noncommissioned officers of the first three grades. Noncommissioned officers of the fourth grade and below, however, were reduced to private when transferred.[5]

When noncommissioned officers of the first three grades returned to the States in grade for discharge, they were carried in grade during the transfer period on detached service from their organizations until the actual expiration of their term of enlistment, or receipt of notification of discharge.[6]

When lower-ranking noncommissioned officers and privates first class were reduced to private or stripped of their specialist ratings before transfer to the United States, this enabled overseas commanders to fill immediately, by promotions from within their own command, the vacancies thus created. Some exceptions to this rule were made among noncommissioned officers of the finance department who were not disrated before transfer. Overseas vacancies in that department were filled by men sent out from the States in grade. Noncommissioned officers and privates first class returning to the States for medical observation or treatment were also not reduced or disrated, unless warranted by their own misconduct. Specialists, however, could be disrated at the discretion of their own commanding officers.

Because of the highly specialized nature of their training, noncommissioned officers of the fourth grade (sergeant) in the air corps, quartermaster corps, signal corps, medical department, chemical warfare service, and the cavalry were also transferred in grade overseas. However, only the first three grades (1st, master, and staff sergeant) of the infantry, field artillery, corps of engineers, and ordnance enjoyed this privilege. The first three grades of the coast artillery, with the exception of those 1st sergeants who had been appointed to that rank overseas, and master and staff sergeants (supply) and staff color sergeants, were transferred in grade. These exceptions were reduced to sergeants fourth class prior to return to the States.

The Army, however, did attempt to ameliorate somewhat this regulation's impact by creating the rank of acting noncommissioned officer for the period of the transfer. This rank was bestowed upon a man scheduled for return, thereby enabling him to return in grade to the United States. The appointment did not authorize payment of a noncommissioned officer's pay and allowances while in transit. However, the men were allowed to wear the insignia of their grade and were to be obeyed and respected by subordinates as if they were actually holding that rank. The appointments remained in effect until revoked by the commanding officer of the discharge and replacement depot upon departure or discharge, unless terminated sooner because of misconduct or inefficiency.

Dissatisfaction soon surfaced over the more onerous inequities inherent in those aspects of the regulation that impacted unequally upon noncommissioned officers of similar grades among the various arms and services. Interestingly enough, it was the commanding general of the Panama Canal Department who first brought the matter to Chief of Staff General Douglas MacArthur's attention. Early in 1932, he observed in a letter to the Chief of Staff that he did not

> consider it fair to a soldier of the line who has gained the grade of sergeant while serving in this Department to be returned to the States as a private while another man who has gained the grade in the supply corps [quartermaster] returns to the United States in grade. It is a discrimination against the fighting man in favor of the noncombatant. I earnestly recommend that steps be taken to remedy this condition.[7]

On the instructions of the Chief of Staff, the adjutant general canvassed the chiefs of the various arms and branches to determine their views concerning this recommendation. From the chief of the chemical warfare service came the observation that "if noncommissioned officers of the fourth grade and below, who had been appointed by the overseas commander, were replaced in grade it would eliminate many promotion opportunities in units on foreign duty."[8]

An even more negative position was taken by the chief of the coast artillery corps, who pointed out that inasmuch as "52.2 percent of the sergeants 4th grade in the Coast Artillery Corps are on foreign service, the reasons given for not replacing all noncommissioned officers of the first three grades in grade as, for example, master and staff sergeants (color) & (supply) apply equally to the 4th grade." For example, replacement of the fourth-grade personnel in grade would be even more detrimental to morale than in the case of noncommissioned officers of the first three grades, because while the latter were entitled to transportation of their dependents, those of the fourth grade were not. Moreover, many men in the latter grade often had considerable service and were married with one or more dependents.[9]

Moreover, a larger proportion of the noncommissioned officers of the first three grades in the coast artillery corps were serving overseas than in any other arm or branch. For example, only 20.75 percent of the 1st sergeants of the field artillery and 25.3 percent of those of the infantry were on foreign service compared with 52.6 percent of the 1st sergeants of the coast artillery corps.

On this basis, the chief of the coast artillery pointed out, if replacements from the States were furnished in grade for all of the men listed, noncommissioned officers would remain in the States for less than two years before again being ordered to foreign service. This would not only have been manifestly unfair to the men concerned in that it would cause considerable hardship and inconvenience to them and their families, but it would also seriously interfere with the training and efficiency of coast artillery units in the United States.[10]

Of the sixty-three coast artillery 1st sergeants then on foreign service, twenty-five, or 39.7 percent had been sent in grade from the United States. Since there were at that time only fifty-seven coast artillery 1st sergeants in the United States, they spent approximately two years out of every six on foreign service, provided no extensions of tours were granted. This meant that coast artillery 1st sergeants spent more time on foreign duty than those from any other arm of the service.

The chief of the coast artillery corps therefore recommended that preferential treatment be given those 1st sergeants who, although originally appointed to that grade while on foreign duty, had satisfactorily held the grade for a number of years. Replacements for such men from the States should, he declared, be furnished in grade, since this would tend to counterbalance the attrition on foreign service among those who had originally been appointed to that grade in the United States. This would, the chief concluded, keep the number sent in grade from the United States approximately constant. He recommended no changes be made in the regulations governing the return of coast artillery noncommissioned officers of the first three grades.[11]

From the chief of engineers came a similar response. But he added a suggestion that contained the possibility of at least a partial solution to the problem perceived by the commanding general of the Panama Department. That was to adopt a policy of limited mutually agreed-upon transfers between men in the States desiring foreign duty and those overseas wishing to return in grade to the United States.[12]

Nevertheless, the policy proposed by the commanding general of the Panama Canal Department posed problems for the engineers as well. Each engineer regiment in the United States would, the chief pointed out, have to furnish annually from seven to thirteen noncommissioned officers of the fourth grade as replacements for foreign service. This meant the transfer of from one to two sergeants annually from each company and would have resulted in a complete turnover of that grade every four to seven years, with consequent detriment to the units involved.

In urging the Chief of Staff to reject the proposal, the chief of engineers fell back on a classic declaration of the Army's image of the noncommissioned officer as being essentially the company commander's man. "The morale and discipline of a company are helped," he declared, "by reserving to the company commander the initiative in the appointment and promotion of all noncommissioned officers in his unit, and are correspondingly hurt by his having to receive even a part of them by transfer." Furthermore, since neither quarters nor travel allowances for dependents were authorized for the fourth grade noncommissioned officers, many of whom were married, they would suffer real hardship if they were ordered to overseas stations in grade.[13]

Although he did not concur in the proposal to transfer noncommissioned officers in grade, the chief of engineers recommended modification of the existing regulation to permit mutually agreed-upon transfers among sergeants of the fourth grade and to provide for the return to the United States, in grade, of sergeants who had volunteered for foreign service, with a provision for their absorption in the organization to which assigned. The engineers placed a two-month limit on each man's retention in grade while waiting for a vacancy in the unit to which he was being assigned. If no vacancy occurred during this time, the man would be reduced to private. Such an arrangement would, the chief of engineers observed, "give sergeants who desire foreign service an opportunity to get it without losing their grade. Also the prospect of transfer in grade to another organization in the United States would encourage sergeants who attain their grade while on duty abroad to remain in the service."[14]

Only one branch of the service, the field artillery, had been perceptive enough to recognize the basic problem—that of inequitable treatment of career noncommissioned officers. After all, most of the former had made career commitments equally as binding as those made by officers. Yet the careers of noncommissioned officers were hedged about with administrative fiat that belied their reputed status as "backbone" of the Army. After studying the problem, the chief of field artillery concluded that the most equitable system for the first four grades ought to parallel that in use for commissioned officers. He recommended the establishment of two foreign service rosters, one mandatory, the other voluntary. Similar to those maintained by the War Department for commissioned officers, such rosters would have made no distinction between married and single men and would have been decentralized through the adjutant general to the various corps area headquarters.[15]

While the adjutant general, the services, and arms tried to resolve the problem of transfers in grade, many noncommissioned officers themselves managed, with the adjutant general's approval, to develop a practice first suggested by the chief of engineers—mutually agreed transfers. This served as a partial solution to the problem until a new system could be developed. An example of how the mutually agreed-upon transfer system could work is that of Master Sergeant Robert Goodwin. In February 1934, Goodwin, then of the 15th Infantry stationed in Tientsin, China, worked out a mutual transfer through the intermediary of the assistant adjutant general with a Master Sergeant Nicholas Shaffer of the 21st Infantry in Hawaii.[16]

There were many variations on this practice. In December 1938, for example, two staff sergeants then stationed at Ft. Monroe, worked out a mutually agreed transfer whereby Staff Sergeant Thomas H. Clements, under orders to Ft. Banks, Massachusetts, but preferring foreign duty, arranged to change places with Staff Sergeant Howard G. Hatch, who had orders for foreign service but preferred to remain in the States. The chief of coast artillery found no objection, and the transfer was satisfactorily arranged.[17] Through an extensive intrabranch sergeant's network, hundreds of similar transfers took place. This remained an *ad hoc* practice among many noncommissioned officers until World War II.

Meanwhile, by mid-1938, the question of the replacement of noncommissioned officers of the first four grades on foreign service had become acute. A survey of the regular Army showed that 66 percent of the men of the first four grades and 88 percent of the men of the first three grades were married. For example, at Ft. Bragg, North Carolina, then a field artillery post, it was determined that 133 of the 143 noncommissioned officers stationed there had dependents. Yet because of the shortage of quarters for married noncommissioned officers at overseas garrisons, and the high cost of suitable off-post accommodations for married enlisted men, the detail of married noncommissioned officers to foreign service was greatly restricted. The Army staff considered it undesirable, however, from the viewpoint of the Army as a whole, to exempt any category of men from foreign-service duty.[18] One possible solution to the problem, in the words of Major General Van Horn Moseley, then commanding general of the IV Corps, would have been to require the Hawaiian Department "to develop its own noncommissioned officers [corps] with the understanding that they may all be busted upon return to the states."[19]

However, this would have perpetuated a class of professional soldiers permanently tied to foreign duty stations, as had already occurred in the Philippines. Many soldiers stationed there had married native women and after retirement remained abroad. Not only Army policy, but also state law, as for example California's, had this effect when combined with the Asian exclusion legislation that forbade immigration of Filipino women. Author Charles Willeford, then stationed at Clark Field in the Philippines, knew some of these men and commented poignantly on their fate. His unit's first sergeant had been stationed at Clark Field ten years at the time Willeford served under him, was married to a Filipino woman, and had had six children by her. Willford wrote that

> he could never go back to the States because of this mixed marriage. He came from Sacramento originally . . . and was doomed by his marriage to stay in the Philippines

> until he died. There were two retired soldiers married to Filipino women, who lived like natives in Sloppy Bottom [a barrio adjacent to Clark Field], and the First Sergeant would end up like them someday, scrounging cigarettes or a glass of gin from soldiers when they came over to the barrio.[20]

Because of a chronic shortage of quarters at all foreign duty stations, it had been Army policy since January 1936 to send overseas only single noncommissioned officers of the fourth grade and below, or those who were willing to sign a statement that their families would neither accompany them nor would join them later overseas. As a result, unmarried sergeants went on foreign service more frequently than every four years. For example, in the coast artillery, unmarried sergeants found themselves on overseas duty every two years. Faced with an average of only 45 percent of sergeants in all branches unmarried, the adjutant general was unable to make sufficient replacements in overseas garrisons with only single sergeants who possessed the needed qualifications.[21]

To solve this problem the staff considered two possible solutions: one was to replace in grade sergeants of the fourth grade and require them to go on foreign service when selected, regardless of their marital status; or alternatively, to discontinue their replacement in grade and allow foreign service commands to continue to fill such vacancies locally, but revoke them upon return of the enlisted men to the States.

Commanding generals of all overseas departments, as well as the chiefs of all arms and services, unanimously opposed the first solution because it would have been detrimental to morale. On the other hand, the alternative, with certain exceptions and modifications, had worked well in the past. The immediate problem of implementing it was how to absorb those sergeants fourth grade presently on foreign duty and eligible to be returned to the States in grade without causing complete stagnation in promotions for the next several years. Nevertheless, with the exception of the commanding general of the Panama Canal Department, the chief of the army air corps, and the Army surgeon general—who depended upon a viable promotion policy to retain qualified men—all department commanders and chiefs of arms and services favored this alternative.[22]

By June 1939, a decision had been made for the second alternative. Effective July 1, sergeants fourth grade of the air corps, medical department, detached enlisted men's list (DEML), and the 2d Signal Service Company, were to be sent overseas in grade. Sergeants fourth grade of other arms and services who had been ordered to foreign service prior to this date were to be returned in grade for assignment to duty stations without replacement.*

In order to absorb these sergeants as they returned from overseas, promotions to sergeant fourth grade were frozen in the infantry, field artillery, coast artillery, the corps of engineers, the quartermaster corps, the chemical warfare service, the

*The cavalry and finance at that time had no sergeants overseas in this grade and were thereby not included in this order.

signal corps (except the 2d Signal Service Company), and ordnance department. This policy proved short-lived, however, because in September 1939, as war clouds loomed on the horizon in Europe, the War Department took another look at the promotion freeze and lifted all restrictions on promotions to that grade within the United States.[23]

There was yet another category of noncommissioned officers whose transfer involved certain inequities. These were men assigned to the DEML as orderlies for general officers. When generals transferred from one post to another they usually took along with them some trusted noncommissioned aides. This was done by requesting the adjutant general to transfer a particular enlisted man to the DEML of orderlies for general officers in the grade of private. This done, the general making the request immediately restored him to his former grade or, in many cases, promoted him. An example of how this worked is the case of Staff Sergeant Edward S. Smith, of Headquarters Company, Washington, D.C. At the request of General Pershing on March 5, 1930, Sergeant Smith was transferred in the grade of private to the DEML. Effective the same date he was promoted to technical sergeant and continued his duties as Pershing's orderly. However, not all transfers to or from the DEML were as advantageous to the men involved—most noncommissioned officers undergoing similar transfers usually lost seniority when restored to their former rank.[24]

The chief of engineers next took up the cudgels on behalf of noncommissioned officers whom he considered were being unfairly treated. He recommended a change in the pertinent Army regulation (615-5) because of the manifest unfairness of the present method of transfers of noncommissioned officers from organizations to the DEML, where "reduction from higher grade to that of the 4th Grade is mandatory." To prevent loss of seniority, he recommended that

> a noncommissioned officer who is transferred and reduced for the convenience of the government, and who is reappointed to the same or lower grade the same day the reduction is effective, will be given a warrant as of the date of the previous warrant for the grade, or if reappointed to a lower grade, as of the date of his previous warrant in the lower grade.[25]

Strong opposition to this recommendation came from the chief of ordnance, who pointed out that the proposed change "would provide seniority to men to which they are not entitled or qualified," and jeopardize their branch's promotion system. For example, in the ordnance department, promotions to master sergeant were made only from the grade of ordnance technical sergeant, and promotion to the latter grade only from staff or 1st sergeants of ordnance companies. Appointments to staff sergeant were made from any branch of the service only after the men had demonstrated their qualifications in a written examination and been recommended by their commanding officer as possessing the necessary personal qualifications for such an appointment.

The chief of ordnance added that it would be unfair to those men already on the ordnance staff sergeants' list to place newly appointed ordnance staff sergeants ahead of them because they had held the same or higher grade in some other arm or branch or whose warrants had been antedated in accord with the proposed change in the regulations. He concluded that staff, or even technical sergeants in other branches or arms had always been willing, even anxious, to receive appointment as ordnance staff sergeants with date of warrant the same as their date of appointment in the department and saw no reason at all to change this practice.[26]

From the chiefs of the combat arms came similar criticism of the engineers' proposal. The chief of cavalry, for example, pointed out that it was not "fair to enlisted men who remain within their own arm or service for a considerable period of time, to have some soldier who had transferred to another arm or service return to his original arm and reassume the seniority he had prior to his transfer." Furthermore, he observed, it would be unfair to enlisted men of the gaining organization if new men were given a rank senior to that held by others who, through years of service with the unit, had attained seniority in their respective grades. Instead of helping morale, he concluded, this practice would only crush the esprit of those men who had remained with the same unit many years.[27]

These arguments, all in behalf of discouraging a uniform policy of transfers throughout the service, eventually prevailed. The adjutant general pointed out that under then-existing Army regulations, transfers involving loss of grade or loss of seniority in grade were made only at the soldier's request. Usually such requests were motivated by an expectation on the soldier's part that he could better himself through such a transfer. If, on the other hand, a soldier were transferred arbitrarily from the DEML, he was transferred in grade, unless he was transferred in a lower grade at his own request.

In the adjutant general's opinion, the change proposed by the chief of engineers would tend to encourage the "floater" type of soldier—a man given to frequent transfers in a restless search to improve his position. The Army preferred the steadier type who chose to remain with a particular unit for his entire career. The recommended change in AR 615-5 would have placed such men at a disadvantage. This and similar arguments carried the day with the adjutant general, and the original recommendation of the Panama Department was rejected.[28]

Nevertheless, on the eve of World War II adjustments to the needs of such arms as the coast artillery and the growing Army Air Corps, with their special requirements, resulted in an *ad hoc* extension of the authority to transfer men in grade. The exercise of this authority, nevertheless, remained greatly restricted by the "interests of the service" principle and was also limited to the "authority competent to appoint thereto."[29]

The mid-thirties success of the rapidly growing Army Air Corps in obtaining a measure of control over intrabranch transfers in grade of noncommissioned officers is illustrative of this change. Both the coast artillery and the relative new air corps required by their very nature, a high degree of technical specialization in their noncommissioned officers. Therefore, these organizations needed the authority to move them about when and where required "for the good of the service." This fact undoubtedly accounted for the Army Chief of Staff's ready acceptance of a proposal from the commanding general of the air corps for a change in paragraph 11(a) of AR 615-200 to permit the commanding general of the air corps "to transfer enlisted men [in grade] to, from, and within the Signal Corps, Quartermaster Corps, Finance Department, Medical Department, Ordnance Department, and Chemical Warfare Service."

The Chief of Staff agreed that "it would be desirable to extend the authority of the commanding general [air corps] to permit him to transfer enlisted men [without loss of rank] to, from, and within, all arms and services in his command." This action considerably enlarged the career flexibility and opportunities of Army Air Corps noncommissioned officers, particularly the specialists. The senior representative of each of the services on the staff of general headquarters, air corps, however, did have the opportunity to make recommendations and to express his views and that of his service in each transfer involving it.[30] This allowed the several service chiefs to maintain some measure of control over intrabranch transfers by determining the qualifications of fitness of the men recommended for transfer.

In spite of these practices, transfers of enlisted men within one arm or branch in the U.S. Army, right up to the outbreak of World War II, were usually made only in the grade of private. In special cases, however, if in the interest of the service, many transfers in grade above that of private could "be made to existing vacancies by an authority competent to appoint thereto, and authorized . . . to make transfers."[31]

As had happened with the entry of the United States into the First World War, as the nation once again took up arms in global conflict, the exigencies of mobilization and expansion forced upon the Army a radical liberalization of regulations governing transfers in grade of noncommissioned officers. By 1943, all transfers were in grade, except in unusual circumstances,[32] the emergency situation having won out over tradition and a radical step, albeit reluctantly and in the face of world crisis, had been taken toward enhancing career mobility for the noncommissioned officer. No longer would he be doomed to leave his stripes behind as Army regulations had long required. He had moved a step closer to an Army-wide career pattern, an advantage the commissioned officer had always enjoyed. Concurrent with this change, enlisted men were also about to acquire other privileges hitherto reserved only for the officers such as an equitable retirement system that would permit retirement with less than thirty years' service, and retirement for disability.

TOWARD A MORE EQUITABLE RETIREMENT

Not only the privilege of transfer in grade, but a more equitable retirement vis-à-vis commissioned officers had long been withheld from career enlisted men. A basic reason for this was the perceived essential difference between the commissioned and noncommissioned officers' relationship to the Army. An officer coming into the service usually brought with him a college education, or its equivalent, and a potential middle-class earning power. Upon his acceptance of a commission, it was assumed that he had adopted the service as a career. Once in, the government could in effect hold him indefinitely. Most enlisted men, on the other hand, entered the service under relatively short service contracts (usually three- or five-year enlistments) renewable at the option of the government. In most cases a recruit did not consider that he was entering upon a lifetime career, and in normal times only a relatively small percentage did in fact reenlist.[33]

Even for those enlisted men who chose to make a career of military service, their status was hedged about with restrictions. Unlike their officers, noncommissioned officers lacked the same security or tenure in office. Those men who failed to reenlist within a specified time following completion of their enlistment lost their noncommissioned warrants. Further, a noncommissioned officer returning to the United States on detached service for discharge by reason of expiration of his term of service could not be reenlisted in grade. Moreover, even excellent service and character in a past enlistment did not always secure for a man an absolute right of reenlistment.[34]

A new retirement law reducing the service required for enlisted retirement from thirty to twenty-five years was first proposed in Congress in September 1919. Before World War II, legislation had been introduced on at least nine other occasions to permit enlisted men to retire after twenty-five years' service or on disability, as had long been the custom with commissioned officers. In each instance the War Department successfully opposed the adoption of such legislation on the grounds that it would load the Army's retired list with able-bodied men, and that traditionally, disabled veterans had been cared for through the Veterans Administration pension systems.[35]*

The War Department admitted there was a great disparity between pensions paid men disabled during wartime service and those with a similar degree of disability incurred during peacetime. In the mid-1930s, for example, the rate for permanent disability incurred during peacetime was only $45.00 per month—hopelessly inadequate even then. Nevertheless, the Army staff, while acknowledging the inequity, believed that the remedy lay not in disability retirement under War Department auspices, but rather in the hands of the Veterans Administration.[36]

Traditionally, enlisted men who became disabled in line of duty had been honorably discharged. Thereafter, they became eligible for a pension under one or more of the several pension laws administered by the Veterans Bureau and the Bu-

*The Veterans Administration was established as an independent agency by Executive Order 5398 of July 21, 1930, in accordance with the Act of July 3, 1930, which also authorized the president to consolidate the U.S. Veterans Bureau, the Bureau of Pensions, and the National Home for Volunteer Soldiers into one agency.

reau of Pensions. Eligibility for retirement and retired pay from the Army came only after the completion of thirty years of service, including credit for double time given for foreign service, or combat duty prior to 1912. In the eyes of the Army staff, such retirement was a suitable reward for those who had spent their lives in the service, but it was quite a different thing from those compensation rights or pensions due enlisted men whose physical disability had terminated or precluded the renewal of an enlisted contract then in force.[37] The War Department believed that the compensation paid a man who had suffered an impairment to his earning capacity through injury or disease incident to his military service should be based on the degree of impairment rather than on a fixed percentage of his pay received at the time of discharge, as would have been the case if enlisted men were granted disability retirement like commissioned officers.

In fiscal terms, it made no difference whether the enlisted man's name appeared on the Army's retired list or the pension list. In any case, the government in one way or another compensated disabled enlisted men. But under the regulations then in force, the amount of such compensation was determined by the individual's degree of disability and was not affected by his length of service, the rates being fixed by the Congress. In the War Department's opinion, Congress should have removed the discrimination against men disabled in peacetime service. Since such discrimination had an adverse affect on the morale of enlisted men, its removal would have assured fairer treatment and better provision for disabled enlisted men of the regular Army.[38]

There were other arguments in favor of providing both for a twenty-five-year retirement and for disability retirement for enlisted men. Toward the end of the interwar period, many senior noncommissioned officers with long and faithful service were finding it increasingly difficult to adjust to rapidly changing technological and structural conditions in the service, and consequently could no longer be placed in positions commensurate with their rank. Others were in such poor physical condition that they could no longer properly perform their assigned duties. Yet because retirement on a surgeon's certificate of disability would have entitled these men to only a pittance dispensed by the Veterans Administration as compensation for their years of service, most commanders felt compelled to keep them on duty and assign them tasks more in keeping with their physical and mental capabilities. Adoption of the twenty-five-year retirement with provisions for disability retirement might have resolved some of these problems.[39]

Nevertheless, the War Department steadfastly opposed the use of the Army retirement system as a means of caring for disabled men. Yet at that time the Coast Guard permitted the retirement of enlisted men who, by reason of a service-connected disability, were no longer able to perform their duties and were placed on the retired list or dropped from the service. In 1938 there were 715 such men with less than thirty years' service who constituted 67 percent of the Coast Guard retired list.

Although neither the Army nor the Navy adopted such a practice, the Army nevertheless did work closely with the Administrator of Veterans Affairs to secure a revision of existing pension rates to provide more adequately for disabled peacetime veterans. By 1938 the Veterans Administration finally agreed to recommend to Congress the inclusion of retirement features in determining pension rates providing for increases in pensions for length of service over ten years. On this basis the War Department once again decided to deny its support to legislation calling for twenty-five-year retirements and retirements for disability, this time on the grounds that the measures recommended to Congress by the VA would solve the problem.[40]

The solution, long in coming, resembled earlier proposed legislation more than it did that recommended by the VA. However, the senior noncommissioned officers had to wait until the eve of World War II before they would obtain some redress. Not until 1941, in an act passed on June 30, did Congress finally acknowledge that enlisted men of long service who had suffered disability in the line of duty were entitled to retirement benefits similar to those that for many years had been granted to officers. Under this act an enlisted man with twenty years or more of service permanently incapacitated for active duty due to physical disability incurred in line of duty would be placed on the retired list with 75 percent of the average pay received over the six months prior to retirement. A monthly allowance for subsistence, clothing, and quarters would also be authorized. If a man had less than twenty years' service, however, he would be honorably discharged and compensated through the pension system administered by the Veterans Administration.[41]

Following World War II, Congress further liberalized enlisted retirement. Through the Armed Forces Voluntary Retirement Act of 1945, enlisted men of the regular Army and the Air Force were permitted to transfer to their respective enlisted reserves upon completion of not less than twenty nor more than twenty-nine years of active federal service. Once placed on the retired list, the enlisted man received an annual pay equal of 2.5 percent of the average pay received for the six months preceding retirement, multiplied by the number of years of active service. The soldier remained, however, a member of the enlisted reserve, subject to recall to active duty, until completion of twenty years of service.[42]

DECLINE AND RENAISSANCE OF THE WARRANT OFFICER CORPS

Not only were changes taking place in the U.S. Army's retirement practices for noncommissioned officers, but the grade of warrant officer went through significant changes during the decade of the 1930s.

When in the late thirties the House Armed Services Committee queried the War Department about the role of the warrant officer, the department replied that the warrant officer corps was a category of personnel for which the Army no longer had a requirement. Nevertheless, the Army continued to use the grade as it had in the 1920s, as a means of rewarding deserving noncommissioned officers. By the end of the decade, however, it found that even this latter purpose had been found unsound and unsatisfactory.[43]

With the outbreak of World War II and the enormous demands of general mobilization, however, the warrant officer corps gained a new lease on life. In 1936, because of the depletion of the original lists, competitive examinations had been held to replenish the lists of eligibles for regular Army warrant officer appointments. Until the beginning of the war, appointments against vacancies were made from this list. In 1939 warrant officers who had been qualified as pilots were declared eligible for appointment as lieutenants in the air corps, regular Army. The following year the Army authorized warrant officers of the finance department to act as disbursing agents. Although warrant officer appointments now began to occur in significant numbers for the first time since 1922, total strength of the corps nevertheless reflected a decrease until 1942. This was the result of the transfer of large numbers of warrant officers to active duty as commissioned officers.[44]

In 1941, on the eve of America's entry into the war, Congress passed legislation that proved the most significant since the original law creating the warrant officer corps in 1918 in terms of the status of the warrant officer grade. The new act created two warrant grades: chief warrant officer and warrant officer junior grade. Flight pay was authorized for those whose duties involved aerial flight.

Significantly, the legislation also provided that warrants might be assigned to such duties as were prescribed by the secretary of war. When these duties necessarily included those normally performed by commissioned officers, warrant officers were vested with the power to perform them, under regulations prescribed by the president. Finally, when serving as an assistant adjutant of any command, the warrant officer was authorized to administer oaths for all purpose of military administration. Consequently, for wartime purposes, the warrant officer became sort of a commissioned specialist—a far cry from the original concept advanced for the creation of this grade in the early years of the twentieth century.[45]

COMMISSIONED OFFICERS' PERCEPTIONS OF THE NONCOMMISSIONED OFFICER

While in both peace and war the career enlisted man was slowly drawing abreast of the commissioned officer in terms of intraservice transfer and retirement privileges, there was little indication of change taking place in the officer's perception of the noncom.

So often described as "the backbone of the Army," the NCO was seldom discussed as such in the annual reports of the secretary of war. An examination of those reports between the years 1927 and 1941, for example, indicates that the noncommissioned officer was the invisible man—not viewed by the Army staff as a member of a group separate from all other enlisted men. These reports make no mention of him, although each had something to say about the Army mule.

This omission can be explained mainly because traditionally the regular Army saw itself as consisting of only two elements—officers and men. Unlike the British army (and for that matter all the other armies of the western world), which saw itself composed of three elements—officers, noncommissioned officers, and other ranks—the United States Army saw the noncommissioned officer as simply an enlisted man, temporarily elevated at his officer's pleasure to a supervisory rank. This fact seems to suggest that historically noncommissioned officers enjoyed a more clearly defined image and role in those armies raised from societies far more structured and hierarchical than that of the United States.

Another way of determining the noncommissioned officer's image within the regular Army during the interwar years is to examine the recollections of retired senior officers, who recalled with nostalgia those faithful and able sergeants who had patiently and skillfully guided their footsteps when they, as young lieutenants, reported to their first duty stations. Such recollections abound in expressions of fond appreciation, and when taken together, amply support Kipling's oft-quoted image of the noncommissioned man.[46]

Each interviewee recalled the noncommissioned officers of his youth who were often combat-tried veterans, wise, shrewd, and rich in common sense. In the words of one retired general officer, they were "very dedicated people, and you could depend on them, damn it." Most of these men had twenty years or more of service and had earned their stripes slowly, because in those days an enlisted man had to count on at least four to five years of service before he could hope to get any stripes at all. Postwar reductions imposed on the Army had the effect of freezing promotions for many worthy men and denying them for many years their deserved advancement. Nevertheless, many senior officers agreed that most of these men had a degree of integrity and professionalism lacking in many noncommissioned officers of the post–World War II era.[47]

For the most part, these pre–World War II noncommissioned officers had perforce spent many years with the same units and had developed special relationships with their men, relations commissioned officers, subject to frequent transfer, had never acquired. Consequently, the noncommissioned officer in such units enjoyed a great deal of prestige and authority. As far as disciplinary measures were concerned, he could withhold passes, confine men to the barracks, and put them on work details.

Even commissioned officers felt in many subtle ways the force of this prestige and authority. One retired general who had once served in the cavalry observed that these sergeants had

> developed a great deal of pride in the troop and part of the source of [that] pride was the officers of the troop. And if they got a young lieutenant in the troop who was inefficient or couldn't get the job done or . . . got into trouble or anything of that nature, well, they felt that it reflected on the troop. So they felt a real responsibility to try and get the lieutenant to shape up. If you were amenable to their instruction,

> well, you got along fine with them, but if you tried to buck them, well, the next thing you knew, you got a lousy horse assigned to you, or they would change orderlies on you, and you would have one of the eight balls out of the troop as your orderly and so on.

Yet another retired general officer recalled that when reporting as a young lieutenant to an infantry regiment

> You found that the Non-Coms did take over and run it [the company] just as you read of it in the Old Army. The only problem was that you had to have a little pride or pretty soon the Non-Coms would be running you completely. This became a game for the new lieutenant to know how to play the Non-Com to get the most out of him, without becoming his servant. My company commander had been General Summerall's aide for twelve years, including his period as chief of staff. The First Sergeant of Easy Company in the 29th Infantry had been a company officer with my company commander in World War I. This was quite a combination to crack, because the First Sergeant would call you at your quarters, and would say, "The lieutenant will report at such and such a place at such and such a time." Then you would have to say, "Sergeant Davis, who says that I will report?" This was the sort of thing that went on constantly. Most of us learned very quickly. I think that it was good training for us; because it was a contest of wills. Most of the sergeants, once they learned that you were going to be the officer, really appreciated it, but if they could run it on you they would.

In many respects these senior noncommissioned officers also functioned as a kind of quasi-permanent middle-management group for each regiment. Again, a retired general described the system as it worked in the 12th Cavalry Regiment:

> Sergeant Henry [1st sergeant of B Troop] sort of ran the internal administration of the troop, and the troop commander paid the soldiers on payday, and he took them out on tactical exercises and that sort of thing. But the day-to-day management of the soldier and the care and feeding of the soldier was sort of the first sergeant's problem. When we went out on a field exercise there was always a PX tent set up; and in the evening after all the horses and the troopers had been fed and everything, well, the senior NCOs, usually the regimental sergeant major and the first sergeants, would all assemble at the PX tent, and they would chip in and buy a case of beer, and then they would sit around and talk. And one of the things they talked about, you know, was how well their lieutenants were doing and whether Lieutenant Smith had screwed up a tactical problem or not and so forth and so on. So, there was a great deal of pride amongst those men about their officers.
>
> But Sergeant Henry, our first sergeant, taught me a great deal during the time I was in B Troop and I really feel indebted to him for the interest he took in me and for the advice and counsel. I always knew when I had done something wrong, because he would wait until the day's work was finished and the horses were on the picket line or back in the stables and the troop had been released and he would say, "Begging the lieutenant's pardon, but could I have a word with the lieutenant?" And I would say, "Yes, sergeant," and then we would go off some place out of earshot, and then he would tell me what he thought I had done wrong and suggest what to do to correct it.

Most interviewees shared doubts that the post–World War II noncommissioned officers had either the same depth of experience or the attachment to one unit to develop similar relationships with their officers. Some senior officers who, so to speak, had grown up on Army posts, saw their relationships with older noncommissioned officers, most of whom were considerably older than the junior officers of that time, as almost that of father to son. One of these retired generals told of a senior noncommissioned officer who had greatly impressed him when he was a young lieutenant. That was a Sergeant Collins, sergeant major in the 9th Infantry "when I was adjutant of it." Collins was, the old general declared, "a magnificent man."

Conscious, as were many of the generals interviewed, of their early youth and inexperience, this officer too had turned willingly to his senior noncommissioned officers for advice and help in administrative matters. As a company commander, most of whose noncommissioned officers were his senior in years, this officer recalled a time when his unit was beset with numerous small problems. When after investigation everything seemed to point to one duty sergeant as the source of these problems, the company commander "consulted with Sergeant Waite [his 1st sergeant]. And right then the sergeant said, of the duty sergeant, 'He's a troublemaker. Get rid of him, bust him,' which I could do with the colonel's approval, and the thing stopped like that."

No less a personality than General of the Army George C. Marshall, when a colonel commanding Ft. Screven, Georgia, placed a similar value on his 1st sergeants. When he was asked what men he could spare for duty with the newly established Civilian Conservation Corps, Marshall replied, "Leave my post surgeon, my commissary officer, my post exchange officer, and my adjutant, and I will run this command with First Sergeants."[48]

There were other aspects to this relationship. Young officers attending the student officer course at Ft. Benning learned to appreciate their sergeant instructors as a necessary part of their military education. There were those, in the words of another retired general, who

> were trying to make a big impression [and] wouldn't listen to the noncoms, and would invariably get lost because all our sergeants knew where they were anywhere on that reservation [Ft. Benning], they'd been in the outfit for ten or fifteen years and they knew where each tree was in respect to post headquarters. And, if the students listened to them they would never get lost. But, if the students wouldn't listen to them, the sergeants would frequently turn signs around and things like that just to confuse the student officers. Pretty good hazing formation.

Yet most of these sergeants, as close as their duty relationships were to the commissioned officers, lived in separate worlds. As one retired officer put it, they "neither attempted nor desired to call any officer 'friend.' " They usually found all they wanted out of life "by bearing that proud title of soldier."[49]

As fondly as these retired generals remembered those "magnificent men," most seemed to agree that the noncommissioned officers of the World War II era were better educated and better trained. They might not have been as dedicated as those old-timers, one officer observed, "and in many cases they don't have the certain type of shrewdness that they had to make the military machine operate. But today's noncommissioned officers are better because they've had a much broader experience . . . been to many schools."

There was, however, another aspect to the Army's perception of noncommissioned officers in the so-called brown-shoe, interwar force. Recalling his duty as a young platoon leader, a retired general observed that rivalry among units, particularly regiments, for athletic prestige in the peacetime Army was "ferocious and frequently influenced noncommissioned officer selection and promotion." His battalion commander thought that it would be a good idea if he promoted one of his men, a Private Ward—who happened to be an outstanding athlete—to private first class.

> I stacked him up with the other people in the platoon and I said "Never will I make him a PFC, he's not good enough, he hasn't earned it." Well, needless to say, the company commander made him a PFC. Then six years later, I was athletic officer . . . in the 21st Infantry, I used to meet all the athletes coming in at the boat, and behold, who arrived but PFC Ward, so I told Plooky Shute [the regimental commander] we had a first-class pitcher now in the regiment. He said, "What's his name?" I said, "PFC Ward." Plooky said, "You go over and tell his company commander I want him made a sergeant by tomorrow morning." He'd never even thrown a baseball in Hawaii. I was the guy who had to go over and tell Captain McGraw, "I'm sorry, Captain, but the boss says he would like to see Ward make sergeant. A man with all that service should be made a sergeant, he said."

Frequently the question has been asked whether this period was indeed the noncommissioned officer's golden age, as many of these recollections seem to suggest. Without denying that there were many "magnificent men," loyal, able, and shrewd, among the noncommissioned officers of the interwar Army, one must admit that the Army, chronically starved for funds especially during the Depression years, harbored, as one writer described it, "a sizable residue of muddle-headed noncommissioned veterans who had been treading water in the military manpower pool since the Great War." The lack of provision for disability retirement during those years tended to support this. Furthermore, there were "more hoodlums . . . wearing chevrons in 1939 than the Army's leaders would care to admit," or, one might add, than many retired generals would care to recall.[50]

Yet at the same time one has to respect those older men. Another general observed that "the NCO corps has grown with the increased responsibilities that they have had to accept and which have been thrust on them as our Army became more modern and more sophisticated not only in its equipment, but in the many other factors to be dealt with." It was, one interviewee added, "a very relaxed Army that we had in the thirties, it was a poor man's Army." Declared another, "Some of the sergeants were bums, but . . . most of the first sergeants were pretty good men . . . when you got to first sergeant, you got a good man." Recalled another, "Very few of those soldiers had any high school education at all. They had at best a grammar school education, and came almost exclusively from the lower strata of our society. They . . . were much more amenable to the external discipline and never questioned anything. They just did what they were told." Apparently this was sufficient for the infantry and horse cavalry of the 1930s, for in those arms there was as yet little advanced technology to be concerned with.

Whatever its virtues or vices, insofar as the fabled "Old Army" was concerned, it "died almost unnoticed at 2:15 on a Tuesday afternoon and was laid to rest by a host of khaki-clad amateurs," when on August 27, 1940, President Franklin D. Roosevelt, by executive degree federalized the National Guard, and on December 16 signed the nation's first peacetime selective service act. During 270 days in 1942–1943, over 3.5 million civilians in uniform inundated the small professional regular Army. Although the prewar noncommissioned officers formed a major part of the training cadre that helped to make soldiers of these millions "with remarkable success, considering the circumstances," few of them became the noncommissioned combat leaders in the divisions deployed overseas, for most of them were too old, and their numbers too few to match the vast needs of the wartime Army.[51]

CHAPTER 14

WORLD WAR II

CHALLENGES AND CHANGES

On September 8, 1939, one week after the German army invaded Poland and began the Second World War, President Franklin D. Roosevelt declared a limited national emergency. By executive order he increased the regular Army's strength by 17,000 to 227,000, and authorized an additional increment of National Guard units, thereby raising the Army's total strength to 235,000 men. A year later Congress authorized a 370,000-man regular Army. Meanwhile, the War Department planned to raise by October 1941 a field army of one million men, two million by January 1942, and four million by April the same year.[1]

During that first year recruits moved directly into existing regular Army divisions to raise them to authorized strength. This confronted the Army's officers and noncommissioned officers with the formidable tasks of simultaneously providing basic training and conducting advanced field exercises. Later, after both the regular Army and the National Guard units had been brought up to full strength and training camps constructed, recruits were no longer sent directly from reception centers to tactical units but instead to replacement training centers, where they received thirteen weeks of basic training, much of it conducted by regular Army noncommissioned officers. Following this period the newly minted soldiers were sent through three additional phases of training—small-unit, combined-arms training, and finally large-scale maneuvers involving divisions. It was during this latter period that many of these citizen soldiers earned their first chevrons.[2]

WARTIME EXPANSION AND CHANGE WITHIN THE NCO CORPS

With the coming of the war the United States Army found itself faced with essentially the same problems in the selection and training of thousands of noncommissioned officers it had during the First World War. This time, however, the numbers involved were significantly larger than in 1917, and the duration of service would be much longer.

World War II mobilization not only greatly increased the numbers of noncommissioned officers but produced an unprecedented inflation of noncommissioned grades. For example, during World War II the chief of infantry increased the eight-man squad to a twelve-man squad and elevated the squad leader to the rank of sergeant, with the corporal—the erstwhile leader of the squad—as second in command. Consequently, this doubled the noncommissioned officer requirements in the 23,328 rifle squads belonging to the 288 infantry regiments ultimately on duty by the end of the war. Calculating the needs of squads organic to the 70-plus separate battalions of armored infantry, Rangers, etc., the final tally of squads requiring an additional noncommissioned officer (sergeant) rose well past the 25,000 mark.[3]

In addition to greatly increasing the numbers and grades of noncommissioned officers, the wartime emergency necessarily also widened the authority for their appointment and promotion. For example, within the technical services promotion of noncommissioned officers was normally controlled by the service chief's office. But general mobilization, as well as the exigencies of wartime expansion of the Army, brought about rapid and widespread decentralization of authority for promotion of temporary noncommissioned officers in the technical services, including privates first class, to regiments, separate battalions, and even companies.[4]

With the decentralization of promotion authority within the technical services came change for all noncommissioned officer promotions. As of June 11, 1941, warrants in all arms and services issued after July 1 of that year were henceforth to be temporary. Regular Army noncommissioned officers, who received temporary warrants in a wartime grade, however, were allowed to retire at the higher grades even though they were temporary wartime promotions.[5]

The whole system of noncommissioned officer and specialist ratings remained remarkably stable up to the time of the World War II expansion. There was only one change in the list of military specialties after 1923, and that had come in 1930 with the addition of the classification of "instrument operator." One of the main reasons for this stability had been that the personnel-classification system, developed in 1917–1918, fell into complete disuse during the interwar years. Consequently, interest in the problem of classifying personnel for proper assignment waned. Thus, when in 1938–1939 the Army staff made a survey of occupational and military classifications, it revealed a considerable lack of uniformity in the assignment of enlisted grades and ratings for the same job, and a multiplicity of terms used to describe the same job. World War II overtook the work of the survey group, but some of its conclusions apparently affected the planning for reorganization of the enlisted grade structure in 1942.[6]

During the period of prewar expansion (1939–1941), the Army continued to get

AUTHORIZED CHEVRONS, 1920–1948*

Design	*Dates of Authorization*	*Rank*
	1920–1948	Master Sergeant
	1920–1948	Technical Sergeant
	1920–1942	1st Sergeant
	1920–1948	Staff Sergeant
	1920–1948	Sergeant
	1920–1948	Corporal
	1920–1948	Private First Class
	1942–1948	1st Sergeant
	1942–1948	Technician 3rd Grade
	1942–1948	Technician 4th Grade
	1942–1948	Technician 5th Grade

*After Emerson, Table 7-3

along under the 1920 system of grades and ratings. However, early in 1942, in an effort to simplify the structure for administrative convenience, Congress established a new system in the Pay Readjustment Act of June 16. Under this act, technicians were generally selected from the various grades where they had been embedded since 1920, shifted to grades three, four, and five, and given chevrons marked with a "T" in addition to the stripes of those grades (see the accompanying illustration). Technicians in these grades ranked immediately below the staff sergeants, sergeants, or corporals of the line, as the case might be. Thus a technician third grade outranked a sergeant who was in grade four, although in a body of men, the men wearing the "T" with their chevrons had no authority to command if there were line noncommissioned officers present.

Looking back over the World War II years, the personnel division of the Army staff attributed the change to the new system to a desire to clarify lines of promotion among the lower grades and to simplify pay procedures. In spite of its adoption as a hasty wartime measure, the new system endured until 1948.

The congressionally mandated Pay Readjustment Act of June 16, 1942, also raised enlisted pay considerably over the 1920 levels. The monthly base pay for a man in the first grade (master and 1st sergeant), was set at $138.00; second grade (technical sergeant) $114.00; third grade (staff sergeant) $96.00; fourth grade (sergeant) $78.00; fifth grade (corporal) $66.00; sixth grade (private first class) $54.00; and seventh (private) $50.00. On July 1, 1943, an additional 20 percent differential was added across the board for overseas service.

Under the authority granted in the act, the Army advanced 1st sergeants to the first pay grade and added another arc to their chevrons, placing them on the same level as master sergeants. In the same manner, the company supply and mess sergeants and the technical supply sergeants of the U.S. Army were advanced from the fourth to the third grade, that is, to staff sergeant.

Important as these changes in pay and grade structure were, an even more significant managerial innovation was adopted by the Army during the war. This was the military occupational specialty (MOS) system as a means of identifying the many complex skills required throughout the Army. This system consisted of a three-digit numbered code to identify each position in each of the hundreds of separate tables of organization and equipment. Personnel administrators were now able to determine from the overall number of each type of skill required within the Army and to establish the proper grade for each position. Personnel classification in World War I had extended only to the initial classification of men in terms of their civilian vocational skills. But the MOS system adopted during World War II went a step further, for it also provided means for identifying the *need* for these skills within the military structure. Without this valuable managerial tool, the Army could not have handled the vast complexities of wartime personnel classification and assignment.

Valuable though it was, the system had its defects. Two of the more important of these were that it reflected the needs for specialists far better than it did for noncommissioned leaders and, moreover, it made no distinction between these two categories of men. Furthermore, it was overspecialized and tended to degenerate into a hodgepodge of unrelated numbers as each branch organization developed its own series of specialist numbers.

By mid-1943, however, there arose considerable concern within the Army staff over the extent to which a large influx of technicians had produced a general inflation of noncommissioned officer ranks—to the detriment of the prestige and role of genuine combat leaders. Behind this concern lay changes authorized in December 1943 promoting line combat unit platoon sergeants from staff to technical sergeant, section leaders from sergeant to staff sergeant, and squad leaders and assistant squad leaders from corporal to sergeant. Moreover, battalion sergeants major moved from staff to technical sergeant and one half of the privates became privates first class.

As a result of this influx of technical grades and the increase in the grades of line noncommissioned officers was a steady inflation in the noncommissioned officer ranks during World War II. For example, the rank of corporal came to mean very little in a line organization, though the corporal was in theory and by tradition a combat leader. Further evidence of this is that in December 1941 only 20 percent of the enlisted ranks consisted of noncommissioned officers, but by June 1945 the proportion had increased to nearly 50 percent. The increase in the numbers in the first three grades was hardly less marked than in the lower ones.*

In any case, one of the consequences of this increase in noncommissioned ratings throughout the war was to give late arrivals in the Army an opportunity to climb the promotion ladder more rapidly once the chances of gaining a commission had diminished as the war moved to a close. Under these circumstances, the better pay, freedom from menial, irksome tasks, privileges of quarters or passes, and the badge of success symbolized by noncommissioned officer chevrons offered inducement and prestige to the common soldier of World War II. Then, too, there was always the human feeling that further advancement could be made by men who held any grade or rank at one given moment.

Another result of this rapid promotion was that whereas 48 percent of the regular Army privates thought that most of their noncommissioned officers were the best that could have been picked, this view was shared by only 35 percent of conscripted privates during the war. One of the latter commented:

> The noncommissioned officers are not efficient enough to operate in war. There are so many who have received stripes and don't know what the score is. Anybody can be an NCO. Under the present Army no tests are given, you are just told that you have been made a corporal, sergeant, or what have you, and that is all.[7]

*Nevertheless, it is worth noting that if the total number of specialists of all classes in 1939 was included in the number of noncommissioned officers, the actual percentage of men with grades and ratings in that year would have been just slightly smaller than the 1945 percentage.

In general, wartime studies by the Research Branch, Information and Education Division of the Army Staff, disclosed that privates were more likely to approve behavior on the part of noncommissioned officers that reflected intimate social relations with their men; lenient interpretation of rules and regulations, and sympathetic, indulgent policies in the supervision of their men; and lack of emphasis, in social and working relations, or formal status of differences between themselves and their men. On the other hand, War Department analysts found that officers preferred a more "official" point of view of the noncommissioned officer.

While, as in previous wars, there were many difficulties centering on the ability or failure of men to fill noncommissioned positions adequately, other problems were closer to the question of a satisfactory grade structure in the war years. For instance, a substantial number of men who had been transferred into the infantry divisions as replacements for privates and privates first class during 1944 and 1945 were noncommissioned specialists from other branches. This produced a large surplus of noncommissioned officers in most divisions. This influx of specialist noncommissioned officers had an adverse effect on the morale of old-timers, who after working long and hard for advancement, now found further promotion blocked by the presence of these men possessing many stripes but little experience in line positions. Demoralization was also rife among the newcomers whose specialist ratings did not prevent them from being required to serve in the ranks as riflemen—often under men who wore fewer stripes but were hardened veterans of combat.

After a period of orientation, the noncommissioned newcomers were usually given a trial in infantry positions corresponding to their specialist ratings. Some of them made good, others were reduced to privates—a costly procedure in terms of casualties. "This . . . played hell with their morale," one division G-3 declared, "and they haven't made good riflemen. It's too much to expect us to take mavericks and make doughboys out of them in three months."

The appointment of so many new noncommissioned officers in the Army of the United States overwhelmed the relatively small corps of regular Army noncommissioned officers. Thousands of soldiers, many of them trained by these older men, won chevrons within months that it had taken the regulars years to earn. Yet it was these citizen soldiers, drafted, trained, and promoted during the hectic months of 1942 and 1943 who ironically assumed the leadership roles in combat for which many of the regulars had prepared themselves during the lean interwar years. With few exceptions, it was the citizen soldier and not the long-service career noncommissioned officer who led the squads and platoons, sometimes even companies, in some of the hardest fighting ever encountered by the U.S. Army.

How professionally and courageously they carried out their duties has been eloquently portrayed in many personal accounts of combat in World War II. Descriptions of some of these men are to be found in Charles B. MacDonald's account of Company I, 23rd Infantry. They were such men as 1st Sergeant Steven Neubert, Staff Sergeant Raymond Meads, Technical Sergeant Frederick

Weber and Sergeant Raymond Savage, all draftees with temporary wartime warrants.[8]*

Illustrative of the combat capabilities of most wartime noncommissioned officers, whether in Europe or the Pacific, were the experiences of three from the 350th Infantry of the 88th Division, who were faced with their first firefight during the spring offensive in Italy. One was bold to the point of heroism, while the other two were exceedingly, but understandably cautious in the face of their first exposure to enemy fire.

Their regiment had led the II Corps' main effort on the Fifth Army's front on May 11, 1944—the first day of the Allied spring offensive aimed at Rome. Shortly after midnight, when machine-gun fire brought the advance of one of Company F's platoons to a halt, the platoon leader, Staff Sergeant Charles W. Shea, continued forward alone to attack the enemy guns. Crawling up to one gun, he tossed grenades into the position, forcing four enemy soldiers to surrender. He then attacked a second, capturing its two-man crew. Though a third gun took him under fire, he rushed it as well, firing all the while, and killed all three Germans in the position. With these guns silenced, his platoon and then the entire company advanced. The battalion's attack soon gathered momentum and quickly gained its objective.[9]†

On another part of the regimental front neither Staff Sergeant Peter Pyenta or his men were as aggressive. Moving forward at a trot, Pyenta and his group of twenty men soon encountered some unexpected barbed wire. As they sought a bypass, fire from automatic weapons emplaced to the west of a ridge, along which the men were moving, cut down half the group. Fighting back with rifles and grenades, the survivors managed to silence the enemy guns, but with only nine men left and no information concerning the rest of the company, Pyenta withdrew his men to a point about 150 yards north of the Minturno cemetery—their starting point.

Another group, led by 1st Sergeant Paul N. Eddy, came under several short rounds of supporting artillery fire and ran into brief fire fights with individual enemy skirmishers along the ridge road, but continued to advance until halted by machine-gun fire, apparently from the same guns that had decimated Pyenta's group. Failing to silence the guns with rifle grenades, the infantrymen dug in. They vainly awaited reinforcements until nightfall on the 12th, when they too withdrew to the Minturno cemetery, where they found Pyenta and his men.

In spite of such temporary setbacks—regular parts of most military operations—Pyenta and Eddy ultimately led their men to their objectives. Noteworthy, however, is that such acts of individual heroism as that of Staff Sergeant Shea were not always the most desirable characteristic of an outstanding small-unit

*The last-ditch defense of Bataan and Corregidor in the Philippines and the early operations in North Africa were two most noteworthy opportunities the regular Army NCO had to prove his worth in combat.

†Shea received the first Medal of Honor awarded in the 88th Division and was later commissioned a second lieutenant.

leader. The most effective noncommissioned officers led their men, kept them under control, and directed their movements under fire until the objective was gained. It was, therefore, the noncommissioned officer as team leader rather than the individual hero—often a loner—grappling with the enemy far in front of his unit, who was typical of the draft Army's noncommissioned officers in every theater of operations during the war. Admittedly, sometimes one man by his rash courage could do the work of twenty men, yet the latter, when well led, were more dependable and could, when successful, occupy and hold ground that the lonely hero, who often sacrificed his life, could not.

Nevertheless, these men were often the catalysts who carried a stalled attack to success. One was Sergeant Charles E. Mowrer of Company A, 34th Infantry, 24th Division, in an attack against Japanese positions near Capoocan, Leyte on November 3, 1944. Mowrer was an assistant squad leader in an attack against strongly defended enemy positions on both sides of a stream running through a wooded gulch. As the squad leader attempted to advance through concentrated enemy fire, he was killed, and Mowrer immediately assumed command of the squad. In order to better direct fire on the enemy, Mowrer started to lead his men across the stream already churned by machine-gun and rifle fire, but was severely wounded before reaching the opposite bank. After signaling his men to halt, he realized that his own exposed position was the most advantageous point from which to direct the attack. Half submerged, gravely wounded, but refusing to seek shelter or aid of any kind, he continued to shout and signal to his squad as he directed it in the destruction of two enemy machine guns and numerous riflemen. Discovering that the intrepid man in the stream was largely responsible for the successful action against them, the surviving Japanese concentrated the full force of their firepower upon Mowrer. While still urging his men on, the sergeant succumbed to the onslaught. Sergeant Mowrer was posthumously awarded the Medal of Honor.[10]

On the other side of the world, at Utah Beach on D-Day, Sergeant Harrison Summers of the 502d Parachute Infantry Regiment, 101st Airborne Division, won the Distinguished Service Cross as another "lonely hero" in an assault against some German coastal fortifications. Although this task had originally been assigned to a battalion, Summers, with twelve men, none of them from his own unit, moved out against the enemy's positions. When they encountered heavy fire from the first building, the twelve men fell back, leaving Summers to continue the assault alone. He did not hesitate but ran up to the first position, kicked open the door and killed the enemy within at their firing positions. When a captain from the 82d Airborne Division joined him, the enemy gunned the officer down before he had taken ten steps. A lieutenant attempted to join Summers, but he too fell to enemy fire. Still alone, Summers continued down the row of stone buildings, killing the enemy within as he went.[11]

It is not surprising that noncommissioned officers—sergeants—garnered more Medals of Honor during World War II than any other category of Army personnel—100 as compared with 95 won by privates, privates first class, corporals, and technical sergeants to technicians fifth class combined; and 67 won by commissioned officers. Of the 195 Medals of Honor won by Army enlisted men, however, it is noteworthy that only nine of them were won by regular Army noncommissioned officers—that is, by men who had earned their stripes in the regular Army prior to the adoption of selective service.

Such statistics, however, do not disparage the prewar noncommissioned officer: They serve to illustrate the point that most of these men had fulfilled their major wartime roles not as combat leaders of small units, but rather as teachers and trainers of men in the vast training centers that supplied the replacements and fillers for the thousands of tactical units. In any case, many of the prewar noncommissioned officers who had seen service during the interwar years were, by 1944, too old for front-line duty. These factors help to explain their rare appearance in combat.

The major exceptions to this observation were the noncommissioned officers of the Philippine garrison. This was a conglomeration of units composed of individuals ranging from old noncommissioned officers with thirty years' service to green recruits who had arrived in the Philippines just before the war. The latter's plight was worsened when many of the senior noncommissioned officers were taken away to serve as instructors and advisers for raw Philippine army units. This left the regular Army garrisons often at only two-thirds strength, with only one or two commissioned officers per unit and heavily dependent on the leadership of the remaining noncommissioned officers. Nevertheless, these units fought on with skill and determination until overwhelmed by the Japanese forces.[12]

ATTEMPTS TO IMPROVE THE ROLE AND STATUS OF THE NCO

Despite the many outstanding noncommissioned officers produced during the war, there were problems. The Army learned again, as it had late in the First World War, that the practice of simply grafting the prewar *ad hoc* selecting and training of noncommissioned officers onto the body of a multimillion-man conscript force left much to be desired in producing both the quality and quantity of noncommissioned officers needed for a modern army. This was especially true of the combat arms. In most cases, many of these men had been selected and trained by commissioned officers who were themselves citizen soldiers, temporarily elevated to officer rank either through the officer candidate schools, ROTC, or the National Guard. Consequently, even as the war raged on, the Army took steps to improve selection and training of the noncommissioned officer. As it had during the last months of the First World War, so it was in the midst of the second that the War Department urged upon all commanders the necessity of improving their noncommissioned corps.

That in both world wars the department had failed to publish such exhortations at the beginning of the conflict, when organization and training of units and men were just getting under way, suggests that it was essentially reacting to demonstrated deficiencies revealed during the course of operations rather than anticipating perceived needs. "It has been clearly demonstrated in this war," the secretary of war observed, "that the noncommissioned officers are the backbone of the Army." Certainly not an original statement, but nevertheless a somewhat belated recognition that success in combat depended upon the character and qualifications not only of commissioned but also of noncommissioned officers, leading small units such as weapons sections, squads, and platoons.[13]

Army Chief of Staff General George C. Marshall later observed that, unlike their German counterparts who with few men would fight on as if a lieutenant general were in command, the American sergeants "when new at the game would think somebody ought to come right away and reinforce them or take over."[14] But how were sufficient men of such caliber as these to be developed? Army tradition and doctrine placed upon the unit commanders—usually the company or battalion commanders—the responsibility to develop and maintain a thoroughly competent corps of noncommissioned officers in their units. In practice, and through hallowed custom, the noncommissioned officer had been essentially the unit commander's man. A capable commander saw to it that his noncommissioned officers were regularly used as channels of command as well as communications, thereby enhancing their authority and prestige. During the First World War General Pershing, as indeed many of America's allies, had also urged upon the Army the extension to the noncommissioned officers of traditional European prerogatives such as additional liberties, separate messes and quarters, and recreational rooms and facilities that would enhance both their prestige and personal appearance.

Yet for all the emphasis placed on the unit commander's role in noncommissioned officer training and development, the War Department from the beginning of the war enjoined the establishment and maintenance at the regimental or division level of appropriate schools for the training of noncommissioned officers. These schools were to be staffed with the best officers of the command. Where practicable, noncommissioned officers attending such schools were to be relieved from other duties and quartered and messed together at some distance from their place of normal duty. These schools were not to be the informal study groups, meeting after duty hours in the mess hall or orderly room as in the past, but formal educational exercises devoted solely to noncommissioned officer training—a modest step in the direction of earlier Uptonian recommendations made almost seventy years before and a first step toward what would eventually develop into the noncommissioned officer academies established in the post–World War II years.

In spite of War Department encouragement, such schools were uncommon during the hectic days of general mobilization in 1940–1941 because it was a rare unit that had either the time or manpower to afford the luxury of one. Moreover, many commanders were urged to send potentially able noncommissioned officers, who were not performing well, to such schools and then upon graduation transfer them to another organization. Generally, however, instead of being sent to the schools such men were more often transferred in grade to organizations requiring fillers or replacements just prior to movement overseas, or as cadre for units being formed.

The War Department also drew attention to a problem chronic in many units, namely the status and role of noncommissioned officers in units with a commissioned overstrength. While seldom a problem with combat units, it was nevertheless true that in many other organizations such overstrengths led to a tendency to permit surplus officers to usurp the authority and duties of noncommissioned officers. The practice undermined the latter's status and prestige, for it violated the historic principle that officers ought to deal with enlisted men through the appropriate noncommissioned command channels. A competent commander, the War Department declared, would create innumerable situations in which his noncommissioned officers exercised initiative and leadership. Unit commanders, moreover, were enjoined to consult with the appropriate noncommissioned officers in planning the implementation of directives. If it was perceived by their enlisted subordinates that they were integral parts of the unit's planning and command structure, the noncommissioned officers' image and status would be enhanced. However, such exhortations to commanders were perennial. It remained to be seen whether, after the war, the noncommissioned officer's image and role would change significantly.

RELATIONSHIP BETWEEN NCO AND SPECIALIST

There was another problem, notably that of defining the relationship between the noncommissioned officer as leader and the specialist with a critical skill but no leadership responsibilities. This problem had been of chronic concern to the Army staff before World War I and continued to challenge the staff throughout World War II and after. Actually, as the number and variety of specialists increased, the problem became ever more acute, for with the increasing pace of technological change there came the requirement for men with the skills to use and service the new and often complex equipment.

During World War II approximately one third of the fourteen million enlisted men in the armed services received some form of specialist (as distinguished from NCO) training. By war's end the military occupational specialty (MOS) had become an integral and accepted part of the military personnel system. Between the two wars the Army established in the enlisted ranks a system of differential pay for enlisted specialties in order to attract and hold highly skilled men. However, the conditions of mass conscription during World War II, which gave the armed services highest priority for available skilled manpower resources, enabled the Army to eliminate that system. This was, as one student of the period has put it, "to condition military personnel practices for a decade or more in the post war period."[15]

Many aspects of the wartime personnel system, however, were institutionalized following the war. This enabled the Army to retain virtually the full range of enlisted specialist positions that had been established to meet wartime needs. As the mechanical, technical, and white-collar enlisted military occupational specialties increased, there were corresponding reductions in the older military skills. Continuation of the draft in any case assured an adequate supply of higher aptitude personnel for training and assignment in these skills, and enabled the Army to staff these positions without difficulty throughout the 1950s and 1960s.[16]

While there was no problem obtaining qualified men for specialist/technician positions as long as the draft lasted, there remained, nevertheless, some problems in defining the relationship between them and the line noncommissioned officers within the command structure. As mentioned earlier, the Army attempted in mid-1942 to solve these problems by deciding that technicians were to be regarded as noncommissioned officers. Henceforth, technicians of the third, fourth, and fifth class were to be addressed as sergeant or corporal, depending on their pay grade.[17]

But confusion and lowered morale among many noncommissioned officers caused the Army to reverse itself by late 1943 and decide that technicians would no longer have noncommissioned officer status. The rapid growth of the Army, together with an increasing variety of weapons and equipment, resulted in the appointment of specialists/technicians without any training or qualifications for leadership. As long as these men were accorded noncommissioned officer status a typical rifle company had only one private first class and seventeen privates without noncommissioned rank. This placed an impossible burden of fatigue and guard duty upon too few men. To correct this problem the Army decided that all technicians were to rank between PFCs and corporals, with sleeve insignia distinguishing them clearly from line noncommissioned officers. As a possible solution, all specialists/technicians appointed after December 1, 1943 would rank with privates, wear arabic numerals on their sleeves designating their grade, but draw the pay of technician of the third, fourth, and fifth class.[18] This requirement that arabic numerals be worn to designate rating was never implemented, however.[19]

The result of these changes produced not only instant confusion, as one officer observed, but

> all regulations and orders relating to command authority applied to technicians/specialists in the same manner as to other noncommissioned officers. In some units the situation bordered on the absurd when, for example, in an infantry division 60% of the men in its signal company ranks as noncommissioned officers. Eventually, haphazard selection, premature promotion, and incompetent training of noncommissioned officers would take a terrible toll. In February 1944, the then Army Chief of Staff, General George C. Marshall notified the Secretary of War Stimson that "the outstanding deficiency noted in our divisions is the number of noncommissioned of-

> ficers who are below satisfactory standards of intelligence and qualities of leadership."[20]

In response, in late 1944 the War Department shifted twenty-five thousand specialists from service forces to the ground training arms for training as line noncommissioned officers. This move gave the noncommissioned officer corps a needed shot in the arm, so that slowly and against ridiculous odds a new breed of noncommissioned officer at last began to take shape. "What emerged after 44 months in the crucible and 34 battle streamers on the Army flag was seasoned, tough, and professionally accomplished through and through."[21]

WARRANT OFFICER DEVELOPMENTS

Not only did the ranks of the specialists swell to meet the demands of new wartime technologies, but by 1942 warrant officer appointments had also expanded to include forty occupational areas. For the first time, these included areas other than commanding of mine-planter ships, leading bands, administration, and supply—the original occupational areas for warrant officer assignments. The new areas were not incorporated into the MOS structure but were identified by number and title of the examination required for appointment. In late 1942 temporary warrant officer appointments were decentralized to major commanders, and appointments by quota were made in the forty occupational areas for the remainder of World War II. These decentralized appointments were generally used as a selection device. Rather, they consisted of examination by a board for those candidates who met the statutory requirements.[22]

In January 1944 the Army authorized the appointment of women to warrant officer, and the first four appointments were made in March of that year. By the end of the war there were forty-two women warrant officers on active duty.

By early 1946 the forty warrant officer occupational areas had been incorporated into the same MOS structure as that used for noncommissioned officers, thereby raising a question as to the corps' purpose. After the war the Department of the Army answered this question by using the warrant officer appointment as an *incentive* to able noncommissioned officers rather than as a *reward*. For a time, the Army envisioned the warrant officer as a capstone rank into which outstanding enlisted personnel could routinely expect to advance in connection with a postwar enlisted career guidance program. Before World War II the Army's original use of the warrant officer grade as a suitable reward for outstanding noncommissioned officers—too old to be commissioned and who could otherwise look forward to no further advancement—and the postwar decision to use the grade as an incentive, resulted in its extension into so many areas of mixed utilization that in practice warrant officers became largely interchangeable with junior commissioned officers or senior enlisted personnel.

▪ ▪

As with all the wars in the nation's history, World War II brought both progress and change, but not without accompanying confusion and unresolved problems. The small regular Army noncommissioned officer corps, its prewar homogeneity shattered beyond repair, never reverted to its interwar pattern. New managerial techniques, realization of wartime shortcomings, and the need to correct them in the face of the challenges of the Army's global responsibilities combined to produce what in time became the foundations for revolutionary changes in the noncommissioned officer corps.

CHAPTER 15

POSTWAR RETROSPECTION, CHALLENGE, AND EVALUATION

LIGHTS IN A DARK AND DREARY NIGHT

In spite of the Army's triumph over the Axis land forces, the immediate postwar years were to be, as had been the case following all the nations' wars in our history, years of challenge and change. They were made even more difficult by two forces pulling the Army in opposite directions. The first was the traditional national demand to dismantle and retrench, and the second the growing Cold War tensions that would make for expansion and continuation of the wartime draft and eventually war itself.

The more traditional forces found their focal points in two prestigious boards that were called into being to examine conditions, first within the wartime Army and second, within the nation's armed forces as a whole. The first of these was the Doolittle Board, chaired by the wartime hero who led the first air raids over Tokyo. Formed in the spring of 1946, this board examined adverse personnel conditions within the Army brought to light in the immediate postwar period. The second was the Womble Board, which met in the shadow of the Korean War seven years later, in the spring of 1953. This board addressed itself to the conditions affecting career choices for qualified men in all of the armed services and how these conditions affected enlistments.

The forces making for expansion and continuation of the draft gradually gathered strength during the first decade following the victory over the Axis. These years of growing international tension with the Soviet Union ultimately led to confrontation and war with two of its client states—North Korea and the Peoples Republic of China. During these years of cold followed by hot war, forces were set in motion that eventually produced considerable change within the Army and the noncommissioned officer corps itself.

In World War II, conscription, in the words of one observer, diluted the old regular Army noncommissioned officer corps "to a point of nonexistence, so that we had a people's army; and the noncommissioned officers were appointed and had no tradition, and weren't very skilled."[1] Consequently, as had happened during

World War I, company-grade officers became accustomed to taking over many duties traditionally entrusted to the noncommissioned officer.

Not only had the noncommissioned corps been diluted, but the officer corps as well. Both relatively inexperienced commissioned and noncommissioned officers had been temporarily elevated to positions of authority to which they were largely unaccustomed. They were placed in a close but at the same time authoritarian relationship with men, often men of superior social and educational backgrounds—men who were less than tolerant of their nominal superiors' shortcomings. This created situations during the war that the news media could, and ultimately did exploit, once the wartime censorship was lifted.

The Army, the service that had taken the overwhelming number of draftees, quite understandably bore the brunt of much of this criticism. Most of it was aimed at the Army's hierarchical caste system and its alleged abuse by both commissioned and noncommissioned officers, many of whom admittedly lacked the competence and skills needed to deal with many types of enlisted men drawn into the service through military conscription. With the rapid increase in demobilization following the victory over the Japanese empire, a crescendo of criticism of the armed forces swept over the land through radio and press as thousands of often embittered soldiers returned to their homes.

Even within the Army there was little unanimity of opinion. In the immediate postwar period, as criticisms of the wartime Army's personnel and administrative practices mounted, both commissioned and noncommissioned officers of the regular Army speculated on what had gone wrong with the wartime system of personnel management. Officers who had administered the classification policies during the war observed that the fault lay less in the system than in a lack of cooperation and understanding among opinionated or tradition-bound commanders. Others stressed that the entire regular Army had to share the blame, for it had formulated the personnel policies and supervised the training and operation of the huge "democratic" Army that was now under fire. Senior noncommissioned officers pointed to such things as the wartime classification system, inexperienced junior officers, and the concept of a democratic army as all contributing to the "demasculinization" of the noncommissioned officer.[2]

This state of confusion could be, at least in part, laid at the door of Army regulations, for they had given little guidance concerning the status and role of the noncommissioned officer, his selection, and training. His duties had been outlined in only the most general way. He was, for example, "to be carefully instructed in [his] duties as such." Squad leaders were to be responsible for seeing to it that their men's clothing and equipment were properly cared for. Little, however, was said about the squad leader's responsibility for training his men and of his role as their tactical leader in combat.[3] Thousands of temporary wartime officers found this insufficient guidance in the selection and use of their noncommissioned officers.

At war's end the Army expressed its concern, through changes in regulations, over criticism of noncommissioned officer selection and training. First, greater emphasis was to be placed upon selection and schools or academies were established at the division level to deal with training. Noncommissioned officers found unsatisfactory and whose deficiencies could not be corrected through training were to be removed promptly. At the same time, capable men were to be given public recognition of their importance and accomplishments in the hope of enhancing their prestige both within the service and in the outside community.

The Army hoped through these measures to overcome some of the unfavorable stereotypes created during the war years. Commanders were urged to delegate to their noncommissioned officers "all authority rightfully theirs and create increased opportunities for them to exercise command and initiative." Furthermore, commanders were "to consult with their noncommissioned officers in the planning and implementation of directives dealing with enlisted personnel."[4]

Essentially this change was no change at all. It simply sought to remind commissioned officers of what the status and role of the noncommissioned officer had always been. If accepted, many of the duties and responsibilities that had been his before the war but had been lost or neglected during the wartime expansion, would be restored to him.

THE DOOLITTLE BOARD

To examine wartime experience and to deal with the mounting criticism of the Army, Secretary of War Robert P. Patterson in March 1946 appointed a board chaired by Lieutenant General James H. Doolittle. After two months of hearing testimony from scores of witnesses and reading even more testimony from hundreds of veterans and journalists, the board submitted its report in May of that year. While most of the testimony had been critical of the abuse of rank and privilege on the part of commissioned officers, all witnesses nevertheless agreed that an army, in order to accomplish its objectives, must have discipline and must retain authority and privilege that accompany ascending levels of rank. The latter were generally conceded to be necessary inducements for qualified men to seek military careers. Although the board focused its attention on the relationships between commissioned officers and enlisted men in general, some attention was also devoted to the role and status of noncommissioned officers within the military hierarchy.

The embarrassingly high visibility that rank, pay, and privilege had generally given incompetent commissioned officers often all but obscured much of the ancillary testimony given the board concerning the shortcomings of many noncommissioned officers in the maligned military hierarchy. For purposes of discussion, such testimony is divided into two broad categories: Criticism of the abuse of rank and privilege by many noncommissioned officers; and criticism of a system that was frequently perceived as being as inequitable to noncommissioned officers as it was to the rank and file of the Army.[5]

In the first category some witnesses declared that they had seen more tyranny exercised by a tough noncom over his men than between officers and enlisted men: "The average private had bigger bones to pick with the noncom than with an officer." Nevertheless, most of the better noncommissioned officers, witnesses agreed, exercised their authority through strength of will or character. They, unlike commissioned officers, could not fall back on hallowed customs and traditions of the service. For example, when a commissioned officer entered a barracks custom required that the troops be called to attention by the first individual to notice the officer's presence. No similar courtesy was extended the senior noncommissioned officer, although his contact with the men was closer and more direct.

Nevertheless, some witnesses recalled those outstanding senior noncommissioned officers who by the very strength of their personality and leadership had impelled a respectful silence when they strode into a barracks. Such courtesy, witnesses declared, was accorded not merely because of rank but from a respect that such able men had earned. In some cases respect was mingled with fear on the part of many soldiers toward a particularly strong and dominating noncommissioned officer, a feeling vividly evoked in lines from Dennis Murphy's postwar novel, *The Sergeant*:

> At six o'clock he [1st Sgt. Callan] came out of his office and walked down the wooden sidewalk. They were already quiet as he approached, forming their lines without an order, but even when he came opposite them he waited as if it would become more quiet.[6]

To a certain extent this relationship required, as it did with commissioned officers, that the sergeant maintain a certain reserve and distance between himself and his subordinates. One witness, a former 1st sergeant, confirmed this by observing that:

> It was soon apparent to me as a noncommissioned officer . . . that I could not go out at night, drink, play cards, be a good fellow with the men in my squad or platoon, and expect them to obey my commands the next day. It just would not follow—the men felt justified in expressing how they felt about fatigue details, certain drill schedules and training. They thought I should still be the good fellow and march them off to some place where they could loaf on the job, or otherwise carry out activities to their liking. I also found that it was difficult to show the impartiality required in the Army, where I was on terms exceedingly friendly with the men under my command. This was bound to affect my recommendations for promotions—for fatigue details—for ceremonies—for certain activities that were pleasing to all men. I found that I could treat all men friendly, fair, and impartially, and have their confidence, admiration, and respect. This was merely training for battle, when unquestioned leadership is of the highest importance.

On the other hand, observations of the second category suggested that many commissioned officers failed to give their noncommissioned counterparts the respect due their position and experience. Some witnesses observed that noncommissioned officers were frequently victims of an inequitable system that permitted some to be "busted" when they should not have been, and others not demoted when they should have been. Incompetence, however, was the most widely cited grounds for demotions of noncommissioned officers. Yet witnesses added that many officers equally incompetent were not demoted. One witness remarked that it should be "as simple and easy to demote an incompetent officer as it is an [incompetent] noncommissioned officer," and conversely as difficult to break the latter as it was to reclassify the former. This witness added that he had "seen an extremely competent old staff sergeant broken to private because a general saw him chewing gum," and lieutenant colonels "who had screwed things up from hell to breakfast transferred and made colonels just to get them out of the way."

The noncommissioned officer's stripes were also at hazard from another direction—that old problem of transfer in grade. Although in recent years this problem seemed generally to have been solved, there were still exceptions. One witness observed that

> when a man is transferred to another organization at the specific request of the officer to whose command or office he is being transferred, that officer is expected to advance the man one grade; if the man is being transferred at his own request, he has no real right to keep his stripes.

Some witnesses placed much of the blame for most leadership and personnel problems on the Army's rapid expansion in the fall of 1940. Because of this expansion the Army had been forced to rely heavily on reserve and National Guard officers who frequently went directly to duty with troops without having had refresher courses in their particular arm or service. Consequently, the conscripts who were to become the source of the majority of the company-grade commissioned and noncommissioned officers often received their original training from many officers who, through no fault of their own, were themselves unprepared for the tasks thrust upon them.

Likewise, throughout the months leading up to the entry of the United States into the war, the Army had been handicapped by the nation's divided mood and by political considerations that often made the task of training soldiers virtually impossible. When the nation finally entered the war the Army expanded even more rapidly than before, with a consequent increase in these problems. During World War II this often left the Army with no choice but to draw heavily for its officer candidates and its senior noncommissioned officers from among men with little military experience. Although the Army recognized that leadership was a qualitative not a quantitative matter, the demands of war made quantity an overriding necessity, and quality consequently suffered.

A widely expressed opinion that ran like a thread through much of the testimony, both written and oral, was that the Army should reorganize its personnel system. Such a reorganization would, it was hoped, eliminate the official gap or line of demarcation between officers and enlisted men. This gap had been the basis for much of the criticism concerning commissioned officer relations with enlisted men. Some witnesses expected that a reformed or reorganized personnel system would eliminate the distinction between commissioned and noncommissioned personnel and would substitute a gradual gradation from the lowest to the highest ranks in the Army, with each step up the scale involving an increase in duties, responsibilities, authority, and pay. Furthermore, selection of individuals for any position in this scale would involve complying with specific requirements and passing examinations. This would, these witnesses claimed, permit a more effective placement of technically trained individuals, i.e., specialists. Each specialist should also be trained in military practice and organization but not given command responsibility unless leadership qualified.

Although these witnesses were most likely ignorant of the organization of sixteenth-century armies of Western Europe, what they urged upon the board bore an uncanny resemblance to it. In those long-vanished armies there had been no clear distinction between commissioned and noncommissioned officers; rather from the corporal to the captain general or the field marshal there was a progression in rank through which a surprising number of able careerists rose to prominence. Except for the private soldier, all ranks were officers of the military organization, differing only in their degree of authority and responsibility.* Needless to say, even the Doolittle Board was unreceptive to such a radical reorganization of the Army.

Many witnesses also urged that the pay scale should correspond to that which prevailed in the most advanced personnel management systems in business and industry—the pay being commensurate with larger responsibilities and duties. They advocated that traditional monetary allowances should also be on a graduated scale, but factors other than solely rank should govern the amounts paid at each level. Such a system would, it was believed, provide incentive for advancement, a motivation to follow the military as a career, and hopefully reduce the possibility of incompetence getting into positions of authority and responsibility. Of course adoption of such a plan would have involved considerable change in the existing statutes, the abandonment of many hallowed customs and traditions, and a complete rewriting of most Army regulations.

Although the board's wide-ranging recommendations did not go so far as to accept all of the concepts included in the voluminous testimony, they did include much that, if adopted, would have constituted one of the most thorough-going reforms of the Army ever undertaken. While these recommendations focused on the relationships between commissioned officers and enlisted men, their adoption quite naturally would also have had a profound effect on the status and role of the noncommissioned officer. Inherent in both the recommendations of many wit-

*See Chapter 1.

nesses and those of the board itself were concepts concerning military justice, training, military education, promotion, and retirement that in later years came to influence reform and change throughout the postwar Army.

Among the board's recommendations were that greater emphasis be placed on the moral character, knowledge, and competency of those in the service or those planning to enter it. The board also recommended that the selection of men for positions of responsibility up the promotion scale be based on the most advanced practices in personnel selection found in industry, business, and government, as well as those developed by the Army. Furthermore, the board recommended, such a system should be established on a basis of merit, making it possible to advance especially competent individuals ahead of any seniority average.

Turning to the retirement system that had long been an object of criticism because of its inequitable treatment of enlisted men, as compared with officers, the board also called for the establishment of a system where for shorter periods of service, such as ten and twenty years, all personnel, commissioned and enlisted, would have the privilege of retirement as well as an assurance of some degree of security for having devoted a significant part of their lives to the Army. Disability retirement should likewise be extended to all ranks. Such changes in the retirement system were, in the board's eyes, desirable because all ranks in the Army of the future should be composed of younger men who in general were regarded as better able to cope with the new technology then emerging. The retention of older men should be only on the basis of their proven capability to accept and adapt to these ideas.

Despite the Doolittle Board's sweeping recommendations for reform, mainly in the relationship between commissioned officers and enlisted men in other than its judicial aspects, the Army staff ignored most of them. The board's judicial recommendations, however, were eventually embodied in major changes made in the Uniform Code of Military Justice (UCMJ). Essentially they curtailed the power of local commanders "to use military courts as personal disciplinary weapons." In 1950 Congress enacted legislation that incorporated these changes into a new UCMJ. No major revisions were made in this code until 1969.[7]

As for the board's recommendations that the staff rejected, many years and two more wars passed before any of the concepts inherent in the report became integral parts of the Army's structure. Some of these concepts included greater recognition on the part of the Army of the noncommissioned officer's professional status and a pay scale more in keeping with the pay of highly skilled foremen in civilian life. Enhancement of noncommissioned status would have been a step toward the historical traditions of European armies and a more clearly defined relationship between noncommissioned officers and the rank and file. One might ask, therefore, what the board's real significance was for improving the status and role of the noncommissioned officer in the immediate postwar period, other than laying the foundation for a revised UCMJ. Its importance lay in the fact that for the first time the officer-enlisted relationship was laid bare in public and thoroughly analyzed. In the 1960s, there emerged concepts for the reform and reorganization of the Army's personnel system out of this examination. These in turn became goals that the Army set for itself in the 1970s.

INTERWAR REFORM AND NEGLECT

When, at four A.M. on Sunday, June 25, 1950, thousands of North Korean troops attacked across the demarcation line between North and South Korea, the U.S. Army faced its first real battle test since the Japanese had laid down their arms in August 1945. Not only for the Army but for the nation, the Korean War was a unique challenge. By assuming the leadership of the United Nations forces in Korea, the United States adopted a war policy new for itself but not to its allies. As an agent of the United Nations, the United States was charged with fighting a war for limited objectives, and was governed by the concept of controlled violence as a means to an end. For this kind of war it has been noted, Americans "were not ready in body or in spirit."[8]

Not only was the U.S. Army fighting a war for limited objectives determined for it by an international rather than a national agency, but it was also facing its first combat encounter since the reforms of the Uniform Code of Military Justice recommended by the Doolittle Board. As one observer has remarked, "The U.S. Army since 1945, had, at the demand of the public, been civilianized. The men in the ranks were enlistees, but they were a new breed of American regular who, when they took up the soldier, had not even tried to put aside the citizen."[9]

Because of the fears generated by the so-called Cold War, the U.S. Army had not been allowed as it had following World War I to revert to the small, elite professional force it had been in 1939. Then noncommissioned officers had been exclusively troop leaders—"a hard corps elite, set apart from their fellow men; washboard-knuckled Buck Sergeants, the scourge of barracks and field, ruled platoons in despotic grandeur, and corporals held sway over squads."[10]

Like it or not, before World War II, many noncommissioned officers were in effect "married" to their men for richer or poorer, for better or worse, in sickness and in health. These noncommissioned officers knew their men like the backs of their own hands. Living for the most part in the barracks, they were on tap around the clock, ministering to basic needs, maintaining good order and discipline, and keeping a sensitive thumb on the unit pulse seven days a week. These noncommissioned officers were on top of the heap, proud, prestigious, and professional. Theirs was the power and the glory, the authority supreme.

By 1950 this selfless professionalism had been allowed to decay. Devotion to duty above family and self had become rare enough to elicit special attention. After all, a large percentage of "new army" noncommissioned officers were married and no longer lived in the barracks with their men. A new mood, a national frame of mind, had infiltrated the Army. This could not, however, be laid at the door of the Doolittle Board reforms. Although they had somewhat restricted the powers of the company commander, good commanders and professional noncommissioned officers still had the means at hand to forge a hard-fighting outfit out of the malleable recruits supplied them by the postwar draft.

What changed was not so much the relevant Army regulations but rather how they were viewed by the postwar Army, cautiously sensitive to a media and public ever ready to censure. As one officer described it,

> Sergeants—once chosen to sit at the right hand of God because of a singular ability to soldier and make jar-head privates see things the Army way—now shrank from shouting at psychoneurotic yardbirds because it might get them in a jam. Under a smoke screen of simpers and silly smirks, they simply chided roughnecks for being rude, and sent them on their ways.[11]

Not only did the nation tolerate—indeed, insist upon—less rigid standards of behavior and discipline for the Army, it also indicated that it was willing to provide no more than 600,000 men to carry the burden of America's global military responsibilities. Successive secretaries of defense reasoned that any army charged with a larger-than-ever peacetime role and supported by a peacetime draft had to march in step with popular sentiments and therefore had to be made over into the likeness of those sentiments. Since Americans were historically egalitarian in sentiment, the Army too must be remade in that image.[12]

Among other things, this meant breaking down the walls of tradition and custom that the Old Army had erected between the sergeants and the enlisted multitude. Short of a court-martial, the company officer's power to inflict punishment had been reduced. It also became increasingly difficult to dispose of ineffective noncommissioned officers. However, the real effect of the Doolittle Board had been largely psychological. While the officers had not been shorn of all their authority to enforce discipline and good order among the troops, many felt as if they had. By the time the Korean War began, the professional officer corps had not yet learned to live with the new code. What the Doolittle Board had in small measure tried to do was bring the professional Army into the new postwar society. What it could not do in 1946 was foresee the future.[13]

Not only was the Army being reshaped by changing national mood and sentiment, but there were other problems as well. Some of these were of the Army's own making. As a result of Army personnel policies the top noncommissioned officer grades were heavily overstrength. Below the level of master sergeant, noncommissioned grades were frozen. A reduction in grade, therefore, became almost permanent. Yet when the Army's postwar overall strength reached its low-water mark in mid-1948, noncommissioned officer ranks were bursting at the seams. Nevertheless, much practical training had been neglected, and commissioned as well as noncommissioned officers had been permitted to forget their battle drill. Consequently, when the Korean War burst upon a startled world, as one career officer remarked,

> The pampered, undisciplined, egalitarian army that U.S. society had forced upon us, was unveiled as a soft, hollow shell. Out-numbered, out-maneuvered, out-gunned, and out-trained, most senior noncommissioned officers, however, stuck by their guns, but many younger ones melted away. Crew-served weapons were abandoned to the foe, and dead and wounded comrades left behind. This was the legacy of a lack of training and discipline.[14]

RENAISSANCE OF THE CORPS

The first weeks of the war in Korea were indeed replete with panic, poor combat leadership, and lack of discipline as was to be expected from the general malaise that spread throughout the occupation forces in Japan. Yet in the midst of this, some genuine noncommissioned leaders, mature veterans of World War II who still remembered some of their combat lessons, stood out like shining lights in a dark and dreary night of defeat and despair. Against war's shattering experiences only superbly trained and conditioned troops, knowing almost from rote what they must do, can carry out their tasks under all conditions. The knowledge that they were so trained brings pride to men, "pride in their own toughness, their own ability," and this pride held them true in Korea when all else failed.[15]

However, among those troops suddenly plucked from their comfortable billets in Japan, this confidence was sadly lacking. Company A, 34th Infantry, which early came under enemy attack, illustrates this problem. When Platoon Sergeant Ray E. Collins shouted to his men, "Commence firing! Commence firing!" only two other men, veterans of World War II, took up the shout and opened fire. Although the men of Company A from their hilltop position could plainly see the North Koreans advancing on them, hardly anyone fired. Sergeant Collins then turned to the two riflemen in his own foxhole: "Come on, you got an M-1, get firing! Come on!" he added, jabbing one of them sharply. Most of the men, however, stood slack-jawed, staring at the advancing enemy as if unwilling to believe that they were really trying to *kill* them. For many minutes only the squad and platoon leaders did any shooting, and more than half the men never got off a single round.[16]

It was indeed fortunate for Collins's men that in him the flame of combat leadership continued to burn brightly during this first engagement. If it had not been for his example, picked up by the other noncommissioned officers, the enemy might have overrun and destroyed the platoon. Following this action, Collins tried to determine why his men had failed to fire against the enemy. Of thirty-one members of his platoon, twelve complained that their rifles were either broken or dirty or had been assembled incorrectly. Collins sorted out the defective weapons, dropped them in a nearby well, and secured new ones for his men. Inasmuch as the sergeant had joined the platoon just a few days before, he could not be blamed for the lack of weapons maintenance.[17]

There were other leaders, such as Master Sergeant Travis Watkins of Company

H, 9th Infantry. In line near Yongsan, Korea, Sergeant Watkins distinguished himself by conspicuous gallantry when an overwhelming enemy force broke into his company's position and isolated thirty men of the unit. Watkins at once took command, established a perimeter defense and directed a fire fight that repelled a series of fanatical enemy assaults. During this action he moved from foxhole to foxhole, exposing himself to enemy fire, giving instructions, and offering encouragement to his men. Later, when the need for ammunition and grenades became critical, he shot two enemy soldiers fifty yards outside the perimeter and went out alone to gather up their ammunition and weapons. As he did so, he was attacked by three others and wounded. Returning their fire, Watkins killed all three. He then gathered up their weapons and ammunition as well and returned safely to his own lines.

During a later assault, six enemy gained a defiladed position and from there began hurling grenades into the perimeter, making it untenable. Watkins rose from his foxhole to engage them with rifle fire. As he did he was hit with a burst of machine-gun fire, but he continued firing until he had killed the six grenade throwers. With this threat eliminated, Watkins collapsed, paralyzed from the waist down by his latest wounds. Nevertheless he encouraged his men to hold on and refused all food, preferring to give it to his able-bodied comrades. When it finally became apparent that his men could no longer hold the position, Watkins ordered them to withdraw but to leave him behind so as not to impede their escape. Before they left, one soldier, at Watkins's request, laid his carbine on his chest, the muzzle pointing toward his chin. Watkins put his hand around it and, grinning at the men standing about, wished them good luck. For his gallant leadership and bravery, Master Sergeant Travis Watkins received a posthumous award of the Medal of Honor.[18]

As the war dragged on, many of the more experienced noncommissioned officers, like Watkins, became casualties, and junior noncommissioned officers emerged to prove themselves able leaders. Such a situation developed in Company G, 23d Infantry, 2d Infantry Division, during the fighting for Heartbreak Ridge in October 1951.

Company G and its commander, First Lieutenant Raymond W. Riddle, was assigned a supporting role in the battalion attack against the ridge. Hill 520 along the ridge was the company's objective. Because he had so few men, Riddle decided to mass his forces and attack the objective frontally. His two remaining platoons, the 1st and 3d—the 2d platoon had been wiped out in the fighting and Riddle had divided its survivors between the remaining formations—deployed in a line of skirmishers. There was nothing unusual about this operation, except that one platoon was commanded by a corporal and the other by a private. Corporal David W. Lamb commanded the 1st platoon and Private Cliff R. High the 3rd. Before beginning their advance, both platoon leaders selected six men to support them with machine guns as a base of fire during the assault. After calling off their long-range supporting fire, Lamb and High led their men in a line of skirmishers toward the enemy objective some two hundred yards away. Within three hours the men of Company G captured and secured their objective.[19]

Among the Allied forces noncommissioned officers also upheld honored tradition in adversity. It must be remembered, however, that for the most part, Allied units, unlike the American, were composed largely of professionals. When, for example, the British 1st Battalion of the Gloucestershire Regiment was ordered to withdraw from a hill it had held for sixty hours against furious enemy attacks, the British had no choice but to fight their way through the surrounding enemy forces. Under the circumstances, there was, however, no hope of evacuating sixty seriously wounded men. Among those who volunteered to remain behind to care for them were the battalion commander, Lieutenant Colonel Carne, the surgeon, the chaplain, and Sergeant Major Hobbs, the father figure and keeper of good order and discipline. Both Colonel Carne and Sergeant Major Hobbs had spent most of their adult lives with the regiment, and it was unthinkable in the tradition of the "Glosters" that they would abandon their men in their hour of need. Of such men are great leaders and great regiments made.[20]

Not all the problems faced by American units in Korea can be traced to inexperienced small-unit leaders and inadequately trained and disciplined troops. Some of the blame must be assigned to the Army's *ad hoc* replacement system, more or less improvised in the heat of battle. Officers, noncommissioned officers, and men were often sent forward to units shortly before they were to go into action, as had been the case with Sergeant Collins or, as was frequently the case, even during an operation. This meant that many squads, platoons, and even companies in combat were not functioning teams, for replacements at any grade cannot be fitted effectively into a unit within two hours of an operation. Even the best leader needs some time in order to get to know his men before they face the enemy together. As one historian of the war has asked, "Who follows an unknown leader wholeheartedly, or puts his life in the hands of a virtual stranger? Cooperation among friends is the rule, among strangers it is news."[21]

As in earlier wars, capable noncommissioned officers took over command when a unit—company or platoon—commander became a casualty. Another example of this occurred during an action conducted by D Company, 8th Engineer Combat Battalion, in an attack on the summit of Ka-san, September 4, 1950. Colonel R. D. Palmer, 8th Cavalry, to whose command the 8th Engineers had been attached, considered the operation so important he had his intelligence officer accompany the engineers in their attack on Ka-san. Although Platoon Sergeant James N. Vandygriff of the 2d Platoon, D Company, doubted the wisdom of the mission, he immediately took over command of his platoon when his lieutenant collapsed because of illness. Sergeant Vandygriff's platoon then led the company to the objective. Shortly after reaching it, Colonel Palmer, recalled to his command post, left Company D to face a North Korean attack just after dawn the following day. The engineers repulsed the enemy but suffered some casualties.

During the attack enemy fire destroyed Vandygriff's radio, forcing him to use runners to communicate with his company commander.

Shortly after the battalion commander reinforced Vandygriff's platoon with one from E Company, the North Koreans attacked again. Unfortunately, the reinforcements had brought no mortar with them. This left Vandygriff with no choice but to use a 3.5-inch rocket launcher (bazooka) to fire into the approaching enemy formations. The North Koreans apparently thought that this fire came from either a mortar or a 75mm recoilless rifle and broke off their attack. Meanwhile the resourceful Sergeant Vandygriff checked his platoon and found that it was just about out of ammunition, so he ordered his men to gather up from the enemy dead all the weapons and ammunition they could. In this manner the men of the 2d Platoon obtained about thirty to forty rifles, five machine pistols, and some hand grenades.

At 1:30 P.M. the 8th Cavalry received orders to withdraw. This order failed to reach anyone in Company D. Nevertheless, exercising their own judgment, Sergeant Vandygriff and the sergeant commanding the platoon from E Company and the remaining platoons of D Company, decided to withdraw, having sustained over 50 percent casualties. This they did successfully, without losing any more men.[22]

In another instance, after the commander of G Company, 34th Infantry, was killed along with the leader of his 3d Platoon, Sergeant Junius Poovey, a squad leader, took command of the platoon and continued to lead the men in combat for several hours. By late afternoon Poovey had only twelve effectives and seventeen wounded left in his platoon. With his ammunition almost exhausted, Poovey requested and received permission to withdraw to the main G Company position. After dark, the twenty-nine survivors, three of them on stretchers, escaped from their exposed position by timing their departure from the hill with the arrival of supporting tanks, which engaged the enemy and thereby diverted their attention from the beleaguered men on the hilltop. Sergeant Poovey and his men then managed to make their way to the main company positions half an hour before midnight.[23]

These incidents and many more that could be cited demonstrated that although both commissioned and noncommissioned officers had over the five years since the end of World War II neglected to refresh their battle wisdom gained during that experience, they quickly relearned it, albeit at considerable cost to themselves and others. As Brigadier General S.L.A. Marshall described it, top noncommissioned officers, having been repressed for half a decade, quickly bounced back. Nearly all of these men were mature, combat-hardened veterans, less disposed than their World War II predecessors "to wait for official approval before taking local decision in an emergency situation."

Consequently, the ranks ultimately received better personal direction and commissioned officer time was less monopolized by attention to small details as able noncommissioned officers emerged from the trial of battle. Combat studies made during the conflict demonstrate that without exception, in every outstanding performance of an infantry company, there was conspicuous participation by a number of noncommissioned leaders. This strong participation in small-unit actions was, again in Marshall's words, "the most encouraging aspect played by junior leadership." During the Korean conflict the noncommissioned officer, when compared with his junior officers, emerged more prominently as a battle leader than he had in World War II. The record was convincing to the point that "strengthening the prestige of the upper bracket of noncommissioned officers within the combat arms contributed more directly than all else to an uplift of the fighting power of the Army."[24]

General Marshall believed that much of this improvement in noncommissioned officer leadership in the line derived from the quality of the junior officers. Without "their understanding and sympathetic support, no such advance would have been possible." For a comparable relationship between officers and noncommissioned officers, one would have to look back to World War I, for a "comradely and mutually supporting" relationship that did not border on familiarity. This relationship proportionately advanced the "leadership dynamic of both groups, particularly during combat."[25]

As the Korean conflict continued, evidence accumulated which showed a radical increase in the percentage of individual participation in the fire fight, as compared with operations in World War II[26] and in the early days of the Korean conflict. Some of this change was undoubtedly attributable to the practice of junior officers and noncommissioned officers moving about among their men during a firefight and remaining with an individual until he began to use his weapon. Consequently, in an average infantry company in Korea, a large percentage of the men not only participated actively in the firefight, but exercised varying degrees of initiative in on-the-spot leadership and personal action of a type that improved the unit's position and induced cohesion.[27]

Influencing this development was stronger and more clearly defined squad action, as compared with World War II engagements. Enhancement of squad operations owed much to the highly compartmented nature of the Korean terrain—deeply eroded hills, ridges, narrow valleys, and deep gorges—that forced units to advance as squads, withdraw as squads, or get cut off as squads. This may have accounted somewhat for the high percentage of corporals and sergeants who won the Medal of Honor during the Korean War. Out of a total of fifty-five awards, these two ranks, including those in the Marine Corps, accounted for the largest number awarded in that conflict.[28]

This marked improvement in small-unit leadership after December 1950, when the Eighth Army was near total defeat and its spirit dragged bottom, to mid-1951, when the Army's infantry gained a moral ascendancy, derived from a regained confidence in their leadership and weapons. This enabled the individual soldier to accept with relative calmness of spirit the prospect that local surprise might be achieved by a numerically superior opponent. These individual soldiers, as organized into units, "were well disciplined and physically conditioned troops, measured against our best standards," Marshall observed. They were now well led and took an active interest in the job at hand. "They engaged strongly and took their losses in admirable spirit. Even in defeat, as for example, the withdrawal from the Yalu, they acquitted themselves like men."[29]

In spite of these improvements, as the war sputtered to an end there remained perennial organizational problems that would plague the career-minded noncommissioned officer in the postwar years. As had been the case during previous periods of rapid wartime expansion, temporary enlisted promotions were authorized during the Korean War without regard to local grade vacancies or major command promotion ceilings, provided time-in-grade or time-in-service requirements had been met.

Rifle companies promoted squad leaders to sergeant first class (E-7) as the once-honored rank of corporal sank into oblivion. Rifle companies lost all but three corporals, a trio of machine gunners, who doubled as assistant squad leaders in each of the weapons squads. Eventually, as the process ran its course, almost half of an infantry company, as in World War II, was classified as noncommissioned officers. This in turn tended to undermine the hard-won authority that thousands of noncommissioned officers had regained on the battlefield. As an observer of the Army during that period remarked, "as in World War II, a lot of soft-shoe artists who couldn't tell an aiming stake from a rusty field range got stripes just because they were there."[30]

THE WOMBLE COMMITTEE REPORT

Widespread advocacy within the media for many of the reforms inherent in much of the earlier testimony given the Doolittle Board in 1948 quickly diminished in the face of the growing concerns engendered by World War II and the harsh realities of the Korean War. With the end of the latter, however, there emerged once more, in an even more virulent form than after World War II, a chronic lack of respect for the military life both inside and outside the armed services. When combined with bitter public debate over the inconclusive outcome of the Korean War, this lack of respect produced a widespread mood that soon manifested itself in a "growing lack of concern among armed forces personnel in military service as a worthwhile and respected career."[31]

The Joint Chiefs of Staff were particularly concerned over the implications of this lack of respect, for undoubtedly it adversely affected the future proficiency of the military services. On April 30, 1953, President Eisenhower informed Congress that he too shared this concern and had therefore directed the secretary of defense to study the problem and recommend solutions. The Womble Committee, chaired by Rear Admiral J. P. Womble, Jr., with senior representatives from the other services, was the result.

As had been the case with the Doolittle Board, attendant publicity soon attracted hundreds of letters from active and retired military personnel as well as from the general public. After examining this correspondence, together with voluminous testimony obtained from the several military departments, the committee took note of the national mood by declaring in its final report, submitted in October 1953, "that military service as a career that will attract and hold capable and ambitious personnel had deteriorated alarmingly in comparison with other fields of skilled endeavors."[32]

The committee quite naturally focused its attention on career personnel—the professional officer (including reservists on extended active duty) and the noncommissioned officers of the regular forces, since these represented the foundation on which the armed forces rested. The committee set about to determine "why has military service lost much of its attractiveness as a lifetime career for inherently capable personnel and what corrective measures are necessary?"

As had been the case with the Doolittle Board seven years before, the Womble Committee learned that there existed a widespread indifference, even hostility, on the part of much of the citizenry toward things military. Many career personnel felt this hostility and were sometimes influenced by it to resign. Much of this hostility seemed to stem from public controversy not only over the recent conflict in Korea but also the continued operation of the Selective Service. The committee observed that able and conscientious men would not likely continue in a profession thus dishonored by public criticism.

There were other problems as well. For example, the postwar posture of United States foreign policy meant that the U.S. Army now had global tasks involving not only garrisons but operations in distant lands. These meant that professional soldiers were required to accept a career that prohibited, or made difficult, normal family life—an added obstacle to recruiting and holding first-rate men in military careers.

Furthermore, greater demands for industrial manpower subsequent to the outbreak of hostilities in Korea had greatly increased the number of inexperienced personnel, particularly within the Army, and had resulted in a significant dilution of experienced career leaders. This dilution was further exacerbated by losses of experienced personnel who no longer found the military service an attractive and satisfying career. Most important, in terms of its impact on the noncommissioned officer, dilution of experienced personnel as a result of the war necessitated increasing centralization of authority and control. Not only did this diminish the status of the company commander somewhat, but also significantly undermined the prestige and authority of his noncommissioned officers. Consequently, oversupervision became a hallmark of the Korean War and post–Korean War period.

Indirectly, the committee also sharply criticized what it perceived to be the pernicious influence of the Doolittle Report, observing that certain post–World War II "reforms" designed primarily to force officers and enlisted men into a common pattern by diminishing differences in rank served instead only to reduce pride in service, inhibit effective discipline, reduce incentive, and ultimately encourage careerists to leave the service. Deterioration in discipline, moreover, led to a decline in professional standards. In the committee's eyes, much of the blame for this could be traced to the adoption of the Uniform Code of Military Justice, with its unwieldy legal procedures. This, in turn, the committee declared, made the maintenance of military discipline more difficult.

In sum, these shortcomings had inhibited the development and maintenance of that essential quality of *esprit*. Without collective pride in organization and mission it was difficult for men to identify themselves with a particular military unit and mission. Yet throughout the immediate postwar years shortages of experienced personnel resulted in frequent reassignments and excessive turbulence in command and personnel that made such identification difficult.

The committee disclosed yet another factor as adding to the problems facing the military services—the decline in leadership skills. The rapidly increasing importance of technology and its servant, the specialist, were perceived by the committee as detrimental to the development of the needed skills of command and leadership as the primary criteria in promotion policy. This led, the committee observed, to the promotion of many officers and noncommissioned officers solely on the basis of technical skills, inasmuch as their ability to lead and to command had never really been tested. Military command and technical astuteness were regarded by the committee as two separate and distinct fields of endeavor and had to be so recognized in promotion procedures.

The committee therefore concluded that professional standards of leadership and command had to be restored if the military service were to be made more attractive to able men. The prestige and authority of commissioned and noncommissioned officers alike had to be restored. Their authority and responsibility had to be increased, incompetents ruthlessly demoted, over-supervision—caused by a shortage of able leaders—be eliminated, and a premium placed on the development of leadership and command abilities, especially among junior officers and noncommissioned officers. This would, perhaps, reverse the pendulum put in motion by the reformist demands embodied in the Doolittle Board's report, the Womble Committee opined. However, almost two decades and another war in Asia would pass before these goals came even close to realization.

There were of course other aspects to solving the problem of how to restore the attractiveness of military careers. These included such things as improvement in pay, living conditions, and retirement. The committee observed that recent increases in service pay had neither approximated increases in the cost of living nor even increases in pay afforded federal civil service employees.

In the meantime there had also been alarming decreases in compensatory benefits traditionally enjoyed by military personnel for their relatively low pay. These two trends combined to place career military personnel, especially many noncommissioned officers, in the position of being unable to live even modestly on their pay or to provide adequately for their families.

Not only did the career soldier find it increasingly difficult to make ends meet while on active duty, in retirement the challenges were even greater. The formerly unique advantages once enjoyed by military personnel were rapidly disappearing in the postwar years, as industry adopted retirement plans often exceeding those offered by the armed forces, which had pioneered in this area. The Womble Committee therefore concluded that retired personnel had to share in any pay readjustments made for those on active duty.

To such improvements in the lot of the career soldier, the committee declared, had to be added better provisions for dependents, including improved housing, education and survivor's benefits. If the armed services were to compete with the burgeoning postwar civilian economy for capable personnel they should, the committee stated, provide compensation adequate to the sacrifices demanded by the military way of life. Nothing less would assure the armed services of that hard core of expert career personnel capable of training and leading soldiers in the event of another total mobilization, as in 1941–1942. Although the Womble Committee's report dealt alike with commissioned and noncommissioned officers, all of its conclusions impinged on the role and status of the careerists upon whom the structure of a battle-worthy army rested—the noncommissioned men.

Like the Doolittle Board, the Womble Committee served to draw attention to serious and chronic problems affecting the professional soldier. While its deliberations and conclusions solved none of the problems, in years to come the lot of the professional soldier, especially the noncommissioned officer, improved somewhat, partly through belated adoption of many of the committee's recommendations.

The Doolittle Board, the early setbacks of the Korean War, and the Womble Committee all in one way or another threw light on many of the Army's internal shortcomings and strengths that were revealed during the first decade following World War II. It was against the background of these disclosures that the U.S. Army took up the formidable tasks of organizing the military occupation of Germany and Japan. Concurrently, with the accomplishment of these tasks, the Army faced the growing challenges of the Cold War and a second war in Asia.

CHAPTER 16

TRAIN US TO LEAD

FIRST ARMYWIDE STEPS TO IMPROVE NCO EDUCATION

As the U.S. Army undertook its postwar occupation missions in Europe and Japan and confronted the early challenges of the Cold War, the need for numerous, well-trained noncommissioned officers remained just as critical and apparent as it had in the early days of World War II. To meet this need, the Army began work on two programs.

The first of these programs, a career-guidance program, originated at the Army staff level and expanded rapidly. Although the Korean War temporarily brought the program to a halt (see Chapter 15), it was later revived, but in a greatly changed form. The significance of this program was that it represented the first step toward what almost twenty years later evolved into a servicewide enlisted personnel career management and training program resembling that long in use for the commissioned officers.

The second program—an Armywide system of noncommissioned officer academies—had its beginnings in the field as an *ad hoc* effort within what was to become U.S. Army, Europe (USAREUR). Despite some continuing problems, the academy concept also spread throughout the Army, and its operational standards were eventually standardized by service regulations.

As had happened following earlier wars, the United States after World War II rapidly demobilized its armed forces, and the Army, being the largest, bore the brunt of the demobilization and its attendant problems. From a total of over eight million men, the U.S. Army (including the Army Air Corps) was reduced to 1,950,000 by June 1946, and 1,070,000 by the following July. These reductions were only partially offset by modest increases in the strength both of the National Guard and the organized reserves. By June 1950, the former numbered 324,761 in 4,597 ground-force units, and 176,541 officers and men in 10,629 units of the organized reserves. An additional 390,961 men were carried on the rolls of the reserves, but were unassigned.[1]

By prewar standards, these figures seem impressive, yet in view of the widely perceived growing Communist threat to Central Europe and East Asia, the U.S. Army was woefully weak and inadequate for the implementation of a defense policy directed at checking this threat. In response to presidential urging and the ominous portents of Soviet-sponsored expansion, Congress agreed to a temporary extension of the Selective Service Act to March 31, 1947. However, after that date it allowed the act to lapse until June 1948, when the Communist coup in Czechoslovakia and increased Cold War tensions stirred the legislators to revive the draft. By that time the Army had shrunk to two-and-one-third divisions spread thinly in occupation garrisons in Austria, Germany, Japan, and Korea.

It was therefore to the development of an Armywide systematic educational and selection program aimed at developing better noncommissioned officers that successive chiefs of staff and commanding generals of the Army Ground Forces—later the Continental Army Command (CONARC)*—directed their attention from 1947 into the 1960s. While armed conflict in Korea and Southeast Asia delayed the fulfillment of this program, it nevertheless served to demonstrate a need for it.

DEVELOPING A CAREER GUIDANCE PLAN

The experience of mass mobilization and of war itself had earlier convinced the Army of the need to give greater emphasis to the development of Armywide standards for noncommissioned officer selection and training. This conviction grew out of wartime developments that impacted significantly on the noncommissioned officer's role and status in the Army. Among these were a rapid increase in the use of complex fire and improved communications equipment, the application of scientific management techniques to personnel and supply administration, and the proliferation of the service support forces. Taken together, these developments made the Army a far more complex organization than it had been at the beginning of World War II. To illustrate this point, by war's end in 1945, 64 percent of the Army's total enlisted strength had been engaged in technical and administrative specialties and only 36 percent in strictly military-type occupational specialties.[2]

Out of this spectacular increase in technical specialization there emerged a need for a more workable classification system for the numerous skills spawned by swelling wartime technological developments. In turn, this led, it will be recalled, to one of the most significant managerial innovations to emerge from the war—the introduction of the military occupational specialty (MOS) system. While this system was not without some shortcomings, personnel managers ultimately so refined its application until it became one of the most important tools of their trade, pro-

*CONARC was responsible for all the army commands within the continental United States, in contrast to the overseas army headquarters.

viding a means of identifying rapidly and accurately requirements for a host of complex skills.

During World War II, a large influx of noncommissioned officer technicians, together with the inevitable increase of line noncommissioned officers, had so inflated overall noncommissioned ranks as to greatly diminish the prestige and position of genuine enlisted combat leaders. At the beginning of the war noncommissioned officers made up only 20 percent of the enlisted ranks, but by June 1945, with the increase in enlisted specialists who were also considered noncommissioned officers, the proportion had more than doubled, rising to 50 percent.

One of the first problems, and one that proved to be a major part of the revamping process, was a search for an Army-wide educational and promotion plan for career enlisted men. It proved to be a search that continued for three decades before a satisfactory and workable plan was finally devised. During this period the Army terminated the occupations of Germany and Japan, fought two wars in Asia to unsatisfactory conclusions, and established at the army and corps command level a series of loosely coordinated noncommissioned officer academies. All of these activities in one way or another provided valuable experience and training for noncommissioned officers. Nevertheless, the Army staff early realized that only an Armywide, standardized educational, selection, and promotion system for career enlisted men would produce the quantity and quality of noncommissioned officers required by any army with global responsibilities. The career-guidance plan for warrant officers and enlisted personnel, published in 1947, was one of the first steps toward this goal.[3]

However, this plan proved to be only a tentative and informative statement submitted by the War Department to its subordinate commands for comment. By September 1947, these comments and recommendations had been returned to the Chief of Staff. They contained a cross section of ideas from commissioned, warrant, and senior noncommissioned officers concerning the plan's adequacy as well as suggestions for improvements in its procedures.

The plan's ultimate purpose was to build broadly qualified, well-rounded warrant and noncommissioned officer corps that, in time of emergency, could provide a trained cadre for mobilization as well as augment the regular Army officer corps. The Army expected this would avoid repetition of its experience in the early months of both World War I and II, when rapid and large-scale expansion had greatly diluted both the commissioned and noncommissioned corps.

The guidance plan provided for regular career progression, with promotions to be based on competitive examinations rather than position vacancies. All jobs were to be graded with established Armywide uniformity, providing equal pay for similar jobs. This would include an overhauling of the enlisted grade structure within the existing seven–pay-grade framework.

As a first step in preparing a new pay-grade structure, the Army dropped all technical ratings. Personnel in each pay grade, whether troop leaders or specialists, were given the same insignia of rank. However, to distinguish between the two categories of noncommissioned officers, men with troop leader assignments were given insignia with dark blue chevrons on a gold background and were to wear green cloth tabs on each shoulder loop.* Noncombat specialists would wear gold chevrons on a blue background and no tabs on the loops.

The plan had three principal elements. The first was to determine what jobs were necessary for the accomplishment of the Army's mission and to set the standards and grades needed to fill these jobs. The second was to devise a training system for qualifying personnel for these jobs, and the third to create a system of personnel procedures for getting the right man into the right job.

It will be recalled that a policy established by the War Department Circular 303 of August 5, 1920 had first introduced the rank of staff sergeant. The circular had also established the seven enlisted grades and chevrons that for the most part, remained in effect until the July 1958 change. It had also prescribed that chevrons would henceforth be worn on the left sleeve only. This latter provision had lasted only until March 16, 1921, when War Department Circular 72 directed that chevrons be worn once more on both sleeves.[4] The career-guidance plan also provided in each job field for a progression of "career ladders," outlining the possibilities for development and promotion of career enlisted men to the highest position on each job "ladder." There were also provisions for lateral transfers to related job ladders. When adopted, this plan was to establish a system providing an overall pattern of job fields offering the widest opportunities within a particular field, yet at the same time the system would provide opportunity within the broad career fields for narrower specialization when needed for mobilization or for civilian components. A pay grade was established for each job to assure that equal skills received equal pay, regardless of the type of unit to which the soldier was assigned.

Testing for promotion under this plan was based on the premise that each man was first a soldier, then a specialist. Therefore, all personnel progressing from the seventh to the sixth pay grade had first to demonstrate proficiency as soldiers by passing a test in general military subjects. To assure the desired uniformity of standards throughout the Army, this test was prepared by the War Department and distributed to all unit commanders.

As a gesture to tradition, administration of the tests and promotions for grades seven through three were left in the hands of the unit commanders. However, the commanding generals of the Army Air Corps, Army Ground Forces, overseas commands, continental armies, and designated Army Air Corps commands, and chiefs of administrative and technical services for class II installations (those not

*The shoulder loop is the strip of cloth affixed to the shoulders of military shirts and jackets worn as outer garments, usually secured under the collar with a button. Loops are used to display a variety of items, including rank and unit heraldic insignia. Shoulder loops are often confused with "shoulder straps," embroidered cloth devices secured at right angles to the shoulder on officers' blue dress uniform coats and intended only for the display of rank insignia.

under the command of a general officer), were authorized to centralize, where necessary, promotions from the fourth to the third grades in order to give equality of consideration to those soldiers on detached duty and in isolated stations. Promotions from the third to second grades (the senior grades), however, were to be made exclusively by these commanding generals.

Finally, the War Department was to fill Armywide vacancies in the first grade, based on the candidate having had eighteen months' service in grade two, and at least five years' total active service, and passing the appropriate servicewide competitive MOS test. Moreover, only those enlisted soldiers who had been recommended by their immediate commanders and had fulfilled all requirements for advancement would be permitted to compete for promotion to the next higher grade. Provision was also made for personnel entering the third grade to take tests for the Officer's Reserve Corps (ORC). Those men who qualified were to be given reserve commissions without having to attend officer candidate school (OCS) in their particular arm or branch of service. Once having received a reserve commission, the soldier might volunteer for a tour of extended active duty as a commissioned officer, and while on duty, compete for a regular Army commission. Thus did the career-guidance program for enlisted men open for the first time a programmed career ladder that could lead all the way from recruit to a regular Army commission.

From the point of view of the noncommissioned officers, the plan's most important provision was an attempt to abolish on-the-job training (OJT). Fallen into disrepute because of the nonstandardized training provided, OJT nevertheless had long been the traditional method of training noncommissioned officers. Quite understandably, the quality of the training provided depended largely on the skill and ability of the individual noncommissioned or (in some cases) commissioned trainer.

Apprentice training was substituted for OJT in the expectation that it would differ little from formal school training, except in the method of instruction. Apprentice training was expected to stress actual performance of the tasks under conditions that had been standardized throughout the Army.

As for formal schooling, its adoption was to depend on completion of a department-ordered job analysis program that would determine the extent to which formal school training should be a prerequisite for advancement. In brief, if the particular MOS could best be taught in a classroom environment, it would be. As an additional means of instruction, that old ideal of self-study was revived. To this end, commanders were to use their troop information and education (TI&E) officers to inform enlisted personnel about the numerous correspondence courses then offered by the United States Armed Forces Institute (USAFI) at Madison, Wisconsin. These could be used as preparation for many of the specialist MOS examinations.

As a part of the Army's goal to upgrade the quality of noncommissioned officer training, the career-guidance plan also provided for retesting senior noncommissioned officers in their respective MOS. Six months after the announcement that henceforth all promotions would be based on MOS tests, as outlined in the plan, all personnel in the first through third grades were to be prepared to be retested to determine their proficiency in grade and in their primary job field. However, to protect longtime careerists, the plan exempted from retesting those soldiers with ten years or more of service in their present or higher grade, as well as Medal of Honor recipients.

Noncommissioned officers who failed the tests for retention in their present grade were to be reduced to the next lower one. After six months these men could be required to pass the test for that grade, or face another reduction to the next lower grade until, presumably, they had found their level of competence. The War Department hoped thereby to purge the first three grades of unqualified and incompetent personnel. Before adoption, the plan was reviewed by the major commands, and their comments and recommendations in turn reviewed by the staff. Following this review, the final text of the plan was published in January 1948.[5]

Actually, comments and recommendations from the field produced very few changes in the original Circular 118. The new circular mainly defined the plan's purpose more precisely. In its own words, it was

> to establish in the Army an orderly and systematic plan of assignment, training, and promotion for enlisted men and warrant officers so as to make service in the Army a dignified and attractive career for the American citizen who desires to serve his country, and to permit his advancement to the highest grades and rank limited only by his ability, integrity, and initiative.[6]

As shown in this statement, the new circular also served as a partial rejoinder to postwar criticism of Army training policy. Since the end of the war there had been frequent complaints of lack of professional knowledge on the part of many infantry noncommissioned officers. Among the latter were all too few of the more capable combat leaders of World War II, most of whom had elected not to remain in the service. Those who did remain often suffered from a lack of focused or structured training for their military occupational specialties. Many of these men ran through a variety of assignments over the years ranging from cook, mess sergeant, truckmaster, platoon sergeant, military police sergeant, honor guard noncommissioned officer, or perhaps inspector or instructor.

When assigned as infantry squad or platoon sergeants, these men often faced insuperable difficulties in meeting their professional responsibilities. They were expected to lead, train, command, and instruct men who might know more about the task at hand than they did. Nevertheless, they were expected to perform in a professional manner tasks for which they had not been prepared. During the period when the draft provided the bulk of the Army's manpower, many noncommissioned officers frequently found themselves attempting to train men with far more formal education than they had. Only a far-reaching program of high-level professional military training could enable noncommissioned officers to surmount these shortcomings.[7]

The revised circular as published was expected to help provide guidelines for such training. As in the original, apprentice training was to be used to the maximum in place of OJT to advance the individual soldier after completion of his basic training. As for the self-study program, there was to be no further reliance on the United States Armed Forces Institute (USAFI). Instead, the Army would itself prepare self-study pamphlets for each MOS to aid the individual soldier in preparing himself for a qualifying examination in his MOS. (In this provision can be seen the conceptual origins of the skill qualification test of the 1970s.) Formal instruction at service schools would continue to be used as a training vehicle for those MOSs best taught in that format, but it would not be used as the sole means for awarding an MOS for advancement.

Examinations in basic military subjects were to be administered at the discretion of the training division commanders while annual testing for the first three grades and semiannual examinations for grades four and five were to be administered on dates specified by the Department of the Army. Promotion authority, however, remained unchanged from the previous draft circular. The seven enlisted pay structure was retained by dropping the rank of sergeant, fourth grade—the venerable three chevrons of the so-called buck sergeant, which had designated that rank since 1833—but adding the grade of recruit. Grade four was then redesignated corporal, with three chevrons.

The complete package set up an enlisted grade structure as follows:

Grade	*NCOs*	*Privates*
E-7	M/Sgt.	—
	1st Sgt.	—
E-6	Sgt. 1st Cl.	—
E-5	S/Sgt.	—
E-4	Cpl.	—
E-3		PFC
E-2		Pvt., E-2
E-1		Rct., E-1

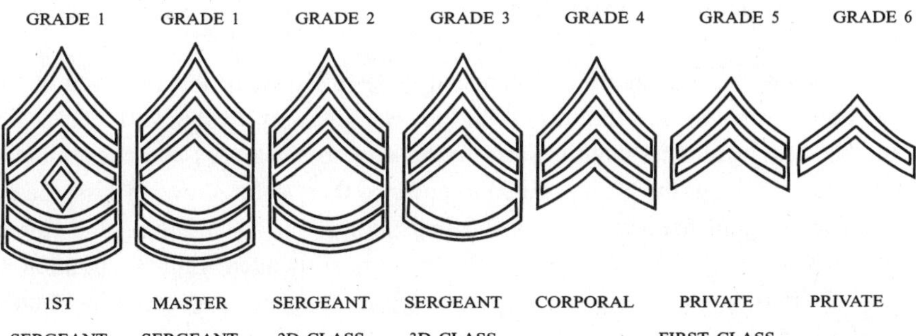

The new circular also outlined changes in traditional recruiting practices. Henceforth, recruitment was to be by career field rather than by arm or service. There were other changes to come.

Drawing up the new grade structure had not been without its problems. General Bruce C. Clarke, then representing the Army Ground Forces commanded by General Jacob Devers, tells of a briefing that the G-1 gave to General Omar Bradley, Chief of Staff in 1948.

> The G-1 started, "E-7 will be a master sergeant." General Bradley nodded his head. "E-6 will be a sergeant first class." General Bradley again nodded approval. Continuing, The G-1 said, "The E-5 will be known as sergeant second class." General Bradley's fist hit the desk. He said, "Get out of here, and come in with a new name. There may be second-class sergeants in the Army, but we are not going to call them that." When the G-1 came back the name had been changed to "staff sergeant."[8]

Observing that the most important changes to the enlisted grade structure in this century seem to have taken place in the summertime (August 1920, August 1948), one career noncommissioned officer commented,

> Is it coincidence that all these sweeping peacetime changes have been made in the summer months? Are staff officers more ingenious in the summer? Is it, perhaps, that they have less work to do in the summer and can use their time then to concentrate on those thorny problems that have to be shelved during busier times of the year?[9]

In 1949 the Career Compensation Act reversed the old order for numbering the enlisted grades that dated from 1920. Henceforth, the top grades—master sergeant and 1st sergeant—were designated as E-7, and recruit would be E-1.

Contrary to expectations, postwar revampings of the wartime personnel management system seemed actually to have favored the enlisted specialists over the line noncommissioned officers, because it eliminated all distinctions in pay and rank between the two categories. In 1950 the two different types of chevrons designating troop leaders and specialists by different colored background cloth were incorporated into one basic design, thereby ending much confusion in distinguishing rank.

Abolition of the category of technician in 1948, however, left unsolved one of the basic problems that prompted the postwar changes in the first place. The number of noncommissioned officers in the same basic grades had been substantially increased, but the change failed to enhance their status. Nevertheless, the enlisted career-guidance system limped along until 1950, when, during the Korean War expansion, it collapsed completely and was suspended. Enlisted promotions then reverted back to the former practice of filling position vacancies in units as they occurred.

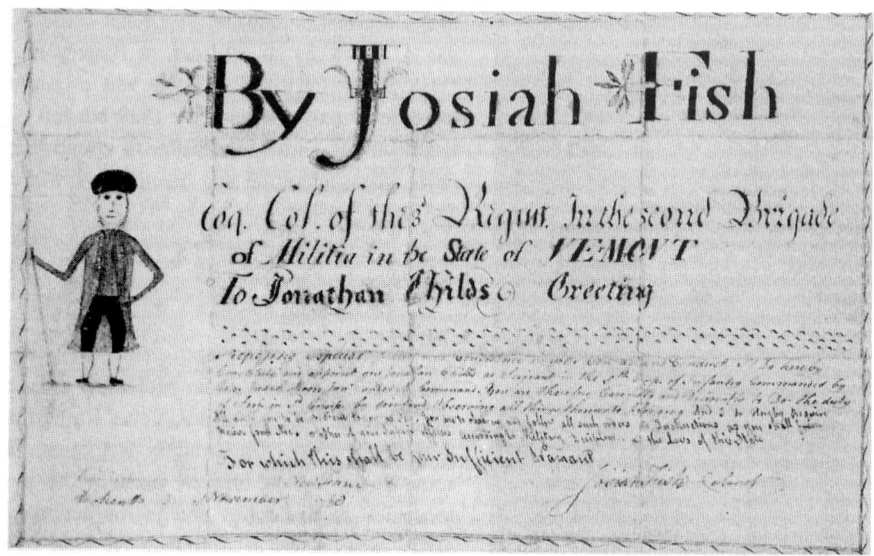

By Josiah Fish

of Militia in the State of VERMONT

To Jonathan Childs Greeting

For which this shall be your sufficient Warrant

Revolutionary War certificate of promotion for Sergeant Jonathan Childs, signed by Colonel Josiah Fish, Esquire, is one of the earliest examples of a noncommissioned officer warrant signed by a regimental commander. (SMITHSONIAN INSTITUTION)

Civil War Commissary Sergeant William McKinley served in Ohio's 23 Infantry Regiment commanded by Col. Rutherford B. Hayes. Both men became president of the United States. (WESLEY DAY COLLECTION)

Infantry Sergeant S. D. Quint is wearing the M1881 dress uniform with spike helmet, both of which reflect German influence on the U.S. Army, which followed Germany's 1871 military victory over France. (ARMY MUSEUM OF THE NONCOMMISSIONED OFFICER)

U.S. Cavalry First Sergeant C. E. Warren and corporal, 1888, on American frontier duty. NCOs of this period often led small, independent units on operations that today would be called peacekeeping duty. (ARMY MUSEUM OF THE NONCOMMISSIONED OFFICER)

In 1898, First Sergeant William Clark of Company F, 12th Regiment of Pennsylvania Volunteers, had a key role in his company's mobilization during the Spanish-American War. He is shown here wearing the M1895 service hat with clover emblem of the Second Army Corps. (MONTOUR COUNTY HISTORICAL SOCIETY AT USAMHI)

With more than thirty-three years of regular Army service, First Sergeant Samuel Woodfill was proclaimed "the greatest American soldier of the [First] World War." He held both the Medal of Honor and the French Legion of Honor. (SMITHSONIAN INSTITUTION)

In World War II, Staff Sergeant Audie Murphy was one of America's most highly decorated soldiers. He held the Silver Star, the Distinguished Service Cross, and the Medal of Honor, all awarded for heroism. (COURTESY OF STAN SMITH)

In the Korean War, Medal of Honor winner Master Sergeant Ola L. Mize distinguished himself by heroic action against the enemy in Surang-ni on June 10–11, 1953. (U.S. ARMY)

Sergeant (then private first class) Clarence Sasser was awarded the Medal of Honor for medical heroism and heroic leadership while himself severely wounded during a North Vietnamese ambush in Ding Thoung Province in the Republic of Vietnam. (U.S. ARMY)

Sworn in on July 11, 1968, Sergeant Major of the Army William Wooldridge was the first to hold the post as the Army's most senior noncommissioned officer. The position was created both to improve the quality of enlisted advice to the Army's senior leaders, as well as to enhance the role of noncommissioned officers following the low point in enlisted leadership during the Vietnam War. (U.S. ARMY)

Command Sergeant Major Yzetta Nelson of the Women's Army Corp Center was the first woman appointed to this rank, March 20, 1968. With CSM Nelson is CSM Curtis S. Ramey, also appointed on that date. (U.S. ARMY)

An Army engineer for most of his career, Sergeant Major of the Army Leon L. Van Autreve was the first SMA who was not from the combat arms. He was also the first who had not served in Vietnam, and the first foreign-born (Belgium). He served in the post from 1973 to 1975. (U.S. ARMY)

The old and new SMA rank insignia. The new insignia was first presented to, and worn by, SMA Richard Kidd in 1994. (U.S. ARMY)

New rank insignia, a unique collar insignia, and now a new flag for the SMA, indicate the Army's desire to further enhance the prestige the of the noncommissioned officer corps. The flag was presented to SMA Robert Hall in 1999. (ASSOCIATION OF THE U.S. ARMY)

The Number One NCO mission in the twenty-first century—individual soldier training—begins with the drill sergeant in basic training and continues in the unit until the soldier is promoted to noncommissioned rank. (ROBERT MELHORN, SOLDIERS MAGAZINE)

In spite of the failure of the enlisted guidance plan to greatly improve the professional and leadership quality of the noncommissioned officer corps, the Army staff continued to seek solutions to this problem throughout the post–Korean War period. To some extent, it had some success. In the late fifties and early sixties, as one observer remarked, "when there was some stability and the draft was running well, the Army was refitted and became fairly professional again." During that period the Seventh Army in Europe "reached probably the highest point of professionalism since World War II." The Army in the sixties, this observer concluded, would work its way back "toward a higher level of professionalism, and the noncommissioned officer corps was gaining strength."[10] Unfortunately, the demands and the attrition of the war in Vietnam soon aborted this process.

CONSOLIDATION OF THE WARRANT OFFICER PROGRAM

As an adjunct to the career-guidance program and to provide further career incentives for enlisted personnel, the Department of the Army held competitive examinations through its various commands beginning in 1948 and continuing into 1949 to select for appointment approximately six thousand regular Army warrant officer personnel.[11]

Appointments were made in forty-seven MOSs and four special (classified) occupational areas. These regular Army warrant officer selections and appointments numbered approximately 4,500 in the general Army examinations given in 1948 and approximately 1,500 the following year. Most of the appointments made as a result were as unit administrators. Approximately one half of the overall total of 6,000 appointees, however, were chosen from the ranks of non-regular Army commissioned rather than noncommissioned officers on extended active duty under reserve commissions. This called into question the Army's original intent to use the warrant officer grade as a career incentive for senior noncommissioned officers. In any case, the 1947 career-guidance program was expected to provide a far better goal than the rank of warrant officer.

In late 1948 the Army authorized a considerable number of duty positions in line units for warrant officer use. However, in spite of these increased requirements, continuing budgetary restrictions denied the additional appointments needed to implement the broadened concept of warrant officer utilization.

In 1950 approximately 900 warrant officer appointments were made, using eligibility lists based on the 1948 and 1949 examinations. The following year temporary appointments were decentralized to major commands which made approximately 1,400 appointments in sixty MOSs. In practice, however, the use of the warrant officer corps as a haven for reserve officers dropped from extended active duty proved inflationary and made a mockery of the grade's original purpose. In order to bring appointments in line with actual requirements and to restore that grade's original purpose, the Army attempted once again to establish warrant officer positions—instead of regular Army commissions—as logical career caps for all enlisted military occupational specialties, in keeping with the incentive envisioned in the original career guidance circular of 1947. Despite the corps expansion that resulted from the demands of the Korean War, the program eventually faltered because of lack of spaces.

THE FIRST NONCOMMISSIONED OFFICER ACADEMIES

As already mentioned, the noncommissioned officer academy concept originated as an *ad hoc* response to a perceived need in the field. When the U.S. Army settled down in 1947 to occupation duties in the American Zone of Germany, a division-sized force, the U.S. Constabulary, took up patrol duties along the border between the American and Russian zones. Rapid expansion during World War II had, it will be recalled, diluted the prewar noncommissioned corps' prestige and authority to a point of nonexistence. Consequently, company-grade officers had become accustomed to taking over many of the duties formerly entrusted to sergeants in the prewar army. To remedy this situation, the commander of the U.S. Constabulary, General I. D. White, established training courses "to enhance their [the officers' and noncommissioned officers'] military education so as to become properly oriented and prepared to assume their proper respective responsibilities in the postwar army."[12]

Noncommissioned officers of the constabulary received their training at an academy established in 1947 at Sonthofen, Germany. This appears to have been the first postwar noncommissioned officer academy. However, congressionally imposed budgetary limitations as well as suspension of the training circular authorizing such remedial training caused discontinuance of these courses and the closing of the Sonthofen academy in July 1948, just one year after its establishment. Noncommissioned training that could not be accomplished as OJT in the field was merged with such existing programs as the sergeants major and 1st sergeant's courses at the European Command (EUCOM) Signal School at Ansbach, and the supply sergeant's course at the quartermaster school at Darmstadt.[13]

Despite this contraction of noncommissioned training facilities, it soon became apparent to General White that traditional OJT for noncommissioned officers was failing to produce either in quality or quantity the leaders required by the U.S. forces in Germany. General White managed to secure the necessary funding and directed then–Brigadier General Bruce C. Clarke, commanding general of the 2d Constabulary Brigade, to open a new school for noncommissioned officers so that they might be trained more systematically than was possible in the field or in combination with technical training. General Clarke, whose thinking was already running along similar lines, established such a school at Munich, and the first class enrolled on December 17, 1949. Two years later, the U.S. Seventh Army absorbed the functions of the constabulary, and the school, with increased funding, was redesignated the Seventh Army Noncommissioned Officers' Academy.[14]

Years later, General Harold K. Johnson, former U.S. Army Chief of Staff, observed that the creation of this academy "had been major breakthrough in strengthening and improving the lot of the noncommissioned officer," and that General Clarke deserved full credit for it. Unlike the now-abandoned service-wide career guidance plan, the noncommissioned officer academies continued to operate throughout the Korean War and after.[15]

Up until this time the constabulary and later the Seventh Army acted on their own initiative, setting up a noncommissioned officers' academy because, as yet, there had been little guidance from the Army staff on this matter. Yet the Army was becoming aware that few of the many outstanding noncommissioned officers who served during the Second World War had remained in the service, and the practice of simply grafting the prewar *ad hoc* system of selection and training noncommissioned officers of the combat arms onto an army engaged in confrontation with the Communist powers of Europe and Asia left much to be desired. This system failed to produce noncommissioned officers of both the quality and quantity needed for a modern atomic-age army. In late June 1957, eight years after General Clarke established the academy at Munich, the Department of the Army for the first time published a regulation establishing a "standard pattern for the Noncommissioned Officers' Academies in the United States Army," whose purpose would be "to broaden the professional knowledge of the noncommissioned officer and instill in him the self-confidence and sense of responsibility required to make him a capable leader of men."[16] Thus, over eighty years after General Emory Upton urged upon the Army a similar move, it undertook a modest program of systematic and formal education for noncommissioned officers of all arms.

With the publication of this regulation, however, the Army did not abandon traditional on-the-job methods of training noncommissioned officers of the combat arms. Rather, it authorized but did not require commanding generals of divisions or commanders of major installations, with the approval of the appropriate echelons of command, to establish such academies *if they so desired*; if so, the regulation spelled out the standard pattern of training, curriculum, programming, budgeting, funding, and administration they were to follow.

These regulations set a minimum of four weeks for each course of instruction, leaving it to the local commander to determine the number of such courses to be offered annually. Although the course content for both senior and candidate noncommissioned officers was to be similar, commanders were encouraged to conduct them separately in the interest of maintaining the prestige and authority of the former. Only the most outstanding noncommissioned officers who themselves had completed a course of instruction at an academy were to be used as instructors.

The curriculum, in the words of the regulation, was to stress "the increased responsibility of noncommissioned officers under the new concepts of atomic warfare," an obvious reference to the assumed characteristic of an atomic battlefield with many scattered units and fire teams operating often in isolation from one another. In all phases of instruction, however, emphasis was to be placed "on *how* to teach the material presented rather than on mere presentation of information." The noncommissioned officer was thus perceived as essentially a teacher and therefore needing the skills required of good teachers. Consequently, methods of instruction occupied the largest single block in the curriculum, with a minimum of thirty hours. Map reading—a chronic deficiency among inexperienced troops—ranked next with a minimum of twenty hours. Tactics and problems of command were left to the discretion of the division or installation commander and depending on the emphasis he placed on leadership, might take up even more of the student's four weeks at the academy than methods of instruction.

On October 24, 1958, the Seventh Army Noncommissioned Officer Academy graduated its 236th class at the Jensen Barracks in Munich. This was the last to graduate at the Munich site and brought the academy's total of graduates to 45,000 men. The academy then moved to Flint Kaserne, at Bad Tölz, where the first class matriculated on November 8 of that year.[17]

As part of the overall U.S. Army, Europe–Seventh Army school system, the academy generally prospered or declined according to the budgetary or administrative restrictions affecting the command as a whole. In the autumn of 1958, two classes were cancelled because of the move to Bad Tölz. Nevertheless, 3,352 men graduated during fiscal year 1959, and for the next year, with larger and better facilities at the new location, the school's quota was increased to 3,799. The noncommissioned officer academy and the combined arms school at Vilseck were the only two of the command's nine schools to receive an increased quota for the next fiscal year. This gave some indication of the worth the theater command placed on the academy's curriculum. Even the newly formed West German *Bundeswehr* sent several students to the academy for training during fiscal year 1958.[18]

SOME PROBLEMS OF THE ACADEMY

There were some serious problems, however, in this otherwise bright picture. Foremost was the large percentage of men who failed to complete the course of instruction. Investigation determined that failure was caused primarily by unit commanders who did not select properly motivated and qualified men to attend. To remedy this, commanders were encouraged to select career men who, upon completion of the course, would benefit not only their units but ultimately the entire Army. Those men failing the course were to be reduced in grade upon returning to their units.[19]

By October 1958, concurrent with the shift of the academy from Munich to Bad Tölz, Seventh Army accordingly attempted to tighten the selection criteria for personnel attending. At first, senior noncommissioned officers (first three grades) and men with over twelve years' enlisted service were either exempted from the program or sent to the academy only as exceptional cases. When attendance fell, Seventh Army made an important change in policy by establishing attendance quotas on the basis of actual unit needs rather than on school capacity. This resulted in quotas of 185 spaces per course, for a total possible annual output of 4,255 students, a considerable increase over the previous year. Since it had been USAREUR policy that there be no mandatory quotas set for the USAREUR service-school system, including the Seventh Army Noncommissioned Officer Academy, it was no surprise to that Army's G-3 that attendance continued to decline, and for fiscal year 1960 Army units in Europe submitted requests for only 2,442 student spaces, or approximately 125 students per class.

Consequently, the commanding general of the support command (SUPCOM) informed the Seventh Army commander in November 1958 that his technical service unit noncommissioned officers had special needs for leadership training to supplement their narrow specialist training, and was quickly assured that all nominations of senior noncommissioned officers for the academy would be accepted regardless of earlier restrictions. At the same time the Army commander extended these assurances to all corps, division, group, or separate regimental commanders who might have similar needs. However, as the Seventh Army G-3 suspected, most combat-unit commanders were reluctant to release their key senior noncommissioned officers for the academy, especially during maneuver periods. Therefore, in spite of Seventh Army's efforts, enrollment in the academy continued to decline, reaching a low point in March 1959. This development moved the Army commander to consider two alternatives: either make the earlier quotas of 185 per class mandatory, or close the school. He chose the former, in spite of USAREUR, and the input of students began to increase, albeit slowly.[20]

In April 1959, Lieutenant General Francis W. Farrell took command of the Seventh Army. Turning his attention to the academy's flagging enrollment, he decided to expand the student base by accepting PFCs as students. Previously, attendance had been restricted to noncommissioned officers, specialists who were to become noncommissioned officers, and men who had been accepted for officer candidate schools.

Despite the expansion of the student base, enrollment failed to rise substantially, and the rate of failures continued to increase. All signs pointed to the fact that many unit commanders were continuing their practice of sending poorly motivated or unqualified men. This was a puzzling situation. Army surveys continued to show a high regard among its graduates and their commanders for the academy and its program of instruction. Moreover, the Department of the Army had employed the academy's standards as the model for the basic regulation establishing noncommissioned academies throughout the Army.

Hoping to offset the problem of poor motivation on the part of some students, Seventh Army adopted a policy of voluntary attendance, but at the same time urged upon senior commanders the need to stress the value of the academy's training program in developing capable noncommissioned officers. In March 1959 the

Army Chief of Staff gave the academy both recognition and encouragement when he asked it to develop a leader's reaction course. Adopted in April of that year, the course eventually proved a useful testing vehicle for noncommissioned leaders Armywide. Consisting of a number of simulated combat situations to be solved by a team of students under the supervision of a member of the cadre who rated each student, the course proved a valuable tool in testing noncommissioned officer leadership ability. This course was a forerunner of what was to become, years later, the very popular and useful "adventure-training" concept.[21]

REEVALUATION OF NONCOMMISSIONED OFFICER ACADEMIES

Although since 1947 the academies had been attempting with varying degrees of success to improve training, a surprisingly large number of capable noncommissioned officers never attended one. Moreover, motivation to do so was low because many commissioned as well as noncommissioned officers had never attended one or, considered the curriculum too narrow and the academic standards too low to really meet the challenge of improving the corps.[22]

Despite the Army regulations setting standards for the establishment and operation of the academies, there was little Armywide standardization. Some academies were commanded by a brigadier general or a colonel, others by a second lieutenant. Some improvised classrooms with Rube Goldberg–type mockups in abandoned mess halls. One had an enrollment of only twenty students, another twelve times that. Some courses lasted for sixteen weeks, others for only two. Yet all courses completed gave equal credit to the individual's record, regardless of the size or quality of the academy attended. Although the relevant Army regulation forbade any graduate of a recognized academy from attending another, because of indifferent record keeping in many units, numerous noncommissioned officers attended three or four courses while one luckless sergeant at Ft. Benning endured seven.[23]

Nevertheless, fixed quotas and misplaced command pressure often dragooned students into each class regardless of qualification or desire. In 1960, the Third Army reported that "attitudes of incoming students varied from bitterness to complacency." Seventh Army reported that most of its students were good soldiers, but "we get some real duds in every class." The report added that "some units are having to scrape the bottom of the barrel in order to meet their quotas." There were other problems as well. As late as 1966, nearly 80 percent of all students at the Seventh Army academy were specialists rather than line noncommissioned officers. Nearly three quarters of these were from dissimilar technical services. Understandably, the Seventh Army report concluded, "numerous superior NCO's eschew these expensive, time-consuming schools which promise scant professional remuneration in return."[24]

By the spring of 1962, this situation moved one despairing noncommissioned officer to write, "I have been unable to find the reason why our academies have not been improved and geared to the needs of our times. I have even seen how they sometimes are closed for lack of funds."[25] Yet as we have noted, many deserving and capable men were never touched by these schools. A random sample of one stateside airborne infantry battalion in 1964 disclosed that only sixty-two of its 167 sergeants had ever attended an academy of any kind; none of its corporals had. A battalion of the 35th Infantry of the 25th Infantry Division had 194 noncommissioned officers, grades E-5 through E-9, assigned in October 1966. Of these only twenty-seven had graduated from a recognized noncommissioned officer academy. Half of the twenty-seven had diplomas from division-level academies where the facilities had been very austere. At the same time the 1st Brigade, 101st Airborne Division, with a strength of 5,165, had a mere 200 noncommissioned officer academy graduates.

Perhaps the best evaluation of the Seventh Army NCO Academy is to be found in the subsequent careers of the men who attended. One unique individual was SP4 (later Command Sergeant Major) Paul W. Muuss, III, who attended the Bad Tölz Academy in March and April 1959. In 1980, as a command sergeant major, he returned there as its commandant.

"I had almost four years of service, had been reduced from E-4 to E-3 and had just made E-4 back when I was selected to go," Sergeant Major Muuss recalls.[26] Two other men from Muuss's platoon had been sent to Bad Tölz before him but both had washed out and his platoon sergeant's "ass was on the line to send someone who would make it!" Muuss did not let his platoon sergeant down, graduating sixth in a class of 133, missing selection as an honor graduate by only one tenth of a point—beat out by a master sergeant undergoing the course as a prerequisite for assignment there as a cadre.*

A typical day at Bad Tölz began at 0500 with reveille at 0600. After breakfast the candidates attended classes until noon. Classes resumed after lunch and lasted until 1700. After supper the candidates prepared their uniforms for the next day and studied. Although Lights Out was at 2200, the men continued their studies until midnight, often by candle or flashlight. Under these circumstances, morale and esprit were very high.

> Everyone cared and we helped each other! Cooperate and graduate was our motto—if someone didn't help others and was out for himself—he was history! We had young soldiers (E-2 and up) who were trying to get to OCS. We also had higher ranking NCO's (E-6/E-7) who were going through to become cadre so we were all together. There was no separation of any students. We started together and finished together.

*Every enlisted member of the cadre went through the course as a student, regardless of his grade, before assignment to the academy staff. This ensured that each tactical sergeant was himself a graduate of the academy.

The commandant in Muuss's day was the senior officer at Flint Kaserne, the commander of the 10th Special Forces Group. This officer delegated the day-to-day operations to a lieutenant colonel. "I never saw him," Muuss recalls, "and that was good because he was the last one you saw on your way out the door [as a washout] or you saw him at graduation."

There were two student companies at the academy in 1959, Company A, about 200 strong, and Company B, with approximately 150 candidates. The courses ran in tandem, two weeks apart with a one-week break between cycles. During the one-month course there were no holidays observed. The first two weekends the candidates were restricted to barracks; the third they were required to help the incoming class; the final weekend before graduation the candidates were on their own.

The academy cadre were all enlisted men and it was they who were responsible for course content.

> The emphasis was on both learning and teaching. We learned how to march and then were graded on teaching our squad how to march. We also taught our squad how to do a PT exercise but the emphasis was on teaching, not physical fitness. We were inspected by the TAC and later in the cycle we inspected our squad and were graded on how we performed . . . we were taught map reading because most junior NCO's just didn't know how to read a map! Most of [the instruction] was doctrine and not needing discussion. But underlying it all was *discipline*! We couldn't discipline others if we couldn't discipline ourselves!

Each prospective instructor at the academy was required to undergo a "murder board" before he could be considered qualified to teach. The board consisted of other cadre playing roles: There was the "smart aleck," the "know-it-all," the "sleeper," and the "talker," all stereotypes every instructor is required to deal with in the classroom. Muuss continued this practice when he became commandant years later. "As a result, the instructors were top-drawer and couldn't be beat. But they were somewhat one-dimensional. Take them out of their safe environment and they were out of luck—not many 'real-world' NCOs there—more like professional instructors."

Many of the men who attended the Seventh Army NCO Academy in the late fifties and early 1960s went as a prerequisite for acceptance at officer candidate schools, hardly a proper utilization of a noncommissioned officer academy, but when years later Sergeant Major Muuss met some of these graduates, then full colonels, they were proudly displaying their hard-earned Seventh Army NCO Academy diplomas on their office walls.

As a master sergeant in 1967, Muuss was assigned as an instructor at the United States Military Academy at West Point, where he taught plebe map reading. "It was a breeze," he recalls, "because of what I learned at Bad Tölz." He remembers a particular nighttime exercise:

> We were trucked to a field, broken up into threes, given a flashlight, a compass and a sheet with azimuth and distance and we were to walk behind each other. The first

> man had compass on azimuth, the second counted paces and the third made sure we didn't hit a tree. Well, I was teamed with two cooks who couldn't find the mess hall at noon! The only thing we found was the hood of the deuce-and-a-half after they blew the horn for us for twenty minutes. If I had done well on the night map reading course I'm sure I would have graduated with honors. Neither cook graduated!

Men who failed to graduate from the academy often found themselves treated with disdain when they returned to their units. Muuss was certain that if he failed to graduate it would mean reduction to PFC again. As it turned out, some months after graduation he was granted an exceptional waiver to the time in grade requirement and promoted to sergeant, E-5. "The 7th Army NCO Academy was the cornerstone of my career," he writes. "It stood me in good stead until I was selected to attend the Sergeants Major Academy in July 1975."

Other graduates remember their time at the Seventh Army NCO Academy with equal intensity:

> The day before graduation, at a practice graduation exercise, I walked across the stage and Command Sgt. Maj. Muuss was standing there to shake my hand for "making it." I was charged with emotion and my eyes were misty. I figured he might chew me out, but I was going to tell that academy command sergeant major just how damned proud I was to be a part of the NCO corps. I said it just that way and he looked me right in the eyes (without looking at my name tag), and said, "Sgt. Hawes, I know just how you feel."[27]

SUGGESTED ALTERNATIVES

To further improve the NCO education system, in 1962 the Infantry School at Ft. Benning queried noncommissioned officers of the Infantry Center's 2d Infantry Brigade and the XVIII Airborne Corps, using a "formidable array of interviews and forums" to obtain their thoughts concerning improvement of noncommissioned officer education. These men recommended a three-tiered system, comprising elementary, high school, and college levels. They suggested noncommissioned officer academies as they then existed could best be employed to train noncommissioned officer candidates, E-4 and below. Intermediate-level training, the surveys showed, could be supplied by career courses, conducted for E-5s (sergeants) and E-6s (staff sergeants) through their respective branches. This was not to be specialist training, however, but comprehensive survey courses, giving a feel for actions across the branch spectrum.

The college-level training would be offered by a single noncommissioned officer college, the pinnacle of all enlisted learning. At this school, selected E-7s (sergeants first class) and E-8s (master sergeants) could be trained to take over the top enlisted positions in command posts from company to field army. Admission to this course—of from twelve to fifteen weeks' duration—all agreed should be limited to truly outstanding enlisted leaders with fourteen or more years of service and a secondary school diploma. There should be no quotas and selection should be made at Department of the Army level.

From other noncommissioned officers came such suggestions as establishing career academies—centralized academies for each branch—as a means of providing the needed professional training for noncommissioned officers. Some believed such training would help bridge the gap between commissioned and noncommissioned officers attending the same branch school by giving both groups an opportunity to share their knowledge and to exchange ideas while at the school. Uniform, service-wide standards for such training might "reinforce the backbone [of the Army] before it cracks or splits."[28]

A modified version of this scheme appeared in mid-1967, when eighteen of the Army's twenty-one branch schools began to offer career-development correspondence courses for conscientious noncommissioned officers, and CONARC prepared a command and general staff college-level extension course for the top two grades of noncommissioned officers. As well intentioned as these measures were, they were not practical for noncommissioned officers caught up in a fifteen-hour day, as well as those in combat in Vietnam. Experience had demonstrated that extension courses, even when accompanied by organized group study, were poor substitutes for resident instruction.[29]

THE ACADEMIES AND ON-THE-JOB TRAINING

In spite of command encouragement from headquarters, U.S. Army, Europe, noncommissioned academies in that command had not been wholeheartedly accepted as a substitute for OJT at the unit level. Traditionally, most regular Army officers believed "that [on-the-job] training is the best means of developing the noncommissioned and potential noncommissioned officers."[30]

Learning by imitation and doing—following the example of senior noncommissioned officers in the unit—was the traditional training method in the U.S. Army. But despite its long history of use, OJT had many disadvantages in the post–World War II Army such as a lack of suitable facilities and insufficient training time. After all, a unit's primary mission was not noncommissioned officer education. Consequently, that training often took place at the expense of unit training. For example, soldiers with no training in the use of the command voice conducted periods of company drill; untrained instructors attempted to teach; and squad leaders lost their men in maneuver areas because they had insufficient training in map reading. For all this the unfortunate unit commander frequently bore the major share of the blame. The fastest and most efficient means of training noncommissioned officers was, many still believed, the academy, but this augmentation of the harried unit commander's efforts to train his noncommissioned officers was not always available because, as pointed out earlier, the regulations did not require its establishment.

In spite of their obvious advantages over unit-centered OJT, the question remained whether the academies were actually providing the background and training required by the noncommissioned officer as the Army entered the decade of the 1960s. Some of the academies' more prominent disadvantages were widely discussed in the service. For example, generally there were still no minimum prerequisites for attendance and, despite Army regulations, there was no standardization of instruction. Moreover, the academies had not fully integrated reserve and National Guard noncommissioned officers into the system and, as then structured, the normal four-week leadership training course was all of that type of training most noncommissioned officers could expect to receive during an entire career. Furthermore, most curricula did not provide an overall program of noncommissioned officer development, nor, in many cases, did they provide the separate training of potential noncommissioned officers and senior noncommissioned officers.

In any case, the divisional organization was considered to be too lean to support properly a noncommissioned officer academy. All things considered, it was apparent to many that the noncommissioned officer academies, as then constituted, were not fully preparing the students for duties and responsibilities required of them. Something more was needed.

BEGINNINGS OF THE DRILL SERGEANT CONCEPT

Meanwhile, the "father" of the USAREUR–Seventh Army Noncommissioned Officers' Academy, General Bruce C. Clarke, now commanding general, Continental Army Command (CONARC), continued to search for new ways to strengthen the academies and to better train the noncommissioned officer as an instructor. In October 1958, responding to a directive from General Clarke, the Third Army established an Army trainer academy (ATA) at Ft. Jackson, South Carolina. This course concentrated on training men to train others. General Clarke's experiment, for such it was, proved to be short-lived, however. On March 3, 1959, the ATA reverted to its role as the Third Army Noncommissioned Officer's Academy.

General Clarke's concept, however, resurfaced in 1963 with the enthusiastic support of Secretary of the Army Stephen Ailes, when a pilot drill sergeant's course, conducted this time by CONARC, opened at Ft. Jackson as an adjunct to the noncommissioned officers' academy already in operation there. The first course took place from May 25, to June 26, 1964. Now encouraged by the results, CONARC directed the establishment of a second drill sergeants' school at Ft. Dix, New Jersey, as a part of the existing noncommissioned officers' academy.

Two years later, in an effort to upgrade the new drill sergeant program, CONARC directed each of the six Army training commands to select ten noncommissioned officers to attend the Marine Corps' Drill Instructor's Course at Parris Island, South Carolina. The next year, CONARC expanded the drill sergeants' program with the establishment of a drill sergeants' assistants' course as an adjunct to the Third Army Noncommissioned Officers' Academy.

Meanwhile, General Clarke continued his efforts to improve the quality and effectiveness of the noncommissioned academies and to voice his concern over the lack of uniform standards in the operation of the academies within the continental United States. In June 1965, he directed the six continental, U.S. Army commanders to establish within each of their commands a single CONARC-programmed and -funded noncommissioned academy, thereby eliminating the many post and divisional academies that had sprung up largely on an *ad hoc* basis and were the sources of many of the admitted shortcomings of the program. Two years later, also at CONARC's direction, the Infantry School at Ft. Benning discontinued its basic noncommissioned officers' course and redesigned its senior course as a vehicle for preparing better instructors for the six Army academies.

Although these academies had for over a decade partially supplied the Army's requirements for skilled noncommissioned leaders and trainers, they were not what the Army staff had had in mind when, in April 1946, it had approached CONARC's predecessor, Headquarters, Army Ground Forces, for its opinion concerning "the advisability of establishing a career-guidance program of progressive education for noncommissioned officers of the first three grades."[31]

The immediate postwar years were for the Army and its noncommissioned corps a period of planning and experimentation. Faced with an unforeseen need for an army capable of dealing with the demands of increasing postwar tensions, the Army staff desperately sought to maintain a force in spite of rapid demobilization qualitatively equal to that which emerged victoriously from the war with Germany and Japan. Although most of its veteran soldiers were returning to civilian life, the Army was helped by resumption of the draft after June 1948 in filling its ranks with many able men capable of being professionally trained.

Realizing that most of the veteran noncommissioned officers had left the service, the Army staff turned its attention to how best to train another noncommissioned corps to conduct this training. The two plans that emerged—the career-guidance program and the noncommissioned academies—were both unable to realize their full potential before the Korean War pushed them aside for the duration. Moreover, when that war ended, an even more pressing demand, improving pay and the grade structure, emerged to consume the interests of the staff. The next chapter examines Army efforts to deal with these problems even while facing a second war in Asia.

CHAPTER 17

DAY OF THE SUPERGRADES

IMPROVING PAY AND GRADE STRUCTURE

The post–Korean War years left the noncommissioned corps with several burdens, none of its own making. Frustrating for many because it blocked normal promotions, was the glut of noncommissioned officers left over after the war, especially in the higher grades. Equally frustrating to able and conscientious noncommissioned officers as it was to the commissioned officers was an excessively high percentage of substandard men to be molded into soldiers. Most burdensome, however, was a pay scale eroded by inflation and hopelessly out of step with the times.

As was the case following each of the nation's major wars, the end of the Korean War left the Army with a surplus of both commissioned and noncommissioned officers. Dealing with this problem meant drastic and often undesirable consequences for the individuals and for the service. In fiscal year 1955 alone, more than five thousand reserve officers on extended active duty (EAD) were passed over for promotion to the grades of captain, major, and lieutenant colonel, and were released from active duty. To ease the burden of interrupted careers somewhat, the Army offered the ousted officers whose service began prior to March 22, 1948, automatic appointments as master sergeants. Those with later entry dates were offered noncommissioned ranks one grade lower. Unfortunately, this well-intentioned policy to ameliorate the large-scale reduction in force resulted by 1955 in glutting the top enlisted ranks with "cheerless commissioned rejects who filled every room at the inn," as one officer described it.[1]

This heavy infiltration of the upper enlisted ranks continued until April 1957; thereafter, subsequent rejects did not fare so well—they were fortunate to get an E-5 (sergeant or specialist five) appointment. Nevertheless, by February 1958, the Army had by percentage more master sergeants and sergeants first class than at the height of World War II. Yet at the same time budget restrictions had reduced enlisted strength by nearly one half.

Ironically, this surfeit of noncommissioned officers was no assurance that a well-trained and disciplined rank and file would be created. In July 1957, Lieutenant General Bruce C. Clarke observed that nearly 28 percent of his command—the U.S. Seventh Army in Germany—was composed of virtually untrainable "eightballs" in Category IV, the lowest mental category eligible for military service. At the same time, the servicewide percentage was 28.2 percent.

By 1963, as the conflict in Vietnam began to take shape, most of the first three grades on active duty were products of these years of ignominy and despair. But help was on the way. With the activation in October 1964 of the U.S. Army Recruiting Command (USAREC), at Ft. Monroe, Virginia, the quality of the ranks was expected to rise phoenixlike from the ashes of the late 1950s.

UPGRADING THE CORPS

Following the war in Korea, the Army resumed tentative efforts to create a more viable career-management system for enlisted men. These efforts initially took form in studies at the defense and departmental levels and reaffirmed the truths of over half a century before—namely, that until a military compensation system more in keeping with the demands of modern technology and its wartime utilization could be devised, efforts to significantly upgrade the professional noncommissioned corps would remain less than satisfactory.

Although efforts aimed at improvements in the selection and training of able noncommissioned officers were critical to the creation of a modern army, adequate compensation was recognized as the key to obtaining and retaining such men as career professionals. A pattern that had emerged around the turn of the century reemerged in the decade after 1945. Fifty years before there had been much discussion in Army circles about how better to select and train the type of noncommissioned officer required by a twentieth-century army. As this discussion continued there developed an awareness that until enlisted pay scales more accurately reflected the growing value placed on the skilled worker in an industrial society, the prospects of either obtaining or retaining the quality of noncommissioned officer needed for modern warfare seemed rather dim. Out of this realization on the part of the Congress and the armed forces there had emerged the Pay Bill of 1908. This legislation had supported the Army throughout the mobilization, expansion, and challenges of World War I.

Now, in the 1960s, after a second world war and a bitter limited war in Asia, there was even greater awareness that a rapidly changing weapons and communications technology had wrought (and were continuing to do so) many changes in both tactical organization and operational concepts. These changes placed even greater emphasis on the noncommissioned officer's role as a small-unit combat leader. The pentomic concept, with its inherent requirements for greater dispersion, increased mobility, and a vastly enlarged battle area demanded far more than ever before of the small-unit fire team and its leader—the sergeant.

Increased technology had brought not only requirements for better-trained combat leaders but for highly skilled technicians—specialists—whose skills were also in ever-increasing demand by industry. Although technicians were not normally troop leaders, their skills nevertheless required the Army to compete with industry for their services and to recognize that they merited pay at least comparable to that of line noncommissioned officers.

It will be recalled that in 1953 the Womble Committee studied, among other things, the problem of enhancing the noncommissioned officer's status and prestige. The committee recommended that only those enlisted men with demonstrated command potential, as opposed to those with technical skills or aptitudes, be considered for noncommissioned appointments. This left unresolved the question of what to do with the technician/specialist—how was he to be compensated and ranked vis-à-vis noncommissioned officers?

In 1954 the Army Chief of Staff approved a plan for distinguishing the line noncommissioned officers from the technicians/specialists within a revised seven-grade pay structure. The following year the Army implemented this grade structure. Henceforth, the line noncommissioned officers ranked above the specialists/technicians in order of precedence, regardless of pay grade. This was expected to increase noncommissioned status and prestige as enlisted troop leaders by distinguishing them in meaningful terms from the enlisted technical or administrative specialist. One of these terms was to be a more easily distinguishable badge of rank. Line noncommissioned officers retained their traditional chevrons with the arcs *below* the bars, while specialists were to wear an American eagle in gold against a green background with rank being indicated by arcs *above* the eagle.

REFORMING THE PAY SCALES—THE CORDINER COMMITTEE

Three years after the Womble Committee made its recommendations, the armed services finally got down to the task of actually reforming the now outdated pay scales. To this end the secretary of defense appointed yet another committee—this one to approach the problem of enhancement of the enlisted careerist's status and prestige through an improvement of compensation. Known officially as the Defense Advisory Committee on Professional and Technical Compensation, it was chaired by Ralph J. Cordiner—hence the name by which it has been known ever since. Appointed in March 1956, this committee presented its final report to the secretary of defense in May 1957.

Current pay scales, the committee observed, were based on a historically established principle of longevity. For over one hundred and fifty years military pay had provided for periodic increases for cumulative years of service. This principle had been well adapted to the congressional tradition of drastically reducing the size of the armed forces between wars, with resulting long periods of promotion stagnation for all personnel, commissioned and noncommissioned. Under the conditions that prevailed in 1956, this meant that a soldier reached E-7 (master sergeant) in about twelve years, leaving him a future of eight to eighteen years in that grade before retirement at twenty or thirty years of service. While a limited few could take advantage of the warrant officer program, the majority had, in spite of a postwar career-guidance program, no further opportunities available to them.

Faced with Cold War challenges on a global scale, a complex arsenal of modern weapons, and continuing competition with industry for skilled technicians, the country's military compensation system, the committee acknowledged, was out of date. The current system placed too much emphasis on survival on the job and in fact encouraged mediocrity with a deleterious effect on the noncommissioned officer, especially in the higher grades.

For thirty-five years prior to the committee's creation, enlisted pay had been geared to a seven–pay grade system, yet in that time industry had expanded its pay scales in recognition of increased levels of competence and responsibility caused by growing technological complexity. The committee concluded that the present military compensation system was clearly out of step with the times: inadequate to meet the needs of technically advanced military operations, and contrary to all that had recently been learned concerning personal motivation.[2]

Although the Cordiner Committee examined the question of professional and technical compensation for officers, enlisted men, and civilians in all of the armed services, the most significant impact of its report was upon the enlisted grade structures—especially as they related to the skilled noncommissioned officers and specialists whose retention was of primary concern to the services, particularly the Army.

The committee's basic objective was to propose "a modern system of manpower compensation for the Armed Forces." Its recommendations, therefore, were "to provide the kinds of incentives and conditions needed for motivation and retention of sufficient numbers of professionally skilled officers, enlisted personnel, and civilians required by our Armed Forces today and for the foreseeable future."

Accelerating technological change in society and on the battlefield, when it came to public attention around the turn of the century, caused many then in the Army to question traditional ways of doing things, including the selection and training of noncommissioned officers and specialists. Fifty years later the Cordiner Committee faced essentially the same challenge in its deliberations. In the committee's words,

> the machinery of modern defense (and offense) is becoming ever more fantastically complex. No weapons system of today can safely be considered more than a transient stage in the headlong rush of technological discovery and development. Vastly improved weapons which will comprise the armament of tomorrow are now on the drafting boards and in the research laboratories. Our opponents are searching, developing, and producing with equal speed and consummate skill . . . changes in strategy and tactics geared to the pace of technological change and the dynamic world situation had created an unprecedented need for increasingly effective management in the armed forces.

Although the Korean War was essentially an infantryman's war, by its close, the committee pointed out, "the percentage of technicians and mechanics as a portion of the total enlisted force had increased from 34% to 41%. By 1956 this ratio had increased to 44%. With this growing requirement for skilled men, the Army's manpower problem had become one of obtaining and retaining quality rather than quantity." The committee found, however, that in the post–Korean War period, despite a greater sense of professionalism among the noncommissioned corps than had been the case during the war itself, the armed services were unable to keep, challenge, and develop "the kinds of people needed for the period of time necessary for those people to make an effective contribution to the operation of the force." The committee continued, "We must move forward from a concern with numbers to a deeper concern for quality and for retention of skilled personnel for an extended period of productive service."

The Cordiner Committee confirmed what had been known for some time. In its own words, the compensation practices of the armed forces were

> so clearly out of step with the times, so clearly inadequate to the needs of a technically advanced form of national defense, and so of a technically advanced form of nation defense, so clearly contrary to all that had been learned about human motivations that they can unmistakably be identified as a major impediment to national security. [Modernization of compensation is] the basic problem to be attacked immediately.

An examination of the history of the armed forces', particularly the Army's, pay systems since the Pay Bill of 1908, disclosed that percentage increases in military compensation since then had had the effect of steadily reducing the spread between the pay of the highest and the lowest enlisted grades. This compression of compensation came about through pay increases for those at the low end of the scale and constant resistance at the political level against increasing the pay of those at the top beyond certain rigid ceilings. Consequently, during the fifty years since then, the committee found that pay of the lowest enlisted grade had increased by almost 800 percent, while the compensation paid an Army master sergeant or a Navy chief petty officer had increased by only about 300 percent.*

The effect of this compression within the compensation system was traced to a continuing decline in the ultimate economic opportunity offered by a military career. Relief from this compression was to be one of the Cordiner Committee's most significant recommendations.

The problem of pay inequities was reflected in the fact that since the beginning of the 1950s Army reenlistment rates had been erratic. Before the Korean War, the U.S. Army, with a mixed volunteer-draft strength of 1.5 million men, reenlisted about 60 percent of its personnel. But after the war, the reenlistment rate fell to

*Over the same period, the pay of a major general/rear admiral had increased only about 60 percent. All of these figures include allowances payable in lieu of rations and quarters.

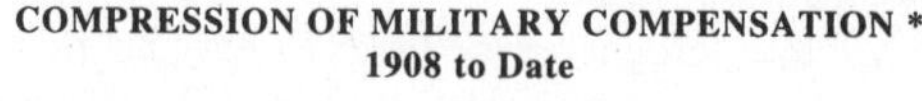

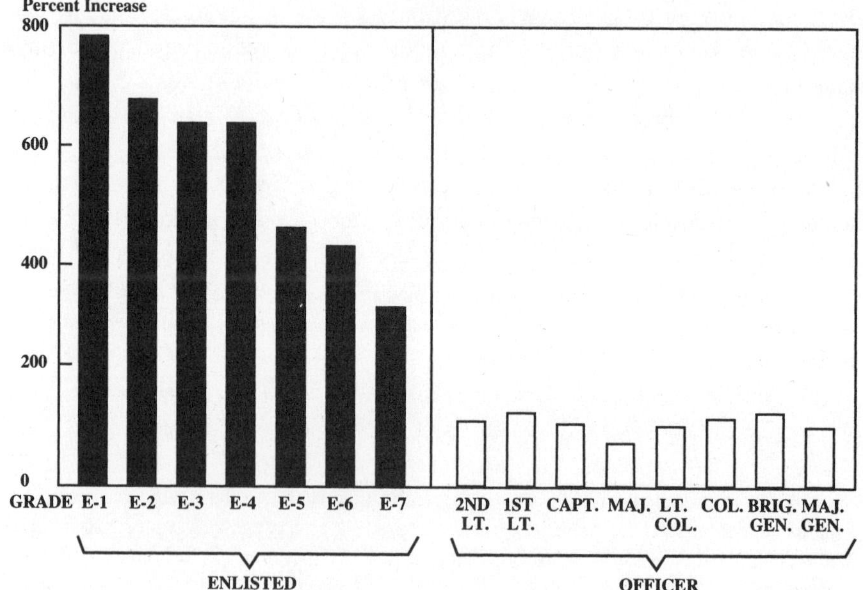

* Reflects 1955 Career Incentive Act Increases

about 18 percent at its lowest point, and below the minimum required to maintain a reasonable stable force. This alarming situation set off a flurry of legislative proposals, commencing with the passage of legislation increasing reenlistment bonuses in July 1954. On the heels of this action, Congress enacted into law seven proposals for a career-incentive legislative program (1955–1956). These measures laid the foundation for vigorous programs in the armed services to increase retention rates for trained and experienced personnel. As a result, overall reenlistments rose from the low of 18 percent to about 43 percent by the end of fiscal year 1956.

As welcome as this rate of increase was, it still fell short of enabling the Army to attain the balanced force structure desired. For example, men in the so-called "hard" skills—occupational specialties requiring long lead-time training—reenlisted after their first term of service at one half the rate of those in the short lead-time skills. With an increasing emphasis on technology and the growing complexity of weapons systems, the military requirements for technicians, mechanics, and skilled leaders were still in excess of the numbers apparently willing to embrace a military career. In the Cordiner Committee's opinion, this imbalance in first-term reenlistments was the crux of the enlisted personnel problem in 1957.

CREATING TWO NEW GRADES

The major result of the committee's deliberations and recommendations was the Military Pay Bill of 1958. In addition to correcting some of the inequities of pay, one of the most significant aspects of this legislation in terms of noncommissioned prestige was the creation of two additional pay grades, E-8 and E-9. According to the text of the bill,

> the purpose of establishing the two new enlisted pay grades E-8 and E-9 [was] to provide for a better delineation of responsibilities in the enlisted structure. Today for practical purposes the first two enlisted pay grades merely mark a transition period for an enlisted man in his first term of service. This leaves only five pay grades to provide for delineation of some 275 different skills and skill levels in the enlisted work force.
>
> The result is that a situation exists wherein E-7's supervise E-7's who supervise other E-7's. The establishment of the pay grades of E-8 and E-9 will make it possible to distinguish properly between the different levels of responsibility and at the same time provide the necessary monetary recognition for the jobs being performed by those who hold the grades.

In recognition of supervisory ability the House bill provided that not more than 1 percent of the total enlisted members could hold the grade of E-9 and not more than 2 percent could hold the grade of E-8. Further, the House bill provided that in order to be advanced to the military rank and pay of an E-8 or E-9 (excluding proficiency pay advancement), an enlisted man must have completed eight years of cumulative service for E-8 and ten years for E-9.[3]

This bill served also to ease the grade compression to which the Cordiner Committee called attention, and to give substantial pay increases to all personnel with over two years of service. For its part, the Army hoped thereby to improve incentives for reenlistment and to add stability to the noncommissioned corps.

Armed with this legislation, the Army authorized the upgrading of selected and highly qualified E-7s to E-8 and E-9. This upgrading was accomplished in three phases. The first sought to identify those military occupational specialties (MOS) in the noncommissioned area that warranted positions in the new grades. The second phase identified suitable positions in the technical fields for upgrading, while the third consisted of further review and job analysis to assure that the new grade structure would remain realistic and current.

The establishment of a new grade and stripe structure, however, brought objections from the corps with the creation of new insignia of rank to identify the new grades. The Army reacted to these objections by publishing Change 4 to AR 670-5 which authorized E-5s, E-6s, and E-7s who had held their grades on May 21, 1958 to continue wearing the insignia and using the titles appropriate to these grades, unless promoted or reduced. This latter exemption led to a situation where for a time the Army had master sergeants in pay grades E-7 and E-8, sergeants first class in grades E-6 and E-7, and staff sergeants in grades E-5 and E-6.[4] The following table illustrates this situation:

Pay Grade	*NCOs*	*Specialists*	*Privates*
E-9	Sergeant Major of the Army Sergeant Major	Not Authorized	
E-8	1st Sergeant Master Sergeant	Not Authorized	
E-7	Sergeant First Class† Platoon Sergeant	Specialist Seven*	
E-6	Sergeant First Class† Staff Sergeant	Specialist Six*	
E-5	Sergeant	Specialist Five*	
E-4	Corporal	Specialist Four*	
E-3			Private First Class
E-2			Pvt. E-2
E-1			Pvt. E-1

In dealing with problems inherent in such a transition, the Army demonstrated more than ever before a far greater degree of sensitivity to noncommissioned officer morale. If, after July 1, 1958, the Army had immediately required all noncommissioned officers to make the change to the new stripes, over 192,000 men would have been affected. Therefore, the Army decided to delay the change since, in the minds of many noncoms, changing to the new chevrons would have seemed a demotion—for example, a master sergeant, E-7 would have lost a "rocker" when converting to the new sergeant first class chevron. Change 4 to AR 670-5, even though creating considerable confusion by allowing men to retain their old insignia for a while longer, was designed to help the men make the transition with less damage to their morale.

By 1965, however, the Army decided that the time had come at last to make the big switch, but reaction from the noncommissioned corps was still so adverse that the Army staff decided to let the matter rest a bit longer. When the ax finally fell on June 30, 1968, the total number of men affected had been reduced to only 6,600 through attrition and retirement. By then—the midst of the Vietnam War—most noncommissioned officers had decided that the time was ripe to make the change anyway.

The new grades were expected to add considerable incentive and prestige to

*For rank and precedence all specialists fall immediately below the rank of corporal.
†Transitional title for those who held this grade continuously since May 31, 1958.

CATALOG NUMBERS FOR CHEVRONS FOR MALE PERSONNEL OTHER THAN SPECIALISTS 1951–PRESENT*

Design	*Catalog Number*	*Dates of Authorization*	*Rank*
	400	1951–present	Master Sergeant
	401	1951–present 1958–present	Sergeant First Class or Platoon Sergeant
	403	1951–1958 1958–present	Sergeant Staff Sergeant
	404	1958–present	Sergeant
	405	1951–present	Corporal
	406	1951–1968 1968–present	Private First Class Private (E-2)
	413	1951–present	1st Sergeant
	442	1951–1968 1968–1971 1971–present	Sergeant Major Staff Sergeant Major Sergeant Major
	444	1968–present	Command Sergeant Major
	446	1968–present	Private First Class
 	470	1979–1994 1994–present	Sergeant Major of the Army

*Official width is three inches; actual widths may vary by one eighth of an inch.

CATALOG NUMBERS FOR SPECIALIST CHEVRONS 1955–PRESENT*

Design	*Catalog Number*	*Dates of Authorization*	*Rank*
	430	1955–1959† 1959–1961† 1960–present‡	Specialist Third Class Specialist Four Specialist Four
	431	1955–1959† 1959–1961† 1960–1985‡	Specialist Second Class Specialist Five Specialist Five
	432	1955–1959† 1959–1961† 1960–1985‡	Specialist First Class Specialist Six Specialist Six
	433	1955–1959† 1959–1961† 1960–1978‡	Master Specialist Specialist Seven Specialist Seven
	434	1959–1965‡	Specialist Eight
	435	1959–1965‡	Specialist Nine
	436	1959–present§	Specialist Four
	437	1959–1985§	Specialist Five
	438	1959–1985§	Specialist Six
	439	1959–1985§	Specialist Seven
	440	1959–1985§	Specialist Eight
	441	1959–1985§	Specialist Nine

*NOTE: Women's insignia (430 through 435) are two inches wide; men's insignia (436 through 441) are three inches wide.
†All personnel. ‡Women personnel only. §Men only.

those noncommissioned officers now holding them. The new pay grades for the first sergeant and sergeant major established them at the top of the enlisted structure in terms of responsibility and pay. Commanders were now authorized to waive the fifteen- and eighteen-year service requirement for up to 20 percent of all promotions to grades E-8 and E-9. This allowed outstanding and aggressive noncommissioned officers with between eight and fifteen years of service to advance more rapidly in rank. And on July 1, 1958, the Army once again authorized permanent enlisted promotions, thereby providing added stability and recognition to noncommissioned officer and specialist grades then held on a temporary basis.[5]

Another step, this one toward Armywide personnel management for enlisted careerists, and one that resembled that used for commissioned officers, was also taken at this time. It provided for name assignment of grades E-8 and E-9 at departmental level against requisitions from the field. These assignments were based on the enlisted qualification record (Department of the Army Form 20) and an assignment-preference card.

With the adoption of Armywide selection and assignment procedures for the newly created top two enlisted grades, the Army staff faced the task of overcoming tradition-based resistance and suspicion on the part of many commanders in the field. The prospect of having their top enlisted men selected for and assigned to them by staff divisions outside their units did not appeal to many unit commanders from battalion to division level. To counter this concern, the staff took steps in 1959 to assure commanders in the field that they would receive the very best and most qualified noncommissioned officers available, given the manpower restraints placed on the Army. The deputy chief of staff for personnel (DCSPER) refined the assignment procedures for these men to "insure accurate and timely reporting by field commanders of appointments to these positions and subsequent changes in the individual's status and qualifications."[6]

These selection and assignment procedures worked something like this: six months prior to the loss of an incumbent, the using unit submitted a special personnel requisition to the Department of the Army for a replacement in grade E-8 or E-9. Requisitions were consolidated at the major command level and then forwarded to the adjutant general, where a qualification record for each E-8 and E-9 in the Army was now maintained. The adjutant general then selected for assignment to fill a specific requirement from among those considered best qualified and eligible "with consideration of the individual's background, experience, physical qualifications, and assignment preferences."

Thus, assignments of the top two enlisted grades were now controlled by the adjutant general and made on a unit-to-unit basis in much the same way assignments had long been made for commissioned officers. Centralized assignment procedures also made it possible to employ an automatic data processing system for this task.

During 1960 permanent appointments were made for the first time for E-8s, and the time in grade requirements for appointment to E-9 were raised to match those required for E-8—sixteen months. Of the 5,346 temporary promotions allocated by the adjutant general for the grade of E-8 in 1960, however, only 100 were allocated as permanent promotions.

With the creation of the grade of E-9 there also arose, somewhat belatedly to be sure, the question of how such individuals should be addressed. In the British army the custom of addressing men holding the senior noncommissioned positions as "sergeant major" had greatly enhanced their role and prestige. Consequently, it was expected that a similar custom might have a salutary effect in the U.S. Army. In 1962, Army Chief of Staff General George H. Decker decided that all personnel holding the rank of E-9, regardless of MOS, should bear the title of sergeant major. This decision was confirmed with the publication of Change 3 to AR 600-20 on January 28, 1963.[7]

Admirable though it was, the decision to give the title to all personnel holding the grade of E-9 had actually created an incongruous situation. What started out to be the senior enlisted position within a TOE (combat) or TDA (support) unit was now subverted to that the title no longer enjoyed its former prestige. As more men were promoted into this grade there were far greater numbers than had been originally anticipated. Although only one E-9 in any one color-bearing unit could actually be the senior enlisted man, each staff section also had one E-9 because as yet there had been no move to authorize specialists in this pay grade.

As a first step to clear up this situation the Army staff created identifying MOSs for E-8s and E-9s so that each sergeant major could at least be distinguished by his occupational specialty. On March 9, 1959, DCSPER approved these revised MOSs and grade standards. Because the exercise of leadership and supervision were vital for these grades, DCSPER believed it important to readily identify them with suitable military occupational skill codes.

The following year the Army staff addressed itself to the status of specialists in the higher grades. On January 25, 1960, the AG sent a directive to all MOS monitors with proposed criteria for the identification of master sergeants and sergeants major in primarily specialist positions. This action provided higher pay but not rank for men with technical skills but whose tasks involved minimal supervisory or leadership functions. Thus it was hoped to settle the question of how to distinguish between the master sergeant and sergeant major leader and their technical or specialist counterparts.

However, adverse reaction to this directive soon surfaced within headquarters, USCONARC. The opposition stemmed from long-standing differences in philosophy concerning the rating of specialists with noncommissioned officers. CONARC conceded that specialists paid at E-8 and E-9 rates ought to be actually advanced to those two grades and, when promoted, carried on the rolls as noncommissioned officers rather than specialists. A letter from retired General Bruce C. Clarke to the commanding general, CONARC, sparked this reaction. General Clarke, however, went beyond even CONARC's initial reservations by calling into question the basic NCO-specialist program. He recommended that "all enlisted men above the grade E-5 be considered noncommissioned officers and that no upgrading of specialists take place." The Chief of Staff thereupon directed the adjutant general to restudy the entire directive concerning rating specialists.

Meanwhile, October 30, 1963, Lieutenant General Vittrup, DCSPER, directed that efforts be made to identify additional positions that might become candidates for upgrading to E-9. By June 30, 1964, the active Army was projected to have four thousand individuals in that grade and was thereafter to add one thousand each year until the statutory 1 percent of enlisted strength had been reached. This would have produced ten thousand sergeants major by fiscal year 1967, five thousand more than the 1964 strength. This would also fly in the face of one of the Army's original purposes in creating this grade—to emphasize the position of the sergeant major as the senior noncommissioned officer in the unit and not to create a broad group of senior noncommissioned officers, calling them all sergeants major.

Another original objective in creating the so-called "supergrades," relief of the pay compression within the grade structure, had been achieved by adding the two new grades and reducing by an equal amount the authorized strength of E-7s in the Army. The additional grades were also envisioned, it will be recalled, as enhancing enlisted career opportunities. But the Chief of Staff's decision in 1962 that all E-9s, regardless of position, should be addressed as "sergeant major" created a problem because initially the staff did not expect that all E-9s would be given that title. The staff expected that the title sergeant major would continue to be reserved for the senior enlisted men of a battalion or higher organization. Diffusion of the title across an increasingly wide spectrum of MOS positions created dissatisfaction among the nominal sergeants major as well as confusion among military personnel as to which individual was actually the unit's senior noncommissioned man. This diffusion also created a certain amount of contempt for the new grade. A novelist writing about this period years later expressed it like this:

> Despite the hooting and occasional catcalls that greeted Riley's remarks, things would have been all right if he had not made the disastrous mistake of referring to the new ranks by an expression that was only then becoming current: "supergrades."
>
> Upon hearing this word, Jack jumped up and shouted, "Hey, Sarge, we'll call the E-nine 'Super Senior Sarge,' and he'll be issued a lined cape and two E-sevens just to keep it off the ground as he inspects the garbage cans behind the second platoon's barracks!"[8]

Increasingly, sergeants major throughout the service were growing critical of the system that allowed individuals in basically administrative or operational positions to be addressed as sergeant major. This criticism grew more widespread as more E-9s were created. However, most of the criticism focused on the more visible aspects of identification—the lack of differentiation in the insignia—rather than address, the basic question of which was, What really was the role and position of the sergeant major as opposed to other E-9s?

Military personnel of grade E-9 generally acknowledged that granting the title of sergeant major to those individuals who were not the senior enlisted men of a color-bearing unit did, nevertheless, add to the prestige of their positions. Moreover, once a noncommissioned officer had actually been designated as sergeant major in a battalion, brigade, or division, his reversion to the position of operations or administrative sergeant was tantamount to a reduction in position and responsibility, even though the individual's pay and actual rank remained unchanged. Most complaints from the field found this situation unacceptable to senior noncommissioned officers and a major bone of contention among men who occupied the position of unit sergeant major.

Whereas the comparable position among master sergeants of the company or battery 1st sergeant retained its prestige as well as its traditional lozenge, the fact that the chevrons with a star in the field identified all E-9s as sergeants major also tended to degrade the traditional senior soldier's position in the minds of most careerists. To correct this situation, the Army staff recommended that the title of sergeant major be restricted solely to those individuals in grade E-9 who were actually occupying the position of senior noncommissioned officer of a color-bearing unit. As for the other E-9s, other titles should be devised for those in administrative, operational, and specialist MOSs. The most important aspect of the staff's recommendation was that individuals who had served in the position of sergeant major at battalion or higher be considered for repetitive assignments in similar positions within their MOS field. This returned the program to its original intent: to create a corps of senior noncommissioned officers from which to draw men to be assigned to the position of sergeant major. Thus would these men be clearly distinguished from others of similar pay grade but holding what were essential specialist positions.

By the mid-sixties, as the troop buildup got under way in Vietnam, the position of the unit sergeant major (E-9) had at last been clearly defined and recognized within the enlisted grade structure. His tasks are best described by a former sergeant major who, as he said of himself, was "a man of two worlds; his success depending upon how well he straddled them."[9] The sergeant major's basic responsibility is toward his commanding officer: to serve him well and loyally. This must also be his relationship with the staff, to counsel them wisely in matters relating to the commander's feelings. Yet he is at the same time the senior enlisted man in the unit, with responsibilities toward the troops. The sergeant major's service to these three constituencies are best described, albeit somewhat ideally, by the man himself:

> To his CO the sergeant major is the one person close to him—other than his wife—who without fear of retribution by efficiency report can voice a completely candid opinion or a popular sentiment that runs counter to the commander's known or suspected feelings. Like the boy in the fable, the sergeant major can say, "Look! The King has no clothes!"
>
> The sergeant major is an opinion-maker, and interpreter, and at times an apologist. He can, and will, explain the commander to the troops in language they can understand.

The first definition of a sergeant major I ever heard was from PFC Neff, while giving a squad of us our recruit training on the golf course at El Morro Castle in San Juan in 1940. Neff pointed out Master Sergeant Fath, sergeant major of the 27th Engineer Battalion, and told us, "He is the eyes, the ears, and the voice of the Old Man."

One sergeant major I know used to get up at 5 A.M. daily while in garrison. He checked the MP desk blotter and took notes on incidents of the night before. He stood behind reveille formation at a different company each day. He ate breakfast at a different mess hall each day. At 0730 daily this sergeant major was standing tall in front of the general with a list of things that had happened the night before. At 0800 the general was on the phone to his commanders questioning them about things in their own outfits of which they were still ignorant. Finky? Some thought so for sure! The important thing is that the general used his "eyes" the way he wanted and he got exactly the results he wanted. A sharp outfit!

The sergeant major is an alarm bell. A good one lets the staff know when it is propitious to put forward an idea. He keeps constant tabs on the Old Man's needs and warns the staff or encourages them, as the case may be. Sometimes he becomes protective in this and tries to spare the commander; but allowing for his split loyalties, he is a good judge of timing.

In all his dealings with the staff, the sergeant major is trying to make them look good to the commander. He is trying to solve the petty problems before they reach the Old Man, and he is trying to make the command look good to outsiders—and to those in it.

To the troops—the sergeant major is a port in a storm, a refuge in time of need, an appeal to Caesar. He embodies approachable, sympathetic wisdom. He is a grizzled old head who knows people and regulations. His advice and counsel can prevent a lot of grief.

The sergeant major is a symbol of leadership. The men should be proud of him, proud that he is their sergeant major. He must have dignity, command presence and intelligence; he must be the best leader in the unit and have the most thorough knowledge of leadership principles.

The sergeant major is a disciplinarian. It is he who should keep the troops straight on such matters as haircuts, uniforms, saluting, and attitude. The sergeant major is the only person who can properly take a senior noncommissioned officer aside and tell him his frayed uniforms aren't going to make it to retirement. It's the sergeant major who first knows and first counsels the noncommissioned officer who is hitting the bottle—or his wife. It's the sergeant major who helps the private collect the ten bucks he shouldn't have loaned in the first place.

The sergeant major is a representative of the men of the front office. He is there to look after their interests. He is an enlisted conscience among the brass. A union leader without strike powers. He is duty-bound to speak out in behalf of the men. He does so at the risk of failing to disfavor himself.

To himself—The sergeant major is torn apart. His sympathies extend in two directions. He lives by principle, searching his conscience daily and making decisions based on tolerance, humility, understanding, and real affection for all the men and officers concerned. He wants to perform well in the role that time has written for him.

More than any other person, the sergeant major respects the fitness and necessity of the status quo. At the same time, he burns to see change and adjustment benefit the individual soldier. Deaf ears in both the officer corps and the enlisted ranks have

> thrust him into the role of interpreter. He belongs to two worlds. How well he does his job depends upon how well other people understand what it is.[10]

Another ex-professional defined the role of the ideal sergeant major like this:

> Sergeant Major Billy George Oates possessed that rare ability, found only in the smallest handful of enlisted leaders of an army, really a sixth sense, that enabled him to size up a man almost by looking at him. After a few words with a private soldier, Oates could tell if he'd been paid on time, had family problems, was getting along with his squad and platoon leaders, or gave a hang one way or another about the army. Oates could go into any rifle company in the division and, after an hour of talking with its men, tell the company commander who his problem children were and which of them he could rely on as his best enlisted soldiers. He was a constant source of amazement to the officers and a pure inspiration to the enlisted men.[11]

THE COMMAND SERGEANT MAJOR PROGRAM

Having established the primacy of the sergeant major as the senior noncommissioned position in a color-bearing unit, as compared with other personnel in the same pay grade, the Army staff now turned its attention to the problem of determining a title that would truly set the sergeant major apart from the other sergeants major as the enlisted adviser to the commander.

The result of these deliberations was the command sergeants major program to which Army Chief of Staff General Harold K. Johnson gave his approval on July 12, 1967. Its purpose was to provide an additional career goal but no extra pay for the Army's most experienced senior noncommissioned officers. The program was expected to improve "the caliber and effectiveness of sergeants major occupying the top enlisted positions in the major commands of the army that they could serve as the principal enlisted assistants to the commanders at all levels, from battalion through headquarters, Department of the Army."[12]

As envisioned by the senior enlisted control branch of the DCSPER, the command sergeants major program would in time create a small body of selected sergeants major for ready assignment to all major commands of the Army. This more clearly distinguished those E-9s assigned as a commander's enlisted assistant from the other E-9s.

Screening, selection, assignment, and career management of these individuals was to be controlled by the Department of the Army in a manner similar to that employed for general officers. The screening selection board established at departmental level was similar for the selection board used for colonels. The former made its selection from a list of sergeants major recommended by the major commands throughout the Army. All sergeants major on active duty with a date of rank effective prior to January 1 the year the board convened were considered within the zone of consideration. In the staff's words, these candidates must "possess the highest qualifications of leadership, integrity, dedication, and professionalism." These were no idle words, for in exchange for taking part in the CSM program a successful noncommissioned officer undertook to accept far greater responsibility and work with no extra pay. It demanded, therefore, men truly dedicated to the Army.[13]

Some idea of the eventual magnitude of the program can be gained by noting that of the 5,228 sergeants major in the Army as of March 31, 1968, 1,230 occupied positions suitable for command sergeants major at various levels from battalion to department. This figure was reached in several stages. The first stage had been divided into three increments. The first increment was completed on December 29, 1967, with the adjournment of the first board convened to consider nominees for appointment. Of 214 men nominated Armywide, the board selected 192.*

A second board completed the next increment on March 20, 1968, selecting 321 out of 411 nominees. With the adjournment of the third selection board on July 5 of the same year, the third increment of 717 out of 1,046 nominees was completed.

With the completion of this increment a second phase in the selection process began. This provided candidates for appointment to make up for losses through normal attrition and to select additional men to fill authorized positions not filled earlier; some men, for various reasons, declined appointments. Nominations in the second phase were made, in most cases against positions outside the nominating command, thus requiring commanders to nominate only those men whom they would be willing to accept as their own command sergeant major. During this phase all sergeants major, even those assigned to small or remote organizations, received consideration.

Even as the CSM program was under way, some criticism was expected within DCSPER. The most significant harked back to tradition-based objections to the whole concept of centralized selection, promotion, and assignment of noncommissioned officers. These objections claimed to defend the division commander's traditional privilege of selecting from among the best of his battalion or regimental noncommissioned officers his own man for the post of senior noncommissioned officer in the division. Instead, an outsider's choice would now be foisted upon him. This view overlooked the fact that Armywide selection, promotion, and assignment would pit each candidate not just against his peers within his own unit, whether battalion or division, but against his peers throughout the Army.[14] It also ignored the likelihood that the best qualified in most units would be within the zone of consideration in any case. Therefore, a general's preference might be competing against his peers within his own division. Nevertheless, all commanders were assured that only the best men the Army had available at the time would be selected.

*The honor of being the first man selected to be a CSM went to Sergeant Major Theodore Dobol, a World War II veteran of the 1st Infantry Division.

There remained however one major problem—identifying by MOS those men deemed best qualified for the position of command sergeant major. For example, under the MOS system in existence during the late 1960s, command sergeants major, as had been the case with sergeants major before, could not be distinguished from other E-9s. As a consequence, the Army's chief of personnel operations determined that he could not effectively manage the careers of this important category of noncommissioned officers. There were more than 78 MOSs in which a noncommissioned officer could attain the rank of E-9, and after appointment to command sergeant major, he continued to hold his same MOS. This could be the same as other E-9s occupying such positions as operations sergeant major or intelligence sergeant major. The magnitude of the problem lay in the fact that as of March 31, 1967, of the 5,228 sergeants major in the Army, approximately 1,500 were filling command sergeants major positions.[15] DCSPER finally settled the problem by specifically creating a new MOS, 000Z, command sergeant major, for the command sergeants major.[16]

Concurrently with the establishment of a new MOS was the task of creating a distinctive insignia of rank for the command sergeant major. At this time all sergeants major, regardless of position, wore the same insignia—three chevrons up, three arcs below, with a star in the middle. The only visual means of distinguishing a command sergeant major from any other was the combat leader's green felt tab worn on the shoulder loops of the shirt or blouse by combat or combat support sergeants major at corps headquarters or below. There was no way at all of distinguishing the CSM of the noncombat arms or commands higher than corps headquarters. The insignia finally adopted was the same as that for the sergeant major but with a laurel wreath surrounding the star in the center field.

To make assignments, manage careers, and maintain records for the growing corps of CSM, DCSPER established a command sergeants major control section. This consisted of one officer, one senior noncommissioned officer, and one typist. This staff had the mission of phasing the CSM into the major commands of the Army, filling the forty-nine top commands first, and placing the remainder in CSM training positions where they were prepared for the top-level jobs.[17]

Controls of the CSM program remained throughout at Department of the Army level and were administered through the DCSPER. As with commissioned officer and sergeant major promotions and assignments, this program too was centralized and administered Armywide. Only the Department of the Army was authorized to assign sergeants major and command sergeants major from lists prepared by Army selection boards. No major command could assign men from these lists to another position in the same command without prior approval of the chief of personnel operations, DCSPER. An exception to this rule was made for combat zone commanders, who could delegate authority to assign sergeants major to division and separate brigades. Ultimate authority to appoint men to the position of CSM, however, remained with DCSPER. Combat zone commanders had to report such assignments to him for approval.[18]

For overseas assignments all command sergeants major were selected by name. Commanders had to submit a requisition to DCSPER in order to fill a CSM vacancy. Pending arrival of the replacement, the commander could assign the incumbent sergeant major to an appropriate vacancy within the command provided that the incumbent had not previously been selected by the board for appointment to a CSM position. The commander might also report the incumbent sergeant major to the chief of personnel operations for reassignment. A third choice open to the local overseas commander was to allow his sergeant major to remain in the CSM position provided another CSM was not serving in a subordinate unit of that command.

In 1974 the Army extended the CSM program to the Army Reserve and National Guard. On March 18 of that year the Department of the Army Reserve Components Command Sergeants Major Selection Board convened to consider nominees for appointment as CSM in both the Reserve and the Guard. The board adjourned on March 22 after selecting 74 men out of the 139 nominees considered. As with the regular Army, these men had been nominated by their commanders.[19]

ATTEMPTS TO DEFINE THE CSM'S ROLE

In summary, much of the difficulty in implementing the command sergeants major program and in defining the role and status of the command sergeant major as opposed to others in the E-9 pay grade stemmed from the fact that the Army had not yet officially defined the roles of the sergeant major and the CSM as well as their relationship to the rest of the noncommissioned officers. Despite strong command initiative, especially in overseas commands (Germany and Korea), to enhance the prestige of the CSM by defining his duties as essential to combat effectiveness, many commanders failed to rely on their CSMs as their "eyes and ears" and thus failed to use them properly.[20]

In the words of the one theater commander, the CSM was "the vital connection in the noncommissioned officers' channel of communications and an advisor to the subordinates and superior." Nevertheless, many officers continued to question whether senior noncommissioned officers could discharge their responsibilities, as envisioned in the command sergeants major program. Was there indeed a distinct line of authority that flowed down from the sergeant major through the first sergeants to the platoon sergeants and squad leaders? Would it interfere with the traditional chain of command? These were some of the questions that challenged the secretary of the army, Martin R. Hoffman and senior Army commanders as they gathered in conference at General William E. DePuy's headquarters, Training and Doctrine Command (TRADOC) in December 1975. The focus of their discussion turned on the Army's perception of the role of the CSM in the overall context of the noncommissioned officer's role and status in the service and the theory behind such perception.

During the conference there developed a consensus that "noncommissioned officers are *directly* responsible for a wide range of routine duties." The conferees also agreed "that the command sergeants major, first sergeants, and platoon sergeants or chiefs of gun sections were directly and personally responsible for the standards of performance of the soldiers and the noncommissioned officers in the line below them." All of the general officers taking part in the discussion agreed that these responsibilities were not universally understood and in fact that the average company, battery, or troop commander would not agree that the battalion sergeant major had *any* responsibility for the performance of anybody in his unit. This point of view took Secretary Hoffman somewhat by surprise, for he had assumed, based on his previous service with the 101st Airborne Division, that the active role, functions, and responsibilities of the CSM were understood, accepted, and in operation throughout the Army.

A part of the difficulty lay perhaps in the weak and waffled wording of Army Regulations 600-20 (Personnel—General, Army Command Policy and Procedure, 25 October 1974) definition of the noncommissioned officer duties and responsibilities. On the one hand, the regulation specified that the noncommissioned officer channel is one of communications and exchange of information. On the other, it stated that the noncommissioned officer channel is often used to accomplish "certain routine but important tasks and responsibilities." The foregoing, in concert with the last sentence, set up only a *permissive* policy rather than a *requirement* that all commanders use their noncommissioned officers to do these tasks. Therein lay much of the problem, although there were, and remain, deep-seated differences in viewpoint among commissioned officers regarding the role and status of the noncommissioned officer within the Army command structure.

The conferees agreed, however, that the line of authority from the CSM down through the noncommissioned echelons must be clear and understood by all. Although the traditional chain of command is the final authority, the noncommissioned line of authority must be permitted, indeed, must be required to operate. The conference host, General DePuy, summed up the issue rather forcefully.

> Unless the whole Army moves to such a policy in concert under the direction of the Chief of Staff and with the full support and understanding of the major commanders, it will not be possible to move very far at all. Inherent in the system of NCO responsibility/authority is the requirement for commanders at every echelon to understand, support, and enforce it.

To illustrate this point, DePuy then gave an example of a unit with a rule that all soldiers would have clean weapons, all authorized ammunition, and helmets with them at all times. Therefore,

> [if a] battalion, brigade, or division commander wishes to inspect for compliance with this rule, he should be accompanied only by the command sergeants major in

> the line of NCO authority and responsibility and the NCOs below the sergeant major (first sergeants, platoon sergeants). If shortfalls are found, it must be regarded as a failure on the part of the battalion sergeant major, the first sergeant, and the platoon sergeant. It must not be regarded automatically or even primarily as a failure on the part of the company commander. However, it is *secondarily** the responsibility of the . . . commanders who have failed to *require* or *permit* the NCO line of authority to operate . . . we have almost a cultural problem—compounded by our recent past.

The recent past to which General DePuy referred was the so-called full-up "people program era of the Modern Volunteer Army" that was eventually to replace the draft during the operations in Southeast Asia. At that time the noncommissioned corps was frequently described as an obstacle "to communicate better." This was often both the perception and practice during the war in Vietnam, when many of the junior company-grade officers were closer in age, background, and attitudes to the average soldier than was the older career noncommissioned officer whose experience frequently extended back to the closing months of World War II or to the Korean War.

According to General DePuy, this approach to the noncommissioned officer corps nearly put it "out of the game." "It was," he observed,

> "an astounding concept—an Army without sergeants. We have come a long way," he added, "but we have a long way to go. My personal guess is that we get less than 50 percent of their potential from our command sergeants major. We could bring that up to 80 or 90 percent if we were willing to tackle the formidable problem of changing the Army's perception and practice in the use of the NCO line of authority and responsibility."

To this, commander in chief, U.S. Army, Europe, General George S. Blanchard, added his own standard for the command sergeant major:

> He must *seek*† responsibility and at the same time see that the other NCOs of the command have their responsibilities clearly defined and are accepting and performing in accordance with these responsibilities . . . the CSM must reflect the image of the NCO Corps and demand that his fellow noncommissioned officers do the same.

While the commanding generals of major Army commands sought to more clearly define the role and status of the command sergeant major in particular and the noncommissioned officer corps in general, Army Chief of Staff Harold K. Johnson in 1967 took a major step toward enhancing the corps' prestige by creating a new position on the Army staff—that of Sergeant Major of the Army. His role was similar to that of the CSM—more work and responsibility but no more pay than any other E-9.

*Emphasis added.
†Emphasis added.

A DECISION REGARDING WARRANT OFFICERS

In August 1953 Army plans for a force reduction following cessation of hostilities in Korea disclosed that total warrant officer requirements would also have to be reduced by one third to conform with the fiscal year 1954 budget authorization of approximately 12,400 positions. A year before, in March 1952, fiscal limitations forced termination of all warrant officer appointments. Except in very limited cases, there were no further appointments made after that date, until the acceleration of the missile programs in the mid-1950s. This situation led to a searching analysis by the Army between 1952 and 1957 of the warrant officer program to determine whether the corps should be continued and if so, what its future role and purpose should be.

When Congress passed legislation in 1958 creating the enlisted supergrades, the Air Force, scarcely nine months later, discontinued procurement of warrant officers, deeming that these new enlisted grades would take their place. A prime consideration for this action was a perceived need to eliminate what was regarded by the Air Force as an unnecessary layer of supervision between officers and noncommissioned officers. The Air Force thereupon merged warrant officer authorizations with those of commissioned officers, and the rank of warrant officer disappeared from that service.

The Army, on the other hand, was not so quick to reach a decision regarding the warrant officer. As the Army staff saw it, the issue turned on whether the rank augmented or duplicated the enlisted/officer grade structure. Although most noncommissioned officers agreed at the time that it represented unnecessary layering, the Army waited until 1965 before canvassing the major commands on this question. At that point, more than two thirds of the replies stated that the warrant officer grades did not duplicate either the enlisted or officer grade structures. Of this, a majority believed that the structure augmented both the enlisted and commissioned grade structures and therefore served as a bridge between the two. A few replies saw the augmentation applying only to the commissioned grade structure while an even smaller number saw it as limited to the enlisted structure. The latter viewed the warrant officer more as a specialist or a technician than as an officer. Yet the warrant officer was generally perceived as having a higher grade level of competence and experience than that expected of an enlisted specialist.

Army assignment policies enabled the warrant officer to provide greater stability and continuity than either officers or noncommissioned officers. Furthermore, the structure of the Army's aviation and missile arms, to mention but two, was considered too heavily dependent on the depth of training and experience found with the warrant officer corps to tolerate its disbandment. Clearly, the Army was not prepared, as was its sister service—the Air Force—to abandon the warrant officer grade. In retaining it, however, the Army did once and for all drop the corps' original concept as a cap or goal for able senior noncommissioned officers.

Henceforth the warrant officer corps existed as a grade structure in and of itself, with no ties to the noncommissioned corps.[21]

In one respect this decision served to throw the noncommissioned corps back upon itself. From now on senior noncommissioned officers considered the new grades of E-8 and E-9 as their career goals. In terms of pay and prestige, these new grades came to rival the position of the warrant officer.

Even as all this was happening, events were taking shape halfway around the world in Vietnam that were to embroil the Army and the nation in a war so bitterly controversial that both would be left changed and deeply wounded but unbowed and in many ways stronger than before.

CHAPTER 18

VIETNAM

THE CRISIS OF THE CORPS

Scarcely had the reforms of the late 1950s—the Pay Bill of 1958 and the attendant changes in the enlisted grade structure—been received and digested than the escalating challenges of military operations in Southeast Asia confronted the Army.

These challenges changed in character and intensity as the war dragged on and on. They were not exclusively military, as might have been expected, but in the latter years of the war became more and more influenced by deteriorating morale on the home front. When combined with the professional challenges of meeting and defeating elusive enemy forces, both regular and irregular, on unfamiliar terrain, the impact on the Army of lack of direction and confusion on the political front placed enormous strains on leadership from sergeant to general. These strains manifested themselves through a series of crises at various periods in the war and at various levels of command. One of the most serious in terms of its threat to the integrity of the Army was what has been called the "crisis of the noncommissioned officer corps." Manifesting itself rather late in the war, this crisis continued on into the postwar period, during the early phase of the adoption of the all-volunteer Army, until further reform and change restored morale and brought the situation at last to an end.

The crisis of the NCO corps had many causes. One, according to a general officer, could be laid at the door of the commissioned officer corps of the U.S. Army. It was during this period, mainly in the second half of the war (after 1968), that because of a chronic shortage of experienced noncommissioned officers, many officers, especially at the company level, resumed the practice of bypassing their noncoms when dealing with the troops. As had happened before, this practice eroded the sergeant's proper role as a small-unit leader and pushed him to the sidelines in many units where he became a spectator instead of the focus of the action, as he was meant to be. This astounding development—an Army without sergeants—seriously undermined the role and morale of the noncommissioned corps. Ironically, this occurred exactly at a time in the Army's operational history when, because of the nature of the tactics employed in Vietnam, the small-unit leader was more vitally needed than ever before.[1]

Unlike World War II and, to a lesser extent, the Korean War, Vietnam was not a senior commander's war involving large formations and great expanses of terrain. It was a junior leader's war, limited to small areas with the brunt of much of the fighting falling on the noncommissioned troop leader. It was indeed a war of the platoon sergeant, squad, patrol, and fire-team leaders. Because of this as well as other factors peculiar to operations in Vietnam, units were forced to endure a shortage of experienced noncommissioned officers.

Regular Army divisions, i.e., the 1st Infantry, began their Vietnam operations with "a lot of good sergeants," but lost most of them through the twelve-month rotation policy and normal combat attrition. One of this division's later commanders, General William E. DePuy, observed that small units, bereft of experienced noncommissioned leaders, just weren't being properly trained and in consequence, were frequently "stumbling into battles." In General DePuy's view, the problems were found down in the squads and platoons.[2]

By 1966, another observer declared, "the attrition of combat, one year tours in Vietnam, the 25-month stabilized tour in the rotation base, and the administrative erosion of separation and retirement combined to reduce the flow of qualified [noncommissioned] replacements to a trickle."[3]

A decision had already been made in Washington that the organized reserve units were not to be called up in support of operations in Vietnam. This left the Army with no choice but to draw upon its own considerable resources, supported as it was by a stepped-up draft. In any case, during the first years of the involvement the regular Army managed to sustain operations without an increase in the draft call-up. But by 1967, the weekly turnover rate among noncommissioned officers in the combat arms had risen to two hundred. Heretofore, most of the impact of the gradual buildup in support of widening hostilities had been absorbed by the regular noncommissioned officer corps. But in the face of attrition and expansion, the Army's demand for experienced small-unit leaders eventually exceeded the supply. This finally forced the Army to set aside for a time those personnel policies that seemed no longer capable of providing sufficient noncommissioned officers for its operations in Southeast Asia.

THE NCOCC PROGRAM

The Army's response to this need was to establish in the United States noncommissioned officer candidate courses (NCOCC) to train young men to serve in the combat arms—infantry, armor, artillery—for the need was greatest there. The first of these courses was offered at the infantry school at Ft. Benning; the second and third were established at the armored school at Ft. Knox and the artillery school at Ft. Sill, respectively.

There were some not unexpected parallels between the long-established officer candidate schools (OCS) that had served the Army so well during World War II and the NCOCC. Candidates for both were volunteers and were promoted to corporal upon assignment to their respective schools. There were other parallels as well. Upon graduation following a twenty-three-week course, the OCS candidate received a commission as a second lieutenant. The NCOCC graduate, after an intensive ten-week course, was promoted to the rank of sergeant (E-5).* An additional ten weeks of practical training in grade followed as assistant instructors and tactical noncommissioned officers in a basic training center—a total of twenty weeks of training before the new noncommissioned officers were sent to prove themselves in combat.

The course length was designed to make maximum use of a conscript soldier's two-year tour of active duty. Because of the length of time required for basic and advanced individual training (AIT), plus the necessary leave and travel time, and the twelve-month limitation on in-country service in Vietnam, Army planners settled on twenty-one to twenty-two weeks as the optimum time to produce a noncommissioned officer—about the same length of time it took to produce a commissioned officer.

On June 22, 1967, Army Chief of Staff Johnson approved the NCOCC plan, and the first class began training at Ft. Benning on September 5 of the same year. After completing the first half of its training in November, graduates of this class reported to several training centers for the practical application phase of the course. By mid-February 1968, this class had completed the second phase and was ready to report for duty in Vietnam.

General Johnson's decision concerning NCOCC had been no spur of the moment remedy to a growing problem. He had been considering such a program for some time. He reasoned that if the Army managed to produce good platoon leaders through a twenty-three-week OCS, it ought to be able to produce good fireteam leaders in twelve to thirteen weeks. As logical as this program seemed, General Johnson found that resistance to the idea at lower levels had served to delay adoption of the program. As he was later to observe,

> I could never quite get that idea accepted by General [Paul L.] Freeman [CG, CONARC April 2, 1965–June 30, 1966] and his headquarters staff, and as a consequence, we didn't start the program until after General [James K.] Woolnough [CG CONARC, July 1, 1967–October 31, 1970] went down there, because I didn't want to have a program that was going to get "lip service" from the people who were responsible for carrying it out. And that is what I was concerned with at the time. We might get "lip service," and we simply had to have a very substantial effort if we were going to turn out good noncommissioned officers. I guess we are still uncertain in regard to how that program came out, but without it, I don't know what we would have done. In querying noncommissioned officers in Vietnam in April 1968, I found enthusiastic support for the program. One criticism was that the young noncommissioned officer graduate of the NCOCC did not assume non-duty hour disciplinary

*The top 5 percent of graduates were promoted to staff sergeant (E-6).

> responsibility, although technically proficient. He wanted to be one of the boys and engage in the off-duty cut-up activities prevalent among the young.[4]

In the words of a general officer who had commanded a division in Vietnam, adoption of the NCOCC represented a "bold departure from previously accepted military training policies." These earlier policies rested on a tradition of slow progression through the ranks, mainly through on-the-job-training or *ad hoc* unit schools for selected men. While these policies nevertheless had produced some fine noncommissioned officers, they were suitable primarily to maintain a small peacetime army but not a million-man force deployed on a global scale.

Virtually all of the junior officers interviewed by a team of investigators sent to Vietnam from the Department of the Army spoke highly of the young sergeants and staff sergeants of the combat arms turned out by the NCOCC and judged them "essential to the successful completion of their combat missions."[5]

On the other hand, some senior noncommissioned officers denigrated these men as inexperienced, overly familiar with their subordinates, lacking in military bearing, and tolerant of the use of drugs by the troops. Middle-grade noncommissioned officers—sergeants and staff sergeants who had spent up to ten years earning their rank—particularly resented those they scornfully referred to as "Shake 'n' Bake" or "Instant NCOs."* Yet the alternative to the NCOCC would have been to require mid-grade noncommissioned officers to go on short tours to Vietnam more frequently and remain there longer, or to continue the former practice of requiring a platoon leader faced with the loss of a sergeant to select the brightest PFC he had and declare him sergeant and entrust the lives of a dozen men to his care. To most senior noncommissioned officers, these were unacceptable alternatives. So the NCOCC remained in effect for the balance of the war.

Actually, when older sergeants were questioned specifically concerning their younger colleagues, their response was generally, "Well, Sir, now I've got three of them in my platoon, and they're working hard—fine young men—and they really know the equipment we're using." And from a rifle platoon sergeant in an infantry company there came a somewhat more cautious comment that he had "good results with the 'shake and bake' type NCOs I have assigned to my platoon. I presently have six assigned to my platoon—four are good NCOs, the other two we are in the process of having them reduced because of their negative attitudes and cannot [*sic*] control their troops."

So widespread were such responses that an investigative team sent to Vietnam by the Department of the Army concluded that the NCOCC program had been a great success.† Yet there remained three problems with the program that were never satisfactorily solved: to win from senior noncommissioned officers final ac-

*After popular quick-food products of the day.

†A 1968 distinguished graduate of the Ft. Benning NCOCC, Thomas J. Ridge, who won the Bronze Star for Valor as a staff sergeant with the Americal Division in Vietnam, is today serving as a U.S. congressman from Pennsylvania's 21st District.

ceptance of the NCOCC graduates; to train and persuade the best among them to make a career of the Army; and to identify those combat arms noncommissioned officers who were either physically or emotionally unfit to serve any longer in their primary specialties and retrain them or eliminate them from the service.

There had also been some problems with the implementation of the NCOCC. The most troublesome was an unusually high attrition rate of 34 percent in the original class of 200 candidates at the Infantry School. In time this rate was lowered considerably through more careful selection of students. Attrition was less a problem with the other two combat arms, for with much smaller enrollments in their classes they could be more selective. The Artillery School at Ft. Sill, for example, enrolled only 48 candidates every two weeks, while the Armor School at Ft. Knox accepted 120 candidates every three weeks.

Not only did Vietnam provide young graduates of the NCOCC with rapid promotion, but the exigencies of the conflict, as in all wars, meant unaccustomed advancement for other ranks as well. Battle and non-battle losses plus the one-year rotation system stretched the Army in Vietnam thin in both the younger commissioned and middle noncommissioned grades. Consequently, promotion to the ranks of captain and major on the one hand and staff and platoon sergeant on the other came more rapidly than in peacetime. A lieutenant could attain captain's rank in two years; noncommissioned officers deployed to Vietnam as sergeants (E-5) could, if they survived, expect to reach staff (E-6) or platoon (E-7) sergeant within the same length of time. In the post-Vietnam period, this rapid inflation of grades returned to haunt the Army.

CHANGING ATTITUDES AND THEIR CONSEQUENCES

A significant phenomenon in military sociology, especially as it related to the status of the noncommissioned officers, also manifested itself in the latter stages of the war in Vietnam. This phenomenon represented an apparent reversal in attitudes of enlisted men toward officers and noncommissioned officers as had happened in World War II. One student of military sociology has pointed out that almost without exception, a *Leitmotif* in the novels describing military life during World War II was the social void that separated the commissioned officers from the enlisted men.[6]

While the Vietnam-era enlisted man generally despised the authoritarian military system as much as any of World War II, writers of Vietnam war novels often describe enlisted men as forming strong informal ties to the leaders in their immediate unit—both noncommissioned officers and other ranks. The soldier's adaptation to military life is described as depending upon these strong primary relationships with his comrades. Rarely was anything comparable perceived as developing between enlisted men and their officers in the novels of World War II.

Gradual changes in these attitudes had been recognized as early as the so-called Cold War, in the 1950s, when the focus of enlisted animosity began to shift toward the "lifer," the noncommissioned careerist. Novelists of this period frequently portrayed the career soldier—the noncommissioned officer—as someone who had found a "home in the Army" because he was seen as incapable of coping with civilian life or life "on the outside." During the war in Vietnam this shift in attitudes gradually displaced the earlier World War II hostility toward officers.[7]

James Webb captured this shift of mood in his classic Vietnam war novel, *Fields of Fire*. As he describes Lieutenant Robert E. Lee Hodges reacting to the men (and they to him) of his new command in Vietnam, Webb, who won the Navy Cross in Vietnam combat, is delineating a common experience of the Vietnam war that cut across the normally inviolable borders of military service and unit.

> But he felt an immediate, visceral kinship with most of them, and sensed that it was mutual. . . . Bagger brought Hodges a cookie from a package his wife had sent, and then used the occasion to display a whole string of pictures. In five minutes Hodges had a history of their whole love affair, beginning with their first date after a football game his junior year in high school.[8]

Among the forces in Vietnam, the college-educated enlisted malcontent, however, is frequently portrayed by novelists as being far more alienated from his enlisted peers of lower socioeconomic background than he was from his junior officers, with whom he was presumed to share a similar class background. This resulted in an untraditional phenomenon of junior officers having a greater affinity for many of their enlisted men than they had for field-grade officers and senior noncommissioned officers since the rank and file were generally drawn from the same groups that at home were sharing a general tolerance of, if not addiction to, the growing drug culture within the United States.

On the other hand, senior noncommissioned officers (E-7 through E-9) whose career commitment to the Army matched that of the senior officers, found in Vietnam that their shared commitment to the military life and its ideals overrode the earlier status differences between officers and enlisted men. This group—senior officers and noncommissioned officers alike—viewed with increasing dismay and frustration the widespread manifestations of insubordination on the part of many conscripts toward their lawful leaders, and at home of civilian youth toward the administration in Washington. Consequently, in Vietnam the traditional hostility toward commissioned officers, as a group, began in the war's later years to yield to a growing animosity between lower-ranking enlisted men and senior sergeants, especially the 1st sergeants, whom the former came to regard as the source of all their woes.

As the buildup continued in Vietnam, many officers observed with dismay a growing polarization between the professional noncommissioned officers and their junior enlisted men. Two classes were perceived as emerging within the ranks. On the one side were the privates (E-1) through junior sergeants and specialists (E-5), and on the other the senior noncommissioned officers, a "magnificent few" who held it all together, as a former Sergeant Major of the Army observed. There developed a gradual deterioration in communication between the two groups. Junior or company-grade officers often tended to identify with the first while the second group generally found itself either siding with the attitudes of the senior officers or sometimes in isolation, believing that they had been scorned or unsupported by their commanders. In this situation, unit discipline became an ultimate casualty.[9]

Not only were traditional attitudes toward the noncommissioned officer corps changing, but the corps' composition was also undergoing significant change. During the Vietnam years the Army, sustained by a selective service system that tended to defer men from the more affluent classes and to conscript those less fortunate, experienced a growing proportion of blacks reenlisting after their initial term of service. As their hash marks increased in number, these men rose to noncommissioned rank. Consequently, in some units there came to be a preponderance of black enlisted leaders. As this occurred, there arose some problems among noncommissioned officers themselves. As a former Chief of Staff described it,

> At Fort Bragg, in the 82d Airborne Division, in the fall of 1964 or early 1965, the black noncommissioned officers had achieved numbers to the extent that they and their wives had assumed control of the noncommissioned officers' club. We had instances of white noncommissioned officers moving off post because they felt they were really being put into an intolerable situation on post by their black neighbors . . . now this thing carried over as we began to rotate people into Vietnam. Here you had a substantial number of black noncommissioned officers, and they had risen to these positions. And a substantial number, a significant part, of our casualties in Vietnam, especially in the early days were among these noncommissioned officers. You had a very high attrition rate. Now this, I think, stemmed from two things. Number one, the noncommissioned officer had to demonstrate, partly to himself, that he was, in fact, a leader, and by leading, he was out there exposing himself and perhaps more than other people for whom he was responsible. And second, in those early stages there was not the caution that later began to grow as people became more battle-wise.[10]

When the element of racial tension was added to the factor of increasing polarization between senior noncommissioned officers and junior enlisted men—against a background of company officers bypassing their older noncommissioned officers—the Army in Vietnam had all the ingredients of a serious crisis on its hands.

Incidents of insubordination and violence toward senior noncommissioned officers and sometimes company commanders abound in the inspector general's records for that later period, and they tell a tragic tale. This is not to imply that the Army was rife with insubordination or that the sergeants had lost control of their men, but these incidents were numerous enough to create an atmosphere of frustration and despair among many experienced senior noncommissioned leaders. The impact this had upon the morale of these important professionals became in time so pervasive as to shake the foundations of the corps and hence the integrity of the Army itself.

THE BELEAGUERED SERGEANTS

Illustrative of the hostility or, in some cases, the isolation of older noncommissioned soldiers from the younger men (and in some cases their officers as well) is the testimony given investigators concerning the murder of a master sergeant at Quang Tri Combat Base, Vietnam, in May 1971.[11]

The master sergeant was shot by a person or persons unknown while serving as acting 1st sergeant of his company, a combat support unit. Interrogation of the former company commander disclosed that he regarded the sergeant as "a soldier of the old Army, and he sought his goals in that manner . . . he believed in blind obedience, and communication was usually one-way." To allegations that he failed to support or back the sergeant in his efforts "to establish discipline of personnel in the unit," the captain replied that he had "backed Sgt. Craig as much as possible through counseling, command interest, administrative eliminations, and military justice. Many Articles 15 [nonjudicial punishment authorized under Article 15 of the Uniform Code of Military Justice] and courts-martial were administered or approved at his request."

The company commander went on to explain that he had had some problems with replacements who didn't want to go to Quang Tri and "gave the NCOs a hard time." They were disrespectful to the NCOs, cursing them and addressing rude remarks to them. Apparently the captain did not or was unable to stop this practice that undoubtedly provoked the 1st sergeant into some harsh language toward the offenders. The captain observed that the murdered sergeant had belonged in spirit to the "brown shoe army." Soldiers of that era—one that neither the captain nor his 1st sergeant had little direct experience with—were, in his words, "blindly obedient to a superior, and if they stepped out of line or got in some kind of trouble, the NCOs or somebody would physically beat them or something of this nature. In other words, they weren't allowed to question any order or anything that affected [them]." With a commanding officer as ignorant as this one, no wonder the 1st sergeant was frustrated and angry toward the men who were insubordinate.

If the 1st sergeant saw something wrong or something struck him as being wrong, the company commander added, "he would immediately begin yelling at the individual or individuals who were involved without evaluating the situation first." At one time, the captain stated,

> the troops came in from the field and one of the men was wearing a head band—a practice that was becoming popular in Vietnam at the time. The First Sergeant spotted the man in the mess hall and told him to take it off. The man had a tray of food in his hands and replied that he would take if off when he got to his table. The old sergeant naturally expected and demanded instant obedience and when the man refused to lay down his tray and remove the head band the sergeant became angry.

In this case the company commander supported the 1st sergeant and gave the insubordinate soldier an Article 15 at the sergeant's urging.

Incidents of this sort, the captain explained, strained the sergeant's relations with the men and alienated them from him. Yet the officer admitted that his 1st sergeant "kept the paperwork flowing and unit details functioning." The captain testified that he had frequently counseled the 1st sergeant to be more flexible. He was "slowly, very slowly changing his traditional thoughts . . . he used to make the statement that the Army was going to pot, and he always left you with the impression that he was way behind." He was, his commanding officer concluded, unable to change his thinking to incorporate "new ideals and new Army policies."

Corroboration that the company commander hesitated to fully support his noncommissioned officers came from additional testimony offered by the other sergeants in his unit. Admittedly, they were close companions of the slain 1st sergeant, but the pattern on the part of the negligent captain was a familiar one. Among the 1st sergeant's comrades was a sergeant first class who, under interrogation, testified that morale in the unit had steadily declined under the captain.

> First he took the leadership responsibilities away from the noncommissioned officers by writing letters of reprimand over trivial matters . . . when he was giving an Article 15 he would grin at them, almost laughing at them. There was nothing serious about giving an Article 15 . . . general attitude—he didn't care about the troops. He set up command reveille once a week, and he wouldn't even monitor it himself. Also he set up a command information class on Mondays, and we only had one or two of these, and they were spaced three or four weeks apart.

In answer to the question, Was the captain derelict in maintaining discipline in the unit after arrival at Quang Tri? The sergeant first class replied yes. He gave a similar answer to the query, Had the captain failed to back his first sergeant's efforts to maintain discipline in the unit?

In the opinion of the other noncommissioned officers of the company, even though their murdered 1st sergeant was an "old soldier" whose biases and prejudices made it difficult "to change to the younger ways," the failure of a young and inexperienced company commander to check the use of drugs and to support his subordinate in maintaining discipline created conditions that resulted in the sergeant's murder.

From one of the company officers, however, there emerged a somewhat different picture of the company commander. Nevertheless, it also corroborated the picture given by the noncommissioned officers of their late 1st sergeant. The company, in the words of the lieutenant, had more than its share of "undesirables," men who were insubordinate and who were addicted to drugs. This officer described the drug scene as "very intense in the company. Anytime you have a portion of your unit taking drugs, it's going to affect the atmosphere, morale, and discipline of the unit." Under these conditions, the 1st sergeant's task was especially difficult. He met the problem head-on, requiring the troops to stand in formations and to follow dress regulations and general discipline. He was, the lieutenant added, "a strong-willed first sergeant . . . required the men in the unit to perform their duties as soldiers." The 1st sergeant "required the men to get haircuts when they came in from the field—what any normal soldier was expected to do . . . the first sergeant required the men to do these things, and they resented it." The officer giving testimony in this case, instead of questioning whether the company commander backed up his 1st sergeant, questioned whether the captain received the proper support from higher authority.

Far more frequent than shootings were the so-called "fragging" incidents in which fragmentation hand grenades were used by angry subordinates and drug-addicted men against officers and noncommissioned officers toward whom they harbored real or imagined grievances.[12]

Typical of such cases were the seven incidents that occurred in one combat battalion during the period April 2 to December 28, 1969. Lack of discipline, lack of command support for noncommissioned officers, and cumbersome administrative procedures involved in handling lawless elements within the ranks all combined to create an atmosphere in which these incidents could occur.

Illustrative of this situation was the Army's inability to convict and incarcerate all but the most hardened criminals. The insubordinate and malingering soldier—popularly referred to as a "dud," tended, under the conditions obtaining in Vietnam, to become a freewheeler, drifting from one place to another under the pretext of "appointments with the Inspector General, the Staff Judge Advocate, Medical authorities, and Reenlistment offices," to name a few of the excuses used. By this means these individuals managed to prolong the mechanics of punishment or discharge and got themselves and others into more trouble along the way.

Under the appointment system that existed in Vietnam, combined with the desire of rear-area hospitals to unencumber themselves of the tasks of controlling personnel, a "dud" was relatively free to move about in the rear. Unfortunately, most units generally had neither the time nor the capability to track down these individuals and return them to some degree of control. Under judicial rulings then in force, pretrial confinement was virtually impossible. Most responsible officers and noncommissioned officers believed that only a radical change in these rulings would make it possible to deal effectively with these undesirables.

With the social ills of a strife-torn, permissive society foisted on the Army in the 1960s, it is not surprising that insubordination and lawlessness were rife in many units. Fraggings and other acts of violence were only the more radical manifestations of soldiers influenced by this strife. The inspector general observed that

> at every echelon, we must convince the soldier that a society will remain a good society [only] as long as the law is upheld. Anything else will produce chaos. . . . the Army too must retain and support commanders at every level who are willing to punish swiftly and impartially. The positive impact of a hard-nosed commander is dramatic. Knowing that punishment is sure to come is one of the greatest deterrents available to prevent crime.

Testimony given during investigation of the fragging incidents already referred to gave further evidence of hostility toward the senior noncommissioned officers from certain elements within the battalion. One noncommissioned witness declared that, in his opinion, the fragging incidents stemmed partly from

> a lack of communication between section chiefs [staff sergeants] and personnel . . . they were fighting the guard situation, and the blame for this commitment [was] being placed on the first sergeant. I experienced the same resentment after taking charge of the platoon. I found this resentment throughout the company when I took over as acting first sergeant. [I relieved the tension somewhat] by conducting individual briefings and encouraging section leaders to explain why the heavy guard commitment was necessary.

That a partial solution lay in an improved quality of leadership was underscored by another witness, this one a commissioned officer. Of the three morale factors, racial tensions, poor environment, and leadership, the first two, while troublesome, were not, in his opinion, critical. The critical factor, in this officer's estimation, was poor leadership. Environmental factors were admittedly grim, considering the constant threat of enemy attack and the monsoon rains.

As for the guard commitment, the infantry battalions with 14 percent of the base camp strength pulled 41 percent of the guard. When this figure was reduced to the people who actually served regularly as sentinels on the bunkers (E-5s and below), the line battalions were admittedly pulling 76 percent of the guard duty. It was unfortunate that the men worked all day and stood guard all night, but given the tactical situation, it was not altogether abnormal. What was not normal, in the view of this officer, was the lack of leadership at brigade level—the commander's total inability to communicate "with subordinates resulted in a command that was a smoldering volcano . . . by way of written messages, radio calls, and rumors, his life too was threatened."

Conditions in the last years of the war continued to deteriorate to such an extent that many responsible commissioned and noncommissioned officers were in danger of being fragged. One witness observed of his company that "the inability of investigators to determine who throws a grenade has caused it to become a favorite weapon of would-be assassins."

The conditions producing a fragging incident seemed to fall, in this particular situation, into two readily identifiable categories. The first was when an attempt was made to bring a group of "duds" to justice. The second was when a command effort was made to close in on users or pushers of narcotics and other stimulants. Whenever an attempt was made to tighten discipline within such a unit, the pinch was felt by all, but especially those living on the periphery of the law. In varying degrees, those men caught in the squeeze lashed out at those in authority.

Witnesses observed that intimidation of responsible officials in civilian life had been so successful that the practice had made significant inroads into military life. These malcontents were well aware that the burden of proof lay with the commander attempting to court-martial them. Realizing that the difficulty of gathering sufficient evidence and witnesses to convict was difficult under the circumstances in Vietnam, the lawbreaker or dissident usually resorted to intimidation. In one battalion it was bruited about that "contracts" had been put out to kill or maim the company commander, the acting 1st sergeant, and one platoon sergeant. Weak officers and noncommissioned officers often gave in to such threats, and the rabble had its way. Firm commanders faced the possibility of being killed or maimed by the fraggers, as did the company commander and the 1st sergeant in this case.

The criminal investigation division investigated these incidents but rarely came up with conclusive evidence. In this case the investigation was terminated, a final report rendered, and no one was ever brought before a court-martial.

Despite sensational coverage in the media, very little was known precisely about this situation until 1976, when a systematic study of these crimes was undertaken.[13]

Actual frequencies of these crimes had been difficult to determine. An unofficial source reported that from 1968 to 1972 there had been approximately 500 fraggings with 86 deaths. Yet another source reported that between 1970 and 1972 there had been 363 assaults involving explosive devices with another 118 cases termed possible assaults resulting in 45 deaths. It was evident from the foregoing that an objective study of this problem was needed. Consequently, two behavioral scientists assigned to the U.S. Army Disciplinary Barracks at Ft. Leavenworth, Kansas, undertook the collection and collation of a wealth of unique data from prisoners confined at the disciplinary barracks.

Their report focused on the military and personal characteristics of the offenders, the environment in which the incidents occurred, and the characteristics of the victims as reported by the offenders. One must keep in mind, however, that in most cases offenders were rarely identified or prosecuted; consequently, this study was based on interviews with only twenty-four inmates. Originally twenty-eight men had been selected but two were released, one paroled prior to the interview period, and a fourth refused to participate.

Most of the interviewees believed themselves to have been singled out and made scapegoats for others, in terms of their treatment by their superiors. Furthermore, most of the men (83 percent) judged their unit to be a support rather than a combat unit. Half of those interviewed stated that they had worked daily at duties "not directly related to their primary or secondary military occupational specialty" for which they had received special training prior to being assigned to Vietnam.

The investigators found that 80 percent of the assaults occurred at a base camp; 91 percent in darkness; and that 67 percent of the offenders claimed they had done nothing to avoid apprehension. However, in view of the fact that very few perpetrators were ever identified or brought to trial, this statement suggests that the interviewers were speaking to an unrepresentative sample. Obviously, this sample represented a minority—those who had been apprehended and convicted. Not surprisingly, the overwhelming number of offenders admitted to having been under the influence of alcohol or drugs at the time of their crime. Less than 10 percent of this sample reported that racial tensions had anything to do with the offense, but slightly more than one third admitted that there were disciplinary actions pending against them at the time of their crime.

As to the identity of the victims, nearly twice as many officers (62.5 percent) as enlisted men had been primary targets of these assaults. Captains (company commanders) were the most frequent targets (70 percent), while a similar percentage of the enlisted targets were noncommissioned officers (E-6 and above). Ironically, although the target percentages were the same, more enlisted men fell victim to the attacks than officers. Another finding that tended to support the statements that racial tensions played a minor role is that 75 percent of the incidents involved white offenders and white victims, but that no nonwhite offenders reported a nonwhite victim.

Offenders generally described their perceptions of their victims' attitudes as "insensitive to the frustrations of the men" and as tending to single out certain individuals for restrictions and special treatment. If these perceptions had any validity whatever, it would suggest a certain deficiency in leadership and in handling and motivating subordinates.

While the majority of the men declared that military life had not lived up to their expectations, most stated they had enjoyed their work. However, this statement flies in the face of previous declarations attributed to half of the offenders, namely that they "worked daily at duties not directly related to their primary or secondary military occupational specialties." A quarter of these men also averred that before their conviction they had planned on making the military a career. One wonders how suitable such men could be for career service in the Army inasmuch as very few of them had "felt remorse and still did not at the time of the study." Eighty percent of them, however, indicated that they would not repeat the offense if given the opportunity.

Faced with the serious problem of fragging, the Army's initial response was to restrict access to grenades to personnel in combat who had a demonstrated need for them. Yet this problem far transcended such a response, because it was only symptomatic of a far more serious condition—the crisis of small-unit leadership, especially in combat support and rear-area units, that developed during the war in Vietnam.

THE CRISIS OF LEADERSHIP

This crisis, though chronic and widespread, was not evident to a significant degree in combat units forward of battalion. This was a conclusion by a team composed of two officers and one noncommissioned officer sent to Vietnam in April/May of 1971 by the Chief of Staff on behalf of Lieutenant General G. I. Forsythe, his special assistant on the modern volunteer army (MVA). The team's objectives were to determine the successful leadership techniques "which both accomplish the mission and tend to retain outstanding personnel in the Army," and to identify the reactions of company/battery-level personnel to planned and ongoing actions of the modern volunteer army.[14]

The study was based on group interviews with small combat units throughout U.S. Army, Vietnam. The study group interviewed a total of 1,167 officers and men from the 1st Cavalry Division, the 5th Mechanized, the 101st Airborne, and the 23d Infantry divisions as well as 1st Squadron, 10th Armored Cavalry, the 173d Airborne Brigade, and the 765th Transportation Battalion. In addition to the above units, their support units were visited as well.

Armed with knowledge gleaned from the civilian news media and from many field-grade officers that combat units could be characterized by extensive use of drugs in the field; avoidance of contact with the enemy; misrepresentation of their real locations to higher commanders; and the occurrence of major racial problems, the investigators found that conditions were not nearly as grim in the combat units as they had been led to believe. They found that while in the field (and they emphasized this point), infantry units did not in general use any drugs because the troops policed their own ranks. The investigators discovered two occasions in which the members of platoons had beaten offenders so badly that they had been hospitalized.

However, there had been two major exceptions to these findings of drug abstinence during operations. Two battalion-sized units visited were found to be using all types of drugs while in the field. Although their officers had attempted to control the problem, they had failed because the men themselves, unlike those in most other combat units, did not regard drug use as a threat to their safety. Both units, however, were limited to small-unit pacification operations.

During its study trip, the team found only five platoons that were "papering missions," that is, avoiding contact and reporting false locations. In every case the investigators determined that this had occurred when the platoon leader was strongly opposed to the war and used this as a rationale to avoid contact. Three of these five platoon leaders were all found to be in one battalion and could have been easily detected and eliminated by a commander with open channels of communications down to his troops.

The team of investigators also determined that "the degree of aggressiveness demonstrated by units in contact, varied directly as a function of leadership and not as a function of troop reliability." Vigorous personal leadership still resulted, as it always had, in aggressive performance from U.S. combat troops. The team contrasted this kind of leadership with that occasionally observed, where troops operating on dispersed missions referred to the company commander and the 1st sergeant as "they" whom they never or rarely saw. Although there were undoubtedly persuasive reasons for a commander at any level to remain in a fixed position where his radio communications gave him good control of his units, if the subordinate leaders (the noncommissioned officers) "do not directly see his influence, he will lose personal [control]."

With very few exceptions, the team declared that generally it found few racial problems of any magnitude "forward of combat battalion headquarters." While in the field, soldiers of both races worked very well together. However, when a company-sized unit returned to fire base, in almost every case the black soldiers separated themselves from their white comrades during off-duty hours. This, however, was not perceived by either racial group as a problem. There were, nevertheless, exceptions to this observation. The troops of one battalion, for example, were found poised on the brink of open racial conflict. This situation stemmed from a combination of hard-core black militants, a total lack of communications between the races that further aggravated fear and distrust, and a battalion commander who, while technically competent, had nevertheless refused to take corrective action in the hope that the problems would eventually go away.

Racial problems, where encountered, were generally found in brigade fire-support bases or rear areas where disciplinary cases awaiting trial or administrative action could, because of a lack of preventive detention, move freely throughout a large area and make contact with other hard-core types. When combined with a ready access to drugs and with noncommissioned leadership partially intimidated by the threat of physical retaliation, this situation frequently produced, as the inspector general reports illustrate, dangerous and volatile conditions. The investigators found several examples of this intimidation. In one a medical service corps lieutenant had been physically beaten for several minutes in his orderly room by two black soldiers while other soldiers, including his 1st sergeant, looked on and did nothing. In another incident a soldier in a crowded mess hall struck an adjutant-general major in the face six times with a radio, and in still another case, a company commander was beaten and then shot by one of a group of militant blacks. Accounts of these relatively few outbreaks of criminality were widely circulated by all ranks within a unit. This resulted in further intimidation of the leadership and further emboldened the relatively few militants. Incidentally, during the same period similar conditions were reported by the *Army Times* to have occurred in the army in Europe.

Another serious problem with adverse effect on small-unit leadership, especially that provided by noncommissioned officers, stemmed from "a simple lack of communication between the leaders and the led." This lack in turn caused many soldiers to form distorted perceptions of reality with adverse effect on morale.

The most prominent example of this distortion was found in the area of the Uniform Code of Military Justice and the procedures for administrative discharge of undesirables. During their visit to the army in Vietnam, the investigating team found that "almost without exception the entire noncommissioned officer corps and most company grade officers believe that the judicial machinery of the armed forces had totally collapsed [as a result of the Doolittle reforms] and is unresponsive to their needs." In general, the team determined that the junior leaders, and this included the noncommissioned officer corps of the army in Vietnam, believed that the system of military justice as then constituted was unworkable. Once this belief became widely held, the system indeed came under considerable strain—the junior leaders became hesitant about enforcing regulations concerning personal appearance, use of drugs, disrespect for authority, refusal to take part in combat or in any army work. In countless incidents the team reported, they encountered "infuriated platoon sergeants" who insisted "that discipline was totally gone in the Army."

On the other hand, the investigators found that the majority of effective soldiers were not influenced in their behavior by "the absence of speedy, visible punishment." It did, however, have an adverse effect on the conduct of weak and mediocre combat leaders. While most junior leaders visited and communicated effectively with their men, some glaring examples were found among company-grade officers and noncommissioned officers who, while technically competent to be leaders in terms of their knowledge of how to do a job, still got less than satisfactory performance from their men because of a gap in communications.

The investigators were surprised to learn that the great majority of commanders and noncommissioned officers regarded the so-called human relations councils as an effective supplementary avenue of communications where and when used. Senior noncommissioned officers, moreover, did not consider these councils as a threat to their authority, and in many cases at least one noncommissioned officer served on a council. By and large the most effective leaders were found to be those who practiced the age-old principles of leadership—technical competence combined with an active and intelligent concern for the welfare of their subordinates.

Illustrative of these principles were a company commander and the 1st sergeant of a truck company committed to the resupply of beleaguered Khe Sanh combat base. Their men consistently referred to them as people who really "looked out for the troops" and "took care of them." Although the officer never had direct control or contact with his entire unit at any one time, he and his 1st sergeant made the rounds of the base-camp bunker line each night, talking to the drivers who had been deployed during the day. The key phrase most often heard by the interviewer from the men was they "talked to them and listened to what they had to say."

A phrase most frequently mentioned by successful younger officers and noncommissioned officers was "persuasive leadership" (a new name for an old leadership principle) to successfully accomplish missions while retaining a high degree of troop morale. Nearly all of these young commanders were fully confident that they were always in firm control of their units, and that when they gave an order it would be obeyed. They did not equate persuasive leadership with permissiveness or being forced to task their soldiers to perform their duties. In nearly all of these small units the investigators found a very low level of formality to command. On some occasions this method of leadership became a crutch for young leaders who were basically unprepared emotionally for the "responsibility and lonesome aspects of command."

The pressure seemed greatest on the young E-5s (the graduates of the NCOCC) and the inexperienced lieutenants. Some could walk the fine line to be one of the boys and yet be the recognized leader, but many could not. The problem was perhaps best summed up by a senior noncommissioned officer with several tours of service in Vietnam. "Most noncommissioned officers," he observed, "plodded onward using the old tried and true common sense approach to leadership noncoms have always used, and got the job done."[15]

MEETING THE CRISIS

Perhaps the most serious immediate problem identified by the team in Vietnam was the necessity to rebuild and retrain those elements of the noncommissioned officer corps that had been greatly discouraged and weakened by seven years of war (1965–1972). Key mid-level managers, the E-6 and the E-7, were no longer present in sufficient numbers in infantry companies. In unit after unit the pattern that emerged was that platoon sergeants and staff sergeants were often no longer serving with rifle units. Among the reasons for this were the increasing absorption of senior noncommissioned officers by brigade and division staff elements; proliferation of positions that were peculiar to the war in Vietnam—namely "Green Line" NCO-in-charge, division courtesy patrol, NCO-in-charge of the malingerers at battalion firebases—and the very prevalent factor of "hip-pocket" profile (limited-duty medical certificates).

Commenting on the scarcity of mid-level enlisted leaders in the field, a rifle platoon sergeant declared,

> Many NCOs (E-6s and E-7s) with profiles indicating they have varying assignment limitations are carrying the profile slips in their wallets. Copies of these revised profile slips, however, are not in the individual's parent organization nor in his servicing personnel office. This is the reason we have little [*sic*] or no E-6s and E-7s out in the field with the combat soldier. They [these sergeants] are not performing their duties; instead they have some so-called sham job in the rear area. I feel that these personnel should be reclassified into some other MOS and have their profiles posted in their 201 files at Department of the Army. This would prevent personnel from coming out on the DA promotion list with hip-pocket profiles and not performing their duties.

Illustrative of this situation was that in many, if not in most company- or battery-sized units the soldiers, because of their dispersion in combat units over large areas, rarely saw their 1st sergeants except at the time of their arrival or departure from Vietnam, or in the event of disciplinary action. Eventually, most 1st sergeants became merely the resupply noncommissioned officer and an overseer of malingerers left behind in the rear areas, where they were vulnerable to the criminal activities of these men.

The absence of these senior noncommissioned officers in the field served to further increase the alienation of the noncommissioned officer corps from both the junior officers and the enlisted ranks. Many troop units were thus deprived of the tremendous advantages of the influence of these mature and experienced leaders. Moreover, in rear areas noncommissioned officers were seen as segregating themselves from the young soldiers they led during off-duty hours. This resulted in a further deterioration in intercommunication, and the men tended to scornfully look upon the senior sergeants as "lifers" instead of professionals.

A second problem, one of equal magnitude at least in the eyes of the noncommissioned officers, emerged as the team widened their interviewing activity. This involved the noncommissioned cadre of combat support and combat service units. Fully 95 percent of these senior noncommissioned officers felt that they lacked the technical competence necessary to be fully effective low-level managers of the men and the machines they serviced. Most of those interviewed in this category declared that they sorely needed periodic refresher training in their military occupational specialties. Many, especially those in pay grade E-8 (master sergeant) in all types of units, after years of dealing mainly with problems of direct leadership, frequently found themselves grossly unprepared for the administrative and managerial challenges of the command sergeant major or 1st sergeant position. For example, a platoon sergeant in a maintenance battalion observed,

> It's been 12 years since I was in any kind of an Army School. There have been many changes, and the equipment is much more sophisticated now. The young men coming into this maintenance battalion are much more knowledgeable on the weapons systems and vehicles because they have been school trained. They show up here with the latest poop and we NCO's stand around wondering what the hell is going on. Sure, we can dig a lot of it out of the TMs [technical manuals], if they are available, but it does not compare with the technical training these young men are getting.

Part of the reason for this situation was simply that there were not many advanced schools for these noncommissioned officers to attend.

Interviews uncovered other complaints especially among mid-level noncommissioned officers. One was the twelve-month limitation that the Army had placed on assignments to Vietnam. While this policy admittedly had a favorable effect on individual morale and had greatly reduced the incidence of combat fatigue, it had a deleterious effect on many noncommissioned officers who found themselves repeatedly returning to Vietnam. On the other hand, the two-year conscripts had only one twelve-month tour to look forward to. In time, family responsibilities and demands frequently conflicted with these repeated assignments and, when combined with other factors, caused many otherwise fine noncommissioned officers to leave the service at the end of their enlistments rather than return to Vietnam. This was a significant loss to the Army and another cause of the shortage of experienced enlisted leaders in many combat units.[16]

The exigencies of the Vietnam experience disclosed other problems as well.

One was that of accelerated promotions of younger men, especially graduates of the NCOCC, to pay grades E-5, E-6, and E-7, all within a two- or three-year period without taking into account the individual's length of service.

Quite understandably, this policy caused considerable resentment among older noncommissioned officers who had worked many years to reach similar grades. One 1st sergeant of a rifle company declared that most of these younger men were lacking in

> both maturity and experience, and are promoted to supervisory or leadership positions on the basis of knowledge in a very limited field in which they are working at the time of recommendation. This results in many individuals being promoted who lack the leadership, responsibility, experience, initiative, and discipline required of personnel in these grades [E-5 and E-6].

Some of these critics, however, seemed to have forgotten that they had earned their stripes in a similar fashion in World War II or in Korea.

Another problem was the application of a recently adopted personnel quality-control policy—popularly designated the "Up or Out" program. Under this program, if a soldier failed to qualify for promotion after the normal interval, he would be forced into retirement by being denied the opportunity to reenlist in the case of enlisted men, and in the case of commissioned officers simply retired.

Frustrating as these problems were to many, as the war in Vietnam drew to an end, there loomed over all the U.S. government's decision—one that in 1973 enjoyed wide public support—to terminate the draft after almost thirty years of use and return to a volunteer army—the modern volunteer army or MVA. As its designation "modern" seemed to suggest, it was not to be a return to the so-called "Old Army" of the 1920s and thirties, but was rather to be a force built on the most modern principles of personnel management, motivation, and training.

Therein lay the seed for future problems, for initially the officer corps and most of the noncommissioned officer corps had differing perceptions of what the new army would mean to them. Until these perceptions had been reconciled, the crisis of morale within the noncommissioned officer corps continued into the post-Vietnam period.

CHAPTER 19

SERGEANT MAJOR AT THE SUMMIT

The latter years of the war in Vietnam witnessed the nadir of noncommissioned officer morale, yet during those years the Chief of Staff elevated a senior enlisted man to a key position within his personal staff for the first time in the Army's long history. At first glance, it seems that in creating the position of the Sergeant Major of the Army, General Harold K. Johnson created a position somewhat analogous to that of the command sergeant major at a subordinate headquarters, and to a certain extent, this was true. Yet as the office of the Sergeant Major of the Army evolved, it has become something far wider in scope and more significant in function than any other enlisted appointment in the Army.

The Sergeant Major of the Army has been variously described as an ombudsman for the enlisted personnel of the army, the enlisted spokesman on the staff, and the enlisted member in the Chief of Staff's personal retinue. He is of course all of these things, yet something more. He represents, as does the Chief of Staff himself, the pinnacle of the hierarchy of rank—in this case, the noncommissioned rank structure to which each enlisted soldier may aspire.

The first incumbent of that office, Sergeant Major William O. Wooldridge, was sworn into that unique position on July 11, 1966, by the Chief of Staff, General Harold K. Johnson.[1]

General Johnson's original concept of the office included coordination with the other armed services to establish similar positions. On their behalf, Congressman Mendel L. Rivers introduced legislation to establish the positions of Sergeant Major of the Army, Master Chief Petty Officer of the Navy, Sergeant Major of the Marine Corps, and Chief Master Sergeant of the Air Force.[2]

This bill, however, never got out of committee, apparently because neither the Army legislative liaison staff nor the committee's staff had checked first to see what, if anything, had already been done by other services. When they did investigate, they found to their embarrassment that the Marine Corps had had a Sergeant Major of the Corps (the equivalent of Sergeant Major of the Army) since 1957. On May 23 of that year the Corps' commandant, General Randolph McCall

Pate, had named Sergeant Major Wilbur Bestwick to the position of Sergeant Major of the Marine Corps with duties quite similar to those envisioned by General Johnson for the Sergeant Major of the Army. This left the remaining three services free to proceed on their own without legislative action to establish the position of senior noncommissioned officer of their respective services.

While the Marine Corps had led the way in creating the position of senior enlisted adviser to the Commandant, the Navy and the Air Force followed the Army in that order. On January 13, 1967, Gunner's Mate Delbert D. Black was named as the Master Chief Petty Officer of the Navy, and in April of the same year the Air Force named Master Sergeant Paul W. Airey as its first Chief Master Sergeant of the Air Force.

When questioned some years later as to his reason for establishing the position of Sergeant Major of the Army, General Johnson observed that the position had been established "on the premise that if we were going to talk about the noncommissioned officers being the backbone of the army, there ought to be established a position that recognizes that this was in fact the case." Yet, he added—somewhat cryptically—that "the people who tended to mouth the cliché [the noncommissioned officer is the backbone of the Army] the most frequently were the very people who resisted the creation of the position most."[3] General Johnson believed that most of the resistance arose out of concern over the position's possible affect upon the command channel.

As the Chief of Staff pondered his decision to create the position of Sergeant Major of the Army, some serious problems had to be considered. Here was a position—command sergeant major and its counterpart at departmental level, the Sergeant Major of the Army—that "at each echelon of command . . . does not have a legal responsibility, does not have responsibility that you can place on an individual in a technical sense and as a consequence . . . can't provide the position with much authority either." On the other hand, General Johnson observed,

> there is a sort of a *de facto* responsibility that arises out of it [the position] and an assumed authority, assumed two ways; the people below it who, looking at the position, see someone of substantial stature and consequently substantial authority. The individual himself, in that position, is going to tend to take things into himself, if the opportunity arises. So there had to be a very careful relationship established between that office and the Office of Personnel Operations, specifically, but even more broadly with the office of the Deputy Chief of Staff for Military Personnel (DCSPER) . . . because the Sergeant Major of the Army is basically dealing with people.

This is also the DCSPER's job, and he was concerned that the Sergeant Major of the Army's office might possibly intrude into the assignment function and through an "old-boy network" of senior noncommissioned officers put sand in DCSPER's assignment machinery by arranging for transfers and assignments out of regular channels. To meet this concern General Johnson placed a requirement upon the sergeant major that every request for transfer received by his office be handled only through DCSPER. Under no circumstances was he to deal directly with personnel operations and direct a transfer from the Chief of Staff's office.[4] General Johnson intended that the Sergeant Major of the Army, like the command sergeant major of any unit, be an adviser and not an operator, as DCSPER feared. "What we created," General Johnson observed, "was what might, for want of a better term, be called an *ombudsman*. He was to be a spokesman at the highest echelons of the uniformed side of the Army . . . to provide a recognition for the enlisted ranks of the Army, and I think from that point of view it has been very useful."[5]

Unlike the first command sergeant major, the first Sergeant Major of the Army was selected not by a board but rather by the Chief of Staff himself, assisted by members of his personal staff. General Johnson canvassed by letter each of the major commands, describing the new position and "asking each one of them to nominate, from his command, someone who would be suitable for the position." All nominations received (and all commands responding) were listed on a "spread sheet with different qualities and characteristics of the individuals." The Chief of Staff then reviewed the entire list. As they became available, additional information, checks, and inquiries were added to the list for a second review. The DCSPER was consulted but played little part in this phase of the selection process. General Johnson later remarked that "there was a good bit of exchange between my personal staff, essentially my ADC's, and myself" during this process.

Of all the names on the list, only one was then on duty in Vietnam, Sergeant Major William O. Wooldridge. Inasmuch as Vietnam was the major command in which American soldiers were then engaged in operations against hostile forces, Wooldridge's name caught everyone's attention. Sergeant Major Wooldridge's name had been brought to General Johnson's attention by Major General Jonathan O. Seaman, former commander of the 1st Infantry Division, then commander of II Field Force in Vietnam. General DePuy, then commanding general of the 1st Infantry Division, supported General Seaman's recommendation. General Johnson later observed that he had seen Wooldridge several times and that "he was a fine figure of a man." Because of the background investigations, Johnson was well aware of certain shortcomings in Wooldridge's past—minor brushes with the law and some instances of drunkenness—and this continued to trouble the Chief of Staff throughout the selection process. But all this the general was willing to "lay to the exuberance of youth." General Johnson was not a man to close his mind against anyone he regarded as a good soldier because of a few mistakes in his past. "Once a man had paid the price," General Johnson later declared, "you don't forever hold him to account for that, particularly where subsequent service has been exceptional in nature and so recognized."

However, he was so anxious that the first Sergeant Major of the Army be above reproach, that on the evening before he made his decision he gave the entire file to his aides with the remark, "I want you to keep this overnight, and I want you to make any other checks that you think we should be making to be sure that we don't have something in the individual's background here that's going to come up and haunt us in the years ahead."

General Johnson was later to learn that there had been some investigations in Europe concerning Wooldridge but news of them, having been blocked by Major General Carl Turner, the Army provost marshal, reached neither the general staff nor the Department of Army. In any event, the allegations were never proved. Later, when allegations were made concerning favored assignments arranged by the sergeant major's office, General Johnson was confident that these too would prove groundless, for he was certain that the safeguards—requests for transfers to be handled only through DCSPER—he had established at the time he had created the office would prevent this sort of thing from occurring. Johnson was not disappointed, for to meet DCSPER's concerns the Chief of Staff had prescribed a special form that had to go through the DCSPER on its way to the office of personnel operations before any senior enlisted transfers could be made.

There seems to be no basis for allegations made in the media at that time of so-called "improper transfers" of personnel arranged through the office of the Sergeant Major of the Army. However, SMA Wooldridge was later to observe that one of his recommendations for assignment while "innocently made and correctly handled would combine with other circumstances to later incriminate me."[6]

When General Johnson selected Sergeant Major Wooldridge for the post of Sergeant Major of the Army in 1966, the Chief of Staff had already served two years of what would eventually become a four-year term. Both Johnson and Wooldridge assumed that the sergeant major would step down when his Chief of Staff's term of office was over. Since at the time of General Johnson's retirement Wooldridge had still two years to serve before his retirement, he requested reassignment to Vietnam upon the Chief of Staff's retirement. General Johnson agreed to this request.

Wooldridge not only gained General Johnson's assent to being allowed to serve out the remainder of his enlistment with Military Assistance Command, Vietnam, but carried with him, as a sign of the Chief of Staff's approbation, an award of the Distinguished Service Medal "for exceptionally meritorious service in duty of great responsibility."[7] This was the first award of this medal to an enlisted man. Later, as Sergeant Major Wooldridge took up his duties in Vietnam, and as the media boiled with stories of his alleged misdeeds there, Johnson's successor, General William Westmoreland, revoked the award on August 14, 1969, six days after a subcommittee of the U.S. Senate began an investigation of the charges made against Wooldridge.

Charges against Sergeant Major Wooldridge surfaced while he was still assigned to the 24th Infantry Division in Germany. Later investigation by the Senate Permanent Investigation Sub-Committee, after he had returned to Vietnam following service as Sergeant Major of the Army, disclosed that Wooldridge had been the leader of a group of senior noncommissioned officers whom a member of the committee (Senator Charles Percy of Illinois) dubbed "the khaki Cosa Nostra." This group had been accused of skimming thousands of dollars from enlisted-club slot machines in U.S. garrisons in Germany. In April 1967 the Army CID charged Wooldridge with trying to smuggle liquor into the United States. As noted above, this information, and suspicions concerning his actions with the 24th Division, failed to come to the Chief of Staff's attention after the provost marshal of the Army, Major General Carl Turner, blocked further investigation into Wooldridge's activities. General Turner was later removed from his position and retired from the Army.[8]

During Sergeant Major Wooldridge's tenure as Sergeant Major of the Army there seems to have been no evidence of any wrongdoing on his part. However, when General Johnson retired and Wooldridge was reassigned at his own request to Vietnam, many of the sergeants associated with his earlier service in Germany also transferred to Vietnam, moving "around in flocks like blackbirds migrating up to South Dakota," as Senator Karl Mundt of South Dakota, a member of the subcommittee, observed.

After he had spent some months in Vietnam, further investigations disclosed that Sergeant Major Wooldridge, together with three other sergeants, had invested over $5,000.00 in a company under the name of Maredem. Headed by a so-called sergeants' syndicate, this company had control of negotiating contracts with vendors in Southeast Asia supplying enlisted clubs in Vietnam, including those of the 1st Infantry Division, Wooldridge's former unit. These operations involved kickbacks and other forms of graft that netted the syndicate thousands of dollars in illegal payments.

In his appearance before the Senate subcommittee, Wooldridge steadfastly and with a dignity that impressed many observers refused to answer questions by invoking the Fifth Amendment thirty-eight times. As one reporter noted, "All present, in some way, must have felt the tragedy of the scene. It was without question a dreary day for the United States Army."

On February 17, 1971, Sergeant Major Wooldridge was indicted by an Army court-martial on various charges of having feloniously received monies from contractors dealing with the Army. Nevertheless, he was retired on February 1, 1972 with full pension and benefits. On May 29, 1973, he was sentenced by a civil court to five years' probation, to turn over most of his cash assets to the United States, and to work without pay for three years for charitable causes. In spite of this tragic episode, the office of Sergeant Major of the Army survived under Wooldridge's successor, Sergeant Major of the Army Dunaway.

Eventually an agreement reached between Wooldridge and the U.S. Department of Justice, as part of the final resolution of the charges against him, did not substantiate any wrongdoing on his part for the period of time (as SMA) for which the distinguished service award had been given. The award, however, was not restored to him.[9]* Perhaps the major oversight in General Johnson's otherwise careful selection process was that he and his advisers, in spite of some misgivings, had made their decision on "Old Army" standards of picking a "hero" with all the virtues and some of the shortcomings of an old-time sergeant.

General Johnson nevertheless laid the foundation for how later incumbents would be employed by their chiefs of staff. His purpose in limiting the sergeant major's tenure to that of the Chief of Staff who had selected him had been to give each chief the freedom to select his own man for the office.

Furthermore, the Sergeant Major of the Army henceforth enjoyed a highly visible position—often at the Chief of Staff's side—as Sergeant Major Wooldridge accompanied General Johnson on inspection visits to the various Army commands throughout the world. His very presence with the Chief of Staff enhanced the sergeant major's prestige—a symbol of the importance the Army attached to the senior representative of the enlisted personnel. The Sergeant Major, in this capacity, conveyed the Chief of Staff's greetings to the troops of the units visited, and through personal conferences and meetings with the men, sounded out the noncommissioned officers and, indeed, all enlisted personnel on matters of concern to them. Wooldridge later set up his own travel schedule and made the rounds quite independently of the Chief of Staff, but always with his authorization. Moreover, during his brief tenure, he did gain the trust and confidence of a substantial body of the enlisted population of the Army, and became, as General Johnson had originally envisioned he would, an ombudsman. In his opinion, the Chief of Staff was gratified that most senior noncommissioned officers regarded the creation of the office of Sergeant Major of the Army as "one of the finest things that had happened to the noncommissioned officers corps in recent memory."[10]

Establishment of the office of Sergeant Major of the Army also introduced a new staff element whose functions within the general staff structure evolved through the collective experience of a series of incumbents. The charter that set up the office envisioned the incumbent as a member of the Chief of Staff's personal suite, not a member of the Army staff. The sergeant major was to serve the Chief of Staff as his senior enlisted adviser and consultant on enlisted affairs, and, in so doing, help to identify problems affecting enlisted personnel and to recommend appropriate solutions to these problems. As General Johnson observed at the time, such a position "had no precedent in the United States Army."

As might have been expected, such a radical step generated some resistance within both the staff and in the Army quite independently of the legal problems of Sergeant Major Wooldridge. Although General Johnson clearly stated that the Sergeant Major of the Army would "serve as a personal assistant to me on matters relating to enlisted personnel," by 1970 the office of the Sergeant Major of the

*AR 672-5-1, June 20, 1977, states that once an award has been presented, it may be revoked "if facts subsequently determined would have prevented original approval of the award, had they been known at the time of the award."

Army, under General Westmoreland, Johnson's successor, found itself under the direct supervision of the secretary of the general staff rather than under the Chief of Staff.[11] Although this change was made to enable the former to provide guidance, counsel, and assistance without in any way diminishing the sergeant major's access to the Chief of Staff, it had nevertheless placed him in a definitely subordinate position, compared with other members of the Chief of Staff's personal staff. Under this arrangement, the sergeant major now had considerably less prestige and authority vis-à-vis the staff than did a command sergeant major in either a brigade or a division.[12]

Those within the staff, largely in DCSPER, who had never wholeheartedly supported the idea of a Sergeant Major of the Army now took advantage of the position's increased vulnerability in public opinion (especially following the Wooldridge affair) to launch two proposals that, if adopted, would have adversely affected the position's future status as originally envisioned by General Johnson. These proposals were either to disestablish the position of Sergeant Major of the Army altogether, or to bury it in relative obscurity in the enlisted personnel division (EPD) of DCSPER. Fortunately for the prestige of the noncommissioned officer corps within the Army, neither of these proposals was approved. General Westmoreland rejected both, and the office of the Sergeant Major of the Army survived its first real challenge.

The value of the office of the Sergeant Major of the Army was now widely perceived as enhancing the status not only of the noncommissioned officers but indeed of all enlisted personnel within the Army. The office provided a highly visible sounding board at departmental level for enlisted sentiment and transmitted directly to the Chief of Staff grass-roots views from the ranks without interfering either with the chain of command or the prerogatives of either the staff divisions or the Chief of Staff. Acceptance of either of the earlier proposals to diminish the status of the Sergeant Major of the Army would have run counter to the Army's increasing concern with improving the role and status of the noncommissioned officer.

During his term of office SMA Wooldridge managed to accomplish some significant innovations designed to enhance the role and status of the noncommissioned corps. One of these was the establishment of the annual command sergeants major conference. Shortly after taking office in July 1966, Wooldridge submitted to General Johnson a suggestion that in conjunction with the annual army commanders' conference held in Washington, the army commanders be asked to bring along their command sergeants major so that they could hold concurrent conferences on matters relating to enlisted personnel. Wooldridge believed that important recommendations would come out of such a meeting that he, in turn, could submit to the Chief of Staff for consideration.[13]

General Johnson approved this suggestion, and in November of the same year a total of twenty-one command sergeants major from the Army's major commands throughout the world accompanied their commanders to Washington to confer with one another and with the Army staff. This large-scale input of enlisted concern direct from the field was unique in Army annals and a tradition eventually timed to coincide with the annual meeting of the Association of the United States Army in October. Some of the participants in these first conferences themselves later became Sergeants Major of the Army, thus helping to secure a tradition of these annual meetings.[14]

While acknowledging the significance of the establishment of the command sergeant's major conferences, Sergeant Major Wooldridge rated the establishment of the command sergeant's major position itself as the most significant measure affecting the role and prestige of noncommissioned officers during his tenure. When Wooldridge became Sergeant Major of the Army in 1966, the office was generally recognized as a position and not as an enlisted rank in itself. As a sergeant major, Wooldridge received the same pay as all other sergeants major in the Army. Proficiency pay was the only means of compensating the SMA or indeed of any other sergeant major for his added responsibility. But this was no solution to the problem. To compensate somewhat for this inequity in terms of prestige but not in pay, the Army staff established the rank of command sergeant major in May of 1967.[15] By creating this rank, the Army made a distinction between sergeants major serving mainly in staff sections and those men serving as the commander's enlisted assistant.

A study of the CSM program prepared by DCSPER in June 1967 evolved into a proposal to improve the caliber and effectiveness of sergeants major occupying the top enlisted positions in the Army's forty-nine major commands. In July of that year, the Chief of Staff met with his advisers to consider the problems of administering the CSM program. At that meeting General Johnson directed that the CSM's insignia be changed to make them readily identifiable. The result was a modification of the E-9's chevrons. The star in the field was to be surrounded with a wreath to designate the rank of command sergeant major.[16]

As General Johnson prepared to retire in July 1968, Wooldridge, who still had two years to serve before his own retirement, declined General Westmoreland's request that he remain in office for another two years because of his prior understanding with General Johnson. Westmoreland agreed to Wooldridge's request to return to Vietnam but asked him to remain as SMA until August during the transition of offices for the Chief of Staff.[17]

During this interval the new Chief of Staff asked Wooldridge for his recommendation as to his replacement. He recommended Sergeant Major George W. Dunaway, a wartime veteran with the 517th Parachute Infantry, who had been serving with the 101st Airborne Division in Vietnam since December 1967. General Westmoreland thereupon selected Dunaway, who had only two years to go before mandatory retirement.

It was in 1969, during Sergeant Major Dunaway's tour as Sergeant Major of the Army, that centralized promotions for the top two enlisted grades, E-8 and E-9, went into effect. For the first time in Army history selection and assignment orders for all senior noncommissioned officers were prepared at Army staff level. Concurrently with this innovation the department adopted an Armywide standardized promotion-scoring system. This involved a new procedure that established qualification point values by which all senior noncommissioned officers would be rated. This enabled competing enlisted personnel to compare their individual standing with those of their contemporaries throughout the service.

The original general order that established the position of Sergeant Major of the Army had, it will be recalled, envisioned his tenure coinciding with that of the Chief of Staff. At that time the latter position had been only two years with the option to extend it at the pleasure of the president. Both Wooldridge's and Dunaway's tenure in office had been two years. Even though General Johnson and General Westmoreland served for four years, SMA Dunaway recommended to General Westmoreland that a two-year limit be placed upon the SMA's tenure of office. Sergeant Major Dunaway pointed out that such a limit would assure the Chief of Staff of a continuous flow of fresh ideas from the senior noncommissioned officers. At the same time, Dunaway also recommended that the present *ad hoc* system of selecting the Sergeant Major of the Army be changed to include a screening board presided over by a general officer. Westmoreland approved both recommendations.

Instead of the Chief of Staff canvassing the major commands for names of candidates, a worldwide message was sent announcing the appointment of a selection board composed of a lieutenant general chairman, two colonels, two lieutenant colonels, and, significantly, the incumbent Sergeant Major of the Army. Of the two lieutenant colonels, one represented the command sergeant major career-management section in the office for personnel operations. At the same time as the announcement, DCSPER sent a backchannel message to the major commands soliciting nominations for the positions.[18]

After the board received the nominations from the field it began a screening process to include review of intelligence dossiers to determine the nominee's security clearance. Final selection screening was based upon a clean record—no letters of reprimand, Article 15s, or summary courts-martial. This thorough screening process of necessity eliminated from consideration many otherwise able and eligible noncommissioned officers. But after the Wooldridge episode, the Army was taking no chances. The board then presented five or six remaining candidates to the Chief of Staff, who made the final selection following personal interviews with the candidates. It was in this manner that General Westmoreland selected Sergeant Major Silas L. Copeland to succeed Sergeant Major of the Army Dunaway. A fifty-year-old veteran of twenty-seven years' active service, Sergeant Major Copeland at the time of his selection in October 1970 was the command sergeant major of the 4th Infantry Division in Vietnam.

To allow Copeland to serve until his retirement, General Westmoreland, who retired in June 1972, extended his tenure one year—for a total of three years. But this was an exception. Although eligible to retire with thirty years' active service in February 1973, Sergeant Major Copeland, at his own request, remained in office through June, to allow General Westmoreland's successor, General Creighton Abrams, more time to make his selection for the Sergeant Major of the Army. The new sergeant major would then have more time to acquaint himself with his job before meeting with the command sergeants major at their annual fall Washington conference.[19]

Before making his selection, General Abrams changed the makeup of the screening board to include senior commanders rather than staff officers as in previous boards. To chair the new board, General Abrams selected Lieutenant General Melvin Zais, three major generals, and SMA Copeland. Abrams believed such a board would have a better knowledge of the eligible senior noncommissioned officers in the field. To this day the board continues to be made up of one lieutenant general, three major generals, and the incumbent Sergeant Major of the Army.

On the basis of examination of records, recommendations, and personal interviews with candidates, the board presented the Chief of Staff with a list of five names. Following personal interviews with these men, General Abrams selected Sergeant Major Leon L. Van Autreve, then sergeant major, U.S. Army Alaska. For the first time since the position had been established, the Sergeant Major of the Army came from outside the Vietnam theater of operations. And for the first time he was selected from outside the combat arms, for most of Van Autreve's assignments had been with the engineers.*

Prior to Van Autreve's selection, the new Chief of Staff had decided that the Sergeant Major of the Army should also be a married man. Although the first three holders of the office fit this requirement, it had not been a prerequisite for their selection. Yet the groundwork for Abrams's decision had already been started during Westmoreland's and Dunaway's tenure of office. In General Abrams's words, the sergeant major's marital status was to be not only a requirement for social purposes, but also an assurance that the sergeant major's wife accompany him on some of his inspection trips to the major commands. On such trips she could visit and consult with the wives of enlisted personnel and share with her husband some of her insights into the needs of enlisted men and their families that might not otherwise have been brought to his attention. Here too, SMA Dunaway paved the way for this development by requesting through General Westmoreland that the comptroller fund travel expenses incurred by the SMA's spouse during official trips. This was approved, thereby paving the way for Abrams's action.[20]

Like his predecessors, Sergeant Major Van Autreve stressed the need for first-rate performance on the part of noncommissioned officers, and the necessity on the part of their supervisors to allow them to perform their assigned duties. This

*He was also the first foreign-born SMA, having been born in Ekloo, Belgium. Sergeant Major Van Autreve's academic record of 111 hours of college-level study and his commission in the Army reserves as a major also set him apart as the most highly educated of the men who had held the position up to that time. SMA Van Autreve had served as sergeant major in Alaska from July 1969 to June 1973.

was especially important on the heels of the war in Southeast Asia, during which a policy of zero defects had caused many officers to deny to their noncommissioned officers opportunities to fulfill their proper roles in the unit lest any failure on their part be laid at their commander's door. This meant that many noncommissioned officers had virtually sunk to the status of mere spectators of operations in their units. That Van Autreve managed to achieve some success in this direction is apparent. At midpoint in his tenure he observed with some accuracy that "squad leaders, platoon sergeants, and first sergeants . . . create the leadership environment in which today's Army concepts thrive or expire."[21]

It was during Van Autreve's tenure as SMA under General Creighton Abrams that the noncommissioned officer's progressive career educational system (NCOES) gained its capstone with the establishment of the sergeants major academy. This institution would, in a sense, become the combined war college and staff college for the noncommissioned officers' corps.* Henceforth, the career enlisted soldier could—as did commissioned officers—advance through basic leadership courses all the way to a war college–type of environment—the sergeants major academy at Ft. Bliss, Texas. An upsurge in the quality of noncommissioned officers, in Van Autreve's words, was the result of these programs.

Sergeant Major Van Autreve's contemporaries saw in him "a tough taskmaster, a strictly no-nonsense type who was trying to revitalize the noncommissioned officer corps and restore the lost faith of many noncommissioned officers in the Army—a faith lost largely in Viet Nam." In the words of one, he "took the Noncommissioned Officer Corps by the collar and shook some sense into it . . . for he has led us a mighty long way in the past year and a half."[22] Coupled with such praise was a request on behalf of many senior noncommissioned officers that Van Autreve's tour be extended. However, the new Chief of Staff, General Frederick C. Weyand, who had taken over upon General Abrams's untimely passing, was reluctant at the time to change the two-year limitation placed earlier on the sergeant major's tenure of office.

As Sergeant Major Van Autreve's tour drew to an end in the spring of 1975, the selection board, with Van Autreve as a member, selected nine sergeants major to be interviewed by the new Chief of Staff in his quest for a successor to Van Autreve. The man eventually selected, William G. Bainbridge, was unique in many respects. A veteran of World War II, captured during the Ardennes campaign, he was the first to come directly from the Army's educational system, in this case, the sergeants major academy, where Bainbridge had been serving as its first command sergeant major. Earlier Sergeant Major Bainbridge served as General Ralph Haines's CSM before the latter took over command of CONARC. General Haines had been so impressed with his CSM that when CONARC established the sergeants major academy in 1972, he selected Bainbridge to serve as its first CSM

*Planning for the academy, however, had been under way since SMA Dunaway's tenure.

Over the next few years Sergeant Major Bainbridge played an outstanding role in getting the academy off to a successful start.[23]

Sworn in on July 1, 1975, Sergeant Major Bainbridge was to serve in the office the longest, for midway in his tour, General Weyand decided to make the SMA's tour three instead of two years. This was because Bainbridge had "earned the confidence, respect, and admiration of the Army's leadership as well as its soldiers, during his service as the Army's senior enlisted member." In November 1977, General Weyand's successor, General Bernard W. Rogers, decided to extend Bainbridge's tour an additional year.[24]

Sergeant Major Bainbridge's observations concerning the office of the Sergeant Major of the Army are worth noting, for not only are they the comments of one who served long in that office, but also because during his time the prestige of the office reached its highest level since its inception. In an interview given during the last months of his term of office, Sergeant Major Bainbridge remarked that "over these past . . . years I have seen this office move from a coordinating office with largely perfunctory and obligatory involvement into an integral element of the Army staff." He was speaking from his own experience as SMA, for during Bainbridge's tenure of office the secretary of the army directed that the Sergeant Major of the Army be included as a member of the Army policy council. The Chief of Staff directed that he also be made a member of the Army staff council and more recently that he become a member of the general staff council (commonly referred to as the staff principals).

The SMA, no longer under the supervision of SGS, had become a full-fledged member of the Chief of Staff's staff. His added exposure to the Army hierarchy paid tremendous dividends across the board in terms of credibility. It is understood by all in no uncertain terms that the SMA does, in fact, have the eyes and ears of both the Chief of Staff and the secretary of the army on enlisted matters. This made it certain that any action or development that impacted on enlisted personnel from a policy standpoint would be routinely coordinated with the Sergeant Major of the Army. His opinion is now considered essential before an action is sent on the CSA.[25]

Some idea of the significance and magnitude of these developments as well as how far advanced the Army's view of the noncommissioned officer corps had become, especially over the four-year period represented by Sergeant Major of the Army Bainbridge's tenure of office, is disclosed by an exchange of letters in 1935 between the then–Secretary of War George Dern, and a congressman, J. H. Hoeppel, then of the House Military Affairs Committee. Mr. Hoeppel noted in a letter to the secretary of war that in the preparation of legislation pertaining to military and naval affairs very little consideration was ever given to the problems peculiar to enlisted men. Congressman Hoeppel observed that both the War and Navy Departments had supplied commissioned officers who acted as liaison and advisers to the chairmen of the Senate and House Military Affairs Committees, but no one qualified to speak from actual and continuing experience as such for the enlisted men of the services.[26]

Congressman Hoeppel, then a well-known advocate of servicemen's interests, requested that Secretary Dern assign an enlisted man as liaison to the House Military Affairs Committee, whose chairman was an enthusiastic supporter of the idea. Hoeppel was also prepared to recommend for that post a competent and qualified soldier to represent the enlisted viewpoint.[27]

In his reply, the secretary of war stated that he had read the congressman's letter with interest (although the letter had been received in the Secretary's office on February 11 and he had waited until October before replying). Oblivious to his rather cavalier handling of the congressman's query, Secretary Dern replied that because of a commissioned officer's "broader training and wider experience" he had sufficient understanding of the enlisted men's needs to represent them well before a congressional committee. Mr. Dern added, playing somewhat loosely with the facts, that "many of the officers have been enlisted men before they were commissioned officers." This was hardly descriptive of general staff officers of the Army in the 1930s.[28]

Moreover, Dern assured the congressman, officers of the inspector general's office, during their visits to the various units, heard all valid complaints from enlisted men. Therefore, any legislation that might affect enlisted personnel would receive the serious and sympathetic consideration of commissioned officers not only familiar with but deeply interested in their welfare.

Taking aim directly at Hoeppel's concept of enlisted representation at the command level, the secretary of war added that it had never been Army policy "to have enlisted men participate in a council of officers." He went on to reject firmly any suggestion that officers could not be as "much interested or as adequately informed on the problems of enlisted personnel as an experienced enlisted man." Dern concluded with the traditional paternalistic note that good officers knew best how to insure proper consideration of legislation affecting the interests of enlisted men.

What a contrast between this view and that embodied by outgoing Sergeant Major of the Army Bainbridge some thirty-four years later! A world war and two limited wars, as well as revolutionary changes in society and military technology, were to take place before the Sergeant Major of the Army would become a member of the Army's policy council, and be made a member of the general staff council.

When, in July 1979, Army Chief of Staff General Edward C. Meyer named William A. Connelly to be the next Sergeant Major of the Army, he picked for the first time a graduate of the sergeants major academy at Ft. Bliss.* Sergeant Major Connelly was also the first to enter upon his office for an officially established

*Concurrently, the commanding general of TRADOC and FORSCOM selected academy graduates to be their command sergeants major.

three-year tenure. While both Copeland and Bainbridge had served two years and eight months and four years respectively, theirs had been results of *ad hoc* extensions.

As Sergeant Major Connelly began his duties, the Chief of Staff gave him two rather broad guidelines. The first was in the long-established pattern for a command sergeant major, that is, to be the eyes and ears of the commander—in this case, the Chief of Staff—in matters concerning the enlisted personnel of the Army. The second was of a more general nature, but equally challenging. That was to provide the Chief of Staff with additional ideas and concepts for further professional development of the noncommissioned officers' corps. The latter change was to come to fruition in December 1980, with the publication of Army Regulation 350–17, entitled "The Noncommissioned Officer's Development Program" (NCODP).[29] During his term of office SMA Connelly also devoted himself to improving communications with both the troops and the civilian communities. As vehicles for the first, Connelly created a service-wide newsletter, *Down-Range*, as well as numerous videotapes for Armywide circulation. The second community was reached through frequent testimony given before congressional committees as a spokesman for the needs of the Army's enlisted men, and through numerous talks before civilian organizations in efforts to enhance public awareness of the Army's role.[30]

With the establishment of the office of the Sergeant Major of the Army the Army at last had two parallel lines of action and leadership extending from top to bottom. One is headed by the Chief of Staff, who as senior commissioned officer exercises command over the entire Army. The second is headed by the Sergeant Major of the Army, who as senior noncommissioned officer represents the enlisted personnel of the Army, including the noncommissioned corps that runs it on a day-to-day basis.

CHAPTER 20

INSTITUTIONALIZING PROFESSIONALISM

RETURN OF THE NONCOMMISSIONED OFFICER

Like a juggler trying to keep several objects in the air simultaneously, the Army faced several major manpower challenges in the mid-1960s but without the support of all-out mobilization. Operations in Vietnam consumed increasing quantities both of men and matériel, and field armies in Western Europe and in Korea also placed heavy demands upon both training and maintenance facilities. As might be expected, these challenges made great demands of junior leaders, especially of noncommissioned officers. To improve the professional capabilities of these leaders, it will be recalled, the Army earlier developed one personnel program after another to meet the need for better-trained enlisted leaders and specialists. Yet in themselves none of these programs seemed capable of solving the problem of more dependable professional leadership at the noncommissioned officer level. Meanwhile, with the termination of operations in Southeast Asia, Army strength fell like a barometer before a storm—from 1.5 million to about 800,000.

With the beginning of the 1970s, the drawdown from Vietnam, the near certainty of an end to the draft, and the emergence of an all-volunteer army, it became evident that the various piecemeal personnel-management programs that had been tried and often found wanting over the past decade had to be reexamined if the Army was to become truly an all-professional force. Accordingly, in the summer of 1973, after having withdrawn completely from Vietnam, the Army under Chief of Staff, General Creighton W. Abrams's direction began a major review of existing systems of enlisted professional development.[1]

This review was made by the Training and Doctrine Command (TRADOC) formerly CONARC, in partnership with the U.S. Army's Military Personnel Center (MILPERCEN). General Abrams's directive gave them the task of molding the several existing programs of enlisted training, evaluation, classification, and promotion into an integrated servicewide system. Overseeing this task was a steering committee composed of general officers representing personnel, operations, force development, major commands, reserve components, and other agencies with an interest in the development of particular career fields. General Abrams also invited his newly selected Sergeant Major of the Army, Leon L. Van Autreve, to sit as a member of this prestigious committee.

Behind this review of personnel management policies and practices lay a realization on the part of the Army staff that the shift from a draft-supported to an all-volunteer army now required a radical change in enlisted career management if the Army were to attract and hold a truly professional enlisted force. The core of such a force would be, it was generally agreed, a thoroughly professional corps of noncommissioned officers. But to create such a core the Army enlisted personnel managers must first solve the problems of how to attract the needed skilled and talented men and women and, having done so, to efficiently utilize and retain them. The roots of this problem lay partly in the widespread unpopularity of the war in Vietnam, but mainly in the decision to terminate the draft and to establish an all-volunteer army. This latter was itself a policy change that arose out of swelling adverse public reaction to the war and the Army.

For the Army, an end to the draft in the midst of a period of the development of increasingly sophisticated technology as well as high employment placed great demands upon an enlisted force that could be expected to be less endowed in talent and skill than one supported by a cross section of the entire eligible male population. To ease somewhat these demands, the Army staff considered a number of possible measures. In particular, two appeared to be potentially and politically feasible: a more efficient utilization of the talents and skills already at hand and improvement of service attractiveness through other than monetary means. For the first, training time might be shortened, thereby obtaining longer use of a soldier's acquired skills during his term of enlistment. Furthermore, career management fields (CMFs), those functionally related MOSs in which a soldier might be expected to spend his entire career, could be redesigned to allow greater suitability among related MOSs, thereby improving the matching of a man with his job. The grouping of grades within skill levels might also be standardized for all CMFs, thereby facilitating substitution between CMFs when necessary. Finally, for those MOSs (or CMFs) that were out of balance between the Continental United States and the overseas commands, "crosswalks" might be created, supported by special training programs. These crosswalks would enable individual career soldiers to serve in different career fields on alternate tours in different commands without loss of efficiency.

The second measure would depend upon the results of a search for improved nonmonetary incentives, if the Army were to meet its recruiting goals, because Congress had denied an increase in both enlistment and reenlistment bonuses. This search depended upon finding answers to the following questions: What factors (other than a need for a job or money) attracts nineteen-year-olds to enter the Army; what attracts twenty-two-year-olds to sign on for another three to six years; and what attracts twenty-five to twenty-nine-year-olds to make at least a twenty-year career commitment? Having reached a point of diminishing returns with monetary bonuses granted a soldier on successive reenlistments, the Army now prepared to reexamine the enhancement of professional standards that might both attract and hold a soldier. This approach the staff designated as "increasing professionalism."

While it could not be denied that throughout the Army's past many outstanding noncommissioned officers who were professionals in every sense of the word had served in its ranks, there had not clearly existed defined servicewide standards and procedures for systematically identifying, training, and educating such men. Such training had, with few exceptions (among them the noncommissioned officer academies), been almost always on-the-job varying in both quality and quantity and depending upon the whims and skills of the local unit commander and of the noncommissioned officers who actually did most of the day-to-day training. However, in 1973 the Army stood on the threshold of the creation and adoption of a servicewide enlisted personnel-management system that was to assure the professional education and training of the noncommissioned officer corps. The staff expected adoption of this system to result in the professionalization of the noncommissioned officer corps on as far-reaching a scale as had the establishment of the military academy at West Point for the professional education and training of commissioned officers some 170 years before.

This new system did not spring like Minerva fully developed from the brow of a Jovian staff, but rather represented a pulling together or integration of several existing strands or programs of enlisted education and management that had already been developed and put into practice or had been discussed as concepts or, in some cases, had reached the planning stage. In the late fifties and early sixties, it will be recalled, the Department of Army initiated measures toward what would ultimately become a part of the new enlisted personnel-management system. Among them was an enlisted evaluation system that provided an objective procedure for evaluating enlisted personnel in their assigned military occupational specialties against Armywide standards. Promotion qualification, based upon this rating system, was used as a basis for temporary promotions to ensure that only the best-qualified men were promoted to and within the noncommissioned officer ranks. Furthermore, the adoption of the principle of proficiency pay provided a monetary incentive to noncommissioned officers in pay grades E-4 and above. In addition, the Department of Army believed that the creation of grades E-8 and E-9 in the Pay Bill of 1958 had relieved the grade compression that formerly existed within the E-7 grade and therefore provided a better delineation of authority and responsibility for noncommissioned officers.

The Army staff also expected that the new enlisted personnel-management system (EPMS) would encourage educational self-development for all enlisted personnel. This represented a revival of traditional Army practice, but with the difference of a significantly broadened opportunity for such development. Henceforth, a soldier would be encouraged to further his education through off-duty participation in U.S. Armed Forces Institute (USAFI) correspondence courses or group-study classes at an Army educational center, usually located on an Army post. In addition, the enlisted college-training program, though open to all enlisted personnel, seemed especially applicable to noncommissioned officer career advancement, for at no cost to themselves these men would be able to participate in a college- or university-level program while on active duty.

By January 1973, the director of military personnel management, Department of Army, and the commander of the Military Personnel Center (MILPERCEN) agreed upon the design of a new EPMS. Staff work began the following month to develop a thoroughly revised EPMS concept. This proved to be a fortuitous decision—at the same time, the secretary of defense also requested that the Department of Army submit a comprehensive enlisted force management plan by the end of fiscal year 1973. Meshing this requirement with the earlier decision to redesign EPMS, the office of the deputy chief of staff for personnel (DCSPER) and MILPERCEN formed a working group for this purpose. This group completed the enlisted force management plan first, which the Chief of Staff approved in June and submitted to the secretary of defense in July. The plan would provide the general guidelines under which EPMS planning would take place.[2]

By October 1975, the DCSPER announced the completion of the new enlisted personnel-management system. By redesigning each career management field (CMF) the staff expected that a "logical and visible road map" would be provided to guide motivated career soldiers along the most direct route from E-1 to E-9. The staff also expected that the new system would help to eliminate promotion bottlenecks and afford fair promotion opportunities to all enlisted men and women. Soldiers' skills would be broadened, their assignments made more flexible, and greater career challenges provided by decreasing the number of MOSs through eliminating some and combining others at the lower grades and merging others at the higher grades. Finally, the staff viewed the new system as a means of providing continuous professional training throughout a soldier's career.[3]

As was to be expected there were several significant differences between the revised EPMS and the system that it was about to replace. The first of these was a division of entry-level training for recruits between the basic training centers and schools, where the drill sergeants reigned supreme, and the units to which the newly minted soldiers were initially assigned. For example, in the combat arms and in many mechanical and administrative service career management fields, initial training subsequent to basic combat training (BCT) might be conducted at the same training base where the recruits had received their basic training. The commander of the recruits' first unit following BCT would give them "augmentation training" in the subject schedule of their MOSs and then rate their performance in the required skills. He would then award the individual soldiers a skill level 1 (apprentice) in their respective MOS. This would be a prerequisite to promotion to PFC and the first step in the soldier's military career. The Army expected that by shifting this part of the soldier's MOS training to his first unit commander morale and discipline would be enhanced, the commander's responsibility and authority reinforced, and, most important, the role of the unit's noncommissioned officers, who would actually do the training, strengthened.

There were only two exceptions envisioned to this pattern. First was training in those so-called hard skills that required a technical proficiency on the part of the private/private first class at a level comparable to that of his immediate noncommissioned officer supervisor. Hard skills, requiring long, advanced individual training, would be restricted to those that could not be taught in the unit but in special schools. Second, there were to be contingency plans in wartime to shift those elements of individual training taught by the unit back to the training center.

POSTSCRIPT TO THE NCO ACADEMIES

Even as the Army began laying the groundwork for the revised enlisted personnel-management system, the noncommissioned officer academies lingered on, but, as always, they remained outside the Army's formal school system. As the Army moved into the era of the modern volunteer format, some of the academies were found to have an educational approach—spit and polish and an "angry" style of leadership, typical of OCS—that was believed to be out of step with the professionalism and respect for individual dignity that the staff expected the modern volunteer Army to cultivate.[4]

Nevertheless, many of the academies had accomplished their mission in a highly professional manner. Moreover, most students who graduated from them seemed satisfied with the course of instruction they had received. However, the Army's plans for the noncommissioned officers education system (NCOES) would eventually diminish the role of the academies. For, in spite of their admitted accomplishments, they had, in the staff's opinion, proven inadequate to fulfill the entire Armywide requirements for noncommissioned officer education.[5]

Yet in the post-Vietnam era the academies continued to play a role. Their mission then was to train sergeants, staff sergeants, and specialists (E-5 and E-6) to be leaders or supervisors in a garrison-type environment—to offer career-education opportunities especially for younger noncommissioned officers. Many of these were products of the wartime NCOCCs, returning from Vietnam rich in combat experience but lacking in the skills needed for day-to-day training and administration in a peacetime situation. Each continental army commander was required to maintain within his army area one CONARC-funded and programmed noncommissioned officers' academy, until the NCOES had displaced it. Training at U.S. Army noncommissioned officers' academies in CONUS would continue until the basic and advanced NCOES courses were under way. At that time TRADOC planned to gradually phase out the academies, which were then located at forts Knox, McClellan, Hood, Riley, and Lewis.[6]*

*The academy at Ft. Hood, however, was scheduled to be phased out by July 1, 1971, in conjunction with transfer of the Fifth Army's functions to Fourth Army. The former's facility would then be combined with the Fourth Army's academy at Ft. Riley.

The noncommissioned officer education system, a subsystem of the enlisted personnel-management system, had been implemented, it will be recalled, during the last half of fiscal year 1971. It consisted of three levels of training, reminiscent of an earlier three-tiered system discussed in the 1960s and similar to that long in use for commissioned officers. The first, or basic-level course, provided technical training leading to qualification at skill level 4 of an MOS. Training was conducted within a military occupational specialty to qualify individuals to command comparatively small groups of enlisted personnel with a similar MOS. This course, it will be recalled, emphasized basic leadership skills and a knowledge of those military subjects needed to effectively command enlisted personnel at the team, squad, section, and comparable levels.

Advanced level courses within NCOES provided technical training designed to award the graduate a primary or secondary MOS above the fourth or advanced skill level. The emphasis in these advanced courses was placed upon the development of leadership skills and knowledge of military subjects but, at this level, aimed at qualifying men to perform the duties of a first sergeant and a sergeant major at the company, battalion, brigade, or comparable levels of homogeneous units.

The objectives of the senior level NCOES course, at whose apex now stood the sergeants major academy, were to prepare selected noncommissioned officers in the grade of E-8 to perform duties as key sergeants major at division and higher headquarters. This course provided these noncommissioned officers with an understanding of the functions of Army, joint, and combined commands, and developed the intellectual depth and analytical abilities needed for assignments at those levels. As might be expected, this course was branch immaterial and oriented toward broad professional development.

PLANNING FOR THE REVISED EPMS

Although there were several suitable ongoing training and personnel programs such as NCOES, on which the staff planned to build an enlisted personnel-management system, there were problems to be solved before these programs could be integrated into a successful servicewide system of enlisted professionalization. One of the first was a problem perceived by the staff as a major weakness in the Army's ability to retain men with excellent career potential. This was a loss of noncommissioned officer prestige and status that resulted from the overly liberal promotion policies adopted during the Vietnam era. While such policies may have then been necessary to provide leadership grades for wartime expansion and to provide a living wage to the junior leader in the face of rising inflation, these reasons were no longer valid in the mid-1970s.[7] But simply slowing down the rate of promotions could not by itself enhance noncommissioned officer status and prestige. Instead, the staff envisioned a system whereby each promotion henceforth would be earned in a visibly difficult and, therefore, a prestige-conferring manner. The system proposed was derived in part from current Army practice and in part borrowed from the Navy and Air Force as well as from British and Canadian systems. It was designated as "increased professionalization of the career soldier."

This new approach, however, contradicted the long-accepted distinction that Samuel P. Huntington had made in his landmark work *The Soldier and the State*. Professor Huntington's observation that commissioned officers constituted the "profession of arms," while noncommissioned officers were the nonprofessional "tradesmen," was now perceived by the staff to be a holdover from an earlier and less technical era. Possibly only in the case of the combat arms did this concept still have any relevance, and even there the staff regarded it as counterproductive. In other words, whether or not Huntington's view of the noncommissioned officer remained valid or not in civilian terms, the all-volunteer professional Army could no longer afford to so regard him. In the modern volunteer Army the noncommissioned officer must have his own sense of professionalism, and the Army's personnel policies must encourage it.

In the words of one general officer who had much to do with the development of EPMS, there had been "good reason for failure on the part of the commissioned officers to recognize that the noncommissioned officer was also a professional military man." This failure stemmed from the fact that unlike the officer corps, the noncommissioned officer corps never had a formal servicewide system of professional career development. There had never existed a prescribed career pattern of the sort that commissioned officers had long taken for granted when embarking upon an Army career. There has never been explicit career guidance for noncommissioned officers such as commissioned officers had long received from their particular branches. Noncommissioned officers also lacked a feature that provided milestones in a commissioned officer's professional development—a system of career-long training and education.[8]

Some observers have remarked that one of the reasons for the failure to develop such a system earlier could be found in the Army's dependence upon the draft since World War II. Thanks to the Selective Service, the Army enjoyed an almost limitless source of relatively talented manpower during these years. As General William A. Patch remarked, "each year's draft call brought in an abundance of high school and college graduates, men easily trained in the complex technology of a modern army." Not many reenlisted, to be sure, but those who did provided the Army with a pool of talent and skill that an all-volunteer force would most likely not provide.

Because of this situation, skill development had been concentrated in the first two-year terms of service. During the early postwar years the Army processed an average of fifteen thousand men each month. Upon induction these men were given a battery of tests whose results were then fed into a complex matching process against advanced individual training spaces. These spaces were themselves determined by forecasting Army requirements in terms of MOSs. In the course of this large-scale training and assignment of recruits, professional training went largely unmanaged. Consequently, as the individual soldier rose in rank and responsibility he went from one assignment to another, gradually acquiring the knowledge and skills required through on-the-job training or experience.

During the 1960s this unstructured process, it will be recalled, became the subject of a number of Army-sponsored studies concerning the enlisted grade structure, career-progression patterns, and noncommissioned officer training. All of these reached similar conclusions—if the Army wished to make the best use of the skills of its career soldiers, it must develop a comprehensive system of professional career management and development. While none of these studies produced such a system, they nevertheless pointed to the fact that, as the war in Vietnam drew to a close, and the end of the draft became apparent, one would be needed.

In addition to the development of an enlisted career-management system, the staff pointed out that three more changes ought also to be considered in order to truly professionalize the noncommissioned officer corps. The first two of these changes would eventually become Army policy, while the third failed to meet widespread acceptance within the service. Adoption by the Army of the regimental system—the first of the three changes—the staff argued, would help to give the noncommissioned officers a more "definable universe in which to have an impact and in which to establish a reputation." If noncommissioned officers were treated as merely Armywide assets, they could hardly be expected to regard themselves as individuals in a professional sense. Under the proposed regimental system, modeled on that long in use within the British army, whenever a career soldier was reassigned from one theater to another, he would be assigned if at all possible, within the regimental-level unit he had served in during a previous tour in that theater.

The second proposed change was to find a way to restore noncommissioned pre–World War II responsibilities by taking them back from the junior officers, who during World War II and after had gradually assumed them. For too long, it seemed, the Army had paid only lip service to the cliché that the noncommissioned man was the "backbone of the Army." Instead, action adhered to a policy "if it's important, get an officer to do it." Some of the corrective measures suggested were to delete the position of unit executive officer in peacetime and allow the 1st sergeant to administer—but not command—the company. Furthermore, such duties as mess, motor, and supply—long among the additional duties of many junior officers—could be turned over to noncommissioned officers without loss of efficiency. Moreover, much of the unit training could be conducted by noncommissioned officers.

A final proposal was to abolish the term "enlisted man." Over the years in both military and civilian circles the term had acquired a derogatory connotation. After World War II the Navy, Marines, and Air Force abandoned the use of this term in favor of Sailor, Marine, and Airman respectively. The staff believed that the Army might do well to designate its men by a title, which, however it is regarded outside the military, is an object of honor within—soldier. In some respects this suggestion harked back, albeit unwittingly, to the sixteenth and seventeenth centuries, before there existed a clear distinction between commissioned and noncommissioned officers; as has been shown, all ranks then were simply gradations of authority within a military hierarchy that ran from corporal up to general.

As radical for their time as some of these proposals seemed to be, the winds of change were already rising within the staff of Army personnel management. For several years there had been a massive redesign of officer career patterns underway by the officer personnel-management system (OPMS). Therefore, it was not surprising when in January 1973, the Army decided also to take a fresh look at enlisted career management. Ultimately, this fresh look entailed nothing less than a total restructuring of enlisted personnel management under the enlisted personnel-management system (EPMS).

In July of that year Army Chief of Staff General Creighton W. Abrams forwarded to the secretary of defense the requested enlisted force management plan (EFMP) that provided a set of numerical objectives and practices for the Army in the coming decade. This plan provided an authoritative basis for a detailed examination and redesign of its enlisted management policies and procedures. Out of this examination ultimately emerged a career management plan that assured all soldiers a clearly stated, understandable, and rewarding career management system while in service.[9]

But even before the secretary of defense approved the EFMP, the Army staff devoted considerable time and effort toward the improvement of enlisted personnel policies. It will be recalled that during the 1960s, under successive chiefs of staff the Army created several programs related to enlisted career management. Among them were the career management fields (CMFs); centralized and semicentralized promotion systems; a qualitative management program (QMP); a noncommissioned officers education system (NCOES); reenlistment and reclassification controls; and an enlisted evaluation system (EES). As important as each of these programs had been, they had not yet been integrated into an overall system of career management for the noncommissioned officer corps. The task of accomplishing this integration fell to General Abrams and his successor.

To design such a system DCSPER now formed an enlisted personnel-management system task force within the Enlisted Personnel Directorate of the U.S. Army Military Personnel Center (MILPERCEN). With the Chief of Staff's directive in hand, this task force formed a partnership with its counterpart at headquarters Training and Doctrine Command (TRADOC) to undertake a major review of the Army's system for professional development of the enlisted force. The newly augmented task force's mission was to mold existing programs of training, evaluation, MOS classification, and promotion into an integrated Armywide system. Its work was supervised by a steering committee of general officers, representing personnel, operations, force development, the reserve components, and major commands, as well as other agencies with interest in particular career fields.

The Chief of Staff also selected the Sergeant Major of the Army, Leon Van Autreve, to serve on this committee.[10]

After a year's work, the joint committee developed a personnel-management system through which a soldier's career would indeed become a highly visible and easily comprehended series of achievement levels. Existing subsystems of training, evaluation, classification, and promotion would become more closely integrated, thereby enabling the Army to achieve major savings through a shift in peacetime of much of the entry-level MOS training (except for the so-called hard skills) from basic training centers to troop units. A resulting reinforcement of the noncommissioned officer's authority, gained through training their own subordinates with skills acquired through NCOES, was expected to have a positive impact upon servicewide discipline and morale. The revised enlisted personnel-management system that eventually emerged from the committee was the enlisted counterpart of the officers' personnel-management system and involved the entire active Army.

Throughout the months of planning and development, MILPERCEN/TRADOC conducted briefings and interviews at command and installation level throughout the United States and overseas to tap the views of both officers and men, particularly those of noncommissioned officers whose careers would be most profoundly touched by the EPMS. During fiscal year 1974, MILPERCEN/TRADOC briefed groups at twenty-seven locations in the continental United States and at forty-three locations in Europe and the Pacific. Over 100,000 noncommissioned officers, as well as several hundred commissioned officers, provided the necessary feedback, which in turn influenced the content of the EPMS that eventually emerged from the joint MILPERCEN/TRADOC committee.[11]

The review of EPMS began in fiscal year 1974 and continued into fiscal year 1975 with a shift in emphasis from the conceptual to the developmental and implementation phases. The Army staff continued to use as a basis for this review the long-range numerical manpower objectives contained in the earlier enlisted force-management plan as a standard for measuring progress toward achieving the enlisted force strength objectives. The review indicated that considerable progress had been made toward achieving the total force and top six enlisted grade strength goals in the desired percentages. In addition to providing a numerical basis for the review, the Defense-sponsored enlisted force-management plan also provided a rationale for the top six grade strength in the fiscal year 1976 budget request. One important objective of EPMS had been to bring the top six grade authorizations down to budgeted levels, and this, the review disclosed, had been accomplished by applying the EPMS standards of grade authorization.[12]

As EPMS approached its implementation phase in fiscal year 1975, it seemed to many in DCSPER that the new system would not be as radical a change from current practices and procedures as had first been anticipated. To a certain extent this was true, for EPMS, as will be recalled, was built upon existing programs and policies, integrating them into a coherent Armywide system of personnel management. EPMS, as it eventually emerged from the hands of MILPERCEN-TRADOC committee, was essentially a thoroughgoing "product improvement" of the current enlisted personnel-management system.

On August 23, 1974, the then–acting Chief of Staff, General Fred C. Weyand, approved EPMS. In January 1975, Department of Army began distribution of EPMS-implementing instructions to field commanders to commence changing authorization documents and the reclassification/conversion of personnel to reflect a designed career management field/military occupational specialty structure for the first of the MOSs/CMFs designated to be overhauled. These were: CMF 11 (Maneuver Combat Arms); 16 (Air Defense); 63 (Mechanical Maintenance); 74 (Automatic Data Processing); and 95 (Law Enforcement). The Department of Army at the same time directed that this first phase of EPMS be completed by the end of the first quarter of fiscal year 1976. Completion of this phase was expected to affect some 188,000 soldiers, with the remainder of the enlisted force to come under EPMS at six-month intervals. Complete implementation of the new system was scheduled for October 1977.

As implementation of the EPMS got under way, four constraints, only one of which was of the Army's own making, impinged upon the operation of the new system. The first of these was the overall size of the Army, determined by congressional, not by Army action. The second was the political decision to end the draft on December 31, 1972, a decision that fortunately the Army had long anticipated with steps already taken to prepare for an all-volunteer force. The third was the grade inflation caused by the large number of noncommissioned officers who had been promoted through the accelerated promotion policy adopted during the war in Vietnam. Many of these had decided to remain as careerists in the Army. The fourth, and in many ways the most challenging of these constraints, was the Defense Department's budget estimate based upon a post-Vietnam defense policy. This budget placed the Army in a fiscal vise. Consequently, fiscal restraint and not military need would largely determine the grade structure.

Thus, the slots in the top six enlisted grades were determined by the Department of Defense and not by the Army. Although the Army's force structure in the early 1970s called for 72 percent of all enlisted positions to be in the top six enlisted grades (E-4 to E-9), the Army was seldom able to realize this goal. On the basis of revised projections, the Defense Department approved instead a top six ceiling of 63 percent. Fortunately, this proved sufficiently high to provide reasonably good promotion opportunity and the career progression necessary to sustain the noncommissioned enlisted force in line with the Army's budgeted grade structure.

However, a problem lay in the fact that this figure left the Army with a grade structure that had about sixty thousand E-3 (private first class) spaces and a corresponding decrease in top six spaces. In addition to those ceilings, the Defense Department had also set a minimum time in service required for promotion—the percentage of soldiers who might be selected for promotion from the secondary zones of consideration—and the amount of time in service that might be waived for promotion purposes. All of this confronted Army personnel planners with manning documents calling for more than sixty thousand soldiers to be paid for jobs in the top six grades for which there was neither Defense authorization nor money. Consequently, one of the Army's objectives through EPMS was to bring its manning documents into alignment with the Defense Department grade authorizations—a task comparable to attempting to put a quart of water into a pint jar.

This then was the EPMS's first task—to balance the grade structure through improved managerial practices rather than through a meat-ax approach. These improved managerial practices, it was expected, would enable a qualified soldier to move from the bottom to the top without concern for lack of spaces in a job that appealed to him (or her). These better promotion opportunities were provided by restructuring each and in a similar manner. Training in these would be supported by the previously established noncommissioned officers education system (NCOES). Five levels of training made up this system: basic combat training (BCT) and advanced individual training (AIT), upon which rested four additional levels of the system; primary, basic, including the primary technical course for specialists; advanced; and senior levels. Each was tied to a skill level.

The unit commanders had responsibility for the primary and basic levels. The primary phase, or PNCOC, was to be of approximately four weeks' duration. This course was to be branch immaterial and would train soldiers for key combat duty positions in grade E-5 (sergeant or specialist five). Successful completion of this course was the prerequisite for promotion in the combat arms. Attendees for this course were selected by field commanders. The basic course, or BNCOC, that had pre-dated EPMS, would continue to prepare E-5s for key jobs as E-6s (staff sergeants). In the combat arms, training for this course would be given at the installation/division level. Combat support/service MOS training at the BNCOC level for the primary technical course would be conducted as a four-week course at the service schools.

The ten-week advanced course (ANCOC) was also continued under the revised EPMS. The major change under EPMS was that only E-6s would be considered for attendance to train for the key duty positions of sergeant first class (E-7). Selection of soldiers to attend this course was to be made at departmental rather than at field level. The fourth level—the senior course—would be a series of courses conducted at installation/division level in some type of nonresident mode to prepare sergeants first class for the duties of master sergeant (E-8). The final course—not actually an integral part of the five-tiered NCOES—was the sergeants major academy, at the apex of the noncommissioned officers education system, the soldier's premier school. It would continue to function as before.

While attendance and successful completion of these courses was to prepare the soldier for the skill level required at the next higher grade, it would not in itself guarantee promotion eligibility. This depended upon the *quality of performance* that ultimately determined the individual's readiness for promotion.

Under the pre-EPMS practice it had been difficult to determine whether one soldier was better qualified than another, especially when both had attended the same schools and had completed the same courses. Professionalism and mediocrity were lumped together in the same box. As Sergeant Major Don Weber of the DCSPER EPMS task force described it, "the old system was like a compass that pointed to the ground instead of to the north. It told the soldier where he was—not where he was capable of going." The problem, Weber added, "was like a fifteen-man squad suited up for a basketball game. All fifteen men can play basketball, but only five of them can play on the first team."[13]

This evaluation of the performance process under EPMS replaced the former MOS test. Developed at TRADOC under General William E. DePuy, and designated the skill qualification test or SQT, the new procedure helped the Army distinguish the starters from the bench warmers. The SQT was divided into three parts: the written test; the hands-on test; and the unit commander's certification that the individual had attained a certain level of skill. While periodic pre-EPMS evaluations of all soldiers were continued, a new feature had been added that was expected to promote excellence—the requirement that the next higher skill level must be reached *before* promotion.

Testing of each soldier in his primary MOS was reduced from an annual affair to every other year, and testing for the secondary MOS from every year to just once in a soldier's career. These skill qualification tests were to be used to determine the skill level at which the individual soldier was qualified. Underlying the SQT concept was the "soldier's manual" that told him exactly what he must be able to do at each skill level. Mastery of this manual, of which there was to be one for each career management field, would be the key to passing the SQT.

Commenting on the implementation of EPMS and the SQT, General DePuy said that he wanted

> the command sergeants major, through the first sergeants and the platoon sergeants, to be sure that the first-line supervisors, the squad leaders, the chiefs of section, and the tank commanders and scout leaders . . . understand that it is their responsibility to see to it that every soldier, in fact, is trained in accordance with this Soldier's Manual. [This will] bring the sergeants back to their functions of 1939 which was to be the first-line trainer of the individual in the army, as opposed to the unit. Henceforth, the commissioned officers would be expected to command the *unit*, and the noncommissioned officers the *soldiers*.[14]

In general, the EPMS-engendered evaluation system was expected to work in the following manner: upon promotion to E-4 (corporal) the soldier would be tested every other year on the test designated as a requirement for the next higher grade. That is, E-4s would take the E-5 SQT, E-5s the E-6 test, and E-7s the E-8/9

SQT. The score made on the SQT would then be used for two purposes—verification of the skill level corresponding to the soldier's current grade or his attainment of the skill level corresponding to the next higher grade. Test scores were then combined with a weighted average of the soldier's efficiency reports and converted to a normative score for such purposes as superior performance pay and reenlistment controls. Since each MOS was tested annually, even though an individual soldier took the test only on alternate years, a soldier who wished to try for a higher score could volunteer to retake the test the next year. Essentially the SQT measured each soldier's potential to perform at the next higher grade. This would enable the Army to recognize and to advance professionalism as soon as it was identified in the individual.

Classification was the third cornerstone of EPMS. It is, observed Sergeant Major Weber of the EPMS Task Force at MILPERCEN, "the real glue which brings professionalism together through EPMS."[15] Under EPMS the classification policy would show supervisors and managers where a soldier is going in his career, not where he'd been. Unit commanders were given the authority to promote through pay grade E-4. The Department of Army would influence promotions to grades E-5 and E-6 through published promotion cutoff scores and other measurable promotion-qualification guidelines. However, promotion to sergeant first class (E-7) and above would be determined by Department of Army selection boards.

EPMS also provided an alternate means of advancement to those soldiers not selected for formal NCOES training that was more in line with former practices. Such men could prepare for higher skill classification through on-the-job experience (OJE). OJE or OJT (on-the-job-training) meant that a soldier had served for a certain period of time in his primary MOS and demonstrated that he could do the job. In order to qualify for the skill level of the next higher grade, the OJE- or OJT-qualified soldier must pass the prescribed SQT. He must also complete a period of six months OJE/OJT to qualify for skill levels 2 and 3 and one year for skill levels 4 and 5. If the OJE/OJT-trained soldier failed the SQT, he had one year to study and prepare himself to retake the test the following year.

Following successful completion of the SQT, actual promotion, whether through NCOES or OJE, was the final step. For this purpose, the Army established three levels of promotion authority: decentralized; semicentralized; and Army Department selection boards. The first of these three levels remained, as has been noted, with the unit commander, who retained authority to promote through pay grade E-4. Semicentralized promotion authority lay with promotion boards convened by field commanders to consider soldiers for advancement to grades E-5 and E-6, sergeant and staff sergeant respectively. Promotion points for an individual soldier would be recorded through such achievements as the amount of education accomplished, military schools attended, MOS scores, awards, and most importantly, individual performance ratings. A soldier could also receive points by appearing before locally convened promotion boards. The sum of all these points determined eligibility for promotion. At this point the Department of Army again entered the picture and controlled the number of promotions to E-5 and E-6 through announcements of monthly promotion cutoff scores for each MOS. Those soldiers with sufficient points to match or to exceed the scores were then promoted.

This procedure put all professional soldiers in similar CMFs or MOSs, into competition with one another on a servicewide basis. Essentially EPMS, unlike the former system, integrated both personnel and training management in order to measure *both* performance and potential. It had taken the mechanics of the former promotion system and added an essential ingredient—proof of performance.

On this foundation would be developed, the Army staff now anticipated, a professional army that could offer its members both pride in service and an opportunity for career advancement. To attract and retain the quality of soldiers to man such a force and to maintain the training and discipline needed for a combat-effective force, demanded a noncommissioned officer corps of unprecedented excellence. The system of professional development provided by the enlisted personnel-management system would, the staff expected, help to achieve that excellence. Thus would the noncommissioned officer resume his status and role as "the backbone of the Army."[16]

RETURN OF THE NONCOMMISSIONED OFFICER

While the adoption of the EPMS institutionalized noncommissioned officer professionalism within the Army, there were other programs adopted at the major command level that reinforced and extended NCO professionalism in areas not covered by EPMS. Even as Army Chief of Staff General Weyand approved implementation of EPMS in August of 1974, commander in chief, U.S. Army, Europe (USAREUR), General Michael S. Davison, launched a commandwide program to which he gave the designation USAREUR Noncommissioned Officer Professionalism Program (NCOPP). Its aim he declared, was "to create conditions that will enable each noncommissioned officer to reach his, or her, full potential both professionally and in terms of self-development." General Davison expected this in turn to improve USAREUR's operational readiness and combat capability.[17]

General Davison provided staff guidance for a USAREUR professional NCO advisory group that held its first meeting at headquarters, USAREUR, on August 15, 1974. Membership in this first group was selected by the CSM of USAREUR, Robert S. Ham, who restricted the initial group to seven CSMs and one SFC simply to get the project underway as quickly as possible. However, he left himself the option of expanding its numbers later, if necessary. An increase in membership was not long in coming. At its first quarterly meeting the advisory group invited four more CSMs to join. With this increase in membership, the group's designation was also changed to that of a board in time for its December meeting. Henceforth, it would be known as the noncommissioned officers' professional advisory board, or PAB.

One of the board's first tasks was to identify those conditions that General Davison had noted were necessary. The board's prestigious makeup, chaired by USAREUR's CSM and consisting of the command's senior noncommissioned officers, gave DCSPER assurance that meaningful recommendations would soon be forthcoming.[18]

At its inception the PAB seemed to be most concerned with what might be termed the administrative irritants of military living in Europe, such as housing, facilities, and assignments. In December 1974, at the advisory board's second quarterly meeting, its members gave first priority in its recommendations to DCSPER to noncommissioned officer housing, second priority to giving greater authority and responsibility to noncommissioned officers in the chain of command, and third and fourth priorities, respectively, to assignments and promotions. Part of the reason for this was, in CSM Frederick K. Tracey's words, that the first advisory group suspected that the NCOPP was a publicity gimmick. These CSMs felt they had been professional NCOs all along, and consequently "the initial surge was to identify the administrative irritants to the noncommissioned officer; what was the army doing that affected the NCOs in such a way as to irritate them." Hence the initial priorities.[19] On the other hand, from the commander's side the mission of the PAB was perceived as recommending ways in which noncommissioned officer professionalism might be enhanced by allowing the NCO greater authority and responsibility within the chain of command.

Although rating last in PAB's priorities, the promotion policy for enlisted personnel, then embodied in EPMS, had been a subject of considerable confusion. This seems to have been responsible for the high rate of dissatisfaction over promotion policy (60 percent) expressed by respondents in an opinion survey of USAREUR's noncommissioned officers. The same survey also disclosed a significant difference in opinions concerning these policies between junior officers and senior noncommissioned officers.

The PAB did, of course, continue to push all three issues, and by March, 1975, 75 percent of the advisory board's recommended changes to regulations, designed to give noncommissioned officers greater responsibility and authority, had been accepted by commander in chief, USAREUR. Nevertheless, as with many of the earlier EPMS provisions, the impact of these changes ultimately depended upon the cooperation of the local unit commanders—company, battery, and troop—for it was they who really determined whether or not the noncommissioned officers would be properly utilized in accordance with changed USAREUR regulations.

In 1974 changes had also taken place in Army regulations concerning noncommissioned officers in support of the thrust envisioned by the EPMS. These changes specifically charged commanders and their staffs at all echelons of command, "with the responsibility of ensuring equitable delegation of authority and responsibility . . . to noncommissioned officers by their superiors, whether officer, warrant officer, or other noncommissioned officer."[20]

At its March 1975 quarterly meeting, the board enthusiastically welcomed these changes by recommending that they be required reading for all commissioned officers. This recommendation was not as quixotic as it seemed, for earlier additional clout had been given the board when the deputy commander in chief, USAREUR admonished the staff not to treat the noncommissioned officer professionalism program lightly.

In spite of departmental and command changes in regulations, resistance to giving the noncommissioned officers the opportunities to function at their fullest capacity lingered on at the unit level. Four years after these regulations were published, and the NCO professionalism program had been launched, General George S. Blanchard, successor to General Davison as commander in chief, USAREUR, complained bitterly that battery and company commanders were still "spending too much time (14–15 hours per day) on the job supervising and do not allow the NCO to run the unit." However, Blanchard admitted that part of this problem could be laid at the door of those battalion command sergeants major who had failed to convince battalion, company, and battery commanders to let their NCOs run the unit while they commanded.

Some months later, still voicing concern over the excessive amount of time unit commanders were spending supervising their men, General Blanchard declared "we must educate our NCOs and officers at every level of command concerning the proper role of the noncommissioned officer . . . commanders have no choice (under USAREUR Regulation 600-1) but to trust and have confidence in their noncommissioned officers." It was, he concluded, "the responsibility of the CSM's and the 1st Sergeants to get this across to their commanders." To this, General Bernard W. Rogers, then U.S. Army Chief of Staff, added, "the noncommissioned officers are the best judges on the ground. Commanders should use their wisdom and know-how to improve things."

Despite these ambitious programs and command initiatives, ultimately the local unit, where the average noncommissioned officer spent most of his professional career, remained the arbiter of whether or not these programs and initiatives would achieve their goals. There were some indications, even one year after EPMS and the USAREUR noncommissioned officer professionalism program had been implemented, that something was amiss—something standing in the way of the full realization of the goals of servicewide professionalism. A commentator writing at the time in the pages of the widely circulated *Army Times* noted that

> the Army has gone all out to promote NCO pride and professionalism. Incentives include basic and advanced NCOES, the Sergeants Major Academy, leadership and management courses, centralized promotions, direct assignments and increased opportunities for higher civilian education. But these fine programs lose their glitter at

> unit level where the action is. It is at the unit level, where these people work, that NCO professionalism is discouraged. How can that be?[21]

Brigadier General Robert B. Hankins, then commander of the 56th Field Artillery Brigade in Europe, was quoted as observing in answer to this query that "a lot of the problem lies within the officer corps. Today's young officers had not learned how to properly manage their NCO's. . . . too often, they fail to respect and take advantage of the years of practical knowledge their NCO's have accumulated."

Another general officer remarked that "our helicopter and tactical communications have developed to the point where a brigade commander can direct squads if he wants to, and many did in Vietnam because [in a zero-defects Army] their careers depended upon how well their small units performed." The result was, he added, "a generation of junior officers and NCO's who are accustomed to having people looking over their shoulders to make sure they don't make any mistakes."

Yet the commander in chief, USAREUR declared that mistakes made by junior officers and noncommissioned officers should be used by commanders as training vehicles to correct those errors by showing their subordinates how to avoid them in the future. Responsibility was, in General Blanchard's words, the key word in the NCO professionalism program. Repeatedly he urged all commanders to give their noncommissioned officers mission-type orders and to allow them to function as they should, even while allowing for mistakes. For example, a sergeant should be allowed to make sergeant-type mistakes, but *not* corporal-type mistakes. A noncommissioned officer learned by functioning as a leader and supervisor of men. According to Joe D. Offut, CSM of the Berlin Brigade, "professionalism and prestige are not attributes that can be awarded the NCO like a Good Conduct Medal or issued him in generous helpings according to some phase plan."[22]

There was yet another obstacle out of the Army's immediate past that was to frustrate at times the best intents of the EPMS and the NCOES to enhance noncommissioned officer professionalism. That was a long-standing practice on the part of many unit commanders of sending only dispensable personnel to school or on extended temporary duty when confronted with quotas for NCO academies. In many cases the indispensable or better junior noncommissioned officers remained with their units while less-deserving personnel accumulated the additional educational points for promotion under EPMS. Therefore, when the time for promotion came around, frequently those individuals with several schools and varied assignments to their credit, regardless of how well they had performed in their MOS at the unit level, had the advantage over those who had remained in their assigned units, where they had performed outstandingly but had not received the added school credit in their records.

To illustrate this problem, the Army personnel chief, Lieutenant General Harold G. Moore, declared that "a lot of senior NCO's and company and battery commanders were not sending their best people to the NCO Basic Course [BNCOC]." Many units, he added, were "holding back, keeping them [their good NCOs] down in their motor pool or supply room and not filling the spaces. This practice hurts the army, and it hurts the soldier's career [under EPMS]." Sergeant Major of the Army William G. Bainbridge provided statistical reinforcement to this charge by observing that the Army "had failed to meet its fiscal year basic NCO course quota by nearly 2,100 and was 600 people short of meeting FY 1976 quotas."[23]

THE "SERGEANT MORALES PROGRAM"

Just as the noncommissioned officer professionalism program was General Davison's contribution to noncommissioned officer professionalism in USAREUR, so was the "Sergeant Morales" Club Program General Blanchard's addition to noncommissioned officer improvement in the command. The origins of this program are to be found in General Blanchard's tour of duty as commanding general of the 82d Airborne Division, prior to his coming to Europe as commanding general of VII Corps in 1974. His concept of the program undoubtedly owed something to the fact that in 1939 he had been a highly successful buck sergeant in charge of an artillery section at Ft. Bliss, Texas. He knew from experience the sergeant's business, his authority and responsibility, and what it took to be a good noncommissioned officer.[24]

The "Morales" idea grew out of one of General Blanchard's tours of inspection in the 82d Airborne Division area. As Blanchard described it, the commander of an engineer company introduced one of his sergeants to the commanding general with the observation that "the Sergeant was leaving us after three years as a squad leader . . . and he has had no AWOL's in his squad during the entire time."

Impressed by the sergeant, General Blanchard invited him to his headquarters that same afternoon to discuss his concept of noncommissioned leadership. After a two-hour discussion, General Blanchard described his leadership characteristics. "First of all," Blanchard remarked, "he led by example; he got his hands dirty; was good not only in the personal aspects of counseling soldiers and that sort of thing, but also in the field and in army training tests and so on. No matter how you looked at it, [he] was just a great leader." He was moreover, short of stature and slight in build, and his accent was Hispanic. Nevertheless he was able to perform as an outstanding leader.

When in 1973 General Blanchard took command of VII Corps, he considered ways to enhance General Davison's noncommissioned officer professionalism program. Talking over the matter with his CSM, William Strickland, Blanchard expressed his concern over the need to improve the noncommissioned officer corps in the immediate post-Vietnam period. During these conversations, CSM Strickland suggested the formation of a "club" to recognize those individuals who had proven themselves to be outstanding leaders for an all-volunteer army. General Blanchard agreed, but in the interval discovered that he had forgotten the outstanding sergeant's name. Selecting one that sounded similar to the original, General Blanchard dubbed the club the "Sergeant Morales Club."

At first, VII Corps placed no grade limitations on the noncommissioned officers who might be nominated for membership. Later it was limited to the pay grades of E-4 and E-5. The entire selection process was handled through the noncommissioned officer chain. Evaluation of individuals nominated was first made by the battalion sergeant major, his recommendation then went on to brigade and finally to division. In instances where there was no tactical chain or there were no tactical units in the community, the selection and review process was accomplished on a community basis. Above the division, or the community, the selection boards consisted of command sergeants major. After several men had been selected and inducted into the club, they too were invited to sit on the selection boards. Eventually the selection rate in VII Corps was one "Sgt. Morales" for every thousand noncommissioned officers.

After selection, the candidates were brought to corps headquarters where they were inducted into the club by the corps commander and given a certificate of membership and a membership card. Later, when General Blanchard became commander-in-chief USAREUR, he expanded the program to cover all of USAREUR. Successful candidates were brought to the Heidelberg headquarters for formal induction. This was followed by luncheon with the commanding general, and, over a three-day period, there followed a series of visits with the USAREUR staff and briefings similar to those given general officers and other dignitaries upon arrival at headquarters, USAREUR.

General Blanchard expected that these outstanding noncommissioned officers would return to their units and there, by example, help to improve the quality of performance and leadership. Therefore, he insisted that the Sergeant Morales selectees be returned to their original units and not moved elsewhere by their unit commanders for publicity or prestige purposes. The commander in chief, USAREUR, did not object, however, when he visited a unit on inspection that a "Sergeant Morales" was selected as his escort. Furthermore, during the Reforger exercise sergeants "Morales" were among those assigned as escorts to visiting dignitaries. These noncommissioned officers fully justified their selection for these duties, for the selection and induction process into the "Sergeant Morales Club" was a fine learning and maturing experience for these young men and women. "A Sergeant Morales," General Blanchard later observed, "exemplified the type of noncommissioned leadership needed in the modern army." Through their example, these men and women, then numbering in the hundreds, helped to raise the level of noncommissioned officer professionalism within USAREUR and proved a suitable complement to General Davison's ongoing noncommissioned officer professionalism program.

Out of these two USAREUR programs there emerged a concept of the noncommissioned officer's role that blended the traditional with the modern and thus established a pragmatic basis for redefining the noncommissioned officer's role and status two centuries after General von Steuben first defined it for the Continental Army at Valley Forge during the War of Independence.

CSM Frederick Tracey, General Blanchard's CSM during his tenure as commander in chief, USAREUR, outlined what was expected of a noncommissioned officer in USAREUR in 1975. The NCO Tracey said,

> has four basic duties or responsibilities, and if they're executed properly, they spell success. The first responsibility is toward the soldier, his appearance, and that's what he looks like when you first break him out in the morning until he goes to bed at night. From the tip of his shoes to the top of his hair, and we also include his waistline. That means you've got to keep him physically fit, [he] has got to be ready and has to look good. The second one is that the soldier's property, all of his equipment, is properly recorded and kept serviceable, functional, and ready for use, and that's everything from a M-60 tank to the blankets on his bunk, it's all got to be charged, recorded, and ready for use. And the third one (we don't do too well on that one), that's the one I call USAREUR in motion; the accountability for the soldier during the given duty day, where's he at, what he's doing, who told him to go there, who brought him back . . . in other words, the immediate supervisor has to know where that soldier is, at all times . . . and the fourth one, which we will always have, the responsibility (and it really blossomed out with the Skill Qualification Test) that the noncommissioned officer is fully responsible for the individual training of the soldier. If we do these four things, we'll have a great army, and that's what we're doing, and its moving in the right direction.

Although less eloquent than the language of the eighteenth-century infantry drill regulations, the similarity of CSM Tracey's statement to that of General von Steuben almost two centuries earlier is remarkable.[25]

If the noncommissioned officer's responsibilities and duties have changed so little through the centuries, what indeed has changed? Perhaps the most significant change regarding the role and status of the noncommissioned officer within the Army has occurred since the Vietnam War. This is the servicewide institutionalization of professionalism for the noncommissioned officer corps. The careers of noncommissioned officers are now managed in a fashion quite similar to that long in use for the commissioned officers. This in turn has established an important change in the relationship between the commissioned and noncommissioned officer—a recognition that the noncommissioned officer is truly a professional partner in arms, different in function but coequal in importance. The commissioned officer must trust his professional colleague to do his job—and let him do it. "Sir, these are *my* duties!"[26]

CHAPTER 21
REAPPRAISAL AND RESTORING PROFESSIONALISM

With the withdrawal of U.S. forces from Vietnam, the Army at last turned its full attention to making the transition from dependence on the Selective Service for manpower to an all-volunteer force. One of the major tasks in this transition was to gain the full support of the noncommissioned officer corps. Initial reaction from many senior noncommissioned officers had been extremely hostile. They saw the modern volunteer army (MVA) concept as yet another step toward a more civilianized and therefore permissive institution "in which their years of service would not be recognized and their already tenuous authority further undermined." These attitudes had been fostered partly through adverse publicity given the MVA concept in the pages of such periodicals as the *Army Times*. For example, an interview with the commanding general of the Continental Army Command (CONARC) entitled "Old Sarge—Big VOLAR Hang-up," had had a devastating impact on the morale of a large number of noncommissioned officers—mainly platoon sergeants—by lumping many of them together as part of the problem rather than the solution, as indeed they were.[1]

Many noncommissioned officers also interpreted the MVA concept as an institutionalization of permissiveness, as reported in the *Army Times* through such articles as, "Beer Can Now Flow in Barracks and Messes."[2] These and other articles in this widely read newspaper caused many senior sergeants to perceive top-level leadership as being indifferent to their problems and personal futures. The Department of the Army was able to dispel much of this discontent and concern through careful and detailed explanation of the aims and policies of the MVA program as it developed. After a good deal of the earlier adverse publicity was demonstrated to have been misleading, the overwhelming majority of the noncommissioned officers began to express relief that the Army was not plotting its own—and their—destruction. One 1st sergeant declared, "Look, I've been in this Army in three wars. The Army has always been changing, and I've always changed with it. I'm still running the Army."[3]

Several other programs scheduled for adoption by the MVA also aroused particular interest among noncommissioned officers. The prospect of stabilized tours through the "home post" concept had from its inception appealed to all noncommissioned officers interviewed. They also expressed enthusiasm for some system of retraining older combat arms noncommissioned officers at the end of their useful service, but before they were required to be retired. Most realized, as a result of their experiences in Vietnam, that service limited to company-sized units was a road that led to civilian life at the end of a ten-year military career with no transferrable skills.

Junior noncommissioned officers generally viewed the announced MVA program with favor also. On the other hand, as a group, the mid-level noncommissioned officers, as operations in Vietnam had drawn down, felt themselves increasingly excluded from the respect and responsibilities given the noncommissioned corps. Most of these men were graduates of the noncommissioned officer candidate courses for the combat arms—men who had proven themselves for the most part capable leaders of small units, to include platoons. Remarks such as: "Look, Sir, I'm an E-5 and I've been running a rifle platoon [normally an E-7's responsibility] for eight months. Why don't I get the stripes and the pay to go with the job? How come all the E-7s come out of the woodwork when we get back to the States? Then I get treated like some . . . damn private!" In the face of such sentiments, the Army was challenged to retain the most capable of these men through faster promotion and follow-on training in the post-Vietnam period. It was found that many of the best of these younger noncommissioned officers had plans to leave the service upon their return from Vietnam unless this situation was corrected, and quickly.

Combat operations during the seven years of war in Vietnam (1965–1972) had heavily depleted the noncommissioned corps, particularly in the infantry. To replenish the corps the Army somehow had to retain and continue the training of the younger generation of noncommissioned officers, especially those graduates of the NCOCC who had proven themselves capable combat leaders. Yet at the same time the Army had to convince the older noncommissioned officers that their leadership still had a place for them in the modern volunteer Army. With proper care they too could be expected to become part of the solution, for completion of the transition from a draft to a volunteer army depended on the cooperation of a well-trained corps of noncommissioned officers. An all-volunteer army simply could not exist without thoroughly professional enlisted trainers and leaders.

However, in order to create and retain such a corps of men, the Army had first to sell them on the MVA program. To do this involved, among other things, overcoming the flood of adverse publicity concerning the program, much of which came from the *Army Times*. Since the inception of the MVAP, this newspaper had been a regular critic and much of this criticism, as noted above, had had a devastating impact on noncommissioned morale.

Yet another challenge was a widely held perception on the part of a majority of company-grade officers and senior noncommissioned officers alike that the

Uniform Code of Military Justice had failed them as an effective disciplinary tool. Whether or not this perception was accurate, it nevertheless had a detrimental effect on the retention rate of junior officers and many noncommissioned officers. To overcome this perception, punishment for serious offenders henceforth was made more visible, speedy, and certain. A failure to retain able junior leaders and commanders would further tarnish the Army's image, following the long and increasingly unpopular war in Vietnam.

As will be recalled from Chapter 18, Lieutenant General Forsythe, special assistant to the Chief of Staff, MVA, sent an interview team to Vietnam to look into matters of morale and training. Some of the recommendations made by this team were eventually adopted by the MVA as it replaced the draft-supported Army following withdrawal of combat forces from Vietnam.

Among the team's recommendations was one that CONARC open a permanent noncommissioned officer academy for the purpose of providing outstanding sergeants and staff sergeants returning from Vietnam with needed additional training. Although these men had graduated, many with distinction, from combat arms noncommissioned officer candidate courses and had performed well as small-unit leaders in combat, most lacked the training needed for them to serve effectively as noncommissioned officers in a peacetime garrison. Actually, instead of creating a new academy as recommended, CONARC acted on this recommendation by providing the needed training for these men at existing academies, of which there were several.

Another recommendation that directly concerned noncommissioned training pointed toward a permanent noncommissioned officer academy for the training of platoon and master sergeants. These noncommissioned officers were to receive at such an academy training mainly in the administrative and management responsibilities of the 1st sergeant and command sergeant major. About one year after these recommendations had been made, General Ralph E. Haines, then commanding general, CONARC, submitted to the Army Chief of Staff a plan calling for a permanent-change-of-station course of approximately twenty-three weeks' duration to prepare senior master sergeants for duty in key noncommissioned positions at division and higher headquarters while developing their intellectual depth and analytical ability.

On May 17, 1972, General William Westmoreland, then Army Chief of Staff, approved the creation of a school offering what was, by then, the senior level of the noncommissioned officer education system (NCOES) at Ft. Bliss, Texas. The approved course was to involve a PCS move, and classes were to be conducted on a frequency of two per year. Although a name had not yet been selected for the school, the CSA requested recommendations suggesting that it be designated an academy. In time it would become the sergeants major academy.

As far as the crisis of the noncommissioned corps was concerned, the war in Vietnam had been both a genesis and a revelation. Largely a small-unit commander's war, operations in Vietnam had taken an inordinate toll among mid-level noncommissioned officers and had led the Army to adopt the NCOCC program; on the other hand, it created a new generation of combat-experienced enlisted leaders who introduced a leavening influence into the ranks of the noncommissioned corps during the postwar period.

As these causal factors combined to confront the Army and the noncommissioned corps with new problems, several shortcomings in the training and education of small-unit leaders were revealed. Solutions to these problems required a completely new service-wide career management system to raise and maintain the corps' professional standards. Stabilization and retraining of the corps in the postwar years became integral steps in the creation of the modern all-volunteer Army.

To some noncommissioned officers, these difficult years seemed not only years of crisis but in some respects the "Dark Ages" of the corps. Yet as one veteran senior noncommissioned officer of those years has observed,

> We called this period the Dark Ages because of a tendency among all soldiers of all ages to declare, "Boy, did we ever have it bad in them days!" That's just another way of saying, I'm tough. I came through. And in the end, that's the best epitaph I can think of for the noncommissioned officer of that era.[4]

Even as the corps struggled to survive amid the many corrosive and debilitating influences abounding during operations in Vietnam, the Army nevertheless took significant steps toward enhancing the role and status both of the individual noncommissioned officer and of the corps. These were bright lights in that dark age. One of the first of these had been lighted in 1966, approximately one year after the commitment of the first U.S. Army ground combat units in Vietnam, when Chief of Staff General Harold K. Johnson appointed the first Sergeant Major of the Army, William Wooldridge.

This action had, it will be recalled, marked an increased awareness on the part of the staff of the noncommissioned officer's importance to the Army. Further acknowledgement occurred in 1968, when the CSA approved a centralized system similar to that for commissioned officers authorizing the temporary promotion of enlisted men to the pay grades of E-8 and E-9 on a service-wide basis. This was followed in 1969 by the development of the enlisted personnel centralized-management system (EPMS). Henceforth, there was to be a career-management program, again similar to that in use for the officers, for enlisted careerists and administered at the departmental level. This system included a noncommissioned officer educational development program (NCOEDP) that embraced basic, advanced, and senior levels of career instruction for noncommissioned officers. Ultimately, the noncommissioned officers educational system (NCOES) came to embody this program.

Now, with the Sergeant Major of the Army (SMA) to perform the vital role as spokesman for the ranks, the Army undertook to reassure the Army's senior enlisted leadership both in word and deed that it was in fact the "backbone of the Army," without which neither the corps nor the Army itself could survive.

It was not until 1970, with the certainty of the adoption of an all-volunteer force, that the Army undertook a serious in-depth study of how to improve genuine professionalism within the service. In January 1970, Chief of Staff Gen. William C. Westmoreland directed the Commandant of the Army War College at Carlisle Barracks, Pennsylvania, to undertake "an analysis of current leadership principles and techniques with a view to determining the type of leadership that would be most appropriate" as the Army's personnel sustainment procedures changed from reliance on the draft to all volunteer accessions. This involved critical examination of the appropriateness of the Army's institutional concept of leadership.[5]

Although the study was to concentrate on the commissioned corps, the role of the noncommissioned officer was considered as well for the study's central theme was

> that both the Army and the soldier must see themselves as parties to an informal contract. In this informal contract, the Army expects proficiency and disciplined response from the soldier. The soldier, on the other hand, expects fairness, worthwhile work, and sufficient pay from the Army. If each party to this informal contract meets the expectations of the other, a mutually satisfactory relationship will exist—a relationship which will create the loyalty and dedication which are the cornerstone of true discipline.

Before beginning the study, the eighteen-man research team agreed that there would be no questioning of the traditional, essentially authoritarian mode of the military organization. Using a scientifically designed questionnaire and group interview techniques, the team managed to collect data from 1,800 individuals representing a broad base of Army leadership up to and including 8 to 10 percent of the Army's general officers. The findings demonstrated that "the Army's time-honored principles of Leadership were accepted overwhelmingly by leaders at all levels as appropriate for the coming decade" (the 1970s). However, the data further showed that within the command structure there were "serious deficiencies in the application of these principles."

The Army War College study disclosed what many in the Army had long observed, that far too many commanders at all levels looked upward to please superiors rather than downward to fulfill the legitimate needs of subordinates. Across the board, the study found the officer corps "lacking in their responsibilities of looking out for the welfare of their subordinates."

Loyalty, the study observed, applied to personnel at both ends of the command structure, and was based upon mutual trust and respect. But undermining this traditional sense of trust, loyalty, and concern for one's subordinates and, at the same time reinforcing a self-centered concern for one's own aggrandizement, were several strong influences. The first of these had its origins outside the Army. It was a widespread acceptance within the civilian society from which the Army drew its personnel of "me-tooism," or "what's in it for me?" The other two were endemic within the Army. One was the "zero-defects" approach to command, an all-pervasive attitude that motivated perhaps a majority of the commissioned officers during the 1960s. Another was servicewide personnel turbulence—rapid and frequent change of commands and transfers—that made it difficult to develop or to maintain unit cohesiveness and loyalty. True loyalty could not be developed overnight, as the history of the Army demonstrated.

The study recognized these problems by noting, among other things, that "everyone is afraid to make a mistake with someone always looking over his shoulder." As a result, authority and ability were diluted at every level of responsibility. Although junior officers and noncommissioned officers were more intelligent and capable than ever before, they were so afraid of making mistakes that they hesitated to make decisions lest they lose respect or be "clobbered" by their seniors on their efficiency reports.

Further study by the War College disclosed that junior officers and noncommissioned officers, whose leadership experience was limited to the war in Vietnam, generally regarded themselves as ill-prepared for peacetime leadership responsibilities in an all-volunteer Army. The new study recommended the establishment of an extensive and progressive program of academic and technical education for all career noncommissioned officers. In this recommendation can be seen the genesis of the noncommissioned officers education system (NCOES).[6]

Not only was there the problem of the transition from a wartime to a peacetime environment, but the Army now also had to prepare to adjust to an all-volunteer basis. Over the past two decades Army leadership and policy had developed within an environment dependent on the draft. There was good reason, therefore, to believe that reversion to an all-volunteer force would present the Army with leadership challenges sufficiently different to warrant some modifications of existing leadership practices. Junior officers and noncommissioned officers with primarily Vietnam experience were well aware that leadership in a peacetime garrison environment was more complex than in combat. Consequently, these men were expected to be receptive to efforts on the part of the Army to prepare them for garrison duty.

THE EMERSON BOARD

Looking ahead to possible solutions to the challenges posed by a return to an all-volunteer army, Chief of Staff Westmoreland called upon General Ralph E. Haines, commanding general, CONARC, to join him in short- and long-term efforts to improve leadership within the Army, because there was an "evident need for immediate attention by the chain of command to improving our leadership techniques to meet the Army's current challenges." To this end, Westmoreland proposed that CONARC form a board consisting of "selected young leaders" to study the subject of leadership and to formulate a leadership improvement program.

In response to the Chief of Staff's instructions, General Haines appointed a board chaired by General Henry E. Emerson, and composed of fifteen commissioned officers and seven senior noncommissioned officers, including two command sergeants major, one 1st sergeant, two sergeants first class, and two staff sergeants. Retired General Bruce C. Clarke, one of the Army's most distinguished trainers and commanders, acted as a consultant to the board as it formulated a program to review the fundamentals of leadership and examine techniques to handle such contemporary problems as dissent, race relations, and drug abuse.[7]

The Emerson Board incorporated the method and findings of the earlier Army War College study on leadership into a seminar program designed to disseminate its findings throughout CONARC. During the summer and early autumn of 1971, traveling teams from the board held leadership seminars, sponsored by installation commanders for senior commanders and command sergeants major. In turn, selected installation representatives held leadership workshops for junior officers and noncommissioned officers. The general purpose of these was to obtain the cooperation of leaders at all levels of command to reflect on the specific problems and opportunities of leadership as the Army prepared to move toward an all-volunteer force.

In addition to the seminars, the board recommended a long-range program to improve leadership and command instruction through the Army school system—from the basic NCO course to the Army War College. In doing this the board observed that "the Army has tended in the past few years to neglect long-term human goals by placing too much emphasis on short-term organization goals." To be sure, the concept of improved leadership was based on the accomplishment of the organizational mission but, while doing so, preserving the dignity of the individual and insuring his welfare. Leadership behavior had therefore to be flexible in technique and personal in application in order to motivate the individual, promote, and maintain a high state of discipline, and foster *esprit de corps*.

In its final recommendations and findings, the board subjected the Army's entire system of leadership training to a thoroughgoing criticism. For example, it found leadership instruction in service schools to be inadequate to meet both current and future needs. An examination of service schools, noncommissioned officer academies, and ROTC training disclosed that about one half of noncommissioned courses contained no instruction on counseling or motivation of personnel.

The board included a recommendation that pointed toward the soon-to-be-implemented NCOES. This was that officer and noncommissioned officer leadership instruction should be designed by levels so that instructional programs could be developed to give the student knowledge and skills commensurate with his gradually increasing leadership responsibilities. To this end the board developed six outlines of progressive programs of instruction containing fifty-two learning objectives with supporting scopes for schools ranging from NCOES to the Command and General Staff College.

Most installation representatives attending the seminars and leadership courses drew attention to a serious need for more training of the noncommissioned officers and the necessity of giving senior sergeants responsibility for training junior noncommissioned officers as well as opportunities for doing so. The board also concluded that more division-level noncommissioned academies were needed with teaching emphasis on development of leadership. General Clarke had drawn attention to the paucity of school-trained noncommissioned officers at division level. Not surprisingly, the board also found that the Army's leadership manual (*Field Manual 22–100*) needed a thorough revision as it was out of date in terms of current needs.

On the heels of CONARC's implementation of leadership guidance throughout the command, came the Army Chief of Staff's June 30, 1971, directive establishing a policy of decentralized training. Mandatory subjects prescribed by higher headquarters were to be eliminated, and training guidance provided battalion headquarters through mission-type instructions (general rather than specific instructions) rather than detailed directives.

General Westmoreland wished by means of this directive to encourage more dynamic training in combat units. Such training was to be tailored to the particular unit's needs—needs that were better known to commanders and leaders, both commissioned and noncommissioned—at the battalion or lower level. With training responsibility returned to the unit commander, training was expected to be more imaginative, innovative, and professionally challenging on the part of the trainer as well as more zestful and satisfying for the individual soldier. Implemented at the company and platoon level, or even at the squad or fire-team level, this policy was to give the junior leaders far greater responsibility for individual and unit training and thereby greatly enhance the role and status of these leaders.[8]

Once in place, however, this new training policy was slow getting started. Junior commanders and leaders failed at first to develop and conduct dynamic training in part because they were products of "a culture which gave them more passive, receiving experiences, such as watching television" as opposed to active, accomplishing experiences, such as hiking or hunting, as had been enjoyed by previous generations of young Americans. Many junior officers and some noncommissioned leaders were found lacking the experience, training, and imagination for conducting the dynamic training envisioned in the Chief of Staff's directive. This problem proved to be Armywide and second only to that of the chronic shortage of personnel for unit training.

Not only were many junior leaders lacking in experience necessary to conduct dynamic training, many were also unreceptive to such training, for the reasons just enumerated but also because they came from a society more permissive and antimilitary than the one that produced their fathers and older brothers. As noted when we discussed leadership in Vietnam, these men tended to identify with their subordinates as equals rather than the traditional senior-subordinate relationship of the military service.

Furthermore, the personnel turbulence and rapid promotions associated with the Vietnam years produced an abundance of junior officers and younger noncommissioned officers who had never served in a peacetime training environment. These faced further problems in the implementation of a decentralized, dynamic training policy. Yet the demands placed on company commanders and platoon leaders in training as well as combat had become more complex than ever.

In improving leadership through greater emphasis on professional development, the Army faced still more problems. For example, career development schooling for noncommissioned men of all grades was, until the implementation of NCOES, virtually nonexistent. The Army's numerous noncommissioned officer academies had been found (see Chapter 16) to vary widely as to goals, requirements, and number of students allowed to attend. Because of these varied standards and requirements, many junior sergeants had little motivation to attend any additional schooling after they completed advanced individual training.

THE BOARD FOR DYNAMIC TRAINING

To remedy this situation, a CONARC-created group designated the Board for Dynamic Training was convened at Ft. Benning, Georgia. This board recommended several measures to increase the professionalism and prestige of the noncommissioned officer corps. The first was to provide periodic classes that would be directed primarily at the junior noncommissioned officer. They would stress job proficiency and leadership and in most cases be taught by senior noncommissioned officers.

Furthermore, the board recommended noncommissioned officer promotions be based on demonstrated ability and not doled out because allocations were available. In addition to job performance, promotion to E-6, for example, should be predicated on successful completion of a course at a noncommissioned officer academy at division level or higher. Under such conditions the wartime noncommissioned officer candidate courses could be discontinued at the earliest possible opportunity.

The board also concluded that senior noncommissioned officers must be teachers as well as leaders. The board therefore recommended reeducation of senior noncommissioned officers as to their responsibilities for teaching their subordinates.

To achieve these goals the board recommended that schooling be standardized throughout the Army. However, the board did not recommend a command and general staff college equivalent school for the noncommissioned ranks. Specifically, it was recommended that this schooling should include attendance at a division-level noncommissioned officer academy for a four-week course as a prerequisite for promotion to staff sergeant. A six-week course, branch immaterial, offered at Army-level noncommissioned officer academies, was thought requisite for sergeants first class and master sergeants. Academies at this level would offer noncommissioned officers the chance to associate with colleagues from other arms and technical services. The students would gain thereby a broader perspective of the Army as a step toward becoming a "total soldier." The board recommended that future sergeants major should be selected from the lists of graduates of these courses.

Eventually an analysis of these and similar recommendations and studies resulted in the second post-Vietnam policy—the creation of a servicewide system of career management for all enlisted personnel. This policy was expected to greatly enhance the quality of the enlisted career force in an all-volunteer army. In such an army the individual must establish his eligibility to remain in service as a careerist by developing, through career-progression programs, his potential, and by demonstrating his efficiency. There would, under this policy, no longer be a place in the Army for that traditional figure, the "yardbird," or permanent private. There would be no place, as in years past, for the mere time server.[9]

In many ways, the military reforms of the 1970s represented, especially for noncommissioned officers, some of the most progressive measures ever adopted by the U.S. Army for their enhancement, education, and status. Yet as one student of military sociology has observed, it also represented a "partial reversion to traditional forms," to a more conventional and authoritarian social organization.[10]

As with most reform movements, there was in the Army an undercurrent of resistance to the new concepts as advanced by General Westmoreland and the Army War College studies. There remained "a steadfast reluctance by some competent, dedicated, professional commanders to decentralized training. Consequently, brigade and division staffs often rewrote SOPs in order to maintain control over all training from brigade or division level. Such actions and attitudes not only greatly restricted the exercise of initiative by company commanders, but tended to ignore or bypass the noncommissioned officers in the chain of command with quite understandably adverse effects on their morale."[11]

It was, therefore, not surprising that many noncommissioned officers continued in spite of all the service reforms to feel that they were being overlooked by the staff in the transition to an all-volunteer force. Generally, these men felt betrayed by a perceived lack of trust on the part of their superiors. This sense of betrayal was all the more keen because most noncommissioned officers believed that they were performing an essential role in the defense of the nation. Therefore, when they believed that they would not be given the opportunity to fulfill their perceived duties and responsibilities, they began to harbor doubts whether the Army really considered them to be essential. These doubts in turn led to a loss of pride and confidence among many of them.

General Forsythe, however, did not consider that the issue of noncommissioned morale had become a problem of major proportions. Nevertheless, he believed that the Chief of Staff should give the matter his immediate attention. Much of this discontent arose, Forsythe believed, from a widespread misunderstanding of the goals and projects of the modern volunteer army concept. Once they were properly explained, the noncommissioned officers would react positively, he maintained. He went on to declare, and General Westmoreland agreed, that the noncommissioned officers of the U.S. Army had earned a well-deserved pat on the back as well as more visible roles in implementing the Army's transition to the all-volunteer force. Both officers knew that if it were to succeed, it could only do so with their full cooperation. General Haines, the commanding general, CONARC, put it more bluntly when he declared that the all-volunteer concept was headed for failure "unless we can convince our platoon noncommissioned officers that the Army is doing the right thing."[12]

As if to underline his continuing emphasis on noncommissioned professionalism and to assure these men that the modern volunteer army would fully recognize their proper status and role as leaders and teachers of men, General Westmoreland sent a memorandum to all major commanders in May 1971 urging them to grant their noncommissioned men broader authority. Pointing out that the success of any unit depends on its sergeants, he asked all commanders to accord them a larger voice in the operation of their units. Westmoreland listed fourteen specific guidelines for officers to follow in developing the leadership capabilities of noncommissioned officers under their command. Noncommissioned officers throughout the Army immediately hailed these guidelines as "The Noncommissioned Officer's Bill of Rights."[13]

Inasmuch as these fourteen points provided the doctrinal platform on which the MVA was to erect an edifice of noncommissioned professionalism, they are worth repeating here. Officers were urged to:

1. Give NCOs sufficient authority to carry out their assigned responsibilities.
2. Not assign specialists to NCO jobs.
3. Stress the responsibility the NCO has for welfare, training, and morale of personnel. Give him a voice in their assignment, reassignment, promotion, reduction, responsibility, and demonstrated performance.
4. Issue more mission-type orders and fewer detailed instructions.
5. Acknowledge the key role of the NCO by according him privileges commensurate with his position, responsibility, and demonstrated performance.
6. Keep NCOs informed and insist they, in turn, keep their subordinates informed.
7. Recognize outstanding NCO performance, especially at the junior level.
8. Expand the NCO's education through wise counseling and by affording him opportunity to attend NCO academies, NCO refresher courses, and off-duty educational programs.
9. Set high but practical standards of cleanliness, neatness, and readiness, and demand compliance.

10. Make inspections meaningful and practical, not harassment. Note excellent as well as substandard performance.
11. Insist upon economical use of all resources—especially manpower.
12. Avoid excessively early deadlines, just to assure that a unit or project is ready well ahead of time.
13. Supervise but avoid taking over the NCO's job. Counsel him as to the quality of his performance.
14. Initiate appropriate action to replace and reduce those NCOs who consistently demonstrate their inability to maintain proscribed standards of performance or personal conduct.

As significant as they were, these guidelines had been long in appearing, for the need for them had been pointed out rather succinctly five years before, by a veteran commander of World War II.

> It would be a fine thing if the NCO went back to work as such . . . the NCO will develop and flourish only if he is given appropriate responsibility. Over the years too much of that responsibility has been withdrawn, putting the NCO often in a position of a highly paid private. . . . All sorts of effort had been made to increase the prestige of the NCO's—this is a good idea, but it is a goal that will not be reached by building fatter and flossier NCO clubs. It will come only by getting the officer out of the NCO's job and making the NCO do it, by returning some meaning to various grades of NCO and by assigning specialists, not NCOs to jobs inappropriate to the title.[14]

General Westmoreland expected these goals would be accomplished by his recently published guidelines. Unfortunately, they proved in themselves insufficient to attain the goal of a truly professional noncommissioned officer corps. Consequently, Westmoreland's successor, General Creighton W. Abrams, building on his predecessor's work, had to direct his attention to further measures to improve noncommissioned professionalism.

CHAPTER 22

DEFINING THE NONCOMMISSIONED OFFICER'S ROLE

Although noncommissioned officer professionalism has been institutionalized through increasingly centralized selection, training, and promotion procedures for the higher grades, the Army noncommissioned corps continues to be plagued by a legacy of the Vietnam years. This legacy is a frequently widespread practice on the part of platoon and company commanders to squeeze the noncommissioned officers to the sidelines in their concern to win the approbation of their superiors.

By the late 1970s many of these younger officers had become battalion commanders. They and their subordinates continued to perform duties that were more appropriately accomplished by the noncommissioned officers, whose proper role had become increasingly controversial and misunderstood since Korea and during the course of the war in Southeast Asia. The duties of the command sergeant major, for example, had often been determined more by the perception of individual commanders than by approved and widely understood Army doctrine. There was also another aspect of this problem. As had been the case during the Vietnam conflict, age-group identification between junior company officers and junior noncommissioned officers all too frequently continued to disenfranchise senior noncommissioned officers. Furthermore, lines of authority between command sergeants major and 1st sergeants were variously understood and practiced from unit to unit.

This servicewide failure to clearly define the roles of noncommissioned officers frequently resulted in overworked officers (working at the wrong tasks) and underutilized noncommissioned officers. In turn this led to lessened job satisfaction with low morale as well as decreased efficiency on the part of both commissioned and noncommissioned officers.[1]

As with so many events that would eventually have wide repercussions, the decision to reexamine and redefine once and for all the role and status of the noncommissioned officer in the U.S. Army stemmed from a chance observation by the then–Secretary of the Army Martin R. Hoffmann to a group of generals at a meeting in headquarters, TRADOC at Ft. Monroe in December 1975. The secretary observed with some feeling his debt to those senior sergeants who had eased his transition as a young lieutenant from OCS to active duty. His host, TRADOC Commanding General William E. DePuy, acknowledged the usefulness of sergeants to young officers, but went on to point out that the United States Army didn't understand how to use its sergeants major. There were plenty of sergeants major, but the Army had never decided how to best utilize them. This had given rise to a serious morale problem among them.[2]

General DePuy then pointed out that the overwhelming number of captains commanding companies, batteries, or troops in the Army rejected the claim of the sergeant major to any authority at all over unit noncommissioned officers, stating that they were responsible for their units 100 percent of the time and for 100 percent of what they did. Moreover, they refused to yield to any sergeant at battalion, brigade, or division headquarters any authority "with my NCOs." These young captains felt that way because that's what they had been told, DePuy added. Secretary Hoffman replied that he was shocked—indeed shattered—to hear that and that something would have to be done to change that state of affairs.

Once in a while, General DePuy continued, one can find a battalion commander who charges his sergeant major with the maintenance of standards among the noncommissioned officer corps. This, the general declared, is what a sergeant actually does. He doesn't command anybody, for there's only one sergeant in the Army who commands anybody—he's the squad leader or tank commander. What are all the rest there for? DePuy asked rhetorically. Answering his own question, he continued, "They're deputies, like a platoon sergeant; they're assistants to the company commander, like the first sergeant; they're sergeants major. What do we have them there for?"

General DePuy went on to say that it was difficult to explain to company commanders that there are two chains of communication, for "we all know that one chain of command is the final authority," for it has an override over any other so-called chain of communications. Legally only officers have certain authorities, but, he added,

> if there isn't a chain of command, or a chain of something, from the sergeant major down to the first sergeants and platoon sergeants and the squad leader . . . doing all those things you don't want officers to do, then we don't need any sergeants major in the Army. We certainly don't need any ambassadors out with the troops. That's nonsense—the biggest waste of manpower that you can imagine.

From the foregoing it seemed that General DePuy was trying to define what would eventually be designated the noncommissioned officer support channel, but at that time he was uncertain whether the concept of two channels, command and noncommissioned officer, lay "outside the culture of the United States Army or not . . . it may be that American officers by nature and by the customs of our society operate in such a manner that they can't tolerate that system. We know,"

DePuy continued, "that in some units the two channels work marvelously . . . a lot of good sergeants major make it work, and a lot of other sergeants major don't even try." In order to try to illustrate to Secretary Hoffman just how he envisioned the two channels worked, General DePuy described his experience in Vietnam as commander of the 1st Division.

> I explained that I wanted the officers lying awake at night trying to figure out how to fight better, how to run better operations, and I didn't want them wasting their time on the thing that sergeants ought to do. A sergeant in the Army, if he's a squad leader or tank commander, is a commander just like an officer. No difference whatever. It's just the smallest tactical element. If he's a sergeant major or platoon sergeant or a first sergeant, his responsibility is to see to it that the soldiers all do the things they're supposed to do, that are done the same every day, or that they are done exactly the way it had been directed.

Drawing upon a comparison with the building trades, DePuy pointed out that noncommissioned officers were like foremen building a building, they put the wires and the plumbing exactly where the blueprints say they should be. They make the bricklayers always lay the bricks straight and adhere to those standards. As long as they do that, the officer can be cast in the role of the construction engineer or the architect. That's what an officer is paid for.

General DePuy followed up this conversation with a letter to Army Chief of Staff, Fred C. Weyand, dated December 24, 1975. In this letter he developed some of his ideas concerning the role of the sergeant major within the context of the role of the noncommissioned officer—ideas that he had discussed with the secretary—as a basis for a thorough analysis and possible revision of AR 600–20 (Army Command Policy and Procedure).

During the modern volunteer army's early days, General DePuy wrote to the Chief of Staff,

> It was sometimes asserted that the NCO Corps was an obstacle to communications with the soldiers, that is, the junior officers could communicate better. This nearly put the NCO Corps out of the game. An astounding concept—an Army without sergeants. We have come back a long way [referring to the progress made since the end of hostilities in southeast Asia]. We have a long way to go. My personal guess is that we get less than 50% of their potential from our command sergeants major. We could bring that up to 80 or 90% if we are willing to tackle the formidable problem of changing the Army's perception and practice in the use of the NCO line of authority and responsibility.[3]

It is interesting to note that while the secretary of the Army, the Army Chief of Staff, and commanding general, TRADOC wrestled with revisions to AR 600–20 and attempted to redefine the role and status of the sergeant major and of the noncommissioned officer corps, successive USAREUR commanders, such as

General Michael S. Davison and George S. Blanchard, had previously sought to accomplish these tasks with commandwide noncommissioned officer development programs. These rested upon a well-defined and clearly understood role for the command sergeant major, as holding the position on "the right of the line" and as the "vital connection in the Noncommissioned Officer's channel of communication and an advisor to subordinates and superiors."[4]

Meanwhile, in response to General DePuy's suggestion, General Fred C. Weyand directed DCSPER to undertake an examination of the role of the noncommissioned officer in the Army. To do so, DCSPER solicited comments from all MACOMS, selected general officers, and, through the Sergeant Major of the Army, the views of a large number of senior noncommissioned officers.[5]

Not surprisingly, in view of General DePuy's earlier findings, DCSPER found there were "distorted perceptions by both officers and enlisted men concerning the role, duties, and authority of the NCO, and that clarification of his role was necessary." In particular, both junior officers and noncommissioned officers did not fully understand their proper relationship to one another—a chronic problem since World War II.

While there appeared to be general agreement that some revision of AR 600–20 was needed, the views of commanding officers varied widely as to what, if anything, should be included in such a revision. There was a similar diversity of views regarding the command sergeant major's role. In terms of Department of Army policy, it was agreed that his role should be flexibly and broadly defined, inasmuch as his duties and responsibilities ought to be left to the discretion of the commander to whom he was assigned. Moreover, there was no widespread sentiment for a Department of Army–prescribed list of responsibilities for noncommissioned officers.

Taking note of this, the Chief of Staff assured DePuy that while he had his full support for any effort to strengthen noncommissioned officer authority and responsibility, commander in chief, TRADOC should be careful that any policy or doctrinal changes involving the NCO corps "should be accomplished only after careful study and deliberation."

Meanwhile, response to TRADOC/DCSPER's earlier survey concerning the role and status of the noncommissioned officer continued to confirm General DePuy's observation that there was Armywide misunderstanding and confusion not only over the sergeant major's role, but over the role of the noncommissioned officer corps as a whole. Many placed the major part of the blame for this situation upon the officer corps, especially the company-grade officers who generally were characterized within the staff as not really understanding the role of the noncommissioned officer in the Army.[6]

The causes of this misunderstanding were perceived by some to be a failure on the part of the Army's educational system to emphasize the noncommissioned officer's role, a failure on the part of many noncommissioned officers to assert their responsibilities at the company operational level where the officer begins his formative years, and finally a failure on the part of senior officers to remedy this state of affairs that had been increasingly apparent to many since the Korean War.

Others, after canvassing the views of their own noncommissioned officers, determined that while noncommissioned officer authority traditionally derived solely from the commanding officer, the former now perceived the Department of Army as the source of at least a part of his authority since the commanding officer no longer promoted or arbitrarily reduced (at senior grades) noncommissioned officers. This argued for more specific definitions of the noncommissioned duties, responsibilities, and obligations, and for the Department of Army to spell out more clearly the limits of noncommissioned officer authority.

Another aspect of the problem pointed to the earlier-perceived generational or communication gap between senior noncommissioned officers and the very junior enlisted men. This resulted in widespread acceptance by junior officers of the belief that the gap would be better closed by the age proximity of the lieutenant to the junior enlisted man. In turn, this caused a generation of lieutenants, who felt themselves better able to communicate with the soldiers, to cut the senior noncommissioned officer out of the communications channel. By the end of the 1970s these junior officers had become commanders, and, in some instances, junior majors. In their new roles, they continued to harbor the approach to junior enlisted men which they had developed with the advent of the modern volunteer Army. The senior noncommissioned officer sensed this and saw it as a real but almost unidentifiable force, hampering him in the performance of his traditional role. This suggested a real need for the reeducation of the commissioned officer corps in the proper use of the noncommissioned officer.[7]

There also appeared to be a consensus among senior noncommissioned officers that very few battalion, brigade, and division commanders had really analyzed AR 600–20 as it related to the role and function of the command sergeant major in particular, and those of other noncommissioned officers in general. Yet few commanders would admit or acknowledge that they didn't know what to expect from their noncommissioned officers.

On the other hand, there appeared to be some doubt among the noncommissioned officer corps as well as to its proper role and status. While most senior noncommissioned officers probably understood their role, there seemed to be some doubt among them and confusion as to just what authority the command sergeant major and other noncommissioned officers actually had since the advent of the MVA concept in the early 1970s. Since then so many restrictions had been placed upon them in their relations with the soldiers that many noncommissioned officers believed their role had become dormant as to severely diminish their authority in the eyes of the young soldiers.

Among themselves, noncommissioned officers had long recognized a distinct line of authority and communication extending from the sergeant major through the 1st sergeants to platoon sergeants and squad leaders. Yet its distinctness had depended a great deal upon the individual commander and varied from unit to unit. In many instances commanders restricted this line lest it usurp the traditional and only legal chain of command. This was certainly one of the main reasons for the noncommissioned officer corps' difficulty vis-à-vis the commissioned officer.

If the latter recognized and used the noncommissioned line of communication to their own advantage, most noncommissioned officers agreed they would find it of paramount importance in mission accomplishment. But before this recognition could come about, noncommissioned officers believed that greater stress must be placed on understanding the proper role and status of the noncommissioned officer—beginning with the officers' basic course, all the way up to the Army War College.

As might be expected, some of the most perceptive comments on the noncommissioned officer came from one of their number—specifically, the command sergeant major of headquarters, TRADOC, J. F. La Voie. He outlined one of the clearest expressions of the differing role of commissioned and noncommissioned officers by declaring that

> the routine daily business of the Army is noncommissioned officer business, that is to say, execution of established policies and standards pertaining to the performance, training and conduct of enlisted personnel is the responsibility of the Noncommissioned Officer Corps. The establishment of those policies and standards is the responsibility of the officer corps.[8]

Turning to the oft-criticized and frequently neglected AR 600–20, Sergeant Major La Voie observed that it "encourages this utilization of the Noncommissioned Officer but leaves it to each commander to decide how and even if the Noncommissioned Officer is to be allowed or required to meet the responsibility of executing the daily business of the Army." The resulting utilization of noncommissioned officers varied so much from unit to unit that there was perhaps only a 60 to 70 percent Armywide utilization of the noncommissioned officer potential. This 30 to 40 percent loss resulted in the officer corps doing tasks that the NCO corps should be responsible for, with the simultaneous derogation of officer performance and growth, La Voie maintained.

In reviewing the comments of many commanders and their command sergeants major, CSM La Voie had been impressed by the rather close agreement of all concerning the role and function of the noncommissioned officer. Misunderstandings, he found, arose "when it comes to whether the NCO line of authority is, or should be that, or a line of communication." While many commanding officers assigned their CSM (and thereby the noncommissioned officer corps) the responsibility for the performance of the enlisted force, most commanders remained adamant that there is only one command channel that was fully supported by AR 600–20 and that the NCO channel was primarily for communication or exchanging information. Consequently, in practice, responsibility at each level fell usually to the officer corps, with the single exception of the squad leader, who is in the chain of command, and, on special occasions, upon the platoon sergeant when there is no assigned commissioned platoon leader.

What was needed, CSM LA Voie wrote, was a doctrine formalizing and legalizing noncommissioned officer responsibilities to the commanding officers of those command sergeants major who did not understand or were reluctant to require the noncommissioned officer corps to execute its rightful responsibilities. This doctrinal change, La Voie continued, could be accomplished by changing AR 600–20 so that the "NCO line of responsibility and authority is defined and commanders [are] required to use it." If past Army experience was an example, it would take more than doctrinal change to affect individual behavior, because Army doctrine, like church doctrine, was sometimes more honored in the breach than in the observance.

CSM La Voie concluded his comments with a recommendation for changes or revisions to AR 600–20. Although as TRADOC CSM La Voie carried considerable weight, there were other voices, namely those of the staff and faculty at the Command and General Staff College (C&GSC) at Ft. Leavenworth, that carried even more weight. Their review of the role and status of the noncommissioned officer led them to conclude "that AR 600–20 probably does not need revision." Their conclusion stemmed from responses from command sergeants major who expressed their acceptance of the disputed AR 600–20 and an understanding of their role as outlined therein. The staff at C&GSC also claimed to have a found a "great similarity between major command local interpretations of the role of the CSM." Of these C&GSC planned to issue the USAREUR version to support resident instruction on this subject during the academic year 1976–1977.[9]

As was to be expected, the uniformed academicians at the U.S. Military Academy at West Point approached the analysis of the noncommissioned officer's role in a somewhat different manner than had the faculty at the Command and General Staff College at Ft. Leavenworth. First of all, in the opinion of the West Point faculty, the command sergeant major was not to be considered as the direct counterpart of the British army's sergeant major. Rather, he should be regarded as "a role model and goal for noncommissioned officers, and a boundary role personality between the commissioned and noncommissioned officers."[10]

In the opinion of the West Point faculty, the CSM, in this latter role, performed several significant tasks:

> As a coding and filtering agent; acting almost as a translator between the officer and enlisted soldier . . . he filters, interprets, and passes on information from the commander along a path parallel to the channels of command [this was the first suggestion of a legitimate, parallel relationship between the chain of command and the NCO channels].

The academic faculty further saw the CSM as representing the noncommissioned officer establishment to the commissioned officer and, in some cases, to society at large. He might also function as a buffer between the two estates, "absorbing, deflecting, and protecting the enlisted chain of information and responsibility from the transient impulses of the commanding officer, and often blocking disruptive energy from below before it troubles the commander."

Yet in the eyes of the academy faculty, there were several shortcomings perceived in these roles. First among them was that "the very presumption of a need for an agent at the boundary [between commissioned and noncommissioned estates] may in some cases serve to widen that gap." It seemed doubtful, the academy response continued, "that any device which created or dramatized such a gap might be more destructive in the long run than a simple dialogue between the commander and his soldiers . . . not his officers and enlisted—a gap that does not reflect parallel distinction in the societal base [of the Army]." Further, the assumed parallel lines of information flow—battalion to company commander to platoon leader to platoon sergeant to squad leader, and command sergeant major to 1st sergeant to squad leader—were superfluous and counterproductive, for any increase in the number of exchanges of information from one recipient to another was seen as merely increasing the number of opportunities for confusion and misinterpretation. Clarity would best be served by a reduction, not an increase, in the number of transactions. In combat a CSM "with undefined or arbitrary and perhaps maladaptive duties at the boundaries [of this gap] might sow confusion where he would be expected to reap order and efficiency." Nevertheless, the faculty concluded, for all its shortcomings the "present CSM program while it has developed through the influences of increasingly divergent tradition and social/organization reality . . . is probably still institutionally desirable, and should be retained."

This renewed focus in the late 1970s on the role of the noncommissioned officer in the Army disclosed that unless good intentions were followed up by concrete behavioral change on the part of both commissioned and noncommissioned officers, the problem of obtaining servicewide agreements as to the role of the noncommissioned officer would continue to plague the Army. Despite the fact that since the Korean War the Army had launched numerous programs designed to enhance the prestige of the noncommissioned officer, each program for a number of reasons had more or less failed to achieve its goal.

The single most important reason seemed to be that the commissioned and noncommissioned officer corps had failed to follow with behavioral changes the ideas that had been adopted in directives or verbally. Any change in the noncommissioned officers' role and status had to have the commitment of all concerned, and such commitment had to be accompanied by identifiable behavioral change.

But such change required support at the highest levels of the Army. TRADOC commanding general William DePuy initiated a servicewide review of the noncommissioned officers' role, but this review only served to disclose widely differing opinions and slight consensus. If the high command truly intended to redefine the noncommissioned officer's role, it would have to accept certain risks in the endeavor. Senior commanders would have to display enough trust in their senior noncommissioned officers as to indicate that they were willing to accept responsibility and accountability for the noncommissioned officers' performance of clearly specified duties. This did not mean, however, that commanders should abrogate their ultimate responsibility, but rather that they be willing to delegate to their noncommissioned officers the authority to undertake certain actions. Yet few commanders indicated their willingness to do so.

Commitment on the part of commanders to eliminating instances of officers performing noncommissioned officers' jobs involved considerable reorganization and abolition of a significant number of officer jobs. This would have provided noncommissioned officers with a large increase in responsible tasks, together with an increase in status and prestige arising from their accountability for these tasks. This could have accomplished more in the way of constructive change than a myriad of publications extolling such a need. In effect, what seemed to be needed was not only a redefinition of the noncommissioned role, but some redefining of the commander's job as well.

As for the role of the command sergeant major, nearly all respondents to TRADOC's original questionnaire commented that the sergeant major's role was not clearly enough defined. Instead, it had more or less variously evolved as a result of the interaction between each commanding officer and his sergeant major. This had raised a fundamental question whether the Army could afford to leave almost totally undefined the role of its senior noncommissioned officers. If so, this in turn raised the question as to the need for such a position. However, rather than eliminate the grade, it seemed that the wiser course of action would be to prescribe certain tasks and responsibilities for the command sergeant major. This would assure all sergeants major of a modicum of critical tasks to perform, and yet in no way prevent individual commanders from delegating accountability to their sergeants major beyond these limits. The commanding general, TRADOC, therefore, recommended that the Sergeant Major of the Army develop guidance regarding the framework of these tasks, and that such guidance also be applied throughout the service school system for commissioned as well as noncommissioned officers.[11]

General DePuy also regarded the introduction of the soldier's manuals and the SQTs at the same time the Army was reexamining the role of the noncommissioned officer as fortuitous. In his eyes, a noncommissioned officer's central role was that of a first-line supervisor. As such, General DePuy wrote, the noncommissioned officer had two responsibilities: the first, "to accomplish an assigned group of collective missions as, for instance, those given to squad, tank crew, or artillery sections"; the second, "to supervise the training of the individual soldiers in that squad, section, or crew." This task, he concluded, "should be almost an exclusive responsibility of the first-line supervisors under the direction of and with the support of platoon sergeants, first sergeants, and command sergeants major."

The time had come, DePuy continued, "to put the noncommissioned officer corps back to work on its vital responsibility for training young soldiers, and to do so clearly and unequivocally. The time is right because we can now (thanks to CMF and NCOES) define soldier jobs and tell noncommissioned officers what standards to apply to performance, and where to find the wherewithal for training." The tools needed for this mission, DePuy believed, were the soldier's manuals and the skill qualifications tests. In his opinion, they provided a training program for soldiers, conducted by the thousands of intervals of time available. It was, General DePuy insisted, "a training program tailored for NCO's." He did not, however, underestimate the difficulty of bringing either officers or NCOs to accept this division of labor. This involved "a cultural change in the army" that could not be solved by issuing a peremptory order from the Department of the Army, TRADOC, or FORSCOM. Acceptance of these roles for the noncommissioned officer would, DePuy observed, entail an educational process.

There was another aspect of the noncommissioned officer's duties that General DePuy had failed to mention. That was as exemplar or role model for the junior enlisted men. As such, noncommissioned officers had a moral as well as a technical responsibility for their men.

It was against this background of servicewide discussion and analysis that the commanding general, TRADOC, tasked the commandant of the sergeants major academy at Ft. Bliss "to develop a course of instruction for officer and NCO service schools at all levels teaching the duties, responsibilities, and authorities of the NCO and the interplay and relationship of these duties, responsibilities and authorities of officers that make for mission accomplishment, readiness, and team play." At the same time the sergeants major academy was to formulate appropriate Army doctrine on the duties and responsibilities of the noncommissioned officer. The academy's task was to be completed in mid-1977.[12]

By June 1977 the Sergeants Major Academy Task Force, set up to complete the project, had produced a draft FM 22–600–20 that included a block of instruction relating to commissioned and noncommissioned officers and their relationship to one another. Entitled *The Duties, Responsibilities, and Authority of NCO's and the Interplay and Relationship with the Duties Responsibilities and Authority of Officers—Doctrine and Methodology*, this field manual was to be used to teach both groups at the Army service schools. The commandant of the sergeants major academy sent copies of the completed draft for comment to the Armor, Infantry, Ft. Lee, and Ft. Leavenworth schools. While noncommissioned officers at the schools were generally impressed with the draft, the faculty at Ft. Leavenworth, as they had earlier, continued to question the need for such material.

In spite of the Command and General Staff College's and the Combined Arms Center's poor reception of the draft FM 22–600–20, General DePuy was pleased with it and directed that the doctrine and methodology associated with it be taught in all service schools as well as the basic and advanced noncommissioned officers course, including the sergeants major academy. The commanding general, TRADOC also directed that the field manual be printed and distributed to the field by Christmas 1977. He was confident, he observed, that the new doctrine would be accepted and would result in a more effective army. Shortly after taking this action, General DePuy retired.[13]

Unfortunately for DePuy's expectations, with his retirement the project passed into other, less receptive, hands. When a copy of the draft FM 22–600–20 reached General Edward C. Meyer, then DCSOPS (Deputy Chief of Staff Operations), he reviewed and commented adversely upon it before passing it on to Chief of Staff General Bernard W. Rogers. Apparently neither General Rogers nor Meyer thought that the manual, as then drafted, was suitable for the use of new corporal or sergeant. They had something less detailed and far more basic in mind than had General DePuy.[14]

The Sergeants Major Academy Task Force, set in motion by General DePuy's verbal instructions to the academy commandant, included a detailed study of the historical roots of the relationship between commissioned and noncommissioned officers in the United States Army. Acknowledging that in the republic's early years the distinction between the two groups had rested largely upon the fact that the former were drawn from the propertied classes of colonial American society and the latter from the rural yeomanry and town craftsmen, the draft went on the observation that this had been an outgrowth of the eighteenth-century English class system. The founding fathers who had drawn up the Constitution of the United States retained this class idea in terms of commissions or appointments by the president for the avowed purpose of allowing the propertied class to maintain its traditional influence over the Army. With the passage of time, however, a more practical reason for presidential commissioning of officers had emerged. This had established a legal basis for the president of the United States to appoint and have direct control over qualified people to act as his legal agents and to assist him in carrying out his duties as commander in chief of the nation's armed forces. Since then the class-based idea of possession of property as a qualification for commissioned officers had become irrelevant, but a requirement for a high degree of education and literacy continued.[15]

Another continuing tradition was the commissioned officers' "direct relationship" with the president—the chief executive. It is this direct tie with the president, as commander in chief, that since the adoption of the Constitution has been the basis of the commissioned officer's legal authority, his power to exercise command, as well as his position within the military hierarchy of rank that gives him authority over both warrant and noncommissioned officers.

On the other hand, senior noncommissioned officers are selected and promoted by Department of Army boards divided between commissioned and noncommissioned officers. E-5s and E-6s are promoted by boards composed exclusively of other noncommissioned officers. Promoted from the ranks, all noncommissioned officers are charged with duties that assist and complement the officer's in the discharge of their own, a relationship somewhat analogous to that of the commissioned officer to the president. From this relationship is derived, in large measure, the basis for the noncommissioned officers' own legal authority.

By means of this outline—together with further analysis—the academy's task force hoped to provide an analytical methodology and thought process that could be used "at all levels within the Army to assist in proper assignment of tasks to officers and noncommissioned officers, to superiors and subordinates . . . related to and complemented by the requirement for proficiency in the skills identified in the TRADOC effectiveness model for military personnel."

Unfortunately, as already indicated, this analysis proved to be far more detailed than the Army Chief of Staff had had in mind for a revision of AR 600–20. While this draft had been intellectually stimulating to students at the sergeants major academy and other service schools, it was, General Meyer believed, more than a newly minted sergeant (E-5) could handle or find immediately useful. It was hardly something that he would carry with him for handy reference as he went about his daily duties. The draft document nevertheless represented a significant attempt to analyze and understand the relationship between commissioned and noncommissioned officers in the U.S. Army.

In a letter to General Donn A. Starry, who had succeeded DePuy as commanding general, TRADOC, the Chief of Staff expressed his own thoughts concerning the draft field manual. It was, first of all, Rogers observed, "pitched at a theoretical level which some of our NCOs, particularly the more junior ones, may not fully comprehend." The manual, Rogers added, "should contain practical information"—implying that the original draft had not done so—such as explaining facets of a sergeant's job that may not be clear to him. Rogers wanted a new training manual that would become the dog-eared reference book that the 1st sergeant hands to the newly appointed corporal or sergeant.[16]

In sharp contrast with DePuy when he had launched the projects to prepare a draft TM 22–600–20, Rogers had very definite ideas about what he wanted the field manual to do and to what level of professionalism it should be directed. Needless to say, many of these ideas were at variance with those of General DePuy. For example, General Rogers seemed reluctant to give the noncommissioned officers in his staff much authority to screen "special category" messages for him, although as it turned out, he eventually had to allow them to do it, since it was too time-consuming for him.[17]

The essence of what the Army Chief of Staff and the DCSOPS had in mind for the manual was perhaps best expressed in the following guidelines that the Chief of Staff, in a letter of December 28, 1978, presented to the new commanding general, TRADOC, General Starry. These, General Rogers wrote, were points that must guide the manual's final form.

> The manual's primary purpose is to provide Noncommissioned Officers with a practical reference book and performance guide regarding their legal and inherent duties, responsibilities, and authority. . . .
>
> Pitch the document to all Noncommissioned Officers, but give particular emphasis to the junior grades (E-5 and E-6).
>
> Flavor the manual in a positive, practical, down-to-earth tone . . . avoid discussion of theoretical concepts, except where necessary to explain a practical technique for performance of duties.

Specify and explain the NCO's broad responsibilities and authority in both a legal and traditional sense. Discuss the NCO's role and responsibilities as a leader, counselor, trainer, supervisor, and manager.

Provide guidance and standards to the NCO pertaining to individual training, soldier welfare, the maintenance of equipment, and other specific duties. (Consider providing special guidance to the NCO who finds himself in unique roles, such as a Drill Sergeant or instructor in a training center.)

Discuss the relationships between NCO's and soldiers. Avoid lengthy discussions of what officers should and should not do. [This had been particularly troubling to the Ft. Leavenworth faculty.]

Discuss the NCO's moral and ethical responsibilities to his country, his commanders and his subordinates.

Provide practical tips to the NCO in carrying out troop leading functions as well as performing effectively in organizations.

Provide some assistance to the NCO in dealing with complex matters of race relations and women in the Army.

Provide advice for professional development.[18]

Although at that time General Rogers expressed the hope that the manual would be printed within six or seven months, it was not published until March 1980—almost two years later. That a field manual of such significance—seeking as it did to delineate the role and status of the noncommissioned officer and his relationship to the commissioned officer—required an additional two years before its publication (four years from inception) suggests that even at that late date the Army was not yet of one mind on the role and status of the noncommissioned officer. Therein lies a tale of differing concepts and philosophies of command that divided the officer corps until well into the 1980s, with adverse consequences for Army operational readiness.

The version of FM 22–600–20 that finally emerged in March 1980 was a fifty-two-page document as opposed to the eighty-nine-page manuscript draft prepared by the task force at the sergeants major academy. Reflecting mainly the views of General Rogers and General Meyer rather than those of DePuy and the academy, FM 22–600–20 nevertheless retained some guidelines that appeared in the original draft.[19]

One of the key elements of the commissioned and noncommissioned officer relationship brought out in the earlier academy draft and retained in the published version was a clear explanation of the relationship between the commissioned officer chain of command and the noncommissioned officer support channel. There is, FM 22–600–20 pointed out, but one chain of command in the Army, however,

> it is paralleled and reinforced by the noncommissioned officer support channel. Both are channels of communication used to pass information through the unit [from commanding officer to squad leader]. Neither, however, is a one way street; nor are the two entirely separate. For in order for the chain of command to function, the noncommissioned officer support channel must be operating. Officers and noncommissioned officers must work together to accomplish the unit's mission in peace and war.

Prior to the December 20, 1976, interim change to AR 600–20, the noncommissioned officer support channel had been considered as only an informal communications channel. The change as outlined in FM–22–600–20, not only formalized this channel, but further expanded its functions, making it directive in nature within established command policies and directives. This seems to have been FM 22–600–20's most significant doctrinal contribution.

ORIGINS OF THE NONCOMMISSIONED OFFICERS DEVELOPMENT PROGRAM (NCODP)

While this doctrine was taking shape, other elements of the Army staff had been concerned with improving the process of leader development both among the commissioned and noncommissioned officers. For the latter this concern was focused upon assuring the noncommissioned officer opportunities to put into practice, through on-the-job experience, those skills he had acquired through BNCOC and ANCOC to further enhance his particular career skills.

In 1975, even as General DePuy was developing his concepts for the noncommissioned officer guide, the deputy chief of staff for personnel (DCSPER) tasked the U.S. Army Administration Center (ADMINCEN) "to develop a single leadership model to provide for progressive leadership instruction, identity, and include leadership training requirements from precommissioning to senior staff college levels." Although this had been focused upon commissioned officer training, the conclusions arrived at ultimately laid the groundwork for change in noncommissioned officer development as well. The leader-development plan model that eventually emerged from ADMINCEN served to demonstrate that leader development occurred as "a result of the systematic interaction of four primary components: motivation (attitudes), skills, knowledge, and opportunity."[20]

While the Army's service schools provided leaders with "a base for development of the requisite skills and knowledge necessary to perform effectively in future assignments," the model demonstrated that "such skill and knowledge were not the exclusive purview of the Army school system." Unit commanders, therefore, were responsible not only for on-the-job training (OJT) but also for assuring that their subordinates, both commissioned and noncommissioned, were afforded opportunities to apply skills acquired either through the formal school system or through on-the-job training in the performance of unit missions. A breakdown of these latter two components—manifested through inadequate skills and knowledge or through lack of opportunity—could adversely affect attitudes and commitment on the part of all junior leaders, including noncommissioned officers. Although the service schools were acknowledged to have an essential role, the ADMINCEN study determined that "organizational climate in units ultimately determines the effectiveness of leader development."

There were two reasons for this: the first, the greater part of a soldier's career is spent in a unit rather than in a school; second, unit commanders have traditionally had responsibility for the development and practical application of leadership skills among their subordinates. Only unit commanders through assignment and utilization of personnel could provide opportunities to their subordinates—either commissioned or noncommissioned—for continued leadership development through on-the-job experience. Skills learned in the classroom must be followed by support and reinforcement through the chain of command, if they were to be retained by the individual. The study concluded that "motivated leaders, provided with appropriate skills and knowledge *and* afforded opportunities to practice them are likely to experience self-improvement and leadership development."*

Undoubtedly the concept of a leader development model, which embraced leadership training from noncommissioned officers to general officers, and earlier plans, such as General Davison's noncommissioned officer professionalism program, as well as General Blanchard's "Sergeant Morales Club" for noncommissioned officers in USAREUR, served as background for the concept of a professional development for Army noncommissioned officers as now adopted by Army Chief of Staff General Edward C. Meyer. In December 1979 Meyer tasked his newly appointed Sergeant Major of the Army, William A. Connelly, "to initiate and coordinate a positive, timely, and effective professional development program for Army noncommissioned officers."[21]

This program's ultimate purpose was, as had been General Davison's earlier NCOPP, "to increase Army combat readiness by strengthening the NCO through improved professionalism, prestige, responsibility, and potential." Unit development, responsive to unit needs, was to be the focus of the new program. By focusing on the unit, the program drew upon the findings of the ADMINCEN's earlier conceptual Leader Development Study and Plan that, in turn, emphasized Army tradition that placed responsibility for noncommissioned officer development in the unit commander's hands.

On the other hand, the program also established servicewide policy for the administration of unit programs for noncommissioned officer professional development by placing the entire program on the foundations created by the enlisted personnel-management system (EPMS) and the noncommissioned officer educational system (NCOES). This latter proviso assured that Armywide management of noncommissioned officer careers was not jettisoned as the focus of noncommissioned officer training now shifted back to the unit. For unlike USAREUR's earlier programs, the Chief of Staff's concept transferred overall responsibility from DCSPER to DCSOPS. Furthermore, as had been the case with the CSM of USAREUR, the Sergeant Major of the Army monitored, advised, and assisted DCSOPS in the establishment of the noncommissioned officer development program. The Sergeant Major of the Army also chaired, as had CSM USAREUR, an advisory board of senior noncommissioned officers representing the Army in the field. This board met periodically to review the program's progress.

*Emphasis added.

By April 1980, DCSOPS together with the SMA had prepared a draft of a new Army Regulation 350–17, which outlined the noncommissioned officer development plan (NCODP) in response to Chief of Staff's charge to DCSOPS and the SMA in 1979. Following study, revision, and approval by General Meyer on October 3, 1980, the regulation was published and distributed to the service on December 1. Not surprisingly, the new regulation incorporated the Chief of Staff's charge to SMA Connelly, "to monitor the program and to advise and assist the Deputy Chief of Staff for Operations (DCSOPS) in the program's implementation."[22]

This provision, as were several others, was so similar to General Davison's NCOPP as to establish the latter as a legitimate forerunner of the Chief of Staff's concept for the Armywide NCODP. However, AR 350–17 went beyond Davison's earlier directive in assigning to the SMA a key role in the implementation of the noncommissioned officer development program. He was, for example, to act "as the focal point for required DA NCODP actions which do not otherwise define themselves by functional staff responsibility." The SMA would likewise serve as the "focal point for all Headquarters, Department of the Army, agencies and their field operating agencies on decisions which impact upon noncommissioned officer development and NCODP policies." Finally, the SMA was to submit to the Chief of Staff an annual report "on the state of the Army's NCO Corps," including "an assessment of the implementation of NCODP in the major army commands (MACOMS), the Army National Guard (ARNG), and the U.S. Army Reserve (USAR)."

Most significantly, the NCODP complemented but did not supplant the enlisted personnel management system and the noncommissioned officer education system (NCOES). NCODP therefore represented a program that enabled the noncommissioned officer to put into practical application in his own unit the schooling and skills acquired through EPMS and NCOES. It would be this "doing" phase of noncommissioned officer training that would, General Meyer expected, enable "soldiers to achieve their goal of becoming a truly professional noncommissioned officer."

A former SMA has observed that the NCODP (AR 350–17) both complemented and supplemented NCOES right on up through the sergeants major academy. The new regulation directed unit commanders to support NCOES by assigning their best men to attend the appropriate courses at the right time in their careers. They would, of course, be assisted in this endeavor through the enlisted personnel-management system. Furthermore, NCODP had removed NCOES from DCSPER and placed it under DCSOPS since it was, after all, a training program. Under the latter staff agency the several noncommissioned officer training programs were pulled together. This would prevent such abuses as allowing sergeants to attend a noncommissioned officer academy several times simply because the local unit commander had to send someone he believed could pass the course, or someone whom he could spare at the time. Henceforth, NCODP would encourage unit commanders to insist that the noncommissioned officer considered best qualified attended either the sergeants major academy or the 1st sergeant's course. It was expected this would put an end to the permissiveness that too often had allowed senior noncommissioned officers to decline opportunities to attend these schools. However, until such schooling had been made a prerequisite for promotion, even AR 350–17 could not put teeth into this requirement. Only a stringent application of EPMS and NCOES as career-management tools for those staff divisions responsible for noncommissioned officer careers could do this.[23]

As the 1970s came to an end, it seemed as if the Army now had in place all the structural, institutional, and doctrinal programs needed to produce the quantity and quality of noncommissioned officers needed for the modern volunteer Army. Yet there remained some unresolved problems. Eventually these would come to the attention of the Senate Armed Services Committee, which had instructed the General Accounting Office to make a review of U.S. Army training to determine whether the noncommissioned officers were indeed fulfilling their role as trainers of soldiers, as outlined in FM 22–600–20.

UNRESOLVED PROBLEMS

Despite servicewide career management for the upper enlisted grades, and such features as FM 22–600–20, NCOES, and the command-sponsored NCODP, the goals of proper utilization of noncommissioned officers and their fulfillment of the highest professional standards seemed, at the beginning of the 1980s, to have been only partially realized. Concern over this shortfall found expression in the press and eventually aroused the interest of Congress—particularly that of Senator Sam Nunn of Georgia, chairman of the Subcommittee on Manpower and Personnel of the Senate Committee on the Armed Services.[24]

The Senate Armed Services Committee was especially concerned about "the loss of a large number of quality NCO's from the services"* for the long-recognized technological revolutions within the armed services had brought in their train increased competition with industry for qualified men and women. Consequently many highly trained noncommissioned officers were leaving the services for well-paying civilian jobs, mainly in highly skilled technical areas. In turn, this raised an additional concern whether those noncommissioned officers who remained in service were of the same quality level as those leaving. Focusing upon this latter concern, Senator Nunn requested the General Accounting Office to make a trend analysis of each service in order to find an answer to this question.

For the purpose of its study, the GAO directed its attention to fiscal years 1977–1979. Interestingly, none of the services had any means of determining the relative quality difference between reenlistment eligibles who reenlist or separate. Once it was determined that a noncommissioned officer was eligible to reenlist, that individual was considered to be fully qualified.

*Although the Armed Services Committee was interested in all four services the focus of the following discussion is on the Army.

For each of the three years analyzed, the General Accounting Office study determined that the group leaving the military service had a larger proportion of mental category I and II personnel than did the group remaining. While consistent, this quality gap was found to be relatively small—in most cases, 5 percent or less. In the Army, the differences were determined to be greater among those leaving with less than five years of service, but less among those noncommissioned officers leaving with five to ten years of service.

Summing up its findings, the GAO reported that although more noncommissioned officers with higher mental aptitudes were then leaving the service than remaining, there was little difference in the educational levels of those leaving and those reenlisting. Furthermore, those staying were generally of the slightly higher pay grades than those leaving. In the opinion of the GAO, these relatively minor differences were not of such magnitude as to justify further analysis of the relative quality issue, and therefore the committee's initial question was not considered as serious as first believed.

EVALUATING THE NONCOMMISSIONED OFFICER AS TRAINER

Of far greater impact upon the role and status of noncommissioned officers had been the Army's decision in the mid-1970s to change its skill-training philosophy for individual soldiers. Anxious to reduce the cost of formal schooling for MOS training and at the same time make the training programs more specific, the Army shifted its emphasis from the formal school environment to the operating unit and designated specific tasks to be trained for at each level. Consequently, to the present day most training now takes place at the unit level where the noncommissioned officer functions as the primary trainer of the individual soldier. In 1980–1981, the effectiveness of such training became the subject of yet another General Accounting Office study prepared at the request of Congress.[25]

To accomplish this review the General Accounting Office studied training at ten active units in the continental United States and five in Europe and administered questionnaires to more than 6,300 soldiers throughout the Army.

Prior to 1977, individual training in the Army had been poorly defined. Soldiers had acquired their skill training within a general framework at one of the Army's advanced individual training (AIT) schools. Thereafter, upon assignment to a unit, they were trained in those tasks deemed critical by their noncommissioned officers. During the training, there was no assurance that the soldiers having the same job would be trained in the same tasks.*

*This had been a chronic problem in the Army. However, in some instances it led to the individual soldier receiving valuable on-the-job training in a number of diverse fields—medical, signal, law enforcement. These often enhanced the soldier's overall knowledge of the Army, thus giving him the self-confidence acquired through the mastering of a variety of complicated tasks.

In 1977, however, General DePuy, then commanding general of TRADOC, had implemented the skill qualification test (SQT) based upon the soldier's manual concept. In this manual the critical tasks for each military occupational specialty (MOS) as well as the performance conditions and standards for each of the tasks were listed. A companion document, the commander's manual, designed for use by unit commanders and noncommissioned officers, had also been prepared by TRADOC schools. The latter manual listed each task shown in the soldier's manual and designated who, school or unit personnel, was responsible for providing the needed training. Actually, the majority of the individual job training under this concept was the responsibility of the unit. The purpose of the General Accounting Office review, therefore, was to determine how effectively the unit was providing this training.

After making its review of Army training, the General Accounting Office investigators concluded that although the soldier's manual had provided "the most specific and probably the best training guidance ever developed by the Army," many soldiers had not received the unit training that would enable them to perform all tasks the Army considered critical for proper job performance and survival in combat, and that unit commanders themselves considered critical to mission accomplishment. The results of a questionnaire used by GAO disclosed that 54 percent of noncommissioned officers believed that less than half of the soldiers they supervised were "adequately trained for combat duty in their military occupational specialty (MOS)." Furthermore, at each of the forty-three companies/batteries visited, the GAO inspectors asked soldiers to tell whether they could perform each of the tasks in their soldier's manual. Their replies showed that the soldiers could not perform "a significant number of the tasks the army considered critical for proper job performance." At the squad and section level the GAO study disclosed that "soldiers were not being trained in all Soldiers Manual tasks considered critical for their MOS."

Detailed review of fifteen units confirmed this finding. Soldiers questioned stated that neither their noncommissioned officers nor officers had "implemented training programs to provide soldier training in all occupational and combat tasks." Noncommissioned officers and commanding officers of units visited added that there was "no incentive at the battalion or company level to emphasize individual skill training in all the Soldiers Manual tasks." They also believed that higher headquarters placed no "emphasis on individual training in all Soldiers Manual tasks," and that commanders generally were not evaluated on the effectiveness of individual training programs. In turn, this had created a perception that individual training was less important than other unit activities.

Despite the adoption by the Army in April 1977 of the TRADOC-initiated skill qualification test (SQT) with accompanying soldier's manual as a means of measuring individual proficiency in MOS tasks and to determine eligibility for promotion, many officers and noncommissioned officers had chosen not to use it. One of the reasons for this situation may have been growing criticism of the SQT program from field commanders, Congress, and the General Accounting Office.[26]

Unlike the old military occupational specialty (MOS) test system that was a written examination, an SQT, in addition to a written test, also required a soldier to actually demonstrate that he could perform selected MOS tasks. However, fewer than 20 percent of the noncommissioned officers at the units inspected by the GAO teams said they used SQT results to determine those tasks that required additional training. Throughout the Army only 23.9 percent of the noncommissioned officers said that they used the SQT result to determine training needs.*

Not only were many noncommissioned officers failing to properly employ the SQTs for individual training, but inspections of several FORSCOM units by GAO also disclosed that in many instances noncommissioned officers were not properly supervising their men; poor weapons maintenance was widespread; soldiers were found loitering in post facilities and wandering around the installation during duty hours; and noncommissioned officers were not making use of available time for what GAO described as "opportunity training"—that is, to make use of all nonscheduled time for training purposes.

General Accounting Office investigators determined that one reason opportunity training was not fully utilized and perhaps why scheduled training classes were frequently canceled, was that many noncommissioned officers did not feel themselves qualified to teach all MOS tasks. Yet the recently published *Noncommissioned Officers Guide*, FM 22–600–20, urged all noncommissioned officers "to study Field and Technical manuals, practice tasks set forth in Soldiers Manuals and in Army Training and Evaluation Programs."[27]

Nevertheless, throughout the Army only 35 percent of the noncommissioned officers indicated that they felt themselves to be qualified to teach all the tasks in their own MOS. This fact reduced the incentive of many noncommissioned officers to make use of "opportunity time" and contributed to a widespread indifference toward individual training at the unit level, in spite of the fact that Army doctrine stated that the noncommissioned officer's duties "as a trainer must be high on the list of things [the noncommissioned officer] needs to be able to do very, very, well."[28] Clearly, in spite of all servicewide programs for noncommissioned officer development there seemed to be a lack of an adequate number of experienced and qualified noncommissioned officers to serve as trainers.

The reasons for the first were determined to be low pay, the declining value of Army benefits, decreasing standards of discipline, the low quality of many re-

*While there was considerable praise for the SQT, many soldiers criticized it as neither an adequate measure of skill nor a realistic indicator of performance. One noncommissioned officer complained that in his MOS—71L Administrative Supervisor—one was tested over such a broad spectrum that "the only way you could prepare was to study a shelffull of regulations." Many noncommissioned officers spent a great deal of time doing just that, thereby becoming proficient at test-taking in fields where they lacked practical experience in applying the theory they had learned.

cruits, and the Army's rotation system—personnel turbulence in most units. As for the second reason, more than 25 percent of the "trainers" had not attended an Army leadership school, and only 39 percent had attended the battalion training management system workshops, established in February 1979 and designed to reemphasize the importance of individual skill training and provide basic assistance to commissioned and noncommissioned officers in conducting this training. Furthermore, a GAO servicewide questionnaire had disclosed that 39 percent of the noncommissioned officers were not receiving training in their MOS tasks, and 35 percent stated that they did not feel qualified to teach all of these tasks to their subordinates.

From the foregoing it was evident that the Army had not yet fully evaluated the effect of the change in the mid-1970s from a school-oriented to a unit-oriented approach to individual training. Such an evaluation, however, was needed to determine this change's impact on the noncommissioned officers' capability to train individual soldiers, and whether it would be more effective to continue skill training at the unit level or to provide the soldier more formal skill training at a school prior to being assigned to a unit.

An attempt to make such an evaluation was made in mid–1979 when the Department of Army inspector general's office established a training-management inspection division to conduct servicewide inspections of training. The first major inspections by this division took place in late 1979 and early 1980, and the results were presented to the Army Chief of Staff in mid-1980. The GAO review, however, found that this system was not adequate for a proper evaluation.

All General Accounting Office reviews continued to reinforce the fact that the properly qualified noncommissioned officer remained the key to effective individual training, which was acknowledged to begin at the lowest supervisory level—the squad leader. Unfortunately, the GAO inspectors found that many of these junior noncommissioned officers were unable to perform some of the tasks for which they were responsible. Because many unit commanders were well aware of this situation, they failed to hold them responsible for many of the training management principles taught in the workshops. In both instances the end results were similar—training principles were being formally taught, but many soldiers were not being trained according to them.

When GAO brought this matter to the attention of the Department of Army, the acting assistant secretary for manpower and reserve affairs acknowledged that while the Army was aware that "sufficiently qualified noncommissioned officers [were] critical to the success of the individual training effort," it faced severe shortages of such men in the combat MOSs. To help remedy this situation the Chief of Staff, General Meyer, directed in September 1980, "a crossleveling [shifting] of noncommissioned officers between Europe and CONUS that should provide some improvement in strength for CONUS-based units." Furthermore, the Army believed that recently approved promotion policies for the junior-level noncommissioned officer grades should provide more of the needed noncommissioned officers; this in spite of the fact that the GAO report indicated that the problem lay not with numbers but with a lack of properly trained noncommissioned officers. However, the Army believed that the expanding noncommissioned officers' educational system (NCOES) would eventually improve noncommissioned officer professionalism, and the recent servicewide noncommissioned officer development program (NCODP), initiated by General Meyer would "provide the basis for better noncommissioned officer professional development in units."[29]

FUTURE DIRECTIONS

Even as the Army sought by means of FM 20–600–20 to codify the duties of the noncommissioned officer and his relationship with the commissioned officer, as exemplified in the parallel chain of command and the noncommissioned officer support channel, the traditional two-class system—commissioned and enlisted—came under critical scrutiny.[30] Although such analysis did not do so, it could have drawn upon historical experience. In the fifteenth- and sixteenth-century military organizations in Europe, there had been, as we saw in Part I, originally no distinction made between commissioned and noncommissioned categories. All ranks represented ascending stages in an organized hierarchy. The tradition of dividing the hierarchy of rank into two classes or two estates—commissioned and noncommissioned—developed gradually during the seventeenth century as European monarchs, seeking to bind their often defiant nobility more closely to the crown, reserved for them the higher ranks in their armed forces. Thus, the two-class system became an integral part of European military organizations and eventually was exported to the United States of America.*

In time, however, rationales were developed in support of the system other than the historical one—namely to bind the noble, or propertied, classes more closely to the throne or to give them control of the armed forces as in Britain. Professor Richard Rosser has drawn attention to four of them. The first is that the system "has withstood the test of time"; the second, that it is needed "to maintain standards of authority and discipline"; the third, it "represents functional differences" and "differences in class, education, skill, and experience"; and finally "the separation is necessary because special awards and privileges must be offered to get competent people to join the military—specifically, to get officers."[31]

After dismissing each of these rationales as being no longer relevant for a twentieth-century military force, Rosser proposes a new organization which he designated a "meritocracy." In this system "almost everyone would begin at the lowest rank and progress upward according to his ability and ambition; rank would depend on responsibility, skill, and function." Promotions would be "radically accelerated for promising individuals." Lateral entry at higher grades, based upon

*See: Part I, Chapter 1, European Beginnings.

age and experience, somewhat analogous to the federal civil service, would be permitted with no break between the "two categories of rank as now exists."

Whether such an organization would ever be adopted by the United States armed forces, especially the Army, is questionable. But if historical experience may point the way, it is of interest to note that variants of Rosser's proposal served Europe well for several centuries.

It will also be recalled that for many years the armies of several European states have permitted, indeed encouraged, noncommissioned officers upon their retirement, generally after twelve to eighteen years' service, to enter the lower grades of the civil service of their respective states. This practice is quite old in some cases, for the kings of Prussia, Frederick William I and his successors, frequently employed retired or invalided noncommissioned officers as village schoolmasters. Prussian kings considered these men, veterans of many campaigns, able leaders and teachers of young men, to be ideally qualified as teachers and trainers of sometimes unruly farm boys.

In early 1983 there were to be seen more immediate portents of change in the U.S. Army's noncommissioned officers' role and status. Among them were appointments of retired senior noncommissioned officers to positions in the civil service commensurate with their professional experience. Although for years many retired noncommissioned officers of the United States Army have obtained positions in such agencies as, for example, the United States Postal Service, and civil service positions at the municipal, county, state, and federal level, they have done so only after twenty to thirty years' service and then carried with them the denigrating epithet of "double-dippers." American opinion has, through the years, steadfastly resisted the European practice of formal integration of retired soldiers through lateral entry into the civil service, in spite of the fact that Americans have for many years enthusiastically raised generals and other military figures to high public office. Recently, however, there have been some portents of change in attitudes. In early 1983, the Department of Defense, at the request of the administrator of the Veterans Administration, loaned Sergeant Major Samuel J. Walsh, a senior noncommissioned officer with considerable experience in the secretary of the Army's office, for service in a very responsible position in the Veterans Administration.* Shortly thereafter, the administrator appointed newly retired Sergeant Major of the Army William Connelly, to a senior position in the same agency. Moreover, since 1979, following his retirement, Sergeant Major of the Army William E. Bainbridge has been a member of the commissioners as director, member services, of the Soldiers and Airmens Home in Washington, D.C. Whether or not these are simply isolated examples of recognition of outstanding senior noncommissioned officers or genuine portents of changing status and a more rational utilization of the experience and talents of senior noncommissioned officers following their retirement remains to be seen.

*Sergeant Major Walsh was an exception, however, for he was on active duty, on "loan from the Department of Defense for a two year period." Walsh has since joined the staff of AMVETS.

▪ ▪

As this history of the noncommissioned officer comes to a close, one must conclude that the events of the years since 1775 have demonstrated that the evolution of the role and status of the noncommissioned officer has been an evolutionary process through time. After almost a century, noncommissioned officer professionalism has been institutionalized at the Department of Army level, as had long been the case with commissioned officers. This has included the establishment of a systematic educational system paralleling that long available for commissioned officers, centralized career management, promotion boards chaired by general officers for senior noncommissioned officers, and noncommissioned officer positions at the right hand of every commanding officer from the platoon leader to the Chief of Staff.

And yet, as with commissioned officers, the role and status of the noncommissioned officer, as congressional studies have shown, continues to depend upon Army doctrine and practice (or institutional behavior) as applied from the Chief of Staff on down the chain of command. For, as one senior noncommissioned officer has aptly observed, "as a basic rule, the noncommissioned officer is always the same, but the corps as a whole in the Army is what the officers want it to be."[32]

AFTERWORD

The noncommissioned officer corps as a whole
is what the officers want it to be.
—Command Sergeant Major Nathaniel McElroy

Command Sergeant Major McElroy spoke a historic truth. Since the activation of the United States Army over two centuries ago, the individual noncommissioned officer has been both trainer and leader of men in war and peace, in the field and in garrison. What has changed through the years, as this book demonstrates, is how the Army regarded the noncommissioned officer corps as seen through the methods developed for its selection, training, promotion, and assignment. Originally a creation of his company commander and subject to his whims and humors, the noncommissioned officer has acquired from the Army, often grudgingly, a professional career status resembling that of the commissioned officer. That this has come to full fruition through two world wars and two limited wars in Asia is evidence of the historical momentum of the sociomilitary revolution in the Army's view of the noncommissioned officer corps.

While initial selection and appointment of junior noncommissioned officers remains in the hands of the unit commander, promotions to the middle grades are by boards at the brigade and division level and to the top three grades by boards at the Department of the Army, similar to the practice with commissioned officers. Senior sergeants now scan the periodic promotion lists as avidly as do the commissioned officers. Today, one of their number, the Sergeant Major of the Army, is the personal adviser to the Chief of Staff on enlisted matters, functioning as his eyes and ears, just as the command sergeants major do at the battalion, brigade, and division levels.

No longer can a company commander arbitrarily "bust" a noncommissioned officer for some infraction of military regulations. The disciplining of noncommissioned officers, like their commissioned counterparts, is based upon clearly defined procedures that assume the noncommissioned officer is a professional and that he is to be treated as such.

Since the Army's first years, specialists such as farriers, wagoners, cannoneers, medical aids, musicians, and signalmen have enjoyed noncommissioned status and pay. Over the years as military technology became more complex, the Army sought to differentiate between the tactical noncommissioned officer and the growing number and variety of specialists. After considerable experimentation, it developed two hierarchies of rank—noncommissioned officers and specialists; but, even then, there was considerable overlap between them. Eventually, in October 1985, this overlap was eliminated and 40,000 specialists five and six were converted to sergeant and staff sergeant respectively. There remained only one specialist rank (the former specialist four) as a relic of a rank structure that traces back to before World War I.

In addition to abandoning the specialist rank structure, there were changes in the rank insignia of the Sergeant Major of the Army (SMA). The first change in rank insignia was developed by Sergeant Major of the Army William G. Bainbridge, who designed a SMA insignia having two stars instead of one to differentiate it from the rank of command sergeant major. The second change occurred under Sergeant Major of the Army Richard Kidd in 1994, which added the federal eagle to the two stars on the insignia of rank. Finally in 1999, the office of the Sergeant Major of the Army received its own unique colors. These seemingly minor changes are actually profound signs of the Army's long-sought goal to recognize the enhanced status of its noncommissioned officer corps and should be viewed as capstone events in NCO recognition.

Changes in NCO selection and training continued as the staff reacted to chronic dissatisfaction from the field with the military occupational specialty (MOS) skill qualification test (SQT) program. With the support of Sergeant Major of the Army Julius Gates and Chief of Staff Carl Vuono, SQTs for privates first class, specialists, corporals, and sergeants were eliminated in 1990 in favor of skill development tests (SDT) based on the Soldier's Manual. The SDT was linked to the Noncommissioned Officer Education System (NCOES) and to diagnostic tests to assist school commandants and command sergeants major in assessing the leadership skills of soldiers being sent to schools. Once again, responsibility for preparation and testing was placed upon the shoulders of the individual noncommissioned officer, thereby reviving the traditional self-study practice for the soldier aspiring for advancement.

In spite of the Chief of Staff's endorsement problems arose. One of the areas dramatically affected by the post-1991 force reduction was a large decline in the number of TRADOC school-house doctrine writers. As a result, it became increasingly more difficult to maintain the currency of the SDT. It was finally decided that the SDT could no longer be supported, and in December 1994, the TRADOC commander, General Hartzog, eliminated SDTs after a consensus among major command command sergeants major found them to be a redundant paralleling of the NCOES.

Since then, and especially after 1998, the command-approved Noncommissioned Officer Education System—with its progressive schooling from basic and advanced noncommissioned officer courses capped by the Sergeants Major Course—has continued to be the foundation of the noncommissioned officer leadership development process.

Although still valid doctrinally, Field Manual 22-600-20 has been superseded by Training Circular 22-6, *The Noncommissioned Officer's Guide.* Embodied in this doctrine are three new principles: (1) Establishment of a noncommissioned officer support channel for communication and reinforcement among NCOs from squad leader to command sergeant major; (2) the assignment to noncommissioned officers of the primary role in training and developing individual soldier skills; and (3) the strengthening of the Primary Leadership Development Course (PLDC) as the NCOES entry course required for promotion to the rank of sergeant. Thus, the basics of leadership that the Army has struggled with over the centuries—training the leaders who teach the soldiers—has been resolved. Sergeants now have the responsibility and means for training themselves in the NCOES, and for training the American soldier from his entry into the Army until his departure or promotion into the noncommissioned leadership ranks.

Thus, the basics of noncommissioned officer leadership training and performance standards have been established as the requirement for career progression in today's Army, and the noncommissioned officer can go about his or her duties creating the U.S. Army of the twenty-first century on a solid basis of doctrine, leadership development, and authority.

The twentieth century did not end without some changes and surprises at the top of the Army's noncommissioned officer structure. Sergeant Major of the Army Gene C. McKinney was relieved in February 1997 following allegations of misconduct. After a seven-month interim, the post was filled by Sergeant Major of the Army Robert Hall. At his July 2000 retirement, Chief of Staff General Eric Shinseki thanked Sergeant Major Hall for his steady leadership of the Army's NCO corps, but also reminded his listeners that "we have the most competent and professional noncommissioned officer corps in history."

In July 2000, Jack L. Tilley was selected as the twelfth Sergeant Major of the Army and the first of the twenty-first century. In this position Tilley will oversee all United States Army enlisted personnel in 25 countries. In remarks following his induction, Tilley declared, "I am going out to talk to the soldiers." Thus, the Army's senior noncommissioned officer will continue to be the eyes and ears of the Army on issues affecting the rank and file. Sergeant Major Tilley also set a continuing challenge for the modern U.S. Army noncommissioned officer—to be one that: "leads by example, trains from experience, maintains and enforces standards, takes care of soldiers, and adapts to a changing world."

NOTES

CHAPTER 1: EUROPEAN BEGINNINGS

1. G. Teitler, *The Genesis of the Professional Officer Corps*, London & Beverly Hills: Sage Publications, 1977, p. 186; William H. McNeill, *Technology, Armed Force, and Society Since A.D. 1000*, Chicago: University of Chicago Press, 1982, p. 117.
2. G. Teitler, p. 183; Johann Jacobi von Wallhausen, *Manuale Militare*, Frankfurt: 1616, pp. 125–28 (The Folger Library, Washington, D.C.).
3. André Corvisier, *Armies and Societies in Europe, 1494–1789*, translated by Abigail T. Siddall, Bloomington, Indiana: Indiana University Press, 1917, pp. 146–49.
4. Ibid., pp. 163, 170.
5. Ibid., pp. 156–59.
6. Ibid.
7. Austin Lane, *Obligations of Society in the XII and XIII Centuries*, Oxford: Clarendon Press, 1946, p. 34; Chapter 4; Sir Charles Oman, *A History in the Art of War in the Sixteenth Century*, New York: E. P. Dutton, 1937, p. 377.
8. Ibid (Oman), p. 377.
9. Hauptmann a.D. Ferdinand Freiherr von Ledebur, *Die Geschichte des Deutschen Unteroffiziers*, Berlin: Junker und Dünnhaupt Verlag, 1939, pp. 1–10.
10. Francis Grose, *Military Antiquities Respecting a History of the English Army*, new edition, 2 vols., London: Stockdale, 1812, Vol. I, pp. 1, 172–73; John Keegan, *The Face of Battle: A Study of Agincourt, Waterloo, and the Somme*, New York: Viking, 1976, pp. 318, 321.
11. Michael Powicke, *Military Obligations in Medieval England*, Oxford: Clarendon Press, 1962, pp. 27, 33–34.
12. von Ledebur, pp. 1–18.
13. Raymond de Beccarie Pavie, Sieur de Forquevaux, *Les Instructions sur le Facit de la Guerre*, ed. by G. D. Kerson from the original work published in Paris, 1548, London: Athelone Press, 1954, pp. 13–14.
14. Grose, p. 198.
15. Sir John Smythe, Knight, *Certain Discourses to the Nobilities of the Realme of England*, London: May 1590, unnumbered pages (STC), Folger Library, Washington, D.C. (Sir John [1539–1607], a military writer and diplomat, saw service in the Netherlands as well as in France and Spain.); McNeill, *Pursuit of Power*, p. 126.
16. Werner Lahne, *Unteroffiziere, Gestern–Heute–Morgen*, 2nd edition, Herford Bonn: Verlag Offene Worte, 1974, pp. 20–25.

17. Ibid., pp. 544–45.
18. Robert Barret, *The Theorike and Practike of Moderne Warres; Discourses in Dialogue Wise*, London: Printed for Wm. Ponsonby, 1598, pp. 16–19.
19. Johann Jacobi von Wallhausen, *Militia Gallicia, oder Frantzoische Kriegskunst*, Hanau: 1617, pp. 13–17.
20. Barret, pp. 16–19.
21. Ibid., pp. 16–19.
22. von Wallhausen, *Militia Gallicia*, IV. Kapitel.
23. Captain Gerat Barry, *A Discourse of Militarie Discipline*, Brussels: 1634, pp. 12–16.
24. Robert Ward, *Animadversions of Warre*, London: John Dawson, 1639, pp. 196–7; Barret, pp. 16–19.
25. Ward, pp. 196–97; Barret, pp. 18–19.
26. Ibid. (both).
27. Ibid.
28. Ibid.
29. Sir John Smythe, *Observations, and Orders Mylitarie Requisite for all Chieftaines, Captaines, and higher and lower men of change, and officers to understand, knowe and observe*, London: Richard Johns, 1595, pp. 44–45, Folger Library, Washington, D.C.
30. Barry, pp. 12–16.
31. "Sergeants' Pikes," *Journal of the Society for Army Historical Research*, Vol. X., pp. 255–56.
32. Oman, pp. 377–78.
33. Barret, pp. 16–19.
34. von Wallhausen, IV. Kapitel.
35. Barret, pp. 16–19.
36. Henry Hexham, *The Principles of the Art Militarie Practiced in the Wars of the United Netherlands*, Delft: 1637, p. 2.
37. Ibid.
38. Ibid.
39. Sir James Turner, *Passas Armata, Military Essayes of the Ancient, Grecian, Roman, and Modern Art of War*, London: Printed by M.W. for Richard Chiswell, 1683, pp. 218–19.
40. George Clayton, *The Approved Order of Martiall Discipline, with every particular officer, his office, and duty*, London: I. C. Abraham Kitsonne, 1591, p. 40 (original at Cambridge University Library, photo facsimile at Folger Library, Washington, D.C.).
41. Barret, pp. 18–19.
42. von Ledebur, p. 14.
43. Hexham, p. 8.
44. Ibid.
45. Ibid.
46. Barret, pp. 18–19.
47. Hexham, Part 2, p. 5. (Unless otherwise cited, the following are based on this reference.)
48. von Wallhausen, pp. 13–17.
49. Hexham, Part 2, p. 7; von Wallhausen, *Manuale Militarie*, IV. Kapitel.
50. Theodore Ropp, *War in the Modern World*, Durham, N.C.: Duke University Press: 1962, p. 32n.
51. *The Four Books of Flavius Vegetius Renatus*, translated by John Sadler, London: 1572, p. 17A (STC).
52. Lindsay Boynton, *The Elizabethan Militia (1558–1638)*, London: Routledge & Kegan Paul, 1967, pp. 218, 246.

53. Grose, Vol. I, p. 38; J. R. Western, *The English Militia in the Seventeenth Century*, London: Routledge & Kegan Paul, 1965.
54. Ibid. (Grose and Western). See also Barret.
55. Maurice, Comte de Saxe, *Reveries, or, Memories Concerning the Art of War*, Edinburgh: 1776, p. 41.

CHAPTER 2: BUILDING ON THESE BEGINNINGS

1. Samuel Huntington, *The Soldier and the State*, Cambridge, Mass.: Harvard University Press, 1957, pp. 17–18.
2. *Social Survey*, New York: 1970, pp. 112–13. See also Lindsay Boynton, *The Elizabethan Militia, 1558–1638*, London: Routledge & Kegan Paul, 1967, p. 12.
3. Correlli Barnett, *Britain and Her Army, 1509–1970*, New York: William Morrow & Co., 1970, p. 112.
4. Charles M. Clode, *The Military Forces of the Crown, Their Administration and Government*, Vol. I, London: John Murray, 1869, p. 40.
5. George Townshend, *A Plan of Discipline for the Use of the Militia of the County of Norfolk*, London: 1659.
6. James Ripley Jacobs, *The Beginning of the U.S. Army, 1773–1812*, Princeton, New Jersey: Princeton University Press: 1949, pp. 1–12.
7. Eberhard Kessel, "Die Preussische Armee, 1640–1866," in *Deutsche Heeresgeschichte*, ed. Karl Linnebach, Hamburg: Verlag Offene Worte, 1939; Townshend, p. xxviii, pp. 27–30; Part III, pp. 1–2. Unless otherwise noted, the following is based upon this reference.
8. Major General James Wolfe, *General Wolfe's Instructions to Young Officers, also his orders for a battalion and an army*, etc., 2nd edition, London: 1780.
9. Ibid., pp. 1–96.
10. Barnett, pp. 170–71, 223.
11. Letter, Gen. Nathaniel Green, to Gov. Cooke, December 4, 1776, *American Archives, Fifth Series*, Peter Force, ed., Vol. III, Washington, D.C.: Government Printing Office, 1853, pp. 1071–72.
12. Humphrey Bland, *A Treatise on Military Discipline*, 4th edition, London: S. Buckley, 1740; 9th edition, London: R. Baldwin, 1762.
13. James Ripley Jacobs, *The Beginning of the U.S. Army, 1783–1812*, Princeton, N.J.: Princeton University Press, 1943, pp. 1–12; Charles K. Bolton, *The Private Soldier Under Washington*, Port Washington, New York: Kennikat Press, 1902 (reprint 1964), pp. 109–10.
14. *The Writing of George Washington (From Original Manuscript Sources), 1745–1799*, thirty-nine volumes, Vol. I, 1745–1756, edited by John C. Fitzpatrick, Washington, D.C.: The George Washington Bicentennial Commission, Government Printing Office, 1931–1944, pp. 177–78 (henceforth cited as Washington).
15. Bolton, pp. 127–29.
16. Ibid.
17. Charles Royster, *A Revolutionary People at War: The Continental Army and the American Character, 1775–1783*, Chapel Hill, N.C.: University of North Carolina Press, 1979, pp. 25–30.
18. Bolton, p. 128.
19. Washington, Vol. I, p. 353.
20. Ibid., pp. 450–51.
21. Washington, Vol. II, pp. 111–12.

22. Russell F. Weigley, *History of the U.S. Army*, New York: Macmillan, 1967, pp. 23–27.
23. *Enlisted Grade Structure Study*, Vol. VI, Section I, Annex E, "Historical Review of the Enlisted Grade Structure of the U.S. Army, 1775–1976," Department of the Army, Deputy Chief of Staff for Personnel, July 1976. Unless otherwise stated, the following is based on this reference.
24. See also Robert K. Wright, Jr., *The Continental Army*, U.S. Army Lineage Series, Washington, D.C.: Center of Military History, Department of the Army, 1983, pp. 13–15.
25. Washington, Vol. III, p. 497; Vol. IV, pp. 89–90, p. 499.
26. Ibid., Vol. IV, general order, Cambridge, Oct. 31, 1775.
27. Ibid., Vol. V, p. 238.
28. Ibid., p. 337; *Enlisted Grade Structure Study*, Vol. VI, Section I, Annex E, p. 4.
29. Washington, Vol. III, general order, Headquarters, Cambridge, July 23, 1775, p. 357.
30. Washington, Vol. XXIV, general order, May 14, 1782, p. 254; Vol. XXV, general order September 10, 1782, p. 144.
31. Allen Bowman, *The Morale of the American Revolutionary Army*, Washington, D.C.: The American Council on Public Affairs, 1943, p. 13.
32. Washington, Vol. III, p. 406.
33. Bowman, pp. 13–16; Royster, pp. 50–51.
34. Ibid.
35. Bowman, pp. 14, 23–25, 70–71; Royster, pp. 50–51.
36. Emory Upton, *Military Policy*, Washington, D.C.: 1912, p. 33.
37. Werner Lahne, *Unteroffiziere, Gestern–Heute–Morgen*, 2nd edition, Herford-Bonn: Verlag Offene Worte, 1974, pp. 51–71.
38. Ibid.
39. Hauptmann a.D. Ferdinand Freiherr von Ledebur, *Die Geschichte des Deutschen Unteroffiziers*, Berlin: Junker und Dünnhaupt Verlag, 1939, p. 78.
40. Von Ledebur, p. 24; Christopher Duffy, *The Army of Frederick the Great*, London: David & Charles, 1974, p. 201.
41. Bowman, p. 31.
42. Upton, p. 54.
43. Bolton, p. 59.
44. Ibid.
45. Ibid., pp. 60–62.
46. Ibid., pp. 33–34.
47. von Steuben, *Regulations for the Order and Discipline of the Troops of the United States*, Philadelphia. 1779. (Hereafter cited as Steuben.)
48. Ibid., pp. 63–73.
49. Ibid., p. 136.
50. Ibid.
51. Ibid., p. 137.
52. Ibid., p. 141.
53. Ibid., p. 142.
54. Ibid., p. 144.
55. Ibid.
56. Ibid., p. 145.
57. Ibid., p. 148.
58. Alvin R. Sunseri, "Fredrick William von Steuben and the Reeducation of the American Army: A Lesson in Practicality," *Armor*, March–April 1965, pp. 40–47.

59. Washington, Vol. V, p. 351; Vol. VI, p. 110.
60. Ibid., Vol. VI, pp. 110–11.
61. Ibid., Vol. VII, pp. 426.
62. Steuben, p. 136.
63. Bolton, pp. 96–97; Maj. Edward C. Baynton Harrison, compiler and editor, *General Orders of George Washington issued at Newburgh on the Hudson, 1782*, New York: 1783.
64. Bolton, pp. 96–97.
65. Steuben, p. 1.
66. Washington, Vol. XVIII, pp. 45–46.
67. Ibid., pp. 46–47.
68. Ibid., Vol. XVIII, p. 76; Vol. XVIV, p. 476.
69. Steuben, pp. 75, 80, 85.
70. Washington, Vol. XXVI, pp. 328–39; Vol. XXIV.
71. Washington, Vol. XXVI, p. 332.
72. Ibid.
73. Ibid.
74. Ibid., Vol. XXVI, pp. 448–49.
75. Ibid.
76. Weigley, pp. 78–79.
77. John M. Palmer, *America in Arms, the Experience of the United States with Military Organization*, New Haven, Conn.: Yale University Press, 1941, p. 3.
78. Wright, pp. 180–82.
79. Ibid.

CHAPTER 3: ADOPTION OF NEW PRINCIPLES

1. Report of the Field Manual Review Board, Annex B., *Evolution of the United States Army Field Manual: Valley Forge to Vietnam*, Washington, D.C.: Government Printing Office, 1966, pp. 7–9.
2. Ibid.
3. Lois G. Schwoerer, *No Standing Armies: The Antiarmy Ideology in Seventeenth-Century England*, Baltimore: The Johns Hopkins University Press, 1974, p. 200.
4. Ibid., p. 195.
5. *The Writings of George Washington (from original manuscript sources), 1745–1799,* Vol. XXVI, June 26, 1783, edited by John C. Fitzpatrick, Washington, D.C.: The George Washington Bicentennial Commission, Government Printing Office, 1931–1944, pp. 374–96. (Hereafter cited as Washington.)
6. Washington, Vol. 26, pp. 392–93.
7. See J. R. Western, *The English Militia in the Eighteenth Century: The Story of a Political Issue, 1660–1802*, London: Routledge & Kegan Paul, 1965.
8. Ibid., pp. xv, 112, 199, 205.
9. Brevet Major General Emory Upton, *The Military Policy of the United States*, 3rd impression, Washington, D.C.: U.S. Government Printing Office, 1912, p. 69.
10. John M. Palmer, *American in Arms*, New Haven: Yale University Press, 1941, pp. 3–5.
11. James Riley Jacobs, *The Beginnings of the U.S. Army, 1783–1812*, Princeton: Princeton University Press, 1947, p. 51; Upton, p. 75; Thomas M. Exley, *A Compendium of the Pay of the Army from 1785 to 1888*, Washington, D.C.: Government Printing Office, 1888, pp. 50–51.
12. Upton, p. 79.

13. Ibid., pp. 80–81.
14. Jacobs, pp. 132–36, 145–71. Unless otherwise noted, the following is based on this reference.
15. Russell F. Weigley, *History of the U.S. Army*, New York: Macmillan, 1967, p. 93; Upton, p. 83.
16. Jacobs, p. 192.
17. Weigley, pp. 107ff.
18. Jacobs, pp. 198–99, 260–62. Unless otherwise noted, the section following is based on this reference.
19. William Addleman Ganoe, *The History of the U.S. Army*, New York: D. Appleton, 1924, pp. 83, 106; Jacobs, pp. 261–62.
20. Jacobs, pp. 282–83.
21. Ibid., pp. 236–37.
22. Maurice Matloff, *American Military History, Army Historical Series*, Washington, D.C.: Office, Chief of Military History, U.S. Army: 1969, pp. 117–18.
23. Weigley, p. 195.
24. Ibid., pp. 115–16.
25. Col. Brooke Nihard, USMC, "A Humorous Account of a Militia Muster Circa 1807," *The Journal of the Company of Military Collectors & Historians*, Vol. X, Spring 1958, pp. 11–14.
26. Weigley, pp. 129–30.
27. William Duane, *Regulations for the Discipline of the Infantry*, 9th edition, Philadelphia: 1814. Unless otherwise noted, the following is based on this reference.
28. Capt. C. Hartell's Company Book, 27th Infantry, 1814–1815, entry 265, NARA, Old Military Records Division. Unless otherwise noted, the following is based on this reference.
29. Orders, The Adjutant, Sackets Harbor, 9th Military District, October 21, 1812, 1812–13, Vol. 390, NARA, Old Military Records Division.
30. Weigley, p. 130.
31. *Rules and Regulations for the Field Exercise and Maneuvres of Infantry, Compiled and Adapted to the Organizations of the Army of the United States Agreeably to a Resolve of Congress, dated December 1814*, New York: 1815 (shorter title, *U.S. Army Infantry Drill Regulations, 1815*). Unless otherwise noted, the following is based on this reference.
32. *Regulations*, Articles XI, XIII, XXII, Washington, D.C.: 1841.
33. Ibid.
34. Franz Koehler, *Coffee for the Armed Forces: Military Development and Conversion to Industry Supply*, QMC Historical Studies, Series II, No. 5., Washington, D.C.: Office, Chief of Military History, U.S. Army, 1958, pp. 8–9.
35. Ibid., p. 10.
36. *General Regulations for the Army*, Washington, D.C.: 1835, pp. 10–11, 17.

CHAPTER 4: ENHANCING THE NONCOMMISSIONED OFFICER CORPS

1. Maurice Matloff, *American Military History*, Army Historical Series, Washington, D.C.: Office, Chief of Military History, U.S. Army, 1969, p. 148.
2. Thomas M. Exley, *A Compendium of the Pay of the Army, from 1785 to 1888*, Washington, D.C.: Government Printing Office, 1888; Order Book of a Rifle Regiment, the northern army, Headquarters 9th Military District, 1813–1815, enclosure GO, Adjutant

& Inspector General's Office, July 24, 1815, Vol. 439, NARA (Old Military Records Division).

3. Russell F. Weigley, *History of the U.S. Army*, New York: Macmillan, 1967, p. 195; Matloff, p. 149.
4. Weigley, pp. 140–43.
5. Order Books, Company H, 1st Infantry Regiment, July 12, 1821–1822, Vol. 476, NARA (Old Military Records Division).
6. Captain Ferdinand A. Amelung's Company Book, 1st Infantry Regiment, 1818–1820, Vol. 76, NARA. (Unless otherwise noted, the following is based on this reference.)
7. *Enlisted Grade Structure*, Vol. VI, Annex E, p. 6.
8. Ibid.
9. Ibid.
10. *General Regulations of the Army or, Military Institutes*, Washington, D.C.: 1821 and 1825, p. 35. (Unless otherwise noted, the following is based on this citation.)
11. *Enlisted Grade Structure*, Vol. VI, Annex E, pp. 6–10.
12. Ibid.
13. William A. Ganoe, *History of the United States Army*, New York: Appleton-Century, 1936, pp. 146–60; *Enlisted Grade Structure*, Vol. VI, Annex E, p. 7. See also William K. Emerson, *Chevrons, Illustrated History and Catalogue of U.S. Army Insignia*, Washington, D.C.: Smithsonian Press, 1983.
14. Ganoe, p. 180.
15. Letter, Maj. Gen. Jacob Brown to Sec'y of War, HQ of the Army, Washington, D.C., Nov. 17, 1825, in *American State Papers, Military Affairs*, Vol. III, p. 111. (Unless otherwise cited, the following is based on this reference.)
16. Ganoe, pp. 183–84; see also, *An Act Establishing Rules and Articles for the Government of the Army of the United States with the Regulations of the War Department Respecting the Same*, Albany, 1812; and *Enlisted Grade Structure*, Vol. VI, Annex E., p. 7.
17. *U.S. Army General Regulations*, 1832, Article XV (ordnance sergeants), pp. 34–36; *Enlisted Grade Structure*, Vol. VI, Annex E, p. 8.
18. This correspondence, as well as all other citations from official dispatches in this chapter (through endnote 38) may be found on Microcopy #567 (letters received by the Office of the Adjutant General, main series, 1822–1860), NARA (Old Military Records Division).
19. Letter, BG George M. Brooke, CO, 3d Mounted Rifles, St. Louis, Mo., to AG BG R. Jones, Washington, D.C., Feb. 17, 1846.
20. Letter, BG Brady, Comdg. Hqs. 4th Military District, Detroit, Michigan, March 21, 1846, to AG R. Jones, BG, Washington, D.C.
21. Letter, BG Geo. M. Brooke, Comdg. Hqs. Western Div, New Orleans, LA, April 11, 1848, to Col. Geo. Talcott, Ord. Dept., Washington, D.C.; Memo, AG BG Jones to Secy. War Marcy.
22. Letter, Jeremiah Beck, Ord. Sgt. Ft. Wood, La., April 20, 1848, to Gen. Brooke, Comdg. Western Division.
23. Letter, 1st Lt. H. W. Wessels, Recruiting Rendezvous, Utica, N.Y., to Lt. Col. N. S. Clark, Sup. Recruiting Service, New York City, Jan. 29, 1846.
24. Letter, Capt. T. Z. Garden, Comdg. Co. B, HQs, 4th Arty, Ft. Brook, Tampa, Fla., Dec. 17, 1849, to AG T. Jones, Washington D.C.
25. Letter, B. C. Smead, Capt, 4th Arty, Comdg., Co. D to Maj. H. Brown, Comdg., 4th Arty Regt., Toluca, Mexico, May 8, 1848.

26. Letter, W. R. Wilson, Recruiting Sergeant, Richmond, Va., July 11, 1847, to the Hon. W. L. Marcy, Secy. of War.
27. Ibid.
28. Letter to AG Jones, Washington, D.C., with Application for Ord. Sgt., from R. T. Jackson, Hqs, 6th U.S. Infantry, Mexico, Oct. 27, 1847.
29. Letter (Application for Post of Ordnance Sergeant), Sgt. Wm. Smith, Co. H. 1st Arty Regiment, City of Mexico, Nov. 15, 1847, to Brig. Gen. R. Jones, Adjutant General U.S. Army, Washington, D.C.
30. Letter, John B. Gibson, Capt., 1st Arty & Comdg. Co. H., City of Mexico, Nov. 10, 1847, to AG, Brig. Gen. R. Jones, Washington, D.C.
31. Letter, Bvt. Major J. Dimick, Comdg. 1st Regt. of Arty, Citadel of the City of Mexico, Nov. 16th, 1847, to Brig. Gen. R. Jones, AG, U.S. Army, Washington, D.C.
32. Letter, Jno. Love, 1st Lt. 1st Dragoons, Washington, D.C., Nov. 10, 1848, to Col. E. V. Sumner, Comdg. 1st Dragoons, Jefferson Barracks, Mo.
33. Letter, Gen. A. Shields, Washington, D.C., March 17, 1848, to Adjutant General R. Jones's Application for Ordnance Sergeant.
34. Letter U. H. La Motte, Capt. Co. C, Hqs. 1st Infantry, Ft. Brown, Texas, to AG R. Jones, Brig. Gen. Washington City.
35. Letter, F. F. Flint, 1st Lt., Hqs. Ft. Smith, Ark., March 27, 1848, to Adjutant General R. Jones, Washington, D.C.
36. File containing letter, Hqs. 4th Artillery, Ft. Monroe, Va., June 1, 1846 to AG R. Jones, Washington, D.C.; Ltr. Sgt. Chas. Bussell to President of the United States, and General Winfield Scott, U.S.A., June 1846, Newport, Va.
37. Ibid.
38. Letter, 1st Lt. Robt. Allen, 2d Arty Hqs., Principal Depot, Ft. Columbus, N.Y., May 7, 1846, to AG R. Jones, Washington, D.C.; Msg. AG R. Jones, Washington, D.C., May 8, 1846.
39. *Messages*, War Department, 1845, U.S. Army Center of Military History, Washington, D.C., p. 209.
40. Col. Paul R. Goode, *The United States Soldiers Home: A History of Its First Hundred Years*, Richmond, Va.: privately published, 1957, pp. vii, 1, 15–19. Similar homes were also established in Kentucky and Mississippi but were eventually closed.
41. *Regulations, 1861*, pp. 11–12; *Sec War Report, 1853*, p. 150.

CHAPTER 5: PROMOTIONS FROM THE RANKS

1. *Recollections of the U.S. Army, a Series of Thrilling Tales and Sketches*, by an American Soldier [written during a period in the service since 1830], Boston: James Munroe & Co., 1845, pp. vii–ix. (Unless otherwise cited, the following is based on this reference.)
2. Russell F. Weigley, *History of the U.S. Army*, New York: Macmillan, 1967, pp. 153–54.
3. American State Papers *(Military Affairs)*, Vol. IV, p. 683 (No. 471, 21st Congress, 2d Session). Washington, D.C.: Gales & Seaton, 1861.
4. Idem., No. 511 (22d Congress, 1st Session). Emphasis added.
5. Idem., No. 713 (24th Congress, 2d Session). Unless otherwise noted, the following is based on this reference.
6. *Report of the Secretary of War*, Message of the president to Congress, Washington, D.C.: Government Printing Office, 1854, p. 150.
7. Terry W. Strieter, "An Army in Evolution: French Officers Commissioned from the Ranks, 1848–1895," *Military Affairs*, December 1978, pp. 177–79.

8. Twenty-Ninth Congress, Sess. II, Ch. 61, 1847, Sect. 17, Brevets to Noncommissioned Officers, approved March 3, 1847.
9. Ibid.
10. Letter, D. E. Twiggs, to CO, 2d Dragoons, Metamora, Mexico, June 30, 1846, to Lambert Tree, Washington City, in letters received by the office of the Adjutant General, Main Series, 1822–1860. Microcopy No. 567 in NARA, Old Military Records Division. (The correspondence hereafter cited in this section is in this series.)
11. Letter, Lambert Tree, Washington City (n.d.) to the Hon. Cave Johnson.
12. Letter, James Herring, New York, June 18, 1846, to William L. Marcy, Secretary of War, Washington, D.C.
13. Letter, Lt. A. Lowry, 2d Dragoons, Jan. 29, 1847, to Capt. H. W. Merrill, Comd. B. Company, 2d Dragoons.
14. Letter, Capt. H. W. Merrill, 2d Dragoons, Comdg. B. Comp., Dragoon Encampment on the Rio Grande River, Texas, Jan. 30, 1847, to Adjutant General, U.S.A., Brig. Gen. R. Jones, Washington, D.C.
15. Letter, John Wentworth, Chicago, Ill., Nov. 6, 1846, to Secretary of War, Wm. L. Marcy
16. Letter, Capt. Bainbridge, Hqs. 3d Inf., Victoria, Mexico, Jan. 6, 1847, to Adjutant General of the Army, BG R. Jones, Washington, D.C.
17. Letter, Commanding Officer Recruiting Party (1st Lt. 3d Artillery), May 5, 1847, Pittsburgh, Pennsylvania, to Assistant Adjutant General, Washington, D.C.
18. Letter, John W. Tibbits, Col., 16th Inf., Camp Near Monterey, Mexico, Sept. 1, 1847 to Major W.W.S. Bliss, Ass't Adjutant General, Washington, D.C.
19. Letter, Officers of the 6th Infantry Regt., City of Mexico, Sept. 26, 1847, to BG R. Jones, Adjutant General, U.S.A.
20. Letter, Capt., 2d Artillery Regiment, Tacubuya, Mexico, Aug. 24, 1847, to the Adjutant General, U.S.A.
21. Letter, Capt. J. J. Archer, City of Mexico, Sept. 30, 1847, to T. P. Andress, Col. Comd'g U.S. Regiment of Voltigeurs.
22. Letter, Major Montford S. Stokes, Hqs. 1st Regiment of So. Carolina Vols. Cessvalvo, Mexico, June 11, 1847, to James K. Polk, President of the United States.
23. Letter, Chas. I. Biddle, Capt. Voltigeurs, Hqs. Toluca, Mexico, May 21, 1848, to T. P. Andrews, Col. Comdg. Regiment of Voltigeurs.
24. Ibid.
25. Letter, AG U.S.A., Brig. Gen. R. Jones, Wash., D.C., to Hon. Wm. L. Marcy, Secretary of War, Jan. 19, 1848.
26. Letter, Wm. L. Marcy, Secretary of War, June 27, 1848, to President of the United States.
27. Letter, Bvt. Maj. Braxton Bragg, 3d Arty, Comdg. Light Company C, camp near Monterey, Mexico, June 27, 1847, to Maj. W. W. Bliss, Asst. Adjutant General of the Army.
28. Letter, M. Hamilton, Lt. Col. Comdg. 2d Dragoons, Monterey, Mexico, to Maj. Bliss, Asst. AG, July 13, 1847.
29. Letter, Capt. T. W. Sherman, 3d Arty, Comdg. Light Co. E, Light Arty, Camp Buena Vista, Mexico, July 9, 1847, to Major W. W. Bliss, Asst. Adjutant General.
30. Letter, James Duncan, Bvt. Col. Light Arty Co. A, Mexico, Sept. 26, 1847, to Asst. AG Capt. H. L. Scott.
31. *Selected Manpower Statistics*, Department of Defense, Washington Headquarters Services, Directorate for Information, Operations, and Reports, March 1979, Table P225, p. 28.

32. *Report of the Secretary of War, Messages*, "Report of the Commanding General of the Army," Washington, D.C.: Government Printing Office, 1854, p. 150.

CHAPTER 6: DIVERSITY AND LEADERSHIP

1. K. Jack Bauer, *The Mexican War, 1846–1848*, New York: Macmillan, 1974, pp. 397–98.
2. *Sec. War Rpt.*, 1858, p. 3.
3. *Report of the Secretary of War*, "Messages from the President of the United States to the Two Houses of Congress, Nov. 23 and Dec. 3, 1854," in Report of the Maj. Gen. Commanding the Army, Washington, D.C.: Government Printing Office, 1854, pp. 130–32, 309 (hereafter cited as "Messages").
4. Russell F. Weigley, *History of the U.S. Army*, New York: Macmillan, 1967, p. 158.
5. Augustus Meyers, *Ten Years in the Ranks, U.S. Army*, New York: The Stirling Press, 1914, p. 22.
6. Muster & Receipt Rolls of Captains T. J. Robeson and W. Coles; Companies of the 3d Rifles, 1814–1815; Approved Company Book for the Army of the United States (1814–1817), Captain Henry K. Craig's Company of Light Artillery, Company I. (These records are in the Old Military Records Division of the National Archives and Records Administration [NARA], Washington, D.C.)
7. Meyers, pp. 18–19.
8. Ibid.
9. Weigley, p. 168; Francis Paul Prucha, *The Sword of the Republic: The U.S. Army on the Frontier, 1783 to 1846*, New York: Macmillan, 1969, pp. 326–28.
10. Ella Lonn, *Foreigners in the Union Army and Navy*, Baton Rouge, La.: Louisiana University Press, 1951, pp. 270–71. (Unless otherwise noted, the following is based on this source.)
11. *Sec. War Rpt.*, 1858, p. 3, 1860, Vol. UU, pp. 1–5.
12. Robert M. Utley, *Frontier Regulars—The United States Army and the Indian: 1866–1891*, New York: Macmillan, 1973, p. 342.
13. Weigley, pp. 161–62.
14. "Messages," Dec. 1844, Washington, D.C. (Rpt. of the Commanding General of the Army, Dec. 3, 1844.)
15. *Sec. War Rpt.*, 1859, Vol. II, p. 3.
16. Utley, p. 8.
17. *Rpt. of Sec. War for 1854* (Rpt of Dept. of Texas, Corpus Christi, May 15, 1854, Persifor F. Smith, Bvt. Maj. Gen. Commanding) pp. 28–29. (Unless otherwise noted, the following is based on this source.)
18. George F. Price, *Across the Continent with the Fifth Cavalry*, New York: Van Nostrand, 1883, pp. 57–93. (Unless otherwise cited, the following is based on this reference.)
19. *Sec. War Rpt.*, 1859, Headquarters, Navajo Expedition, Ft. Defiance, New Mexico, Oct. 17, 1858, Rpt. of D. S. Miles, Lt. Col. Commanding, p. 282.
20. Ibid., p. 258.
21. *Sec. War Rpt.*, Vol. II, 1860, p. 203.
22. *Sec. War Rpt.*, 1859, p. 361.
23. *Sec. War Rpt.*, 1858, p. 22.
24. Percival G. Lowe, *Five Years a Dragoon, and Other Adventures*, Kansas City, Mo.: The Franklin Hudson Publishing Company, 1906, pp. 5, 18, 19, 24–25. Lowe's diary was discovered years later among his papers, which had been given to the University

of Kansas Library. The diary was published by his descendants in 1906. (Unless otherwise noted, the following is based on this reference.)

25. Ibid., p. 46.
26. Eugene Bandel, *Frontier Life in the Army, 1854–61*, translated by Olga Bandel and Richard Jente, ed. Ralph P. Beber, Glendale Ca.: The Southwest Historical Series, The Arthur H. Clark Co., 1932. This book was published years after Bandel's death and consists of translations of letters to his parents in Prussia during his service. (Unless otherwise noted, the following is based on this source.)

CHAPTER 7: NONCOMMISSIONED OFFICERS IN THE CIVIL WAR

1. *Sec. War Rpt.*, 1861, p. 5; Russell F. Weigley, *History of the U.S. Army*, New York: Macmillan, 1967, p. 200.
2. Weigley, pp. 200, 216.
3. Ibid.
4. Weigley, pp. 199–200; *Sec. War Rpt.*, 1861, p. 10.
5. Weigley, p. 226.
6. *Sec. War Rpt.*, 1861; Dennis U. McCarthy Papers (1860–1866) in U.S. Army Military History Institute, Carlisle Barracks, Pa.
7. August Meyers, *Ten Years in the Ranks, U.S. Army*, New York: The Sterling Press, 1914, p. 184.
8. Bruce Catton, "Union Discipline and Leadership in the Civil War," *The Marine Corps Gazette*, Jan. 1956, No. 1, Vol. 40, pp. 18–25; The Ronald D. Boyer Collection of Civil War Papers (Civil War Memoirs of Henry F. Charles); The Sergeant Fergus Elliott Papers of the Civil War (unnumbered pages), in U.S. Army Military History Institute, Carlisle Barracks, Pa.
9. The Frank McGregor Papers in the U.S. Army Military History Institute, Carlisle Barracks, Pa.
10. *Revised Regulations for the U.S. Army*, 1861, p. 499.
11. The Sergeant Fergus Elliott Papers.
12. David Leib Ambrose, *History of the 7th Regiment, Illinois Volunteer Infantry, From Its Muster into the U.S. Service, April 25, 1861, to Its Final Muster Out, July 9, 1865*, Springfield, Ill.: Illinois Journal Co., 1868, pp. 59–60, 276–77. (Unless otherwise noted, the following is based on this source.)
13. *Sec. War Rpt.*, 1861, p. 9; Weigley, p. 231
14. The Frank McGregor Papers.
15. The Griest Family Papers (Alva Clarkson Griest); the Frank McGregor Papers. Both in the U.S. Army Military History Institute, Carlisle Barracks, Pa.
16. Meyers, p. 186.
17. Ibid., p. 173.
18. George F. Price, *Across the Continent with the Fifth Cavalry*, New York: Von Nostrand, 1883, pp. 265–68. (Unless otherwise cited, the following is based on this source.)
19. Ibid., pp. 309–10.
20. Ibid., pp. 404–6.
21. Ibid., pp. 501–2.
22. Ibid., pp. 407–9.
23. Ibid., pp. 529–31.
24. Ibid., pp. 583–85.

25. Brig. Gen. Silas Casey, *U.S.A. Infantry Tactics for the Instructions, Exercise, and Maneuvers of the Soldier, A Company, Line of Skirmishers, Battalion, Brigade, or Corps d'Armée*, Vols. I–III, New York: Van Nostrand, 1862.
26. Ibid., Vol. I, pp. 5–6.
27. Ibid.
28. Bell Irvin Wiley, *The Life of Billy Yank, the Common Soldier of the Union*, New York: Bobbs-Merrill, 1951, pp. 26-27. (Unless otherwise noted, the following is based on this source.)
29. Ibid.
30. Ibid., pp. 50–54.
31. Andrew S. Burt Papers (unnumbered pages), in the U.S. Army History Research Collection, Military History Institute, Carlisle Barracks, Pa.
32. Wiley, pp. 26–27.
33. The Sergeant Fergus Elliott Papers.
34. The Andrew S. Burt Papers.
35. The Frank McGregor Papers.
36. The Sgt. Fergus Elliott Papers, letters written from Bolivar Heights, Va., Nov. 29, 1862.
37. The Fergus Elliott Papers; the Gregory Cace Collection (Tallman Recollections) Book Third, pp. 3, 38, U.S. Army Military History Institute, Carlisle Barracks, Pa.
38. Ernest F. Fisher, Jr., "Muzzle Loader to Breech Loader: The Impact of Weapons Technology on Infantry Organization and Tactics in the U.S. Army from 1775 to 1975," *Acta No. 2*, Washington, D.C.: The International Commission for Military History, 1975.
39. Casey, *Infantry Tactics*, Vol. I; also Maj. Gen. Emory Upton, *The Armies of Asia and Europe*, New York: D. Appleton, 1878, pp. 313–16.
40. Casey, *Infantry Tactics, Vol. I.*
41. Upton, pp. 315–16.
42. The Jonathan P. Stowe Papers, U.S. Army Military History Institute, Carlisle Barracks, Pa.
43. Meyers, pp. 231–33.
44. Casey, Vol. I.
45. Ibid.
46. The Sgt. Fergus Elliott Papers.
47. Meyers, p. 235.
48. Ibid., pp. 273–74, 323.
49. F. N. Boney, "The Conqueror: Sgt. Mathew Woodruff in War and Peace, 1861–66," *The Alabama Review*, July 1970, pp. 193–211. (Unless otherwise noted, the following is based on this source.)
50. The Sgt. John Bailey Papers (*Civil War Times* Collection). Crocker letter of May 8, 1862. On another occasion Rebel cavalry captured the sergeant major of the 66th Ohio Volunteers while he took a sergeant's place by helping to post the guard. Incidents such as this, and that of Sgt. Bailey, suggest a more flexible attitude toward enlisted rank among volunteers than was the case among regulars. (Tallman Recollections, Co. E., 66th Ohio Vols., Book Third, p. 18. Both items in U.S. Army Military History Institute, Carlisle Barracks, Pa.)
51. The Jonathan P. Stowe Papers, *Civil War Times Illustrated* Collection in the U.S. Army Center of Military History, Military History Institute, Carlisle Barracks, Pa. (Unless otherwise noted, the following is based on this citation.)
52. Ambrose, pp. v–vi.

CHAPTER 8: INDIANS, FOREIGNERS, AND REFORM

1. Russell F. Weigley, *History of the U.S. Army*, New York: Macmillan, 1967, p. 265.
2. Ibid., p. 267.
3. George Rex Buckman, "Ranches and Rancheros of the Far West," *Lippincott's Magazine*, May 22, 1882, Vol. III, pp. 425–35.
4. Fairfax Downey, *Indian-Fighting Army*, New York: Scribner's, 1944, pp. 66–74.
5. Don Rickey, Jr., *Forty Miles a Day on Beans & Hay: The Enlisted Soldier Fighting the Indian Wars*, Norman, Okla.: University of Oklahoma Press, 1963, p. 52; George A. Forsythe, *The Story of the Soldier*, New York: D. Appleton & Co., 1900, p. 131.
6. William K. Emerson, "Old Bill," *Armor*, Sept.–Oct. 1978, p. 28
7. Rickey, pp. 58–59.
8. Robert G. Carter, *The Old Sergeant's Story: Winning the West from the Indians and Bad Men in 1870 to 1876*, New York: Hitchcock, 1926, pp. 44, 60.
9. Rickey, p. 60; Forsythe, p. 131.
10. *Medal of Honor, 1863–1968*, Washington, D.C.: U.S. Government Printing Office, 1968, p. 307; Downey, pp. 235–36.
11. Downey, p. 301; *Medal of Honor*, p. 329.
12. J. W. Vaughan, *The Battle of Platte Bridge*, Norman, Okla.: University of Oklahoma Press, 1963, pp. 77–89.
13. Ibid.
14. Robert G. Carter, *The Old Sergeant's Story*, New York: Hitchcock, 1926, p. 126.
15. Rickey, pp. 50, 81.
16. Ibid., pp. 56, 58.
17. Forsythe, p. 87.
18. Ibid., pp. 89–90.
19. Ibid., pp. 51, 91–92.
20. Descriptive Book, 12th Infantry Regiment, 1880–1902, in Modern Military Records Division, NARA.
21. Frazier and Robert Hunt, *I Fought with Custer: The Story of Sergeant Windolph, Last Survivor of the Battle of the Little Big Horn*, New York: Charles Scribner's Sons, p. 4.
22. Descriptive Book, 12th Infantry Regiment, 1880–1902.
23. Descriptive Book, 16th Infantry Regiment, Old Military Records Division, NARA.
24. Descriptive Book, 4th Infantry Regimental Staff and Band; Descriptive Book, 4th Artillery Regimental Staff and Band, NARA.
25. Don C. Rickey, Jr., "Life Since 1888," interview with Reginald A. Bradley, Grass Valley, Col., Jan. 10, 1968. (At the time of this interview Sgt. Bradley was one hundred years old. Unless otherwise cited, the following is based on this source.)
26. Frazier and Robert Hunt, p. 16.
27. Jack D. Foner, *The U.S. Soldier Between Two Wars: Army Life and Reforms, 1865–1898*, New York: Humanities Press, 1970, p. 69.
28. Foner, pp. 70–71; *Acts Approved on 11 June 1878*, Section 2 & 18 June, Section 3; *Regulations of 1863*, Paragraph 22; *Regulations of the U.S. Army & General Orders in Force of 17 Feb. 1881*, Washington, D.C., p. 11.
29. General Orders No. 37, Section 4 (Promotion of Noncommissioned Officers to Second Lieutenants), June 19, 1878, U.S. Army Center of Military History.
30. General Orders No. 62, Promotion of Meritorious Noncommissioned Officers, Aug. 26, 1878.
31. Ibid.
32. General Orders No. 10, January 20, 1890.

33. Foner, pp. 112–13.
34. Foner, pp. 79, 84–87, 94, 113, 120. (Unless otherwise indicated, the following section is based on this source.)
35. Maurice Matloff, *American Military History*, pp. 285–87; Weigley, pp. 281–82.
36. Samuel P. Huntington, *The Soldier and the State: The Theory and Politics of Civil-Military Relations*, Cambridge, Mass.: Harvard University Press, 1959, pp. 222–30; Weigley, p. 271.
37. Weigley, p. 224.
38. Foner, pp. 61–62, 104–16. (Unless otherwise noted, the following is based on this source.)
39. *War Department Report*, Vol. I, 1970, "Report of the I.G. of the Army," U.S. Army Center of Military History.
40. Frank N. Schubert, "The Violent World of Emanuel Stance, Fort Robinson, 1887," *Nebraska History*, Vol. 55, No. 2, Summer 1974, pp. 203–19.
41. Ibid., p. 221.
42. Ibid., p. 217.

CHAPTER 9: IMPROVING THE TRAINING OF NONCOMMISSIONED OFFICERS AND THEIR TESTING IN WAR

1. *Sec War Rpt.*, Vol. I, 1888, pp. 142–43.
2. Ibid., p. 143.
3. Rufus F. Zog'baum, *Horse, Foot, and Dragoons, Sketches of Army Life at Home and Abroad*, New York: Harper & Bros., 1880, pp. 60–62.
4. Ibid.
5. Robert Arthur, *The Coast Artillery School, 1824–1927*, Ft. Monroe, Va.: The Coast Artillery School, 1928, p. 15. See also by the same author, *The History of Fort Monroe*, Ft. Monroe, Va.: The Coast Artillery School, 1930, pp. 145–55.
6. Arthur, *The History of Fort Monroe*, pp. 155–56.
7. Ibid., p. 163.
8. Ibid., pp. 166–67.
9. P. M. Ashburn, *A History of the Medical Department of the U.S. Army*, Boston: Houghton Mifflin Co., 1929, pp. 7–48, 62, 75. (Unless otherwise indicated, the following is based on this source.)
10. Ibid., pp. 247–48.
11. *Historical Sketch of the Signal Corps, 1860–1941*, Ft. Monmouth, N.J.: Eastern Signal Corps Schools, Pamphlet #32, Dec. 10, 1942, pp. 20–21.
12. *Sec. War Rpt.*, 1881, p. 9.
13. *Historical Sketch*, pp. 22–23.
14. Ibid., pp. 20–21.
15. Paul J. Schieps, "Will Croft Barnes and the Apache Uprising of 1881," *Military History of the Spanish-American Southwest, A Seminar*, 1976 (copy in DA/CMH).
16. Sgt. O'Keefe file, in custody of Dr. Paul J. Scheips, DA/CMH.
17. Donald R. Whitnah, *A History of the United States Weather Bureau*, Urbana, Ill.: University of Illinois Press, 1961, p. 62.
18. J. Willard Brow, *The Signal Corps U.S.A. in the War of the Rebellion*, Boston: U.S. Veterans Signal Corps Association, 1896, pp. 279, 281, 286.
19. *Historical Sketch*, p. 30.
20. Letter to HQDA (DAMH-HDS) Washington, D.C. from U.S. Army Communications Command, Ft. Hauchuca, Arizona, April 21, 1977. (The best account of the heliograph

in the Geromino campaign is Bruno J. Rolak, "General Miles' Mirrors: The Heliograph in the Geronimo Campaign of 1886," *The Journal of Arizona History*, Vol. XVI, Summer, 1975, pp. 145–60.)

21. *Historical Sketch*, pp. 25–27. (The best account of the Greely expedition is A. L. Todd's *Abandoned: The Story of the Greely Arctic Expedition 1881–1884*, New York: McGraw-Hill, 1961. Unless otherwise indicated, the following is based on this source.)
22. Emory Upton, Bvt. Maj. Gen., U.S.A., *The Armies of Asia and Europe, Embracing Official Reports on the Armies of Japan, China, India, Persia, Italy, Russia, Austria, Germany, France, and England*, New York: D. Appleton & Co., 1878, p. 123; Stephen F. Ambrose, *Upton and the Army*, Baton Rouge, La.: Louisiana State University Press, 1946, p. 96.
23. Upton, pp. 203–6.
24. Ibid., p. 126.
25. Lt. Gustave A. Wieser, "The Noncommissioned Officer: Their Efficiency an Essential Factor in Our Army," *Journal of the Military Service Institution of the United States*, Vol. 38, Jan.–Feb. 1906, p. 104.
26. 1st Lt. Harvey C. Carbaugh, "The Instruction of Noncommissioned Officers in the Army," *Journal of the Military Service Institution of the United States*, Vol. II, March 1890, p. 222. (Unless otherwise indicated, the following is based on this source.)
27. 1st. Lt. C. W. Farber, "To Promote the Efficiency of Non-Commissioned Officers," *The Journal of the Military Service Institution of the United States*, Vol. XXII, Jan. 1898, p. 101.
28. John M. A. Palmer, *America in Arms*, New Haven, Conn.: Yale University Press, 1941, p. 119.
29. I. B. Holley, Jr., *General John M. Palmer, Citizen Soldiers, and Army of a Democracy*, Westport, Conn.: Greenwood Press, 1982, p. 65.
30. Ibid.
31. Ibid.
32. Spanish-American War Survey, Signal Corps, Diary of Corporal Leland S. Smith, entry of Oct. 20, 1899. In Military History Institute Archives, Carlisle Barracks, Pa.
33. Spanish-American War Survey, U.S. Army Signal Corps, letters of Sgt. A. H. Frazier 1898, in Military History Institute, Carlisle Barracks, Pa.
34. Ardell Stelck, "Sgt. Guy Gillette and Cherokee's 'Gallant Company M' in the Spanish-American War," *Annals of Iowa* pp. 561–78.
35. Ibid.
36. Ibid.

CHAPTER 10: DECADES OF INDIFFERENCE

1. *War Department, U.S.A. Annual Reports, 1907*, Vol. I, Washington, D.C.: Government Printing Office, 1907, pp. 78–80. (Unless otherwise indicated the following is based on this source.)
2. Ibid., pp. 78–80.
3. Ibid., pp. 80–81.
4. Russell F. Weigley, *History of the U.S. Army*, New York: Macmillan, 1967, p. 270.
5. George A. Forsythe, *The Story of a Soldier*, New York: D. Appleton & Co., 1900, pp. 94–95.
6. *Sec. War Rpt.*, Vol. I, 1888, p. 207.
7. Ibid.
8. Maj. Wilmot E. Ellis, "What Is the Cause of the Recent Falling Off in the Enlisted

Strength of the Army and Navy, and What Means Should Be Taken to Remedy It?," *Journal of the Military Service Institution of the United States*, March–April 1909, Vol. CLVIII, p. 173 (hereinafter cited as Ellis). (Unless otherwise cited, the following is based on this source.)

9. Maj. Robert Arthur, *The Coast Artillery School 1824–1927*, Ft. Monroe, Va.: The Coast Artillery School, 1928, pp. 57–58.
10. Memorandum for the Assistant Chief of Staff of the Army from Capt. Shelton, Subject: The Army as a Life for Enlisted Men, Washington, D. C., July 1907 (hereinafter ACOS Memo 1907). In War College Division Correspondence, 1903–1919, #4560, RG 165, Records of the WD General Staff and Special Staff, NARA.
11. Maj. W. P. Evans, "Pay of Noncommissioned Officers," *The Journal of the Military Service Institution of the United States*, March–April 1904, Vol. XXXIV, p. 276ff. (Unless otherwise indicated, the following is based on this source.)
12. *War Department Report*, 1907, Vol. I, p. 17; Vol. III, p. 176; 1908, Vol. I, p. 12.
13. Evans, p. 276ff.
14. Ibid.
15. ACOS Memo, 1907, p. 33
16. Ellis, pp. 175–77.
17. Ibid.
18. Ibid. p. 177.
19. Ibid., p. 103.
20. Ibid.
21. *Regulations for the Army of the United States*, 1908, para. 305, p. 58; ACOS Memo, July 1907. (Unless otherwise noted, the following is based on this source.)
22. *Sec. War Rpt.*, 1907, pp. 96–99.
23. Ellis, pp. 173–74.
24. ACOS Memo, July 1907.
25. Ellis, pp. 173–74.
26. *Sec. War Rpt.*, 1908, "The Report of the Inspector General," p. 445.
27. *Sec. War Rpt.*, 1907, pp. 100–102.
28. Ellis, pp. 100–102. (Unless otherwise noted, the following is based on this source.)
29. *History of the Warrant Officer Corps*, Department of the Army Pamphlet 600–11, July 7, 1977.
30. General Order No. 76, June 1, 1900, established the policy of granting double time toward retirement.

CHAPTER 11: WORLD WAR I

1. John M. A. Palmer, *America in Arms: The Experience of the United States with Military Organization*, New Haven, Conn.: Yale University Press, 1941, pp. 139–40.
2. Memo from War Plans Division, to Chief of Staff, Subject: Status of Noncommissioned Officers on Foreign Service, July 29, 1913, WPD 7881–1, WPD National Archives and Records Administration (NARA).
3. Memorandum for the Chief of Staff, from WPD, Subject: Relief of Regimental Noncommissioned Officers Serving in Colonial Regiments, Nov. 21, 1913, Adjutant General's Office, 2064260, War College Division (later War Plans Division) 7881-5. WPD NARA.
4. Ibid.

5. Memorandum WPD for Chief of Staff, Subject: Status of Noncommissioned Officers on Foreign Service, July 29, 1913, WCD 7881–1, WPD NARA.
6. Notes by General Wothersponn, July 1913, WCD, WPD 7881-4, NARA.
7. Ibid.
8. General Orders 75, War Department, Washington, D.C., August 7, 1918, sgd. Peyton C. March, General, Army Chief of Staff, In Box 483, Record Group 407, NARA.
9. Memorandum from D. W. Ketcham, Col., GS, WPD, to Army Chief of Staff, April 3, 1918, WPD 7431, in NARA.
10. Memorandum for the Inspector General from Brig. Gen. E. A. Helmick, IGD, NA, June 19, 1918, Subject: Suggestions and Recommendations for Improving Disciplinary Drill in Our Army, WPD 7541-116 NARA.
11. There were approximately 20,000 noncommissioned officers in the regular Army at the time.
12. Letter, CG Western Dept. to AG, U.S. Army, Subject: Promotion of Noncommissioned Officers, March 4, 1916, in WCD 9466-18, Box 425, NARA.
13. Memorandum for Chief of Staff, from: Brig. Gen. M. M. Macomb, Chief, War College Division, Subject: Special Training of Selected Noncommissioned Officers, March 24, 1916, in WCD-Bell, NARA.
14. Ibid.
15. Letter, CG Hawaiian Dept. to the AG, Washington, D.C., Subject: Special Training of Selected Noncommissioned Officers, April 18, 1916, WCD NARA. (Unless otherwise noted, the following sections are based upon this citation.)
16. Letter, Adjutant General of the Army to Commandant Coast Artillery School, Ft. Monroe, Va., March 29, 1916, Subject: Special Training of Selected Noncommissioned Officers of the Regular Army to Fit Them for Duties of Commissioned Officers, 1st endorsement, CA School, April 19, 1916, in WCD file, NARA.
17. Letter, the Commandant, Army Service Schools, Ft. Leavenworth, To: The Adjutant General of the Army, Subject: Special Training of Selected Noncommissioned Officers of the Regular Army to Fit Them for the Duties of Commissioned Officers. April 1, 1916, in WCD, file NARA. (Unless otherwise indicated, the following is based upon this reference.)
18. General Order 69, Nov. 16, 1915, outlined the procedure for the appointment of 2d Lts. of the line: (1) Cadets graduated from West Point, (2) Enlisted men by examination, (3) Civilians ages 21–27 by competitive examination.
19. Letter, Col. William A. Glassford, SC, to: CG, Western Department, Subject: Training of Noncommissioned Officers for Commissions, June 23, 1916, in WCD File, NARA.
20. Ibid.
21. Letter, 3d Endorsement, CG, HQ Southern Dept., Ft. Sam Houston, Texas, Sept. 8, 1916, To: The Adjutant General of the U.S. Army, Washington, D.C., In WCD files, NARA.
22. Palmer, pp. 164–64. The Draft Act prepared by the Army War College's Plans Division was based upon the concept of universal compulsory training—essentially Washington's national militia concept. The regular Army would be used primarily for the training of the new reserves, and men so trained would be organized into a national army. However, the draft bill that President Wilson eventually sent to Congress was quite different. It was drawn up by the judge advocate general, Enoch Crowder, and his legal staff. Secretary of War Baker added to it the principle of local draft board control (autonomous local boards of citizens). (*Gen. John M. Palmer, Citizen Soldiers, and the Army of a Democracy*, by I. B. Holley, Jr., Greenwood Press, 1982, pp. 262–66.)
23. *War Department Annual Reports*, Vols. I–III, Washington, D.C.: Government Printing Office, 1917, pp. 166–67, 1918, p. 211.

24. Capt. M. B. Stewart, 8th U.S. Infantry, *Handbook for Noncommissioned Officers of Infantry*, Kansas City, Missouri: Hudson-Kimberly Publishing Co., 1903.
25. *A Manual for NCOs and Pvts. of Infantry of the AUS*, Washington, D.C.: War Department, Government Printing Office, 1917.
26. Memorandum for Chief of Staff, Subject: French Advisory Mission in the United States, Oct. 13, 1917; Memorandum for the COS, Subject: Arrival of Foreign Officers in the United States and Arrangements for Their Assignment, October 10, 1917; Cable No. 5,023, From Military Attaché, London, To: War College Division, Washington, D.C. British Officers as in the U.S. All in WCD 10071–228, Box 593 NARA; R. H. Haigh and P. W. Turner, "World War I and the Serving British Soldier," *Military Affairs/Aerospace Historian*, Manhattan, Kan., 1979, p. 10.
27. Capt Edgar T. Fell, *History of the Seventh Division, U.S.A. 1917–18*, Philadelphia: privately published, 1927, pp. 1–8, 254.
28. Western Union Telegram, CG Cp. Mills, Long Island, N.Y., Nov. 20, 1917, To: AG of the Army, WD, Washington, D.C. In WCD Box 199, 7541-30 to 34, NARA.
29. Maj. Gen. John F. O'Ryan, *The Story of the 17th Division*, New York: Hallenbeck, Crawford Co., p. 125.
30. Haigh & Turner, pp. 6, 8.
31. Letter, from Sec. War to Sec. State, Subject: British and French Officers as Advisors to the United States Forces, Aug. 9, 1917, 7541-30, WCD Box 199, NARA.
32. Memorandum for the Adjutant General, From: Brigadier General H. Jervey, Acting Assistant COS, Director of Personnel, Subject: Intensive Training for Infantry Regiments Not Yet in Divisions, June 8, 1918, in WCD 7431-52, Box 188, NARA.
33. Ibid. N.B.: The Army resisted centralized training because it was dispersed in company-sized units and distances were too great for centralized authority, which only became possible for the first time in the World War I training camps.
34. Headquarters 2d U.S. Infantry, Camp Fremont, Calif., July 12, 1918, Memorandum No. 8, in 7431-52, WCD, Box 188, NARA.
35. Headquarters 308th Cavalry To: The Adjutant General of the Army, Washington, D.C., Subject: Schools for Instruction, August 15, 1918. In 7431-52, WCD, Box 188, NARA.
36. Letter, from Instructor, Noncommissioned Officers' Schools, To: Commanding Officer, 10th Infantry, Subject: Report of Schools, Aug. 21, 1918. 1st Ind. To: The Adjutant General of the Army, Washington, D.C., from: Col. Easton R. Gibson, 10th Infantry. In WCD 7431-52, Box 188, NARA.
37. Fell, p. 8.
38. Leonard Nason Hastings, *Sergeant Eadie*, New York: Nason, Grosset & Dunlap, 1928, p. 100.
39. Eric J. Leed, *No Man's Land: Combat and Identity in World War I*, Cambridge, England: Cambridge University Press, 1979, p. 104.
40. Haigh and Turner, p. 8.
41. Memorandum for Adjutant General of the Army, from: Maj. Gen. Henry P. Jervey, ACOS, April 10, 1920, WCD 1901, NARA. (These and other references to inadequate pay for sergeants suggest that the long-fought-for Army Pay Bill of 1908 sorely needed revision to bring it more in line with the times.)
42. E. Streeter, *Dere Mable: Love Letters of a Rookie*, New York: Frederick A. Stokes Co., 1918, pp. 8, 53.
43. Sgt. Cyril B. Mosher, Correspondence, D Battery, 12th Field Artillery, 2d Division, Letter, 1917, Military History Institute, Carlisle Barracks, Pa.
44. Letter, The Adjutant General of the Army to: The Superintendent, United States Military Academy, West Point, N.Y., Subject: Treatment of Enlisted Men, Feb. 10, 1914, WCD Correspondence file 9466-18-21 (8552-7) NARA, Washington, D.C.

45. George H. English, *History of the 89th Division, U.S.A.* Denver, Colo.: Smith-Brooks Publishing Co., 1920, p. 21; History of the 89th Division (an analytical study prepared in the historical section of the Army War College), MS 1924.
46. Memorandum: The Director of Training, The War College U.S.A. From: The British Military Mission, Washington, D.C., March 20, 1918, Subject: Status of the NCO in the British Army, In WCD 7-65.5, Box 223, NARA.
47. Lt. John D. Clark, Correspondence, WWI, C Battery, 15th FA, 2d Division in World War I Collection, Military History Institute, Carlisle Barracks, Pa.
48. Ibid.
49. Memorandum for Adjutant General of the Army, from: Acting COS, War Plans Division, Subject: Administration of Tactical Divisions, April 22, 1918, WPD 10872-5 in WCD Correspondence files, NARA; note from: Gen. Vignal, French Military Attaché, To: ACOS & Gen. Morrison, Chief/The Training Committee, Jan. 9, 1918 (same location).
50. Ibid.
51. Report from Riggs (B) June 19, 1916, in WCD 6566-35, NARA, Washington, D.C.
52. Maj. Gen. John F. O'Ryan, *The Story of the 27th Division*, New York: Wynkoop, Hallenbeck, Crawford Co., 1921, pp. 287–88.
53. Elmer Frank Straub, "A Sergeant's Diary in the World War: The Diary of an Enlisted Member of the 150th Field Artillery (42d Rainbow Division) October 27, 1917, to August 7, 1919," *Indiana World War Records*, Vol. III, Indianapolis, Indiana: Indiana Historical Commission, 1923, p. 207.
54. Hastings, p. 338.
55. Ibid., p. 9.
56. Cable No. 952-2, April 19, 1918, General Headquarters, ASWAR, Washington, Pershing (NARA); Memorandum for ACOS, from: BG Lytle Brown, Director, WPD, ACOS, in WCD 7431-45 (NARA), Subject: Cablegrams from Gen. Pershing on the Training of Troops Recently Arrived in France, May 10, 1918.
57. Memorandum for the Adjutant General of the Army: Subject: Cablegrams from General Pershing on the Training of Troops Recently Arrived in France, Enc. 1, Office Chief of Staff War Plans Division, 7431-45, May 10, 1918, Peyton C. March, WCD Correspondence, NARA.
58. Holley, p. 374.
59. G. Edward Buxton, *Official History of the 82d Division*, Indianapolis, Ind.: Bobbs Merrill, 1919, pp. 59–62.
60. English, p. 83.
61. Papers of Frank R. Dillman, Cpl., 64th Infantry, 7th Division WWI 1309, 1916–1919. In Military History Institute, Carlisle Barracks, Pa. (Unless otherwise noted the following is based upon this citation.)
62. Diary of World War I, Sgt. James E. Warrell, 112th Infantry, 28th Div., in the Military History Institute World War I Collection, Carlisle Barracks, Pa.

CHAPTER 12: ADJUSTING TO POSTWAR AUSTERITY

1. *Secretary of War Report for 1921*, Washington, D.C.: Government Printing Office; pp. 8–9.
2. Ibid., p. 15. This was an idea that was advocated by Gen. George C. Marshall and John M. Palmer following World War II as well.

3. B. F. Cooling, "Enlisted Grade Structure and the Army Reorganization Act of 1920," *Military Affairs*, Vol. XXI, No. 4 (Winter 1967–1968), pp. 187–94.
4. *History of the Warrant Officer Corps*, Department of the Army Pamphlet 600-11, July 7, 1977; Enlisted Grade Structure Study, Vol. VI, p. E-29.
5. Ibid.
6. *Hearings Before the Committee on Military Affairs on H. R. 12827*, Washington, D.C.: Government Printing Office, 1912.
7. Letter, Chief of Cavalry, to the Adjutant General of the Army, Feb. 18, 1939, Subject: Warrant Officers, U.S. Army, Other Than AMPS and Band Leaders. In AG 221.79 Box 1069, RG 407, NARA.
8. Letter, Sec. War to: Chairman, Committee on Military Affairs, U.S. Senate, May 19, 1920. In OCS WPD 4863, Box 484, RG 407, NARA.
9. Memorandum for the Chief of Staff, Subject: S.1929—Providing for the Promotion of Certain Noncommissioned Officers of the Regular Army, Jan. 27, 1928. In AG 202.1 Box 1062, RG 407, NARA.
10. Letter, Sec. of War to Chairman, Committee of Military Affairs, U.S. Senate, May 19, 1920, in OCS WPD 4863, Box 484, RG 407, NARA; Memorandum for Chief of Staff, Army, Jan. 27, 1928, Subject: S. 1929—Providing for the Promotion of Certain NCOs of the Regular Army, in AG 220.1, Box 1052, RG 507, NARA.
11. Ibid.; "Who Are the Officers of the Army?" *Army and Navy Register*, Vol. 86, Oct. 26, 1929, p. 390ff.
12. Letter, the Chief of Cavalry to the Adjutant General, Subject: Warrant Officers, U.S. Army, Other Than AMPS and Band Leaders, Feb. 18, 1939. In AG 221.79, Box 1069, RG 407, NARA.
13. Memorandum for Chief of Staff, Army, Feb. 18 and Aug. 5, 1929, Subject: H.R. 16217, A Bill to Authorize the Appointment of Quartermaster Corps Clerks as Warrant Officers. In AG 220.1, WO Box 1062, RG 407, NARA.
14. Memorandum for the Chief of Staff, Army, Jan. 7, 1930, Subject: Bill to Make Civilian Clerks Warrant Officers, From: R. J. Andrews. In AG 220.1 Box 1062, RG 407, NARA.
15. Ibid.
16. Letter, the Chief of Cavalry, to: The Adjutant General, Feb. 18, 1939, Subject: Warrant Officers, U.S. Army, Other Than AMPS and Band Leaders. In AG 221.79, Box 1069, RG 407, NARA.
17. Ibid.
18. *History of the Warrant Officer Corps.*
19. *Enlisted Grade Structure Study*, Vol. VI, Annex E., p. E-30.
20. *Army and Navy Journal*, Dec. 4, 1920, p. 205.
21. *Army and Navy Journal*, April 29, 1922, p. 827.
22. Ibid.
23. *Army and Navy Journal*, Vol. XVII, No. 4, Oct. 20, 1920, p. 205.
24. William K. Emerson, *Chevrons: Illustrated History and Catalog of U.S. Army Insignia*, Washington, D.C.: Smithsonian Institution Press, 1983, p. 118.
25. *Stars & Stripes*, edition of June 7, 1918, p. 1.
26. *Stars & Stripes*, edition of July 5, 1918.
27. War Department General Orders No. 36, June 19, 1920.
28. *Enlisted Grade Structure Study*, Vol. VI, Annex E, p. 31.
29. Ibid.
30. Ibid., p. E-34.
31. Memorandum for Chief of Staff, Army from Brig. Gen. Joseph E. Kuhn, Assistant to

the CofS, C/War College Division, Subject: Limited Warrants for Noncommissioned Staff Officers, CAC, June 20, 1917, WPD 1011-11; Memorandum for the AG of the Army, from Maj. Gen. Tasker H. Bliss, Acting CofS, Army, Subject as Above.

32. Memorandum for the Adjutant General from Brig. Gen. E. D. Anderson, Acting Director of Operations, Subject: Order of Precedence of Noncommissioned Officers Who Reenlist Within Three Months After Being Discharged as Commissioned Officers, Jan. 27, 1919. In 10221-2 WPA, NARA.
33. Letter to Chairman, Committee on Military Affairs, House of Representatives, from Sec. of War, February 7, 1918. In WCD 9754-67, AG 011.3 (Misc. Div.), WPD, NARA.
34. WD, JAGO, March 1, 1918, to the Adjutant General. In 220.45 (1-9-25) to (2-22-18), RG the AGO, Box 422, NARA.
35. Russell F. Weigley, *History of the U.S. Army*, New York: Macmillan, 1967, pp. 400–403.
36. Robert K. Griffith, Jr., *Men Wanted for the U.S. Army, America's Experience With an All-Volunteer Army Between the Wars*, Westport, Conn.: Greenwood Press, 1982, p. 66; *Army & Navy Journal*, Nov. 25, 1922, p. 298.
37. Letter, Maj. Gen. C. R. Edwards, HQ I Corps Area, to the Hon. John W. Weeks, Dec. 1, 1922. OCS 8867 in 220.26 (3-21-23) to (9-28-17), Box 407, NARA.
38. Memorandum for the Adjutant General of the Army, from Col. E. D. Anderson, Acting Director of Operations, Subject: Appointment of Noncommissioned Officers, Dec. 9, 1919. In 7618-36, RG 407, NARA.
39. Memorandum for Chief of Staff, Army, Subject: Appointment of Noncommissioned Officers of the Quartermaster Corps, Sept. 15, 1920. In AG 300.33, RG 407, NARA.
40. WD AGO, Subject: Warrants for Noncommissioned Officers, QMC. To: Commanding General, All Corps Areas, Depts. and the District of Columbia, and COs of Exempted Stations, May 16, 1922. In AG 220.14 with Encl. (2-28-25) to (5-9-22), RG 407, NARA.
41. Ibid.; General Orders No. 113, Aug. 22, 1917.
42. War Department Circular No. 7, Jan. 7, 1921.
43. War Department Circular No. 41, Feb. 15, 1921, Appointment of NCOs of the Medical Dept. Medical & Dental & Veterinary Services.
44. Memorandum for the Chief of Staff, Army, from: Brig. Gen. J. H. McRae, ACofS, G1, Subject: Reduction of Noncommissioned Officers and Rated Specialists to Conform to the Reorganization of the Army at Strength of 150,000, Oct. 13, 1923. In AG 220.31, Box 418, RG 407 NARA.
45. Ibid.
46. Memorandum from Chief of Staff, Army, to Acting Deputy CofS, Jan 18, 1922; Memo from MG J. G. Hardbord, Deputy CofS, to ACofS, G1, Feb. 7, 1922. In Box 418, RG 407, NARA.
47. Memorandum for the Chief of Staff, Army, from: Brig. Gen. J. R. McRae, ACofS, G1, Subject: Reduction of Noncommissioned Officers and Rated Specialists to Conform to the Reorganization of the Army at Strength of 150,000, Jan. 21, 1922. In Box 418, RG, 407, NARA.
48. Ibid.
49. Ibid.
50. Senate Calendar No. 917, 67th Congress, 3rd Session, Report No. 931, Subject: Increase in the Percentages of Noncommissioned Officers of the Army, 1922.
51. Ibid.; Memorandum for the Adjutant General of the Army, Subject: Reduction of Surplus Noncommissioned Officers, Dec. 12, 1922; G-1/4317 and War Department

Circular No. 214, Subject: Demotion of Noncommissioned Officers and Disrating of Specialists, Dec. 13, 1922. In AG 220.14, RG 407, NARA.

52. *Army and Navy Journal*, April 1, 1922, p. 725.
53. Ibid., p. 728.
54. Ibid.
55. Memorandum for the Chief of Staff, Army, from Brig Gen. C. H. Martin, Assistant CofS, G-1, Subject: Demotion of Surplus Noncommissioned Officers, Dec. 8, 1922. In AGO 220.26 (12-8-22), RG 407, NARA.
56. AGO, Subject: Reduction of Noncommissioned Officers and Disrating of Specialists, Feb. 23, 1922. In 220.31 (2-7-22), Box 418, RG 407, NARA.
57. Letter, Chief of Engineers, to Adjutant General of the Army, Subject: Changes in WD Circular 275, 1921, Feb. 14, 1923. In 220.31, Box 418, RG 407, NARA.
58. Letter Order, the Adjutant General of the Army, Subject: Reduction of Noncommissioned Officers of the QMC, March 22, 1923. In AG 220.26, Box 418, RG 407, NARA.
59. Memorandum for the Adjutant General of the Army, from MG W. G. Haan, Director, Enlisted Personnel Directorate, ACofS, G-1, Subject: Detail of Noncommissioned Officers and Other Enlisted Men for Duty at Educational Institutions, August 12, 1919. In AG 220.63 and 64 (8-21-17), Box 446, RG 407, NARA.
60. Ibid.
61. Memorandum for Chief of Staff, Army, from BG William Lassiter, AcofS of Militia Bureau, Subject: Sergeant-Instructors Required for the National Guard, Dec. 3, 1921; Memorandum for the Adjutant General from BG Lassiter, Subject: Allowance of Noncommissioned Officers for the National Guard, July 26, 1922. In AG 220.651 (11-8-2), Box 447, RG 407, NARA.
62. Ibid.
63. Memorandum for the Adjutant General from MG George C. Rickards, Chief, Militia Bureau, Subject: Allowance of Noncommissioned Instructors with the National Guard, March 6, 1923; Memorandum for the Adjutant General, from MG William Lassiter, Assistant CofS of Militia Bureau, Subject: Allowance of Noncommissioned Instructors with the National Guard, March 15, 1923. In AG 220.651, Box 447, RG 407, NARA.
64. Memorandum for the Chief of Staff, Army, Subject: Reallotment of Enlisted Grades and Ratings of the Regular Army Under the Act of June 6, 1924, June 25, 1924. In AG 221 (6-25-24), Box 481, RG 407, NARA.
65. Letter, BG E. J. Williams, Executive for Chief, Militia Bureau, to the Adjutant General of the Army, Subject: Increase in Allotment of Sergeant-Instructors for National Guard, June 20, 1924. In AG 220.651, Box 447, RG 407, NARA.
66. Memorandum for the Adjutant General of the Army from: BG H. A. Brum, Subject: Increase in the Allotment of Sergeant-Instructors for the National Guard, July 3, 1924. In AG 220.651, Box 447, RG 407, NARA; and Memorandum to the Adjutant General, From: E. J. Williams, Executive, Chief of Militia Bureau, Subject: Allotment of Sergeant-Instructors, National Guard, Aug. 1, 1923. In MB 220.651 General-15, Box 480, RG 407, NARA.
67. AG Memorandum for ACofS, G-3, April 16, 1923. In AG 220.62 Enl. Box 445, RG 407, NARA.
68. Letter Order, the Adjutant General's Office, to: Commanding Generals of all Corps Areas and the District of Washington, Subject: Detail of Additional Sergeants to Recruiting as Canvassers, July 20, 1923. In AG 220.62 (6-27-23) Enl. Box 445, RG 407, NARA.
69. Memorandum for Chief, Legislative Branch, from: The Adjutant General of the Army, December 27, 1923. In AG 220.62 Enl. Box 445, RG 407, NARA.

70. 67th Congress, 2nd Session, H.R. 12106, June 21, 1922 and 4th Session, H.R. 13418, December 14, 1922.
71. Memorandum for the Chief of Staff, Army, from ACofS, G-1, Subject: Change in Retirement Law for Enlisted Men, June 29, 1922. In AG 220.85, Box 477, RG 407, NARA.
72. Memorandum for the Chief of Staff, Army, Subject: Retirement of Enlisted Men, Jan. 4, 1923. In AG 220.85 (12-22-22), Box 477, RG 407, NARA.
73. Statement of Sgt. Ernest A. Perry in Connection with Activities Toward a Twenty-five Year Retirement, December 31, 1923, U.S. Army Recruiting Station, 239 Market St., Harrisburg, Pa., 12th Ind.; WD, OIG to AGO, January 31, 1924, both items in AG 220.85, Box 476, RG 407, NARA.
74. Memorandum for the Assistant Chief of Staff, G-1, from ACofS, Gen. John J. Pershing, Subject: Retirement of Officers and Enlisted Men, Jan. 15, 1923. In AG 220.85 (1-12-23), Box 476, RG 407, NARA.
75. Memorandum for the Chief of Staff, Army, from C. H. Martin, BG, ACofS, G-1, Subject: Retirement of Warrant Officers, Field Clerks, and Enlisted Men, November 16, 1924. In AG 220.85 (1-12-23), Box 476, RG 407, NARA.
76. Interview with General James K. Woolnough, by Col. Macmillan and Lt. Col. Stevenson, AWC 70-71, Vol. I, at Military History Institute, Carlisle Barracks, Pa.
77. H.R. 5603, in the House of Representatives, June 12, 1919; Letter to Hon. Julius Kahn, Chairman, Committee on Military Affairs, House of Representatives, Aug. 18, 1919, from Newton D. Baker, Sec. War; Letter to the Chairman, Committee on Military Affairs, House of Representatives, May 12, 1921, from: John W. Weeks, Sec. War; Memorandum for CofS, Army, from: BG J. H. McRae, ACofS, G-1, April 14, 1922, Subject: Bill (H.R. 11108), Extending the Provision of Sec. 127a, National Defense Act Re: Retired Pay of Enlisted Men; Memorandum for Gen. Hersey (through the CO, C.D. of Boston, Ft. Banks, Mass.), Jan. 28, 1923. In AG 220.85, Box 476, RG 407, NARA.
78. Memorandum for Assistant Chief of Staff, G-3, From: Adjutant General, Subject: Reduction of Noncommissioned Officers, Dec. 12, 1923. In AG 221, Box 480, RG 407, NARA.

CHAPTER 13: SYMBOLS AND SUBSTANCE

1. James Jones, *From Here to Eternity*, New York: Delacorte Press, 1951, p. 11.
2. Memorandum to Chief of Coast Artillery from Bryan L. Milburn, Capt., CAC, March 21, 1916, AG 220.31, Box 1075, RG 407, Old Military Records Division, NARA.
3. Ibid.
4. See War Department cables, Manila Nr. 3322, Dec. 1926, Sladen to Adjutant General, and Manila Nr. 4188, Feb. 14, 1929, MacArthur to Adjutant General. Both items in AG 220.31, Box 1075, RG 407, NARA.
5. Memorandum for the Assistant Chief of Staff, G-1, War Department General Staff, Washington, D.C., Subject: Replacement of Noncommissioned Officers on Foreign Service, Sept. 16, 1935, Box 1027, RG 407, NARA.
6. AR 615-210, Enlisted Men, Foreign Service, Washington, D.C.: Feb. 20, 1929.
7. Memorandum for the Adjutant General, Jan. 6, 1932, Subject: Demotion of Certain Noncommissioned Officers on Return from Foreign Service, from Brigadier General Andrews Moses, Assistant Chief of Staff. In AG 220.481 (1-6-32), Box 1027, RG 407, NARA.
8. 1st Endorsement, Chief of Chemical Warfare to the Adjutant General, Jan. 11, 1932;

Letter, Adjutant General, to Chief of Chemical Warfare Service, Jan. 8, 1932, Subject: Demotion of Certain Noncommissioned Officers on Return from Foreign Service. In AG 220.481 (1-6-32), Enl. Box 1027, RG 407, NARA.

9. 1st Endorsement, WD OGCA, Jan. 12, 1932, to Adjutant General, Letter, AG to Chief, Coast Artillery Corps, Jan. 8, 1932, Subject: Demotion of Certain Noncommissioned Officers on Return from Foreign Service. In AG 220.481, Enl. Box 1027, RG 407, NARA.
10. 3rd Endorsement, OCCA, MG, John W. Gulicks, Chief of Coast Artillery, Jun. 4, 1932, to the Adjutant General. (Same source as preceding note.)
11. Ibid.
12. Letter, Adjutant General of Chief of Engineers, Jan. 8, 1932, Subject: Demotion of Certain Noncommissioned Officers, etc., 1st Endorsement, Office Chief of Engineers to the Adjutant General, April 8, 1932. In AG 220.481, Box 1207, RG 407, NARA.
13. Ibid.
14. Ibid.
15. Memorandum for the Assistant Chief of Staff, G-1, War Department General Staff, Subject: Replacement of Noncommissioned Officers on Foreign Service, Sept. 16, 1935. In Box 1027, RG 407, NARA.
16. Letter, M/Sgt Robert Goodwin, 15th Inf., Tientsin, China, Feb. 8, 1934, to BG Edgar T. Conlay, Assistant AG, U.S. Army. In AG 220.31. Box 1072, RG 407, NARA.
17. Letter, Chief of Coast Artillery (through CO, Coast Artillery School Detachment, Ft. Monroe, Va.) Dec. 23, 1938, Subject: Mutual Transfer, from: Howard G. Hatch, Staff Sgt. C.A.S.D. In Box 1078, RG 407, NARA.
18. Memorandum for the Chief of Staff, August 23, 1938, Subject: Exchange of Enlisted Men Between Organizations of Foreign Service and Organizations in the United States, from E. B. Collady, Lt. Col., Acting Assistant Chief of Staff. In AG 220.481, Box 1027, RG 407, NARA.
19. Memorandum for the Chief of Staff, May 17, 1938, Subject: Replacement of Sergeants on Foreign Service. In 200.31 (5-1-39), Box 1070, RG 407, NARA.
20. Charles Willeford, *Something About a Soldier*, New York: Ballantine Books, 1986, p. 63.
21. Memorandum for the Chief of Staff, May 17, 1938, Subject: Replacement of Sergeants on Foreign Service, 200.31 (5-1-39), Box 1070, RG 407, NARA.
22. Memorandum for the Chief of Staff from Assistant Chief of Staff, G-1, May 17, 1939, Subject: Replacement of Sergeants on Foreign Service. In AG 220.31 (5-1-39), Box 1070, RG 407, NARA.
23. Letter Order: Chief of Army and Service, Corps Area Commanders, and Commanders of Exempted Stations in the United States, June 5, 1939, Subject: Replacement of Sergeants on Foreign Service, from the Adjutant Service; Memorandum for the Adjutant General, Subject: Replacement of Sergeants on Foreign Service, Sept. 7, 1939. In AG 220.31 (9-7-39), both in Box 1069, RG 407, NARA.
24. Memorandum for Special Orders N. 53, WD, Washington, D.C., March 5, 1930. In AG 220.31. (3-3-3), Box 1075, RG 407, NARA.
25. 2nd Endorsement, Office, Chief of Engineers, April 15, 1931, To: the Adjutant General. In AG 220.2 234/1, Box 1074, RG 407, NARA.
26. 8th Endorsement, WD, Ordnance, Washington, D.C., June 8, 1931, To: the Chief Signal Officer, 00,300.3/815. In AG 220.31, Box 1074, RG 407, NARA.
27. 15th Endorsement, WD, Office of the Chief of Cavalry, Washington, D.C., July 21, 1931, to: the Adjutant General. In AG 220.31, Box 1074, RG 407, NARA.
28. Memorandum, the Adjutant General, Maj. Gen. C. H. Bridges, July 31, 1931. In AG 220.21, Box 1074, RG 407, NARA.

29. AR 615-200, Section I, "Enlisted Men, Transfers," WD, Washington, D.C., Nov. 24, 1939.
30. Ibid., Change Nr. 3, para. 11, July 19, 1938.
31. Ibid.
32. Ibid., March 15, 1943.
33. Memorandum for Chief of Staff, June 15, 1936, Subject: Benefits Received by Enlisted Men, from: Assistant Chief of Staff, Adjutant General's Office. In 220.85 (6-15-36), Box 1105, RG 407, NARA.
34. Letter, Hon. John J. McSwain, Chairman, House Committee on Military Affairs, from Secretary of War, March 12, 1935. In AGO 220.85, Box 1105, RG 407, NARA.
35. Memorandum for the Army Chief of Staff, January 20, 1928, from Brig. Gen. C. King, Assistant Chief of Staff, Adjutant Generals Office. In 220.85 (4-18-24), Box 1106, RG 407, NARA; Memorandum for Chief of Staff, Subject: Benefits Received by Enlisted Men, June 15, 1936, from Brig. Gen. H.E.E. Knight, Assistant Chief of Staff, Adjutant General's Office. In 220.85, Box 1105, RG 407.
36. Ibid., memo of June 15, 1936.
37. Letter, Hon. John J. McSwain, Chairman House Committee on Military Affairs, Aug. 2, 1935, from George H. Dern, Secretary of War. In AGO 220.85, Box 1105, RG 407, NARA.
38. Ibid.
39. Letter, the Adjutant General's Office (through channels), from: C.O. Air Base Hdqrs., Hamilton Field, Calif., 10-8-38, Subject: Provision for 25 Year Retirement for Enlisted Men. In AGO 220.85, Box 1105, RG 407, NARA.
40. Memorandum for the Chief of Staff, Subject: Legislation to Provide Retirement of Enlisted Men of Over 25 Years' Service Who Are Physically Disabled, Nov. 3, 1938, from Brig. Gen. L. D. Gasser, Assistant Chief of Staff. In AGO 220.85 (11338), Box 1105, RG 407, NARA.
41. Manuscript prepared by the Adjutant General's Office, Feb. 3, 1967, "History and Development of the Army and Air Force Retirement System," in the files of the U.S. Army Center of Military History, Washington, D.C.
42. Ibid.
43. Outline, "The Warrant Officer Program," in the U.S. Army Center of Military History files, Washington, D.C.
44. DA Pamphlet 600-11, "History of the Warrant Officer Corps," July 7, 1977.
45. Ibid.
46. Many texts of interviews with retired senior officers are on file at the U.S. Army Military Research Collection, Carlisle Barracks, Pennsylvania. Among them are those with generals Paul D. Harkins, R. J. Wood, Michael C. Davison, Herbert B. Powell, George R. Mather, James K. Woolnough, and Mathew B. Ridgeway. Unless otherwise noted, the following is based on material contained in these interviews.
47. See *Secretary of War Report*, Washington, D.C.: Government Printing Office, 1926, p. 52.
48. Forrest Pogue, *George C. Marshall, Education of a General*, Vol. I, New York: Viking Press, 1963, p. 276.
49. Lt. Col. Will B. Allanson, "The Incomparable Sgt. Reese: Mentor, Loyal First Soldier, But Never a Friend," *Army*, Jan. 1971, pp. 38–41.
50. Col. John M. Collins, "The Lean, Lean Years, Depression Army," *Army*, Jan. 1972, pp. 8–14.
51. Ibid.

CHAPTER 14: WORLD WAR II

1. Russell F. Weigley, *History of the United States Army*, New York: Macmillan, 1967, p. 428.
2. Ibid., p. 429.
3. John M. Collins, "The Care and Cleaning of NCOs: A Critical Survey of Destructive Policies and Practices Which Have Shaped the Army Noncommissioned Officer Corps Since 1939" (thesis, Industrial College of the Armed Forces, March 1967).
4. War Department Circulars 2, Jan. 3, 1940; 3, Jan 4, 1940; and 25, Jan. 23, 1942.
5. WD Cir 25, Jan. 13, 1942.
6. *Enlisted Grade Structure Study*, "Historical Review of the Enlisted Grade Structure of the U.S. Army, 1775–1967, Vol. VI, Annex E, Department of the Army, Deputy Chief of Staff for Personnel, July 1967. (Unless otherwise indicated, the following is based on this reference.)
7. *Enlisted Grade Structure Study.*
8. Charles B. MacDonald, *Company Commander*, Washington, D.C.: Infantry Journal Press, 1947.
9. Ernest F. Fisher, Jr., *Cassino to the Alps*, Washington, D.C.: Government Printing Office, 1977, p. 47. (Unless otherwise indicated, the following is based on this reference.)
10. Maj. Gen. Aubrey Newman, *Follow Me: The Human Element in Leadership*, Novato, Calif.: Presidio Press, 1981, pp. 102–3.
11. Gen. Harold K. Johnson Papers, speech reference file through 1968. Gen. Johnson quoting Gen. S.L.A. Marshall describing reduction of a German coastal battery at Utah Beach on D-Day. File at Military History Institute, Carlisle Barracks, Pa.
12. Gen. Harold K. Johnson Papers, Box 56 (Speech Reference File). In Archives, Military History Institute, Carlisle Barracks, Pa.
13. War Department Circular 70, *Noncommissioned Officers*, Feb. 16, 1944. (Unless otherwise noted, the following is based on this reference.)
14. Marshall interview with Forrest C. Pogue, Feb. 15, 1957, at Pinehurst, North Carolina. In U.S. Army Center of Military History files.
15. Harold Wool, *The Military Specialists: Skilled Manpower for the Armed Forces*, Baltimore, Md.: The Johns Hopkins Press, 1968, pp. 24–25, 175–76.
16. Ibid.
17. War Department Circular 148, Section I, May 18, 1942.
18. Memorandum from Director, Mil. Pers. Div, Subject: Rank and Precedence of Noncommissioned Officers, Nov. 14, 1943. In AG 220.72 (Oct. 6, 43), RG 165, Entry 43, g-1, Box 422, NARA.
19. See Emerson, Chapter 7, and Army Regulations 600-35, March 31, 1944.
20. *The Procurement and Training of Ground Combat Troops*, Washington, D.C.: U.S. Army Center of Military History, Government Printing Office, 1948, p. 18; *The Organization of Ground Combat Troops*, Washington, D.C.: U.S. Army Center of Military History, Government Printing Office, 1947, pp. 179–80.
21. Collins, p. 46.
22. *History of the Warrant Officer Corps*, Chapter II. (Unless otherwise indicated, the following is based on this reference.)

CHAPTER 15: POSTWAR RETROSPECTION, CHALLENGE, AND EVALUATION

1. Interview with General De Puy, Oct. 19, 1976.
2. *Enlisted Grade Structure Study*, Vol. VI, Annex E, DA/DSCPER, July 1967.
3. AR 245–5, June 2, 1942.
4. Change 1 to AR 245–5, 1942 [December 20, 1945].
5. Unless otherwise cited, the following sections are based upon the final report of the Doolittle Board, May 1946, in USA CMH files, Washington, D.C.
6. Dennis Murphy, *The Sergeant*, New York: Viking Press, 1958, p. 31.
7. Charles C. Moskos, Jr., *The American Enlisted Man, the Rank & File in Today's Military*, New York: The Russell Sage Foundation, 1970, pp. 9–10.
8. T. R. Fehrenbach, *This Kind of War: A Study in Preparedness*, New York: Macmillan, 1963, XV–XVII.
9. Ibid.
10. John M. Collins, "The Care and Cleaning of NCOs: A Critical Survey of Destructive Policies Which Have Shaped the Army Noncommissioned Officer Corps Since 1939" (thesis, Industrial College of the Armed Forces, March 1967). (Unless otherwise indicated, the following is based upon this reference.)
11. Fehrenbach, p. 431.
12. Ibid.
13. Ibid.
14. John M. Collins, "The Care and Cleaning of NCOs: A Critical Survey of Destructive Policies Which Have Shaped the Army Noncommissioned Officer Corps Since 1939" (thesis, Industrial College of the Armed Forces, March 1967).
15. Fehrenbach, p. 232.
16. Ibid., p. 113; Capt. Russell A. Gugler, *Combat Actions in Korea*, Washington, D.C.: Combat Forces Press, 1954, p. 9.
17. Gugler, pp. 11 and 29.
18. *Medal of Honor, 1963–1968*, Washington, D.C.: U.S. Government Printing Office, 1968, pp. 801–2; Fehrenbach, pp. 212–27.
19. Gugler, pp. 223–228.
20. Fehrenbach, p. 455.
21. Gugler, p. 222.
22. Roy E. Appleman, *The United States Army in the Korean War, South to the Naktong, North to the Yalu, June–November, 1950*, Washington, D.C.: Office of the Chief of Military History, 1961, pp. 426–29.
23. Ibid., pp. 472–73.
24. S.L.A. Marshall, ORO, *Commentary on Infantry and Weapons Usage in Korea, Winter of 1950–51*, Baltimore: Johns Hopkins University, 1953, p. 51.
25. Ibid.
26. Ibid.
27. Ibid, pp. 4–5, 61.
28. *Medal of Honor, 1963–1968*, Washington, D.C.: U.S. Government Printing Office, 1968, pp. 729–806.
29. S.L.A. Marshall, pp. 7, 35, 64.
30. Collins; *TOE, 7–17 N, Inf. Rifle Co.* December 9, 1947 (*Change 3*, November 15, 1950).
31. *The Womble Report on Service Careers*, October 1953, in USA CMH files. (Unless otherwise cited the following is based upon this report.)
32. Ibid.

CHAPTER 16: TRAIN US TO LEAD

1. Russell F. Weigley, *History of the United States Army*, New York: Macmillan, 1967, pp. 486–87, 501.
2. *Enlisted Grade Structure Study*, Vol. VI, Annex E, "Historical Review of the Enlisted Grade Structure of the U.S. Army, 1775–1976," DA/DSCPER, July 1976, p. E-34.
3. War Department Circular No. 118, May 9, 1947. The plan, however, was not implemented until the following year. (Unless otherwise indicated, the following section is based on this reference.)
4. Sgt. Maj. Dan Cragg, "Don't Juggle GI Grades, Insignia," *Army*, April 1979, p. 61.
5. Department of the Army Circular No. 1, "Career Guidance Plan for Warrant Officers and Enlisted Peronnel," January 1948.
6. Ibid.
7. 1st Sgt. Louis E. Garcia, "Train Us to Lead," *Infantry*, Vol. 52, No. 2, March/April 1962, pp. 23–24.
8. Gen. Bruce C. Clarke, "No Second Class," *Army*, May 1978, p. 50. In this article Gen. Clarke said the meeting took place in "1949," but in reality it must have occurred sometime before June 7, 1948, because DA Cir. 202, which officially announced the new grade titles, does not contain the designation that so offended General Bradley.
9. Cragg, "Don't Juggle GI Grades, Insignia," p. 61.
10. Interview, author with General William DePuy, Oct. 1976 at CONARC HQ, Ft. Monroe. On file at U.S. Army Sergeants Major Academy, Ft. Bliss, Texas.
11. DA Pamphlet 600-11, *History of the Warrant Officer Corps*, July 7, 1977. (Unless otherwise indicated, the following is based on this reference.)
12. War Department Training Circular No. 5, August 12, 1947.
13. *Occupation Forces in Europe Series*, Jan. 1–Mar. 31, 1948 (1st Quarter Report), Vol. II, EUCOM Historical Division. In U.S. Army Center of Military History files, Washington, D.C.
14. HQ Seventh Army Annual Historical Report, Jan. 1–Dec. 31, 1954. In CMH files.
15. Interview, author with Gen. Harold K. Johnson, USA (Ret.), April 6, 1982, Washington, D.C. Filed under Notes for NCO History, U.S. Army Sergeants Major Academy, Ft. Bliss, Tex.
16. Army Regulations 350-90, *Education and Training, Noncommissioned Officers Academies*, Washington, D.C.: Headquarters, Department of the Army, June 25, 1957. (Unless otherwise indicated, the following is based on this source.)
17. HQ Seventh Army Annual Historical Report, Vol. I, July 1, 1958–Dec. 31, 1959. In U.S. Army Center of Military History files. (Unless otherwise cited, the following is based on this citation.)
18. Ibid.
19. Seventh U.S. Army History, FY 1958 (July 1, 1957–June 30, 1958). In U.S. Army Center of Military History files.
20. HQ Seventh Army Annual Historical Report, Vol. I, July 1, 1958–Dec. 31, 1959. In U.S. Army Center of Military History files. (Unless otherwise cited, the following is based on this source.)
21. Ibid.
22. John M. Collins, "The Care and Cleaning of NCOs: A Critical Survey of Destructive Policies and Practices Which Have Shaped the Army Noncommissioned Officer Corps Since 1939" (thesis, Industrial College of the Armed Forces, March 1967), pp. 110–14. (Unless otherwise cited, the following is based on this source.)
23. Ibid.

24. Ibid.
25. Garcia. pp. 23–24.
26. Letter, CSM Paul W. Muuss (USA, Ret.) to Dan Cragg, July 1, 1990. In author's files. (Unless otherwise indicated, the following is based on this source.)
27. William R. Hawes, "Upholding NCO Training Tradition," *The European Stars and Stripes*, March 14, 1983, p. 11.
28. Ibid.
29. Collins, pp. 116–17.
30. Capt. Fred A. Darden, "More Time for Sergeants," *Infantry*, Vol. 51, No. 1, Dec. 1960, pp. 20–23. (Unless otherwise indicated, the following is based on this reference.)
31. Memorandum for the Record, Enlisted Division, G-1 Section, HQ AGF, April 1, 1946, AGF/AG 203, NARA.

CHAPTER 17: DAY OF THE SUPERGRADES

1. John M. Collins, "The Care and Cleaning of NCOs: A Critical Survey of Destructive Policies and Practices Which Have Shaped the Army Noncommissioned Officer Corps Since 1939" (thesis, Industrial College of the Armed Forces, March 1967), pp. 55–72. (Unless otherwise indicated, the following is based on this source.)
2. *A Modern Concept of Manpower Management and Compensation for Personnel of the Uniformed Services*, Volume I, "Military Personnel: A Report and Recommendations for the Secretary of Defense," Defense Advisory Committee on Professional and Technical Compensation, May 1957. (Hereafter referred to as the Cordiner Report.) (Unless otherwise cited, the following is based on this document.)
3. PL 85-422, 85th Congress—H.R. 11470, May 20, 1958 (Senate Report No. 1472, April 25, 1958).
4. Sgt. Maj. Dan Cragg, "Don't Juggle GI Grades, Insignia," *Army*, April 1979, pp. 60–61. (Unless otherwise indicated, the following is based on this citation.)
5. "Summary of Major Events & Problems, FY 1960," Deputy Chief of Staff for Peronnel, Department of the Army. In DA/CMH files. (Unless otherwise indicated, the following is based on this reference.)
6. Ibid.
7. Letter order for HQ, Department of the Army Office of Personnel Operations, To: Commanding General, Continental Army Command, Subject: Designation of Command Sergeant Major's Position, Sept. 19, 1969 with staff study, Assessment of the Sergeant Major, E-9, in the Army. Filed at DA/CMH. (Unless otherwise indicated, the following is based on this reference.)
8. Dan Cragg, *The Soldier's Prize*, New York: Ballantine Books, 1986, p. 7.
9. Sgt. Maj. Robert B. Begg, "The Sergeant Major." (Unless otherwise indicated, the following is based on this reference.)
10. Ibid.
11. Cragg, *The Soldier's Prize*, pp. 103–4.
12. See Army Circulars No. 633-31, Jan. 8, 1968; 611-36, April 15, 1968; 611-40, June 17, 1968; 611-39, Aug. 19, 1968; Change 2 to AR 614-200, Aug. 2, 1971; and AR 135-205, April 6, 1972. In DA/CMH files.
13. Interview, Dr. E. F. Fisher, Jr., with Brig. Gen. Victor Hugo, Department of the Army Chief of Staff, Management Directorate, The Pentagon, Feb. 24, 1982. On file at DA/CMH.

14. Memorandum from Col. Charles L. Crain, Chief, Classification and Standards Division, DCSPER To: General Norris, Subject: Command Sergeants Major Program, May 22, 1967. In DA/CMH files.
15. DCSPER Summary Sheet, Subject: Command Sergeants Major Program, June 20, 1967. In DA/CMH files.
16. Annual Historical Summary, DCSPER, FY 1968. In DA/CMH files.
17. HQ DA, DCSPER Staff Study, Command Sergeants Major Program, May 1967. In DA/CMH files.
18. Change 3, AR 614-200, Aug. 2, 1971. (Unless otherwise indicated, the following is based on this reference.)
19. Department of the Army Circular 611-31, May 14, 1974. In DA/CMH files.
20. Letter from Gen. W. E. DePuy, Commanding General, Training and Doctrine Command, to Gen. Fred C. Weyand, Chief of Staff, U.S. Army, Dec. 25, 1975. In DA/CMH files. (Unless otherwise noted, the following is based on this reference.)
21. *Enlisted Grade Structure Study*, Vol. IX, Annex J, "Command and Staff Comments of Fifteen Essential Elements of Analysis," DA/DSCPER, July 1976, p. J-12.

CHAPTER 18: VIETNAM

1. Maj. Gen. Melvin Zais, "The New NCO," *Army*, May 1968, pp. 72–77. (Unless otherwise indicated, the following is based on this reference.)
2. Interview, author with Gen. William E. DePuy, Oct. 8, 1976, at CONARC HQ, Ft. Monroe, Va. On file at U.S. Army Sergeants Major Academy, Ft. Bliss, Texas.
3. Interview of Gen. H. K. Johnson by Lt. Col. Glover, Interview No. 10, Senior Officers' Oral History Program, Jan. 22, 1973; by Dr. Ernest F. Fisher, Jr., April 6, 1982. In DA/CMH files. (Unless otherwise indicated, the following is based on these references.)
4. Ibid.
5. OCSA-SAMVA memorandum for Lt. Gen. George I. Forsythe, Subject: Visit to USARV From April 7 to May 15, 1971. In file at DA/CMH. (Unless otherwise indicated, the following is based on this reference.)
6. Charles C. Moskos, Jr., *The American Enlisted Man: The Rank and File in Today's Military*, New York: The Russell Sage Foundation, 1970, pp. 5–71. (Unless otherwise indicated, the following is based on this reference.) See also James Jones, *From Here to Eternity.*
7. Peter Archinger, *The American Soldier in Fiction, 1880–1963: A History of Attitudes Toward Warfare and the Military Establishment*, Ames, Iowa: Iowa University Press, 1975.
8. James Webb, *Fields of Fire*, New York: Bantam Books, 1981, pp. 80–81.
9. Conversations Between General Ben Harrell and Colonel Robert P. Hayden, Senior Officers' Debriefing Program, MHI/AWC, Carlisle Barracks, Pa.
10. Interview, Lt. Col. Glover with Gen. Harold K. Johnson, USA (Ret.), Jan. 22, 1973, Interview No. 10, Senior Officers' Oral History Program, MHI/AWC, Carlisle Barracks, Pa.
11. Transcripts of Testimony, Document 71-49, 224-04, IG files, FY 71, USASUPCOM, DaNang. In the Vietnam document collection, Washington National Records Center, Suitland, Md. (For obvious reasons, the identities of the individuals involved in this investigation are not given here; unless otherwise indicated, the following is based on this source.)
12. Transcript of Testimony, 70-64, 224-04, Inspector General Investigative Files, FY 1970,

11/19. In WNRC, Suitland, Md. (Unless otherwise indicated, the following is based on this reference.)

13. Maj. David H. Gillooly, MSC, USA and Thomas C. Bond, M.D., "Assaults with Explosive Devices on Superiors: A Synopsis of Reports from Confined Offenders at the U.S. Disciplinary Barracks," *Journal of Military Medicine*, Vol. 41, No. 10, November 1976. (Unless otherwise noted, the following is based on this source.)
14. OCSA-SAMVA, Memorandum for Lt. Gen. G. I. Forsythe, Subject: Visit to USARV From April 7 to May 15, 1971. On file in DA/CMH. (Unless otherwise indicated, the following is based on this document.)
15. Sgt. Maj. Dan Cragg, USA (Ret.) to author.
16. Interview, Lt. Col. Glover with Gen. Harold K. Johnson, January 22, 1973.

CHAPTER 19: SERGEANT MAJOR AT THE SUMMIT

1. See General Order 29, Headquarters, Department of Army, July 4, 1966: The Sergeant Major of the Army, Position and Duties. Copy in DA/CMH files.
2. See, H.R. 16553, 89th Congress, 2d Session, July 26, 1966.
3. Lt. Col. Glover, interview with Gen. Harold Keith Johnson, Senior Officers Oral History Program, Interview #10, Jan. 22, 1973, Military History Institute, Carlisle Barracks, Pa.
4. Interview, Dr. Ernest F. Fisher, Jr., with General Harold K. Johnson, USA, April 6, 1982.
5. Glover interview. (Unless otherwise indicated, the following is based upon this reference.)
6. Letter, W.O. Wooldridge, USA. (Ret.) to Dr. E. F. Fisher, Jr., U.S. Army Center of Military History, June 6, 1982, in CMH files.
7. Citation of Distinguished Service Medal to SMA William O. Wooldridge, July 1968.
8. *Army Times*, Sept. 17, 1969, pp. 1, 26; Oct. 15, 1969, pp. 1–2; Nov. 5, 1969, pp. 1, 24. (Unless otherwise indicated, the following is based on these references.)
9. Letter, William O. Wooldridge, SMA (Ret.) to Dr. Ernest F. Fisher, Jr., U.S. Army Center of Military History, June 6, 1982, in files CMH, Washington, D.C.
10. Johnson interview, April 6, 1982.
11. See Chief of Staff Regulation 1-5, Nov. 1, 1973.
12. SMA William O. Wooldridge, "First Look at a New Job," *Army Green Book*, Oct. 1966, pp. 43ff; CSM 70-389, 1970, Inclosure to Memo for ACoS, Subject: Policy Regarding Press Conference and Interview by SMA, OCOI, Dec. 9, 1971; Chief of Staff Regulation 1-5, Dec. 11, 1974, placed the office of the SMA under staff supervision of the Director of the Army Staff.
13. Ibid.
14. Letter, William O. Wooldridge, SMA (Ret.) to Dr. Ernest F. Fisher, Jr. June 6, 1982, in files CMH, Washington, D.C.
15. Staff Study, CSM Program, Hq. DA Office of Personnel Operations, May 11, 1967.
16. Letter, W.O. Wooldridge to Dr. Ernest F. Fisher, Jr., June 6, 1982; Memorandum for Record by Col. J.A. LeClair, Jr. Chief, Senior Enlisted Control Branch, CSM Program, July 17, 1967.
17. Letter, Col. R.H. Johnson, XO to Gen. Westmoreland, to SMA Woolridge, May 10, 1968.
18. Letter, Gen. W. C. Westmoreland, to General James H. Polk, CINCUSAREUR and Seventh Army, June 12, 1970; Draft News Release re: SMA, n.d. In files DA/CMH.

19. DA/News Release, August 14, 1970, no. 672-70; Memorandum to General C. Abrams from SGS through General Palmer, Sept. 15, 1972. In DA/CMH files.
20. Letter, General C. W. Abrams to Gen. B. Rogers, January 5, 1973; Memorandum for Executive, ADSCPER, from Col. R. L. Adcock, Ass't Director Military Personnel Management, Subject: Selection of New SMA; Ltr. SMA G. W. Dunaway, USA (Ret.) to Dr. E. F. Fisher, June 7, 1982, both in DA/CMH files.
21. "Where the 'People' Programs Are: The NCO at the Apex," *Army*, October 1974, pp. 17–18.
22. Letter, CSM J. Jones, CSM, U.S. Army Air Defense Center, Ft. Bliss, Tex. to General Frederick C. Weyand, COS, U.S. Army, October 18, 1974, in DA/CMH files.
23. *History of the U.S. Army's Sergeant Major Academy*, July 1, 1972–December 31, 1974, Ft. Bliss, Tex.
24. Letter, Gen. Bernard W. Rogers, U.S. Army Chief of Staff to SMA William G. Bainbridge, Nov. 7, 1977.
25. Interview, Dr. Ernest F. Fisher, Jr. DA/CMH with SMA William G. Bainbridge, May 30, 1979. In file DA/CMH.
26. Letter, J. H. Hoeppel, House of Representatives, U.S. Congress, February 9, 1935, to the Honorable George Dern, Sec. of War, Washington, D.C. Modern Military Records, NARS, Washington, D.C.
27. Ibid.
28. Letter, Secretary of War, George H. Dern, to Honorable J. H. Hoeppel, House of Representatives, Oct. 15, 1935. In Modern Military Records Branch, NARS, Washington, D.C.
29. Memorandum for Record, Interview, Dr. E. F. Fisher with SMA William Connelly, Sept. 4, 1979, in DA/CMH files; Comments by SMA William Connelly on Draft MS Chapter, June 7, 1982.
30. Ibid.

CHAPTER 20: INSTITUTIONALIZING PROFESSIONALISM

1. DCSPER Annual Historical Summaries, FY 1970–1975. In files U.S. Army Center of Military History. (Unless otherwise indicated, the following is based upon these references.)
2. TRADOC Annual Report of Major Activities, FY 1974, p. 288.
3. U.S. Army Personnel Center, *Focus*, No. 14-75, July 30, 1975.
4. Memo from DA/CS for Col. B. F. Harmon, III, Office of Deputy COSPER, Jan. 4, 1971, Subj: NCO Schools. In file DA/CMH; Memo from A. J. Danields, DAC, Volunteer Army Division, for record, Subj: NCO Schools, Jan. 7, 1971. In DA/CMH files.
5. Memorandum for: DCSOPS, CONARC Col. Robert M. Montague, Jr. Deputy Special Assistant for the MVA, Subj: NCO Schools, March 10, 1971; Memorandum for: Deputy Special Assistant for MVA, Subj: NCO Schools undated. In DA/CMH files.
6. Letter from DA Headquarters CONARC, to Commanding General, CONUSA, Subj: NCO Academy Operations and Program of Instruction, Aug. 24, 1970; Memo from Hqs CONARC, for Col. Robert M. Montague, Jr., Deputy Special Assistant for the MVA, Subj: NCO Schools, March 10, 1971. In DA/CMH files.
7. Enlisted Personnel Management System (EPMS) Concept Paper, prepared as an aid to understanding the professional philosophy underlying the analytical work of the EPMS Task Force, 1973. In files USACMH. (Unless otherwise cited the following is based upon this document.)

8. Brig. Gen. William A. Patch, "Professional Development for Today's NCO," *Army*, Nov. 1974, pp. 15–20. (Unless otherwise cited, the following is based upon this reference.)
9. DCSPER, Annual Historical Summary, FY 1973, pp. 19–20.
10. The discussion of EPMS is based upon the following references; EPMS Briefing paper (103-01 EPMS Concepts and Background), Sept. 16, 1974; MILPERCEN/TRADOC Briefing paper, EPMS, 1978; *The DA Scene*, Office, Chief of Public Affairs, HQDA, Summer, 1976, "EPMS: A Way to the Top," *Tip, The Army Personnel Magazine*, Fall, 1975, pp. 31–34; Lt. Col. Robert L. Wendt, USA, "Army Training Development—A Quiet Revolution," *Military Review*, Vol. 58, Aug. 1978, pp. 74–83; SFC Stonie D. Vaughn, "EPMS, Career Management for Professional Soldiers," *Soldiers*, May 1974, pp. 15–19.
11. Annual DCSPER Historical Summary, July 1, 1973–June 1974 (FY 1974), pp. 6, 21–22; July 1974, June 1975 (FY 1975) pp. 12–14. (Unless otherwise indicated, the following is based upon these references.)
12. MILPERCEN EPMS Briefing at TRADOC, 1978. In files DA/CMH.
13. *The DA Scene EPMS: A Way to the Top*, Office, Chief of Public Affairs, HQDA, Summer, 1976, p. 6.
14. EPMS Briefing, Sept. 16, 1974, 103-01, "EPMS Concepts and Backgrounds," copy in DA CMH files; Interview, Dr. E. F. Fisher with General William E. DePuy, Oct. 19, 1976, Ft. Monroe, Va., HQ TRADOC, pp. 8–9. Copy in DA CMH files.
15. Quoted in *The DA Scene*, Summer 1976, p. 7.
16. EPMS Briefing, 103-01, EPMS Concepts and Background, Sept. 16, 1974. EPMS Briefing Paper, MILPERCEN at TRADOC, 1978. Both in DA/CMH files.
17. Note #13, from the CINC, General Michael S. Davison, to Distribution Special A, Aug. 1974. In files DA/CMH.
18. Minutes of the USAREUR NCO Professionalism Program Advisory Board, Aug. 1974 to July 1979. In files DA/CMH. (Unless otherwise indicated, the following is based upon these documents.)
19. Interviews, Dr. E. F. Fisher, CMH, with CSM F. K. Tracey, Oct. 22, 1979, Washington, D.C.
20. Change 5 to AR 600-20, Oct. 25, 1974, *Enlisted Aspects of Command.*
21. S/Sgt. Ed Hill, "NCO Professionalism Pushed," *Army Times*, Sept. 10, 1975, p. 15. (Unless otherwise cited the following is based upon this reference.)
22. Directive, Sgt. CSM Joe D. Offut, Subj: Berlin Brigade's First Line Supervisors' Program, AEBAD-CG, Dec. 3, 1976.
23. "CO's Hurting Good NCO's," *Army Times*, Nov. 26, 1975.
24. Interview, Dr. E. F. Fisher, Jr., with General George S. Blanchard, USA (Ret.) and CSM Frederick W. Tracey, April 11, 1980, Washington, D.C. (Unless otherwise noted the following is based upon this interview.)
25. Frederick Wilhelm von Steuben, *Regulations for the Order and Discipline of the Troops of the United States*, Philadelphia, Pennsylvania, 1779.
26. Gen. George S. Blanchard and CSM F. W. Tracey, "The Return of the NCO," *Army*, Oct. 1977, pp. 46–47.

CHAPTER 21: REAPPRAISAL AND RESTORING PROFESSIONALISM

1. *Army Times*, April 7, 1971, pp. 4, 43.
2. Ibid., Dec. 16, 1970, pp. 1, 24.

3. Memorandum from OCSA-SAMVA for Lt. Gen. G. I. Forsythe, Subject: Visit to USARV from April 7 to May 15, 1971. (Unless otherwise indicated, the following is based on this source.)
4. Sgt. Maj. Dan Cragg, USA (Ret.), to author.
5. *Study on Military Professionalism*, U.S. Army War College, June 30, 1970, AWC Library, UB 147, U 49 C.18; Maj. Gen. Franklin M. Davis, Jr., AWC paper, *Preface for Study on Leadership for the 1970s*, July 8, 1971.
6. *Leadership for the 1970s: A Study of Leadership for the Professional Soldier*, U.S. Army War College, July 1, 1971, pp. 1–3.
7. Gen. William C. Westmoreland, "An Army Taking Stock in a Changing Society," *Army*, Oct. 1971, pp. 19–22; Gen. Ralph E. Haines, Jr., "CONARC is Pace Setter for Army in Transition," *Army*, Oct. 1971, pp. 33–39; Army War College, *Leadership for the 1970s*, etc. (Unless otherwise indicated, the following is based on these references.)
8. Westmoreland, "Taking Stock," etc., pp. 19–22; *Report of the Board for Dynamic Training*, Vol. IV, annexes F-I, Dec. 17, 1971, Ft. Benning, Ga. (Unless otherwise indicated, the following is based on these references.)
9. Westmoreland.
10. Charles C. Moskos, Jr., *The American Enlisted Man: The Rank and File in Today's Military*, New York: The Russell Sage Foundation, 1970, p. 182.
11. Memo from Lt. Gen. George I. Forsythe, SAMVA, to Gen. Westmoreland, Subject: Report on U.S. Army Training Centers, Sept. 16, 1971. (Unless otherwise indicated, the following is based on this reference.)
12. "Old Sarge—Big VOLAR Hangup," *Army Times*, April 7, 1971, p. 43.
13. "Broader NCO Authority Urged," *Army Times*, May 5, 1971.
14. Gen. Hamilton H. Howze, "35 Years," *Army*, April 1966.

CHAPTER 22: DEFINING THE NONCOMMISSIONED OFFICER'S ROLE

1. TRADOC Tasking Statement—Role of the NCO to Commandant, U.S. Army Sergeants Major Academy, Fort Bliss, Tex., et al. n.d. copy in files, U.S. Army Center Military History.
2. Extract of Remarks by General William E. DePuy, USA, TRADOC Commander, at TRADOC Commanders' Conference, Dec. 10–11, 1975, Ft. Monroe, Va. (Unless otherwise indicated the following is based upon this document).
3. Letter, Gen. Wm. E. DePuy, CG TRADOC, to Gen. Fred C. Weyand, USA, Dec. 24, 1975. In file Hqs. TRADOC, copy in DA/CMH.
4. Letter, George S. Blanchard, CINCUSAREUR, to comdrs. USAREUR MACOMS (to Bn. level) Oct. 7, 1975. In file DA/CMH.
5. Letter, Fred C. Weyand, to CG TRADOC, William E. DePuy, April 23, 1976, in file DA CHM. (Unless otherwise indicated the following is based upon this document.)
6. Memorandum from Maj. Gen. H. D. Smith, DCS for Logistics, TRADOC for Maj. Gen. McClellan, DCSPER TRADOC, subj: Role of the NCO, May 25, 1976. In file DAA/CMH. (Unless otherwise indicated, the following is based upon this document.)
7. Memorandum from Col. Briggs, TRADOC AG for Maj. Gen. McClellan, TRADOC DCSPER, Subj: Role of the NCO, June 7, 1976. In file DA/CMH. (Unless otherwise indicated, the following is based upon this document.)
8. Memorandum from CSM J. F. La Voie, TRADOC for DCSPER TRADOC, subj: Role of the Noncommissioned Officer, June 14, 1976. Copy in files DA/CMH.
9. Letter from Col. H. E. Chapman, Secretary, for the Commandant to Commander, U.S.

Training and Doctrine Command, Ft. Monroe, Va. Attn: ATPR-HR-OE, Subj: Role of the Noncommissioned Officer. Copy in files DA/CMH. (Unless otherwise indicated the following in based upon this document.)

10. Letter from Col. Frederick R. Pole, AG for the Superintendent to Commander, TRADOC, Attn: ATPR-HR-OE, Ft. Monroe, Va. Subj: Role of the Noncommissioned Officer, July 16, 1976. In file DA/CHM. (Unless otherwise indicated the following is based upon this document.)
11. Memorandum from Gen. W. E. DePuy, CG TRADOC for SMA William G. Bainbridge, Sergeant Major of the Army, CSM John F. La Voie, TRADOC, Command Sergeant Major, Subj: The Noncommissioned Officer Corps—the Soldier Manual and the SQT, Oct. 20, 1976. In files DA/CMH. (Unless otherwise indicated, the following is based upon this document.)
12. Letter, from Robert C. Hixon, Maj. Gen Chief of Staff, Hqs. TRADOC, to Commandant, U.S. Army Sergeants Major Academy, Ft. Bliss, Tex., et al., Subj: Tasking Statement—Role of the NCO, Jan. 14, 1977. Copy in files DA/CMH.
13. Letter, from Gen. William R. DePuy, Hqs. TRADOC to Gen. F. J. Korensen, CG, U.S. FORSCOM, Ft. McPherson, GA., June 30, 1977. Copy in DA/CMH files.
14. Interview, Dr. Dan Zimmerman, with Col. Joseph Ostrowidzki, Commandant, SMA, June 30, 1983. In file DA CMH.
15. See Draft FM 22-600-20 (Advance Copy) "The Duties, Responsibilities, and Authority of Noncommissioned Officers, and the Interplay and Relationship with the Duties, Responsibilities, and Authority of Officers—Doctrine, and Methodology," June 1977, The Sergeants Major Academy, Ft. Bliss, Tex. (Unless otherwise indicated, the following is based upon this reference.)
16. Letter, from Gen. Bernard W. Rogers, U.S. Army Chief of Staff, to Gen. Donn A. Starry, Commanding General, TRADOC, Dec. 28, 1978. In file, DA CMH. (In this latter expectation, the Chief of Staff may have been harking back to a time when soldiers carried or saved TMs for ready reference. Unfortunately most no longer do this.)
17. Personal reminiscence of Dan Cragg, who as master sergeant, served as Chief of the OCSA Cables Branch during Gen. Roger's term as CSA.
18. Letter, from Gen. Bernard W. Rogers, U.S. Army Chief of Staff to Gen. Donn A. Starry, Commanding General TRADOC, Ft. Monroe, Va., Dec. 28, 1978.
19. FM 22-600-20, *The Army Noncommissioned Officer Guide*, Hqs. DA, Washington, D.C., March 31, 1980. (Unless otherwise indicated the following is based upon this document.)
20. Leader Development Plan, May 1980, from BG Joseph C. Lutz, Director, Human Resources Development, to all MACOMS. (Unless otherwise indicated, the following is based upon this reference.) Copy in File DA CMH.
21. Memorandum from LTG John R. McGiffert, Director of the Army Staff, for Heads of Staff Agencies, Subject: NCO Development Program, Dec. 4, 1979. Copy in DA/CMH files. (Unless otherwise indicated, the following is based upon this reference.)
22. AR 350-17, Noncommissioned Officer Development Program (NCODP), (Effective Jan. 1, 1981), Hqs, Department of the Army, Washington, D.C., Dec. 1, 1980.
23. Interview, Dr. E. F. Fisher, Jr., with SMA William Bainbridge, USA (Ret.), Washington, D.C., July 16, 1980. Copy of interview on file in Sergeants Major Academy.
24. Letter, United States General Accounting Office, Washington, D.C., to the Honorable Sam Nunn, Chairman, Subcommittee on Manpower and Personnel, Committee on Armed Services, United States Senate, Dec. 31, 1980. In files DA/CMH. (Unless otherwise indicated, the following is based upon this document.)
25. *The Army Needs to Improve Individual Soldier Training in Its Units*, Report to Con-

gress by the Comptroller General of the United States, FPCD-81-29, March 31, 1981. In files DA/CMH. (Unless otherwise indicated the following is based upon this document.)

26. See articles in *Army Times*, on Jan. 4, 1982, April 19, 1982, June 1982, and Sept. 20, 1982.
27. See FM 22-600-20 *The Army Noncommissioned Officer Guide*, March 1980, p. 26.
28. Ibid.
29. Letter, William D. Clark, Acting Asst. Secretary for Manpower and Reserve Affairs, to H. L. Krieger, Director, Federal Personnel and Compensation Division, U.S. General Accounting Office, Washington, D.C., Feb. 8, 1981. Copy in DA/CMH files.
30. Richard F. Rosser, "A 20th Century Military Force," *Foreign Policy*, Vol. 12, 1973, pp. 156–75.
31. Rosser, pp. 156–75. (Unless otherwise indicated, the following is based upon this reference.)
32. Interview, Dr. Ernest F. Fisher, Jr., with CSM Nathaniel McElroy, Feb. 9, 1982. Washington, D.C. Copy in files DA/CMH.

AFTERWORD

1. Will Stokes, *Songs of the Services*, New York: Frederick A. Stokes, 1919, p. 58.
2. *Army Times*, "SQTs to be Phased Out," July 16, 1990, p. 3. (Unless otherwise noted, the following is based on this reference.)

BIBLIOGRAPHY

BOOKS AND PERIODICALS

Allanson, Lt. Col. Will B. "The Incomparable Sgt. Reese: Mentor, Loyal First Soldier, But Never a Friend." *Army*, Jan. 1971.

Ambrose, David Leib. *History of the 7th Regiment, Illinois Volunteer Infantry, from Its Muster into the U.S. Service, April 25, 1861 to Its Final Muster Out July 9, 1865.* Springfield, Ill: Illinois Journal Co., 1868.

American Military History, Army Historical Series, Ed. Maurice Matloff, Washington, D.C.: Office Chief of Military History, 1969 (rev. 1973).

Anon. "CO's Hurting Good NCOs." *Army Times*, November 26, 1975.

———. "Where the 'People' Programs Are: The NCO at the Apex." *Army*, Oct. 1974.

———. "Who Are the Officers of the Army?" *Army and Navy Register*, Vol. 86, Oct. 26, 1929.

Archinger, Peter. *The American Soldier in Fiction, 1880–1963: A History of Attitudes Toward Warfare and the Military Establishment.* Ames, Iowa: Iowa University Press, 1975.

Ashburn, P. M. *A History of the Medical Department of the U.S. Army.* Boston: Houghton Mifflin Co., 1929.

Bandel, Eugene. *Frontier Life in the Army, 1856–61.* Trans. Olga Bandel and Richard Jente, ed. Ralph P. Beber. Glendale, Calif. The Southwest Historical Series, The Arthur H. Clark Co., 1932.

Barnett, Corelli. *Britain and Her Army, 1509–1970.* New York: William Morrow & Co., 1970.

Barrett, Robert. *The Theorike and Practike of Moderne Warres; Discourses in Dialogue Wise.* London: 1598.

Barry, Captain Gerat. *A Discourse of Militarie Discipline.* Brussels: 1634.

Bauer, Jack K. *The Mexican War, 1846–1848.* New York: Macmillan, 1974.

Blanchard, Gen. George S. and Tracey, CSM Frederick W. "The Return of the NCO." *Army Green Book*, Oct. 1977.

Bland, Humphrey. *A Treatise on Military Discipline*, 4th edition. London: S. Buckley, 1740; 9th Edition. London: R. Baldwin, 1762.

Bolton, Charles K. *The Private Soldier Under Washington.* Port Washington, N.Y.: Kennikat Press, 1902; reprint edition 1964.

Boney, F. N. "The Conqueror: Sgt. Mathew Woodruff in War and Peace, 1861–66." *The Alabama Review*, July 1970.

Boynton, Lindsay. *The Elizabethan Militia (1558–1638)*. London: Routledge & Kegan Paul, 1967.

Brow, J. Willard. *The Signal Corps U.S.A. in the War of the Rebellion.* Boston: U.S. Veterans Signal Corps Association, 1896.

Buckman, George Rex. "Ranches and Rancheros of the Far West." *Lippincott's Magazine*, May 22, 1882.

Buxton, G. Edward. *Official History of the 82d Division.* Indianapolis: Bobbs-Merrill, 1919.

Carbaugh, 1st Lt. Harvey C. "The Instruction of Noncommissioned Officers in the Army." *Journal of the Military Service Institution of the United States*, Vol. II, March 1890.

Carter, Robert G. *The Old Sergeant's Story: Winning the West from the Indians and Bad Men in 1870 to 1876.* New York: Hitchcock, 1926.

Casey, Brig. Gen. Silas. *U.S.A. Infantry Tactics for the Instructions, Exercise, and Maneuvers of the Soldier, A Company, Line of Skirmishers, Battalion, Brigade, or Corps d'Armée*, 3 Vols. New York: Van Nostrand, 1862.

Catton, Bruce. "Union Discipline and Leadership in the Civil War." *The Marine Corps Gazette*, No. 1, Vol. 40 (Jan. 1956).

C. J. "Sergeants' Pikes." *Journal of the Society for Army Historical Research*, Vol. 10, 1931.

Clarke, Gen. Bruce C. "No Second Class." *Army*, May 1978.

Clayton, George. *The Approved Order of Martial Discipline, with Every Particular Officer, His Office, and Duty.* London: I. C. Abraham Kitsonne, 1591.

Clode, Charles M. *The Military Forces of the Crown, Their Administration and Government*, Vol. I. London: John Murray, 1869.

Collins, Col. John M. "The Lean, Lean Years, Depression Army." *Army*, Jan. 1972.

Cooling, B. F. "Enlisted Grade Structure and the Army Reorganization Act of 1920." *Military Affairs*, Vol. XXI, No. 4 (Winter 1967–1968).

Corvisier, André. *Armies and Societies in Europe, 1494–1789.* Transl. Abigail T. Siddal. Bloomington, Indiana: Indiana University Press, 1917.

Cragg, Sgt. Maj. Dan. "Don't Juggle GI Grades, Insignia." *Army*, April 1979.

———. *The Soldier's Prize.* New York: Ballantine Books, 1986.

Darden, Capt. Fred A. "No Time for Sergeants." *Infantry*, Vol. 51, No. 1, Dec. 1960.

de Beccarie, Pavie Raymond Sieur de Forquevaux. *Les Instructions sur le Facit de la Guerre.* Ed. G. D. Kerson from the original work published in Paris, 1548. London: Athelone Press, 1954.

de Saxe, Count Maurice. *Reveries, or, Memories Concerning the Art of War.* Edinburgh: 1776.

Downey, Fairfax. *Indian Fighting Army.* New York: Scribner's, 1944.

Duane, William. *Regulations for the Discipline of the Infantry*, 9th Edition. Philadelphia: 1814.

Duffy, Christopher. *The Army of Frederick the Great.* London: David & Charles, 1974.

Ellis, Maj. Wilmot E. "What Is the Cause of the Recent Falling Off in the Enlisted Strength of the Army and Navy, and What Means Should be Taken to Remedy It?" *Journal of the Military Service Institution of the United States*, March–April 1909.

Emerson, William K. *Chevrons: Illustrated History and Catalog of U.S. Army Insignia.* Washington, D.C.: Smithsonian Institution Press, 1983.

———. "Old Bill." *Armor.* September–October 1978.

English, George H. *History of the 89th Division, USA.* Denver, Col.: Smith–Brooks Publishing Co., 1920.

Evans, Maj. W. P. "Pay of Noncommissioned Officers." *The Journal of the Military Service Institution of the United States.* March–April 1904.

Faber, 1st Lt. C. W. "To Promote the Efficiency of Non-Commissioned Officers." *The Journal of the Military Service Institution of the United States*, Vol. XXII, Jan. 1898.

Fehrenbach, T. R. *This Kind of War: A Study in Preparedness.* New York: Macmillan, 1963.

Fell, Capt. Edgar T. *History of the Seventh Division, USA, 1917–1918.* Philadelphia: Privately published, 1927.

Fisher, Ernest F., Jr. *Cassino to the Alps.* Washington, D.C.: Government Printing Office, 1977.

———. "Muzzle Loader to Breech Loader: The Impact of Weapons Technology on Infantry Organization and Tactics in the U.S. Army from 1775 to 1975," *Acta Nr. 2*, Washington, D.C: The International Commission for Military History, 1975.

Foner, Jack D. *The U.S. Soldier Between Two Wars: Army Life and Reforms, 1865–1898.* New York: Humanities Press, 1970.

Ganoe, William A. *The History of the U.S. Army.* New York: Appleton-Century, 1924, 1935.

Garcia, 1st. Sgt. Louis E. "Train Us to Lead." *Infantry*, Vol. 52, No. 2, March/April 1962.

General Orders of George Washington Issued at Newburgh on the Hudson, 1782. Ed. Maj. Edward C. Baynton Harrison. New York: 1783.

Gillooly, Maj. David H. and Bond, Thomas C. "Assaults With Explosive Devices on Superiors: A Synopsis of Reports From Confined Offenders at the U.S. Disciplinary Barracks." *Journal of Military Medicine*, Vol. 41, No. 10, Nov. 1976.

Goode, Col. Paul R. *The United States Soldiers Home: A History of Its First Hundred Years.* Richmond, Va.: By the author, 1957.

Griffith, Robert K. *Men Wanted for the U.S. Army: America's Experience With an All-Volunteer Army Between the Wars.* Westport, Conn: Greenwood Press, 1982.

Grose, Francis. *Military Antiquities Respecting a History of the English Army.* New edition, 2 Vols. London: 1812.

Gugler, Russell A. *Combat Actions in Korea.* Washington, D.C.: Combat Forces Press, 1954.

Haigh, R. H. and Turner, P. W. "World War I and the Serving British Soldier." *Military Affairs/Aerospace Historian*, Manhattan, Kansas, 1979.

Haines, Gen. Ralph E., Jr. "CONARC Is Pace Setter for Army in Transition." *Army Green Book*, Oct. 1971.

Hastings, Leonard Nason. *Sergeant Eadie.* New York: Nason, Grosset & Dunlap, 1928.

Hawes, William R. "Upholding NCO Training Tradition." *The European Stars and Stripes*, March 14, 1983.

Hexam, Henry. *The Principles of the Art of Militarie Practiced in the Wars of the United Netherlands.* Delft: 1637.

Hill, S. Sgt. Ed. "NCO Professionalism Pushed." *Army Times*, Sept. 10, 1975.

Holley, I. B., Jr. *Gen. John M. Palmer, Citizen Soldiers, and the Army of a Democracy.* Westport, Conn: Greenwood Press, 1982.

Howze, Hamilton. "35 Years." *Army*, April 1966.

Hunt, Frazier and Robert. *I Fought with Custer: The Story of Sergeant Windolph, Last Survivor of the Battle of the Little Big Horn.* New York: Charles Scribner's Sons, 1947.

Huntington, Samuel P., *The Soldier and the State: The Theory and Politics of Civil-Military Relations.* Cambridge, Mass: Harvard University Press, 1959.

Jacobs, James Ripley, *The Beginnings of the U.S. Army, 1773–1812.* Princeton, N.J.: Princeton University Press, 1949.

Jones, James. *From Here to Eternity.* New York: Scribners, 1951.

Keegan, John. *The Face of Battle: A Study of Agincourt, Waterloo, and the Somme.* New York: Vintage Books, 1976.

Kessel, Eberhard. "Die Preussische Armee, 1640–1866." *Deutsche Heeresgeschichte*, Ed. Karl Linnebach. Hamburg: 1935.

Lahne, Werner. *Unteroffiziere, Gestern–Heute–Morgen.* Herford-Bonn: Verlag Offene Worte, 1974.

Lane, Austin. *Obligations of Society in the XII and XIII Centuries.* Oxford: Oxford University Press, 1946.

Ledebur, Hauptmann a.D. Ferdinand Freiherr von. *Die Geschichte des Deutschen Unteroffiziers.* Berlin: Junker and Dünnhaupt Verlag, 1939.

Leed, Eric J. *No Man's Land: Combat and Identity in World War I.* Cambridge, England: Cambridge University Press, 1979.

Lonn, Ella. *Foreigners in the Union Army and Navy.* Baton Rouge, La.: Louisiana University Press, 1951.

Lowe, Percival G. *Five Years a Dragoon, and Other Adventures.* Kansas City, Mo.: The Franklin Hudson Publishing Company, 1906.

MacDonald, Charles B. *Company Commander.* Washington, D.C.: Infantry Journal Press, 1947.

McNeill, William H. *Technology, Armed Force, and Society Since A.D. 1000.* Chicago: University of Chicago Press, 1982.

Marshall, S.L.A. *Commentary on Infantry Operations and Weapons Usage in Korea, Winter of 1950–51.* Baltimore: Johns Hopkins University, 1953.

Meyers, Augustus. *Ten Years in the Ranks U.S. Army.* New York: The Sterling Press, 1914.

Moskos, Charles C. *The American Enlisted Man: The Rank and File in Today's Military.* New York: The Russell Sage Foundation, 1970.

Murphy, Dennis. *The Sergeant.* New York: Viking Press, 1958.

Newman, Maj. Gen. Aubrey. *Follow Me: The Human Element in Leadership.* Novato, California: Presidio Press, 1981.

Nihard, Col. Brooke, U.S.M.C. "A Humorous Account of a Militia Muster Circa 1807." *The Journal of the Company of Military Collectors and Historians*, Vol X, Spring 1958.

Oman, Sir Charles. *A History of the Army of War in the Sixteenth Century.* New York: E. P. Dutton, 1937.

O'Ryan, Maj. Gen. John F. *The Story of the 17th Division.* New York: Wynkoop, Hallenbeck, Crawford Co., 1921.

Palmer, John M. A. *America in Arms: The Experience of the United States with Military Organization.* New Haven, Conn.: Yale University Press, 1941.

Patch, Brig. Gen. William A. "Professional Development for Today's NCO." *Army*, November 1974.

Pogue, Forrest C. *George C. Marshall, Education of a General*, Vol. I. New York: Viking Press, 1963.

Powicke, Michael. *Military Obligations in Medieval England.* Oxford: Oxford University Press, 1962.

Price, George F. *Across the Continent with the Fifth Cavalry.* New York: Van Nostrand, 1883.

Prucha, Francis Paul. *The Sword of the Republic: The U.S. Army on the Frontier, 1783 to 1846.* New York: Macmillan, 1969.

Recollections of the U.S. Army: A Series of Thrilling Tales and Sketches, by an American Soldier. Boston: James Munroe & Co., 1845.

Rickey, Don C., Jr. *Forty Miles a Day on Beans and Hay: The Enlisted Soldier Fighting the Indian Wars.* Norman, Oklahoma: University of Oklahoma Press, 1963.

———. "Life Since 1888." An interview with Reginald A. Bradley, Grass Valley, Col., Jan. 10, 1968. On file at U.S. Army Military History Institute, Carlisle Barracks, Pennsylvania.

Rolak, Bruno J. "General Miles' Mirrors: The Heliograph in the Geronimo Campaign of 1886." *The Journal of Arizona History*, Vol. XVI, Summer 1975.

Ropp, Theodore. *War in the Modern World.* Durham, North Carolina: Duke University Press, 1962.

Ross, Arthur M. "The Poets' Corner." *Yank*, Feb. 11, 1944.

Rosser, Richard F. "A 20th Century Military Force." *Foreign Policy*, Vol. 12 (1973).

Schieps, Paul J. "Will Croft Barnes and the Apache Uprising of 1881." *Military History of the Spanish-American Southwest: A Seminar, 1976.* Washington, D.C.: Potomac Corral, The Westerners, 1981.

Schubert, Frank N. "The Violent World of Emanuel Stance, Fort Robinson, 1887." *Nebraska History*, Vol. 55, No. 2, Summer 1974.

Schwoerer, Lois G. *No Standing Armies: The Antiarmy Ideology in Seventeenth-Century England.* Baltimore: The Johns Hopkins University Press, 1974.

Smoler, Fredric. "The Secret of the Soldiers Who Didn't Shoot." *American Heritage*, March, 1989.

Smythe, Sir John. *Certain Discourses to the Nobilities of the Realm of England.* London: May 1590.

———. *Observations and Orders Mylitarie Requisite for All Chieftaines, Captaines, and Higher and Lower Men of Charge, and Officers to Understand, Knowe and Observe.* London: 1595.

Stelck, Ardell. "Sgt. Guy Gillette and Cherokee's 'Gallant Company M' in the Spanish-American War." *Annals of Iowa*, pp. 561–578.

Steuben, Friedrich Wilhelm, Baron von. *Regulations for the Order and Discipline of the Troops of the United States.* Philadelphia: 1779.

Stewart, Capt. M. B. *Handbook for Noncommissioned Officers of Infantry.* Kansas City, Missouri: Hudson-Kimberly Publishing Co., 1903.

Stokes, Will. *Songs of the Services.* New York: Frederick A. Stokes, Co., 1919.

Straub, Elmer Frank. "A Sergeant's Diary in the World War: The Diary of an Enlisted Member of the 150th Field Artillery (42d Rainbow Division), October 27, 1917, to August 7, 1919." *Indiana World War Records*, Vol. III. Indianapolis, Indiana: Indiana Historical Commission, 1923.

Streeter, E. *Dere Mable: Love Letters of a Rookie.* New York: Frederick A. Stokes Co., 1918.

Streiter, Terry W. "An Army in Evolution: French Officers Commissioned from the Ranks, 1848–1895." *Military Affairs*, Dec. 1978.

Sunseri, Alvin R. "Fredrick William von Steuben and the Reeducation of the American Army: A Lesson in Practicality." *Armor*, March–April 1965.

Teitler, G. *The Genesis of the Professional Officer Corps.* London & Beverly Hills: Sage Publications, 1977.

Todd, A. L. *Abandoned: The Story of the Greely Arctic Expedition 1881–1884.* New York: McGraw-Hill, 1961.

Townshend, George. *A Plan of Discipline for the Use of the Militia of the County of Norfolk.* London: 1659.

Turner, Sir James. *Passas Armata: Military Essayes of the Ancient, Grecian, Roman, and Modern Art of War.* London: 1683.

Upton, Emory. *The Armies of Asia and Europe, Embracing Official Reports on the Armies of Japan, China, India, Persia, Italy, Russia, Austria, Germany, France, and England.* New York: D. Appleton, 1878.

Vaughan, J. W. *The Battle of Platte Bridge.* Norman, Oklahoma: University of Oklahoma Press, 1963.

Vaughn, SFC Stonie D. "EPMS, Career Management for Professional Soldiers." *Soldiers*, May 1974.

Vegetius. *The Four Books of Flavius Vegetius Renatus.* Transl. John Sadler. London: 1572.

Wallhausen, Johann Jacobi von. *Manuale Militarie.* Frankfurt: 1616.

———. *Militia Gallica, oder der Kriegsdisciplin der alten Frantzösischen Regimenter.* Hanau: 1617.

Ward, Robert. *Animadversions of Warre.* London: 1639

Webb, James H., Jr. *Fields of Fire.* New York: Bantam Books, 1981.

Weigley, Russell F. *History of the United States Army.* New York: Macmillan, 1967.

Wendt, Lt. Col. Robert A. "Army Training Development—A Quiet Revolution." *Military Review*, Vol. 58, Aug. 1978.

Westmoreland, Gen. William C. "An Army Taking Stock in a Changing Society." *Army Green Book.* Oct. 1971.

Western, J. R. *The English Militia in the Eighteenth Century: The Story of a Political Issue, 1660–1802.* London: Routledge and Kegan Paul, 1965.

———. *The English Militia in the Seventeenth Century.* London: Routledge and Kegan Paul, 1965.

Willeford, Charles. *Something About a Soldier.* New York: Ballantine Books, 1986.

Whitnah, Donald R. *A History of the United States Weather Bureau.* Urbana, Illinois: University of Illinois Press, 1961.

Wieser, Lt. Gustave A. "The Noncommissioned Officer: Their Efficiency an Essential Factor in Our Army." *Journal of the Military Service Institution of the United States*, Vol. 38, January–February 1906.

Wiley, Bell Irvin. *The Life of Billy Yank, the Common Soldier of the Union.* New York: Bobbs-Merrill, 1951.

Wolfe, General James. *General Wolfe's Instructions to Young Officers, Also His Orders for a Battalion and an Army, etc.*, 2nd Edition. London: 1780.

Woll, Harold. *The Military Specialists: Skilled Manpower for the Armed Forces.* Baltimore, Maryland: The Johns Hopkins Press, 1968.

Wooldridge, SMA William O. "First Look at a New Job." *Army Green Book*, Oct. 1966.

Zais, Maj. Gen. Melvin. "The New NCO." *Army*, May 1968.

Zog'baum, Rufus F. *Horse, Foot, and Dragoons: Sketches of Army Life at Home and Abroad.* New York: Harper & Bros., 1880.

U.S. GOVERNMENT DOCUMENTS AND PUBLICATIONS

American Archives, Fifth Series, Ed. Peter Force, Washington, D.C.: Government Printing Office, 1853.

An Act Establishing Rules and Articles for the Government of the Army of the United States with the Regulations of the War Department Respecting the Same. Albany, New York: 1812.

American State Papers, Military Affairs. Washington, D.C.: Gales & Seaton, 1861.

Appleman, Roy E. *The United States Army in the Korean War: South to the Naktong, North to the Yalu, June–November 1950.* Washington, D.C.: Government Printing Office, 1961.

Arthur, Robert. *The Coast Artillery School, 1824–1927.* Ft. Monroe, Virginia: The Coast Artillery School, 1928.

———. *The History of Fort Monroe.* Ft. Monroe, Virginia: The Coast Artillery School, 1930.

Collins, John M. "The Care and Cleaning of NCOs: A Critical Survey of Destructive Policies and Practices Which Have Shaped the Army Noncommissioned Officer Corps Since 1939." Industrial College of the Armed Forces Thesis, March 1967.

Comptroller General of the United States. *The Army Needs to Improve Individual Soldier Training in Its Units.* Report to the Congress, FPCD-81-29, March 31, 1981.

Cordiner Report. See Department of Defense, *A Modern Concept*, etc.

Davis, Maj. Gen. Franklin M., Jr. "Preface for Study on Leadership for the 1970s." Paper for the U.S. Army War College, Carlisle Barracks, Pa., July 8, 1971.

Department of the Army. Army Regulations 350-71. *Noncommissioned Officer Development Program (NCODP).* Washington, D.C.: Dec. 1, 1980.

———. Army Regulations 350-90. *Education and Training, Noncommissioned Officers Academies.* Washington, D.C.: June 25, 1957.

———. Army Regulations 615-200. *Enlisted Men, Transfers, Section I.* Washington, D.C.: Nov. 1939.

———. Army Regulations 615-210. *Enlisted Men, Foreign Service.* Washington D.C.: Feb. 20, 1929.

———. Department of the Army Circular 1. *Career Guidance Plan for Warrant Officers and Enlisted Personnel.* Washington, D.C.: Jan. 1948.

———. Department of the Army Pamphlet 600-11, *History of the Warrant Officer Corps.* Washington, D.C.: July 7, 1977.

———. *Enlisted Grade Structure Study.* Vol VI, Annex E, *Historical Review of the Enlisted Grade Structure of the U.S. Army, 1775–1967.* Deputy Chief of Staff for Personnel, July 1967.

———. *Enlisted Grade Structure Study.* Vol. IV, Annex E, *Historical Review of the Enlisted Grade Structure of the U. S. Army, 1775–1976*; Vol. IX, Annex J, *Command and Staff Comments of Fifteen Essential Elements of Analysis.* Deputy Chief of Staff for Personnel, 1976.

———. Field Manual 22-600-20. *The Army Noncommissioned Officer Guide.* March 31, 1980.

———. *Historical Sketch of the Signal Corps, 1860–1941.* Ft. Monmouth, New Jersey: Eastern Signal Corps Schools, Pamphlet #32, Dec. 10, 1942.

———. *History of the Warrant Officer Corps.* Department of the Army Pamphlet 600-11, July 7, 1977.

———. "History and Development of the Army and Air Force Retirement System." Washington, D.C.: The Adjutant General's Office, Feb. 3, 1967.

———. *History of the U.S. Army Sergeants Major Academy, 1 July 1972–31 December 1974.* U.S. Army Sergeants Major Academy: Fort Bliss, Tex.

———. *The Organization of Ground Combat Troops.* Washington, D.C.: 1947.

———. *Report of the Field Manual Review Board, Annex B: Evolution of the United States Army Field Manual: Valley Forge to Vietnam.* Dec., 1966.

———. *The Procurement and Training of Ground Combat Troops.* Washington, D.C.: 1948.

———. *Report of the Board for Dynamic Training*, Vol. IV, Annexes F through I. Ft. Benning, Georgia: U.S. Army Infantry School, Dec. 17, 1971.

———. *Study on Military Professionalism.* Carlisle Barracks, Pennsylvania: U.S. Army War College, June 30, 1980.

Department of Defense. *Report of Board Chaired by Lt. Gen. James H. Doolittle to Secretary of War Robert P. Patterson.* Washington, D.C.: May 1946.

———. *Report of Board Chaired by Rear Admiral J. P. Womble, Jr. to the Secretary of Defense.* Washington, D.C.: Oct. 1953.

———. *Selected Manpower Statistics.* Washington, D.C.: Washington Headquarters Services, Directorate for Information, Operations, and Reports, March 1977.

———. *A Modern Concept of Manpower Management and Compensation for Personnel of the Uniformed Services.* Volume I, *Military Personnel. A Report and Recommendations for the Secretary of Defense.* Washington, D.C.: Defense Advisory Committee on Professional and Technical Compensation, May 1957.

Exley, Thomas M. *A Compendium of the Pay of the Army, from 1785 to 1888.* Washington, D.C.: Government Printing Office, 1888.

General Regulations for the Army. Washington, D.C.: 1832, 1835, 1861, 1863, 1881, 1908.

General Regulations of the Army or, Military Institutes. Washington, D.C.: 1821, 1825.

Koehler, Franz. *Coffee for the Armed Forces: Military Development and Conversion to Industry Supply.* U.S. Army Quartermaster Corps Historical Studies, Series II, No. 5. Washington, D.C.: Government Printing Office, 1958.

Matloff, Maurice. *American Military History, Army Historical Series.* Washington, D.C.: Office Chief of Military History, 1969.

Medal of Honor, 1863–1968. Washington, D.C.: Government Printing Office, 1968.

Messages, Dec. 1844. Report of the Commanding General of the Army. Washington, D.C.: War Department, Dec. 3, 1844.

Messages from the President of the United States to the Two Houses of Congress. Washington, D.C.: Government Printing Office.

Report of the Inspector General of the Army. Vol. I. Washington, D.C.: U.S. Army Center of Military History, 1970.

Rules and Regulations for the Field Exercise and Maneuveres of Infantry. New York: 1815.

Secretary of War. *Reports.* Washington, D.C.: Government Printing Office, 1853, 1854, 1858, 1859, 1860, 1861, 1888, 1907, 1908.

Upton, Bvt. Maj. Gen. Emory. *The Military Policy of the United States.* Washington, D.C.: Government Printing Office, 1912.

U.S. House of Representatives. *Hearings Before the Committee on Military Affairs on H.R. 12827.* Washington, D.C.: Government Printing Office, 1912.

U.S. Senate. *Increase in the Percentages of Noncommissioned Officers of the Army.* Report No. 931, 67th Congress, 3rd Session. Washington, D.C.: Government Printing Office, 1922.

War Department. *Annual Report.* Washington, D.C.: Government Printing Office, 1907.

———. *A Manual for NCOs and Privates of Infantry of the AUS.* Washington, D.C.: Government Printing Office, 1917.

———. *Annual Reports.* Washington, D.C.: Government Printing Office, 1917, 1918, 1921, 1926.

Washington, George. *The Writings of George Washington (From Original Manuscript Sources), 1745–1799*, Vols. 39. Ed. John C. Fitz. Washington, D.C.: The George Washington Bicentennial Commission, Government Printing Office, 1931–1942.

ARCHIVES AND MANUSCRIPT COLLECTIONS

The Army Library, General Orders and Regulations Collection, Military Documents Branch, The Pentagon, Washington, D.C.

The Center for Military History, Department of the Army, Washington, D.C.
The Folger Shakespeare Library, Washington, D.C.
The National Archives of the United States (NARA), Old Military Records Division, Washington, D.C.
The Smithsonian Institution, Museum of American History, Military History Collection.
The United States Army Military History Institute, Carlisle Barracks, Pennsylvania.

INTERVIEWS

These are interviews with senior officers and noncommissioned officers conducted by the author and other persons. Specific citations are contained in the Notes section.

Sergeant Major of the Army William G. Bainbridge
General George S. Blanchard
Sergeant Major of the Army William Connelly
General Michael C. Davison
General William E. DePuy
General Ben Harrell
General Paul D. Harkins
Brigadier General Victor Hugo
General Harold K. Johnson
General George R. Mather
Command Sergeant Major Nathaniel McElroy
Command Sergeant Major Paul W. Muuss
Colonel Joseph Ostrowidszki
General Herbert B. Powell
General Mathew B. Ridgeway
Command Sergeant Major Frederick W. Tracey
General James K. Woolnough
General R. J. Wood

APPENDIX

ENLISTED GRADE STRUCTURE, 1920–2000

1920*	1944	1948	1959	2000
				SMA (E9)
				CSM (E9)
				SGM (E9)
M/Sgt. (1st Grade)	M/Sgt. (1st Grade)	1st Sgt. (Grade 1)	SGM/SP9 (E9)	1st Sgt. (E8)
Tech. Sgt. (2nd Grade)	1st Sgt. (1st Grade)	M/Sgt. (Grade 1)	1st Sgt./SP8 (E8)	M/Sgt. (E8)
1st Sgt. (2nd Grade)	Tech. Sgt. (2nd Grade)	SFC (Grade 2)	M/Sgt./SP8 (E8)	Plt. Sgt./SFC (E7)
Sgt. (3rd Grade)	Sgt./Tech. 3 (3rd Grade) ††	Sgt. (Grade 3)	Plt. Sgt./SFC/SP7 (E7)	SSgt. (E6)
Sgt. (3rd Grade)	Sgt./Tech. 4 (4th Grade) ††	Cpl. (Grade 4)	SSgt./SP6 (E6)	Sgt. (E5)
Cpl. (5th Grade)	Cpl./Tech. 5 (5th Grade) ††	PFC (Grade 5)	Sgt./SP5 (E5)	Cpl./SPC (E4)
PFC (6th Grade) †	PFC (6th Grade)	Pvt. (Grade 6) †	Cpl./SP4 (E4)	PFC (E3)
Pvt. (7th Grade) †	Pvt. (7th Grade) †	Recruit (Grade 7) †	PFC (E3)	Pvt. (E2)
			Pvt. (E2) †	Pvt. (E1) †
			Recruit (E1) †	

* There were six classes of specialists designated within these grades. Personnel qualifying for these classifications drew from as much as $25 per month extra pay for private first class, specialist first class, to $3 extra for private, specialist sixth class.

† No chevron designated for these grades.

†† Equivalent to modern specialist grades.

INDEX

ABOUT THE AUTHOR

Ernest F. Fisher, Jr., graduated from Boston University in 1941 and in World War II served in Europe with the 501st Parachute Infantry Regiment, 101st Airborne Division. He returned to Boston University and received an M.A. in 1947 and a Ph.D. from the University of Wisconsin in 1952. From 1954 to 1959, Dr. Fisher was a historian with Headquarters, U.S. Army, Europe. From 1960 until his retirement in 1986, he was a member of the staff of the Center of Military History in Washington, D.C. He is also a retired colonel in the Army of the United States.